WOMEN'S AMERICA

WOMEN'S AMERICA

AMERICA

REFOCUSING THE PAST

Linda K. Kerber
UNIVERSITY OF IOWA

Jane De Hart Mathews
UNIVERSITY OF NORTH CAROLINA
AT GREENSBORO

New York   Oxford
OXFORD UNIVERSITY PRESS
1982

Copyright © 1982 by Oxford University Press, Inc.

Library of Congress Cataloging in Publication Data

Main entry under title:
Women's America.

Bibliography: p
Includes index.
1. Women—United States—History—Sources—
Addresses, essays, lectures.   2. Women—Employment—
United States—History—Sources—Addresses, essays,
lectures.   3. Women in politics—United States—
History—Sources—Addresses, essays, lectures.
4. Women—Health and hygiene—United States—
History—Sources—Addresses, essays, lectures.
5. Feminism—United States—History—Sources—
Addresses, essays, lectures.   I. Kerber, Linda K.
II. Mathews, Jane De Hart.
HQ1426.W663   305.4'0973   81-2535
ISBN 0-19-502982-8   AACR2
ISBN 0-19-502983-6 (pbk.)

Printing (last digit): 9 8 7 6 5 4 3 2 1

Printed in the United States of America

To our nieces

Carol Anne Coulter and Jane De Hart Coulter

Meredith Harper Epstein, Lauren Elizabeth Epstein,
Elyse Marin Kerber, Erica Beth Kerber

Acknowledgments

One of the most rewarding aspects of working in women's history is sharing the extraordinary collegiality and mutual support provided by others working in this field. There is now a network of historians that spans generations and geographical distance, bonding together those who seek to recapture women's historical experience. We are beneficiaries of that network, and we are deeply grateful to many people who have generously shared their time, energy, and knowledge.

We are especially grateful to Virginia Yans, Douglass College, Rutgers University; Anne Firor Scott and William Chafe, Duke University; and Jacquelyn Hall, University of North Carolina at Chapel Hill, for their cogent criticism of our manuscript in its formative stage. Gerda Lerner, University of Wisconsin; Barbara Sicherman, editor of *Notable American Women: The Modern Period*; Joan Scott, Brown University; Annette Baxter, Barnard College; Myra Dinnerstein, University of Arizona; and Dorothy Ross, University of Virginia, read subsequent versions and made valuable suggestions. Julia Mears of Iowa City gave us the benefit of her legal expertise.

Many colleagues were kind enough to comment on the manuscript and on its usefulness for general readers. We are particularly grateful to Jean Gordon, University of North Carolina at Greensboro; Laura Becker, Clemson University; Carmela A. Karnoutsos, Jersey City State College; Barbara A. Peterson, Honolulu Community College; Sylvia Frey, Newcomb College, Tulane University; G. Cullom Davis, Sangamon State University; Shirley Jackson, Boston College; Michael D'Innocenzo, Hofstra University; and Ellen Widiss of Iowa City. As graduate assistants, Gary Eblen at the University of North Carolina at Greensboro and Jill Harsin, Roseanne Sizer, Jane Roules, and Cynthia Hamilton at the University of Iowa have transformed what were routine chores into labors of love.

From the beginning of this enterprise Nancy Lane of Oxford University Press has played an important role. She encouraged us to write this book, and she monitored every stage of its development, blending patience and impatience in proper proportion. We feel ourselves extraordinarily fortunate to have worked with an editor whose commitment to excellence and whose personal friendship have enriched our lives. Phyllis Deutsch and Mary Wander gave special attention to this book for which we are especially grateful. We are also indebted to Ann Hofstra Grogg, who rashly agreed to copyedit the manuscript before she received the complete version.

We have repeatedly taken advantage of Donald Mathews's formidable knowledge and his genuine interest in women's history. (We acknowledge, of course, that, given his proximity to one of the editors, he could not very well withhold his assistance.)

While the other editor was away from home working on this book, Dick, Ross, and Justin Kerber refined their domestic skills, cheerfully supporting the social transformation that is the subject of this book.

Iowa City, Iowa   Linda K. Kerber
Chapel Hill, North Carolina   Jane De Hart Mathews
October 1981

Contents

WOMEN'S AMERICA

Introduction

Fifty years ago the historian Mary Beard published an anthology called *America through Women's Eyes*. In it she argued that an accurate understanding of the past required women's experience to be analyzed with as much care as historians had normally devoted to the experience of men. Our perspective and our goals in this book are similar to hers.

From ancient Greece to our own day it has been easy for men to write about human experience from their own perspective. *Mankind* is the noun used as synonymous with humanity; women are the specific exceptions to the general experience. "When we speak of mankind," complained one historian, "we mean men and women collectively, but when we speak of womenkind, we mean the ladies, God bless them."[1] This is an easy habit, but it is a lazy one, and its effect is to distort our understanding of the past. It does not take into account the possibility that the characteristics of men and the characteristics of women may differ, or that the experiences of men and women may differ because their gender is different, even if they are of the same race, class, and ethnic group.

Two decades ago the historian David Potter offered a useful, commonsensical rule that echoed Mary Beard's work of a generation before. "When one meets with a social generalization it is frequently worthwhile to ask concretely: Does it apply to women, or only to the masculine component in the population?"[2] Historical phenomena, when viewed through women's eyes and evaluated for the impact they have had on women, often appear to be very different than when evaluated for their impact on men.

In the last fifteen years historians seeking to test old generalizations have refreshed and often changed our understanding of general trends in American history by what they have learned about women's history. Things we thought we "knew" about American history turn out to be more complex than we had suspected. For example, most textbooks suggest that the frontier meant opportunity for Americans, "a gate of escape from the bondage of the past." But it was men who more readily found on the frontier compensation for their hard work; many women found only drudgery. Other generalizations turn out to be equally suspect. We have often assumed that American slaves were provided with at least adequate diets, but the generalization holds better for male slaves than for pregnant women and nursing mothers who found that the slaves' diet meant semistarvation. Differences in experience often worked to women's disadvantage, but they did not always do so. In a success-oriented society, for example, men have been expected to meet the pressures of competition directly;

3

women, however, have been in some measure shielded from these pressures. Upper-middle-class women, freed from the demands of the marketplace, could pursue their own private interests—in the arts, in philanthropy, in horticulture— at their leisure, for the benefit not only of themselves but also of society.

Whether the differences seem advantageous to one sex or the other, the point remains that to consider one sex while ignoring the other is like looking at an old family photograph in which the male members occupy the foreground as distinct figures, while the female members are an undifferentiated blur in the background. Women's history enables us to see the women in that photograph more clearly. It enables us to set women in the context of their distinctive past, deriving from their different biological, economic, and political situation. Women's history enlarges our vision. And with that wider sight, we can hope to readjust generalizations so that our understanding of the whole now takes into account experiences special to each sex.[3]

The final, authoritative history will never be written. We can only approach the reality of the past, constantly refocusing our vision and refining our understanding. "Probably every historian," observes a recent writer, "has at one time or the other day-dreamed about finding a lost trunk of letters which, when opened, would almost automatically revolutionize our historical understanding. What most of us did not know is that we have had that trunk in our intellectual attics for a long time and never thought to look inside. Women's historians, having pried open the lid, invite us now to think in new terms, leading to a new perspective and therefore to a new past."[4]

This anthology will introduce you to that trunk of materials and to the interpretations historians have been making of what they have found there. Like all anthologists, we are enthusiasts. We reprint here essays and documents that we have enjoyed reading and rereading. We think they deserve a wider audience.

Perhaps the most striking conclusion forced upon us by these materials is that public experience and private experience cannot be sharply separated. For example, instead of being at opposite poles, one private and the other public, the home and factory have strongly interacted in the American economic system. In the early stages of industrialization women working in their homes sold carded wool that was spun by factory machinery. As the consumer society developed, women, as part of their role as homemakers, became the chief buyers of manufactured goods. As mothers they have long inculcated in their children those traits of obedience, honesty, and industry that employers expect of their workers. Private activities that women engaged in for their families in their homes had— and continue to have—significant public implications.

Women's history suggests a more complex understanding of traditional categories of historical interpretation. Conventional periodization has used presidential administrations or wars as major guideposts in organizing our description of the past: the Revolutionary Era, the Age of Jackson, the Civil War, the Eisenhower Years. Conventional interpretations have tended to emphasize the accomplishments of men, whether they be presidents, generals, farmers, or ranch hands. But all men had women for contemporaries, and women experienced the same great social phenomena that men did. Certainly women felt the terrible trauma of war. Even in periods when they did not vote, women were citizens who offered allegiance to government and were affected by its policies. If men and women both felt the force of social change, each did so in distinctive ways. Thus, in trying to include most of the major traditional themes of American history from colonial times to the present, we have also tried to show the distinctiveness of their impact on women and the distinctiveness of women's response to them.

This book is divided into three major chronological sections. Because dates that mark major turning points in traditional historical accounts do not automatically coincide with those dates that mark significant changes in the lives of American women, women's history challenges us to reexamine conventional periodization. Our sections are generally congruent with familiar periodization; they also reflect changing realities in women's experience. The dividing date between traditional and industrial America is 1820, by which time forces were in motion that would erode the domestic economy of an agrarian society, slowly transforming women's lives in the process. The long period of industrialization that followed 1820 may conveniently be broken at 1880, by which time large-scale industries in which women were employed were firmly established. By this time, too, women's rights leaders had come to recognize that suffrage would not be granted by the courts on the basis of a fresh interpretation of the Constitution, and they demanded a specific constitutional amendment. The second major period ends at 1920, when the necessary ingredients for emancipation were present. The historian Gerda Lerner has identified these as "urbanization; industrialization with technology permitting society to remove food preparation and care of the sick from the home; the mechanization of heating and laundry; spread of health and medical care sufficient to lower infant mortality and protect maternal health; birth control; . . . and availability of education on all levels to all children."[5] These conditions existed in varying measure by 1920, which was also the year of the passage of the Equal Suffrage Amendment, the first year in which women attended large state universities in numbers comparable to men, and the first year in which more women were working in factories and white-collar jobs than in domestic service.

The study of women's history not only challenges us to reconsider conventional periodization but it also changes traditional history by emphasizing the interrelationship among fields that have often been treated separately. To look at the past through women's eyes is to see the complex interaction of biology (reproduction), economics, politics, and ideology. These essential categories appear and reappear throughout the book. Taken by themselves they are simple divisions that capture part of women's historical experience. Taken as parts of an interacting whole, these categories underscore the peculiarity of women's experience. The key to the interaction is the way in which biology affects the other three categories. An example of this interaction can help explain what this book is about. The mistress of a plantation in pre–Civil War South Carolina could not vote; her dependent political status was dictated by her dependent economic status, which in turn was dictated by law and custom (ideology). She had no property of her own; whatever she had received from inheritance had been vested in her husband when she married. The *economic* facts of her position could have been that she had brought more wealth to the marriage than had her husband; the *political* facts were that only her husband could manage her property and participate in the community by voting and holding office—these were facts that changed the economic "facts" of life for her. The reason for one set of facts altering another set of facts was rooted in biology and the ideological explanation that accompanied the undeniable fact that women gave birth. The economic and political implications of this biological fact need not have dictated women's political role—this we know from the passage of married women's property acts and the Equal Suffrage Amendment (1920). In the nineteenth century, however, the role of women was defined by the ideological expectation that all women bear and care for children; if some did not, they were deviant. Our plantation mistress could best understand herself—in terms of the prevailing ideology—as appropriately deferential to her husband while strict and demanding to her slaves, nurturing and caring to her children. These were the attitudes assigned to her by her "place" in society and that, expressed as the ideology of "true womanhood" (discussed below), celebrated the economic and political dependence of women not because biology actually dictated such dependence but because most people *believed* that it did. Biology, economics, politics, and ideology combined to describe reality. Historical reality, however, is characterized by change. Our antebellum lady's granddaughters would find their reality to be different from hers; changes in each of the four categories would make their world different. Because the complex interaction of these four categories over time is so crucial to understanding women's differing historical experience, each merits fuller discussion.

BIOLOGY

Exploring the past through women, we become aware that history embraces the private sphere of reproduction and domesticity as well as the public sphere of battlefield, court, and legislature. Indeed, changing patterns of reproduction are the key to understanding women's experience; during most of human history, anatomy has been destiny. Without reliable methods of contraception women spent their entire adult lives bearing, rearing, and often burying children, undergoing pregnancy as often as every two years until finally liberated by menopause. So fundamentally has biology defined the stages of women's lives that historians increasingly use the concept of the life cycle—a concept that makes it possible to analyze female behavior by separating women into age and marital groupings (daughters, single women, wives, mothers, grandmothers, widows). Although these stages of the cycle remain constant, the number of years women have spent in each stage has shifted. For example, while women have tended to marry around the age of twenty throughout most of American history, the child-bearing stage of life has changed dramatically. Quaker women in the eighteenth century who could expect to bear children regularly until nearly forty contrast sharply to their mid-twentieth-century counterparts who completed their families by the age of thirty. Since women in the 1950s could expect to live much longer than their colonial forebears and to devote less time to the care of small children, they enjoyed a vastly wider range of choices and were freed, if they chose, to move out of the domestic sphere. Changing degrees of biological constraints have made women's lives—and therefore their history—significantly different from those of men.

Biological differences have also contributed to different assumptions about sexuality. Women have traditionally been regarded as sexual beings. Reference to woman as Eve, the temptress, can be found in much of Western literature. During the nineteenth century, however, assumptions about female sexuality shifted drastically. "Respectable" women came to be seen as passionless creatures whose duty it was to repel the advances of men (who were thought to be more highly sexed by nature) until wifely duty required their submission in the marriage bed. Some historians argue that the Victorian Lady's effort to deny her husband his conjugal "rights" should be seen as an effort to improve women's lot at a time when periodic or even permanent abstinence was often the only reliable form of birth control.[6] (Periodic abstinence in the form of the rhythm method was not effective as a birth control measure in the nineteenth century; only in the 1920s was the ovulation cycle correctly understood and plotted.) Not until the twentieth century and the widespread use of dependable contraceptive devices such as the diaphragm were most Americans able to separate sex from reproduction, to recognize that sexual relations are a valuable and pleasurable part of life for both men and women, and to acknowledge the full dimensions of female sexuality. As historians examine the sermons, marriage manuals, and other writings that told how women were *supposed* to behave and those records that offer evidence as to how they *actually did behave*, we are fast discovering that sexuality has its own history. In that history, too, gender has made a difference.

ECONOMICS

DOMESTIC ECONOMY

To view work through women's eyes provides a new appreciation of the economic function of the home. Homes were—and to an appreciable extent still are— restaurants, nurseries, schools, hospitals, and lodging places. The colonial housewife, for example, was expected not merely to prepare and serve meals but to provide much of the food she brought to the table. The curing of meat and the pickling and preserving of vegetables and fruits were her responsibility, as were the garden, dairy, and poultry yard. Clothing the family was another of her tasks. In the northern colonies and on the frontier this meant not only cutting and sewing various garments but also spinning the thread and weaving and dyeing the cloth that went into clothes, household linens, and quilts. Rag rugs, too, were of her making. While more affluent households might include servants to lighten the physical burdens of the mistress of the house, she had to oversee their training and work, often exercising in the process considerable managerial skills of her own. Wives of poorer men lived more simply, but they, too, were responsible for feeding and clothing their families and—in the case of illness, childbirth, or death—for serving as nurse, pharmacist, midwife, and undertaker who dressed the body for burial.

As the nation developed, women in cities were gradually relieved of some of these tasks. Even in the twentieth century, however, women in rural areas were expected to do arduous household chores, preserve many dozen quarts of food, and also take their turn in the fields as necessity dictated. Because their homes lacked the plumbing and electricity required for use of an electric washing machine, women in 90 percent of the rural households in the United States were still doing laundry by hand as late as 1930. In the tobacco-growing country of the Carolinas and Virginia young girls not only learned household skills but they, along with their brothers, were taught the basics of crop production: how to drop tobacco plants into carefully prepared soil; how to remove worms from the growing plants; how to bind harvested tobacco leaves for curing; and, afterwards, how to tie them into bundles for the trip to market. Although it was usually the man in the family who took the fruits of the harvest to market, whatever the crop, many a prudent farmwife in the eighteenth century as well as the twentieth gathered up her surplus eggs or other foodstuffs to sell or barter. The domestic economy blended unobtrusively into the market economy.

This subtle blending occurred in other ways as well. In hard times women, especially young unmarried daughters, sold their labor, using their pay to sustain the household. Domestic service attracted many women because it involved traditional women's work and, for live-in servants, room and board as well as wages. Those seeking jobs in towns and cities enjoyed a wider range of options: work in a shop often seemed to offer greater independence and dignity. Census takers and many historians perceived these women to be part of the public market economy because they were working for wages. But the women usually thought of themselves as serving the domestic economy. Most regarded wage work as a temporary necessity undertaken in order to help their families in a time of financial stress.

The change in the status of women's work from that of belonging to the family to that of belonging to women themselves was a significant step in their emancipation. Because of economic necessity the change is not yet complete, even in advanced industrialized countries such as the United States. Emancipation is not achieved until the work itself is seen as liberating or until women can spend their income as they wish. It was not until the middle of the nineteenth century that the earnings of a married woman were hers to dispose of as she chose. Although in reality many women did indeed regard their "egg money" as their own, English tradition and colonial practice dictated that when a woman married, control of her earnings automatically passed to her husband. Indeed, all that had been hers was at the wedding transferred to him. Except for certain technical exceptions utilized by the wealthy, everything a woman owned at the time of her marriage and anything she might earn or inherit in the future were her husband's to dispose of as he saw fit, even on the draw of a card or a throw of the dice. The desire of married women to retain or gain control over property that would have been theirs had they been men was an important force in sustaining women's struggle for political rights in the nineteenth century.

MARKET ECONOMY

The location of white women's work in early America was predominantly in the home, as was the case in most preindustrial, rural societies. But even in the colonial period there were many women whose work was performed directly for the market, most notably slave women, who worked on crops destined for sale. Indeed, black women's work has always been part of the market economy in America. For white northern women, however, the pre–Civil War process of industrialization did much to transform work. The spinning of thread, weaving of cloth, sewing of clothes, preserving of foods—all tasks formerly done in the homes as part of a domestic economy—were now done in mills and factories as part of the market economy. Poorer women followed these traditional tasks into the public sector as the economy modernized. They became part of a paid labor force, as did their children, since low wages made it impossible for many families to subsist on the income of one adult worker. Yet, surprisingly, women's work patterns changed less than we once assumed. Work in the public sector, as in the private sector, continued to conform in large measure to family pressure and to traditional role expectations about what women could and should do, to the great financial detriment of women wage earners.

The extent to which female employment patterns in industry were shaped by family needs is apparent in a study of a New England textile factory that employed an average of fourteen thousand workers in the years before World War I. Women were very much a part of that work force. As young girls, they went into the mill to supplement family income, often allowing brothers to improve their job prospects by staying in school; as wives, they withdrew when children were born and returned as mothers of small children when the perilous state of family finances required them to do so; as mothers of grown children, they returned to stay.[7] Thus family responsibilities were a crucial factor not only in determining at what stage in their life cycle women were gainfully employed but also in explaining why their employment patterns differed from those of male workers. (Indeed, it was not until after World War II that the number of working mothers with small children increased dramatically.)

Family responsibilities did much to determine *when* women worked; they also affected *where* women worked. Since employers shared the popular belief that women's primary obligations were familial and their basic talents domestic, female wage earners were persistently channeled into jobs that corresponded with the kind of work done in the domestic sphere or with characteristics long associated with women. Even in colonial times most women who performed services for pay worked as housekeepers, cooks, nurses, or midwives. In the nineteenth century women seeking new avenues through which to gain economic independence laid claim to the teaching and nursing professions by emphasizing that the attributes required for such work were precisely those considered unique to the female sex. Thus nursing, considered in pre–Civil War years an occupation no respectable woman would enter, was eventually touted as a profession eminently suited to women. Providence, after all, had endowed the fairer sex with that "compassion which penetrate[s] the heart, that instinct which divines and anticipates the wants of the sick, and the patience which pliantly bends to all their caprices."[8] As the economy grew more complex, middle-class women infiltrated the ranks of librarians and secretaries. These occupations had been primarily male, but, like teaching and nursing, were redefined so as to emphasize the nurturing, service-oriented qualities ascribed to women—with a corresponding decrease in pay. Newer industries provided new job titles but old work categories. Receptionists, social workers, and stewardesses were hired by employers still convinced that the tasks required in these jobs were consistent with the attributes and skills traditionally associated with women. Because gender rather than individual talent or capability has been the primary consideration, the result of this kind of stereotyping has been to segregate women into certain kinds of work, whether in the professions or in industry. Occupations and professions that for one generation constituted a lifeline have become a chain to the next; once a form of work has been defined as female, it has invariably become associated with low pay and minimal prestige. Pay and prestige have been reserved for those professions remaining overwhelmingly male. It is not surprising that until very recently women in significant numbers have been effectively barred from wielding scalpels, addressing juries, passing laws, or designing buildings.

Working-class women, especially, have been victims of discrimination. Low pay, long hours, and difficult—often dangerous—working conditions have characterized industrial work for both male and female employees during much of our history. Southern mills, where discrimination was based on race as well as sex, afford a classic example of occupational segregation and the inferior position of white and particularly black women. In a typical southern textile mill in the 1930s management positions were reserved for college-educated white males. Men from working-class backgrounds monopolized supervisory and skilled positions. Semiskilled operative positions were divided among white men and women, with men predominating in better-paying jobs in the card room and dye houses. Women predictably took their place in the spinning and sewing rooms. Black men and women divided the manual labor. Opportunities to work up to a better position were confined to a few white males. For factory and mill women, already bearing the brunt of housework and child care, wage labor frequently meant—and still means—insecure employment in hazardous, low-paying, dead-end jobs.

While unionization enabled many working men to better their lot, it has not provided the same benefit for women. Male members, fearing women would work for lower pay and threaten their jobs, often barred women workers from union membership during the early years of organizing. Even in unions that included women, labor leaders sought only limited economic gains for female workers. They, too, thought of the public economy as an essentially male preserve, and they failed to confront the problem of occupational segregation. The basic inequities built into the system have gone unchallenged until very recently, when pressure from the federal government has helped to produce changes.

Thus segregated into jobs associated with low status and low pay, denied equal pay for equal work, burdened doubly as the parent primarily responsible for home and child care, women have experienced work in the public sector differently from men. Viewed through women's eyes, work in the public sector is different. While it has given women a small measure of economic independence, it has not provided the monetary rewards and the avenues to power and autonomy open to some men. The history of women's participation in the labor force is, therefore, a history of marginality.

POLITICS

Most Americans, for much of their history, were convinced that God and nature had decreed that the two sexes inhabit different spheres and have different roles. Men's roles were public and political, women's domestic. Men's activities were defined as distinct from women's activities even when goals were shared, the place of work the same, and the physical effort equally taxing (as John Mack Faragher shows in his description of work on a family farm). To be sure, such distinctions might be temporarily suspended in emergency situations. Women worked together with men in the fields to harvest hay before the crop was destroyed by rain; they worked to replace men in factories, on railroads, and at construction sites during World Wars I and II. When the emergency subsided, however, conventional patterns again prevailed. Given the tenacity of these assumptions about separate roles and spheres, it is not surprising that women seeking to enter the public world were inhibited by a formidable set of expectations about where men and women belonged and how they should behave.

In Anglo-American tradition the right to participate in political activities— jury duty, officeholding, voting—was conditioned on the holding of property. Since married women could not direct the use of their property, it seemed to follow that they could be neither jurors, nor voters, nor officeholders. That politics was considered a male domain, that women were simply not political beings, is an understanding as old as Western civilization. Aristotle, whose classic work provided the basic terms by which Westerners have understood politics, said that men alone realized themselves as citizens. It is no accident that the civic *virtue* he extolled derives from the same root as the word *virile*. Women, Aristotle maintained, realized themselves only within the confines of the household. Their relationship to the world of politics, like their social status, was derivative—through fathers, husbands, and sons.

Colonists brought this understanding with them to the New World. Even the Revolution, in the course of which the relationship of men to the state was radically redefined, did little to reorient the relationship of women to the state. It was left for women of the post-Revolutionary generations to reassess the promise of republicanism and to devise political strategies by which they would demand full inclusion in the republic.

The political history of American women has been out of phase with that of American men. In the early nineteenth century propertyless white men were successful in demanding the vote; following the Civil War black men were en-franchised. After 1880 one of the major political challenges facing men was to mobilize successful coalitions in support of particular candidates and programs. The political tasks that women faced after 1880, however, remained those that men had already accomplished; women still needed to move from petitioners to voters to electable candidates. Only recently have women in increasing numbers begun to run for office and to mobilize political coalitions in support of candi-dates and programs. Thus the political experience of men and women in America has diverged widely.

The political activities of American women have generally fallen into two categories. The first might be called the Politics of Inclusion. It involves all efforts to become part of the political system: suffrage, jury service, officeholding, and the shaping of policies and statutes. A major goal of the Politics of Inclusion has been and still is to secure equal treatment under the law, to change the many statutes that treat men and women differently. Not until 1975, for example, did the Supreme Court require that women be assigned to juries on the same terms as men.

The second category might be called the Politics of Reform. It proposes to achieve a more just and orderly society. Among these goals have been the aboli-tion of slavery, protective legislation for women workers, and racial justice. Also involved have been radical attempts to restructure society along various so-cialist lines.

Women gave their loyalty sometimes to the Politics of Inclusion, sometimes to the Politics of Reform, sometimes to both. For example, Carrie Chapman Catt, who was president of the National American Woman Suffrage Association from 1914 to 1920, placed inclusionary politics first on her own agenda; only after suffrage was achieved did she work primarily in the peace movement. On the other hand, Emma Goldman distrusted the system so much that she felt the vote was inconsequential for the reformed society of which she dreamed. An example of someone who combined the Politics of Reform with the Politics of Inclusion was the temperance advocate Frances Willard, who supported suffrage as a vehicle by which the social reform she was primarily committed to might be achieved.

A distinctive feature of women's reformist politics has been the way in which women have made their *domestic* experience into a *public* issue and, through this transformation, enhanced both their domestic and public roles. Sometimes women justified moving into the political arena by arguing that public involve-ment would permit them to fulfill their domestic responsibilities more compe-tently. Jane Addams made this appeal when she argued that women should have the vote so that they could elect city officials who would see to it that rotting garbage was removed from homes, decaying meat taken out of markets, and polluted water purified; otherwise, the best efforts of mothers to assure their children clean homes and wholesome food were to no avail. Other women supported the Sheppard-Towner Maternity Act of 1921 on the grounds that women had a special interest in maternal health and infant care. In these and similar cases women worked in the public sphere to protect and improve the domestic one. But once they moved into the public life of politics, no matter how much they justified their presence there in traditionalist terms—arguing that they were acting only as partisans of domestic virtue, health, and safety—the fact of the matter was that they had done something quite untraditional.

Women who crusaded for legislation to prohibit the manufacture and sale of alcoholic beverages were a case in point. The women themselves may have *said* in traditionalist phrases that their only concern was with home and children—homes destroyed and children abused by alcoholic fathers—but what they *did* on behalf of liquor-free homes involved public speeches, parades, demonstrations, and even lobbying of public officials. These actions were certainly not traditionalist—at least not for women in the nineteenth century. Nevertheless, traditionalist words, when added to the innovation of widespread and effective political action, were part of a process. Changes within this process were not always anticipated but came as women in the nineteenth century created for themselves a public life not necessarily at odds with domestic life but as an extension of it. By looking at reformist crusades as an opportunity for women to establish a public role, we begin to understand that, whether or not their goals were feminist, the process itself was a liberating one.

IDEOLOGY

Finally, to examine the past with a new sensitivity to women's experience is to discover how profoundly women's lives have been shaped by ideologies that have developed out of their distinctive biological, economic, and political histories. Implicit in the concept of ideology is the emphasis on the fact that ideas are cradled in social experience and, when used to explain that experience, form interworking networks of meaning that have a compelling attractiveness to those who believe them. The word *ideology* can be used in a negative way—to convey the idea that ideologies distort reality—or in a neutral way. We use it in a neutral way, in part because we do not believe that ideas based upon social experience and explaining that experience *necessarily* distort reality. (Historical "reality" is itself often a matter of social consciousness, i.e., defined by the groups explaining it.) Thus by ideology we mean the terms and assumptions by which Americans think about women, the notions they have about what is appropriate demeanor for women, and the ideas they have about the kind of roles it is normal for women to assume and the kind of goals they should have for their lives.[9]

For example, since the early nineteenth century one of the most pervasive ideologies has been what one historian has called the "Cult of True Womanhood," which extolled the virtues of piety, sexual purity, submissiveness, and domesticity. In the sermons they heard and the books they read, women were instructed to internalize these virtues and to dedicate themselves to the private sphere, nurturing and serving their families and transforming their homes into a "Haven in a Heartless World."[10] "Woman's sphere," declared a newspaper in 1850, "is about the domestic altar and within the tranquil precincts of the social circle. When she transgresses that sphere and mingles in the miserable brawlings and insane agitations of the day, she descends from her lofty elevation and becomes an object of disgust and contempt."[11]

Educational theory and practice reflected and perpetuated many of these same assumptions about women's nature, capacities, and proper place. The belief that women's brains and nervous systems simply were not capable of the sustained intellectual effort expected of men and, more important, that women's place was in the home led to the founding of special female academies that emphasized religion and the domestic arts rather than the classical training provided for young men. Too much study of Greek, Latin, philosophy, and logic, it was feared, might make young females unfit for their primary role as wives and mothers. Given women's inferior mental capacity and their delicate emotional system, intense intellectual debate was also considered inappropriate. School texts often disseminated ideas about correct attitudes and proper demeanor.

Dress, too, reflected ideology insofar as it mirrored what people believed themselves to be and what they wanted others to believe them to be. In the nineteenth century, when women of affluence were expected to be both home centered and leisured, their clothing announced that expectation. They wore boned, tightly laced corsets, which inhibited breathing, and hoops or multiple layers of long, heavy petticoats, which made vigorous walking difficult. Fashion seemed to conspire to keep the lady hobbled to her home—to the dismay of radicals who believed that an uncorseted, loose, shorter dress supplemented by bloomers rather than petticoats would improve women's physical and emotional health by making it easier for them to exercise and to move about more freely in the public world.

An ideology that sought to impose on all women a pattern of life only marginally appropriate for middle-class women could also serve to insulate women from a clear understanding of political and economic relationships. Social divisions made it difficult for women to perceive the subordination they shared. The shopkeeper's wife whose divorce from an alcoholic husband deprived her of custody of her children might underpay the immigrant seamstress who made her clothes. Women's perception of themselves as an oppressed group was further masked by the fact that, unlike other minority groups, they lived on intimate terms with their oppressors, deriving their status from fathers and husbands and, in the case of the more fortunate, benefiting from social and economic advantages that distinguished them from other women. (The respect and privileges accorded a married woman often depended—and in some respects still do—on the position of her husband in the community, not on her own accomplishments.) So completely did many women internalize conventional wisdom about women's proper place that they rejected any attempt to change it.

Women did, however, devise methods of coping with the more constraining aspects of their culture. They struggled to gain some measure of reproductive control not only through abstinence from sexual intercourse but also through widespread use of dangerous abortive devices. They subverted legal constraints on their economic independence by recourse to trusteeships and premarital contracts to protect their own property. They sought and found solace and emotional sustenance in the churches, which welcomed them as communicants, offered them the companionship of fellow believers, and lauded their piety. Indeed, women were considered by nature to be more pious than men, a belief that women could exploit to enlarge their sphere of public activity. Religion, for example, confirmed a sense of mission that found expression in the church-related but increasingly secular female reform societies so prevalent in the nineteenth century—organizations such as the Female Missionary Society for the Poor of the City of New York. Out of common needs, experiences, and associations women created what might be called a female culture, characterized by strong affectionate ties among women of the same class and family networks. Although historians have only begun to explore this subculture, the essay by Carroll Smith-Rosenberg is an important introduction to this "female world of love and ritual." Moreover, as women began moving beyond the home, they brought with them these strong emotional ties to other women, thus creating female networks. These networks provided crucial encouragement and support for individuals whose public activities made them out of step with conventional society, whether in battle on behalf of birth control or against "demon rum" or child labor.

While ideology is reflected in newspapers, books, sermons, and even dress, the real test of its power is how we live our lives, what options we believe are open to us, and what choices we make. For poorer women who could not financially afford to devote themselves exclusively to the domestic sphere and the rearing of their children, the Cult of True Womanhood bore little resemblance to the reality of their everyday lives. For many middle-class women who could afford financially *and* emotionally to live their lives in accordance with these ideological dictates, prescription and practice were one. For some women, however, the emotional cost was too high because the constraints seemed too great. Inherent in the nineteenth-century Cult of True Womanhood and in its twentieth-century counterpart, the Feminine Mystique, is the premise that women's lives are determined by their biology and by the gratification that they might find in self-abnegating service to others rather than in the more abstract exercise of the mind or the pursuit of a career in a traditionally male profession. While these beliefs have served in varying measure to limit all women, they have proved particularly burdensome to those individuals endowed with special talents or creativity that they sought to develop fully.

Women who wished to be artists or intellectuals have encountered difficulties not usually experienced by men of equal talent. They discovered that they lived in a society which assumed that women's family obligations must take precedence over all other activities. As late as 1935 Margaret Mead, whose own career in anthropology was one of great productivity and distinction, observed wryly that a woman might identify herself as "a woman and therefore less an achieving individual, or an achieving individual and therefore less a woman." If she chose the first option, the one presumably consistent with her biological destiny, she was more likely to be "a loved object, the kind of girl whom men will woo and boast of, toast and marry." If she opted for the second, however, she lost "as a woman, her chance for the kind of love she wants."[12] The ideological message delivered was quite clear. Although it is impossible to measure precisely how such messages affected behavior, there are various indications suggesting that they did indeed affect women's perceptions of the options open to them.

CHALLENGES TO PREVAILING VIEWS

We also know that women who challenged the piety, submissiveness, and sexual purity associated with "true womanhood" were punished. Women in Puritan Massachusetts could, as Anne Hutchinson learned, be privately pious but not publicly prophetic. While Hutchinson's remarkable personality attracted to her cause men as well as women who believed in her religious vision, she suffered banishment. In nineteenth-century America women whose sexuality was celebrated, like those in the Oneida community, or whose marital patterns were unusual, like those among the Mormons, were able to withstand social disapproval of their deviance only by living in relatively isolated communities. Even those women who assumed for themselves moral responsibilities which were the logical extension of women's piety found that, if they pursued those responsibilities with greater independence and public activism than society deemed appropriate, they, too, could be condemned as unwomanly. Accordingly, southern ladies who openly agitated against lynching in the early twentieth century discovered that one could be opposed to legal violence in theory but not in practice. The much-vaunted protection that the South bestowed upon the fairer sex existed only so long as the ladies obeyed the "rules." To deviate from the norm was to be labeled unfeminine. "Tomboys" might be acceptable; "mannish" women were not. The accusation of "mannishness" was tinged with intimations of being "unnatural"—sexually deviant—or, if one were not too threatening, merely eccentric.

Despite pressures to conform, there have always been individuals who dissented from prevailing beliefs about women's proper role. For some, frustration, doubts, and questions developed slowly, sometimes requiring years before culminating in outright revolt. Ironic as it may seem, those very doubts and questions could be nourished by precisely those institutions that encouraged women to conform to accepted standards of behavior. Religion and education were two-edged swords. Schools conveyed the expectations of society. But inasmuch as people were encouraged to think, the result might be a questioning of those very expectations.

Similarly, organized religion, while reinforcing traditional values, contributed to the very process by which they were slowly eroded. For example, Protestant evangelicalism, in its emphasis on the Christian home and the place of women within it, stressed—as did nineteenth-century society generally—piety, domesticity, and a self-denying submissiveness. However, the evangelical woman, whether she was Baptist, Methodist, Presbyterian, or even Episcopalian, was encouraged to be "useful." Although the initial intent was to discourage frivolity, a woman who was encouraged to be self-disciplined, sober, and reflective—"the mistress of herself and her actions"—could also become a woman who thought for herself.[13] As she participated in church-related activities and the many reform societies that were an extension of the religious impulse, she could discover an institutional framework within which to meet other women in networks of associates as well as develop leadership skills and become competent in dealing with the public. Efforts to improve the plight of others could lead some women to the conclusion that their own condition needed improving. Thus women active in the antislavery crusade of the 1840s and women active in the civil rights movement of the 1960s learned in those movements not only how to be effective organizers and dissenters but how easily those dedicated to achieving the rights of one group could perpetuate the assumptions and practices that denied the very same rights to another. For some women the result, in the mid-twentieth century as in the mid-nineteenth, was to transform reformers into feminists; advocacy of racial justice developed into commitment to sexual equality.

By whatever process women came to question prevailing assumptions about women's place, they expressed their frustrations in many different ways. Those who were unwilling or unable to confront the real source of their distress sometimes found release from conflicting feelings in psychosomatic illnesses or that most common affliction of nineteenth-century women, hysteria. Those who were able to recognize the conflict between society's expectations and their own needs sometimes expressed their dissent privately, thereby escaping the censure society directs toward those who challenge the status quo. Others expressed their dissent more openly, turning to groups sharing their views. Incorporating equality for women into the party's public statements, socialists enlisted thousands of female members in the first decades of this century. Other women gravitated toward explicitly feminist groups that, although initially quite small, were active in the North before the Civil War and grew dramatically in the decades before World War I. But while organized movements for women's rights have flourished intermittently, it was not until the development of the contemporary women's movement of the 1960s and 1970s that women in significant numbers embraced an ideology that radically challenges traditional values and assumptions, an ideology that incorporates not only family and service but ambition and achievement.

FEMINIST AND TRADITIONALIST

Contemporary feminists reject traditional views about women's role and place because they see these views as supporting attitudes and practices that deny women equality. Women, they believe, should be able to define themselves as individuals, choosing work that at least provides economic independence and at best brings personal and professional fulfillment. Women should also be able to express freely their sexuality and sexual preferences; to decide whether and when to marry; to choose whether and when to have children. As today's feminists have injected these concerns into the public consciousness, they have criticized values that define women primarily as reproductive beings who, simply because they bear children, must automatically lead domestic, mothering lives. It is not surprising that feminists also reject the notion that the most significant goal of women's lives is to make themselves attractive to the men who will provide for them. (Nineteenth-century critics were also scornful of the dependent women who exchanged sexual favors for economic support, whether within marriage or outside of it.)

Because feminists value independence and equality, they see as absolutely basic the right of all women to control their own bodies through access to birth control measures and, when necessary, safe, legal abortions. Believing that financial independence is also essential to full freedom and autonomy, contemporary feminists are very concerned with economic status. They have explored ways in which women working solely within the home might receive economic recognition for their labor. They have criticized those factors that account for the inferior position of women who work outside the home. Because such women now constitute a majority of all American women, and because they average in earnings only 60 percent of those received by men, it would be fair to say that a majority of American women as a class are directly discriminated against in the economic system. Therefore feminists attack discriminatory practices on the part of employers who do not pay men and women equal wages for equal work. They point out the occupational segregation evidenced in the fact that 80 percent of all working women are concentrated in 20 of 411 occupations, the vast majority working as nurses, teachers, saleswomen, and secretaries. The socialization that channels many men into high-paying professions and trades and many women into low-paying, "pink-collar" work is especially deplored. This socialization is epitomized by parents who give young daughters nurses' kits and young sons doctors' bags, guidance counselors who urge mathematically talented girls to become bookkeepers and boys to become engineers.

To escape this double bind, feminists use books, toys, and parental example to demonstrate to young girls that they need not limit their aspirations. They also recognize, however, that the young woman who aspires to a high-level business or professional career will in reality have two full-time jobs if she chooses to have a family in a society in which women are still seen as primarily responsible for home and child care.

The effort of contemporary feminists to redistribute the burdens of the domestic economy makes them part of a tradition. A few feminists in the nineteenth century and a few more early in the twentieth, wrestling with precisely this problem, advocated public schemes, such as kitchenless apartment buildings, while urging a new set of private decisions within the family as to who would do various chores.[14] Contemporary feminists call for institutional measures such as low-cost, quality child care facilities, maternity leaves, and flexible work schedules. They also propose changes in attitudes and life styles, believing that couples working in the public sector can reassess responsibilities so that men and women share equally the burdens and pleasures associated with earning a living, maintaining a household, and rearing a family.

Private action, however, is no substitute for the broad institutional changes that many feminists believe will come when women, historically powerless, have the political power necessary to change a society in which sexual inequality has for centuries been a pervasive and persistent reality. In order to become part of the political power structure women, they believe, must no longer be confined—or confine themselves—to housekeeping chores within the political parties. Instead they must seek and hold elective and appointive office at every level commensurate with their numbers. Having women in positions of political power is a dubious gain, however, unless those women are willing to support the kind of changes feminists believe are necessary if all women are to achieve greater reproductive, economic, and political control of their lives. They are convinced that women and men alike must examine existing values and assumptions about what is appropriate for men and especially women to be and do, ultimately putting together and acting upon a set of new values that liberate rather than constrain and oppress. The end result, many feminists believe, must be the re-structuring of both persons and institutions—in short, a feminist transformation.

Challenges to long-standing beliefs and behavior, whether issued now or in the past, have been criticized by traditionalists. They perceive feminists' demands for equality not as an effort to remove discrimination based solely on gender and to expand options for men and women alike but rather as a rejection of cherished norms and values. Men who possess power and privileges they do not wish to share understandably see in feminism a threat. Moreover, many women who believe they have lived useful and admirable lives by traditional rules see feminist attacks on traditional sex roles as an attack on a way of life they have perfected—and hence an attack on them personally. Thus feminist insistence that women should be able to seek fulfillment in the public world of work and power as well as in the private world of home and family is viewed by traditionalists as an egocentric demand that places personal gratification above familial duty. By the same token, the demand that women themselves be the ultimate judge of whether and when to bear children is seen by some not as a legitimate desire to control one's own body but as an escape from maternal obligations that threatens the future of the family and ultimately, therefore, society itself.

To suggest that some women find feminism a route to personal fulfillment while other women find that route in traditionalism is not to suggest that the ideological history of women is bipolar. It embraces many variants. Traditionalist women may be as suspicious of male-controlled institutions as feminists; feminist women may be as "feminine" as traditionalists. Traditional women may be as publicly active on behalf of their goals as feminists; feminists may be as concerned with family as traditionalists. Both groups identify with a sisterhood and see "women's issues" as special ones, although they do not consistently agree as to what they are. Partisans of the two groups may unite or divide along class, occupational, or political lines. But no matter what the issue and the proposed solution, wherever women are on the ideological spectrum they are part of women's history.

"Woman has always been acting and thinking . . . at the center of life," wrote Mary Beard a half century ago; but the significance of women's activities has, until recent years, often been discounted and rarely been understood. The scholarship of the past decades has spotlighted much that had lain in the shadows of history, unnoticed and unappreciated. As we have examined that scholarship, we find ourselves less impressed by sex role constraints—which were very real—than by the vigor and subtlety with which women have defined the terms of their existence. These creative experiences show how the private lives of historical persons can help us understand the rich complexities of change. To study women's history, then, is to take part in a bold enterprise that can eventually lead us to a new history, one that, by taking into account both sexes, should tell us more about each other and, therefore, our collective selves.

NOTES

1. David M. Potter, "American Women and the American Character" (1962), in *History and American Society: Essays of David M. Potter*, ed. Don E. Fehrenbacher (New York, 1979), p. 279.

2. Potter, "American Women and the American Character," p. 280.

3. These issues have been thoughtfully explored by Joan Kelly. See "The Doubled Vision of Feminist Theory," *Feminist Studies* 5 (1979):216–27; and Joan Kelly-Gadol, "The Social Relation of the Sexes: Methodological Implications of Women's History," *Signs: Journal of Women in Culture and Society* 1 (1976):809–24.

4. Donald G. Mathews, 'Women's History/Everyone's History," in *Women in New Worlds*, ed. Hilah F. Thomas and Rosemary Skinner Keller (Nashville, 1981), p. 30.

5. Gerda Lerner, *The Majority Finds Its Past: Placing Women in History* (New York, 1979), pp. 49–50. Lerner's essays in this collection include not only her pioneering contributions to women's history but also her important effort to set the history of women in the general historical context. Her explorations, both narrative and theoretical, of the possibilities inherent in feminist scholarship have done much to shape our own thinking. See also her collection of documents, *The Female Experience: An American Documentary* (Indianapolis, 1977).

6. Nancy F. Cott, "Passionlessness: An Interpretation of Victorian Sexual Ideology, 1790–1850," *Signs: Journal of Women in Culture and Society* 4 (1978):219–36.

7. Tamara Hareven and Randolph Langenbach, *Amoskeag: Life and Work in an American Factory-City* (New York, 1978).

8. *Raleigh* (N.C.) *News and Observer*, November 24, 1904.

9. For discussion of the concept of ideology, see Clifford Geertz, "Ideology as a Cultural System," in *Ideology and Discontent*, ed. David Apter (New York, 1964), pp. 47–76.

10. Barbara Welter, "The Cult of True Womanhood: 1820–1860," *American Quarterly* 18 (1966):151–74; Christopher Lasch, *Haven in a Heartless World* (New York, 1977).

11. *Raleigh* (N.C.) *Register*, 1850, quoted in Albert Coates, *By Her Own Bootstraps: A Saga of Women in North Carolina* (n.p., 1975), pp. 142–43.

12. Margaret Mead, "Sex and Achievement," *Forum* 94 (1935):303.

13. Mary McGehee to John W. F. Burruss, May 29, 1836, in John C. Burruss Papers, Louisiana State University Library, Baton Rouge.

14. See Dolores Hayden, *The Grand Domestic Revolution: A History of Feminist Designs for American Homes, Neighborhoods, and Cities* (Cambridge, Mass., 1981).

I

Traditional America

1600–1820

Most American histories treat the colonial period as a time when government and order were imposed upon a wilderness. The important subjects tend to be Indian wars, international trade, the establishment of legislatures, and rivalries between British colonies and those of other nations. The first woman mentioned is usually Pocahontas, the innocent Indian princess who allegedly saved the life of the hero of Jamestown, Captain John Smith. The second woman who appears is often Anne Hutchinson, who was banished from Massachusetts Bay Colony for heresy. Both met premature and unpleasant deaths. Unaccustomed to the climate of England, where she had been taken to be shown to Queen Elizabeth, Pocahontas died of pneumonia. Hutchinson was massacred by Indians during a raid on her lonely dwelling in what is now Westchester County, New York. The reader who concludes from these examples that women were not very important in colonial America, and that the few women whom we remember are likely to have been troublesome and to have come to a bad end, may be pardoned.

But if we pose Mary Beard's question and ask, What did colonial America look like, seen through women's eyes? the picture changes. More constructive than troublesome, women were among the founders of virtually every colony. Indeed, a settlement counted itself as having passed the stage of a temporary camp only after it had attracted a reasonable complement of women. A sex ratio approaching 100 (that is, 100 women to every 100 men) was taken to be evidence that the settlement was here to stay. Once founded, communities were maintained in large part by women's labor. The productivity of housekeepers is not easily measured, but more than forty years ago Julia Cherry Spruill established the complexity of the tasks performed in frontier households. Housekeeping, after all, provided the context of the employment of nearly half the adult population, both slave and free.

It may be that America seemed to women less radical a change from the Old World than it did to men. The terrors of the ocean crossing and of the wilderness were, of course, shared by all. In the farming communities Europeans planted along the eastern seaboard daily tasks proceeded in the manner of England, whether the agricultural laborer were farmer or farmer's wife. As Catherine M. Scholten's description shows, the rituals of childbirth were transmitted intact from Old World to New, although it may well have been that the rate of survival of mother and infant was better in the American countryside, where the dangers of infection were far fewer than in the towns and cities of Europe. By contrast, the innovations that made the colonies most distinctive from the Old World—especially governmental institutions like town meetings and provincial legislatures—were settings from which women were barred.

One institution in which women were welcome was the church, but despite repeated quotation of St. Paul's rule that "in Christ there is neither man nor woman," believers of every faith were very conscious of gender distinctions. As Lyle Koehler's account of Anne Hutchinson's trials demonstrates, Hutchinson's heresy was compounded by the fact that it was formulated by a woman. Many of the questions in her trial were grounded in the objection that she had stepped out of her proper place. For women, Puritans had special expectations and understood there to be special punishments. When dissenting women like Mary Dyer were delivered of malformed infants, John Winthrop saw no reason to be surprised at the divine punishment. Witchcraft, too, was a religious heresy; it, too, was gender specific, a woman's crime. Although witchcraft accusations normally arose in places where the entire community was troubled, the accusers were usually teen-aged girls, and the "witches" usually women.

English colonists brought with them a system of property rights which assumed that any property held by a woman normally passed to her husband's control when she married. The right to participate in the political system—to vote and to hold office—was conditioned on holding property. It therefore seemed logical to colonists that political rights be granted only to men. Since girls could not grow up to be legislators, or ministers, or lawyers, little care was taken to provide them with any but the most elementary forms of schooling. "How many female minds, rich with native genius and noble sentiment, have been lost to the world, and all their mental treasures buried in oblivion?" mourned one writer.[1]

Like it or not, women were part of the community. What they chose to do or not to do set constraints on men's options. The Revolutionary army, lacking an effective quartermaster corps, was dependent on women for nursing, cooking, and cleaning. The army, in turn, could not march as quickly as Washington would have liked because provision had to be made for the "woemin of the army." The task of the recruiting officer was eased when men could rely on their female relatives to keep family farms and mills in operation, fend off squatters, and protect family property by their heavy labor, often at grave physical risk. We have no simple calculus for measuring the extent to which women's services made it possible for men to act in certain ways during the Revolution, but it is clear that women's work provided the civilian context in which the war was carried on.

When the war was over and the political structure of the new nation was being reshaped in federal and state constitutions, little attention was given to the political role women might directly play. Yet women did have distinctive political interests. For example, if women had had the vote in 1789, they might well have used it to establish pensions for widows of veterans. Women's distinctive needs tended to be discounted as trivial. It was left to women of succeeding generations to accomplish for themselves what the Revolution had not.

NOTE

1. Clio [pseud.], "Thoughts on Female Education," *Royal American Magazine*, January 1774, pp. 9–10.

JULIA CHERRY SPRUILL
Housewives and Their Helpers

One of the greatest barriers to an accurate assessment of women's role in the community has been the habit of assuming that what women did was not very important. Housekeeping has long been women's work, and housework has long been regarded as trivial. Julia Cherry Spruill was one of the first historians who understood that housekeeping can be a complex task and that real skill and intelligence might be exercised in performing it. More significantly, she understood that the services housekeepers performed were an important part of the economic arrangements that sustain the family and need to be taken into account when describing any community or society. Note the differences Spruill found among the work of poor, middle-class, and wealthy housekeepers. She was unusually sensitive to mistress-servant relationships.

Janet Schaw, visiting Carolina in 1775, found there much that was not to her liking; but the women she regarded with admiration. Generally, she observed, they were excellent housewives and mothers, carefully instructing their daughters in "the family duties necessary to the sex," and in "other accomplishments and genteel manners."[1] She praised her Carolina-born sister-in-law for her domestic accomplishments, declaring that her dairy and garden were proofs of her industry;[2] and she thought Mrs. Cornelius Harnett a woman of extraordinary good sense. "They tell me," she wrote, "that the Mrs. of this place ["Hilton," seat of Cornelius Harnett] is a pattern of industry. She has (it seems) a garden, from which she supplies the town with what vegetables they use, also with mellons and other fruits. She even descends to make minced pies, cheesecakes, tarts and little biskets, which she sends down to town once or twice a day, besides her eggs, poultry and butter, and she is the only one who continues to have Milk."[3]

The domestic achievements of other women are on record. Colonel William Byrd of Virginia boasted of his daughters to an English friend: "They are every Day up to their Elbows in Housewifery, which will qualify them effactually for useful Wives and if they live long enough, for Notable Women."[4] Fithian praised the wife of Councillor Robert Carter of "Nomini" as "a remarkable Economist," and several times noted her housewifery activities in his journal. On one occasion, she showed him her stock of mutton and fowl for the winter, observing that to live in the country and take no pleasure in cattle and domestic poultry would be to her a manner of life too tedious to endure. . . . Eliza Pinckney of South Carolina, though distinguished herself for intellectual attainments and agricultural experiments rather than household occupations, nevertheless was

Excerpted from "Housewives and Their Helpers," Chap. 4 of *Women's Life and Work in the Southern Colonies* by Julia Cherry Spruill (Chapel Hill: University of North Carolina Press, 1938). Copyright © 1938 by the University of North Carolina Press. Reprinted by permission of the publisher. Notes have been renumbered and cross-references adjusted.

proud of her daughter's housewifery. Soon
after the daughter's marriage, she wrote
her son-in-law: "I am glad your little Wife
looks well to the ways of her household.
. . . The management of a dairy is an
amusement she has always been fond of,
. . . I find, as you say, she sends her instructions far and near. . . . she has people out gathering simples, different kinds
of snake-root, and pink-root, and is dis-
tilling herbs and flowers."[5]

There were doubtless many other capable housewives. The home was the only
field in which superior women might distinguish themselves. It was by no means a
narrow sphere, but one wherein individual
initiative and executive ability as well as
many other talents might be put to use.
But the fact that the care of a family was
the only career open to them and that it
furnished an opportunity for the expression of broad and varied abilities scarcely
justifies a general assumption that all colonial women lived up to or even realized
the possibilities of their calling. Their domestic activities, like those of women today, varied in accordance with their personal inclinations and capacities as well as
their social and economic position. Wives
of large planters and slaveholders, ladies
in town mansions, women in frontier cabins, and the poorer sort in town, country,
and backwoods naturally had very different employments, and all women of the
same class by no means had the same interest, training, and skill in household affairs.

More is known of the life of the mistress on a large plantation than of other
classes. She usually had a variety of interesting employments, sufficient help to
save her from drudgery, and opportunities
to express many-sided abilities. Her chief
duties had to do with providing food for
her large family and the innumerable
guests enjoying her ever-ready hospitality.
She had not merely to see to the cooking
and serving of food but also to arrange for
her supplies, many of which came from

her own garden, smokehouse, poultry
yard, and dairy. Some idea of the enormous quantity of provisions used in great
houses is indicated in Fithian's report of a
conversation with the mistress of "Nomini." She informed him that her family
consumed annually 27,000 pounds of pork
and twenty beeves, 550 bushels of wheat,
four hogsheads of rum and 150 gallons of
brandy. One hundred pounds of flour
were used weekly by the immediate
household; white laborers and Negroes
ate corn meal.[6]

A feature of social life increasing the
responsibilities of the mistress was the
custom of inviting into her home all persons needing shelter and refreshment,
strangers as well as friends. Beverley
wrote that a traveler in Virginia needed
no better recommendation to the generosity of the people than that he was a "human creature." If he wanted food or lodging, all he need do was to inquire the way
to the nearest gentleman's seat.[7] The other
southern colonies had the same reputation
for hospitality. . . . A visitor in South
Carolina in 1751 wrote that the inhabitants kept Negroes at their gates near the
public roads to invite travelers in for refreshments.[8]

The mistress had not only to be Lady
Bountiful to these strangers within her
gates, but had also to be prepared for unexpected visits from friends and relatives.
Though they sometimes dined out by special invitation, the colonists considered
such formality unnecessary. Whole coach
loads of young and old with retinues of
servants felt no hesitation in descending
without warning upon an unsuspecting
matron, and she was supposed to lodge
and feed them however great their number might be. It is true, however, that she
was not expected to furnish a great deal
in the way of comforts. A place at the table and a half or even a third share in a
bed was all that any guest expected. A bed
to oneself was a rare luxury and a private
room unthought of. . . .

A surprising variety of vegetables appeared on gentlewomen's tables. The colonists paid great attention to their gardens, importing skilled gardeners as well as plants and seeds from the Mother Country, and experimenting extensively with native plants. Dr. Mazzei, who came to Virginia in 1773 to help introduce the cultivation of several agricultural products of Italy and was entertained in many of the best homes, observed that the housewives were very ambitious to place before their guests fruits and vegetables out of season.[9] By successive plantings and the use of greenhouses and hotbeds, the energetic matron made her menus varied and attractive. Beverley declared that kitchen gardens throve nowhere better than in Virginia, where they had all the "culinary plants" that grew in England, besides many more.[10] President Blair of William and Mary wrote in his diary of having asparagus on his table in March and green peas in September.[11] In North Carolina gardens, according to Brickell, were parsnips, carrots, turnips, beets, artichokes, radishes, several kinds of potatoes, leeks, onions, shallots, chives, and garlic. Salads commonly grown were curled cabbage, savoy, lettuce, "round prickly Spinage," fennel, endive, succory, mint, rhubarb, cresses of several kinds, sorrel, and purslane. Mushrooms grew all over the fields, asparagus throve without hotbeds, and celery, coleworts, cucumbers, and squash were plentiful.[12]

In the preparation and serving of food, the colonial mistress had for her guidance not only the verbal instructions handed down from her mother and the manuscript directions exchanged with friends, but also a number of printed treatises. *The Compleat Housewife, The British Housewife, Mrs. Glasse's Art of Cookery,* and other "Bookes of cookery" were mentioned in wills and inventories and frequently advertised in newspapers. Some of these manuals have been preserved, and throw light upon the culinary art and the etiquette of serving at the time. The recipes show that dishes were rich, highly seasoned, and often complicated. Meats were usually boiled, roasted, stewed, fried, fricasseed, or made into a ragout or pie, and were invariably served with rich stuffings, sauces, and gravies. A mushroom sauce highly recommended for fowl was made as follows: "Pick a Pint of Mushrooms very clean, wash them, put them into a Saucepan, and put to them one Blade of Mace, a little Nutmeg, and a small Pinch of Bay Salt; add a Pint of Cream and a good Piece of Butter rolled in Flour; set them on a gentle Fire and let broil some little Time, keeping frequently stirring them; when they are enough lay the Fowl in the Dish, pour this Sauce in, and garnish with Lemon."[13] A gravy for veal cutlets was made of white wine, butter, oysters, and sweet breads.[14] The numerous recipes for cakes, puddings, creams, syllabubs, and tarts, required lavish use of butter, cream, eggs, and spices. "Common Pancakes" were made with eight "newlaid eggs," "a piece of butter as big as a walnut," a quart of milk, and a glass of brandy. "Rich Pancakes" required a dozen and a half eggs, half a pint each of sack and cream, and several spices; and a "Quaking Pudding" called for a quart of cream and twelve eggs.[15] . . .

Besides innumerable recipes, the housewifery manuals furnished the mistress with "bills of fare" and engraved "schemes" for the proper arrangement of her dishes on the table and instructions in the etiquette of serving. Dinner menus comprised many dishes, all of which were placed upon the table at once. When on special occasions two courses were served, each consisted of meats, fowl, fish, and vegetables as well as tarts, creams, cakes, pies, and puddings. An especially ornamental dish or "grand conceit" was used as a centerpiece and the other dishes arranged, preferably in even numbers, on each side and at the ends. A plan for an everyday dinner in winter suggested by *The Com-*

pleat Housewife had in the first course a giblet pie in the center, gravy soup and chicken and bacon at one end, roast beef surrounded by horse-radish and pickles at the other end, and Scotch collops and a boiled pudding on each side. The second course consisted of a tansy with orange in the middle of the table, woodcocks on toast, and a hare with a savory pudding on each side, and a roasted turkey and a buttered apple pie at each end. Dishes were more elaborate and more numerous on special occasions.

The mistress presided over the table and carved and served. Carving was one of the accomplishments in which the English lady took great pride. She was instructed in this just as she was taught to dance and play upon the harpsichord. The variety of terms and the complicated directions for carving lead us to wonder if this were not the most difficult of the arts she had to master.[16] We read of Lady Mary Wortley Montagu, who as a girl presided over her father's table, that she not only had to "persuade and provoke his guests to eat voraciously," but had also to carve every dish with her own hands, carefully choosing the right morsel for every man according to his rank. She was instructed by a carving master three times a week, and on days when there was to be company she ate her dinner beforehand.[17]

In the eighteenth century, the lady's duties in "doing the Honours of the Table" were somewhat modified. A housewifery book much used in the colonies just before the Revolution explained that in a former period it had been considered proper for the lady to help her guests, both because she was supposed to understand carving and to know where the best bits lay, and because it gave her an opportunity to show with what satisfaction she waited upon her friends. The French manner, which later became fashionable, was for every person to help himself to the dishes near him and pass his plate to

be served by the person sitting near whatever he desired. Under the old English plan, the book pointed out, when there was a large company the mistress had little opportunity to taste any food, while in the French fashion she was only one of the company. The French fashion, the author suggested, was suited to great houses where the dishes and guests were so numerous that the mistress could not serve everybody, but in smaller families and on ordinary occasions, the best form was for the lady to help everybody once and then let each person ask for what he wanted.[18]

Wealthy colonial ladies in the eighteenth century were supplied with the equipment necessary for serving meals in the best English manner. Rich mahogany tables, costly damask tablecloths and napkins, handsome silver plate and china adorned their tables. Yet, there were features unattractive to a twentieth-century diner. Food, prepared in an outdoor kitchen by a Negro cook and a retinue of slave helpers, was carried by slave waiters through all kinds of weather into the mansion house. Despite the use of covered dishes, it must often have been tepid and limp by the time it reached the diners. . . .

The colonial mistress was troubled by no concern for a balanced diet. Abundance and variety were the criteria by which her efforts were judged, and the recurrent bilious complaints of her family were not laid at her door but accepted as afflictions from above. Yet, one of her duties was the practice of "Family Physic." She not only doctored and nursed her patients, but sometimes prepared her own medicines, rivaling the apothecaries in the concoction of salves, balms, ointments, potions, and cordials. Receipts for various nostrums were handed down from mother to daughter and exchanged among gentlewomen like recipes for favorite dishes and were usually given an important place in handbooks on domestic economy.[19] The *British Housewife* gave considerable attention to treatment of "the panes of the gout," cholic, agues, and fevers, the "spleen," the "vapours," the "evil," "hysteric fits," and "hypochondriac complaints," which were among the chief ailments in vogue. "Aqua Mirabilis," one of the cordials doubtless often in demand, was alleged to "be excellent in the Cholick, and against that Sickness and Uneasiness that often follow a full Meal." The mere thought of some of its potions must have been sufficient to frighten the most greedy gourmand into temperance. One highly recommended "Stomachick" was made by boiling garlic in sack. Another was of snails, worms, hartshorn shavings, and wood sorrel stewed in brandy and seasoned with spices and herbs.[20]

Unlike northern and frontier housewives, the southern mistress in the settled counties did not generally spin and weave the clothing of her family. The southern planters had a staple agricultural product, which, while it fluctuated in price, always had a direct market, and, living on navigable streams or harbors, they conveniently exchanged their tobacco for English manufactured goods.[21] Many had even their plainer garments made in England. Others imported large quantities of materials at one time, which, as the need arose, were made up by tailors and seamstresses among their indentured servants. It is true that in many houses there were spinning wheels; Negresses were trained as spinners; and, when the price of tobacco sank below the cost of production or foreign wars obstructed trade, cloth was made for domestic use; but ordinarily clothing, blankets, quilts, and such articles were imported.[22]

As towns grew, an increasing number of shops sprang up, which imported and sold fashionable wearing apparel, and colonial tailors, mantuamakers, and milliners made clothing "after the latest London fashion." White seamstresses made the simpler garments. Clothing of slaves, which was sometimes of materials made on the plantation, but oftener of coarse, imported stuffs, was often made by persons employed especially for the purpose. Wives of overseers, white gardeners, and carpenters were sometimes expected to supervise the cutting and help the Negro women make clothes for the slaves on the plantations where their husbands worked, and many white women earned their living by nursing and sewing for slaves.[23]

With the beginning of the conflict with England, coarse stuffs for Negroes, and occasionally even finer materials for the planters' families, came to be made at home. Flax was planted, Negresses were taught to spin, and wheels were set in motion on every plantation. Washington, in response to the urge for homemade goods, hired a white woman to teach his slave girls to spin and built a house especially for spinning and weaving.[24] John Harrower in 1775 wrote in his diary of the activities on another plantation: "This morning 3 men went to work to break, swingle and heckle flax and one woman to spin in order to make course linnen for shirts to the Nigers. This being the first of the kind that was made on the Plantation. An before this year there has been little or no linnen made in the Colony."[25]

Well-to-do housewives were not only generally relieved of the necessity of making the clothing and household linen for their families, but they also had considerable assistance in the procuring of food supplies and the performance of other duties. Unmarried women relatives, who commonly made their homes with their married kin, were expected to aid the mistress. They frequently took over the direction of one or more branches of housewifery, like the dairy or poultry yard, and sometimes assumed the entire responsibility of housekeeper. . . .

Drudgery was done by white indentured servants and Negro slaves, the most intelligent of whom were used as house servants. In the early part of the seventeenth century most of the domestics were white, . . . but toward the latter part of the century Negro domestics became common. At the time of the Revolution wealthy families had an extraordinarily large number of house servants. Chastellux wrote that the luxury of being served by slaves augmented the natural indolence of the Virginia women, who were always surrounded by a great number of Negroes for their own and their children's service.[26] Timothy Ford declared that the South Carolinians, from the highest to the lowest, required a great deal of attendance. From the multiplicity of servants, he felt, rather than the climate, arose the "dronish ease and torpid inactivity so justly attributed to the inhabitants of the southern states.[27] Eliza Pinckney, living very simply and alone in Charles Town after the marriage of her children, wrote of her domestics: "I shall keep young Ebba to do the drudgery part, fetch wood, and water, and scour, and learn as much as she is capable of Cooking and Washing. Mary-Ann Cooks, makes my bed, and makes my punch. Daphne works and makes the bread, old Ebba boils the cow's victuals, raises and fattens the poultry, Moses is imployed from breakfast until 12 o'clock without doors, after that in the house. Pegg washes and milks."[28] Here were six servants for one old lady. And this was a very modest establishment.

Besides bond servants and slaves, the mistress had a surprisingly large number of white helpers who worked for wages. Expert gardeners and experienced housekeepers were common among those in easy circumstances. We find numerous newspaper advertisements like the following:

WANTED IMMEDIATELY

A DISCREET and capable Woman to officiate as Housekeeper in a Gentleman's Family. Such a Person, upon coming well recommended, will hear of a good Encouragement by Applying to the Post Office, Williamsburg.[29]

Washington apparently considered a housekeeper or steward indispensable at "Mount Vernon" not only after his retirement from the presidency, when the large number of visitors made his home a tavern, but also during the first years after his marriage. We find him at one time writing of the departure of his steward and seeking to hire another to "relieve Mrs. Washington from the drudgery of ordering, and seeing the table properly covered, and things economically used." Later he was advertising in the papers and writing his friends for a good housekeeper, declaring that Mrs. Washington's fatigue and distress for the want of one were so great that the matter of salary would be of no consideration.[30]

In addition to the housekeeper, Mrs. Washington and other matrons of her class generally had the assistance of other white women. Washington's letters show that he expected the wives of his overseers and white laborers to help supply provisions for his table and make Negro clothes. An agreement in 1762 between him and Edward Violett, an overseer, indicates that Violett's wife was tending a dairy, for which services Washington allowed her one-fourth of the butter she made;[31] and a letter to his manager sometime later declared that he would insist that another overseer's wife attend a dairy and raise fowls for the table at "Mount Vernon."[32] Newspaper advertisements for overseers and white gardeners often stated that the wives of these employees would be expected to take charge of a dairy or poultry yard, and many notices show that single women were commonly employed for wages at this kind of plantation work. The following is typical of many notices:

A Right good Overseer, having a Wife that can raise Poultry and manage a Dairy, may have Employment and Encouragement from
Andrew Rutledge[33]

The colonial planter also had a share in the responsibilities pertaining to domestic economy. A number of women, during the absence or at the death of their husbands, supervised all the plantation business as well as their household affairs. But generally the mistress had few cares beyond her immediate household, and the master took responsibility for many domestic matters unthought of by most husbands today. The colonial gentleman, whose office was in the precincts of his home, had opportunity to attend to the education of his children, the entertaining of guests, and the ordering of many household affairs. Though his wife probably informed him of the need of provisions and expressed her preferences in the matter of clothing and furnishings, he commonly kept all household accounts and did the buying, giving careful attention to the selection of furniture, draperies, rugs, china, and silverware, as well as to the details of the whole family's wearing apparel. Furthermore, because perhaps of the inadequacy of his wife's education as well as his own sense of domestic responsibility, he took care of the social as well as the business correspondence of the family, writing the notes of invitation, acceptance, and regret, and the usual letters to absent friends and relatives.

Many letters of Washington illustrate the surprising amount of attention which men, occupied with extensive public and private business, gave to the minutiae of household economy. He ordered the clothing of his wife and stepchildren from Europe, and it appears that he and not Mrs. Washington ordinarily bought most of the provisions and selected the furniture, carpets, wall paper, and other furnishings for "Mount Vernon." Even after he became president, when confronted with the various duties of setting a new government to work, he still found time to give minute directions for the remodeling of the Morris house, engaged for his Philadelphia residence, and to attend to the distribution of the rooms among his family, the selection of new furniture, the employment of additional servants, and

other housekeeping arrangements that one might expect to have been left to his wife's supervision. His letters to Tobias Lear, his secretary, are filled with such details as the placing of furniture and ornaments, the color scheme of the curtains, the exchange of laundry equipment with Mrs. Morris, the choice of housekeeper and steward, the making of servants' uniforms and caps, which washerwomen to bring from "Mount Vernon," and whether the cook should or should not make the desserts and have a hand in planning the meals.[34]

Not much is known of the life of the less well-to-do. The wives of smaller farmers in the settled sections, like the matrons on larger plantations, doubtless were concerned largely with procuring supplies and serving food to their families. But, while they often had indentured servants and slaves, they did not have efficient housekeepers, skilled gardeners, and other paid white helpers to relieve them of the supervision of the various branches of housewifery. They did, however, often have the help of one or more kinswomen living in the home and of their daughters, whose few weeks of school each year interfered little with their household tasks. With the aid of these women in her family and of her servants, the farmer's wife cared for her dairy, poultry yard, and garden, cured meats, pickled and preserved, cleaned house, and prepared meals for the household.

Some of the more industrious of this class spun and wove materials, of which they made clothing for their children and servants and furnishings for their homes, and sometimes earned pin money selling their cloths. Brickell found that the North Carolina girls were "bred to the Needle and Spinning" as well as to the dairy and other domestic affairs, which, he declared, they managed with a great deal of prudence. Many of the women, he observed, made a great deal of cloth of their own flax, wool, and cotton, and some were so ingenious that they made up all the wearing apparel for husband, sons, and daughters.[35] Governor Fauquier wrote in 1766 that the Virginia women made the cotton of the country into a strong cloth, of which they made gowns for themselves and children and coverlets for beds, and that sometimes they offered some of their cloths for sale in Williamsburg.[36]

The wives of tradesmen in the towns helped in their husbands' shops, which were usually in the home, and, with the aid of a few servants, cared for their children and housekeeping. Unlike the country housewives, they did not produce their food supplies but bought them in local stores or on the streets. Newspaper advertisements show that grocery shops carried many provisions. Fresh vegetables raised on near-by plantations or in local gardens were sold by slaves, who strode up and down the streets crying out their wares. Butter, eggs, chickens, vegetables, and sometimes jellies, pickles, and preserves were bought from farmers' wives. In the larger towns there were confectionery shops, where pastries, jellies, cakes, tarts, potted meats, and other delicacies were on sale or made to order. For housewives who could afford these services, there were Negro laundresses, cooks, nurses, and chambermaids to be hired by the day, month, or year; tradeswomen to clean and mend their laces, fine linen, and silk hose, quilt their petticoats, stiffen and glaze their chintzes; seamstresses, who would come into the home and sew by the day; and milliners and mantuamakers, who designed and made their best clothes.

It was the housewife of the back settlements who had to depend most upon her own labor and ingenuity. The frontiersman's remoteness from waterways and highways and his lack of a marketable staple crop prevented his trading much with the outside world and made it necessary for him and his wife to produce almost everything consumed in their household. With broadaxe and jackknife, he made his cabin, furniture, and many of the farming implements and kitchen utensils; and with spinning wheel, loom, and dye-pots, she made all the clothing of the family, the household linen, blankets, quilts, coverlets, curtains, rugs, and other such furnishings. She made her own soap and candles, and, to a greater extent than the plantation mistress, had to be doctor and apothecary to her family. From the woods she gathered herbs and roots, from which she made various purges, emetics, syrups, cordials, and poultices. She needed also to understand the use of firearms that she might protect her home from wild beasts and Indians, and kill wild animals for food. William Byrd wrote in 1710 of a well-to-do frontier woman who had entertained him and the other dividing-line commissioners: "She is a very civil woman and shews nothing of ruggedness, or Immodesty in her carriage, yett she will carry a gunn in the woods and kill deer, turkeys, &c., shoot down wild cattle, catch and tye hoggs, knock down beeves with an ax and perform the most manfull Exercises as well as most men in those parts."[37]

The food, clothing, and household comforts of frontier people varied greatly according to the wealth, energy, and skill of the master and mistress of the household. But generally houses were much smaller, furniture and clothing more scanty and crude, and food less varied than in the more populous regions. The backwoods housewife, who had no skilled gardener and no greenhouse where she could raise vegetables out of season and who found it impossible to get the imported delicacies available to the housewives near the coast, supplied her family with a diet which seemed plain and monotonous to refined visitors from older sections. Food in the back country consisted of pork, wild fowl, game, and Indian corn, supplemented in the more industrious families by beef, milk, butter, eggs, domestic fowl, and a few fruits and vegetables. The prevalence of pork was due to the ease with which it was produced. In many sections, hogs roamed about through the woods, feeding on acorns and roots and requiring no attention. Corn, which was raised in little patches near the cabins, was beaten in a hand mortar into coarse hominy or into meal, which was sometimes boiled into a mush and sometimes baked on the hearth as a hoecake. Homemade beer, cider, and brandy were the drinks. . . .

The backwoods women had the reputation of being more given to labor than their husbands. Lawson found them the "most industrious sex" in North Carolina.[38] Byrd, writing of the outlying settlements in Virginia and Carolina, declared that the men, like the Indians, imposed all the work upon the women and were themselves "Sloathfull in everything but getting Children."[39] The women, he observed, "all Spin, weave, and knit, whereby they make good Shift to cloath the whole Family; and to their credit be it recorded," many of them do it very completely."[40] Oldmixon wrote of the Carolina women: "The ordinary Women take care of Cows, Hogs, and other small Cattle, make Butter and Cheese, spin Cotton and Flax, help to sow and reap Corn, wind Silk from the Worms, gather Fruit, and look after the House."[41] Brickell also found the wives of the poorer farmers "ready to assist their husbands in any Servile Work, as planting when the Season of the Year requires expedition."[42]

The colonial housewife of tradition was a person of superhuman attainments, a composite of all the virtues and talents of women of every class and type. Actually, there were different kinds of housewives in colonial days as today, and women's occupations and achievements varied greatly according to their individual abilities and the circumstances of their lives. Superior women in frontier settlements were strong, daring, and self-reliant, as well as skillful and industrious. With practically no help

from the outside world, they fed, clothed, and physicked their large families, made the household furnishings, and on occasion even defended their homes. But they were not supposed to possess drawing-room accomplishments or to maintain the refined standards of living expected of matrons in town mansions and on large plantations. If they had few servants and no markets where they could buy their household necessaries, at the same time they did little entertaining and were expected to supply their families with only the simplest kinds of foods and clothes. Their houses were small, and they had no costly china, furniture, and silver to keep. Housewives in settled communities, on the other hand, were not expected to possess the physical courage and strength necessary to protect their families from Indians and wild beasts or to suffer hardships common to pioneers; and when they had the care of large and luxurious establishments they had a great deal of assistance in the performance of their duties. The plantation mistress of the class to which Martha Washington and Eliza Pinckney belonged was often a person of easy and hospitable manners, industry, and housewifery skill. She directed a large household and entertained numerous guests. Without the aid of canned goods, refrigerator, or near-by markets, she loaded her table with a variety of foods prepared and served in the best taste of the time. She often doctored the sick of her household, sometimes making the medicines she administered, and occasionally, when trade with England was obstructed, she helped to direct the making of clothing for her household. But she did not do all this single-handed. The coöperation of her husband, the efforts of women relatives living in the home, the skill of experienced hired housekeepers and expert gardeners, and the labor of many servants and slaves went into the accomplishments with which she alone has generally been credited.

NOTES

1. Janet Schaw, *Journal of a Lady of Quality* (ed. Evangeline Walker Andrews with Charles McLean Andrews) (New Haven, 1923), pp. 155–56.

2. Ibid., pp. 160–61.

3. Ibid., pp. 178–79.

4. "Letter to John Lord Boyle, February 2, 1726–27," *Virginia Magazine of History and Biography*, XXXII, 30.

5. Philip Vickers Fithian, *Journal and Letters, 1767–1774* (Princeton, N.J., 1900), pp. 61–72; Harriott Horry Ravenel, *Eliza Pinckney* (New York, 1896), pp. 243–44.

6. Fithian, *Journal and Letters*, p. 121.

7. Robert Beverley, *The History and Present State of Virginia* (London, 1722), p. 258.

8. John Gerard William De Brahm, "Philosophico-Historico-Hydrogeography of South Carolina," *Documents Connected with the History of South Carolina* (ed. P. C. J. Weston), p. 178. See also John Hammond, "Leah and Rachel," *Narratives of Early Maryland*, p. 293; Henry Norwood, "Voyage to Virginia," *Tracts & Other Papers, Relating Principally to the Origin, Settlement & Progress of the Colonies in North America* (ed. Peter Force) (Washington, 1836–46) III (No. 10), 48; Francis Louis Michel, "Journey, 1701–1702," *Virginia Magazine of History and Biography*, XXIV, 114–15; Hugh Jones, *The Present State of Virginia* (London, 1724), p. 49; John Oldmixon, *The British Empire in America* (London, 1741), I, 427–29; Lord Adam Gordon, "Journal," *Travels in the American Colonies* (ed. N. D. Mereness), pp. 397–98, 409; John Ferdinand D. Smyth, *Tour in the United States* (London, 1784), I, 65, 66, 69, 70, 71; Thomas Anburey, *Travels through the Interior Parts of America* (London, 1789), II, 314.

9. "Memoirs of the Life and Voyages of Dr. Philip Mazzei," *William and Mary Quarterly*, IX (2d ser.), 168.

10. Beverley, *History and Present State of Virginia*, p. 253.

11. "Diary of John Blair," *William and Mary Quarterly*, VII (1st ser.), 137.

12. John Brickell, *Natural History of North Carolina* (Dublin, 1737), p. 18.

13. Martha Bradley, *The British Housewife* (London, 1770), I, 45.

14. Ibid., II, 75.

15. Ibid., 548, 570, 571.

16. According to a popular seventeenth-century treatise, no lady of quality would say "Cut up that chicken or Hen." The correct terms in handling small birds were: "Thigh that Woodcock, Mince that Plover, Wing that Quail or Partridge, Allay that Pheasant, Untack that Curlew, Disfigure that Peacock, Unbrace that Mallard, Spoil that Hen, Lift that Swan, Rear that Goose." The directions for attacking fish were equally exact: "Chine that Salmon, String that Lamprey, Splat that Pike, Sauce that Plaice, Culper that Trout, Tame that Crab, Barb that Lobster."—Hannah Wooley, *The Gentlewoman's Companion, or Guide to the Female Sex* (London, 1675).

17. Rose M. Bradley, *The English Housewife in the Seventeenth and Eighteenth Centuries* (London, 1912), p. 107.

18. Martha Bradley, *British Housewife*, I, 73–75.

19. An English lady of 1725 wrote her niece, a young housewife in Maryland: "I have sent hear to in this my Great Book of Receipts and with all the Prescriptions that I have ever had from all the Dockters So that if you or any Friend you have has a head that way they may Set up for Great Praktes and do Good that way."—*Maryland Historical Magazine*, IX, 126.

20. Martha Bradley, *British Housewife*, I, 277, 371–72, 612.

21. Hugh Jones declared in 1723 that goods made in London or Bristol were delivered at the private landing places of Virginia gentlemen with less trouble and cost than to persons living five miles in the country in England.—*Present State of Virginia*, p. 34.

22. Philip Alexander Bruce, *Economic History of Virginia in the Seventeenth Century*, 2 vols. (New York, 1896), II, 258–494. See also Rolla Milton Tryon, *Household Manufactures in the United States, 1640–1860* (Chicago, 1917), pp. 19–20, 37–40, 92–122. . . .

23. Advertisements appeared like that of Eleanor Chapman, who offered to live on a plantation, raise poultry, attend a dairy, nurse sick slaves and make Negro clothes.—*South Carolina Gazette*, July 23, 1772.

24. Tryon, *Household Manufactures*, pp. 110–11.

25. "Diary of John Harrower," *American Historical Review*, VI, 103.

26. François Jean Marquis de Chastellux, *Travels in North America in the Years 1780, 1781, and 1782 . . .* (London, 1787), II, 203.

27. Timothy Ford, "Diary . . . 1785–1786, with Notes by Joseph Barnwell," *South Carolina Historical and Genealogical Magazine*, XIII, 142–43.

28. Ravenel, *Eliza Pinckney*, p. 245.

29. *Virginia Gazette*, June 2, 1774.

30. George Washington, *The Writings of George Washington* (ed. Jared Sparks) (Boston, 1837), XII, Appendix, p. 273; Moncure D. Conway, *Washington and Mount Vernon* (Brooklyn, N.Y., 1889), Appendix, pp. 336–39; Jared Sparks, *Letters and Recollections of Washington* (New York, 1906), pp. 219, 229, 243.

31. Worthington C. Ford, *Washington as an Employer and Importer of Labor* (Brooklyn, N.Y., 1889), p. 31.

32. Conway, *Washington and Mount Vernon*, p. 273.

33. *South Carolina Gazette*, August 4, 1746.

34. *Letters and Recollections of George Washington, Being Letters to Tobias Lear* (New York, 1906), pp. 3–4, 5, 8, 9, 11, 12, 14, 19, 23, 25–26, 30, 33, 36, 40, 43, 44, 45, and passim. . . .

35. Brickell, *Natural History of North Carolina*, p. 32.

36. "Letters of Governor Francis Fauquier," *William and Mary Quarterly*, XXI (1st ser.), 170.

37. "Boundary Line Proceedings, 1710," *Virginia Magazine of History and Biography*, V, 10.

38. John Lawson, *The History of Carolina . . .* (London, 1709), p. 142.

39. William Byrd II, *The Writings of Col. William Byrd* (ed. John Spencer Bassett), (New York, 1901), pp. 75–76.

40. Ibid., p. 242.

41. Oldmixon, "British Empire," *Narratives of Early Carolina, 1650–1708* (ed. A. S. Salley, Jr. (New York, 1911), p. 372.

42. Brickell, *Natural History of North Carolina*, p. 32.

LYLE KOEHLER
The Case of the American Jezebels:
Anne Hutchinson and Female Agitation during the Years of Antinomian Turmoil, 1636–1640

The Antinomian heresy threw the colony of Massachusetts Bay into turmoil for years and forced its leaders to reconsider the nature of their experiment. Antinomians placed greater emphasis on religious feeling than did orthodox Puritans. They tended to be suspicious (*anti*) of law (*nomos*) or formal rules and came close to asserting that individuals had access to direct revelation from the Holy Spirit. Historians usually study Antinomianism as a serious religious upheaval in an important colony. In this essay Lyle Koehler reports that the fact that Anne Hutchinson, the leader of the dissenters, was a woman made an important difference in the way courts treated her and in the sort of people who followed her. This information has always been available in the trial records, but until

Excerpted from "The Case of the American Jezebels: Ann Hutchinson and Female Agitation during the Years of Antinomian Turmoil, 1636–1640" by Lyle Koehler, in *William and Mary Quarterly*, 3d ser., 31 (1974):55–78. Copyright © 1974 by Lyle Koehler. Reprinted by permission of the author. Notes have been renumbered.

recently historians tended to pay little attention to it. Koehler emphasizes that many other women were attracted to Hutchinson's cause, so that Antinomianism became the occasion for the expression of widely shared dissatisfaction and uneasiness. When Hutchinson was held up to public ridicule and exiled, explicit dissent by women was firmly squelched in the Puritan community.

Between 1636 and 1638 Massachusetts boiled with controversy, and for more than three centuries scholars have attempted to define and redefine the nature, causes, and implications of that controversy. Commentators have described the rebellious Antinomians as "heretics of the worst and most dangerous sort" who were guilty of holding "absurd, licentious, and destructive" opinions,[1] as "a mob scrambling after God, and like all mobs quickly dispersed once their leaders were dealt with,"[2] and as the innocent victims of "inexcusable severity and unnecessary virulence."[3] Other narrators have called the most famous Antinomian, Anne Hutchinson, a "charismatic healer, with the gift of fluent and inspired speech,"[4] another St. Joan of Arc,[5] a rebel with a confused, bewildered mind,[6] and a woman "whose stern and masculine mind . . . triumphed over the tender affections of a wife and mother."[7]

Almost without exception, these critics and defenders of Ms. Hutchinson and the Antinomians have dealt specifically with Antinomianism as a religious movement and too little with it as a social movement.[8] . . .

That Anne Hutchinson and many other Puritan women should at stressful times rebel, either by explicit statement or by implicit example, against the role they were expected to fulfill in society is readily understandable, since that role, in both old and New England, was extremely limiting. The model English woman was weak, submissive, charitable, virtuous, and modest. Her mental and physical activity was limited to keeping the home in order, cooking, and bearing and rearing children, although she might occasionally serve the community as a nurse or midwife. She was urged to avoid books and intellectual exercise, for such activity might overtax her weak mind, and to serve her husband willingly, since she was by nature his inferior.[9] In accordance with the Apostle Paul's doctrine, she was to hold her tongue in church and be careful not "to teach, nor to usurp authority over the man, but to be in silence."[10]

In their letters, lectures, and historical accounts many of the Bay Colony men and some of the women showed approval of modest, obedient, and submissive females. Governor John Winthrop's wife Margaret was careful to leave such important domestic matters as place of residence to her husband's discretion, even when she had a preference of her own. She was ashamed because she felt that she had "no thinge with in or with out" worthy of him and signed her letters to him "your faythfull and obedient wife" or "your lovinge and obedient wife." Lucy Downing, Winthrop's sister, signed her chatty letters to her brother, "Your sister to commaund." Elizabeth, the wife of Winthrop's son John, described herself in a letter to her husband as "thy eaver loveing and kinde wife to comande in whatsoeaver thou plesest so long as the Lord shall bee plesed to geve me life and strenge."[11]

Winthrop himself was harshly critical of female intellect. In 1645 he wrote that Ann Hopkins, wife of the governor of Connecticut, had lost her understanding and reason by giving herself solely to reading and writing. The Massachusetts statesman commented that if she "had attended her household affairs, and such things as belong to women, and not gone out of her way and calling to meddle in such things as are proper for men, whose minds are stronger, etc. she had kept her wits, and might have improved them usefully and honorably in the place God had set her." Earlier he had denounced Anne Hutchinson as "a woman of a haughty and fierce carriage, of a nimble wit and active spirit, and a very voluble tongue, more bold then a man, though in understanding and judgement, inferiour to many women."[12]

. . . Reverend John Cotton arrived in Boston in 1633 and soon requested that women desiring church membership be examined in private since a public confession was "against the apostle's rule and not fit for a women's modesty." At a public lecture less than a year later Cotton explained that the apostle directed women to wear veils in church only when "the custom of the place" considered veils "a sign of the women's subjection." Cambridge minister Thomas Shepard, one of Anne Hutchinson's most severe critics, commended his own wife for her "incomparable meekness of spirit, toward myself especially," while Hugh Peter, a Salem pastor and another of Ms. Hutchinson's accusers, urged his daughter to respect her feminine meekness as "Womans Ornament."[13]

The female role definition that the Massachusetts ministers and magistrates perpetuated severely limited the assertiveness, the accomplishment, the independence, and the intellectual activity of Puritan women. Bay Colony women who might resent such a role definition before 1636 had no ideological rationale around which they could organize the expression of their frustration—whatever their consciousness of the causes of that frustration. With the marked increase of Antinomian sentiment in Boston and Anne Hutchinson's powerful example of resistance, the distressed females were able—as

this article will attempt to demonstrate—to channel their frustration into a viable theological form and to rebel openly against the perpetuators of the spiritual and secular status quo. Paradoxically enough, the values that Antinomians embraced minimized the importance of individual action, for they believed that salvation could be demonstrated only by the individual feeling God's grace within.

The process of salvation and the role of the individual in that process was, for the Puritan divines, a matter less well defined. The question of the relative importance of good works (i.e., individual effort) and grace (i.e., God's effort) in preparing man for salvation had concerned English Puritans from their earliest origins, and clergymen of old and New England attempted to walk a broad, although unsure, middle ground between the extremes of Antinomianism and Arminianism. But in 1636 Anne Hutchinson's former mentor and the new teacher of the Boston church, John Cotton, disrupted the fragile theological balance and led the young colony into controversy when he "warned his listeners away from the specious comfort of preparation and re-emphasized the covenant of grace as something in which God acted alone and unassisted."[14] Cotton further explained that a person could become conscious of the dwelling of the Holy Spirit within his soul and directed the Boston congregation "not to be afraid of the word *Revelation*."[15] The church elders, fearing that Cotton's "Revelation" might be dangerously construed to invalidate biblical law, requested a clarification of his position.

While the elders debated with Cotton the religious issues arising out of his pronouncements, members of Cotton's congregation responded more practically and enthusiastically to the notion of personal revelation by ardently soliciting converts to an emerging, loosely-knit ideology which the divines called pejoratively Antinomianism, Opinionism, or Familism.[16]

According to Thomas Weld, fledgling Antinomians visited new migrants to Boston, "especially, men of note, worth, and activity, fit instruments to advance their designe." Antinomian principles were defended at military trainings, in town meetings, and before the court judges. Winthrop charged the Opinionists with causing great disturbance in the church, the state, and the family, and wailed, "All things are turned upside down among us."[17]

The individual hungry for power could, as long as he perceived his deep inner feeling of God's grace to be authentic, use that feeling to consecrate his personal rebellion against the contemporary authorities. Some Boston merchants used it to attack the accretion of political power in the hands of a rural-dominated General Court based on land instead of capital. Some "ignorant and unlettered" men used it to express contempt for the arrogance of "black-coates that have been at the Ninneversity."[18] Some women, as we will see, used it to castigate the authority of the magistrates as guardians of the state, the ministers as guardians of the church, and their husbands as guardians of the home. As the most outspoken of these women, Anne Hutchinson diffused her opinions among all social classes by means of contacts made in the course of her profession of midwifery and in the biweekly teaching sessions she held at her home. Weld believed that Ms. Hutchinson's lectures were responsible for distributing "the venome of these [Antinomian] opinions into the very veines and vitalls of the People in the Country."[19]

Many women identified with Ms. Hutchinson's rebellious intellectual stance and her aggressive spirit. Edward Johnson wrote that "the weaker Sex" set her up as "a Priest" and "thronged" after her. John Underhill reported he daily heard a "clamor" that "New England men usurp over their wives, and keep them in servile subjection." Winthrop blamed Anne for causing "divisions between husband and wife . . . till the weaker give place to the stronger, otherwise it turnes to open contention," and Weld charged the Antinomians with using the yielding, flexible, and tender women as "an Eve, to catch their husbands also."[20] . . .

From late 1636 through early 1637 female resistance in the Boston church reached its highest pitch. At one point, when pastor John Wilson rose to preach, Ms. Hutchinson left the congregation and many women followed her out of the meetinghouse. These women "pretended many excuses for their going out," an action which made it impossible for the authorities to convict them of contempt for Wilson. Other rebels did, however, challenge Wilson's words as he spoke them, causing Weld to comment, "Now the faithfull Ministers of Christ must have dung cast on their faces, and be no better than Legall Preachers, Baals Priests, Popish Factors, Scribes, Pharisees, and Opposers of Christ himselfe."[21]

Included among these church rebels were two particularly active women, Jane (Mrs. Richard) Hawkins and milliner William Dyer's wife Mary, both of whom Winthrop found obnoxious. The governor considered the youthful Ms. Dyer to be "of a very proud spirit," "much addicted to revelations," and "notoriously infected with Mrs. Hutchinson's errors." Ms. Dyer weathered Winthrop's wrath and followed Anne to Rhode Island, but her "addictions" were not without serious consequence. Twenty-two years later she would return to Boston and be hanged as a Quaker.[22] The other of Hutchinson's close female associates, Jane Hawkins, dispensed fertility potions to barren women and occasionally fell into a trance-like state in which she spoke Latin. Winthrop therefore denounced her as "notorious for familiarity with the devill," and the General Court, sharing his apprehension, on March 12, 1638, forbade her to question "matters of religion" or "to meddle" in "surgery, or phisick, drinks, plaisters, or oyles." Ms. Hawkins apparently disobeyed this order, for three years later the Court banished her from the colony under the penalty of a severe whipping or such other punishment as the judges thought fit.[23]

Other women, both rich and poor, involved themselves in the Antinomian struggle. William Coddington's spouse, like her merchant husband, was "taken with the familistical opinions."[24] Mary Dummer, the wife of wealthy landowner and Assistant Richard Dummer, convinced her husband to move from Newbury to Boston so that she might be closer to Ms. Hutchinson.[25] Mary Oliver, a poor Salem calenderer's wife, reportedly exceeded Anne "for ability of speech, and appearance of zeal and devotion" and, according to Winthrop, might "have done hurt, but that she was poor and had little acquaintance [with theology]." Ms. Oliver held the "dangerous" opinions that the church was managed by the "heads of the people, both magistrates and ministers, met together," instead of the people themselves, and that anyone professing faith in Christ ought to be admitted to the church and the sacraments. Between 1638 and 1650 she appeared before the magistrates six times for remarks contemptuous of ministerial and magisterial authority and experienced the stocks, the lash, the placement of a cleft stick on her tongue, and imprisonment. One of the Salem magistrates became so frustrated with Ms. Oliver's refusal to respect his authority that he seized her and put her in the stocks without a trial. She sued him for false arrest and collected a minimal ten shillings in damages. Her victory was short-lived, however, and before she left Massachusetts in 1650 she had managed to secure herself some reputation as a witch.[26]

Mary Oliver and the other female rebels could easily identify with the Antinomian ideology because its theological emphasis on the inability of the individual to achieve salvation echoed the inability of women to achieve recognition on a sociopolitical level. As the woman realized that she could receive wealth, power, and status only through the man, her father or her husband, so the Antinomian realized that he or she could receive grace only through God's beneficence. Thus, women could have found it appealing that in Antinomianism *both* men and women were relegated vis-à-vis God to the status that women occupied in Puritan society vis-à-vis men, that is, to the status of malleable inferiors in the hands of a higher being. All power, then, emanated from God, raw and pure, respecting no sex, rather than from male authority figures striving to interpret the Divine Word. Fortified by a consciousness of the Holy Spirit's inward dwelling, the Antinomians could rest secure and self-confident in the belief that they were mystic participants in the transcendent power of the Almighty, a power far beyond anything mere magistrates and ministers might muster. Antinomianism could not secure for women such practical earthly powers as sizable estates, professional success, and participation in the church and civil government, but it provided compensation by reducing the significance of these powers for the men. Viewed from this perspective, Antinomianism extended the feminine experience of humility to both sexes, which in turn paradoxically created the possibility of feminine pride, as Anne Hutchinson's dynamic example in her examinations and trials amply demonstrated.

Anne Hutchinson's example caused the divines much frustration. They were chagrined to find that she was not content simply to repeat to the "simple Weomen"[27] the sermons of John Wilson, but that she also chose to interpret and even question the content of those sermons. When she charged that the Bay Colony ministers did not teach a covenant of grace as "clearly" as Cotton and her brother-in-law, John Wheelwright, she was summoned in 1636 to appear before a convocation of the clergy. At this convocation and in succeeding examinations, the ministers found particularly galling her implicit assertion that she had the intellectual ability necessary to judge the truth of their theology. Such an assertion threatened their self-image as the intellectual leaders of the community and the spokesmen for a male-dominated society. The ministers and magistrates therefore sharply criticized Anne for not fulfilling her ordained womanly role. In September 1637 a synod of elders resolved that women might meet "to pray and edify one another," but when one woman "in a prophetical way" resolved questions of doctrine and expounded Scripture, then the meeting was "disorderly." At Anne's examination on November 7 and 8, Winthrop began the interrogation by charging that she criticized the ministers and maintained a "meeting and an assembly in your house that hath been condemned by the general assembly as a thing not tolerable nor comely in the sight of God nor fitting for your sex." Later in the interrogation, Winthrop accused her of disobeying her "parents," the magistrates, in violation of the Fifth Commandment, and paternalistically told her, "We do not mean to discourse with those of your sex." Hugh Peter also indicated that he felt Anne was not fulfilling the properly submissive, nonintellectual feminine role. He ridiculed her choice of a female preacher of the Isle of Ely as a model for her own behavior and told her to consider "that you have stept out of you place, *you have rather bine a Husband than a Wife and a preacher than a Hearer; and a Magistrate than a Subject.*"[28]

When attacked for behavior inappropriate to her sex, Ms. Hutchinson did not hesitate to demonstrate that she was the intellectual equal of her accusers. She tried to trap Winthrop when he charged her with

dishonoring her "parents": "But put the case Sir that I do fear the Lord and my parents, may not I entertain them that fear the Lord because my parents will not give me leave?" To provide a biblical justification for her teaching activities, she cited Titus's rule (2:3–4) "that the elder women should instruct the younger." Winthrop ordered her to take that rule "in the sense that elder women must instruct the younger about their business, and to love their husbands." But Anne disagreed with this interpretation, saying, "I do not conceive but that it is meant for some publick times." Winthrop rejoined, "We must . . . restrain you from maintaining this course," and she qualified, "If you have a rule for it from God's word you may." Her resistance infuriated the governor, who exclaimed, "We are your judges, and not you ours." When Winthrop tried to lure her into admitting that she taught men, in violation of Paul's proscription, Anne replied that she thought herself justified in teaching a man who asked her for instruction, and added sarcastically, "Do you think it not lawful for me to teach women and why do you call me to teach the court?"[29]

Anne soon realized that sarcastic remarks would not persuade the court of the legitimacy of her theological claims. Alternatively, therefore, she affected a kind of modesty to cozen the authorities at the same time that she expressed a kind of primitive feminism through double-entendre statements and attacked the legitimacy of Paul's idea of the nonspeaking, nonintellectual female churchmember. When the Court charged her with "prophesying," Anne responded, "The men of *Berea* are commended for examining *Pauls* Doctrine; wee do no more [in our meetings] but read the notes of our teachers Sermons, and then reason of them by searching the Scriptures."[30] Such a statement was on one level an "innocent" plea to the divines that the women were only following biblical prescription. On another level it was an attack on the ministers for presuming to have the final word on biblical interpretation. On yet a third level, since she focused on "Pauls Doctrine" and reminded men that they should take another look at that teaching, her statement was a suggestion that ministerial attitudes toward women ought to be reexamined.

At another point Anne responded to Winthrop's criticism with a similar statement having meaning on three levels. The governor had accused her of traducing the ministers and magistrates and, when summoned to answer this charge, of saying that "the fear of man was a snare and therefore she would not be affeared of them." She replied, "They say I said the fear of man is a snare, why should I be afraid. When I came unto them, they urging many things unto me and I being backward to answer at first, at length this scripture came into my mind 29th Prov. 15. The fear of man bringeth a snare, but who putteth his trust in the Lord shall be safe."[31] Once again, her response was phrased as an "innocent" plea to God to assuage her fears, while at the same time it implied that God was on her side in opposition to the ministers and magistrates. Her statement also told women that if they trusted in God they need not fear men, for such fear trapped them into being "backward" about reacting in situations of confrontation with men.

Anne, although aware of the "backwardness" of women as a group, did not look to intensified group activity as a remedy for woman's downtrodden status. Her feminism consisted essentially of the subjective recognition of her own strength and gifts and the apparent belief that other women could come to the same recognition. A strong, heroic example of female self-assertiveness was necessary to the development of this recognition of one's own personal strength. Anne chose the woman preacher of the Isle of Ely as her particular

heroic model; she did, Hugh Peter chided, "exceedingly magnifie" that woman "to be a Womane of 1000 hardly any like to her." Anne could thus dissociate herself from the "divers worthy and godly Weomen" of Massachusetts and confidently deride them as being no better than "soe many Jewes," unconverted by the light of Christ.[32] Other Bay Colony women who wished to reach beyond the conventional, stereotypic behavior of "worthy and godly Weomen" attached themselves to the emphatic example of Anne and to God's ultimate power in order to resist the constraints which they felt as Puritan women.

Fearful that Ms. Hutchinson's example might be imitated by other women, the divines wished to catch her in a major theological error and subject her to public punishment. Their efforts were not immediately successful. Throughout her 1637 examination Anne managed to parry the verbal thrusts of the ministers and magistrates by replying to their many questions with questions of her own, forcing them to justify their positions from the Bible, pointing out their logical inconsistencies, and using innuendo to cast aspersions upon their authoritarianism. With crucial assistance from a sympathetic John Cotton, she left the ministers with no charge to pin upon her. She was winning the debate when, in an apparently incautious moment, she gave the authorities the kind of declaration for which they had been hoping. Raising herself to the position of judge over her accusers, she asserted, "I know that for this you goe about to doe to me, God will ruine you and your posterity, and this whole State." Asked how she knew this, she explained, "By an immediate revelation."[33] With this statement Anne proved her heresy to the ministers and they then took steps to expose her in excommunication proceedings conducted before the Boston church. The divines hoped to expel a heretic from their midst, to reestablish support for the Puritan way, to prevent unrest in the state and the family, and to shore up their own anxious egos in the process.

The predisposition of the ministers to defame Ms. Hutchinson before the congregation caused them to ignore what she was actually saying in her excommunication trial. Although she did describe a relationship with Christ closer than anything Cotton had envisioned, she did not believe that she had experienced Christ's Second Coming in her own life. Such a claim would have denied the resurrection of the body at the Last Judgment and would have clearly stamped her as a Familist.[34] Ms. Hutchinson's accusers, ignoring Thomas Leverett's reminder that she had expressed belief in the resurrection, argued that if the resurrection did not exist, biblical law would have no validity nor the marriage covenant any legal or utilitarian value. The result would be a kind of world no Puritan could tolerate, a world where the basest desires would be fulfilled and "foule, groce, filthye and abominable" sexual promiscuity would be rampant. Cotton, smarting from a psychological slap Anne had given him earlier in the excommunication proceedings[35] and in danger of losing the respect of the other ministers, admonished her with the words "though I have not herd, nayther do I thinke, you have bine unfaythful to your Husband in his Marriage Covenant, *yet that will follow upon it.*" By referring to "his" marriage covenant Cotton did not even accord Anne equal participation in the making of that covenant. The Boston teacher concluded his admonition with a criticism of Anne's pride: "*I have often feared the highth of your Spirit and being puft up with your owne parts.*"[36]

Both the introduction of the sexual issue into the trial and Cotton's denunciation of Ms. Hutchinson must have had the effect of curbing dissent from the congregation. Few Puritans would want to defend Anne in public when such a de-

fense could be construed as supporting promiscuity. Since Cotton had earlier been sympathetic to the Antinomian cause and had tried to save Anne at her 1637 examination, his vigorous condemnation of her must have confused her following. Cotton even went so far as to exempt the male Antinomians from any real blame for the controversy when he characterized Antinomianism as a women's delusion. He urged that women, like children, ought to be watched, reproved Hutchinson's sons for not controlling her theological ventures, and called those sons "Vipers . . . [who] *Eate through the very Bowells of your Mother,* to her Ruine." Cotton warned the Boston women "to looke to your selves and to take heed that you reaceve nothinge for Truth which hath not the stamp of the Word of God [as interpreted by the ministers] . . . for you see she [Anne] is but a Woman and *many unsound and dayngerous principles are held by her.*" Thomas Shepard agreed that intellectual activity did not suit women and warned the congregation that Anne was likely "to seduce and draw away many, Espetially simple Weomen of her owne sex."[37]

The female churchmembers, who would have had good reason to resent the clergy's approach, could not legitimately object to the excommunication proceedings because of Paul's injunction against women speaking in church. Lacking a clearly-defined feminist consciousness and filled with "backward" fear, the women could not refuse to respect that injunction, even though, or perhaps because, Anne had been presented to the congregation as the epitome of despicableness, as a woman of simple intellect, and as a liar, puffed up with pride and verging on sexual promiscuity. This caricature of Anne did not, however, prevent five men, including her brother-in-law Richard Scott and Mary Oliver's husband Thomas, from objecting to her admonition and excommunication.

Cotton refused to consider the points these men raised and dismissed their objections as rising out of their own self-interest or their natural affection for Anne.[38]

In Anne's excommunication proceedings the ministers demonstrated that they had found the means necessary to deal effectively with this rebellious woman and a somewhat hostile congregation. At her examination and her excommunication trial Anne attempted to place the ministers on the defensive by questioning them and forcing them to justify their positions while she explained little. She achieved some success in the 1637 trial, but before her fellow churchmembers she found it difficult to undercut the misrepresentation of her beliefs and the attack on her character. Perhaps fearing the banishment which had been so quickly imposed on her associate, John Wheelwright, she recanted, but even in her recantation she would not totally compromise her position. She expressed sorrow for her errors of expression but admitted no errors in judgment and assumed no appearance of humiliation. When Wilson commanded her *as a Leper to withdraw your selfe out of the Congregation,* Anne rose, walked to the meetinghouse door, accepted Mary Dyer's offered hand, and turned to impugn her accusers' power: "The Lord judgeth not as man judgeth, better to be cast out of the Church then to deny Christ."[39]

During the year and a half following Ms. Hutchinson's excommunciation, the Massachusetts ministers and magistrates prosecuted several other female rebels. In April 1638 the Boston church cast out Judith Smith, the maidservant of Anne's brother-in-law, Edward Hutchinson, for her "obstinate persisting" in "sundry Errors." On October 10 of the same year the Assistants ordered Katherine Finch to be whipped for "speaking against the magistrates, against the Churches, and against the Elders." Less than a year later Ms. Finch again appeared before the Assistants, this time for not carrying herself "dutifully to her husband," and was released upon promise of reformation. In September 1639 the Boston church excommunicated Phillip(a?) Hammond "as a slaunderer and revyler both of the Church and Common Weale." Ms. Hammond, after her husband's death, had resumed her maiden name, operated a business in Boston, and argued in her shop and at public meetings "that Mrs. Hutchinson neyther deserved the Censure which was putt upon her in the Church, nor in the Common Weale." The Boston church also excommunicated two other women for partially imitating Anne Hutchinson's example: Sarah Keayne was found guilty in 1646 of "irregular prophesying in mixed assemblies," and Joan Hogg nine years later was punished "for her disorderly singing and her idleness, and for saying she is commanded of Christ so to do."[40] . . .

The magistrates not only used the threat of a humiliating courtroom appearance and possible punishment to keep female rebels quiet but also levied very stringent penalties on male Antinomian offenders. Anne Hutchinson's son-in-law William Collins was sentenced to pay a £100 fine for charging the Massachusetts churches and ministers with being anti-Christian and calling the king of England the king of Babylon. Anne's son Francis, who had accompanied Collins to Boston in 1641, objected to the popular rumor that he would not sit at the same table with his excommunicated mother and, feeling that the Boston church was responsible, called that church "a strumpet." The church excommunicated Francis and the Assistants fined him £40, but neither he nor Collins would pay the stipulated amounts (even when those fines were reduced to £40 and £20) and therefore spent some time in jail[41] . . .

. . . Bay Colony leaders popularized the idea that the intellectual woman was influenced by Satan and was therefore unable to perform the necessary functions of womanhood. Weld described Mary Dyer's abortive birth as "a woman child, a fish, a beast, and a fowle, all woven together in one, and without an head," and wrote of Anne Hutchinson's probable hydatidiform mole as "30. monstrous births . . . none at all of them (as farre as I could ever learne) of humane shape."[42] According to Winthrop's even more garish account of Mary Dyer's child, the stillborn baby had a face and ears growing upon the shoulders, a breast and back full of sharp prickles, female sex organs on the rear and buttocks in front, three clawed feet, no forehead, four horns above the eyes, and two great holes upon the back.[43] . . .

. . . Weld's opinion that "as she had vented mishapen opinions, so she must bring forth deformed monsters" impressed the people of the Bay Colony, a people who believed that catastrophic occurrences were evidence of God's displeasure. Some Massachusetts residents viewed the births as the products of both the women's "mishapen opinions" and their supposed promiscuity. . . . A rumor reached England that Henry Vane had crossed the Atlantic in 1637 with Ms. Dyer and Ms. Hutchinson and had "debauched both, and both were delivered of monsters."[44] It was also widely rumored that three of the Antinomian women, Anne Hutchinson, Jane Hawkins and Mary Oliver, had sold their souls to Satan and become witches. Anne in particular "gave cause of suspicion of witchcraft" after she easily converted to Antinomianism one new male arrival in Rhode Island.[45]

The promotion of the belief that the Antinomian female leaders were witches filled with aberrant lusts and unable to live as proper women was accompanied by an attack on the masculinity of some of the Antinomian men. Although Anne's husband, William, had been a prosperous landowner, a merchant, a deputy to the General Court, and a Boston selectman, Winthrop described him as a "man of very mild temper and weak parts, and wholly guided by his wife." Clap also felt that William Hutchinson and the other Antinomian men were deficient in intellect and judgment. He expressed surprise that any of the men in the movement had "strong parts."[46]

While Massachusetts gossip focused on disordered Antinomian births, lusty Antinomian women, and weak Antinomian men, Winthrop and Cotton tried to convince their English and New England readers that public opinion had been solidly behind Ms. Hutchinson's excommuication. Winthrop contended that "diverse women" objected to this rebel's example and would have borne witness against her "if their modesty had not restrained them." Cotton supported the governor's claim by construing the relative silence at Anne's church trial to mean that the "whole body of the Church (except her own son) consented with one accord, to the publick censure of her, by admonition first, and excommunication after." By asserting this falsehood and ignoring Leverett's admission that many churchmembers wished to stay Anne's excommunication, Cotton made it appear that any person who complained about her censure was contradicting the near-unanimous opinion of the congregation.[47]

The effort to discredit the Antinomians and Antinomian sentiment in the Bay Colony was quite successful. By the late 1640s Antinomianism, in a practical sense, was no longer threatening; the ministers and magistrates had managed to preserve a theological system they found congenial. "*Sanctification* came to be in some Request again; and there were *Notes* and *Marks* given of a good Estate."[48] The position of Massachusetts women within the religious system remained essentially unchanged, while in Rhode Island and nearby Providence Plantations the status of women was somewhat improved. In Providence and Portsmouth the men listened to the wishes of the women and protected the "liberty" of women to teach, preach, and attend services of their choosing. . . .

After Anne Hutchinson's arrival and throughout the remainder of the century, women taught and preached in public in Rhode Island. Johnson wrote that in 1638 "there were some of the female sexe who (deeming the Apostle Paul to be too strict in not permitting a room [woman] to preach in the publique Congregation) taught notwithstanding . . . having their call to this office from an ardent desire of being famous." According to Johnson, Anne Hutchinson, "the grand Mistresse of them all, . . . ordinarily prated every Sabbath day, till others, who thirsted after honour in the same way with her selfe, drew away her Auditors."[49] This prating was more purposive than Johnson might have been willing to admit, for Anne soon involved herself in a new controversy, this one springing out of the resentment of many of the poorer inhabitants of the settlement toward Judge (Governor) William Coddington's autocratic rule, his land allotment policy, and his efforts to establish a church resembling closely the Massachusetts example.[50] Allying herself with Samuel Gorton, a religious freethinker and a defender of justice for all men, "rich or poore, ignorant or learned," Anne began to attack the legitimacy of *any* magistracy. Together, she and Gorton managed to foment the rebellion of April 28, 1639, in which the Portsmouth inhabitants formed a new body politic, ejected Coddington from power, and chose William Hutchinson to replace him. William, however, also did not believe in magistracy and soon refused to occupy the office of judge. Coddington, who had fled south with his followers to found Newport, then claimed the judgeship by default, was recognized by the Massachusetts authorities, and proceeded to administer the affairs of Rhode Island.[51] Gorton and at least eleven others

responded to Coddington's resumption of power by plotting armed rebellion against him and were ultimately banished from the colony. Anne broke with the Gortonists over that issue, and she and William joined the Newport settlement.[52]

William Hutchinson died at Newport in 1640, and for much of that year Anne was silent. By 1641, however, she had come out of mourning and, according to Winthrop, turned anabaptist. She and "divers" others supported passive resistance to authority, "denied all magistracy among Christians, and maintained that there were no churches since those founded by the apostles and evangelists, nor could any be."[53] Such opinions achieved enough popularity in Rhode Island to contribute to the dissolution of the church at Newport,[54] although not enough to remove Coddington from power. Disgruntled and fearing that Massachusetts would seize the Rhode Island settlements, Anne sought refuge in the colony of New Netherland in 1642, but her stay there was not long. In August 1643 she, William Collins, two of her sons, and three of her daughters were killed by Indians who had quarreled with her Dutch neighbors.[55]

The Massachusetts clergy rejoiced. Not only had God destroyed the "American Jesabel,"[56] but the Lord's vengeance had descended upon her sons and daughters, the poisoned seed. Peter Bulkeley spoke for all the Massachusetts ministers when he concluded, "Let her damned heresies shee fell into . . . and the just vengeance of God, by which shee perished, terrifie all her seduced followers from having any more to doe with her leaven."[57] But her "seduced followers" were horrified only at the reaction of the Puritan clergy. Anne's sister, Katherine Scott, commented that the Bay Colony authorities "are drunke with the blod of the saints," and Anne's former Portsmouth neighbor, Randall Holden, blamed those same authorities for forcing Anne first to Rhode Island and ultimately to her death. He reminded them of her partially successful struggle against authority: "you know . . . your great and terrible word magistrate is no more in its original, than masterly or masterless which hath no great lustre in our ordinary acceptation."[58]

Impervious to such protests, the Bay Colony divines considered Anne Hutchinson's death to be the symbolic death of Antinomianism. To these divines she had been the incarnation of the Antinomian evil, and their accounts of the Antinomian stress in Boston accented *her* beliefs, *her* activities, and *her* rebelliousness. The ministers were not as concerned with the important roles played by Coddington, Wheelwright, Vane, and the other male Antinomian leaders because none of these men threatened the power and status structure of society in the concrete way that Anne Hutchinson did. Anne was clearly not, as the ministers might have wished, a submissive quiet dove, content to labor simply in the kitchen and the childbed. She was witty, aggressive, and intellectual. She had no qualms about castigating in public the men who occupied the most authoritative positions. She claimed the right to define rational, theological matters for herself and by her example spurred other women to express a similar demand. Far from bewildered, she thwarted her accusers with her intellectual ability. Perceiving her as a threat to the family, the state, the religion, and the status hierarchy, the Puritan authorities directed their antagonism against Anne's character and her sex. By doing so, they managed to salve the psychological wounds inflicted by this woman who trod so sharply upon their male status and their

ministerial and magisterial authority. Their method had a practical aspect as well; it helped restore respect for the ministry and curb potential dissent.

Anne's ability to attract large numbers of women as supporters caused the ministers and magistrates some worry but little surprise, since they believed that women were easily deluded. They chided Anne for choosing a female preacher as a role model and refused to attribute any merit to her at times subtle, at times caustic intellectual ability. They could see only the work of Satan in Anne's aggressiveness and not the more human desire for equal opportunity and treatment which this rebel never hesitated to assert by example in the intellectual skirmishes she had with her accusers throughout her trials. The double oppression of life in a male-dominated society, combined with biological bondage to her own amazing fertility, could not destroy her self-respect. Because of the theologically based society in which she lived, it was easy for her to ally herself with God and to express her self-confidence in religious debates with the leading intellectual authorities. Neither Anne's rebellion nor the rebellion of her female followers was directed self-consciously against their collective female situation or toward its improvement. Specific feminist campaigns for the franchise, divorce reform, female property ownership after marriage, and the like would be developments of a much later era. For Anne Hutchinson and her female associates Antinomianism was simply an ideology through which the resentment they intuitively felt could be focused and actively expressed.

Notes

1. John A. Albro, ed., *The Works of Thomas Shepard*, I (New York, 1967 [orig. publ. n.p., 1853]), cxvi–cxvii.

2. Darrett B. Rutman, *Winthrop's Boston: Portrait of a Puritan Town, 1630–1649* (Chapel Hill, N. C., 1965), 121.

3. John Stetson Barry, *The History of Massachusetts: The Colonial Period* (Boston, 1855), 261.

4. Andrew Sinclair, *The Emancipation of the American Woman* (New York, 1966), 23.

5. Edith Curtis, *Anne Hutchinson: A Biography* (Cambridge, Mass., 1930), 72–73.

6. Emery Battis, *Saints and Sectaries: Anne Hutchinson and the Antinomian Controversy in the Massachusetts Bay Colony* (Chapel Hill, N. C., 1962), 9, 50–56, 90, admits that Ms. Hutchinson had a "prodigious memory and keen mind," but he believes that she was "wracked with unbearable doubt" as a result of her inability to find a male "mental director." Her husband could not fulfill this need for he "seems to have lacked the power to provide adequate support and direction for his wife." Ms. Hutchinson's rebellion, according to Battis, grew out of this need for male guidance and was accentuated by the fact that she was experiencing menopause and felt that "her own inadequacy was at least in part responsible" for the death of two of her children. Of these many reasons for Ms. Hutchinson's restlessness Battis substantiates only his conclusion that she was undergoing menopause. His argument is weakened, however, by anthropological research which ties the psychological distress of menopause to the loss of self-esteem that middle-aged women experience in societies where their status deteriorates at menopause. See Joan Solomon, "Menopause: A Rite of Passage," *Ms.*, I (Dec. 1972), 18. Puritan New England was clearly not such a society, for elderly women could serve as deaconesses and, since they were free from the materialistic proclivities of youth, could furnish venerable examples for younger women. See Benjamin Colman, *The Duty and Honour of Aged Women: A Sermon on the Death of Madam Abigail Foster* (Boston, 1711), 11–30.

7. Peter Oliver, *The Puritan Commonwealth. An Historical Review of the Puritan Government in Massachusetts in its Civil and Ecclesiastical Relations* . . . (Boston, 1856), 181.

8. Anne Hutchinson and the Antinomians have been treated sympathetically in Charles Francis Adams, *Three Episodes of Massachusetts History* (Boston, 1892); Brooks Adams, *The Emancipation of Massachusetts* (Boston, 1887); Winnifred King Rugg, *Unafraid: A Life of Anne Hutchinson* (Boston, 1930); Theda Kenyon, *Scarlet Anne* (New York, 1939); Vernon Louis Parrington, *Main Currents in American Thought: The Colonial Mind* (New York, 1927); Eleanor Flexner, *Century of Struggle: The Woman's Rights Movement in the United States* (Cambridge, Mass., 1959); Elisabeth Anthony Dexter, *Colonial Women of Affairs: A Study of Women in Business and the Professions before 1776* (Boston, 1924); Sinclair, *Emancipation of American Woman*; Rufus M. Jones, *The Quakers in the American Colonies* (New York, 1911); Curtis, *Anne Hutchinson*; Barry, *History of Massachusetts*. Critics of Anne and the Antinomians include Henry Martyn Dexter, *As to Roger Williams, and His "Banishment" from the Massachusetts Plantation; with a Few Further Words Concerning the Baptists, the Quakers, and Religious Liberty* (Boston, 1873); George E. Ellis, "Life of Anne Hutchinson with a Sketch of the Antinomian Controversy in Massachusetts," in Jared Sparks, ed., *The Library of American Biography*, 2d Ser., VI (Boston, 1849); John Gorham Palfrey, *A Compendious History of the First Century of New England* . . . (Boston, 1872); Thomas Jefferson Wertenbaker, *The First Americans, 1607–1690* (New York, 1927); Oliver, *Puritan Commonwealth*; Rutman, *Winthrop's Boston*. More balanced treatments are Edmund S. Morgan, *The Puritan Dilemma: The Story of John Winthrop* (Boston, 1958), and Battis, *Saints and Sectaries*.

9. Studies of early seventeenth-century English attitudes about women appear in Georgiana Hill, *Women in English Life from Mediaeval to Modern Times* (London, 1896); M. Phillips and W. S. Tomkinson, *English Women in Life and Letters* (London, 1926); Gamaliel Bradford, *Elizabethan Women* (Boston, 1936); Doris Mary Stenton, *The English Woman in History* (London, 1957).

10. 1 Tim. 2:11–12. St. Paul told the Corinthians: "Let your women keep silence in the churches; for it is not permitted unto them to speak; but they are commanded to be under obedience, as also saith the law. And if they will learn any thing, let them ask their husbands at home; for it is a shame for women to speak in the church" (1 Cor. 14:34–35).

11. Margaret Winthrop to John Winthrop, 1624–1630, *The Winthrop Papers* (Boston, 1929–1944), I, 354–355; II, 165, 199; Lucy Downing to John Winthrop, 1636–1640, Massachusetts Historical Society, *Collections*, 5th Ser., I (Boston, 1871), 20, 25, 27; Elizabeth Winthrop to John Winthrop, ca. June 1636, *Winthrop Papers*, III, 267.

12. James Kendall Hosmer, ed., *Winthrop's Journal: "History of New England," 1630–1649.* Original Narratives of Early American History (New York, 1908), II, 225; John Winthrop, *A Short Story of the Rise, reign, and ruine of the Antinomians, Familists and*

Libertines in David D. Hall, ed., *The Antinomian Controversy, 1636–1638: A Documentary History* (Middletown, Conn., 1968), 263.

13. William Wood, *New Englands Prospect* . . . (London, 1634), 121–122; Hosmer, ed., *Winthrop's Journal*, I, 107, 120; Michael McGiffert, ed., *God's Plot: The Paradoxes of Puritan Piety, Being the Autobiography and Journal of Thomas Shepard* (Amherst, Mass., 1972), 70; Hugh Peter, *A Dying Fathers Last Legacy to An Only Child: Or, Mr. Hugh Peter's Advice to His Daughter* . . . (Boston, 1717), 22.

14. Morgan, *Puritan Dilemma*, 137. McGiffert's introduction to Shepard's autobiography and journal contains a discussion of the Puritans' problems with assurance. See McGiffert, ed., *God's Plot*, 1–32. Puritan attitudes toward the preparation process are treated comprehensively and perceptively in Norman Pettit, *The Heart Prepared: Grace and Conversion in Puritan Spiritual Life* (New Haven, Conn., 1966).

15. John Cotton, *A Treatise of the Covenant of Grace, as it is despensed to the Elect Seed, effectually unto Salvation* (London, 1671), 177. Cotton's subsequent debate with the other ministers appears in Hall, ed., *Antinomian Controversy*, 24–151.

16. The Familists or Family of Love, a sect which originated in Holland about 1540 and spread to England, gained a largely undeserved reputation for practicing promiscuity. Antinomianism was associated in the Puritan mind with the licentious orgies that accompanied the enthusiasm of John Agricola in sixteenth-century Germany. Opinionism was a term often used for any theology that the divines disliked. James Hastings, ed., *Encyclopaedia of Religion and Ethics* (New York, 1908–1926), I, 581–582; V, 319; IX, 102.

17. Thomas Weld, "The Preface," to Winthrop, *Short Story*, in Hall, ed., *Antinomian Controversy*, 204, 208–209; Winthrop, *Short Story*, ibid., 253.

18. J. Franklin Jameson, ed., *Johnson's Wonder-Working Providence, 1628–1651*, Original Narratives of Early American History (New York, 1910), 127.

19. Weld, "Preface," to Winthrop, *Short Story*, in Hall, ed., *Antinomian Controversy*, 207.

20. Jameson, ed., *Johnson's Wonder-Working Providence*, 132; John Underhill, *Newes from America; or A New and Experimentall Discoverie of New England* . . . (London, 1638), reprinted in Mass. Hist. Soc., *Colls.*, 3d Ser., VI (Boston, 1837), 5; Winthrop, *Short Story*, in Hall, ed., *Antinomian Controversy*, 253; Weld, "Preface," to Winthrop, *Short Story*, ibid., 205–206. . . .

21. John Cotton, *The Way of Congregational Churches Cleared*, in Hall, ed., *Antinomian Controversy*, 423, and Weld, "Preface," to Winthrop, *Short Story*, ibid., 209.

22. Hosmer, ed., *Winthrop's Journal*, I, 266; Winthrop, *Short Story*, in Hall, ed., *Antinomian Controversy*, 281; Horatio Rogers, "Mary Dyer Did Hang Like a Flag," in Jessamyn West, ed., *The Quaker Reader* (New York, 1962), 168–175.

23. Jameson, ed., *Johnson's Wonder-Working Providence*, 132; Winthrop, *Short Story*, in Hall, ed., *Antinomian Controversy*, 281; Nathaniel B. Shurtleff, ed., *Records of the Governor and Company of the Massachusetts Bay in New England, 1628–1641* (Boston, 1853), I, 224, 329.

24. Hosmer, ed., *Winthrop's Journal*, I, 270.

25. "The Rev. John Eliot's Record of Church Members, Roxbury, Massachusetts," in *A Report of the Boston Commissioners, Containing the Roxbury Land and Church Records* (Boston, 1881), 77.

26. Hosmer, ed., *Winthrop's Journal*, I, 285–286; George Francis Dow, ed., *Records and Files of the Quarterly Courts of Essex County, Massachusetts, 1636–1656*, I (Salem, Mass., 1911), 12, 138, 180, 182–183, 186; John Noble, ed., *Records of the Court of Assistants of the Colony of the Massachusetts Bay, 1630–1644*, II (Boston, 1904), 80, hereafter cited as *Assistants Records*; Sidney Perley, *History of Salem, Massachusetts, 1638–1670*, II (Salem, Mass., 1926), 50; Thomas Hutchinson, *The Witchcraft Delusion of 1692* (Boston, 1870), 6.

27. "A Report of the Trial of Mrs. Anne Hutchinson before the Church in Boston," in Hall, ed., *Antinomian Controversy*, 365.

28. Hosmer, ed., *Winthrop's Journal*, I, 234; "The Examination of Mrs. Anne Hutchinson at the Court at Newtown," in Hall, ed., *Antinomian Controversy*, 312–314, 318; "Trial of Anne Hutchinson before Boston church," ibid., 380, 382–383.

29. "Examination of Mrs. Hutchinson at Newtown," in Hall, ed., *Antinomian Controversy*, 313–316.

30. Winthrop, *Short Story*, ibid., 268.

31. "Examination of Mrs. Hutchinson at Newtown," ibid., 330.

32. "Trial of Anne Hutchinson before church," ibid., 380. That Ms. Hutchinson chose a woman preacher as a model for her

rebellious behavior, instead of the more popular "Spirit-mystic" and "apostle of Ely,"
William Sedgwick, indicates that Anne had
some level of feminist self-awareness and
suggests that she was not greatly in need of
specifically male guidance. Cotton expressed
the view that she was far from satisfied with
his guidance. "Mistris *Hutchinson* seldome
resorted to mee," he wrote, "and when she
did come to me, it was seldome or never
(that I can tell of) that she tarried long. I
rather think, she was loath to resort much
to me, or, to conferre long with me, lest she
might seeme to learne somewhat from me."
Cotton, *Congregational Churches Cleared*,
ibid., 434. Cotton's testimony may not be
completely accurate, as he was writing to
wash the Antinomian stain off his own
hands.

Little is known about Anne Hutchinson's
role-model, the woman of Ely. Thomas Edwards, a contemporary Puritan divine, remarked that "there are also some women
preachers in our times, who keep constant
lectures, preaching weekly to many men and
women. In Lincolnshire, in Holland and those
parts [i.e., the parts about Holland in Lin-
colnshire] there is a woman preacher who
preaches (it's certain), and 'tis reported also
she baptizeth, but that's not so certain. *In
the Isle of Ely (that land of errors and sectaries) is a woman preacher also.*" See his
Gangraena . . . (London, 1646), Pt. ii, 29,
quoted in Battis, *Saints and Sectaries*, 43n.

33. Winthrop, *Short Story*, in Hall, ed.,
Antinomian Controversy, 273, and "Examination of Mrs. Hutchinson at Newtown," ibid.,
337.

34. A good discussion of the theological
issues surrounding resurrection is provided
in Jesper Rosenmeier, "New England's Perfection: The Image of Adam and the Image
of Christ in the Antinomian Crisis, 1634 to
1638," *William and Mary Quarterly*, 3d Ser.,
XXVII (1970), 435–459. Rosenmeier depicts
Ms. Hutchinson too explicitly as a Familist
without supplying sufficient evidence.

35. Ms. Hutchinson had responded to an
argument of Cotton's with the rejoinder, "I
desire to hear God speak this and not man."
"Trial of Anne Hutchinson before Boston
church," in Hall, ed., *Antinomian Controversy*, 358, 362, 355.

36. Ibid., 372. See Battis, *Saints and Sectaries*, 52n.

37. "Trial of Anne Hutchinson before
Boston church," in Hall, ed., *Antinomian
Controversy*, 369, 370, 365.

38. Ibid., 385–87, 366–368.

39. Ibid., 378, 388, and Winthrop, *Short
Story*, ibid., 307.

40. Richard D. Pierce, ed., *The Records of
the First Church in Boston, 1630–1868*, I, in
Colonial Society of Massachusetts, *Publications*, XXXIX (Boston, 1961), 22, 25; *Assistants Records*, II, 78, 82; Emil Oberholzer,
Jr., *Delinquent Saints: Disciplinary Action in
the Early Congregational Churches of Massachusetts* (New York, 1956), 85; "The Diaries
of John Hull," American Antiquarian Society,
Archaelogia Americana, III (Worcester, Mass.,
1857), 192n.

41. *Assistants Records*, II, 109; Hosmer,
ed., *Winthrop's Journal*, II, 38–40; John
Cotton to Francis Hutchinson, Mass. Hist.
Soc., *Colls.*, 2d Ser., X (1823), 186. In 1633
the Assistants fined Capt. John Stone £100
for assaulting Justice Roger Ludlow and calling him a "just ass." Four years later Robert
Anderson was fined £50 for "contempt," but
no other reviler of authority was fined more
than £20. *Assistants Records*, II, 35, 66.

42. Weld, "Preface," to Winthrop, *Short
Story*, in Hall, ed., *Antinomian Controversy*,
214. Dr. Paul A. Younge's diagnosis of Ms.
Hutchinson's "30. monstrous births" as an
hydatidiform mole, a uterine growth which
frequently accompanies menopause, is
adopted in Battis, *Saints and Sectaries*, 346.

43. Winthrop, *Short Story*, in Hall, ed.,
Antinomian Controversy, 280–281.

44. Weld, "Preface," to Winthrop, *Short
Story*, in Hall, ed., *Antinomian Controversy*,
214; "From Majr. Scott's mouth," Mass. Hist.
Soc., *Proceedings*, 1st Ser., XIII (1873–1875),
132. John Josselyn, a British traveler, wrote
that he was surprised to find "a grave and
sober person" who told him about Mary
Dyer's "monster" on his first visit to Massachusetts in 1639. See his *An Account of Two
Voyages to New England . . .* (London,
1675), 27–28.

45. Hosmer, ed., *Winthrop's Journal*, II, 8.

46. Ibid., I, 299, and "Clap's Memoirs," in
Alexander Young, ed., *Chronicles of the First
Planters of Massachusetts Bay, from 1623–
1636* (Boston, 1846), 360.

47. Winthrop, *Short Story*, in Hall, ed.,
Antinomian Controversy, 307, and Cotton,
Congregational Churches Cleared, ibid., 420.

48. George H. Moore, "Giles Firmin and
His Various Writings," *Historical Magazine*,
2d Ser., III (1868), 150, quoting Giles Firmin,
Πανομργια, *a brief review of Mr. Davis's Vindication: giving no satisfaction . . .* (London, 1693).

49. Jameson, ed., *Johnson's Wonder-Working Providence*, 186.

50. Howard M. Chapin, *Documentary History of Rhode Island*, II (Providence, R.I., 1916), 68, 84. Coddington controlled the dispensation of land titles because the original deed to Rhode Island was issued in his name.

51. Edward Winslow, *Hypocrisie Unmasked: A true Relation of the Proceedings of the Governour and Company of the Massachusetts against Samuel Gorton . . .* (London, 1646), 44, 54–55, 67; Hosmer, ed., *Winthrop's Journal*, I, 297, 299; Chapin, *History of Rhode Island*, II, 56–57; William Coddington to John Winthrop, Dec. 9, 1639, *Winthrop Papers*, IV, 160–161; Robert Baylie, *A Dissuasive from the Errours of the Time . . .* (London, 1645), 150.

52. Chapin, *History of Rhode Island*, II, 68, and Winslow, *Hypocrisie Unmasked*, 53, 83.

53. Hosmer, ed., *Winthrop's Journal*, II, 39.

54. Thomas Lechford, *Plain Dealing: or, Newes from New-England . . .* (London, 1642), reprinted in Mass. Hist. Soc., *Colls.*, 3d Ser., III (Boston, 1833), 96.

55. "Letter of Randall Holden, Sept. 15th, 1643," *ibid.*, I (1825), 13, and Samuel Niles, "A Summary Historical Narrative of the Wars in New-England with the French and Indians, in the several Parts of the Country," *ibid.*, VI (1837), 201.

56. Winthrop, *Short Story*, in Hall, ed., *Antinomian Controversy*, 310.

57. Perry Miller, *The New England Mind: The Seventeenth Century* (New York, 1939), 391. Increase Mather saw the hand of God at work again when Anne's son Edward died from Indian wounds in 1675. "It seems to be an observable providence," Mather observed, "that so many of that family die by the hands of the uncircumcised." "Diary of Increase Mather, 1674–87," Mass. Hist. Soc., *Procs.*, 2d Ser., XIII (1900), 400.

58. Katherine Scott to John Winthrop, Jr., 1658, Mass. Hist. Soc., *Colls.*, 5th Ser., I (1871), 96–97, and "Letter of Randall Holden, Sept. 15th, 1643," *ibid.*, 3d Ser., I (1825), 13–15.

CATHERINE M. SCHOLTEN
"On the Importance of the Obstetrick Art": Changing Customs of Childbirth in America, 1760–1825

Anthropologists have long known that the rituals of daily life can provide important insights into the life of a community. "Common sense" changes from place to place, and from time to time. Catherine M. Scholten's report on the way Americans handled childbirth shows that in the early eighteenth century the "common sense" of the matter seemed to be that women would assist in the birth process. By the early nineteenth century it had become "common sense" that male physicians would be called to the bedside. Scholten suggests that this change is a symptom of an important shift in attitudes toward women as patients

Excerpted from " 'On the Importance of the Obstetrick Art': Changing Customs of Childbirth in America, 1760 to 1825" by Catherine M. Scholten, in *William and Mary Quarterly*, 3rd Ser., 34 (1977):426–45. Copyright © 1977 by the Estate of Catherine M. Scholten. Reprinted by permission of the Estate of Catherine M. Scholten; Pauline Scholten, Executor. Notes have been renumbered.

and as professionals. Despite a few unenthusiastic efforts to teach improved obstetric techniques to midwives, women were usually denied access to training in the newest medical skills. As medicine became more professional, it also became more strictly segregated by gender. Ironically, scientific developments that had the result of making childbirth less risky also increased the dependence of women on male physicians. A similar result accompanied the spread of "twilight sleep" anesthesia in the twentieth century.

In October 1799, as Sally Downing of Philadelphia labored to give birth to her sixth child, her mother, Elizabeth Drinker, watched her suffer "in great distress." Finally, on the third day of fruitless labor, Sally's physician, William Shippen, Jr., announced that "the child must be brought forward." Elizabeth Drinker wrote in her diary that, happily Sally delivered naturally, although Dr. Shippen had said that "he thought he should have had occasion for instruments" and clapped his hand on his side, so that the forceps rattled in his pocket.[1]

Elizabeth Drinker's account of her daughter's delivery is one of the few descriptions by an eighteenth-century American woman of a commonplace aspect of women's lives—childbirth.[2] It is of special interest to social historians because it records the participation of a man in the capacity of physician. Shippen was a prominent member of the first generation of American doctors trained in obstetrics and, commencing in 1763, the first to maintain a regular practice attending women in childbirth.[3] Until that time midwives managed almost all deliveries, but with Shippen male physicians began to supplant the midwives.

The changing social customs and medical management of childbirth from 1760 to 1825 are the subjects of this article. By analyzing the rituals of childbirth it will describe the emergence of new patterns in private and professional life. It shows that, beginning among well-to-do women in Philadelphia, New York, and Boston, childbirth became less a communal experience and more a private event confined within the intimate family. In consequence of new perceptions of urban life and of women, as well as of the development of medical science, birth became increasingly regarded as a medical problem to be managed by physicians. For when Shippen, fresh from medical studies in London, announced his intention to practice midwifery in Philadelphia in 1763, he was proposing to enter a field considered the legitimate province of women.[4] Childbearing had been viewed as the inevitable, even the divinely ordained, occasion of suffering for women; childbirth was an event shared by the female community; and was supervised by a midwife.

During the colonial period childbearing occupied a central portion of the lives of women between their twentieth and fortieth years. Six to eight pregnancies were typical, and pregnant women were commonly described as "breeding" and "teeming."[5] Such was women's natural lot; though theologians attributed dignity to carrying the "living soul" of a child and saluted mothers in their congregations with "Blessed are you among women," they also depicted the pains of childbirth as the appropriate special curse of "the Travailing Daughters of Eve."[6] Two American tracts written specifically for lying-in women dwelt on the divinely ordained hazards of childbirth and advised a hearty course of meditation on death, "such as their pregnant condition must reasonably awaken them to."[7]

Cotton Mather's pamphlet, Elizabeth in

Her Holy Retirement, which he distributed to midwives to give to the women they cared for, described pregnancy as a virtually lethal condition. "For ought you know," it warned, "your Death has entered into you, you may have conceived that which determines but about Nine Months more at the most, for you to live in the World." Pregnancy was thus intended to inspire piety.[8] . . .

Surely women did not need to be reminded of the risks of childbirth. The fears of Mary Clap, wife of Thomas Clap, president of Yale College, surface even through the ritual phrases of the elegy written by her husband after her death in childbirth at the age of twenty-four. Thomas remembered that before each of her six lyings-in his wife had asked him to pray with her that God would continue their lives together.[9] Elizabeth Drinker probably echoed the sentiments of most women when she reflected, "I have often thought that women who live to get over the time of Child-bareing, if other things are favourable to them, experience more comfort and satisfaction than at any other period of their lives."[10]

Facing the hazards of childbirth, women depended on the community of their sex for companionship and medical assistance. Women who had moved away at marriage frequently returned to their parents' home for the delivery, either because they had no neighbors or because they preferred the care of their mothers to that of their in-laws. Other women summoned mothers, aunts, and sisters on both sides of the family, as well as female friends, when birth was imminent.[11] Above all, they relied on the experience of midwives to guide them through labor.

Women monopolized the practice of midwifery in America, as in Europe, through the middle of the eighteenth century. As the recognized experts in the conduct of childbirth, they advised the mother-to-be if troubles arose during pregnancy, supervised the activities of lying-in, and used their skills to assure safe delivery. Until educated male physicians began to practice obstetrics, midwives enjoyed some status in the medical profession, enhanced by their legal responsibilities in the communities they served.

English civil authorities required midwives to take oaths in order to be licensed but imposed no official test of their skills. The oaths indicate that midwives had responsibilities which were serious enough to warrant supervision. They swore not to allow any infant to be baptized outside the Church of England, and promised to help both rich and poor, to report the true parentage of a child, and to abstain from performing abortions. Oath-breaking midwives could be excommunicated or fined.[12]

Some American midwives learned their art in Europe, where midwifery was almost exclusively the professional province of women. Though barber surgeons and physicans increasingly asserted their interest in midwifery during the seventeenth century, midwives and patients resisted the intruders.[13] The midwives' levels of skill varied. Some acquired their medical education in the same way as many surgeons and physicians, by apprenticeship; some read manuals by more learned midwives and physicians; and after 1739, when the first British lying-in hospital was founded, a few were taught by the physicians who directed such hospitals.[14] But more often than not, women undertook midwifery equipped only with folk knowledge and the experience of their own pregnancies.[15]

Disparity of skills also existed among American midwives. Experienced midwives practiced alongside women who were, one physician observed, "as ignorant of their business as the women they deliver."[16] By the end of the eighteenth century physicians thought that the "greater part" of the midwives in America took up the occupation by accident, "having first been *catched*, as they express it, with a woman in labour."[17] The more diligent sought help from books, probably popular medical manuals such as *Aristotle's Master Piece*.[18]

American midwives conducted their practice free, on the whole, from governmental supervision and control. Only two colonies appear to have enacted regulatory statutes, and it does not seem that these were rigorously enforced. In the seventeenth century Massachusetts and New York required midwives, together with surgeons and physicians, not to act contrary to the accepted rules of their art. More specifically, in 1716 the common council of New York City prescribed a licensing oath for midwives, which was similar to the oaths of England though without the provision on baptism. The oath included an injunction—significant for the theme of this article—that midwives not "open any matter Appertaining to your Office in the presence of any Man unless Nessessity or Great Urgent Cause do Constrain you to do so."[19] This oath, which was regularly re-enacted until 1763, suggests the common restriction of midwifery to women, excluding male physicians or barber surgeons, who, in any case, were few and usually ill trained. There are records of male midwives in New York, Philadelphia, Charleston, and Annapolis after 1740, but only one, a Dr. Spencer of Philadelphia, had London training in midwifery, and it was said of another that "he attended very few natural labors."[20]

Though their duties were not as well defined by law, American midwives served the community in ways similar to those of their British counterparts. In addition to assisting at childbed, they testified in court in cases of bastardy, verified birthdates, and examined female prisoners who pleaded pregnancy to escape punishment.[21] Some colonials also observed the English custom of having the midwife attend the baptism and burial of infants. Samuel Sewall reported that Elizabeth Weeden brought his son John to church for christening in 1677, and at the funeral of little Henry in 1685 "Midwife Weeden and Nurse Hill carried the Corps by turns."[22]

The inclusion of the midwife in these ceremonies of birth and death shows how women's relationships with their midwives went beyond mere respect for the latters' skill. Women with gynecologic problems would freely tell a midwife things "that they had rather die than discover to the Doctor."[23] Grateful patients eulogized midwives.[24] The acknowledgment of the services of one Boston midwife, recorded on her tombstone, has inspired comment since 1761. The stone informs the curious that Mrs. Phillips was "born in Westminister in Great Britain, and Commission'd by John Laud, Bishop of London in ye Year 1718 to ye Office of a Midwife," came to "this Country" in 1719, and "by ye Blessing of God has brought into this world above 3000 Children."[25]

We may picture Mrs. Phillips's professional milieu as a small room, lit and warmed by a large fire, and crowded by a gathering of family and friends. In daytime, during the early stages of labor, children might be present, and while labor proceeded female friends dropped in to offer encouragement and help; securing refreshments for such visitors was a part of the preparation for childbirth, especially among the well-to-do families with which we are concerned. Men did not usually remain at the bedside. They might be summoned in to pray, but as delivery approached they waited elsewhere with the children and with women who were "not able to endure" the tension in the room.[26]

During the final stages of labor the midwife took full charge, assisted by other women. As much as possible, midwives managed deliveries by letting nature do the work; they caught the child, tied the umbilical cord, and if necessary fetched the afterbirth. In complicated cases they might turn the child and deliver it feet first, but if this failed, the fetus had to be destroyed. In all circumstances the midwife's chief duty was to comfort the woman in labor while they both waited on nature, and this task she could, as a woman, fulfill with social ease. Under the midwife's direction the woman in labor was liberally fortified with hard liquor or mulled wine. From time to time the midwife examined her cervix to gauge the progress of labor and encouraged her to walk about until the pains became too strong. There was no standard posture for giving birth, but apparently few women lay flat in bed. Some squatted on a midwife's stool, a low chair with an open seat. Others knelt on a pallet, sat on another woman's lap, or stood supported by two friends.[27]

Friends were "welcome companions," according to one manual for midwives, because they enabled the woman in labor "to bear her pains to more advantage," and "their cheerful conversation supports her spirits and inspires her with confidence."[28] Elizabeth Drinker endeavored to talk her daughter into better spirits by telling her that as she was thirty-nine "this might possibly be the last trial of this sort."[29] Some women attempted to cheer the mother-to-be by assuring her that her labor was easy compared to others they had seen, or provoked laughter by making bawdy jokes.[30]

For some attendants, a delivery could be a wrenching experience. Elizabeth Drinker relived her own difficult deliveries when her daughters suffered their labors, and on one such occasion she noted with irony, "This day is 38 years since I was in agonies bringing her into this world of troubles: she told me with tears that this was her birthday."[31] For others the experience of assisting the labors of friends was a reminder of their sex. Sarah Eve, an unmarried twenty-two-year-old, attended the labor of a friend in 1772 and carried the tidings of birth to the waiting father. "None but those that were like anxious could be sensible of a joy like theirs," she wrote in her journal that night. "Oh! Eve! Adam's wife I mean—who could forget her today?"[32]

After delivery, the mother was covered up snugly and confined to her bed, ideally for three to four weeks. For fear of catching cold she was not allowed to put her feet on the floor and was constantly supplied with hot drinks. Family members relieved her of household duties. Restless women, and those who could not afford weeks of idleness, got up in a week or less, but not without occasioning censure.[33]

The social and medical hold of midwives on childbirth loosened during the half century after 1770, as male physicians assumed the practice of midwifery among urban women of social rank. Initially, physicians entered the field as trained practitioners who could help women in difficult labors through the use of instruments, but ultimately they presided over normal deliveries as well. The presence of male physicians in the lying-in chamber signaled a general change in attitudes toward childbirth, including a modification of the dictum that women had to suffer. At the same time, because medical training was restricted to men, women lost their position as assistants at childbirth, and an event traditionally managed by a community of women became an experience shared primarily by a woman and her doctor.

William Shippen, the first American physician to establish a steady practice of midwifery, quietly overcame resistance to the presence of a man in the lying-in room. Casper Wistar's *Eulogies on Dr. Shippen*, published in 1809, states that when Shippen began in 1763, male practitioners were resorted to only in a crisis. "This was altogether the effect of prejudice," Wistar remarked, adding that "by Shippen this prejudice was so done away, that in the course of ten years he became very fully employed."[34] A few figures testify to the trend. The Philadelphia city directory in 1815 listed twenty-one women as midwives, and twenty-three men as practitioners of midwifery. In 1819 it listed only thirteen female midwives, while the number of men had risen to forty-two; and by 1824 only six female midwives remained in the directory.[35] "Prejudice" similarly dissolved in Boston, where in 1781 the physicians advertised that they expected immediate payment for their services in midwifery; by 1820 midwifery in Boston was almost "entirely confined" to physicians.[36] By 1826 Dr. William Dewees, professor of midwifery at the University of Pennsylvania and the outstanding American obstetrician of the early nineteenth century, could preface his textbook on midwifery with an injunction to every American medical student to study the subject because "everyone almost" must practice it. He wrote that "a change of manners within a few years" had "resulted in almost exclusive employment of the male practitioner."[37] . . .

On one level the change was a direct consequence of the fact that after 1750 growing numbers of American men traveled to Europe for medical education. Young men with paternal means, like Shippen, spent three to four years studying medicine, including midwifery, with leading physicians in the hospitals of London and the classrooms of Edinburgh. When they returned to the colonies they brought back not only a superior set of skills but also British ideas about hospitals, medical schools, and professional standards.[38]

In the latter part of the eighteenth century advanced medical training became available in North America. At the time of Shippen's return in 1762 there was only one hospital in the colonies, the Pennsylvania Hospital, built ten years earlier to care for the sick poor. Shippen and his London-educated colleagues saw that the hospital could be used for the clinical training of physicians, as in Europe. Within three years the Philadelphia doctors, led by John Morgan, established formal, systematic instruction at a school of medicine, supplemented by clinical work in the hospital.[39] Morgan maintained that the growth of the colonies "called aloud" for a medical school "to increase the number of those who exercise the profession of medicine and surgery."[40] Dr. Samuel Bard successfully addressed the same argument to the citizens of New York in 1768.[41]

In addition to promoting medical schools, Morgan and Bard defined the proper practitioner of medicine as a man learned in a science. To languages and liberal arts their ideal physician added anatomy, material medicine, botany, chemistry, and clinical experience. He was highly conscious not only of his duty to preserve "the life and health of mankind,"[42] but also of his professional status, and this new emphasis on professionalism extended to midwifery.

The trustees of the first American medical schools recognized midwifery as a branch of medical science. From its founding in 1768, Kings College in New York devoted one professorship solely to midwifery, and the University of Pennsylvania elected Shippen professor of anatomy, surgery, and midwifery in 1791. By 1807 five reputable American medical schools provided courses in midwifery.[43] In the early years of the nineteenth century some professors of midwifery began to call themselves obstetricians or professors of obstetrics, a scientific-sounding title free of the feminine connotations of the word midwife.[44] Though not compulsory for all medical students, the new field was considered worthy of detailed study along the paths pioneered by English physicians.

Dr. William Smellie contributed more to the development of obstetrics than any other eighteenth-century physician. His influence was established by his teaching career in London from 1741 to 1758, and by his treatise on midwifery, first published in 1752.[45] Through precise measurement and observation Smellie discovered the mechanics of parturition. He found that the child's head turned throughout delivery, adapting the widest part to the widest diameter of the pelvic canal. Accordingly, he defined maneuvers for manipulating an improperly presented child. He also recognized that obstetrical forceps, generally known for only twenty years when he wrote in 1754, should be used to rectify the position of an infant wedged in the mouth of the cervix, in preference to the "common method" of simply jerking the child out. He perfected the design of the forceps and taught its proper use, so that physicians could save both mother and child in difficult deliveries, instead of being forced to dismember the infant with hooks.[46]

To Smellie and the men who learned from him, the time seemed ripe to apply science to a field hitherto built on ignorance and supported by prejudice. Smellie commented on the novelty of scientific interest in midwifery. "We ought to be ashamed of ourselves," he admonished the readers of his *Treatise*, "for the little improvement we have made in so many centuries." Only recently have "we established a better method of delivering in laborious and preternatural cases."[47] Smellie's countryman Dr. Charles White reflected in his text on midwifery in 1793 that "the bringing of the art of midwifery to perfection upon scientific and medical principles seems to have been reserved for the present generation."[48]

Some American physicians shared this sense of the new "Importance of the Obstetrick Art." Midwifery was not a "trifling" matter to be left to the uneducated, Thomas Jones of the College of Medicine of Maryland wrote in 1812. Broadly defined as the care of "all the indispositions incident to women from the commencement of pregnancy to the termination of

lactation," it ranked among the most important branches of medicine. "With the cultivation of this branch of science," women could now "reasonably look to men for safety in the perilous conditions" of childbirth.[49] . . .

. . . Social as well as medical reasons account for the innovations in the practice of midwifery in such cities as Boston, Philadelphia, and New York. Physicians received their medical education in cities, and cities offered the best opportunities to acquire patients and live comfortably. Urban families of some means could afford the $12 to $15 minimum fee which Boston physicians demanded for midwife services in 1806.[50] Obstetrics was found to be a good way to establish a successful general practice. The man who conducted himself well in the lying-in room won the gratitude and confidence of his patient and her family, and they naturally called him to serve in other medical emergencies. It was midwifery, concluded Dr. Walter Channing of Boston, that ensured doctors "the permanency and security of all their other business."[51]

The possibility of summoning a physician, who could perhaps insure a safer and faster delivery, opened first to urban women. The dramatic rescue of one mother and child given up by a midwife could be enough to convince a neighborhood of women of a physician's value and secure him their practice.[52] Doctors asserted that women increasingly hired physicians because they became convinced "that the well instructed physician is best calculated to avert danger and surmount difficulties."[53] Certainly by 1795 the women of the Drinker family believed that none but a physician should order medicine for a woman in childbed, and had no doubts that Dr. Shippen or his colleague Dr. Nicholas Way was the best help that they could summon.[54]

Although she accepted a male physician as midwife, Elizabeth Drinker still had reservations about the use of instruments to facilitate childbirth and was relieved when Shippen did not have to use forceps on her daughter. Other women feared to call a physician because they assumed that any instruments he used would destroy the child.[55] However, once the capabilities of obstetrical forceps became known, some women may have turned to them by choice in hope of faster deliveries. Such hope stimulated a medical fashion. By about 1820 Dewees and Bard felt it necessary to condemn nervous young doctors for resorting unnecessarily to forceps.[56]

The formal education of American physicians and the development of midwifery as a science, the desire of women for the best help in childbirth, the utility of midwifery as a means of building a physician's practice, and, ultimately, the gigantic social changes labeled urbanization explain why physicians assumed the ordinary practice of midwifery among well-to-do urban women in the late eighteenth and early nineteenth centuries. This development provides insight into the changing condition of women in American society.

The development of obstetrics signified a partial rejection of the assumption that women had to suffer in childbirth and implied a new social appreciation of women, as admonitions to women for forbearance under the pain of labor turned to the desire to relieve their pain. . . . In his doctoral dissertation in 1812 one American medical student drew a distinction between childbirth in primitive societies and his own. In the former, "women are generally looked on by their rugged lords as unworthy of any particular attention," and death or injury in childbirth is "not deemed a matter of any importance." Well-instructed assistants to women in childbirth were one sign of the value placed on women in civilized societies.[57]

The desire to relieve women in childbirth also signified a more liberal interpretation of scripture. At the University of Pennsylvania in 1804, Peter Miller, a medical student, modified the theological dictum that women must bear in sorrow. The anxieties of pregnancy and the anguish caused by the death of so many infants constituted sorrow enough for women, argued Miller. They did not need to be subjected to bodily pain as well.[58] Reiterating this argument, Dewees bluntly asked, "Why should the female alone incur the penalty of God?"[59] To relieve the pain of labor Dewees and his fellows analyzed the anatomy and physiology of childbirth and defined techniques for the use of instruments.

If the development of obstetrics suggests the rise of a "special tenderness for women" on the part of men, it also meant that women's participation in medical practice was diminished and disparaged. A few American physicians instructed midwives or wrote manuals for them, but these efforts were private and sporadic, and had ceased by 1820. The increasing professionalization of medicine, in the minds of the physicians who formed medical associations that set the standards of the field, left little room for female midwives, who lacked the prescribed measure of scientific training and professional identity.[60]

William Shippen initially invited midwives as well as medical students to attend his private courses in midwifery. His advertisement in the *Pennsylvania Gazette* in January 1765 related his experience assisting women in the country in difficult labors, "most of which was made so by the unskillful old women about them," and announced that he "thought it his duty to immediately begin" courses in midwifery "in order to instruct those women who have virtue enough to own their ignorance and apply for instructions, as well as those young gentlemen now engaged in the study of that useful and necessary branch of surgery." Shippen taught these private lessons until after the

Revolution, when he lectured only to the students at the University of Pennsylvania, who, of course, were male.[61]

At the turn of the century Dr. Valentine Seaman conducted the only other known formal instruction of midwives. He was distressed by the ignorance of many midwives, yet convinced that midwives ought to manage childbirth because, unlike physicians, they had time to wait out lingering labors, and, as women, they could deal easily with female patients. Seaman offered his private lectures and demonstrations at the New York Almshouse lying-in ward, and in 1800 published them as the *Midwives Monitor and Mothers Mirror*.[62] A handful of other men wrote texts at least nominally directed to midwives between 1800 and 1810; some of these, like Seaman's, discussed the use of instruments.[63] In 1817 Dr. Thomas Ewell proposed that midwives be trained at a national school of midwifery in Washington, D.C., to be supported by a collection taken up by ministers. There is no evidence that Ewell's scheme, presented in his medical manual, *Letters to Ladies*, ever gained a hearing.[64]

Seaman and Ewell, and other authors of midwives' manuals, presumed that if women mastered some of the fundamentals of obstetrics they would be desirable assistants in ordinary midwifery cases. In 1820 Dr. Channing of Boston went further in his pamphlet, *Remarks on the Employment of Females as Practitioners of Midwifery*, in which he maintained that no one could thoroughly understand the management of labor who did not understand "thoroughly the profession of medicine as a whole." Channing's principle would have totally excluded women from midwifery, because no one favored professional medical education for women. It was generally assumed that they could not easily master the necessary languages, mathematics, and chemistry, or withstand the trials of dissecting room and hospital. Channing added that women's moral

character disqualified them for medical practice: "Their feelings of sympathy are too powerful for the cool exercise of judgement" in medical emergencies, he wrote; "they do not have the power of action, nor the active power of mind which is essential to the practice of the surgeon."[65]

Denied formal medical training, midwives of the early nineteenth century could not claim any other professional or legal status. Unlike Great Britain, the United States had no extensive record of licensing laws or oaths defining the practice of midwifery. Nor were there any vocal groups of midwives who, conscious of their tradition of practice or associated with lying-in hospitals, were able to defend themselves against competition from physicians.[66] American midwives ceased practice among women of social rank with few words uttered in their defense.

The victory of the physicians produced its own problems. The doctor's sex affected the relationships between women and their attendants in childbirth, and transformed the atmosphere of the lying-in room. In his advice to his male students Dewees acknowledged that summoning a man to assist at childbed "cost females a severe struggle."[67] Other doctors knew that even the ordinary gynecologic services of a physician occasioned embarrassment and violated woman's "natural delicacy of feeling," and that every sensitive woman felt "deeply humilated" at the least bodily exposure.[68] Doctors recognized an almost universal repugnance on the part of women to male assistance in time of labor.[69] Because of "whim or false delicacy" women often refused to call a man until their condition had become critical.[70] It is unlikely that physicians exaggerated these observations, although there is little testimony from women themselves about their child-bed experience in the early nineteenth century.

The uneasiness of women who were

treated by men was sometimes shared by their husbands. In 1772 the *Virginia Gazette* printed a denunciation of male midwifery as immoral. The author, probably an Englishman, attributed many cases of adultery in England to the custom of employing men at deliveries. Even in labor a woman had intervals of ease, and these, he thought, were the moments when the doctor infringed on the privileges of the husband. It would be a matter of utmost indifference to him "whether my wife had spent the night in a bagnio, or an hour of the forenoon locked up with a man midwife in her dressing room."[71] Such arguments were frequently and seriously raised in England during the eighteenth century.[72] They may seem ludicrous, but at least one American man of Dr. Ewell's acquaintance suffered emotional conflict over hiring a male midwife. He sent for a physician to help his wife in her labor, yet "very solemnly he declared to the doctor, he would demolish him if he touched or looked at his wife."[73]

Physicians dealt with the embarrassment of patients and the suspicion of husbands by observing the drawing-room behavior of "well-bred gentlemen." Dewees told his students to "endeavor, by well chosen conversation, to divert your patient's mind from the purpose of your visit."[74] All questions of a delicate nature were to be communicated through a third party, perhaps the only other person in the room, either a nurse or an elderly friend or relative. The professional man was advised "never to seem to know anything about the parts of generation, further than that there is an orifice near the rectum leading to an os."[75]

Physicians did not perform vaginal examinations unless it was absolutely important to do so, and they often had to cajole women into permitting an examination at all. Nothing could be more shocking to a woman, Shippen lectured his students, "than for a young man the moment he enters the Chamber to ask

for Pomatum and proceed to examine the uterus."[76] Doctors waited until a labor pain clutched their patients and then suggested an examination by calling it "taking a pain." During examination and delivery the patient lay completely covered in her bed, a posture more modest, if less comfortable, than squatting on a pallet or a birth stool. The light in the room was dimmed by closing the shutters during the day and covering the lamps at night. If a physician used forceps, he had to manipulate them under the covers, using his free hand as a guide.[77] On this point doctors who read Thomas Denman's *Obstetrical Remembrancer* were reminded that "Degorges, one of the best obstetricians of his time, was blind."[78]

The crowd of supportive friends and family disappeared with the arrival of the doctor. The physician guarded against "too many attendants; where there are women, they must talk."[79] The presence of other women might increase the doctor's nervousness, and they certainly did not help the woman in labor. Medical men interpreted women's talk of other experiences with childbirth as mere gossip "of all the dangerous and difficult labours they ever heard any story about in their lives," which ought to be stopped lest it disturb the patient.[80] Especially distracting were the bawdy stories visitors told, expecting the physician to laugh, too. Medical professors recommended "grave deportment," warning that levity would "hurt your patient or yourself in her esteem."[81] Far from providing the consolation of a friend, the physician was often a stranger who needed to "get a little acquainted" with his patient. One medical text went so far as to coach him in a series of conversational ice breakers about children and the weather.[82]

Etiquette and prudery in the lying-in chamber affected medical care. Physicians were frustrated by their inability to examine their patients thoroughly, for they knew full well that learning midwifery from a book was "like learning shipbuilding without touching timber."[83] Examinations were inadequate, and the dangers of manipulating instruments without benefit of sight were tremendous. Dewees cautioned his students to take great care before pulling the forceps that "no part of the mother is included in the locking of the blades. This accident is frequent."[84] Accidental mutilation of infants was also reported, as the navel string had to be cut under the covers. Lecturers passed on the story of the incautious doctor who included the penis of an infant within the blades of his scissors.[85]

In view of such dangers, the conflict between social values and medical practice is striking. The expansion of medical knowledge brought men and women face to face with social taboos in family life. They had to ask themselves the question, Who should watch a woman give birth? For centuries the answer had unhesitatingly been female relatives and friends, and the midwife. The science of obstetrics, developing in the eighteenth century, changed the answer. Though women might socially be the most acceptable assistants at a delivery, men were potentially more useful.

In consequence of the attendance of male physicians, by 1825, for some American women, childbirth was ceasing to be an open ceremony. Though birth still took place at home, and though friends and relatives still lent a helping hand, visiting women no longer dominated the activities in the lying-in room. Birth became increasingly a private affair conducted in a quiet, darkened room. The physician limited visitors because they hindered proper medical care, but the process of birth was also concealed because it embarrassed both patient and physician.

Between 1760 and 1825 childbirth was thus transformed from an open affair to a restricted one. As one consequence of the development of obstetrics as a legitimate branch of medicine, male physicians began replacing midwives. They began to reduce childbirth to a scientifically managed event and deprived it of its folk aspects. Strengthened by the professionalization of their field, these physicians also responded to the hopes of women in Philadelphia, New York, and Boston for safe delivery. Although they helped some pregnant women, they hurt midwives, who were shut out of an area of medicine that had been traditionally their domain. All these innovations took place in the large urban centers in response to distinctly urban phenomena. They reflected the increasing privatization of family life, and they foreshadowed mid-nineteenth-century attitudes toward childbirth, mother, and woman.

NOTES

1. Cecil K. Drinker, *Not So Long Ago: A Chronicle of Medicine and Doctors in Colonial Philadelphia* (New York, 1937), 59–61.

2. Although births are noted frequently in diaries and letters of the seventeenth, eighteenth, and early nineteenth centuries, the event itself is rarely described. For the most part, information on the medical procedures and social customs of birth analyzed in this article is derived from midwives' manuals, medical textbooks, and lecture notes of medical students. This literature mingles plain observation with partisan advocacy of medical reform. It seems reasonable to accept the physician's evaluations of midwifery as evidence of their desire for change, and their case histories as documents of the actual circumstances of birth. Despite ambiguities, the material provides a glimpse of social change not directly reflected in many conventional sources.

3. Betsy Copping Corner, *William Shippen, Jr.: Pioneer in American Medical Education* (Philadelphia, 1951), 103; Irving S. Cutter and Henry R. Viets, *A Short History of Midwifery* (Philadelphia, 1964), 150.

4. Cutter and Viets, *Short History*, 148–149.

5. For a discussion of childbearing patterns see Wilson H. Grabill, Clyde V. Kiser, and Pascal K. Whelpton, "A Long View," in Michael Gordon, ed., *The American Family in Social-Historical Perspective* (New York, 1973), 392; J. Potter, "The Growth of Population in America, 1700–1860," in D. V. Glass and D. E. C. Eversley, eds., *Population in History: Essays in Historical Demography* (Chicago, 1965), 644, 647, 663, 679; Robert V. Wells, "Demographic Change and the Life Cycle of American Families," in Theodore K. Rabb and Robert I. Rotberg, eds., *The Family in History: Interdisciplinary Essays* (New York, 1971), 85, 88.

When William Byrd II wrote in his diary in 1712, "my wife was often indisposed with breeding and very cross," he used a term common until the nineteenth century. Louis B. Wright and Marion Tinling, eds., *The Secret Diary of William Byrd of Westover, 1709–1712* (Richmond, Va., 1941), 548. "Breeding" was used colloquially and in popular medical literature. The use of the term to describe the hatching or birth of animals parallels its application to humans. The word lingered longest in speech in the American South, where fertile or pregnant black slaves were called "breeding women," an indication of the animality implied in the word. *The Oxford English Dictionary*, s.v. "breeding"; Mitford M. Mathews, ed., *A Dictionary of Americanisms on Historical Principles* (Chicago, 1951), s.v. "breeding." "Teeming," also considered archaic dialect by the *OED*, applied to women from the sixteenth through eighteenth centuries.

6. Benjamin Colman, *Some of the Honours that Religion Does unto the Fruitful Mothers in Israel . . .* (Boston, 1715), 8; Cotton Mather, *Elizabeth in Her Holy Retirement. An Essay to Prepare a Pious Woman for her Lying-in. Or Maxims and Methods of Piety, to Direct and Support an Hand Maid of the Lord, Who Expects a Time of Travail* (Boston, 1710), 3; Cotton Mather, *Ornaments for the Daughters of Zion, or the Character and Happiness of a Woman: in a Discourse*, 3d ed. (Boston, 1741), 2–3. Even a secular medical manual affirmed the curse of Eve: American edition of *Aristotle's Master Piece*, 1766, discussed in Otho T. Beall, Jr., "*Aristotle's Master Piece* in America: A Landmark in the Folklore of Medicine," *William and Mary Quarterly*, 3d Ser., XX (1963), 216.

7. Mather, *Elizabeth in Her Retirement*, 1.

8. *The Diary of Cotton Mather* (Massachusetts Historical Society, *Collections*, 7th Ser., Pt. II [1912]), VIII, 618, 700; Mather, *Elizabeth in Her Retirement*, 2, 6, 7.

9. [Thomas Clap], "Memoirs of a College President: Womanhood in Early America," ed. Edwin Stanley Wells, *The Connecticut Magazine*, XII (1908), 233–239, esp. 235.

10. Drinker, *Not So Long Ago*, 48.

11. Stewart Mitchell, ed., *New Letters of Abigail Adams, 1788–1801* (Boston, 1947), 3–5, 56; Clayton Harding Chapman, "Benjamin Colman's Daughters," *New England Quarterly*, XXVI (1953), 182; Malcolm R. Lowell, ed., *Two Quaker Sisters, from the Original Diaries of Elizabeth Buffum Chace and Lucy Buffum Lovell* (New York, 1937), 1, 12; Drinker, *Not So Long Ago*, 51–60; Mary Vial Holyoke's diary, in George Francis Dow, ed., *The Holyoke Diaries, 1709–1856* (Salem, Mass., 1911), 70, 73, 75, 83, 95, 100, 101, 107; *Diary of Samuel Sewall* (Mass. Hist. Soc., *Colls.*, 5th Ser. V–VII [1878–1882]), I, 11, 40, 110, 166, 222–223, 351, 394, 426, II, 49, hereafter cited as *Diary of Sewall*; Ethel Armes, ed., *Nancy Shippen: Her Journal Book* (Philadelphia, 1935), 122–124.

12. James Hobson Aveling, *English Midwives: Their History and Prospects* (London, 1967 [orig. publ. 1872]), 3–4, 7, 10; E. H. Carter, *The Norwich Subscription Books: A Study of the Subscription Books of the Diocese of Norwich, 1637–1800* (London, 1937), 17–18, 134; facsimile oath of 1661, in Thomas Forbes, *The Midwife and the Witch* (New Haven, Conn., 1966), 145.

13. Cutter and Viets, *Short History*, 5–55; Isaac Flack, *Eternal Eve* (London, 1950), 218–219; Alfred McClintock, ed., *Smellie's Treatise on the Theory and Practice of Midwifery* (London, 1876–1878), II, 248–250, III, 26–27, 298, 317–319; Percival Willughby, *Observations in Midwifery*, ed. Henry Blenkinsop (Wakefield, Eng., 1972 [orig. publ. 1803]), 37, 155.

Save for midwifery, medical practice in England was divided among three guilds of physicians, surgeons, and apothecaries. Physicians, titled "doctor" and usually possessing university degrees, theoretically as gentlemen did not work with their hands. Surgeons, trained by apprenticeship and rarely holding degrees, dealt with structural emergencies. Apothecaries, also apprenticed, sold drugs. These distinctions disappeared in the rural areas and small towns of England, as well as in colonial America, where medical men, usually without formal training and indiscriminately called doctor, engaged in general practice. Even after 1765, the American men who were by strict definition physicians practiced general medicine. Richard Harrison Shryock, *Medicine and Society in America, 1660–1860* (Ithaca, N.Y., 1960), 2–3, 7, 10.

14. Aveling, *English Midwives*, 138–144; Alice Clark, *Working Life of Women in the Seventeenth Century* (London, 1919), 265, 269, 270–275; *The Compleat Midwifes Practice, in the Most Weighty and High Concernments of the Birth of Man* . . . (London, 1656), 119–124; John Memis, *The Midwive's Pocket Companion: or a Practical Treatise on Midwifery* (London, 1765), v–vii; Jane Sharp, *The Compleat Midwife's Companion: or, the art of midwifery improved* . . . , 4th ed. (London, 1725), x–xii; Willughby, *Observations in Midwifery*, ed. Blenkinsop, 73.

15. John Kobler, *The Reluctant Surgeon: A Biography of John Hunter* (New York, 1960), 31; Sharp, *Compleat Midwife's Companion*, introduction; Willughby, *Observations in Midwifery*, ed. Blenkinsop, 102.

16. Valentine Seaman, *The Midwives Monitor, and Mothers Mirror: Being Three Concluding Lectures of a Course of Instruction of Midwifery* (New York, 1800), viii.

17. Ibid. See also Joseph Brevitt, *The Female Medical Repository* . . . (Baltimore, 1810), 6.

18. Beall, "Aristotle's Master Piece," *WMQ*, 3d Ser., XX (1963), 209–210; Seaman, *Midwives Monitor*, ix. Beall's article is the best study of the popular manuals of "Aristotle." The *Master Piece*, which was the creation of an English physician, "W. S.," and a succession of hack writers, first appeared in England in 1684. The numerous later editions were the only works on sex and gynecology widely available to eighteenth-century Americans.

19. Jane B. Donegan, "Midwifery in America, 1760–1860: A Study in Medicine and Morality" (Ph.D. diss., Syracuse University, 1972), 9–10, 12; "A Law for Regulating Mid Wives Within the City of New York," Minutes of the Common Council of New York, 1716, Appendix I, in Claire E. Fox, "Pregnancy, Childbirth and Early Infancy in Anglo-American Culture, 1675–1830" (Ph.D. diss., University of Pennsylvania, 1966), 442–445; Richard Harrison Shryock, *Medical Licensing in America, 1650–1965* (Baltimore, 1967), 3, 16; James J. Walsh, *History of Medicine in New York: Three Centuries of Medical Progress*, II (New York, 1919), 22, 25.

20. Cutter and Viets, *Short History*, 145, 150; *Maryland Gazette* (Annapolis), Sept. 30, 1747; Francis R. Packard, *History of Medi-*

cine in the United States*, I (New York, 1931), 52–53; Shryock, *Medicine and Society*, 11–12; J. Whitridge Williams, *A Sketch of the History of Obstetrics in the United States up to 1860* (Baltimore, 1903), 1.

21. Wyndham B. Blanton, *Medicine in Virginia in the Seventeenth Century* (Richmond, 1930), 166; Packard, *History of Medicine*, I, 52; Julia C. Spruill, *Women's Life and Work in the Southern Colonies* (Chapel Hill, N.C., 1938), 272; Herbert Thoms, *Chapters in American Obstetrics* (Springfield, Ill., 1961), 10.

22. *Diary of Sewall*, I, 40, 114; Sharp, *Compleat Midwife's Companion*, frontispiece of midwife at christening.

23. Aristotle (pseud.), *Aristotle's Compleat and Experienc'd Midwife, in two Parts. I. Guide for Childbearing Women. II. Proper and Safe Remedies for the Curing of all those Distempers that are incident to the Female Sex* . . . , 9th ed. (London, [1700?]), iii.

24. Broadside of elegy to Mary Broadwell, in Francisco Guerra, *American Medical Bibliography, 1639–1783* (New York, 1962), 69.

25. Packard, *History of Medicine*, I, 49.

26. Drinker, *Not So Long Ago*, 51, 52, 54, 59; Dow, ed., *Holyoke Diaries*, 70, 73, 75, 81, 83, 95, 101, 107; *Diary of Sewall*, V, 40, 222–223, 394, VI, 49; Charles White, *A Treatise on the Management of Pregnant and Lying-in Women* (Worcester, Mass., 1793), 19–20.

27. Aristotle (pseud.), *Compleat and Experienc'd Midwife*, 50–51, 56, 57; Nicholas Culpeper, *A Directory for Midwives: or, a Guide for Women in Their Conception, Bearing, and Suckling their Children* (London, 1651), 167; Drinker, *Not So Long Ago*, 60; *Diary of Sewall*, V, 40; Sharp, *Compleat Midwife's Companion*, 81, 82, 124, 125, 128; White, *Treatise on Pregnant Women*, 20, 74; Willughby, *Observations in Midwifery*, ed. Blenkinsop, 4, 11, 13, 19.

28. Seaman, *Midwives Monitor*, 90–91.

29. Drinker, *Not So Long Ago*, 59.

30. William Buchan, *Advice to Mothers on the Subject of Their Own Health* (Charleston, S.C., 1807), 28; *The London Practice of Midwifery by an American Practitioner* (Concord, N.H., 1826), 129; Thomas Chalkey James, "Notes from Drs. Osborne's and Clark's Lectures on Midwifery taken by T. C. James, London, 1790–1791," MS, Historical Collections, College of Physicians of Philadelphia.

31. Drinker, *Not So Long Ago*, 53, 59.

32. Mrs. Eva Eve Jones, ed., "Extracts from the Journal of Miss Sarah Eve," *Penn-*

sylvania Magazine of History and Biography, V (1881), 195.

33. Mitchell, ed., *New Letters of Adams*, 4–5; Jack P. Greene, ed., *The Diary of Colonel Landon Carter of Sabine Hall, 1752–1788*, II (Charlottesville, Va., 1965), 86; Dow, ed., *Holyoke Diaries*, 49, 56, 58, 62, 63, 65, 67, 73, 77, 78, 82, 95, 100, 107; *Diary of Sewall*, II, 51; Sharp, *Compleat Midwife's Companion*, frontispiece drawing of lying-in; McClintock, ed., *Smellie's Treatise*, I, 380.

34. Corner, *William Shippen*, 124; Cutter and Viets, *Short History*, 150.

35. *Kite's Philadelphia Directory for 1815* (Philadelphia, 1815), xi–xii; John Paxton, *The Philadelphia Directory and Register for 1819* (Philadelphia, 1819), n.p.; Robert Desilver, *The Philadelphia Directory and Register for 1824* (Philadelphia, 1824), n.p.

36. Walter Channing (John Ware?), *Remarks on the Employment of Females as Practitioners in Midwifery* (Boston, 1820), 1; *Independent Chronicle and the Universal Advertiser* (Boston), Nov. 8, 1781.

37. William Potts Dewees, *A Compendious System of Midwifery, Chiefly Designed to Facilitate the Inquiries of Those Who may be Pursuing This Branch of Study* (Philadelphia, 1826), xiv.

38. Charles M. Andrews, *Colonial Folkways: A Chronicle of American Life in the Reign of the Georges* (New Haven, Conn., 1919), 147; Maurice Bear Gordon, *Aesculapius Comes to the Colonies: The Story of the Early Days of Medicine in the Thirteen Original Colonies* (Ventnor, N.J., 1949), 156–157, 460–465; Francis Packard, "How London and Edinburgh Influenced Medicine in Philadelphia in the Eighteenth Century," College of Physicians of Philadelphia, *Transactions*, 3d Ser., LIII (1931), 167.

39. Gordon, *Aesculapius*, 465; Packard, *History of Medicine*, I, 181–230; Packard, "How London and Edinburgh Influenced Medicine," College of Physicians of Philadelphia, *Trans.*, 3d Ser., LIII (1931), 163, 166.

40. John Morgan, *A Discourse Upon the Institution of Medical Schools in America* (Baltimore, 1937 [orig. publ. 1765]), 33.

41. Samuel Bard, *Two Discourses Dealing with Medical Education in Early New York* (New York, 1921), 1.

42. Ibid., 10, 16, 19; Morgan, *Discourse Upon the Institution of Medical Schools*, 14–17.

43. Packard, *History of Medicine*, II, 1125–1127; Williams, *Sketch of the History of Obstetrics*, 5–7.

44. *OED*, s.v. "obstetrics"; Packard, *History of Medicine*, II, 1125–1126.

45. Cutter and Viets, *Short History*, 26–28.

46. Ibid., 44–59; John Glaister, *Dr. William Smellie and His Contemporaries* (Glasgow, 1894), 170, 174, 178–179, 187; McClintock, ed., *Smellie's Treatise*, II, 250–251, 339.

47. McClintock, ed., *Smellie's Treatise*, II, 339.

48. White, *Treatise on Pregnant Women*, viii, 70–71.

49. Thomas Dashiell Jones, *An Essay on the Importance of the Obstetrick Art; Submitted to the Examination of Charles Alexander Warfield, M.D., President of the Medical Faculty of the College of Medicine of Maryland . . .* (Baltimore, 1812), 5, 11, 21, 23.

50. Boston Medical Association, *Rules and Regulations of the Boston Medical Association* (Boston, 1806), 4–5. The minimum fee escalated to $15/day case, $20/night by 1819. Boston Med. Assoc., *Rules and Regulations* (1819 ed.).

51. Channing, *Remarks on Employment of Females*, 19; Edward Warren, *The Life of John Collins Warren, M.D., Compiled Chiefly from his Autobiography and Journals*, I (Boston, 1860), 219.

52. Dewees, *Compendious System of Midwifery* (Philadelphia, 1824), 307.

53. Ibid. (1826), xiv.

54. Drinker, *Not So Long Ago*, 51, 54–56, 59.

55. Dewees, *Compendious System of Midwifery* (1824), 307; Drinker, *Not So Long Ago*, 60.

56. Samuel Bard, *A Compendium of the Theory and Practice of Midwifery*, 5th ed. (New York, 1819), v, 176, 289; Dewees, *Compendious System of Midwifery* (1826) xv.

57. Jones, *Essay on Obstetrick Art*, 8.

58. Peter Miller, *An Essay on the Means of Lessening the Pains of Parturition* (Philadelphia, 1804), 340.

59. William Potts Dewees, *Essays on Various Subjects Connected with Midwifery* (Philadelphia, 1823), 24.

60. Channing, *Remarks on Employment of Females*, 6–12; Jones, *Essay on Obstetrick Art*, 20; Joseph F. Kett, *The Formation of the American Medical Profession: The Role of Institutions, 1780–1860* (New Haven, Conn., 1968), 10–30.

61. *Pennsylvania Gazette* (Philadelphia), Jan. 31, 1765.

62. Williams, *Sketch of the History of Obstetrics*, 13; Seaman, *Midwives Monitor*, iii–vii.

63. Bard, *Compendium of Theory and Practice of Midwifery*, iv, 289; Brevitt, *Female Medical Repository*, 149–155; William Buchan, *A Compend of Domestic Midwifery for the Use of Female Practitioners, Being an Appendix to Buchan's Domestic Medicine* (Charleston, S.C., 1815); Samuel Jennings, *Married Lady's Companion, or Poor Man's Friend . . .* (New York, 1808), 135; Seaman, *Midwives Monitor*, 31–32. All of these works were directed entirely or in part to midwives.

64. Thomas Ewell, *Letters to Ladies, Detailing Important Information Concerning Themselves and Infants* (Philadelphia, 1817), vii–viii.

65. Channing, *Remarks on Employment of Females*, 4–7.

66. Aveling, *English Midwives*, 138–144, 153–159; Cutter and Viets, *Short History*, 43; Glaister, *William Smellie*, 32–36.

67. Dewees, *Compendious System of Midwifery* (1826), xv.

68. Channing, *Remarks on Employment of Females*, 16, 17; Ewell, *Letters to Ladies*, 27.

69. Jones, *Essay on Obstetrick Art*, 11.

70. Seaman, *Midwives Monitor*, iv.

71. *Virginia Gazette* (Purdie and Dixon), Oct. 1, 1772; reprinted in *New-London Gazette* (Conn.), Jan. 29, 1773.

72. Elizabeth Nihill, *A Treatise on the Art of Midwifery, Setting Forth Various Abuses Therein, Especially as to the Practice With Instruments* (London, 1760), and S. W. Fores, *Man-Midwifery Dissected* (London, 1793), are outstanding examples of arguments made about the supposed immorality of man midwives. Glaister, *William Smellie*, discusses other examples of such literature.

73. Ewell, *Letters to Ladies*, 27.

74. Dewees, *Compendious System of Midwifery* (1826), 189; Daniel B. Smith, "Notes on lectures of Thomas Chalkley James and William Potts Dewees, University of Pennsylvania, 1826," MS, Hist. Colls., College of Physicians of Philadelphia.

75. *London Practice of Midwifery*, 109.

76. Bard, *Compendium of Theory and Practice of Midwifery*, 181; lecture notes from lectures of William Shippen, Jr., University of Pennsylvania, n.d., MS, Hist. Colls., College of Physicians of Philadelphia.

77. Bard, *Compendium of Theory and Practice of Midwifery*, 181; Dewees, *Compendious System of Midwifery* (1826), 189–190; *London Practice of Midwifery*, 108–109.

78. Thomas Denman, *The Obstetrical Remembrancer, or Denman's Aphorisms on Natural and Difficult Parturition* (New York, 1848 [orig. U.S. publ. 1803]), 46.

79. *London Practice of Midwifery*, 129.

80. Ibid., 129–130.

81. James, "Notes from Osborne's and Clark's Lectures," Hist. Colls., College of Physicians of Philadelphia; notes on Shippen lectures, ibid.

82. Notes on Shippen lectures, ibid.; *London Practice of Midwifery*, 127.

83. Bard, *Compendium of Theory and Practice of Midwifery*, 220; Seaman, *Midwives Monitor*, ix.

84. Dewees, *Compendious System of Midwifery* (1826), 313.

85. Kobler, *Reluctant Surgeon*, 32; *London Practice of Midwifery*, 132–133.

ANNE FIROR SCOTT
Self-Portraits

One of the most striking modern literary images is Virginia Woolf's fantasy: Suppose, she once asked, Shakespeare had had a sister? While Shakespeare was

Excerpted from "Self-Portraits: Three Women" by Anne Firor Scott, in *Uprooted Americans: Essays To Honor Oscar Handlin*, edited by Richard Bushman et al. (Boston: Little, Brown, 1979), pp. 43–76. Copyright © 1979 by Anne Firor Scott. Reprinted by permission of the author. Notes have been renumbered and cross references adjusted.

sent to school and then permitted to go to London to seek his fortune, his sister would have been kept at home. "But she was not sent to school. She had no chance of learning grammar and logic, let alone of reading Horace and Virgil . . . before she was out of her teens she was to be betrothed to the son of a neighbouring wool-stapler." Like her brother she, too, ran away to London. "She stood at the stage door; she wanted to act she said. Men laughed in her face. The manager . . . hinted—you can imagine what. . . . At last—for she was very young, oddly like Shakespeare the poet in her face, with the same grey eyes and rounded brows—at last Nick Greene the actor-manager took pity on her; she found herself with a child by that gentleman and so—who shall measure the heat and violence of the poet's heart when caught and tangled in a woman's body?—killed herself one winter's night and lies buried at some cross-roads."

Anne Firor Scott puts Woolf's question to use by reviewing the lives of women who were closely related to famous patriots. Scott stresses the disparity in opportunities available to the women and to their brothers. Of the Franklins she observes: "At the age of fifteen one ran off to Philadelphia and . . . began his rise to the pinnacle among the Anglo-American intelligentsia. At the same age the other married a neighbor and in a month was pregnant."

Yet even within the constraints set by their society, women like Jane Franklin Mecom displayed strength and wisdom. Eliza Lucas Pinckney, with considerably greater economic resources, managed a complex family economy, arranging things so that her sons were freed to play out their public roles in the Revolution. Her own work in the development of indigo as a commercial product was itself an important contribution to the colonial economy.

[Collections of letters] heap up in mounds of insignificant and often dismal dust the innumerable trivialities of daily life, as it grinds itself out, year after year, and then suddenly they blaze up; the day shines out, complete, alive, before our eyes. . . .
—Virginia Woolf, "The Pastons and Chaucer"

The eighteenth century, to borrow Bernard Bailyn's phrase, was not incidentally but essentially different from the present, and many of the elements of that essential difference can be most clearly seen in

From "The Pastons and Chaucer" in *Collected Essays*, Volume III by Virginia Woolf. Copyright © 1925 by Harcourt Brace Jovanovich, Inc.; Copyright © 1953 by Leonard Woolf. Reprinted by permission of the publisher.

the lives of women. Colonial history has so long been written in terms of high achievement, of political theory, of founding fathers, of economic development, of David-and-Goliath conflict, that it is easy to forget how small a part such things played in most individual lives. Seen from the standpoint of ordinary people, the essential theme of the eighteenth-century experience was not so much achievement as the fragility and chanciness of life. Death was an omnipresent reality. Three children in one family die on a single day from epidemic disease; fathers are lost at sea; adolescents mysteriously waste away; mothers die in childbirth; yet life goes on to a constant underlying murmur of "God's sacred will be done." In these circumstances, how is the meaning of life perceived? What social structures do people build to sustain the spirit? What, in this context, become the central values? What is the texture of daily life?

The life histories of . . . colonial women give some clues.

The . . . women are Jane Franklin Mecom of Boston, . . . and Eliza Lucas Pinckney of Charleston. Taken together their lives cover nearly a century, from 1712 when the first was born to [1792]. . . . Each created a self-portrait . . . in letters. . . . Various depredations have washed out important parts of their life histories; and many things went unrecorded. Yet the documents which have survived bring us into the midst of daily experience, and reveal, from time to time, their most deeply held cultural values.

JANE FRANKLIN MECOM

Jane, youngest of Josiah Franklin's seventeen children, was born in 1712, six years after Benjamin. Because in later life she would become her brother's favorite correspondent, we know more about her than about any other woman of her social class in eighteenth-century Boston.

She was eleven when Benjamin made his famous getaway, breaking his apprenticeship and embarking upon the legendary career which would make him the archetypal self-made American. In old age both looked back with favor upon their early childhood: "It was indeed a Lowly Dwelling we were brought up in but we were fed Plentifully, made comfortable with fire and cloathing, had sildom any contention among us, but all was Harmony: Especially betwen the Heads—and they were Universally Respected, & the most of the Famely in good Reputation, this is still happier liveing than multituds Injoy."[1]

Even allowing for the rosy glow the passage of time creates, the recollections of both brother and sister suggest that the parents were remarkable people, and that such education as children get at home, both had gotten. The things Jane Mecom singled out for recollection were central values all her life: a good reputation and the respect of the community. She always tried to "live respectable," and her fondest hope was that her children should do so.

At the age when her brother had run away to begin his climb to fame, Jane Franklin married a neighbor who was a saddler. Her brother sent a spinning wheel, an appropriate gift for a seventeenth child who could expect no dowry. The best efforts of both spouses would be required to keep up with a growing family, as—for a quarter of a century—every second year brought a new baby. Three died in infancy, but nine survived to be fed, clothed, and trained for self-support.

By the time we catch another glimpse of Jane Mecom she was already thirty, living in a house owned by her father, taking in lodgers and caring for her aging parents. Her twelve-year-old son was learning the saddler's trade, and she was searching for appropriate apprenticeships for the younger ones. Between caring for parents, children, lodgers, and her husband's shop it is no wonder that the only written word of hers which survives from this period is a postscript to a letter her mother wrote to Benjamin. His letters to her began a pattern which would last a lifetime, as he spoke of sending "a few Things that may be of some Use perhaps in your Family."[2]

His help was more than financial. Busy making his own way in Philadelphia, he took time to find an apprenticeship for his namesake, Benny Mecom, who gave some promise of talents similar to his own. There were problems "such as are commonly incident to boys of his years," although, Franklin added, "he has many good qualities, for which I love him."[3] Diligence was not one of those qualities, and Jane Mecom was deeply concerned lest Benny never learn to work. He never

did, at least not steadily, and would continue to cause his mother anxiety as long
as he lived.

We get our next clear glimpse of Jane
Mecom when she was fifty-one and entertaining her brother in her own house.
While he was there she enjoyed what
would ever after be her measure of "suitable Conversation," and shone, however
briefly, in the reflected glory of Dr.
Franklin as Boston admirers paid court to
him at her house. The fact that he chose
to domicile himself with the Mecoms,
rather than with the far more affluent and
equally welcoming "cousen Williams,"
says something about the quality of her
conversation, or, perhaps, about his sensitivity to her feelings.

That interval of pleasure was brief.
Four of the twelve Mecom children were
already dead; now Sarah, at twenty-
seven a "Dear and Worthy child," died,
leaving a husband and four children
who promptly moved into Jane Mecom's
house. Within six months two of the four
grandchildren were dead. She was still
grieving for them when Edward Mecom,
her husband of thirty-eight years, also
died. She wrote one of the two comments
about him to be found in any of her letters: "It pleased God to call my Husband
out of this Troblesom world where he
had Injoyed Little and suffered much by
Sin & Sorrow."[4] Two years later she lost
her youngest and favorite, Polly, at eighteen: "Sorrows roll upon me like the
waves of the sea. I am hardly allowed
time to fetch my breath. I am broken
with breach upon breach, and I have
now, in the first flow of my grief, been
almost ready to say 'What have I more?'
But God forbid, that I should indulge
that thought. . . . God is sovereign and
I submit."[5]

In 1766 she was fifty-five. Of five surviving children the oldest was thirty-
four and the youngest twenty-one, but
none was in a position to support a widowed mother. Two sons had been bred to

the saddler's trade; one had died and the
other gone to sea. Peter, a soap-boiler
like his grandfather, showed signs of the
mental illness which would eventually in-
capacitate him, and the feckless Benjamin
was not earning enough to support his
own wife and children. Her son-in-law
Flagg was an unskilled workman, hard
put to take care of his two children. The
one daughter who still lived with her was
a melancholy and sickly young woman.

Jane Mecom's thoughts turned, therefore, to self-support. She continued to
take in lodgers and her brother sent from
England a small stock of trading goods
which arrived just as Bostonians decided
to boycott English goods in protest of the
Stamp Act. Poverty, she concluded, "is
Intailed on my famely."[6]

She was acutely aware of her dependence on her brother's help. She tried to
repay him with reports on life in Boston.
"The whol conversation of this Place
turns upon Politices and Riligous contry-
verces," she wrote, adding that her own
sentiments were for peace. With his reply
he sent her a set of his philosophical papers, which she proudly read.[7]

Somehow in 1769 she contrived a trip
to Philadelphia, where Franklin's wife
and daughter found her "verey a gre-
abel"—so much so that he was moved to
suggest, from London, that she consider
staying on permanently.[8] But Boston was
home, and back she went into the midst
of the rising conflict with Great Britain.

Her brother, though thoroughly engrossed in the same conflict in London,
took time to write Jane Mecom asking for
detailed instructions as to the making of
"crown soap," a family secret which he
feared might be lost if it were not preserved for the next generation. Here at
last was something she could do in return
for all his help; her instructions were
given in minute detail.

At about this time her letters began to
grow longer and more revealing. Perhaps
her visit to Deborah Franklin had reduced

her awe of her famous brother; perhaps confidence in her own capacities was growing. Whatever the reason, she began to speak more freely, range more widely, and fill out—for us—the scanty self-portrait belatedly begun.

An admirer of Thomas Hutchinson and a lover of peace, Jane Mecom was no early patriot. By 1774, however, "Proflegate soulders" making trouble and harassing citizens on the streets of Boston pushed her closer to the rebel position. The battle of Lexington finished what the soldiers had begun, as she locked her house, packed such goods as she could carry, and took refuge in Rhode Island.

In some ways the war changed her life for the better. Catherine Ray Greene, with whom she stayed at first, became her good friend. Her granddaughter, Jenny Flagg, married Elihu Greene, brother of General Nathanael Greene, a solid farmer, merchant, and entrepreneur. A man of his standing could well have demanded a dowry, but his willingness to marry Jenny for love marked a change in the hitherto unbroken stream of Mecom bad luck.

In the fall of 1774 Franklin came home after a decade in England, and not long after took his sister for a prolonged stay in Philadelphia. His wife, Deborah, had died, and Jane was able to be helpful to him until he went off to France. In two years General Howe's decision to occupy Philadelphia sent her back to Rhode Island to her granddaughter's house, where she was "much Exposed & . . . under constant Apprehensions" that the British would invade.[9]

Yet the British were not as troublesome to her as a personal crisis brought on by wartime inflation. The country woman who cared for her son Peter suddenly demanded more money for that service than Jane Mecom had or could see any way to get. Dependence on her brother was galling enough when he an-

ticipated her needs; now she had to ask for help. Her spirits felt "so deprest" that she could scarcely write, but what else could she do?

The war had disrupted communication and her letter was a long time reaching him. Meanwhile, relief came in a painful guise: Peter died. Accustomed as she was to accepting God's will, Jane Mecom reflected that Peter had been "no comfort to any won nor capable of injoying any Himself for many years."[10] His death was a blessing.

But at the same time she had heard nothing for five months from her daughter Jane Collas in Boston, and began to worry lest this last remaining child might be going the way of her brothers into insanity. Apologizing for burdening a busy and important man, she wrote her fears to Franklin: "It gives some Relief to unbousom wons self to a dear friend as you have been & are to me. . . ."[11]

Her daughter was, it turned out, physically rather than mentally ill, but sick or well she was never able to live up to her mother's standards of energy and enterprise. "You say you will endeavour to correct all your faults," Jane Mecom wrote in 1778 when Jane Collas was already in her thirties, and proceeded to outline in some detail what those faults were: a tendency to look on the dark side of "God's Providence," an inclination to despair and to extravagance, laziness and a lack of ingenuity in working to meet her material needs, an unseemly fondness for a great deal of company. She also tended to lie abed late, which her mother found "a trouble to me on many accounts." To top it off, she aspired to gentility without the means to support her aspiration—a tendency Jane Mecom scorned whenever she encountered it.[12]

Nine children had survived infancy and none had fulfilled their mother's hopes. Most had died in early adulthood. Benjamin simply disappeared during the Battle of Trenton and no trace of him was ever found. Peter's tragic end has already been noted. The fate of her children pushed Jane Mecom to a rare moment of questioning God's will: "I think there was hardly Ever so unfourtunate a Famely. I am not willing to think it is all owing to misconduct. I have had some children that seemed to be doing well till they were taken off by Death. . . ."[13] But there was nothing to be done. One must accept these things or go mad.

In the late seventies the long train of bereavement, displacement, and struggle abated for a while. Her granddaughter Jenny Greene, with whom she was living, was a most satisfactory young person whose conversation and attention to her comfort she much appreciated, and whose husband she respected. Though there was no neighbor for two miles, many visitors dropped in. She herself never left home unless someone sent a carriage (the Greenes owning none) since "I hant courage to ride a hors."[14] She made and sent to Franklin several batches of crown soap which he wanted for his friends in France, took care of Jenny Greene in her successive lyings-in, helped with the babies, supervised the household, and, from time to time, sold "some little matter" from the small store of goods she had brought from Boston in 1775. "My time seems to be filld up as the Famely I am in Increases fast," she wrote. She was sixty-eight and very energetic, though "as I grow older I wish for more Quiet and our Famely is more Incumbered as we have three children Born since I came & tho they give grat Pleasure . . . yet the Noise of them is sometimes troblesom. . . ."[15] She knew "but little how the world goes Except seeing a Newspaper some times which contains Enough to give Pain but little satisfaction while we are in Armes against each other. . . ."[16] In spite of the inflation and the losses the Greenes were suffering as many of their ships were

captured, her life was pleasanter than it had been since childhood. "I contineu very Easey and happy hear," she wrote in 1781, "have no more to trroble me than what is Incident to human Nature & cant be avoided in any Place, I write now in my own litle chamber the window opening on won of the Pleasantest prospects in the country the Birds singing about me and nobod up in the house near me to Desturb me. . . ."[17]

Life had taught Jane Mecom to be wary when things were going well. Ten months after that happy note her granddaughter died, giving birth to the fourth child in four years, and at seventy Jane Mecom was suddenly again the female head of a household of young children who needed, she thought, "some person more lively and Patient to watch over them continualy"; but since there was no one else, she did it anyway.[18] Fortunately she found them a comfort as she grieved for her beloved grandchild, sacrifice to the age's custom of unbroken childbearing. She was too busy to pine, though the war had cut off her communication with Franklin for three years.

His first postwar letter included a "grat, very grat, Present," for which she thanked him extravagantly, adding that his generosity would enable her to live "at Ease in my old Age (after a life of Care Labour & Anxiety). . . ."[19]

By 1784 she was back in Boston, in a house long owned by her brother, where she was able to "live all ways Cleen and Look Decent."[20] It was a great comfort. She had leisure to read and write, a minister she respected with whom to discuss theology and other things, the care and companionship of her granddaughter Jenny Mecom, the regular attention of her nephew-in-law Jonathan Williams. Her grandchildren and great-grandchildren were often a source of pride and pleasure. . . .

A ship captain friend took a favorable

report of her to Philadelphia, for which she was grateful: "The Gratest Part of my time when I am sitting at home I am apt to Imagine as Samson did when He lost his Hare, that I can Arise & Shake my Self & Go forth as at other times but on Tryal Like him I am wofully disapointed & find my Feet cripling & my Breath short, but I am still chearful for that is my Natural Temper."[21]

In January 1788, replying to his request for a "very peticular" account of how she lived, she provided a detailed description:

I have a good clean House to Live in my Grandaughter constantly to attend me to do whatever I desier in my own way & in my own time, I go to bed Early lye warm & comfortable Rise Early to a good Fire have my Brakfast directly and Eate it with a good Apetite and then Read or Work or what Els I Pleas, we live frugaly Bake all our own Bread, brew small bear, lay in a little cyder, Pork, Buter, &c. & suply our selves with Plenty of other nesesary Provision Dayly at the Dore we make no Entertainments, but some Times an Intimate Acquaintance will come in and Pertake with us the Diner we have Provided for our selves & a Dish of Tea in the After Noon, & if a Friend sitts and chats a litle in the Evening we Eate our Hasty Puding (our comon super) after they are gone; It is trew I have some Trobles but my Dear Brother Does all in His Power to Aleviat them by Praventing Even a wish, that when I Look Round me on all my Acquaintance I do not see won I have reason to think Happier than I am and would not change my neighbour with my Self where will you Find one in a more comfortable State as I see Every won has ther Trobles and I sopose them to be such as fitts them best & shakeing off them might be only changing for the wors.[22]

Six more years of life remained to her. The new Constitution was inaugurated, George Washington took office, mer-

chants and politicians concerned themselves with their own and the nation's prosperity, foreign conflicts flamed and threatened. Jane Mecom, for her part, worried about Benjamin Franklin's illness with "the stone," and prayed for his tranquillity in the face of pain. Their correspondence ranged around topics mostly personal and family, and upon reflections on life as they had lived it. "I do not Pretend to writ about Politics," she said, "tho I Love to hear them. . . ."[23]

Franklin's death in 1790 was a blow, but she was now seventy-eight herself, and prepared to be philosophical about this, as she saw it, temporary separation from her best friend. In his will he provided for her, and when she died four years later this woman who had lived so frugally was able to leave an estate of a thousand pounds to Jane Collas (in trust—she still worried about her daughter's extravagance!) and to her fifteen grandchildren and great-grandchildren.

When the historians came to treat the years covered by her life they dwelt on wars and politics, on the opening of land and trade and manufacture, on the economic development of a fertile wilderness, the rapid growth in population, the experiment in representative government.

That all these things shaped Jane Mecom's life experience there can be no doubt. Yet life as she perceived it was mostly made up of the small events of which great events are composed: of twenty-one years of pregnancy and childbirth which, multiplied by millions of women, created the rapid population growth; of the hard struggle to "git a living," and to make sure her children were prepared to earn theirs; of the constant procession of death which was the hallmark of her time; of the belated prosperity and happiness which came to her in old age. What added up to a wilderness conquered, a new nation created, was often experienced by individuals as a very hard life somehow survived. It is only in retrospect that all the separate experiences together create something we call "economic development," or "manifest destiny," or—simply—"history."

The events of Jane Mecom's life might have destroyed a weaker person, but some combination of natural resilience, good health, belief in the virtues of diligence, industry, and ingeniousness, and firm faith that God had good reasons for all the pain and sorrow which befell her, carried her through. Perhaps her final judgment on the whole experience was summed up in that sentence: "Every won has ther Trobles and I sopose them to be such as fitts them best & shakeing off them might be only changing for the wors."

In chapter three of Virginia Woolf's *Room of One's Own* there is a clever and moving fantasy: what if Shakespeare had had a sister as gifted as himself? The end of the fantasy is tragic, for Shakespeare's imaginary sister, born with a great gift, was so thwarted and hindered by the confines of "woman's place" that she killed herself. In Jane Mecom we have a real-life case, for of the sixteen siblings of Benjamin Franklin, she alone showed signs of talent and force of character similar to his. At the age of fifteen one ran off to Philadelphia and by a combination of wit, luck, and carefully cultivated ability to get ahead began his rise to the pinnacle among the Anglo-American intelligentsia. At the same age the other married a neighbor and in a month was pregnant. From that time forward her life was shaped almost entirely by the needs of other people. Like her brother she had a great capacity for growth, though the opportunity came to her late and was restricted by her constant burden of family responsibilities. The Revolution broadened her experience as it did his, yet she was almost never without children to care for, even in her seventies. Her letters showed a steady improvement in vigor of style, and even in spelling. Her lively intelligence kept Franklin writing

her even when he was very busy. Perhaps she had herself half in mind when she wrote in 1786: "Dr. Price thinks Thousands of Boyles Clarks and Newtons have Probably been lost to the world, and lived and died in Ignorance and meanness, mearly for want of being Placed in favourable Situations, and Injoying Proper Advantages, very few we know is able to beat thro all Impedements and Arive to any Grat Degre of superiority in Understanding."[24]

The "impedements" in her own life had been many, some might have thought insuperable, yet clearly by the age of eighty she had arrived at the "superiority in Understanding" which makes her letters a powerful chronicle of an eighteenth-century life. . . .

ELIZA LUCAS PINCKNEY

Born . . . in the West Indies, daughter of an army officer whose family had owned land in South Carolina (or just "Carolina," as the family invariably referred to it) and Antigua for three generations, Eliza Lucas came from more favored circumstances than Jane Mecom. The contrast between Jane Mecom's rough-hewn prose and phonetic spelling, and her equally rough-hewn handwriting, and the elegant language, copperplate penmanship, and ritual formality of Eliza Lucas's early letters is remarkable. While Jane Mecom's friends and relatives included people in almost the whole range of the social scale, . . . with Eliza Lucas we move at once to the top of the scale and stay there.

There had been money to send her "home" to England for a careful education, and when she was seventeen, her father had settled her, along with her mother and her younger sister, on one of his plantations in Carolina while he carried on his duties as governor of Antigua.

. . . We can see Eliza Lucas clearly in her youth, and an astonishing young person she was. As vigorous and enterpris-

ing as the young Franklin or the young
Jefferson, she began at once to administer
the work of three plantations. For five
years she taught the three R's to her sister
and the slave children, experimented with
new plants, dealt daily with overseers and
factors, wrote long letters on business
matters to her father and to his business
associates, taught herself law and used
her knowledge to help her neighbors who
could not afford a proper lawyer, and read
so much in Locke, Boyle, Plutarch, Vergil,
and Malebranche that an old lady in the
neighborhood prophesied that she would
damage her brain.

A touch of humor and of self-deprecation
was all that saved her from being unbearably
didactic when she wrote to her
younger brothers or younger friends. With
older people—especially her much admired
father—she was witty and straightforward.

Given her talents and wide-ranging interests,
it was no wonder that she found
the run of young men dull. "As to the
other sex," she wrote, "I don't trouble my
head about them. I take all they say to
be words . . . or to show their own bright
parts in the art of speechmaking. . . ."[25]

Her father proposed two possible candidates
for her hand. She thanked him but
declined both suggestions, saying of one
"that the riches of Peru and Chili if he
had them put together could not purchase
a sufficient esteem for him to make him
my husband." She hoped her father would
agree that she should remain single for a
few years.[26]

So she continued happily as his agent,
writing dozens of letters, dealing with the
factor and with the agent in England,
supervising planting, instructing overseers,
paying debts and contracting new
ones. "By rising early," said this female
Poor Richard, "I get through a great deal
of business."[27] It was an understatement.

The social life of Charleston appealed
to her less than the work of the plantation.
"I own," she wrote, "that I love the
vigitable world extremely."[28] Loving it
meant study, experiment, and constant attention.
The most visible consequence of
her love affair with vegetables was the
development of indigo as a major export
crop for South Carolina. At her father's
suggestion she began to plant indigo seeds,
and when, after several failures, a crop
was achieved, she worked with servants
he had sent from Antigua to refine the
process by which it was prepared as a dye.

A true exemplar of the Enlightenment,
she believed religion and right reason
could coexist, and said that "the soports
of the Xtian religion" enabled her to view
life's hazards with equanimity. She endeavored
to resign herself to events as
they came, since "there is an all Wise Being
that orders Events, who knows what
is best for us," and she believed in subduing
the passions to reason.[29]

Migraine headaches hardly slowed her
down. It occurred to her to plant oak trees
against the day when South Carolina
might run out of hardwood. In a careful
letter she compared the agriculture of England
and South Carolina, somewhat to
the advantage of the latter, and observed
that "the poorer sort [here] are the most
indolent people in the world or they could
never be so wretched in so plentiful a
country as this." Indolence was, in her
view, pretty close to a deadly sin.[30]

This precocious young woman who
found men her own age a little boring was
intrigued by the intelligent conversation
of a man in his forties, Carolina's first
native-born lawyer, Charles Pinckney. She
had met Pinckney and his wife soon after
her arrival, liked them both, and carried
on a lively correspondence across the ten
miles that separated the plantation from
Charleston. He lent her books, encouraged
her to report to him on her reading, and
enjoyed the discipleship of so eager a
pupil. Once, in 1741, she absentmindedly
signed a letter to him "Eliza Pinckney."[31]

Three years later in December 1744
Mrs. Pinckney died. On May 2, 1745, Eliza

wrote her father thanking him for permission to marry Charles Pinckney and "for the fortune you are pleased to promise me." She also thanked him for the pains and money laid out for her education, which "I esteem a more valuable fortune than any you have now given me." She assured him that Mr. Pinckney was fully satisfied with her dowry.[32]

To a cousin who had warned that she was so particular she was bound to "dye an old maid," she wrote: "But you are mistaken. I am married and the gentleman I have made choice of comes up to my plan in every tittle . . . I do him barely justice when I say his good Sence and Judgement, his extraordinary good nature and eveness of temper joynd to a most agreeable conversation and many valuable qualifications gives me the most agreeable prospect in the world. . . ."[33]

She bore with equanimity the talk of the town about their somewhat precipitate marriage, but was righteously indignant when gossip told it that the late Mrs. Pinckney had been neglected in her last illness. Writing to that lady's sister she said firmly that she would never have married a man who had been guilty of such a thing.[34] As she had earlier striven to please her father, so now she made every effort to please her husband. "When I write you," she told him, "I . . . desire . . . to equal even a Cicero or Demosthenes that I might gain your applause."[35]

Her father seems to have worried lest the strong-minded independence in which he had reared her might not sit well with a husband, and she reassured him that "acting out of my proper province and invading his, would be inexcusable."[36] She and Pinckney apparently agreed that her proper province was a spacious one, since she continued to supervise her father's plantations, assumed some responsibility for Pinckney's as well, and carried forward the experiments with indigo which were in midstream at the time of her marriage. Her self-improving urge was as strong

as ever. She wrote a long list of resolutions, and planned to reread them daily. With God's help she hoped not to be "anxious or doubtful, not to be fearful of any accident or misfortune that may happen to me or mine, not to regard the frowns of the world." She planned to govern her passions, improve her virtues, avoid all the deadly sins, be a frugal manager while extending hospitality and charity generously, make a good wife, daughter, and mother, and a good mistress of servants. At the end of this long list of injunctions to herself for ideal behavior she made a typical note: "Before I leave my Chamber recolect in General the business to be done that day." Good advice for any administrator.[37] Once she noted that "nobody eats the bread of idleness while I am here."[38] It might well have been her lifetime motto.

Her married life was as busy as her single life had been. In ten months Charles Cotesworth Pinckney was born. Perhaps the childlessness of Pinckney's first marriage explains the extraordinary eagerness of both parents to cherish "as promising a child as ever parents were blessed with." Eliza could see "all his papa's virtues already dawning" in the infant. A friend in England was asked to find a set of educational toys described by John Locke, while his father set about designing toys to teach the infant his letters. "You perceive we begin bytimes," Eliza added, "for he is not yet four months old."[39]

A second son was born and died. Then came Thomas and Harriott. Though Eliza Pinckney had slave nurses to suckle her infants, she was intensely preoccupied with the training, education, and shaping of her children.

In 1752 political maneuvering deprived Charles Pinckney of his seat as chief justice of the colony and he left for England to serve as South Carolina's agent there. The family took a house in Surrey and lived much like their neighbors. Eliza Pinckney was appalled at the amount of time the English gentry wasted, especially in playing cards. On the other hand, she loved the theater and never missed a new performance if she could help it. She called on the widowed Princess of Wales, and found her informality, her interest in South Carolina and in "little domestick questions" very engaging. The boys were sent to school, and Harriott was taught at home. It was a good life, and she was in no hurry to return to South Carolina.

Increasingly concerned by developments in the Seven Years' War, fearful that French might take over a large part of North America, the Pinckneys decided to liquidate their Carolina estate and move to England. To this end they sailed the war-infested sea in 1758, taking Harriott and leaving their sons in school. Three weeks after they landed Charles Pinckney was dead. Eliza Pinckney at thirty-five was once again in charge of a large and complex plantation enterprise. It was just as well, she thought, to have so great a responsibility; otherwise the loss of this most perfect of husbands would have undone her.

I find it requires great care, attention and actvity to attend properly to a Carolina estate, tho but a moderate one, to do ones duty and make it turn to account, . . . I find I have as much business as I can go through of one sort or other. Perhaps 'tis better for me. . . . Had there not been a necessity for it, I might have sunk to the grave by this time in that Lethargy of stupidity which seized me after my mind had been violently agitated by the greatest shock it ever felt. But a variety of imployment gives my thoughts a relief from melloncholy subjects, . . . and gives me air and exercise. . . .[40]

In letter after letter she recited Pinckney's virtues; the same ones she had praised when she married him. His religious dedication, "free from sourness and superstition," his integrity, charm, and good temper, "his fine address"—she

thought she would never find his like again.[41]

Fortunately she still loved books, agriculture, and her children. It was for the children she told herself (and them) that she worked so hard, overseeing the planting, buying and selling, writing ceaselessly to England (in several copies since no ship was secure), nursing slaves through smallpox, supervising the education of Harriott. She expected reciprocal effort from her sons. She wrote Charles Cotesworth: ". . . though you are very young, you must know the welfair of a whole family depends in a great measure on the progress you make in moral Virtue, Religion, and learning. . . . To be patient, humble, and resigned is to be happy. It is also to have a noble soul, a mind out of the reach of Envy, malice and every Calamity. And the earlier, my dear boy, you learn this lesson, the longer will you be wise and happy."[42]

She was convinced that happiness for all her children depended in great measure on a "right Education," and she encouraged Harriott; she was "fond of learning and I indulge her in it. It shall not be my fault if she roams abroad for amusement, as I believe 'tis want of knowing how to imploy themselves agreeably that makes many women too fond of going abroad."[43]

She thought highly of female talent. Once a letter from a friend in England came with the seal broken. Perhaps someone had read the letter? No matter; "it may teach them the art of writing prettily . . . and show how capable women are of both friendship and business. . . .[44]

She fell ill, lay four months in her chamber, but was too busy to die. A friend in England wanted seeds of all the trees in Carolina, and she was happy to oblige. The planting at Belmont, her plantation, was following an old-fashioned pattern; she decided to modernize, working harder, she said, than any slave. She revived silkmaking experiments begun when Pinckney was alive, and endeavored to teach the skill to other women. Harriott's education continued to be one of her chief joys: "For pleasure it certainly is to cultivate the tender mind, to teach the young Idea how to shoot, &c. especially to a mind so tractable and a temper so sweet as hers. . . ."[45]

Though she still talked of going back to England, of taking her sons to Geneva for their final polishing, any observer could have foretold that it would never happen. She was busy, and therefore happy, and the boys were doing well. Both, despite their long absence, were ardent in the American cause, and Thomas had astonished his schoolmates by his articulate opposition to the Stamp Act.

In 1768 Harriott at nineteen married a thirty-five-year-old planter, Daniel Horry, and set about replicating her mother's career. "I am glad your little Wife looks well to the ways of her household," Eliza wrote her new son-in-law; "the management of a Dairy is an amusement she has always been found of, and 'tis a very useful one."[46] Harriott was soon running much more than the dairy.

While Harriott was busy in the country, her mother set about planting a garden at the Horrys' town house. In her own well-organized household five slaves had each their appointed tasks; none was idle and none, she said, overworked. She herself was constantly industrious.

In such good order, then, were the family affairs in 1769 when Charles Cotesworth Pinckney at last came home from his sixteen-year sojourn in England, already an American patriot. He was at once admitted to the bar, and in a month had been elected to the South Carolina Assembly. A year or so later Thomas arrived to join him. The children for whom she had seen herself as working so hard were all launched.

Perhaps, though it would have been out of character, other circumstances would have permitted Eliza Pinckney to slow down at forty-five. But public affairs were in turmoil, and in 1775 both her sons were commissioned in the first regiment of South Carolina troops. Their business and financial affairs remained in the hands of their mother and sister, who were quite prepared to carry on while the men went to war.

It was 1778 before the full force of hostilities reached the Pinckneys. They had chosen Ashepoo, the family plantation belonging to Thomas Pinckney, as the safest place for all their valuables. It was a bad guess. Augustine Prevost's forces burned it to the ground on their way to Charleston, leaving Thomas—as he thought—wiped out and his mother's interest severely damaged. Charles Cotesworth wrote from his military post that of course whatever he had left when the war ended would be divided with them. Eliza wrote to Thomas: "Don't grieve for me my child as I assure you I do not for myself. While I have such children dare I think my lot hard? God forbid! I pray the Almighty disposer of events to preserve them and my grandchildren to me, and for all the rest I hope I shall be able to say not only contentedly, but cheerfully, God's Sacred Will be done!"[47]

The loss of Ashepoo was only the beginning. British troops impressed horses, took provisions, commandeered houses. Eliza Pinckney had to take refuge in the country, leaving her town property to who could know what depredations. In the midst of all this stress Thomas was wounded, Charles Cotesworth, already suffering from malaria, was imprisoned, and two grandchildren were born. In 1780 the British captured Charleston and by that time plenty had given way to pinched poverty. She owed sixty pounds to a creditor in England and could find no way at all to pay it. For a while it seemed that the fruit of thirty years' hard work was all lost.

Even before the war ended, however, it was clear that Eliza Pinckney's labors had accomplished much more than the building of a prosperous planting interest. She had created an enormously effective family. Planting and business, important as they were, had always taken second place to the upbringing and education of her children. Now, as adults, the three saw themselves, with her, as almost a single entity. The men, at war, often wrote their mother once, sometimes twice, a day. Harriott, who had been Tom's close friend and confidante before he was married, and whom he had always treated as an intellectual equal, continued after his marriage as his business agent and political adviser. For both brothers she managed plantations (as well as her own, after Daniel Horry died), handled money, looked after their wives and children. They, in turn, took time from their pressing military duties to oversee the education of her son.

After the war, the pattern continued. Both Pinckney men moved into public service. Charles Cotesworth was a member of the Constitutional Convention; Thomas was elected governor of South Carolina by an overwhelming majority and was in office when the state ratified the Constitution. Both were part of the developing Federalist party. Each was to be a foreign envoy, and to give his name to important treaties. These careers were made possible by the labors of their mother and sister.

In 1792 Eliza Pinckney developed cancer, and almost the entire family proposed to accompany her to Philadelphia, where a physician with considerable reputation in that field was to be found. She refused to go if they all came along: she could not risk the whole family on one ship. So, while Charles Cotesworth and his children reluctantly remained in Charleston, Harriott took her to Philadelphia. It was too late. She died and was buried there, George Washington at his own request serving as one of her pallbearers.

Building notable families was one of the things American colonials had to do for themselves when they came away from

England. [The name of] Franklin became well-known . . . because of the work and the public service of Benjamin. Pinckneys, too, became famous as a consequence of the public service of Thomas, Charles Cotesworth, and their cousin, also Charles. But the family was created, sustained, and developed a strong sense of itself as a consequence of the work, the vision, the exhortation, the constant attention of Eliza Pinckney. Her children carried on the vision to the end of their very l ; lives, and it is a measure of their success that a modern historian, dealing with eighteenth and early nineteenth century Charleston, chose to call his book *Charleston in the Age of the Pinckneys*.[48]

REFLECTIONS ON THE MICROCOSM

"As families are such at last the Church and Commonwealth must be," James Fitch remarked in Boston in 1683. More than a century later Chief Justice John Marshall was moved to comment that he had "always believed that the national character as well as happiness depended more on the female part of society than is generally imagined."[49]

It is with similar assumptions that I have tried to learn from the records left by these . . . women what it was like to be an eighteenth-century person. They take us to the heart of daily life: to scenes of childbearing and nerve-racking struggle to keep babies alive, to scenes of mysterious illness and sudden death, of wartime stringencies and dislocations, to the struggle to "git a living" or—at another level —to get rich. Through their eyes we see the chanciness of life, and begin to understand the central role of kinship in providing such security as was possible in a world so filled with uncertainty.

Different as these women were, each put family at the center of life. Eliza Pinckney and her three children viewed the world, not as individuals, but *as a family*. A threat to one was a threat to all; fame and fortune were also shared. They took care of each other's interests, of each other's children, as a matter of course. Tom's rice crop failed and Charles Cotesworth's wife put five hundred pounds at his disposal, "cheerfully," his brother noted. The family wanted Tom to stay in London. Earlier, when the British burned most of the family's movable assets, Charles Cotesworth announced at once that all he had left was to be divided among the rest of them. When the brothers went abroad, Harriott had their power of attorney; she made sure their plantations were cared for, their debts paid. Together they took responsibility for the younger generation. Young Daniel Horry was a spendthrift and showed signs of becoming a monarchist. His grandmother and his uncles tried to set him right, and his debts were settled as a family responsibility. Meanwhile the young women in the family were trained by their aunt and grandmother so that they, too, could run plantations. By the time Eliza Pinckney died the family had a full-fledged "tradition" for many of its activities, and doubtless no one remembered that it had all been created in two generations. . . .

Jane Mecom's life was shaped by her relationship to Benjamin Franklin, but beyond the two of them lay a wide network of Franklin kin, in-laws, cousins in various degrees. Late in life Benjamin asked his sister to send him a detailed and complete list of all their kinfolk in Boston which he could use for reference. He was constantly being asked for help of one kind or another, and he wanted to be sure that he gave the proper priority to blood relations. In-laws were addressed as "sister" and "brother," and were entitled to at least formal statements of affection. They clearly recognized some members of the clan as more "valuable" than others, but blood created a responsibility even for ne'er-do-wells. While historical demogra-

phers argue about nuclear and extended families, we must pay close attention to the actual experience of families, and beware of false dichotomies. . . .

No one who reads these pages will doubt that women's lives were different from those of men. In a day when contraception was all but unknown there is no mystery about a sexual division of labor which allotted men tasks in the public sphere and women those which could be carried out at home. Each of these women was pregnant within a month of marriage, and [Jane Mecom] continued to bear children into [her] late forties. Eliza Pinckney's family was unusually small for the time, but she was widowed at thirty-five. Shortly before his death Charles Pinckney had discussed with the Princess of Wales his plans for his next son.

Nor was it only their own children who kept women close to home. . . . These women were as much involved in raising the second generation as they had been with the first, and Jane Mecom, for a time, was responsible for four great-grandchildren. Grandmothering was an important part of their lifework.

[Both] believed in work as a moral value. They reserved their strongest criticisms for indolence in any form, and [neither] of them saw old age as justification for idleness. . . . Eliza Pinckney's work encompassed the larger world of plantation trade. Through most of her life she was busy with shipments, payments, factors, and the like, while she also planned and supervised the actual production of rice, indigo, silk, and the hundred other products of the relatively self-sufficient plantation. Though nominally working, first for her father, then for her husband, and finally for her children, she seems not to have felt any inhibition about acting in her own name, making her own decisions. The fact that legal ownership belonged to father or husband was of no great operational significance.

Woman's life in the eighteenth century

was fundamentally influenced by marriage. In a day when conventional wisdom had it that for both men and women it was wise to marry close to home, [both] did so. But the luck of the draw varied widely. There is little record of Edward Mecom's life, but circumstantial evidence suggests that Jane Mecom might have done better on her own. . . .

Eliza Pinckney was convinced that Charles Pinckney was incomparable, and despite various offers she never married again. During her marriage she had played the role of the properly subservient wife; her father had written to her husband the directions he had once sent to her; and her time had been much engaged in child-bearing and child care. Widowed, she assumed the role of head of the family, and continued to make vital decisions even when her sons were grown and had families of their own. With their help she created the "Pinckney Family."

These were only [two] of millions of women who lived and worked and died in colonial America. In this age of statistical sophistication, it is a bold historian who builds any case upon [two] examples, yet in these lives we see exemplified cultural values which were those of many of their contemporaries. In their experience we see much of the common life of eighteenth-century woman, no matter what her social class. In another sense, of course, [both] were uncommon women, whose achievements tell us something about the possibilities as well as the probabilities for women in their day and generation.

NOTES

1. Jane Mecom to Benjamin Franklin, Aug. 16, 1787, in Carl Van Doren, ed., *The Letters of Benjamin Franklin*, VII (New Haven: Yale University Press, 1965), 515n. Sparks 296. Note her use of the plural: "Heads."
2. Ibid., p. 52.
3. Ibid., p. 43.
4. Ibid., p. 84.
5. The original of this letter is lost. It is here reprinted from Jared Sparks, ed., *The Papers of Benjamin Franklin*, VII (New Haven: Yale University Press, 1965), 515n. Sparks corrected spelling and punctuation.
6. Van Doren, *Letters*, p. 114.
7. Ibid., pp. 106–107.
8. Ibid., p. 111.
9. Ibid., p. 183.
10. Ibid., p. 189.
11. Ibid.
12. Ibid., p. 174.
13. Ibid., p. 171.
14. Ibid., p. 197.
15. Ibid., p. 208.
16. Ibid., p. 210.
17. Ibid.
18. Ibid., p. 214.
19. Ibid., p. 221.
20. Ibid., p. 245.
21. Ibid., p. 263.
22. Ibid., p. 306.
23. Ibid., p. 322.
24. Ibid., p. 275.
25. Elise Pinckney, ed., *The Letterbook of Eliza Lucas Pinckney* (Chapel Hill: University of North Carolina Press, 1972), p. 27.
26. Ibid., p. 6.
27. Ibid., p. 7.
28. Ibid., pp. 34–35.
29. Ibid., p. 49.
30. Ibid., pp. 29, 19.
31. Ibid., pp. 39–40.
32. Harriott Horry Ravenal, *Eliza Lucas Pinckney* (New York: Scribner's, 1896), pp. 69–70.
33. Ibid., p. 94.
34. Eliza Lucas Pinckney to Miss Bartlett, Manuscript Division, William R. Perkins Library, Duke University.
35. Ravenal, *Pinckney*, p. 90.
36. Ibid., p. 100.
37. Ibid., pp. 115–118.
38. Ibid., p. 245.
39. Eliza Lucas Pinckney to Miss Bartlett, Manuscript Division, William R. Perkins Library, Duke University.
40. Pinckney, *Letterbook*, p. 144.
41. Ibid., pp. 100–102.
42. Ibid., p. 168.
43. Ibid., p. 142.
44. Ibid., p. 152.
45. Ibid., p. 181.

46. Ibid., p. 243.

47. Ibid., p. 276.

48. George C. Rogers, *Charleston in the Age of the Pinckneys* (Norman: University of Oklahoma Press, 1969). The Pinckney Family Papers in the Library of Congress provide ample evidence that the three children of Eliza Lucas Pinckney continued to operate as a family through the rest of their long lives. From Charles C. Pinckney's receipt book we learn that in 1796 Harriott was acting as "attorney for General Pinckney" and paying his bills. It is clear that through the whole time Tom was abroad she took care of both his plantation and his financial affairs. In August 1815 Charles wrote Harriott asking her to look into and inform him about a certain machine he had heard of for the manufacture of cotton goods. As late as 1822 the two of them were cooperating in the search for black-seed cotton to plant. These are only samples of their continued habit of working as a unit. The large number of "My dear Harriott" letters from both brothers would make an interesting book.

49. Eitch is quoted in Edmund Morgan, *The Puritan Family* (New York: Harper, 1966) p. 143. The Marshall quotation is found in Frances Mason, ed. *My Dearest Polly: Letters of Chief Justice John Marshall to His Wife* (Richmond: Garrett and Massie, 1961), p. 140.

DOCUMENT: *Fund Raising for the Revolution*

THE SENTIMENTS OF AN AMERICAN WOMAN

This broadside of 1780 announced a women's campaign to raise contributions for patriot soldiers. Organized and led by Esther DeBerdt Reed, wife of the president of Pennsylvania, and Benjamin Franklin's daughter Sarah Franklin Bache, the campaign was large and effective. "Instead of waiting for the Donations being sent the ladys of each Ward go from dore to dore and collect them," wrote one participant. Collecting contributions this way invited confrontation. One loyalist wrote to her sister, "Of all absurdities, the ladies going about for money exceeded everything; they were so extremely importunate that people were obliged to give them something to get rid of them."* The campaign raised $300,000 paper dollars in inflated war currency. Rather than let George Washington merge it with the general fund, the women insisted on using it to buy materials for making shirts so that each soldier might know he had received an extraordinary contribution from the women of Philadelphia. The broadside itself is an unusually explicit justification for women's intrusion into politics.

* Mary Morris to Catharine Livingston, June 10 [1780], Ridley Family Papers, Massachusetts Historical Society, Boston; Anna Rawle to Rebecca Rawle Shoemaker, June 30, 1780, in *Pennsylvania Magazine of History and Biography* 35 (1911): 398.

Excerpted from *The Sentiments of an American Woman* ([Philadelphia]: John Dunlap, 1780).

country. Animated by the purest patriotism, they are sensible of sorrow at this day, in not offering more than barren wishes for the success of so glorious a Revolution. They aspire to render themselves more really useful; and this sentiment is universal from the north to the south of the Thirteen United States. Our ambition is kindled by the fame of those heroines of antiquity, who have rendered their sex illustrious, and have proved to the universe, that, if the weakness of our Constitution, if opinion and manners did not forbid us to march to glory by the same paths as the Men, we should at least equal, and sometimes surpass them in our love for the public good. I glory in all that which my sex has done great and commendable. I call to mind with enthusiasm and with admiration, all those acts of courage, of constancy and patriotism, which history has transmitted to us: The people favoured by Heaven, preserved from destruction by the virtues, the zeal and the resolution of Deborah, of Judith, of Esther! The fortitude of the mother of the Macchabees, in giving up her sons to die before her eyes: Rome saved from the fury of a victorious enemy by the efforts of Volumnia, and other Roman Ladies: So many famous sieges where the Women have been seen forgetting the weakness of their sex, building new walls, digging trenches with their feeble hands, furnishing arms to their defenders, they themselves darting the missile weapons on the enemy, resigning the ornaments of their apparel, and their fortune, to fill the public treasury, and to hasten the deliverance of their country; burying themselves under its ruins; throwing themselves into the flames rather than submit to the disgrace of humiliation before a proud enemy.

Born for liberty, disdaining to bear the irons of a tyrannic Government, we associate ourselves to the grandeur of those Sovereigns, cherished and revered, who have held with so much splendour the scepter of the greatest States, The Batildas, the Elizabeths, the Maries, the Catharines, who have extended the empire of liberty, and contented to reign by sweetness and justice, have broken the chains of slavery, forged by tyrants in times of ignorance and barbarity. . . .

. . . We are at least certain, that he cannot be a good citizen who will not applaud our efforts for the relief of the armies which defend our lives, our possessions, our liberty? The situation of our soldiery has been represented to me; the evils inseparable from war, and the firm and generous spirit which has enabled them to support these. But it has been said, that they may apprehend, that, in the course of a long war, the view of their distresses may be lost, and their services be forgotten. Forgotten! never; I can answer in the name of all my sex. Brave Americans, your disinterestedness, your courage, and your constancy will always be dear to America, as long as she shall preserve her virtue.

We know that at a distance from the theatre of war, if we enjoy any tranquility, it is the fruit of your watchings, your labours, your dangers. If I live happy in the midst of my family; if my husband cultivates his field, and reaps his harvest in peace; if surrounded with my children, I myself nourish the youngest, and press it to my bosom, without being affraid of seeing myself separated from it, by a ferocious enemy; if the house in which we dwell; if our barns, our orchards are safe at the present time from the hands of those incendiaries, it is to you that we owe it. And shall we hesitate to evidence to you our gratitude? Shall we hesitate to wear a cloathing more simple; hair dressed less elegant, while at the price of this small privation, we shall deserve your benedictions. Who, amongst us, will not renounce with the highest pleasure, those vain ornaments, when she shall consider that the valiant defenders of America will be able to draw some advantage from the money which she may have laid out in these. . . . The time is arrived to display the same sentiments which animated us at the beginning of the Revolution, when we renounced the use of teas, however agreeable to our taste, rather than receive them from our persecutors; when we made it appear to them that we placed former necessaries in the rank of superfluities, when our liberty was interested; when our republican and laborious hands spun the flax, prepared the linen intended for the use of our soldiers; when [as] exiles and fugitives we supported with courage all the evils which are the concomitants of war. Let us not lose a moment; let us be engaged to offer the homage of our gratitude at the altar of military valour, and you, our brave deliverers, while mercenary slaves combat to cause you to share with them, the irons with which they are loaded, receive with a free hand our offering, the purest which can be presented to your virtue, By An American Woman.

LINDA K. KERBER
Daughters of Columbia:
Educating Women for the Republic, 1787–1805

One of the major problems facing the Revolutionary generation was how to prepare the next generation of virtuous citizens. It was agreed that the republican experiment was risky. There had not been an example of a republican government on a comparably large scale since Rome. As everyone knew, the Roman Republic had become the Roman Empire, and civil liberties had slowly eroded. How would America avoid the fate of Rome? Although a few women voiced the wish to be a direct part of the political community, no legislator devised a way of their doing so, and the ancient assumption that women were not political beings persisted. Instead there arose the position that women needed an improved education, which would suit them to be the mothers of the next generation of male citizens.

"I expect to see our young women forming a new era in female history," wrote Judith Sargent Murray in 1798.[1] Her optimism was part of a general sense that all possibilties were open in the post-Revolutionary world; as Benjamin Rush put it, the first act of the republican drama had only begun. The experience of war had given words like "independence" and "self-reliance" personal as well as political overtones; among the things that ordinary folk had learned from wartime had been that the world could, as the song had it, turn upside down. The rich could quickly become poor, wives might suddenly have to manage family businesses; women might even, as the famous Deborah Gannett had done, shoulder a gun. Political theory taught that republics rested on the virtue of their citizens; revolutionary experience taught that it was useful to be prepared for a wide range of unusual possibilities.[2]

A desire to explore the possibilities republicanism now opened to women was expressed by a handful of articulate, urban, middle-class men and women. While only a very few writers—Charles Brockden Brown, Judith Sargent Murray, Benjamin Rush—devoted extensive attention to women and what they might become, many essayists explored the subject in the periodical literature. In the fashion of the day, they concealed their identity under pseudonyms like "Cordelia," "Constantia," or, simply, "A Lady." These expressions came largely from Boston, New York, and Philadelphia: cities which were the centers of publishing. The vitality of Philadelphia, as political and social capital, is well known; the presence of so many national legislators in the city, turning up as they did at dances and dinner parties, was no doubt intellectually invigorating, and not least for the women of Philadelphia. In an informal way, women shared many of the political excitements of the city. Philadelphia was the home of the Young Ladies' Academy, founded in 1786, with explicitly fresh ideas about women's education, and an enrollment of more than a hundred within two years; Benjamin Rush would deliver his "Thoughts upon Female Education" there. The first attempt at a magazine expressly addressed to women was made by the Philadelphia *Lady's Magazine and Repository*. Two of the most intense anonymous writers—"Sophia" and "Nitidia"—wrote for Philadelphia newspapers. And after the government moved to Washington,

Joseph Dennie's *Port Folio* solicited "the assistance of the ladies," and published essays by Gertrude Meredith, Sarah Hall, and Emily Hopkinson. Boston and New York were not far behind in displaying similar interests: in New York, Noah Webster's *American Magazine* included in its prospectus a specific appeal for female contributors; the *Boston Weekly Magazine* was careful to publish the speeches at the annual "Exhibition" of Susanna Rowson's Young Ladies' Academy.

Most journalists' comments on the role and functions of women in the republic merged, almost imperceptibly, into discussions of the sort of education proper for young girls. A pervasive Lockean environmentalism was displayed; what people were was assumed to be dependent on how they were educated. "Train up the child in the way he should grow, and when he is old he will not depart from it"; the biblical injunction was repeatedly quoted, and not quoted idly. When Americans spoke of what was best for the child they were also speaking—implicitly or explicitly—of their hopes for the adult. Charles Brockden Brown, for example, is careful to provide his readers with brief accounts of his heroines' early education. When we seek to learn the recipe for Murray's "new era in female history" we find ourselves reading comments on two related themes: how young women are to be "trained up," and what is to be expected of them when they are old.

If the republic were to fulfill the generous claims it made for the liberty and competence of its citizens, the education of young women would have to be an education for independence rather than for an upwardly mobile marriage. The periodicals are full of attacks on fashion, taking it for an emblem of superficiality and dependence. The Philadelphia *Lady's Magazine* criticized a father who prepared his daughters for the marriage market: "You boast of having given your daughters an education which will enable them 'to shine in the first circles.' . . . They sing indifferently; they play the harpsichord indifferently; they are mistresses of every common game at cards . . . they . . . have just as much knowledge of dress as to deform their persons by an awkward imitation of every new fashion which appears. . . . Placed in a situation of difficulty, they have neither a head to dictate, nor a hand to help in any domestic concern."[3] Teaching young girls to dress well was part of the larger message that their primary lifetime goal must be marriage; in this context, fashion became a feature of sexual politics. "I have sometimes been led," remarked Benjamin Rush, "to ascribe the invention of ridiculous and expensive fashions in female dress entirely to the gentlemen in order to divert the ladies from improving their minds and thereby to secure a more arbitrary and unlimited authority over them."[4] In the marriage market, beauty, flirtatiousness, and charm were at a premium; intelligence, good judgment, and competence (in short, the republican virtues) were at a discount. The republic did not need fashion plates; it needed citizens —women as well as men—of self-discipline and of strong mind. The contradiction between the counsel given to young women and their own self-interest, as well as the best interests of the republic, seemed obvious. The marriage market undercut the republic.[5]

Those who addressed themselves to the problem of the proper education for young women used the word "independence" frequently. Sometimes it was used in a theoretical fashion: How, it was asked, can women's minds be free if they are taught that their sphere is limited to clothing, music, and needlework? Often the context of independence is economic and political: it seemed appropriate that in a republic women should have greater control over their own lives. "The *dependence* for which women are uniformly educated" was deplored; it was pointed out that the unhappily married woman would quickly discover that she had "neither liberty nor property."[6]

The idea that political independence should be echoed by a self-reliance which would make women as well as men economically independent appears in its most developed form in a series of essays Judith Sargent Murray published in the *Massachusetts Magazine* between 1792 and 1794, and collected under the title *The Gleaner* in 1798. Murray insisted that instruction in a manual trade was especially appropriate in a republic, and decried the anti-egalitarian habit of assuming that a genteel and impractical education was superior to a vocational one. She was critical of fathers who permitted their sons to grow up without knowing a useful skill; she was even more critical of parents who "pointed their daughters" toward marriage and dependence. This made girls' education contingent on a single event; it offered them a single image of the future. "I would give my daughters every accomplishment which I thought proper," Murray wrote, "and to crown all, I would early accustom them to habits of industry and order. They should be taught with precision the art economical; they should be enabled to procure for themselves the necessaries of life; independence should be placed within their grasp." Repeatedly Murray counseled that women should be made to feel competent at something: "A woman *should reverence herself*."[7]

Murray scattered through the *Gleaner* essays brief fictional versions of self-respecting women, in the characters of Margaretta, Mrs. Virgilius, and Penelope Airy. In his full-length novel *Ormond*, published in 1799, Charles Brockden Brown imagined a considerably more developed version of a competent woman. Constantia Dudley is eminently rational. When her father is embezzled of his fortune she, "her cheerfulness unimpaired," sells "every superfluous garb and trinket," her music and her books; she supports the family by needlework. Constantia never flinches; she can take whatever ill fortune brings, whether it is yellow fever or the poverty that forces her to conclude that the only alternative to starvation is corn-meal mush three times a day for three months. Through it all, she resists proposals of marriage, because even in adversity she scorns to become emotionally dependent without love.[8]

Everything Constantia does places her in sharp contrast to Helena Cleves, who also "was endowed with every feminine and fascinating quality." Helena has had a genteel education; she can paint, and sing, and play the clavichord, but it is all fashionable gloss to camouflage a lack of real mental accomplishment and self-discipline. What Brown called "exterior accomplishments" were acceptable so long as life held no surprises, but when Helena meets disaster, she is unprepared to maintain her independence and her self-respect. She falls into economic dependence upon a "kinswoman"; she succumbs to the "specious but delusive" reasoning of Ormond, and becomes his mistress. He takes advantage of her dependence, all the while seeking in Constantia a rational woman worthy of his intelligence; eventually, in despair, Helena kills herself.[9]

The argument that an appropriate education would steel girls to face adversity is related to the conviction that all citizens of a republic should be self-reliant. But the argument can be made independent of explicit republican ideology. It may well represent the common sense of a revolutionary era in which the unexpected was very likely to happen; in which large numbers of people had lived through reversals of fortune, encounters with strangers, physical dislocation. Constantia's friend Martinette de Beauvais has lived in Marseilles, Verona, Vienna, and Philadelphia; she had dressed like a man and fought in the American Revolution; after that she was one of the "hundreds" of women who took up arms for the French.[10] Constantia admires and sympathizes with her friend;

nothing in the novel is clearer than that women who are not ready to maintain their independence in a crisis, as Constantia and Martinette do, risk sinking, like Helena, into prostitution and death.

The model republican woman was competent and confident. She could ignore the vagaries of fashion; she was rational, benevolent, independent, self-reliant. Writers who spoke to this point prepared lists of what we would now call role models: heroines of the past offered as assurance that women could indeed be people of accomplishment. There were women of the ancient world, like Cornelia, the mother of the Gracchi; rulers like Elizabeth of England and the Empress Catherine of Russia; a handful of Frenchwomen: Mme. de Genlis, Mme. Maintenon, and Mme. Dacier; and a long list of British intellectuals: Lady Mary Wortley Montagu, Hannah More, Elizabeth Carter, Mrs. Knowles (the Quaker who had bested Dr. Johnson in debate), Mary Wollstonecraft, and the Whig historian Catharine Macaulay.[11] Such women were rumored to exist in America; they were given fictional embodiment by Murray and Brown. Those who believed in these republican models demanded that their presence be recognized and endorsed, and that a new generation of young women be urged to make them patterns for their own behavior. To create more such women became a major educational challenge.

Writers were fond of pointing out that the inadequacies of American women could be ascribed to early upbringing and environmental influences. "Will it be said that the judgment of a male of two years old, is more sage than that of a female of the same age?" asked Judith Sargent Murray. "But . . . as their years increased, the sister must be wholly domesticated, while the brother is led by the hand through all the flowery paths of science." The *Universal Asylum* published a long and thoughtful essay by "A Lady" which argued that "in the nursery, strength is equal in the male and female." When a boy went to school, he immediately met both intellectual and physical challenge; his teachers instructed him in science and language, his friends dared him to fight, to run after a hoop, to jump a rope. Girls, on the other hand, were "committed to illiterate teachers, . . . cooped up in a room, confined to needlework, deprived of exercise." Thomas Cooper defined the problem clearly: "We first keep their minds and then their persons in subjection," he wrote. "We educate women from infancy to marriage, in such a way as to debilitate both their corporeal and their mental powers. All the accomplishments we teach them are directed not to their future benefit in life but to the amusement of the male sex; and having for a series of years, with much assiduity, and sometimes at much expense, incapacitated them for any serious occupation, we say they are not fit to govern themselves."[12]

Schemes for the education of the "rising generation" proliferated in the early republic, including a number of projects for the education of women. Some, like those discussed in the well-known essays of Benjamin Rush and Noah Webster, were theoretical; others took the form of admitting girls to boys' academies or establishing new schools for girls. There were not as many as Judith Sargent Murray implied when she said :"Female academies are everywhere establishing," but she was not alone in seeing schools like Susanna Rowson's Young Ladies' Academy and the Young Ladies' Academy of Philadelphia as harbingers of a trend. One pamphlet address, written in support of the Philadelphia Academy, expressed the hope that it would become "a great national seminary" and insisted that although "stubborn prejudices still exist . . . we must (if open to conviction) be convinced that *females* are fully capable of sounding the most profound depths, and of attaining to the most sublime excellence in every part of science."[13]

Certainly there was a wide range of opinion on the content and scope of female education in the early republic. Samuel Harrison Smith's essay on the subject, which won the American Philosophical Society's 1797 prize for the best plan for a national system of education began by proposing "that every male child, without exception, be educated."[14] At the other extreme was Timothy Dwight, the future president of Yale, who opened his academy at Greenfield Hill to girls and taught them the same subjects he taught to boys, at the same time and in the same rooms.[15] But Dwight was the exception. Most proposals for the education of young women agreed that the curriculum should be more advanced than that of the primary schools but somewhat less than that offered by colleges and even conventional boys' academies. Noah Webster thought women should learn speaking and writing, arithmetic, geography, belles-lettres; "A Reformer" in the *Weekly Magazine* advocated a similar program, to which practical instruction in nursing and cooking were added. Judith Sargent Murray thought women should be able to converse elegantly and correctly, pronounce French, read history (as a narrative substitute for novels, rather than for its own interest or value), and learn some simple geography and astronomy.[16] The best-known proposal was Benjamin Rush's; he too prescribed reading, grammar, penmanship, "figures and bookkeeping," geography. He added "the first principles of natural philosophy," vocal music (because it soothed cares and was good for the lungs) but not instrumental music (because, except for the most talented, it seemed a waste of valuable time), and history (again, as an antidote to novel reading).

Rush offered his model curriculum in a speech to the Board of Visitors of the Young Ladies' Academy of Philadelphia, later published and widely reprinted under the title "Thoughts upon Female Education Accommodated to the Present State of Society, Manners and Government in the United States of America." The academy claimed to be the first female academy chartered in the United States; when Rush spoke, on July 28, 1787, he was offering practical advice to a new school. Rush linked the academy to the greater cause of demonstrating the possibilities of women's minds. Those who were skeptical of education for women, Rush declared, were the same who opposed "the general diffusion of knowledge among the citizens of our republics." Rush argued that "female education should be accommodated to the state of society, manners, and government of the country in which it is conducted." An appropriate education for American women would be condensed, because they married earlier than their European counterparts; it would include bookkeeping, because American women could expect to be "the stewards and guardians of their husbands' property," and executrices of their husbands' wills. It would qualify them for "a general intercourse with the world" by an acquaintance with geography and chronology. If education is preparation for life, then the life styles of American women required a newly tailored educational program.[17]

The curriculum of the Young Ladies' Academy (which one of the Board of Visitors called "abundantly sufficient to complete the female mind") included reading, writing, arithmetic, English grammar, composition, rhetoric, and geography. It did not include the natural philosophy Rush hoped for (although Rush did deliver a dozen lectures on "The Application of the Principles of Natural Philosophy, and Chemistry, to Domestic and Culinary Purposes"); it did not include advanced mathematics or the classics.[18]

In 1794 the Young Ladies' Academy published a collection of its graduation addresses; one is struck by the scattered observations of valedictorians and saluta-torians that reading, writing, and arithmetic were not enough. Priscilla Mason remarked in her 1793 graduation address that while it was unusual for a woman to address "a promiscuous assembly," there was no impropriety in women's becoming accomplished orators. What had prevented them, she argued, was that "our high and mighty Lords . . . have denied us the means of knowledge, and then reproached us for the want of it. . . . They doom'd the sex to servile or frivolous employments, on purpose to degrade their minds, that they themselves might hold unrivall'd, the power and preeminence they had usurped." Academies like hers enabled women to increase their knowledge, but the forums in which they might use it were still unavailable: "The Church, the Bar, and the Senate are shut against us."[19]

So long as the propriety of cultivating women's minds remained a matter for argument, it was hard to press a claim to public competence; Priscilla Mason was an exception. Rush had concluded his advice to the Young Ladies' Academy by challenging his audience to demonstrate "that the cultivation of reason in women is alike friendly to the order of nature and the private as well as the public happiness." But meeting even so mild a challenge was difficult; "bluestocking" was not a term of praise in the early republic. "Tell me," wrote the Philadelphian Gertrude Meredith angrily, ". . . do you imagine, from your knowledge of the young men in this city, that ladies are valued according to their mental acquirements? I can assure you that they are not, and I am very confident that they never will be, while men indulge themselves in expressions of contempt for one because she has a *bare elbow,* for another because she . . . never made a *good pun, nor smart repartee.* . . . [Would they] not titter . . . at her expense, if a woman made a Latin quotation, or spoke with enthusiasm of Classical learning?"[20]

When Gertrude Meredith visited Baltimore, she found that her mildly satirical
essays for the *Port Folio* had transformed
her into a formidable figure: "Mrs. Cole
says she should not have been more distressed at visiting Mrs. Macaulay the au-
thoress than myself as she had heard I
was so sensible, but she was very glad to
find I was so free and easy. You must allow," she concluded dryly, "that this
compliment was elegantly turned." A
similar complaint was made by an essay-
ist whom we know only as "Sophia":

> A woman who is conscious of possessing,
> more intellectual power than is requisite
> in superintending the pantry, and in ad-
> justing the ceremonials of a feast, and
> who believes she, in conforming to the
> will of the giver, in improving the gift, is
> by the wits of the other sex denominated
> a learned lady. She is represented as dis-
> gustingly slovenly in her person, indecent
> in her habits, imperious to her husband,
> and negligent of her children. And the
> odious scarecrow is employed, exactly as
> the farmer employs his unsightly bundle
> of rags and straw, to terrify the simple
> birds, from picking up the precious grain,
> which he wishes to monopolize. After all
> this, what man in his sober senses can be
> astonished, to find the majority of women
> as they really are, frivolous and volatile;
> incapable of estimating their own dignity,
> and indifferent to the best interests of so-
> ciety. . . ?[21]

These women were not creating their
own paranoid images of discouragement.
The same newspapers for which they
wrote often printed other articles insisting that intellectual accomplishment is inappropriate in a woman, that the intellectual woman is not only invading a male
province, but must herself somehow be
masculine. "Women of masculine minds,"
wrote the Boston minister John Sylvester
John Gardiner, "have generally masculine
manners, and a robustness of person ill
calculated to inspire the tender passion."
Noah Webster's *American Magazine*,

which in its prospectus had made a special appeal to women writers and readers,
published the unsigned comment: "If we
picture to ourselves a woman . . . firm
in resolve, unshaken in conduct, unmoved
by the delicacies of situation, by the fashions of the times, . . . we immediately
change the idea of the sex, and . . . we
see under the form of a woman the virtues and qualities of a man." Even the
Lady's Magazine, which had promised to
demonstrate that "the FEMALES of Philadelphia are by no means deficient in *those
talents,* which have immortalized the
names of a *Montagu,* a *Craven,* a *More,*
and a *Seward,* in their inimitable writings," published a cautionary tale, whose
moral was that although "learning in men
was the road to preferment . . . consequences very opposite were the result of
the same quality in women." Amelia is a
clergyman's only daughter; she is taught
Latin and Greek, with the result that she
becomes "negligent of her dress," and
"pride and pedantry grew up with learning in her breast." Eventually she is
avoided by both sexes, and becomes em-
blematic of the fabled "white-washed
jackdaw (who, aiming at a station from
which nature had placed him at a distance, found himself deserted by his own
species, and driven out of every society)."
For conclusion there was an explicit moral:
"This story was intended (at a time when
the press overflows with the productions
of female pens) . . . to admonish them,
that . . . because a few have gained applause by studying the dead languages, all
womankind should [not] assume their Dic-
tionaries and Lexicons; else . . . (as the
Ladies made rapid advances towards manhood) we might in a few years behold a
sweepstakes rode by women, or a second
battle at Odiham, fought with superior
skill, by Mesdames Humphries and Mendoza."[22]

The prediction that accomplishment
would unsex women was coupled with
the warning that educated women would

abandon their proper sphere; the female pedant and the careful housekeeper were never found in the same person. The most usable cautionary emblem for this seems to have been Mary Wollstonecraft, whose life and work linked criticism of women's status with free love and political radicalism. Mary Wollstonecraft's *Vindication of the Rights of Woman* was her generation's most coherent statement of what women deserved and what they might become. The influence of any book is difficult to trace, and although we know that her book was reprinted in Philadelphia shortly after its publication in 1792, it would be inaccurate to credit Wollstonecraft with responsibility for raising in America questions relating to the status of women. It seems far more likely that she verbalized effectively what a larger public was already thinking or was willing to hear; "In very many of her sentiments," remarked the Philadelphia Quaker Elizabeth Drinker, "she, as some of our friends say, *speaks my mind.*"[23]

Wollstonecraft's primary target was Rousseau, whose definition of woman's sphere was a limited one: "The empire of women," Rousseau had written, "is the empire of softness, of address, of complacency; her commands are caresses; her menaces are tears." Wollstonecraft perceived that to define women in this way was to condemn them to "a state of perpetual childhood"; she deplored the "false system of education" which made women "only anxious to inspire love, when they ought to cherish a nobler ambition, and by their abilities and virtues exact respect." Women's duties were different from those of men, but they similarly demanded the exercise of virtue and reason; women would be better wives and mothers if they were taught that they need not depend on frivolity and ignorance. Wollstonecraft ventured the suggestion that women might study medicine, politics, and business, but whatever they did, they should not be denied civil and political

rights, they should not have to rely on marriage for assurance of economic support, they should not "remain immured in their families groping in the dark."[24]

If, in some quarters, Mary Wollstonecraft's work was greeted as the common sense of the matter, in others it was met with hostility. The *Vindication* was a popular subject of satire, especially when, after the author's death in childbirth in 1797, William Godwin published a *Memoir* revealing that she had lived with other men, and with Godwin himself before her pregnancy and their marriage. Critics were then freed to discount her call for reform as the self-serving demand of a woman of easy virtue, as Benjamin Silliman did throughout his *Letters of Shahcoolen*. Timothy Dwight, who had taken the lead in offering young women education on a par with young men, shuddered at Wollstonecraft and held "the female philosopher" up to ridicule in "Morpheus," a political satire which ran for eight installments in the *New-England Palladium*.[25] Dwight called Wollstonecraft "an unchaste woman," "a sentimental lover," "a strumpet"; as Silliman had done, he linked her radical politics to free love. " 'Away with all monopolies,' " Dwight has her say. " 'I hate these exclusive rights; these privileged orders. I am for having everything free, and open to all; like the air which we breathe. . . .' "

" 'Love, particularly, I suppose, Madam [?]' "

" 'Yes, brute, love, if you please, and everything else.' "[26] Even Charles Brockden Brown's feminist tract *Alcuin* concluded with a long gloss on the same theme: to permit any change in women's status was to imply the acceptance of free love. Alcuin, who has been playing the conservative skeptic, concludes that once it is established that marriage "has no other criterion than custom," it becomes simply "a mode of sexual intercourse." His friend Mrs. Carter protests energetically that free love is not at all what she wanted; " 'because I demand an equality of conditions among beings that equally partake of the same divine reason, would you rashly infer that I was an enemy to the institution of marriage itself?' " Brown lets her have the last word, but he does not make Alcuin change his mind.[27]

Dwight had one final charge to make against Wollstonecraft; he attacked her plea that women emerge from the confines of their families. " 'Who will make our puddings, Madam?' " his protagonist asks. When she responds: " 'Make them yourself,' " he presses harder: " 'Who shall nurse us when we are sick?' " and, finally, " 'Who shall nurse our children?' " The last question reduces the fictional Mary to blushes and silence.[28]

It would not, however, reduce Rush, or Murray, or Brown, to blushes and silence. (Nor, I think, would it have so affected the real Mary Wollstonecraft.) They had neither predicted that women would cease their housewifely duties nor demanded that women should. Priscilla Mason's demand that hitherto male professions be opened to women was highly unusual, and even she apologized for it before she left the podium. There were, it is true, some other hints that women might claim the privileges and duties of male citizens of the republic. In *Alcuin*, Mrs. Carter explains her intense political disappointment through the first two chapters, arguing that Americans had been false to their own revolutionary promises in denying political status to women. "If a stranger questions me concerning the nature of our government, I answer, that in this happy climate all men are free: the people are the source of all authority; from them it flows, and to them, in due season, it returns . . . our liberty consists in the choice of our governors: all, as reason requires, have a part in this choice, yet not without a few exceptions . . . females . . . minors . . . the poor . . . slaves. . . . I am tired of explaining this charming system of equality and inde-

pendence." St. George Tucker, commenting on Blackstone, acknowledged that women were taxed without representation; like "aliens . . . children under the age of discretion, idiots, and lunatics," American women had neither political nor civil rights. "I fear there is little reason for a compliment to our laws for their respect and favour to the female sex," Tucker concluded. As Tucker had done, John Adams acknowledged that women's experience of the republic was different from men's; he hesitantly admitted that the republic claimed the right "to govern women without their consent." For a brief period from 1790 to 1807, New Jersey law granted the franchise to "all free inhabitants," and on occasion women exercised that right; it is conceivable that New Jersey might have stood as a precedent for other states. Instead, New Jersey's legislature rewrote its election law; the argument for political competence was taken no further.[29]

All of these were hesitant suggestions introduced into a hostile intellectual milieu in which female learning was equated with pedantry and masculinity. To resist those assumptions was to undertake a great deal; it was a task for which no one was ready; indeed, it is impossible to say that anyone really wanted to try. Instead, the reformers would have been quick to reply, with Brown's Mrs. Carter, that they had no intention of abandoning marriage; that they had every intention of making puddings and nursing babies; that the education they demanded was primarily to enable women to function more effectively within their traditional sphere, and only secondarily to fulfill demands like Priscilla Mason's that they emerge from it. People were complaining that American women were boring, frivolous, spending excessive amounts of money for impractical fashions; very well, a vigorously educated woman would be less likely to bore her husband, less likely to be a spendthrift, better able to cope with adverse fortune. Judith Sargent Murray versified an equation:

Where'er the maiden *Industry* appears,
A thrifty contour every object wears;
And when fair *order* with the nymph
    combines,
Adjusts, directs, and every plan designs,
Then *Independence* fills her peerless seat,
And lo! the matchless trio is complete.

Murray repeatedly made the point that the happiness of the nation depended on the happiness of families; and that the "felicity of families" is dependent on the presence of women who are "properly methodical, and economical in their distributions and expenditures of time." She denied that "the present enlarged plan of female education" was incompatible with traditional notions of women's duties: she predicted that the "daughters of Columbia" would be free of *"invidious and rancorous passions"* and "even the semblance of pedantry"; "when they became wives and mothers, they will fill with honour the parts allotted them."[30]

Rarely, in the literature of the early republic, do we find any objection to the notion that women belong in the home; what emerges is the argument that the Revolution had enlarged the significance of what women did in their homes. Benjamin Rush's phrasing of this point is instructive; when he defined the goals of republican women, he was careful not to include a claim to political power: "The equal share that every citizen has in the liberty and the possible share he may have in the government of our country make it necessary that our ladies should be qualified to a certain degree by a peculiar and suitable education, *to concur in instructing their sons in the principles of liberty and government*." The Young Ladies' Academy promised "not wholly to engross the mind" of each pupil, "but to allow her to prepare for the duties in life to which she may be destined." Miss P. W. Jackson, graduating from Mrs.

Rowson's Academy, explained what she had learned of the goals of the educated woman: "A woman who is skilled in every useful art, who practices every domestic virtue . . . may, by her precept and example, inspire her brothers, her husband, or her sons, with such a love of virtue, such just ideas of the true value of civil liberty . . . that future heroes and statesmen, who arrive at the summit of military or political fame, shall *exaltingly declare, it is to my mother I owe this elevation*." By their household management, by their refusal to countenance vice, crime, or cruelty in their suitors and husbands, women had the power to direct the moral development of the male citizens of the republic. The influence women had on children, especially on their sons, gave them ultimate responsibility for the future of the new nation.[31]

This constellation of ideas, and the republican rhetoric which made it convincing, appears at great length in the Columbia College commencement oration of 1795. Its title was "Female Influence"; behind the flowery rhetoric lurks a social and political message:

Let us then figure to ourselves the accomplished woman, surrounded by a sprightly band, from the babe that imbibes the nutritive fluid, to the generous youth, just ripening into manhood, and the lovely virgin. . . . Let us contemplate the mother distributing the mental nourishment to the fond smiling circle, by means proportionate to their different powers of reception, watching the gradual openings of their minds, and studying their various turns of temper. . . . Religion, fairest offspring of the skies, smiles auspicious on her endeavours; the Genius of Liberty hovers triumphant over the glorious scene. . . . Yes, ye fair, the reformation of a world is in your power. . . . Reflect on the result of your efforts. Contemplate the rising glory of confederated America. Consider that your exertions can best secure, increase, and perpetuate it. The solidity and stability of the liberties of your country rest with you; since Liberty is never sure, 'till Virtue reigns triumphant. . . . Already may we see the lovely daughters of Columbia asserting the importance and the honour of their sex. It rests with you to make this retreat [from the corruptions of Europe] doubly peaceful, doubly happy, by banishing from it those crimes and corruptions, which have never yet failed of giving rise to tyranny, or anarchy. While you thus keep our country virtuous, you maintain its independence. . . .[32]

Defined this way, the educated woman ceased to threaten the sanctity of marriage; the bluestocking need not be masculine. In this awkward—and in the 1790s still only vaguely expressed—fashion, the traditional womanly virtues were endowed with political purpose. A pivotal political role was assigned to the least political inhabitants of the republic. Ironically, the same women who were denied political identity were counted on to maintain the republican quality of the new nation. "Let the ladies of a country be educated properly," Rush said, "and they will not only make and administer its laws, but form its manners and character."[33]

When Americans addressed themselves to the matter of the role of women, they found that those who admired bluestockings and those who feared them could agree on one thing: in a world where moral influences were fast dissipating, women as a group seemed to represent moral stability. Few in the early republic demanded, in a sustained way, substantial revisions in women's political or legal status; few spoke to the nascent class of unskilled women workers. But many took pride in the assertion that properly educated republican women would stay in the home and, from that vantage point, would shape the characters of their sons and husbands in the direction of benevolence, self-restraint, and responsible independence. They refuted charges of free love and masculinization; in doing so they created a justification for woman as household goddess so deeply felt that one must be permitted to suspect that many women of their generation were *refusing* to be household goddesses.[34] They began to make the argument for intelligent household management that Catharine Beecher, a generation later, would enshrine in her *Treatise on Domestic Economy* as woman's highest goal. The Daughters of Columbia became, in effect, the Mothers of the Victorians. Whether Judith Sargent Murray, Charles Brockden Brown, or Benjamin Rush would have approved the ultimate results of their work is hard to say.

NOTES

1. *The Gleaner*, III (Boston, 1798), 189.
2. Montesquieu's comment that republics differed from other political systems by the reliance they placed on virtue is explored in Howard Mumford Jones, *O Strange New World* (New York, 1964), p. 431.
3. August 1792, pp. 121–123.
4. "Thoughts upon Female Education, Accommodated to the Present State of Society, Manners, and Government in the United States of America" (Philadelphia and Boston, 1787). Reprinted in Frederick Rudolph, ed., *Essays on Education in the Early Republic* (Cambridge, Mass, 1865), p. 39.
5. "The greater proportion of young women are trained up by thoughtless parents, in ease and luxury, with no other dependence for their future support than the precarious chance of establishing themselves by marriage: for this purpose (the men best know why) elaborate attention is paid to external attractions and accomplishments, to the neglect of more useful and solid acquirements. . . . [Marriage is the] *sole* method of procuring for themselves an establishment." *New York Magazine*, August 1797, p. 406. For comment on the marriage market, see letter signed "A Matrimonial Republican" in Philadelphia *Lady's Magazine*, July 1792, pp. 64–67; "Legal Prostitution, Or Modern Marriage," Boston *Independent Chronicle*, October 28, 1793. For criticism of fashion, see

American Magazine, December 1787, p. 39; July 1788, p. 594; *American Museum*, August 1788, p. 119; *Massachusetts Mercury*, August 16, 1793; January 16, 1795.

6. *New York Magazine*, August 1797, p. 406; Philadelphia *Universal Asylum and Columbian Magazine*, July 1791, p. 11.

7. Murray, *Gleaner*, I, 168, 193.

8. Charles Brockden Brown, *Ormond; Or the Secret Witness*, ed. by Ernest Marchand (New York, 1799; reprinted 1937, 1962), p. 19.

9. *Ibid.*, pp. 98–99.

10. "It was obvious to suppose that a woman thus fearless and sagacious had not been inactive at a period like the present, which called forth talents and courage without distinction of sex, and had been particularly distinguished by female enterprise and heroism." Ibid., p. 170.

11. For examples of such lists, see: Murray, *Gleaner*, III, 200–219; John Blair Linn, *The Powers of Genius: A Poem in Three Parts* (Philadelphia, 1802); Philadelphia *Weekly Magazine*, August 4, 11, 1798; *Port Folio*, February 12, 1803; September 27, 1806; Philadelphia *Minerva*, March 14, 1795. For the admiration expressed by Abigail Adams and Mercy Otis Warren for Catharine Macaulay, see Abigail Adams to Isaac Smith, Jr., April 20, 1771; Abigail Adams to Catharine Sawbridge Macaulay, n.d., 1774; Mercy Otis Warren to Abigail Adams, January 28, 1775; in L. H. Butterfield, ed., *Adams Family Correspondence*, I (Cambridge, Mass., 1963), 76–77, 177–179, 181–183. For the circle of English "bluestockings," in the 1780s, see M. G. Jones, *Hannah More* (Cambridge, 1952), pp. 41–76.

12. *Massachusetts Magazine*, II (March 1790), 133; *Universal Asylum* and *Columbian Magazine*, July 1791, p. 9; Thomas Cooper, "Propositions Respecting the Foundation of Civil Government," in *Political Arithmetic* (Philadelphia [?], 1798), p. 27. See also *Boston Weekly Magazine*, May 21, 1803, pp. 121–122; *American Museum*, January 1787, p. 59; Philadelphia *Lady's Magazine*, June 1792.

13. J. A. Neale, "An Essay on the Genius and Education of the Fair Sex," Philadelphia *Minerva*, April 4, March 21, 1795.

14. *Remarks on Education: Illustrating the Close Connection between Virtue and Wisdom* (Philadelphia, 1798), reprinted in Rudolph, *Essays on Education*, p. 211. Smith did acknowledge that female instruction was important, but commented that concepts of what it should be were so varied that he feared to make any proposals, and despaired of including women in the scheme he was then devising. "It is sufficient, perhaps, for the present, that the improvement of women is marked by a rapid progress and that a prospect opens equal to their most ambitious desires" (p. 217). The other prizewinner, Samuel Knox, proposed to admit girls to the primary schools in his system, but not to the academies or colleges. Knox's essay, "An Essay on the Best System of Liberal Education," may be found in Rudolph, *Essays on Education*, pp. 271–372.

15. Charles E. Cunningham, *Timothy Dwight: 1752–1817: A Biography* (New York, 1942), pp. 154–163.

16. Noah Webster, "Importance of Female Education," in *American Magazine*, May 1788, pp. 368, 369. This essay was part of his pamphlet *On the Education of Youth in America* (Boston, 1790), conveniently reprinted in Rudolph, *Essays on Education*, pp. 41–78. *Weekly Magazine*, April 7, 1798; Murray, *The Gleaner*, I, 70–71.

17. Benjamin Rush, "Thoughts upon Female Education," in Rudolph, *Essays on Education*, pp. 25–40. See also the comments of the Reverend James Sproat, a member of the Board of Visitors, June 10, 1789, in *The Rise and Progress of the Young Ladies' Academy of Philadelphia; Containing an Account of a Number of Public Examinations and Commencements; the Charter and Bye-Laws; Likewise a Number of Orations delivered by the Young Ladies, and several by the Trustees of Said Institution* (Philadelphia, 1794), p. 24.

18. Benjamin Say, "Address," December 4, 1789, in *Rise and Progress of the Young Ladies' Academy*, p. 33; Benjamin Rush, *Syllabus of Lectures, Containing the Application of the Principles of Natural Philosophy . . .* (Philadelphia, 1787). Rush, of course, was waging his own crusade against the classics as inappropriate in a republic; he argued elsewhere that to omit Latin and Greek would have the beneficial effect of diminishing "the present immense disparity which subsists between the sexes, in the degrees of their education and knowledge." When his contemporaries omitted the classics from the female curriculum it was usually because they thought women's minds were not up to it. Rush, "Observations upon the Study of the Latin and Greek Languages," in *Essays, Literary, Moral and Philosophical* (Philadelphia, 1798), p. 44.

19. Priscilla Mason, "Oration," May 15, 1793, in *Rise and Progress of the Young Ladies' Academy*, pp. 90–95. See also the

valedictory oration by Molly Wallace, June 12, 1792, ibid., pp. 73–79.

20. Letter signed M.G., "American Lounger," *Port Folio*, April 7, 1804.

21. Gertrude Meredith to David Meredith, May 3, 1804, Meredith Papers, Historical Society of Pennsylvania; Philadelphia *Evening Fireside*, April 6, 1805.

22. *New-England Palladium*, September 18, 1801; *American Magazine*, February 1788, p. 134; *Lady's Magazine*, January 1793, pp. 68–72. (The "battle at Odiham" refers to a famous bare-knuckle prize fight, one of the earliest major events in the history of boxing, fought in 1788 by Daniel Mendoza and Richard Humphries in Hampshire, England.) Other attacks on female pedantry, which express the fear that intellectual women will be masculine, are found in the *American Magazine*, March 1788, pp. 244–245 ("To be lovely you must be content to be women . . . and leave the masculine virtues, and the profound researches of study to the province of the other sex"); *New-England Palladium*, September 4, 18, December 4, 1801, March 5, 9, 1802; Benjamin Silliman, *Letters of Shahcoolen, a Hindu Philosophy, Residing in Philadelphia; To His Friend, El Hassan, an Inhabitant of Delhi* (Boston, 1802), pp. 23–24, 62; *American Museum*, December 1788, p. 491; *Boston Weekly Magazine*, March 24, 1804, p. 86 ("Warlike women, learned women, and women who are politicians, equally abandon the circle which nature and institutions have traced round their sex; they convert themselves into men").

23. *Extracts from the Journal of Elizabeth Drinker, from 1759 to 1807, A.D.*, ed. by Henry D. Biddle (Philadelphia, 1889), p. 285. The entry is dated April 22, 1796.

24. Mary Wollstonecraft, *A Vindication of the Rights of Woman, With Strictures on Political and Moral Subjects* (New York, 1891), pp. 23, 149–156.

25. *New-England Palladium*, November 24, 27, December 8, 11, 15, 1801; March 2, 5, 9, 1802. Identification of Dwight as author is made by Robert Edson Lee, "Timothy Dwight and the Boston *Palladium*," *New England Quarterly*, XXXV (1962), 229–239.

26. *New-England Palladium*, March 9, 1802.

27. Charles Brockden Brown and Lee R. Edwards, *Alcuin: A Dialogue* (New York, 1971), pp. 44–88.

28. *New-England Palladium*, March 9, 1802.

29. Brown, *Alcuin*, pp. 32–33; St. George Tucker, *Blackstone's Commentaries: With Notes of Reference, to the Constitution and Laws, of the Federal Government of the United States, and of the Commonwealth of Virginia*, II (Philadelphia, 1803), 145, 445; John Adams to James Sullivan, May 26, 1776, in *The Works of John Adams*, ed. by Charles Francis Adams, IX (1856), 375–379; Edward Raymond Turner, "Women's Suffrage in New Jersey: 1790–1807," *Smith College Studies in History*, I (1916), 165–187. Opposition to woman suffrage apparently surfaced after women voted as a bloc in an unsuccessful attempt to influence the outcome of an Essex County election in 1797.

30. *Gleaner*, I, 161, 12, 29, 191, 190.

31. Rush, "Thoughts upon Female Education," in Rudolph, *Essays on Education*, p. 28 (my italics); "On Female Education," *Port Folio*, May 1809, p. 388; *Boston Weekly Magazine*, October 29, 1803.

32. *New York Magazine*, May 1795, pp. 301–305.

33. Rush, "Thoughts upon Female Education," in Rudolph, *Essays on Education*, p. 36.

34. See, for example, *Boston Weekly Magazine*, December 18, 1802; *Weekly Magazine*, March 3, 1798; *Port Folio*, February 12, 1803, March 3, 1804, April 20, 1805.

II A

Industrializing America

1820–80

To Americans who lived through it, the Civil War was the most traumatic experience of the nineteenth century. The years from 1830 to 1860 have come to be called the *antebellum* period, as though their importance derives from what they preceded rather than what they encompassed. Other familiar labels—the Jacksonian era, the Rise of the Common Man, Freedom's Ferment—suggest the difficulty historians have had in characterizing the period.

In these years the American economy was transformed by the industrial revolution. Railroads and steamboats linked distant parts of the country and simplified economic interaction; during the Civil War the control of transportation networks would be an important ingredient in the North's success. The cotton gin ensured the profitability of the crop and reinforced the system of slave labor in the South. Steam-powered spinning and weaving equipment was placed in northern factories and tended by a new class of wage workers. The distinctive economies of North and South fostered a political dialogue that became increasingly acerbic over the years. The position of legislators on issues as disparate as tariffs or free speech could be linked to the economic interests of their sections and to the distinctive regional cultures. By 1860 institutions that had helped connect the two cultures—political parties, churches, economic networks—had broken down completely.

It has been relatively easy for historians to see that economic and political developments affected men's lives. The right to vote and hold office was extended to virtually every white man, whether or not he held property; after the Civil War it was extended to black men as well. Congress was a national forum for debate among male political leaders; by the 1850s speeches made there were rapidly diffused to the public by cheap newspapers, printed by newly efficient presses and distributed by railroads throughout the nation. A host of new careers opened to men as politicians, journalists, teachers, capitalists, physicians, and reformers. The expansion of the physical boundaries of the country, by treaty and by war, opened new frontiers and created new opportunities for farmers, merchants, civic promoters, and land speculators.

When we look at these developments through women's eyes, we find that women's lives also changed markedly. The transportation revolution, for example, had special significance for women. Single women rarely traveled in the colonial period; long trips meant nights in unfamiliar taverns and lodging houses where accommodations were uncertain and safety could not be assured. The railroad changed that. The women who traveled to raise funds for abolition societies and women's seminaries could not have played that role a century before. After the Civil War Elizabeth Cady Stanton and Susan B. Anthony traveled a regular lyceum circuit throughout the North and Midwest, speaking on behalf of women's rights.

Improvements in the printing technology and distribution of newspapers meant that women as well as men were no longer dependent on local sources of information and political guidance. Even if one's town lacked a temperance society or an abolitionist organization, one could still subscribe to a temperance or abolitionist newspaper. A person who did so was reaching out, past the local notables—ministers, politicians, lawyers—who had shaped opinion in the colonial period, to make contact with a larger political community. Abolition newspapers like the *National Anti-Slavery Standard* (which was, for a time, edited by a woman, Lydia Maria Child) and women's rights newspapers like *Una* or *The Revolution* could come straight to a woman's mailbox, enlarging her political world.

Although women could travel more freely and read more widely, in other ways the new industrial economy constrained their lives. As Gerda Lerner has pointed out, many of the new opportunities for men came in a form that closed options for women. When additional men were granted suffrage, for example, "women's political status, while legally unchanged, . . . deteriorated relative to the advances made by men."[1] When new medical schools offered formal training only to men, "the process of professionalization . . . proceeded in such a way as to institutionalize an exclusion of women. . . . The status differential between male and female practitioners was more obviously disadvantageous and underscored women's marginality."[2]

If we recall David Potter's rule and ask whether established generalizations about the nineteenth century apply to women as accurately as they apply to men, we find that they do not. Several traditional pictures must be refocused.

For example, the great religious revival of the early part of the century is often described as though it affected both men and women with equal force. But careful examination of church records has suggested that women were already church members when the revival began; the new recruits were most likely to be sons and husbands of women who had long since been "saved." Seen in this light, the Second Great Awakening may be better understood as an occasion on which women acted as a catalyst for church recruitment.[3]

Although the experience of slavery has received fresh attention from historians, the distinctive experience of female slaves has been little examined. It is clear that work roles on the plantation were defined by gender as well as by race. Women were especially vulnerable to sexual exploitation and to debilitating chronic ailments incidental to childbearing. As Michael P. Johnson shows, excessive labor requirements affected not only the slave women but their unborn children.

In free households female work—including taking in boarders, washing their clothes, and cooking for them—might account for as much income as working-class husbands gained from their own employment. If the husband's work was seasonal or erratic, the steady income from taking in boarders could be crucial to the family's survival. The story of the work women who took in boarders did ought not to be relegated to the obligatory chapters on "home and family life"; it is central to the history of American labor.

Traditional interpretations of industrialization require refinement. Familiar accounts are likely to ignore the dependence of early mills on women for their labor force, yet even Alexander Hamilton recognized that a crucial factor in the development of new factories was that their owners could count on a steady supply of female workers at low rates of pay. As Barbara Mayer Wertheimer shows, women were among the first self-conscious laborers in America.

Viewed through women's eyes, antebellum America looks different. The common school movement looms even larger than in traditional accounts. As Kathryn Kish Sklar's essay suggests, the story of the building of public schools does not begin and end with Horace Mann and Henry Barnard. The work of Emma Willard and Catharine Beecher also requires attention. A history of education in antebellum America needs to explain how the great gap in literacy between men and women was closed during those years, and it must also find room for the large number of women who worked, even briefly, as schoolteachers at wage rates so low that planners could think it feasible to construct enough classrooms to educate every child in America.

The frontier has traditionally been treated as a metaphor for unbounded opportunity. But the experience of married women in the trans-Mississippi West was likely to be one of hardship encountered at the urging of their husbands, not out of their own initiative and choice.

Finally, in the middle years of the nineteenth century women pressed at the limits of the ways in which nonvoting citizens could influence the political order.

In antislavery petition campaigns, in efforts to persuade legislatures to reform laws dealing with married women's property rights and child custody, in responding to the crisis of the Civil War, in volunteering as teachers for freedmen's schools after the war, women expressed political opinions and sought to shape political events. Some, like Catharine Beecher and Sarah Josepha Hale, began to formulate an interpretation of the republican community which suggested that women could play an important part in it without voting; others, like Elizabeth Cady Stanton, insisted that women's political rights ought to be the same as those of men. But whatever particular solutions they proposed, whether suffragist or not, the way in which women's citizenship was displayed was a significant element on the American political scene.

NOTES

1. Gerda Lerner, *The Majority Finds Its Past: Placing Women in History* (New York, 1979), p. 18.
2. Ibid., p. 20.
3. Mary P. Ryan, "A Woman's Awakening: Evangelical Religion and the Families of Utica, New York, 1800–1840," *American Quarterly* 30 (1978): 602–23.

MARIA PERKINS
"I am quite heart sick"

Because masters understood the connection between literacy and rebelliousness, slaves were rarely taught to read and write. This anguished letter from Maria Perkins is unusual because it was written by an enslaved woman. We do not know whether Perkins's husband Richard managed to persuade his master to buy her and keep the family together. If a trader did buy Maria Perkins or her child, the likelihood of permanent separation was great. Scottsville, mentioned in the letter, is a small town near Charlottesville; Staunton is some forty miles away.

Charlottesville, Oct. 8th, 1852
Dear Husband I write you a letter to let you know my distress my master has sold albert to a trader on Monday court day and myself and other child is for sale also and I want you to let [me] hear from you very soon before next cort if you can I don't know when I don't want you to wait till Christmas I want you to tell dr Hamelton and your master if either will buy me they can attend to it know and then I can go afterwards. I don't want a trader to get me they asked me if I had got any person to buy me and I told them no they took me to the court houste too they never put me up a man buy the name of brady bought albert and is gone I don't know where they say he lives in Scottesville my things is in several places some is in staunton and if I should be sold I don't know what will become of them I don't expect to meet with the luck to get that way till I am quite heartsick nothing more I am and ever will be your kind wife Maria Perkins.

To Richard Perkins

Maria Perkins to Richard Perkins, October 8, 1852, Ulrich B. Phillips Collection, Yale University Library, New Haven.

ROSE
"Look for some others for to 'plenish de earth"

Letters like Maria Perkins's are very rare. Most firsthand evidence of the experience of being a slave comes from narratives prepared by ex-slaves after they were free. Some accounts were published by abolitionist societies before the Civil War; some people were interviewed by agents of the Freedmen's Bureau after the war. A large group of elderly ex-slaves was interviewed in the 1930s as part of the Federal Writers' Project. One of these speakers we know only as Rose.

Abolitionists shrilly accused masters of breeding slaves as they did cattle. Masters denied these charges and claimed that high birth rates among slave women should be taken as evidence of high levels of nutrition and of good treatment. In Brazil, for example, where the treatment of slaves was much more brutal, fewer children survived. There was some truth in this defense. But slave women lacked the normal legal protections against rape, and, as Rose's moving narrative shows, the line between "forced breeding" and "strong encouragement" could be a very thin one.

What I say am de facts. If I's one day old, I's way over 90, and I's born in Bell County, right here in Texas, and am owned by Massa William Black. He owns mammy and pappy, too. Massa Black has a big plantation but he has more niggers dan he need for work on dat place, 'cause he am a nigger trader. He trade and buy and sell all de time.

Massa Black am awful cruel and he whip de cullud folks and works 'em hard and feed dem poorly. We'uns have for rations de cornmeal and milk and 'lasses and some beans and peas and meat once a week. We'uns have to work in de field every day from daylight till dark and on Sunday we'uns do us washin'. Church? Shucks, we'uns don't know what dat mean.

I has de correct mem'randum of when de war start. Massa Black sold we'uns right den. Mammy and pappy powerful glad to git sold, and dey and I is put on de block with 'bout ten other niggers. When we'uns gits te de tradin' block, dere lots of white folks dere what come to look us over. One man shows de intres' in pappy. Him named Hawkins. He talk to pappy and pappy talk to him and say, "Dem my woman and chiles. Please buy all of us and have mercy on we'uns." Massa Hawkins say, "Dat gal am a likely lookin' nigger, she am portly and strong, but three am more dan I wants, I guesses."

De sale start and 'fore long pappy a put on de block. Massa Hawkins wins de bid for pappy and when mammy am put on de block, he wins de bid for her. Den dere am three or four other niggers sold befo' my time comes. Den massa Black calls me

Manuscript Slave Narrative Collection, Federal Writers' Project, 1941, vol. 17, Texas Narratives, part 4, pp. 174–78, Library of Congress, Washington, D.C.

to de block and de auction man say, "What am I offer for dis portly, strong young wench. She's never been 'bused and will make de good breeder."

I wants to hear Massa Hawkins bid, but him say nothin'. Two other men am biddin' 'gainst each other and I sho' has de worryment. Dere am tears comin' down my cheeks 'cause I's bein' sold to some man dat would make sep'ration from my mammy. One man bids $500 and de auction man ask, "Do I hear more? She am gwine at $500.00." Den someone say, $525.00 and de auction man say, "She am sold for $525.000 to Massa Hawkins." Am I glad and 'cited! Why, I's quiverin' all over.

Massa Hawkins takes we'uns to his place and it am a nice plantation. Lots better am dat place dan Massa Black's. Dere is 'bout 50 niggers what is growed and lots of chillen. De first thing massa de when we'uns gits home am give we'uns rations and a cabin. You mus' believe dis nigger when I says dem rations a feast for us. Dere plenty meat and tea and coffee and white flour. I's never tasted white flour and coffee and mammy fix some biscuits and coffee. Well, de biscuits was yum, yum, yum to me, but de coffee I doesn't like.

De quarters am purty good. Dere am twelve cabins all made from logs and a table and some benches and bunks for sleepin' and a fireplace for cookin' and de heat. Dere am no floor, jus' de ground.

Massa Hawkins am good to he niggers and not force 'em work too hard. Dere am as much diff'ence 'tween him and old Massa Black in de way of treatment as 'twixt de Lawd and de devil. Massa Hawkins 'lows he niggers have reason'ble parties and go fishin', but we'uns am never tooken to church and has no books for larnin'. Dere am no edumcation for de niggers.

Dere am one thing Massa Hawkins does to me what I can't shunt from my mind. I knows he don't do it for mean-

ness, but I allus holds it 'gainst him. What he done am force me to live with dat nigger, Rufus, 'gainst my wants.

After I been at he place 'bout a year, de massa come to me and say, "You gwine live with Rufus in dat cabin over yonder. Go fix it for livin'." I's 'bout sixteen year old and has no larnin', and I's jus' igno'mus chile. I's thought dat him mean for me to tend de cabin for Rufus and some other niggers. Well, dat am start de pestigation for me.

I's took charge of de cabin after work am done and fixes supper. Now, I don't like dat Rufus, 'cause he a bully. He am big and 'cause he so, he think everybody do what him say. We'uns has supper, den I goes here and dere talkin', till I's ready for sleep and den I gits in de bunk. After I's in, dat nigger come and crawl in de bunk with me 'fore I knows it. I says, "What you means, you fool nigger?" He say for me to hush de mouth. "Dis am my bunk, too," he say.

"You's teched in de head. Git out," I's told him, and I puts de feet 'gainst him and give him a shove and out he go on de floor 'fore he know what I's doin'. Dat nigger jump up and he mad. He look like de wild bear. He starts for de bunk and I jumps quick for de poker. It am 'bout three feet long and when he comes at me I lets him have it over de head. Did dat nigger stop in he tracks? I's say he did. He looks at me steady for a minute and you's could tell he thinkin' hard. Den he go and set on de bench and say, "Jus wait. You thinks it am smart, but you's am foolish in de head. Dey's gwine larn you somethin'."

"Hush yous big mouth and stay 'way from dis nigger, dat all I wants," I say, and jus' sets and hold dat poker in de hand. He jus' sets, lookin' like de bull. Dere we'uns sets and sets for 'bout an hour and den he go out and I bars de door.

De nex' day I goes to de missy and tells her what Rufus wants and missy say dat am de massa's wishes. She say, "Yous am de portly gal and Rufus am de portly man. De massa wants you-uns fer to bring forth portly chillen."

I's thinkin' 'bout what de missy say, but say to myse'f, "I's not gwine live with dat Rufus." Dat night when him come in de cabin, I grabs de poker and sits on de bench and says, "Git 'way from me, nig-ger, 'fore I busts yous brains out and stomp on dem." He say nothin' and git out.

De nex' day de massa call me and tell me, "Woman, I's pay big money for you and I's done dat for de cause I wants yous to raise me chillens. I's put yous to live with Rufus for dat purpose. Now, if you doesn't want whippin' at de stake, yous do what I wants."

I thinks 'bout massa buyin' me offen de block and savin' me from bein' sep'-rated from my folks and 'bout bein' whipped at de stake. Dere it am. What am I's to do? So I 'cides to do as de massa wish and so I yields.

When we'uns am given freedom, Massa Hawkins tells us we can stay and work for wages or share crop de land. Some stays and some goes. My folks and me stays. We works de land on shares for three years, den moved to other land near by. I stays with my folks till they dies.

If my mem'radum am correct, it am 'bout thirty year since I come to Fort Worth. Here I cooks for white folks till I goes blind 'bout ten year ago.

I never marries, 'cause one 'sperience am 'nough for dis nigger. After what I does for de massa, I's never wants no truck with any man. De Lawd forgive dis cullud woman, but he have to 'scuse me and look for some others for to 'plenish de earth.

MICHAEL P. JOHNSON
Smothered Slave Infants:
Were Slave Mothers at Fault?

The scarcity of written testimony from slaves about what their lives were like has forced historians to search elsewhere. In the following essay Michael P. Johnson shows how biology and economics intertwined. He offers a strikingly original analysis of census data and proposes that one distinctively painful ex-perience to which slave women were vulnerable was being told that they had smothered their own infants by rolling over or "overlaying" the children who shared their beds. What alternative explanation does Johnson offer for the deaths of these babies? What does he deduce about the levels of health and nutrition of slave women? What does he suggest about the quality of these women's lives?

In the South Carolina upcountry district of Abbeville in 1850 a one-month-old slave girl named Harriet was reported to the census marshall Charles M. Pelot as having died in December 1849 because she was "Smothered by carelessness of [her] mother." Similar reports are scattered throughout the mortality schedules of the United States census for the southern states. Allice Burrow, a six-month-old slave girl in Henrico County, Virginia, "was Smouthered by her Mother Lying on her while asleep"; in Tippah County, Mississippi, the two-month-old slave girl Biddy was "Accidentally overlaid by [her] mother in her Sleep"; in Cobb County, Georgia, an eight-month-old slave boy was "Overlaid by [his] Mother"; in Spartanburg District, South Carolina, a five-month-old slave girl was said to have been "Overlaid by [her] mother and smothered."[1] The grim record goes on and on.

In 1860 the slave states accounted for 94 percent of the nation's 2,129 reported deaths by suffocation. Most of these victims "were probably the children of slaves," the published mortality census speculated.[2] . . . According to a calculation in the 1860 published census slaves were nine times more likely than whites to die of suffocation, a larger interracial gap than for any other cause of death.[3] However, all these figures drastically understate the difference between slaves and whites in the reported incidence of smothering. The appropriate comparison is between death rates. The number of smothered slaves per 1,000 living slave infants should be compared with the number of smothered whites per 1,000 white infants. . . . In 1860, according to data from the manuscript mortality schedules of Georgia, Mississippi, South Carolina, and Virginia, slave infants were 53 times more likely to die of smothering than were southern white infants.[4] Between 1790 and 1860 smothering was responsible for the deaths of over 60,000 slave infants.[5]

The reason so many slave children were smothered was quite clear to contemporaries. Slave mothers were careless. As they slept with their infants, they accidentally overlaid and smothered them. The fault was clearly the mothers'. . . . "I wish it to be distinctly understood that nearly all the accidents occur in the negro population," wrote Pelot, adding, "which goes clearly to prove their great carelessness & total inability to take care of themselves."[6] Although many southerners would have considered Pelot's statement an exaggeration, virtually all would have agreed that the smothering deaths were accidental. Again and again census marshals noted "smothered accidentally" or "overlaid by accident." None of the smothering deaths in Georgia, Mississippi, South Carolina, and Virginia in 1860 produced even a hint of infanticide. There was simply no motive. An observer "will see how very prolific the female slaves are," Pelot noted, "which shows conclusively that their minds are at ease & that they are reconciled and satisfied with the station which God has pleased to place them in."[7] A content, sleepy slave mother carelessly rolled over her infant and smothered it.

Of course, carelessness could be compounded by exhaustion. Thomas Affleck, a planter in the hill country of Mississippi, reported in a southern medical journal that "not a few [slave infants] are over-laid by the wearied mother, who sleeps so dead a sleep as not to be aware of the injury to her infant. . . ."[8] Other medical writers concurred about the dangers of hard work for slave women.[9] But none of the census marshals in the states surveyed in this article recorded any remarks that suggested masters contributed to the smothering deaths by working slave women too hard. Yet the census data suggest very strongly that the heavy physical labor masters assigned to slave women—not the carelessness of the slave mothers—was the major reason so many slave infants were "smothered."

In fact, it is extremely unlikely that these slave infants were victims of smothering. Several historians have recently argued that suffocation deaths were caused by Sudden Infant Death Syndrome (SIDS). Todd L. Savitt's pioneering study of the smothered slaves listed in the death registers of twenty-four Virginia counties and two towns between 1853 and 1860 identified "a remarkable epidemiological correspondence [between smothered slaves and modern victims of SIDS], both in age and in seasonal variation." Savitt pointed out that medical scientists do not fully understand the etiology of SIDS, but he suggested that an "important factor" in the large difference between the smothering death rates of slaves and whites was "the marked underreporting of white suffocation deaths . . . , probably due in part to the social stigma associated with child smothering."[10] Robert William Fogel and Stanley L. Engerman offered a similar interpretation, arguing that deaths actually caused by "undisclosed infections" were probably more likely to be "reported as suffocation for slaves than for free men" because of "the jaundiced view of the overseers who reported the death statistics to the census takers."[11] . . . Both studies emphasized that the mothers of the children were not responsible for the deaths.[12] Modern research has demonstrated, as Savitt said, "that children cannot be smothered as long as there is any circulating air available, even when the infant is beneath the covers or wedged against the sleeping mother."[13] . . . In his searching critique of Fogel and Engerman's analysis of slave nutrition, Richard Sutch suggested that "The staggering difference between slave and white infant suffocation rates . . . would appear as reflections of extreme poverty, low birth weights, and poor postnatal care."[14] . . . All these scholars agreed that smothered slaves were actually victims of SIDS but differed sharply over the significance and explanation of the high incidence of smothering among slaves. The conflicting interpretations and their rather narrow empirical base warrant a step-by-step reconsideration of the evidence. . . .

First, consider the evidence of smothering. The remarks of the census marshals suggest that infants whose deaths were attributed to smothering were in fact found dead in bed. Usually census marshals simply recorded the cause of death as "smothered" or "overlaid." But in Fauquier County, Virginia, the marshal reported two slave infants who were "Supposed to have been smothered in bed. . . ."[15] In Carroll County, Georgia, a slave girl three months old was reported "Smothered probably."[16] The tentative nature of these remarks suggests that smothering was not observed or certain but inferred from the circumstances in which the dead child was found. . . . Indeed, according to D. W. Johnson, the marshal in Union District, South Carolina, in 1850, the actual number of smothered slave infants was much larger than that reported: "A very large proportion of the Deaths of Infant Slaves [whose cause of death was] reported as Unknown Sudden were supposed to have been caused by their mothers' overlying them during Sleep. The presumptive evidence of this fact was of the strongest character."[17]

Taken together, these fragmentary notes of the census marshals suggest that slave infants who were reported to have been smothered, suffocated, or overlain by their mothers were actually found dead in bed. Since a mother slept with her infant, she was presumed to be responsible for smothering it. The death was presumed to be accidental because there was no evidence that the child was sick—in which case death would have been attributed to another cause. The slave mother's grief probably persuaded her master that the death was indeed accidental and that she was responsible.[18] And in fact, the slave mother probably felt responsible for the tragedy.

Ex-slave Tabby Abbey's testimony is compelling. Born in Virginia in 1833, Tabby Abbey was sold at the age of sixteen and taken to Mississippi, near Tunica. "I never did work 'round de white folks' house but always done field work, mostly clarin' new groun'," she told her interviewer in 1936. "I had one baby in my life, a long time ago; but I went to sleep one day when I wuz nussin' him and rolled over on him and smothered him to death. I like to went crazy for a long time atter dat."[19] How many other slave mothers "like to went crazy" after their babies were discovered dead in their beds cannot be known. But it is possible to establish that it is extremely unlikely that the slave infants were actually smothered by their mothers.

The mortality data provide three important kinds of evidence that most of the smothered slaves were actually SIDS victims: the circumstances in which the dead child was discovered, the child's age, and the month of death. It is well established that SIDS victims die during sleep and are typically discovered dead in their bed, their parents having had no warning that they were seriously ill or distressed.[20] The same circumstances that led masters and slave mothers to conclude that the slave infants had been smothered strongly suggest, in light of modern medical knowledge, that the infants succumbed to SIDS. But the most conclusive evidence comes from the age distribution of "smothered" slaves.

According to Dr. J. Bruce Beckwith, an authority on SIDS, "The sparing of very young infants, peak incidence between 2 and 4 months, and rapid decline before the age of 6 months are common to virtually all studies [of SIDS]. We are aware of no other condition with this unique age distribution."[21] The age distribution of smothered slaves in all four states was quite close to the unique SIDS pattern. Overall, only 2 percent of the smothered slaves were less than one month old, over three-quarters were between one and six months old, and nearly 90 percent were less than one year old.

The discrepancies between the smothered slaves' age distribution and the SIDS pattern are relatively easy to explain. The ages of smothered slaves were not reported as accurately as the ages of SIDS victims. When an infant dies of SIDS today, its age is reported at the time of death. In contrast, the smothered slave infants' deaths were reported by either the master or an overseer up to a year after the slave infant had died. Even if the precise age of the infant had been known to the master or overseer at the time of death, it is likely that it was remembered less accurately when it was reported to the census marshal. For example, the large proportion of six-month-old smothered slaves is almost certainly an artifact of inaccurate age reporting. Many masters apparently responded to a census marshal's question about the age of a slave infant with, "Oh, about six months." This sort of imprecision in the age reports makes the conformity of the age distribution of the smothered slaves to the unique pattern of SIDS all the more remarkable. Of course, the death of some of the smothered slave infants was probably caused by something other than SIDS. . . . A careful study of 500 such infants in the state of Washington found that 15 percent of the deaths could be explained by causes other than SIDS.[22] Since none of the slave infants was autopsied, there is every reason to expect that at least a similar fraction of their deaths might have causes other than SIDS. That would probably account for many of the smothered slaves who were over one year old. . . .

The similarity of the age distribution of smothered slaves to the unique SIDS age pattern makes it extremely likely that the slave infants were victims of SIDS. If the age distribution does nothing else, it virtually disproves the notion that these deaths were caused by smothering or suffocation. If that was indeed the cause, as is often assumed by laymen even today in SIDS cases, then, as Beckwith notes, "Why is the very young infant spared, at a time when he seems most vulnerable, yet by the time of peak incidence, between 2 and 3 months, good head control has been achieved?"[23] The same question applies to the infanticide interpretation of these deaths.[24] If slave mothers were bent on infanticide, why did they wait so long? In short, whatever caused the deaths of these slave infants, they were not smothered intentionally or accidentally by their mothers.

Additional evidence that these slave infant deaths were caused by SIDS comes from the death-month distribution. "Nearly all workers have observed seasonal variations in SIDS incidence, with fewer cases occurring in the summer months," Beckwith reports.[25] The same pattern characterized the smothered slaves. In each state the summer months had a lower incidence of smothering deaths. . . .

The death-month and age distributions combined with the citations from the census marshals make it very difficult to construct a persuasive case that smothered slaves were not SIDS victims. Instead, the mortality data strongly support the conclusion of Savitt and others that the slaves died of SIDS. Although slave mothers did not literally smother these infants, as contemporaries believed, perhaps they did or neglected to do something else that was responsible for the deaths. How else can one account for the large difference between the death rates of smothered slave and white infants?

One of the possibilities mentioned earlier is that more white infants were "smothered" than the census manuscripts indicate. The twenty-three white smothering deaths reported to the census marshals in Georgia, Mississippi, South Carolina, and Virginia in 1860 conformed closely to the age and death-month distributions of the smothered slaves. Although the number of deaths is too small to conclude with certainty that these white infants died of SIDS, the peak incidence at two months of age and the disproportionate number of wintertime deaths suggest very strongly that they did. Additional evidence comes from Calhoun County, Mississippi, where census marshal W. R. Sykes recorded the death of the two-month-old white infant James W. Smith, whose cause of death was "Smothered by mother," Sykes adding "overlayed by whilst asleep."[26] Other white parents may have refused to admit such deaths to the census marshals, or smothering may have been suspected as a cause of death less often because fewer white mothers slept with their infants. Or maybe white parents attributed the deaths of a "smothered" infant to another cause. If we pursue the hint of census marshal D. W. Johnson that many infants whose deaths were probably caused by "overlaying" were reported as having died suddenly of unknown cause, then it appears that whites were indeed more subject to "overlaying" than is suggested by the data on smothered infants alone. . . .

Nonetheless, slave infants were much more subject than white infants to sudden, unexpected death, whether or not it was called smothering. The death rate for sudden death of unknown cause for white infants was 2.5; the rate for slave infants was five times greater, 12.7. Although this is much smaller than the fifty-three-fold difference between white and slave death rates for smothering, it is clear that slave infants were much more subject to sudden, unexpected death than whites. It is very unlikely that there were enough unreported white deaths to equalize these differences. Instead, being a slave somehow increased an infant's risk of dying suddenly and unexpectedly because it was "smothered" by its mother. But why?

Modern studies have consistently found that "SIDS victims have a greater proportion of young mothers of low socioeconomic and educational level, who live in crowded housing and have little prenatal care."[27] The most recent research also indicates that the SIDS victims are not normal, healthy infants. Instead, SIDS victims exhibit a variety of "neurologic abnormalities" which constitute "multiple evidences of probable neonatal brain dysfunction. . . ."[28] The exact relationship between the SIDS infant's neurological abnormalities and the mother and her environment is not clear. In a report on the most recent research, Dr. Richard L. Naeye points out that four of the six factors that have been identified as contributing to SIDS "have been shown to either damage the fetus or place it at increased risk of damage"; in particular, "(1) a bacterial infection of the amniotic fluid, (2) anemia in the mother and (3) the use by the mother of cigarettes or (4) barbiturates."[29] Although these factors will only account for about a third of all sudden infant deaths, Naeye believes that, "Their greatest significance may be their indication that fetal life is a fruitful area in which to continue the search for the origins of the syndrome." The respiratory control centers in the brain are located in the brain stem which, according to Naeye, "is a particularly vulnerable target for damage during fetal life because it has a higher metabolic rate than other areas of the brain have. Specifically, the brain stem is vulnerable to damage by low levels of both oxygen and glucose in the blood."[30] This modern knowledge of the general significance of fetal neurological development and the specific risks associated with amniotic fluid infections, maternal anemia, and poor nutrition suggests why so many slave infants were "smothered."

The hard physical labor required of pregnant slave women is the most promising explanation for the high incidence of SIDS among slave infants. Recent research has demonstrated that hard work can have serious consequences for pregnant women. Naeye's study of fatal amniotic fluid infections in Ethiopia, for example, found that the frequency of infections "was greater in the poorest gravid women, in those engaged in hard physical labor, and in twins." "Poverty restricts the quantity and quality of food intake in Ethiopian pregnant women while hard physical labor has a caloric cost," Naeye explains, adding that the "nutritional requirements of pregnancy are greater with twins than with single born infants."[31] A similar relationship between hard work and nutrition probably prevailed among pregnant slave women in the antebellum South.

The nutritional value of the slave diet has been the subject of intense controversy.[32] The best recent evidence indicates that the typical slave diet may have been adequate in caloric quantity but deficient in nutritional quality.[33] The nutritional requirements of a pregnant slave woman were obviously greater both in calories and in specific nutrients. In particular, a pregnant woman required about 65 percent more dietary protein, two and one-half times as much calcium, and three hundred more calories per day than a nonpregnant, nonlactating woman.[34] Sutch has pointed out that a slave "could subsist" on a typical slave ration if the assigned work included such " 'light' to 'moderate' " tasks as cooking, house cleaning, hoeing, plowing, or clearing brush. "Heavy" work, including "such plantation-type activities as dragging logs, felling trees, and digging ditches," greatly increased a slave's caloric needs.[35] Although direct evidence of the rations for pregnant slave women is lacking, the high caloric cost of hard work had to have an adverse effect unless the diet was adjusted accordingly. Even if one assumes the very best about the diet of pregnant slave women—namely that they had the same diet as pregnant white women—it is clear that pregnant slave women had to do more hard physical labor than pregnant white women. That was probably why the incidence of SIDS was higher among slave infants.[36]

Several antebellum medical writers commented on the dangers of hard work for pregnant slave women. A Tennessee physician, John H. Morgan, wrote that "the exposure to which negro women are subjected as field hands during menstruation and pregnancy," along with the "promiscuous and excessive intercourse of the sexes" were "among the principal causes of sterility and abortion." "And many diseases to which they are incident arise from the same cause," he added. In particular, he argued that "The functions of menstruation and pregnancy being so peculiarly delicate, negroes suffer seriously during those periods from hard labor and exposure in bad weather, frequently being badly fed and badly clothed. . . ."[37] A Georgia physician, Edmund Monroe Pendleton, wrote that the much greater incidence of abortion and miscarriage among slaves "either teaches that slave labor is inimical to the procreation of the species from exposure, violent exercise, &c., or, as the planters believe, the blacks are possessed of a secret by which they destroy the foetus at an early stage of gestation."[38] . . . To the question, "Are negro women, under the ordinary regime of plantations, as prolific as white?", a Mississippi observer answered: "Yes, more so, when not overworked."[39] These experienced and informed observers clearly recognized the dangers of hard work for pregnant slave women.

Some masters were equally aware of the risks of hard work. James R. Sparkman wrote that on the South Carolina rice plantation he managed "Allowance is invariably made for the women so soon as they report themselves *pregnant* they

being appointed to such light work as will insure a proper consideration for the offspring."[40] Ex-slave Polly Turner Cancer reported that on the Mississippi cotton plantation where she worked around the house "Ole Marster wudn't let de wimmen do no heavy liftin' coz he wanted dem de have big fine babies; he always sed, 'I don't want no runts.' When we picked cotton he always made de men tote de sacks."[41] Lula Flannigan remembered that her Georgia master "wuz watchful ter see dat 'omans had good keer when dey chilluns wuz bawned. Dey let dese 'omans do easy, light wuk towuds de last fo' de chilluns is bawned, en den atter wuds dey doan do nuffin' much twel dey is well en strong ergin."[42] Although slaveowners clearly benefited from the birth of healthy slave children this testimony suggests that those who took steps to limit the work of pregnant slave women did so late in pregnancy, usually in the last trimester and often in the last few weeks. Such practices may have forestalled premature delivery, but they were too late to have had a significant effect on the influence of hard work on fetal development. And according to slaves many masters did not even observe these precautions.

Harry McMillan, a forty-year-old South Carolina field hand, was asked by the American Freedmen's Inquiry Commission in 1863, "The women had the same day's work as the men; but suppose a woman was in a family way was her task less?" "No, sir," McMillan replied; "most of times she had to do the same work. Sometimes the wife of the planter learned of the condition of the woman and said to her husband you must cut down her day's work. Sometimes the women had their children in the field."[43] Madison Jefferson, a slave from a large Virginia estate, reported to the British and Foreign Antislavery Society in 1841 that "He has known women who were *enceinte*, employed in plantation labour until within a few hours of their delivery; and in some cases the children have been actually brought forth in the field."[44] James Lucas told an interviewer in 1936 of his birth 103 years earlier on a big cotton plantation along the Mississippi River, "Trufe is I wuz bawn in a cotton field during cotton pickin time. De wimmin fixed my mammy up so she didn't lose no time."[45] Jennie Webb, another former slave on a Mississippi cotton plantation, recalled, "My ma wuked in de fiel's up to de day I was born. I wuz born 'twix de fiel's an' de cabins. Ma wuz tooken to de house on a ho'se."[46]

Additional evidence of the common practice of working slave women until late in pregnancy comes from slave testimony about whipping. Former Virginia slave Jordan Johnson told an interviewer about Charlie Jones and his wife who were working in a tobacco field together. "Was plantin' tobacco—he was settin' out an' she was hillin'. Annie was big wid chile an' gettin' near her time, so one day she made a slip an' chopped a young shoot down. Ole man Diggs, de overseer, come runnin' up screamin' at her an' it made her mo' nervous, an she chopped off 'nother one. Ole overseer lif' up dat rawhide an' beat Annie 'cross de back an shoulders 'till she fell to de groun'."[47] Lizzie Williams remembered that on the Mississippi cotton plantation where she worked "Is seen nigger women dat was fixin' to be confined do somethin' de white folks didn't like. Dey [the white folks] would dig a hole in de ground just big 'nuff fo' her stomach, make her lie face down an whip her on de back to keep from hurtin' de child."[48] South Carolina slave Solomon Bradley told the American Freedmen's Inquiry Commission, "I have seen a woman in the family way punished by making a hole in the ground for her stomach when she was stretched out for whipping."[49] Clara Young, a former field hand on a plantation near Aberdeen, Mississippi, recalled that her cousin had been whipped so severely by the overseer that she died the next morning. ". . . she was jest sebenteen years ol' and was in de fambly way for de fust time, and could't work as hard as de rest."[50] Although many overseers and masters may not have been so cruel, far too many were. Yet the most significant disclosure in the slaves' testimony is that it was not at all uncommon for pregnant slave women to do the same tasks as other slaves and to be expected to perform them as efficiently.

Annie Coley's mother was a field hand whose master rewarded her for having twelve children by taking her out of the fields and assigning her to weaving. But Annie Coley remembered an incident which proved that slave women did not simply depend on the self interest of the master for their protection:

> But ole Boss Jones had a mean overseer who tuk 'vantage of the womens in the fiel's. One time he slammed a niggah woman down that was heavy, en cause her to hev her baby—dead. The niggah womens in the Quarters jumped on 'im and say they gwine take him to a brushpile and burn him up. But their men hollered for 'em to turn him loose. Then Big Boss Jones came en made the womens go back to the Quarters. He said, "I ain' whipped these wretches fer a long time, en I low to whip 'em dis evenin'." But all de womens hid in the woods dat evenin', en Boss never say no more about it. He sent the overseer away en never did hev no more overseers.[51]

The slave women on Annie Coley's plantation courageously and successfully resisted the overseer's cruelty. Yet it is significant that what aroused their hostility was not that a pregnant slave woman was working in the fields but that she was horribly abused. Even a "reasonable" master like Boss Jones expected pregnant slave women to work hard; the women in his quarters must have realized the futility of protesting that. Many other masters apparently did not lighten the work routine of pregnant slave women soon enough to diminish the effects of hard work on the developing fetus. "All my child hood life I can never remember seeing my pa or ma gwine to wuk or coming in from wuk in de day light as dey went to de fiel's fo' day an' wuked 'til after dark," Jennie Webb recalled. "It wuz wuk, wuk, all de time."[52]

Evidence that "smothered" slave infants were among the consequences of hard work for pregnant slave women comes from the different death rates in the rice, cotton, tobacco, and upcountry regions of the South. In general, where the production of staple crops for market was primary and where gang labor prevailed, the death rates for smothered slave infants were highest. Georgia is an excellent example. In the cotton counties of central and southwest Georgia—which contained 78 percent of the state's slaves and produced 94 percent of the state's cotton—the smothering death rate was almost twice that in the less market-oriented Piedmont and Pine Barrens counties—which produced only 6 percent of the state's cotton although they contained nearly a third of the state's population. This contrast between regions of maximum and minimum staple crop production was not simply the result of a higher overall death rate for slave infants in the cotton counties. The death rate for all slave infants in the cotton counties was only 20 percent higher than that in the Piedmont and Pine Barrens. An even sharper contrast existed between Georgia's cotton and rice counties. In the coastal counties that produced 99 percent of the state's rice, the smothering death rate was less than one-fourth that in the cotton counties.[53] But the coastal counties were not a healthier environment for slave infants; the death rate for all slave infants in the coastal counties was nearly a third higher than that in the cotton counties. Although slaves in both regions were producing staple crops for market, in the rice region their work was organized largely by

the task system, while gang labor prevailed in cotton areas. . . .

In all four states [Georgia, South Carolina, Mississippi, and Virginia], the highest regional smothering death rates were in areas devoted to staple-crop production with gang labor. In rice areas, where the task system was employed, or in regions less intensely devoted to staple-crop production, the smothering death rates were lower. This is a pattern one would expect to find if the hard work that masters assigned to pregnant slave women were the major cause of slave smothering deaths. . . .

If the labor that masters assigned to pregnant slave women was the major explanation for the high incidence of SIDS among slave infants, then the smothering death rates should have dropped dramatically after emancipation. Freedmen and freedwomen successfully resisted the planters' efforts to reestablish gang labor. Black women withdrew from the heavy, closely supervised field work they had done as slaves.[54] The family sharecropping system still required black women to work in the fields. But precisely because the sharecroppers' labor was organized by black family members rather than by masters, pregnant black women could be sheltered from the heaviest, most exhausting tasks. And indeed, after emancipation the smothering death rates plummeted.

According to mortality data collected in the 1880 federal census the death rate for smothered black infants in the South was only one-fifth of that in 1860. The smothering rates along the South Atlantic and Gulf coasts remained lower than those of the interior, but all the rates had fallen precipitously compared to 1860. In fact, they had fallen to a level indistinguishable from rates for blacks in the northern regions, although they remained over four times greater than the white rates. Perhaps part of the decline was caused by black parents' reticence about admitting to a census official that one of their children had been smothered. That possibility cannot be ruled out, but it seems unlikely that reticence alone would account for such a dramatic decrease in the smothering death rate.

Of course, neither slave women nor their masters could have known about the connection between hard work, pregnancy, and smothering. Medical writers agreed, and masters were well aware, that hard work was not good for pregnant slave women. But the large number of smoth-ered slave infants and the testimony of the slaves themselves are powerful evidence that many masters found it easier to ignore the risks of hard work for pregnant slave women than the promise of a cash crop safely harvested. Masters may not have acted any differently had they known better. Not knowing, they easily blamed slave mothers for smothering their infants. Slave women had to do the master's work and to bear the shame and guilt for one of its tragic consequences. At least, Tabby Abbey did.

NOTES

1. All citations are from Manuscript Census Returns, Seventh Census of the United States, 1850, South Carolina, Schedule 3, Mortality, South Carolina Microcopy Number 2, roll 1; and Manuscript Census Returns, Eighth Census of the United States 1860, Georgia, Schedule 3, Mortality, National Archives Microfilm Series T–655, roll 8; Virginia, Schedule 3, Mortality, National Archives Microfilm Series T–1132, roll 5; Mississippi, Schedule 3, Mortality, Mississippi Department of Archives and History Microfilm, roll 2730; South Carolina, Schedule 3, Mortality, South Carolina Microcopy No. 2, roll 1. These are cited hereafter by state, year, and county or district. Quotations in the text are, in order of their appearance, from South Carolina Mortality Schedules, 1850, Abbeville District, frame 3; Virginia Mortality schedules, 1860, Henrico County, 309; Mississippi Mortality Schedules, 1860, Tippah County, 2 (second paged series); Georgia Mortality Schedules, 1860, Cobb County, 162; and South Carolina Mortality Schedules, 1860, Spartanburg District, frame 378.

2. The 1860 published mortality census did not separate slave deaths from white deaths. U.S. Census Office, *Statistics of the United States (Including Mortality, Property, &c.,) in 1860 . . .* (Washington, 1866), 252.

3. The calculation was based on the 1850 federal mortality data and mortality statistics from Kentucky, New York City, South Carolina, and New Orleans. U.S. Census Office, *Statistics of the United States . . . in 1860,* 281–83.

4. The data used in this article were collected from the manuscript mortality schedules of the 1860 federal census of Georgia, Mississippi, South Carolina, and Virginia. The data include every person in each of these states whose cause of death was listed in the 1860 mortality schedules as smothered, overlaid, or suffocated. Most of the victims were reported as having been smothered (77 percent); those reported as having been overlaid or suffocated accounted for 18 and 5 percent respectively. . . .

5. This is a conservative estimate based on the assumption that the 1860 smothering death rate of sixteen deaths per thousand living slave infants was constant from 1790 to 1860. . . .

6. South Carolina Mortality Schedules, 1850, Abbeville District, frames 11–12.

7. Ibid., frames 16–17.

8. Affleck, "On the Hygiene of Cotton Plantations and the Management of Negro Slaves," *Southern Medical Reports,* II (1851), 435. Of course, masters could blame overseers for overworking slave women, as did Thomas Jefferson: ". . . the loss of 5 little ones in 4 years induces me to fear that the overseers do not permit the [slave] women to devote as much time as is necessary to the care of their children: that they view their labor as the 1st object and the raising of their child but as secondary. I consider the labor of a breeding woman as no object, and that a child raised every 2 years is of more profit than the crop of the best laboring man. in this, as in all other cases, providence has made our interests and our duties coincide perfectly. . . . I must pray you to inculcate upon the overseers that it is not their labor, but their increase which is the first consideration with us." Jefferson to Joel Yancey, January 17, 1819, Edwin Morris Betts, ed., *Thomas Jefferson's Farm Book: With Commentary*

and Relevant Extracts from Other Writings (Princeton, 1953), 43.

9. See for example John H. Morgan, "An Essay on the Causes of the Production of Abortion among our Negro Population," *Nashville Journal of Medicine and Surgery,* XIX (August, 1860), 117, 120–21. . . .

10. Savitt, *Medicine and Slavery: The Diseases and Health Care of Blacks in Antebellum Virginia* (Urbana, Chicago, and London, 1978), 124 (first quotation), 126 (second and third quotations). See also Savitt, "Smothering and Overlaying of Virginia Slave Children: A Suggested Explanation," *Bulletin of the History of Medicine,* XLIX (Fall 1975), 400–404.

11. Fogel and Engerman, *Time on the Cross: The Economics of American Negro Slavery* (Boston and Toronto, 1974), 126; cited hereinafter as *Time on the Cross,* I.

12. However, in a note Fogel and Engerman make the confusing statement that "Virtually all of the difference between the free and slave suffocation rates might be explained by what has recently been identified as the 'sudden infant death' syndrome." *Time on the Cross: Evidence and Methods—A Supplement* (Boston and Toronto, 1974), 101, note 4.5.4; cited hereinafter as *Time on the Cross,* II.

13. Savitt, *Medicine and Slavery,* 124.

14. Sutch, "The Care and Feeding of Slaves," in Paul A. David, *et al., Reckoning with Slavery: A Critical Study in the Quantitative History of American Negro Slavery* (New York, 1976), 292.

15. Virginia Mortality Schedules, 1860, Fauquier County, 214.

16. Georgia Mortality Schedules, 1860, Carroll County, 75.

17. South Carolina Mortality Schedules, 1850, Union District, frame 199.

18. Savitt quotes a master's letter to his brother: "Last week Tilla overlaid / when asleep / and killed her youngest child—a boy 6 or 7 months old. This was no doubt caused by her own want of care and attention." *Medicine and Slavery,* 124.

19. George P. Rawick, Jan Hellegas, and Ken Lawrence, eds., *The American Slave: A Composite Autobiography, Supplement,* Series I (12 vols., Westport, Conn., and London, Eng., 1977), Vol. 6, *Mississippi Narratives,* Pt. 1, pp. 3–4. Volumes in this series are cited hereinafter as Rawick *et al.,* eds., *American Slave.*

20. Indeed, "sleep apnea," or the cessation of breathing during sleep, is currently thought to be the final episode before death.

See Richard L. Naeye, "Sudden Infant Death," *Scientific American,* CCXLII (April 1980), 56; and Naeye, "The Sudden Infant Death Syndrome: A Review of Recent Advances," *Archives of Pathology and Laboratory Medicine,* CI (April 1977), 165–67: Maries Valdes-Dapena, "Sudden Unexplained Infant Death, 1970 through 1975," *Pathology Annual,* XII, Pt. 1 (1977), 133; and J. Bruce Beckwith, *The Sudden Infant Death Syndrome* (Rockville, Md., 1975), 27.

21. Beckwith, *Sudden Infant Death Syndrome,* 9.

22. Beckwith, *Sudden Infant Death Syndrome,* 2–3.

23. Beckwith, *Sudden Infant Death Syndrome,* 25. Important early studies that challenged the suffocation interpretation include Paul V. Woolley, Jr., "Mechanical Suffocation during Infancy: A Comment on Its Relation to the Total Problem of Sudden Death," *Journal of Pediatrics,* XXVI (June 1945), 572–75; and Jacob Werne and Irene Garrow, "Sudden Deaths of Infants Allegedly Due to Mechanical Suffocation," *American Journal of Public Health,* XXXVII (April 1947), 675–87.

24. For a refutation of the infanticide interpretation of SIDS proposed by S. S. Asch, "Crib Deaths: Their Possible Relation to Postpartum Depression and Infanticide," *Mt. Sinai Journal of Medicine,* XXXV (May-June 1968), 214–20; see Walter A. Kukull and Donald R. Peterson, "Sudden Infant Death and Infanticide," *American Journal of Epidemiology,* CVI (December 1977), 485–86.

25. Beckwith, *Sudden Infant Death Syndrome,* 11.

26. Mississippi Mortality Schedules, 1860, Calhoun County, 5.

27. Richard L. Naeye, Bertha Ladis, and Joseph S. Drage, "Sudden Infant Death Syndrome: A Prospective Study," *American Journal of Diseases of Children,* CXXX (November 1976), 1210. Of course, this statement should not be misconstrued to mean that all SIDS victims come from poor families. As Beckwith notes, "Despite its greater attack rate among the underprivileged, SIDS is in fact no respecter of class or social position." *Sudden Infant Death Syndrome,* 11. . . .

28. Naeye, Ladis, and Drage, "Sudden Infant Death Syndrome," 1209; quotations in text and this note. In particular, the infants who became SIDS victims exhibited "abnormalities in respiration, feeding, temperature regulation, and specific neurologic tests." However, none of these abnormalities was great enough to allow physicians to identify

the infants who were likely to die of SIDS . . .

29. The other two factors, not specifically related to pregnancy, are infant blood type *B* and crowded housing. The latter has been shown to contribute to mild respiratory infections which "increase the frequency and duration of apneic spells in infants who are prone to apnea." Naeye, "Sudden Infant Death," 60–61; includes quotations both in text and this note. The environmental and demographic characteristics of mothers of SIDS victims are also "associated with excessive fetal injury and perinatal mortality" in general. . . .

30. Naeye, "Sudden Infant Death," 61.

31. Naeye, *et al.*, "Amniotic Fluid Infections in an African City," *Journal of Pediatrics*, XC (June 1977), 969. "Many other factors associated with the [sudden infant death] syndrome appear to lose their high risk in the absence of an infection of the amniotic fluid," Naeye reports. "Sudden Infant Death," 61. . . .

32. See Savitt, *Medicine and Slavery*, 90–103; Fogel and Engerman, *Time on the Cross*, I, 109–15; II, 87–98; Sutch, "Care and Feeding of Slaves," 231–301; Leslie H. Owens, *This Species of Property: Slave Life and Culture in the Old South* (New York, 1976), 50–69; Eugene D. Genovese, *Roll, Jordan, Roll: The World the Slaves Made* (New York, 1974), 62–63, 540–49, 603–604, 638–39; John W. Blassingame, *The Slave Community: Plantation Life in the Antebellum South* (New York and other cities, 1972), 158–59; Kenneth M. Stampp, *The Peculiar Institution: Slavery in the Ante-Bellum South* (New York, 1956), 282–89.

33. Savitt, *Medicine and Slavery*, 92; Sutch, "Care and Feeding of Slaves," 233–82; Kenneth F. Kiple and Virginia H. Kiple, "Slave Child Mortality: Some Nutritional Answers to a Perennial Puzzle," *Journal of Social History*, X (Spring 1977), 294–99.

34. Savitt, *Medicine and Slavery*, 92.

35. Sutch, "Care and Feeding of Slaves," 267–68.

36. Modern studies have uniformly reported a higher incidence of SIDS among blacks. For example, a recent study of SIDS in North Carolina found that the SIDS death rate for whites was 1.23 per thousand live births, while that for blacks was 3.75. Other studies have reported similar differences. However, there is no evidence to suggest that this is the result of a specific genetic heritage. Jack H. Blok, "The Incidence of Sudden Infant Death Syndrome in North Carolina's

Cities and Counties: 1972–1974," *American Journal of Public Health*, LXVIII (April 1978), 367–72. . . .

37. Morgan, "An Essay on the Causes of the Production of Abortion among Our Negro Population," 117 (first and second quotations), 121 (third quotation).

38. [Pendleton], "On the Susceptibility of the Caucasian and African Races to the Different Classes of Disease," *Southern Medical Reports*, I (1850), 338.

39. Affleck, "On the Hygiene of Cotton Plantations and the Management of Negro Slaves," 434.

40. Sparkman to Benjamin Allston, March 10, 1858, J. Harold Easterby, ed., *The South Carolina Rice Plantation as Revealed in the Papers of Robert F. W. Allston* (Chicago, 1945), 346. Italics in the original.

41. Rawick *et al.*, eds., *American Slave*, VII: *Mississippi Narratives*, Pt. 2, p. 350.

42. Ibid., III: *Georgia Narratives*, Pt. 1, p. 248.

43. John W. Blassingame, ed., *Slave Testimony: Two Centuries of Letters, Speeches, Interviews, and Autobiographies* (Baton Rouge, 1977), 380.

44. Ibid., 221. Italics in the original.

45. Rawick *et al.*, eds., *American Slave*, VIII: *Mississippi Narratives*, Pt. 3, p. 1337.

46. Ibid., X: *Mississippi Narratives*, Pt. 5, p. 2250.

47. Charles L. Perdue, Jr., Thomas E. Barden, and Robert K. Phillips, eds., *Weevils in the Wheat: Interviews with Virginia Ex-Slaves* (Charlottesville, 1976), 160.

48. She also reported that "Lots o' times de women in dat condition [pregnant] would be plowin', hit a stump, de plow jump an' hurt de child to where dey would loose it an law me, such a whippin as dey would get!" Rawick *et al.*, eds., *American Slave*, X: *Mississippi Narratives*, Pt. 5, p. 2337.

49. Blassingame, ed., *Slave Testimony*, 372. For other instances, see ibid., 220, 380.

50. Rawick *et al.*, eds., *American Slave*, X: *Mississippi Narratives*, Pt. 5, p. 2402. For another similar incident, see ibid., 1927.

51. Ibid., VII: *Mississippi Narratives*, Pt. 2, pp. 441–42.

52. Ibid., X: *Mississippi Narratives*, Pt. 5, p. 2250. See also ibid., 2199.

53. The obvious climatic difference between the regions does not appear to be a likely explanation for the different smothering death rates. Modern studies have discounted the effect of climate on SIDS. . . .

54. See Jonathan M. Wiener, "Class Structure and Economic Development in the

American South, 1865–1955," *American Historical Review*, LXXXIV (October, 1979), 973–76; Wiener, *Social Origins of the New South: Alabama, 1860–1885* (Baton Rouge and London, 1978), 36–38, 42–47, 66–69; Herbert G. Gutman, *The Black Family in Slavery and Freedom, 1750–1925* (New York, 1976), 167–68; Roger L. Ransom and Richard Sutch, *One Kind of Freedom: The Economic Consequences of Emancipation* (Cambridge and other cities, 1977), 44–47.

JOHN MACK FARAGHER
The Midwestern Farming Family, 1850

The folklore of rural America suggests that farm people understood intuitively that female work was central to the domestic economy even if the full extent of women's labors were little appreciated. Male farmers spoke of the need to marry a "good strong woman," and folk songs expressed the same understanding. "There was an old man who lived in the woods," runs one song, who wagers that

> he could do more work in one day
> Than his wife could do in three.

She leaves him with a list of her tasks and goes off to do his plowing. When the farmer tries to do her work, he comes to grief; even milking presents unforeseen difficulties:

> But Tiny hitched, and Tiny switched,
>   And Tiny she cocked her nose,
> And Tiny she gave the old man such a kick
>   That the blood ran down to his toes.

By the time the song ends the old man is swearing

> by all of the stars in heaven
> That his wife could do more work in one day
> Than he could do in seven.*

    As long as anyone could remember, farmers had ordered their lives by work patterns strictly defined by gender. Historians and anthropologists can now see

* Jean Ritchie, *The Swapping Song Book* (Oxford, 1952), pp. 54–55. © 1952 Jean Ritchie, Geordie Music Publishing Co. Suggested by Laura Becker, Clemson University.

that both sorts of tasks were central to the maintenance of the economic health of the family farm. As John Mack Faragher shows, what was missing was a convenient set of measures for female productivity; in the absence of these, women's work tended to be undervalued.

The dominant paradigm of farm life was the cycle: the recurrence of the days and seasons, the process of growth and reproduction.[1] Hand-power technology did not deceive men into thinking they could overcome nature; their goal was to harmonize man's needs with natural forces as best they could. The length of the working day, for example, was largely determined by the hours of sunlight. Candles and grease lamps were common but expensive, and the hearth's flickering light was too dim for more than a little work after dark.[2] So most work was largely confined to daylight: up and at work by dawn, nights for sleeping. And in keeping with this daily round, midwesterners told time by the movements of the sun, not the clock. There was a variety of time phrases so rich they nearly matched the clock in refinement; the hours before sunrise, for example, were distinguished thus: long before day, just before day, just comin' day, just about daylight, good light, before sunup, about sunup, and, finally, sunup. Each period of the day was similarly divided.[3]

The seasons imposed the same kind of rule as the sun. The farm's work demands were primarily shaped by the seasons, each quarter calling upon husbandman and housewife to perform appointed tasks. The farming year opened in mid-March when thaws called the tenants outside. Land had to be cleared, drained, manured, and plowed, fields sown, gardens planted. Sheep, grown woolly, needed washing and shearing, geese plucking. In the hardwood stands farmers might spend a few days collecting and rendering maple sap, or searching out and hiving bees.

As the sun approached summer solstice, the work load increased with the day's length. The corn needed cultivation and hilling until it was strong enough to compete successfully with the weeds and "laid by" till harvest. There was hay to make, garden crops to nurture, gather, and replant, and often a winter wheat crop to harvest and thresh. In August, with the corn laid by and harvest coming, men took the opportunity for a respite; there were the dog days when "onery" farmers took long naps and "progressive" farmers mended fences. But August was soon overwhelmed by the frantic pace of September's harvest. Summer grain had to be cut, bound, and shocked within a critically short period, the corn picked, the last round of garden vegetables safely packed away in cold storage while still fresh.

Days continued to shorten, but after harvest the pace of work slowed as well. Still the grain needed threshing, the corn husking and cribbing, there was perhaps fruit to pick, dry, or preserve in a variety of ways, possibly pickles and kraut to make. These and other activities prepared the way for the winter: sowing the winter wheat, making firewood, daubing the cracks in old cabins, barns, and outbuildings, banking dirt around foundations to keep out some of the cold, and butchering enough hogs for salted and smoked meat until the spring again provided a larder of milk, eggs, and poultry.

Summer's activity was counterbalanced by winter's leisure. The daily chores of the farm—tending livestock, hauling wood and water, the domestic routine—continued. There were also numerous tasks to keep an industrious farmer busy: fences to mend, manure to haul and spread, trees to girdle and later fell, roads to maintain. But there was comparatively little opportunity for productive activity in the winter, aside from work in the woodlot. So winter months were occupied with general farm repair and improvement, visiting neighbors, trading the surpluses that summer's labor had produced. In late winter farmers would begin to plan the plantings of the next season, setting out planting dates in traditional fashion by carefully determining with the farm almanac the timing of the phases of the moon and the rising and falling of astrological signs.

Encouraged by their subordination to the natural world, the people of the Midwest held to a traditional animistic conception of the universe: the inanimate world was infused with will, feeling, and spirit.[4] "The world was a huge kaleidoscope, whose bewildering pieces fell by the twist of analogy or contrast into beautifully logical patterns of form, direction, texture, quality, process—patterns to cover everything that might happen, from evening to evening and from spring to spring."[5] As William Oliver, an English visitor and resident of Illinois in the 1840s, wrote, "There is a good deal of superstition or belief in witchcraft, omens, lucky times, etc."[6] The world could be best understood by analogy (if an animal disturbed the afterbirth, that baby would take on some trait of the beast) or contrast (cold hands, warm heart) or the rule of "firsts" (if a woman cries on her wedding day she will cry throughout her married life). Many of the beliefs were employed in a half-embarrassed way, perhaps pulled out only in times of emergencies like sickness, death, disaster; others were the stock-in-trade of midwestern life.[7]

The cycle of the seasons encouraged a traditional view of work as well. Work was the expenditure of human energy to meet given tasks. When wheat was ready for harvesting, for example, men would readily work fifteen-hour days to bring it in before the precious grain was shed on the ground. On the other hand, when seasonal demands slackened, as in winter, a man might quit early without qualms, and few worried when a winter storm closed in the family for a few days. The persistent pace of modern labor, measured not by natural cycles but by the clock, was almost unknown to midwesterners. By the same token, work was understood not as the opposite of leisure but as life's requirement for all creatures, regardless of sex or age. Men, women, and children would share life's burdens. "The rule was," William Howells remembered of his farm life, "that whoever had the strength to work, took hold and helped."[8]

The common work of the farm was, then, divided among family members, but the principal division of work was by sex. Men and women worked in different areas, skilled at different tasks, prepared and trained for their work in different ways. In an economy based on the family unit, women and men in midwestern society achieved common goals by doing different jobs.

Sex and gender is a foundation of individual and social identity in all human societies.[9] As Michael Banton puts it, gender roles "are related so closely to the performance of most other roles that the sex of a party can be concealed only in the most restricted situations."[10] The differences of sex are the starting place for gender roles: each person is given a polar label, either man or woman. Sex implies general natural potentials and limitations, to be sure, but the biological distinctions alone have never been sufficient social determinants of distinctive gender roles; sex differences have always had to be elaborated by patterned cultural forms. "Natural features are never translated directly into social ones. They are always dressed in cultural clothing."[11]

If gender roles are essentially cultural constructions, it follows that the notion of what constitutes the masculine and the feminine will vary greatly from one culture to another and from one time to another. Men and women play their gender roles according to a cultural script outlining the appropriate activities and tasks (the sexual division of labor) as well as the attitudes and personality (the character) of the two sexes.[12] People appear most obviously in society and history as players of their gender roles.

For historians (as well as other social scientists), the proper place to begin an understanding of gender roles is by reconstructing and examining the customary ways in which men and women divided the work of society among themselves.[13] This priority makes methodological sense if for no other reason than because outward behavior is what historians can best determine, and broad areas of behavioral uniformity suggest the presence of roles.[14] These patterns then establish a context of human action for the evaluation of what men and women thought.[15] Such an approach employs an active, concrete concept of gender roles: gender roles are social regularities observed in what men and women do and the ways they think and feel about what they do, as well as how and why they do what they do. In this study both behavioral and attitudinal facts must be derived from the same subjective sources—the diaries and recollections. But even with such documents of personal experience the behavioral regularities are readily exposed and pieced together to form a whole pattern.

The functional principles of the general divisions of work by sex on the midwestern farm were quite clear and quite strict in application.[16] In only a few areas did the work of men and women overlap. Most clearly, men were occupied with the heaviest work. First, they had responsibility for work with the broadax. If the family was taking up new wooded ground—

as many Oregon emigrants would be doing, for example—the land had to be cleared. Frequently a farmer would gird the trees with his ax the first season to kill foliage, felling trees and removing stumps in the following winters. Logrolling, when the men of the neighborhood joined together to clear a field belonging to one of them, was a common late-winter social event for men. Construction, including making fences, was also a male job, as was the ongoing work in the family woodlot. Wood was chopped, hauled and stacked, or dumped near the house.

Men also controlled work with the plow. For new land a breaking plow, drawn by several yoke of oxen, was often needed, especially in prairie sod. Working improved acres was easier, but still hard, heavy work. And within the limitations of available labor and marketability, men were usually itching to put new land to the plow, so the plow was associated with work of the heaviest sort and understood to be male. Work in the cleared and plowed fields, where grain or corn grew, also fell to male control and supervision. Men plowed in spring or winter, sowed their wheat broadcast (until the 1850s), and planted their corn in hills. Men and boys harrowed and weeded until harvest, when they picked the corn together and cooperated in bringing in the wheat, men cradling and boys binding. Fieldwork kept men extremely busy. Two mature men on fifty acres of corn and wheat land spent three-quarters of the whole growing season plowing, planting, and harvesting, exclusive of any other work.[17]

There was plenty of other work to do. Men were responsible for upkeep and repair of tools, implements, and wagons and care of the draft animals, the oxen, mules, or horses. Hogs and sheep, both pretty much allowed to roam, were herded, fed, and tended by men and boys. Finally, men were responsible for cleanup and maintenance of the barn, barnyard, fields, and woodlot. This meant ditching and trenching, innumerable repairs on all the things that could—and did—break, laying down straw and hay, and hauling manure.[18]

Less important in fact, but work which nonetheless played an important role in male thinking, was hunting. For the early pioneers game provided most of the protein in the family diet. By mid-century those pioneer days had passed in the Midwest. But the rifle remained in its central place over the door or mantle long after the emergencies that might call it out had gone the way of the forests. Hunting remained, if only as an autumn sport or shooting match, a central aspect of male identity. "Even farmers," says Buley, "at certain seasons felt a peculiar restlessness."[19] The hunting legacy had one practical consequence for male work loads: men had primary responsibility for slaughtering and butchering large farm animals. Indeed, when hogs ran wild, they were sometimes picked off by rifle shot. Hunting was the male activity that most embodied men's self-conceived role—keystone of the hearth, defender of the household, and main provider.

In fact, women were more centrally involved in providing subsistence for the farm family than men. Nearly all the kinds of food consumed by farm families were direct products of women's work in growing, collecting, and butchering. An acre or so of improved land near the house was set aside for the domestic garden. After husbands had plowed the plot, farm women planted their gardens. Housewives began by setting out onions and potatoes in early April, following up later that month by planting lettuce, beets, parsnips, turnips, and carrots in the garden, tomatoes and cabbages in window boxes indoors. When danger of late frosts had passed, the seedlings were moved outside and set out along with May plantings of cucumbers, melons, pumpkins, and beans.

Women also frequently laid down a patch of buckwheat and a garden of kitchen and medicinal herbs—sage, peppers, thyme, mint, mustard, horseradish, tansy, and others.[20]

The garden required daily attention. At first the seedlings needed hand watering. Then crops required cultivation, and the everlasting battle against weeds began. Garden harvesting could commence in late April and was a daily chore throughout the summer, supplying fresh vegetables for the family table.

Wives and daughters were also traditionally responsible for the care of henhouse and dairy. After a dormant winter poultry came alive in the spring. The farm-wise woman carefully kept enough chickens to produce both eggs for the kitchen and to set hens for a new flock of spring roasters. From late spring to late fall the family feasted regularly on fresh-killed rooster, selected and usually butchered by the housewife. Daughters and young boys gathered the eggs that were another mainstay of the summer diet. Women's responsibility for the henhouse extended even to cleaning out the manure by the bucket load.[21]

Cows were sheltered in whatever served as a barn, and men's general supervision there relieved women of having to shovel the stalls. But women milked, tended, and fed the animals. The milking and the manufacture of butter and cheese was one of their central tasks. Cows were milked first thing in the morning and the last thing at night; housewives supervised the milking but parceled the job out to children as soon as they were able. Boys, however, with their father's sanction would rebel from milking; "the western people of the early days entertained a supreme contempt for a man who attended to the milking."[22] Making good butter was a matter of pride among farm women. The churn had to be operated with patience and persistence if the butter was to come.

Come butter, come;
Come butter, come;
Little Johnny's at the gate,
Waiting for his buttered cake.
Come butter, come.[23]

The meter marked the up and down of the churn. When it had come, the butter was packed into homemade, hand-decorated molds, and pounds of it consumed each week. Cheesemaking was less general; ripened cheeses were the product of a minority. Nearly all women, however, were trained in the manufacture of cottage cheese and farmer's cheese. Dairy production was especially important to the household and central to the definition of women's work. In 1839 a Springfield, Illinois, newspaper reprinted with horror a report that New England women were pressuring their husbands to take over the milking.[24]

There were some areas of food production where women's and men's operations overlapped, but these were the exceptions. When hogs were butchered in fall, men from several farms might work together; it was mainly when it became necessary to supplement the meat supply that women helped men to slaughter and dress the animal. In any event, women were always a part of the butchering, there to chop the scraps and odd pieces into sausage, prepare the hams for curing, and cook the ribs immediately. At other social and almost ritual occasions of food preparation—making cider or apple butter, rendering maple sugar—men and women regularly worked side by side. All of the work of the orchard was often a joint project.

The sexes also sometimes combined their energies during planting. If not preoccupied with field planting, men might help to set out garden seed. More likely, however, field planting would fall behind the schedule set by zodiac or moon, and men called their womenfolk out to help. Women most often assisted in the cornfield. "Tarpley made a furrow with a sin-

gle-shovel plow drawn by one horse," Iowa farm woman Elmira Taylor remembered of the 1860s. "I followed with a bag of seed corn and dropped two grains of seed each step forward."[25] A farmer with no sons worked his daughters in the fields at planting time without a second thought.[26]

Food preparation was, of course, women's work, and by all reports midwestern men kept women busy by consuming great quantities at mealtime.[27] Wives were responsible for preparing three heavy meals a day; most farm wives spent their entire mornings cooking and tried to save afternoons for other work. Included in the daily midwestern diet were two kinds of meat, eggs, cheese, butter, cream (especially in gravies), corn in one or more forms, two kinds of bread, three or four different vegetables from the garden or from storage, several kinds of jellies, preserves, and relishes, cake or pie, and milk, coffee, and tea. Making butter and cheese were only two of the innumerable feminine skills needed to set the farm table. . . .

Women cooked on the open hearth, directly over the coals; it was low, back-breaking work that went on forever; a pot of corn mush took from two to six hours with nearly constant stirring.[28] Cast-iron, wood-burning cook stoves were available in Illinois in the mid-1840s, and by 1860 most midwestern women had been given the opportunity to stand and cook.[29] The next great improvement in domestic technology was the general introduction of running water in close proximity to the kitchen. But throughout the antebellum Midwest, water had to be carried to the house, sometimes from quite a distance, and that invariably was women's work. Domestic work—housecleaning, care of the bedding, all the kitchen work, in addition to responsibility for decorating and adding a "woman's touch"—was a demanding task under the best of circumstances, and farms offered far from the best. The yard between the kitchen and barn was always covered with enough dung to attract hordes of summer houseflies. In those days before screen doors kitchens were infested; men and women alike ignored the pests. In wet months the yard was a mess of mud, dung, and cast-off water, constantly tracked into the house. A cleanly wife had to be a constant worker.[30]

A farmer was said to be a jack-of-all-trades. But women's work outdistanced men's in the sheer variety of tasks performed. In addition to their production of food, women had complete responsibility for all manufacture, care, and repair of family clothing. During the first half of the nineteenth century, domestic manufacture gave way to industrial production of thread and cloth, but in the Midwest, from 1840 to 1860, while home manufactures declined, they remained an important activity for women. On the Taylor homestead in southeastern Iowa, for example, the assessed valuation of household manufactures declined from $73 in 1850 to $50 in 1860, but this marked a decline, not an end to the use of the wheel and loom: in 1861 Elmira Taylor spun her own wool, took it to a mill to be carded, and wove it into cloth throughout the winter on her mother-in-law's loom.[31]

Midwestern homespun was mostly of flax and wool, supplemented by a little homegrown cotton or purchased cotton thread. A few sheep and a quarter-acre of flax were enough to supply the largest family. Farm wives sowed flax in March, harvested it in June (replanting immediately with a sterile-soil crop like potatoes), and prepared it that summer by soaking and sun-drying it to rot the outer coating.[32] Men lent a hand by crushing the flax on the flax break to remove the inner fibers and washing and shearing the sheep, but from that point it was a woman's operation. Spinning wheels were in universal use; each household required

separate wheels for wool and flax. Wheels were precision tools, but families could get them rather cheaply from the wheelwright, and according to William Oliver, "spinning wheels and a loom are very general items in a farmer's establishment."[33] Wool had first to be carded into lean bunches, then spun on the great wheel; the spinner paced back and forth, whirling the wheel with her right hand, manipulating the wool and guiding the yarn on the spindle with her left. Two miles of yarn, enough for two to four yards of woven wool, required pacing over four miles, a full day's work. An excellent spinner, sitting at the smaller flax wheel, could spin a mile of linen thread in a day.[34]

The yarn was woven into wool and linen cloth or more commonly combined into durable linsey-woolsey on homemade looms. If cotton was available it was woven with wool warp to make jean. The giant loom dominated cramped living quarters when in use; it was knocked down and put away when weaving was completed.[35] The cloth still had to be shrunk and sized (fulled)—a job usually put out to the fulling mill if one were nearby—and dyed, sometimes from home dyes, but increasingly with commercial dyes bought at local stores. Nearly all farm clothing was cut from this cloth. Coarser tow cloth, made from the short-fiber, darker parts of the flax, was used for toweling, bandage, menstrual cloth, rags, or rough field clothing. Pillows and mattresses were made of tow and stuffed with the down women collected from the geese and ducks in their charge. The finest homespun, the pure linen bleached scores of times till it reached its characteristic color, was reserved for coverlets, tablecloths, appliqué, and stitchery. For their annual clothing a family of four would require a minimum of forty yards of cloth, or at least two full weeks at the wheel and loom for an experienced housewife. This work was, of course, spread throughout the available time, and one could expect to find women spinning or weaving at almost any time of the day, at every season of the year.[36]

Itinerant weavers first made their appearance in the Midwest during the 1840s, their Jacquard looms offering what seemed incredible detail in patterns. For most farm families, however, everyday cloth remained home-produced until the general availability of low-cost factory-produced dry goods. It was during the commercial shift in midwestern agriculture that family looms and then wheels gave way to cheap commercial cloth. Until the Civil War, however, a good deal of all midwestern clothing, and most clothing on emigrant backs, was homespun.[37]

Every wife was a tailor, fitting and cutting cloth for her own slip-on dresses and those of her daughter, her son's and husband's blouses and pantaloons, and the tow shirts of the younger ones. If there was "boughten" cloth available— cotton or woolen broadcloth, gingham or calico—it was used for dress-up clothing, home-tailored of course. Socks, mittens, and caps were knit for winter wear, but every adult went sockless and children barefoot in summer. Underclothes were not manufactured or worn, for they were considered an unnecessary extravagance.[38]

Women were personally involved in clothing manufacture, from sowing the flax seed to sewing the garment. Homespun "could not be lightly cast aside after so much toil and patience, on account of being slightly or considerably worn."[39] So worn pants and shirts were continually mended, garments too worn to be used saved for patches, and every scrap of every kind of cloth that passed through the house was saved for that special purpose it would one day find. As an old Kentucky woman remembered,

You see you start out with just so much caliker; you don't go to the store and pick it out and buy it, but the neighbors will give you a piece here and a piece there, and you will have a piece left every time you cut out a dress, and you take what happens to come and that's predestination. But when it comes to cuttin' out why you're free to choose your patterns. You can give the same kind o' pieces to two persons, and one will be a *Nine Patch* and one'll make a *Wild Goose Chase* and there'll be two quilts made out o' the same kind of pieces, and jest as different as they can be, and that is just the way with livin'. The Lord sends in the pieces, but we can cut 'em out and put 'em together pretty much to suit ourselves.[40]

Sewing was the consummate feminine skill, a domestic necessity but one practiced and refined until in the hands of many it achieved the status of an art form. Girls were taught to sew before they were taught to read, and started on a four- or nine-patch quilt cover as soon as they could hold a needle. Coverlets, counterpanes, crocheted samplers, and most especially the elaborate patchwork or appliqué front pieces for quilts were the highest expression of the material culture of women. With patchwork, appliqué, and quilt stitchery, utility was a secondary consideration; these were primarily modes of creative artistry for women. One farm woman testified to the importance of this avenue for her: "I would have lost my mind if I had not had my quilts to do."[41]

On a more mundane level, clothes had to be washed, and women made their own soap for both the clothes and the family who wore them. Women loaded hardwood ashes into the ash hopper, poured water over, and collected the lye in the trough below. They boiled kitchen fats and grease, added the lye, and if everything was going well the soap would "come" after long, hot hours of stirring. They poured the hot soap into molds or tubs and stored it. Soapmaking was a big, all-day job, done only two or three times a year.[42] Monday, by all accounts, was the universal washday. Rainwater was used for washing, or alternately a little lye was added to soften well water. The water was heated in the washtub over hearth or stove, soap added, and clothes were pounded against a washboard, then rinsed, wrung out by hand, and hung. The lye, harsh soap, and hot water chapped and cracked the skin; women's hands would often break open and bleed into the tub. In the winter, the clothes were hung outside where sore, wet hands would freeze painfully, or inside, draped over chairs or lines, steaming up the windows and turning the whole place clammy.[43] Ironing and mending were also allocated one day each week.

To women fell a final task. Women bore the children and nursed them for at least the first few months, and in this they worked completely alone. Even after weaning, farm women remained solely responsible for the supervision of young children; both boys and girls were under their mother's supervision until the boys were old enough to help with the fieldwork, at about ten years, at which time they came under their father's guidance.[44] Girls, of course, remained apprenticed to the housewife's craft. Farm mothers put their charges to work "almost as soon as they could walk," and although they could not contribute materially until they were five or six, the correct work attitude had by then been instilled.[45] There was plenty that children could do around the garden, dairy, and henhouse; they watered, fed the animals, collected eggs, milked, hauled water, weeded, and performed innumerable other chores that housewives could never have finished but for the work of their children.

Midwestern farm mothers had relatively large families. The mean family size in the Midwest in 1850 was 5.7.[46] Mean family size of the overland emigrants in this study was a little less, 5.0, mainly because there were so many newly-weds; otherwise the size of emigrant families was very typical of the population at large. The mean size of emigrating families in their full childbearing phase was 7.6. In her lifetime, then, a farm woman could expect to raise five or six children of her own. These children helped significantly with the burden of farm work, but not without the expenditure of a great deal of physical and emotional energy by their mothers.

To determine the full occupations of women, their total work load, we must consider the social effects of childbearing as well as childrearing. Miscarriages, stillbirths, birth accidents, and infant mortality took a terrible toll on the energies and spirit of women. Counting infant deaths alone, one in five children died before its fifth birthday, and prenatal losses were at least as high.[47] Childbirth certainly was a central experience for farm women. It was no occasional or unique event but occurred with demanding regularity. To assess women's reproductive burdens fairly we can measure women's fertility. The mean age of marriage for emigrant men and women was 25.1 and 20.5, respectively. Some women, of course, married earlier than the average and were pregnant before their twentieth birthdays. The peak childbearing years were from age twenty to thirty-five, during which time emigrant women bore over four out of five of their children. Fertility declined precipitously after thirty-five as a combined effect of lowered male and female fecundity, although some mothers continued to bear children into their late forties.

Let us translate abstract fertility into the real terms of farm women's lives: childbearing had to be a dominant fact. Over half the emigrant women gave birth to their first child within their first year of marriage, another quarter the second year, and fully 98 percent by the end of the third. Thereafter a mean of 29.0 months intervened between births throughout a woman's twenties and thirties. For their most vital years farm women lived under the dictatorial rule of yet another cycle, a two-and-a-half-year cycle of childbirth, of which nineteen or twenty months were spent in advanced pregnancy, infant care, and nursing. Until her late thirties, a woman could expect little respite from the physical and emotional wear and tear of nearly constant pregnancy or suckling.

Given the already burdensome tasks of women's work, the additional responsibilities of the children were next to intolerable. Women must have searched for some way of limiting the burden. It is possible that mothers introduced their babies to supplemental feeding quite early and encouraged children's independence in order to free themselves from the restrictions of nursing, which had to seriously limit their capacity to work.[48] There is almost no mention of child-feeding practices in the literature, but there are some indirect indications that babies were soon consuming "bread, corn, biscuits and pot-likker" right along with their parents.[49] On the other hand, there was a prevalent old wives' notion that prolonged nursing was a protection against conception. To achieve a twenty-nine-month cycle without practicing some form of self-conscious family limitation, women would have had to nurse for at least a year.[50]

Short of family planning, there was no easy choice for women in the attempt to reduce the burden of child care. Other groups had practiced family limitation before this time, but the need for labor may have been a mitigating factor here. It comes as no surprise, then, that as soon as it was possible, children were pretty much allowed and encouraged to shift for themselves, to grow as they might, with relatively little parental or maternal involvement in the process. We will find children little mentioned in overland diaries and reminiscences.

By no means were men the "breadwinners" of this economy. Both women and men actively participated in the production of family subsistence. Indeed, women were engaged in from one-third to one-half of all the food production of the farm, the proportions varying with regional and individual differences.[51] Of the farm staples—meat, milk, corn, pumpkins, beans, and potatoes—women produced the greater number as a product of their portion of the division of labor. Women were also likely to be found helping men with their portion at peak planting time. To this must be added the extremely important work of clothing manufacture, all the household work, and the care of the children. To be sure, men and women alike worked hard to make their farms produce. But one cannot avoid being struck by the enormousness of women's work load.

In 1862, in its first annual report, the Department of Agriculture published a study by Dr. W. W. Hall on the condition of farm women. "In plain language," Hall proclaimed, "in the civilization of the latter half of the nineteenth century, a farmer's wife, as a general rule, is a laboring drudge. . . . It is safe to say, that on three farms out of four the wife works harder, endures more, than any other on the place; more than the husband, more than the 'farm hand,' more than the 'hired help' of the kitchen."[52] In his recommendations for improvements in women's condition, Hall's report supplements our view of farm work. The practice of many farmers of letting their wives cut the firewood and haul the water, especially in the cold of winter, needed correction. Men should be responsible for providing a root cellar for potatoes and other vegetables, otherwise wives were compelled to go out in the cold "once or twice every day, to leave a heated kitchen, and most likely with thin shoes, go to the garden with a tin pan and a hoe, to dig them out of the wet ground and bring them home in slosh or rain." Equally perilous for women were the extremes of heat and cold encountered in washing and hanging the winter laundry; men were stronger and should take that job. "The truth is, it perils the life of the hardiest persons, while working over the fire in cooking or washing, to step outside the door of the kitchen for an instant, a damp, raw wind may be blowing, which coming upon an inner garment throws a chill or the clamminess of the grave over the whole body in an instant of time." . . .

Hall lamented the lack of attention to women's needs and recommended to men that they adopt a more sympathetic attitude. "There are 'seasons' in the life of women which, as to some of them, so affect the general system, and the mind also, as to commend them to our warmest sympathies. . . . Some women, at such times, are literally insane. . . ." Husbands had to be patient and affectionate or risk driving their wives to a "lunatic's cell." In addition, a man should realize that his wife loved finery and beauty and should supply her "according to his ability, with the means of making her family and home neat, tasteful and tidy." Hall reminded the farmer that "his wife is a social being; that she is not a machine, and therefore needs rest, and recreation, and change." If hands were to be hired perhaps help in the kitchen was worth considering. Women should be allowed to get out of the house once in a while to do a little visiting with other people; in fact, it was a good idea for both husband and wife to dress up and step out for the day now and then. . . .

Hall's report was a mixture of constructive suggestions and temporizing platitudes; it is unlikely that many farmers or farm women ever saw, let alone heeded, its advice.[53] In the end it is more important for what it suggests concerning the working relations of husbands and wives than for its proposed reforms. Hall implicitly leveled a harsh indictment against farmers: that they were insensitive to the

work load of their wives and drove women past reasonable limits; that they did not comprehend the natural or phychological needs of their wives; that they refused to give women the respect and authority that was their due. Hall attributed the problem to calculations of profit and loss which ignored social and emotional needs (although he made his appeal to men on the very same basis: "no man will ever lose in the long run").

The report adds depth to what we have thus far seen and suggests that the division of labor was structured in favor of men, that it exploited women, and that it was perpetuated, in part, by a masculine attitude of superiority. Daniel Drake, who visited the Midwest in the late 1830s, concluded that the farmer's wife was one who "surrounded by difficulties or vexed with hardships at home, provided with no compensation for what she has left behind, pines away, and wonders that her husband can be so happy when she is so miserable."[54] The true inequity in the division of labor was clearly expressed in the aphorism, "A man may work from sun to sun, but a woman's work is never done." The phrase has a hollow ring to us today, but it was no joke to farm women, who by all accounts worked two or three hours more each day than the men, often spinning, weaving, or knitting late into the dark evening hours.[55]

There are some areas of women's participation in farm life that suggest a higher status. Cross-cultural studies indicate that the responsibility for exchanging goods and services with persons outside the family tends to confer family power and prestige. "The relative power of women is increased if women both contribute to subsistence *and also* have opportunities for extra domestic distribution and exchange of valued goods and services."[56] In the Midwest, the products of dairy, henhouse, garden, and loom were often the only commodities successfully exchanged for other family necessities. Powder, glass, dyes, crockery, coffee, tea, store cloth, metal utensils, and sugar were bought on credit from the local merchant; butter, cheese, eggs, vegetables, homespun, and whiskey were the main items offered in trade to pay the tab.[57]

However, while it was true that women traded, the proceeds were not credited to them individually, but to the family in general.[58] Commodity exchange in corn and grain surpluses, on the other hand, was most frequently used for male economic pursuits: paying off the farm mortgage, speculating in new lands, and as innovations in technology became available, experimenting with new farm equipment. Men's product was for male use; women's product was for the family. It has been claimed that "there was no doubt of her equality in those days because she showed herself equally capable in all the tasks of their life together, and she was proud to know that this was true. Her position and dignity and age-old strength was that of the real help-mate in everything that touched the welfare of the family and the home."[59] From a modern perspective equal work may seem a first step toward sexual equality, but the question of power is not only a question of what people do but also of the recognition they are granted for what they do and the authority that recognition confers. There is little evidence to suggest that men, for their part, gave women's work a second thought. That it was a woman's lot to work that hard was simply taken for granted.

Indeed, one theme of midwestern folksongs was the lament of the husband wronged by the wife who refused to perform her appointed tasks.

> Come all you wary bachelors,
> Come listen unto me
> Come all you wary bechelors,
> Who married once would be.

> Before my wife was married
> She was a dainty dame.
> She could do all kinds of cunjer work,
> Like butter, cheese an' cream.

> She'd weed her father's oats an' flax,
> And milk the cows I know;
> And when she would return at night
> She could spin a pound of tow.

> But since my wife got married,
> Quite worthless she's become.
> An' all that I can say of her
> She will not stay at home.

> She will wash herself, an' dress herself,
> An' a-visiting she will go;
> An' that's the thing she'd rather do
> In place of spinning tow.[60]

One looks in vain for evidence of songs that sang the praises of women's diligence. Even the woman accomplished at all of her duties was likely to fall short in male estimation.

> She could wash and she could brew,
> She could cut and she could sew,
> But alas and alas! she was dumb,
>   dumb, dumb.

> . . . .
> She could card and she could spin,
> She could do most anything,
> But alas and alas! she was dumb,
>   dumb, dumb.

> She was pretty, she was smart,
> An' she stole away my heart,
> But alas, in the door she was dumb,
>   dumb, dumb.[61]

Men and women were locked into productive harmony. The farm could not exist without the cooperative labor of both sexes. Yet men gave women minimal recognition for their work. Women, fully equal in production, were not granted the status of equality.

Despite its interdependence, the character of men's and women's work was essentially different. Woman's work was dominated by the omnipresent awareness of the immediate usefulness of her product, be it milk, cabbage, eggs, or flax. Whatever processing was required she herself performed. Her view was inward, to her household and family. For them she was not simply to provide food and clothing and keep up the house, but to do these things with imagination and care: by gardening industriously, by preserving, drying, and storing to overcome the limitations of nature, by preparing the season's fare with distinction, by dyeing, bleaching, and cutting clothes in ways to please, and by keeping not only a clean but a well-appointed house. The joys of women's work lay in the satisfactions of accomplishment—of bread well made, butter nicely molded, quilts intended for heirlooms—and in the variety of skills each woman had to master. Women who worked up to this standard were good wives; those who failed on these counts were cast in male folklore as improvident slatterns.[62]

Men, for their part, worked long, monotonous, solitary hours at a single pursuit in the fields, plowing row after row, hoeing hill after hill. Hamilton remembered work in the cornfield: "Usually you cultivated the corn with a hired man or two. But you each had your own 'land,' maybe two dozen rows each was working on, a row at a time. So you did not pass close as the two or three crossed and recrossed the fields, stopping, uncovering corn, pulling cockleburrs."[63] Such work would produce, it was hoped, quantities of staple grain great enough to sustain the

family and provide a surplus, but there was little satisfaction in the immediate labor. The flavor of male work was quantitative: acres, fields, bushels—all measured a man's work. Neither the corn nor the grain was immediately consumable but required processing; the connections between production and consumption—the full cycle of work—was not embodied in a man's own activity. The cyclical nature of farm women's work might allow her to see in a flowering field of blue flax the linen for next summer's chemise. For men the fields would yield not usable, tangible articles—bread or hominy—but bushels; quantities, not things.

On the self-sufficient farm, or farms approaching self-sufficiency, the character of men's work was a powerful link between the field and the house. The housewife converted the corn to hominy, the grain to bread, while the farmer looked on: only woman could realize the product of man. But the somewhat abstract nature of men's work enabled them to envision another mode within which they were not dependent upon their wives to fulfill their labor. The market could connect men's work to a larger social process and renumerate them in the tokens of commerce. In order to qualify as social labor, work had to have this characteristic: to be able to reach out and connect the family to the larger social world. Woman's work, always cyclical, always looking inward, did not qualify; it was hidden by domestic draperies. Men's work, even in the precommercial Midwest, encouraged a kind of economic vision women could not ordinarily achieve.

NOTES

1. The following section is based on numerous sources, but see especially Logan Esarey, *The Indiana Home* (Crawfordsville, Ind.: R. E. Banta, 1943); Rodney Loehr, "Minnesota Farmers' Diaries," *Minnesota History* 18 (1937):284–97; Eric Sloane, *Seasons of America Past* (New York: Wilfred

Funk, 1958); Henry C. Taylor, *Tarpleywick: A Century of Iowa Farming* (Ames: Iowa State University Press, 1970); and Carl Hamilton, *In No Time at All* (Ames: Iowa State University Press, 1975).

2. Kerosene lamps came into wide use during the early 1860s; Evadene Burris,

"Keeping House on the Minnesota Frontier," *Minnesota History* 14 (1933):265–67.

3. W. O. Rice, "The Pioneer Dialect of Southern Illinois," *Dialect Notes* 2 (1902): 233.

4. "Animistic" is used here in its general sense—the belief in spirits—and is not meant to imply more specific forms like ancestor worship, object worship, and so on.

5. Frank R. Kramer, *Voices in the Valley: Mythmaking and Folk Belief in the Shaping of the Middle West* (Madison: University of Wisconsin Press, 1964), p. 107. . . .

6. William Oliver, *Eight Months in Illinois* (Chicago: W. M. Hill, 1924; original ed. 1843), p. 71.

7. Kramer, *Voices in the Valley*, p. 70.

8. William Cooper Howells, *Recollections of Life in Ohio from 1813–1840* (Cincinnati: Robert Clarke, 1895), p. 157.

9. I distinguish between the terms *sex* and *gender* by limiting sex to the biological status of a person, either male or female; gender is the culturally assigned status of a person in regard to what is deemed masculine or feminine behavior or belief. Gender roles, then, consist of attributes, beliefs, and behaviors appropriate for masculine men and feminine women. See Resca M. Vaughter, "Review Essay: Psychology," *Signs* 2 (1976): 122 n.

10. Michael P. Banton, *Roles: An Introduction to the Study of Social Relations* (London: Tavistock Publications, 1965), p. 71.

11. Banton, *Roles*, p. 19. Is there any longer any need to cite references for the assertion that biology is *not* destiny? See Eleanor Emmons Maccoby, ed., *The Development of Sex Differences* (Stanford: Stanford University Press, 1965), and Maccoby and Carol Nagy Jacklin, *The Psychology of Sex Differences* (Stanford: Stanford University Press, 1974), for both text and bibliography. Simone de Beauvoir, *The Second Sex* (New York: Random House, Vintage Books, 1974), remains the best general discussion after several years of remarkable feminist writings.

12. Harriet Holter, *Sex Roles and Social Structure* (Oslo: Universitetsforlaget, 1970), p. 55; Letha Scanzoni and John Scanzoni, *Men, Women and Change: A Sociology of Marriage and Family* (New York: McGraw-Hill, 1976), p. 16; Thomas C. Cochran, "The Historian's Use of Social Role," in Louis Gottschalk, ed., *Generalization in the Writing of History* (Chicago: University of Chicago Press, 1963), p. 103.

13. . . . The best work on gender roles continues to be done in anthropology, where field observation of behavior determines the focus; this tradition runs from Margaret Mead, *Male and Female: A Study of the Sexes in a Changing World* (New York: William Morrow, 1949), to Ernestine Friedl, *Women and Men: An Anthropologist's View* (New York: Holt, Rinehart, and Winston, 1975). For an excellent symposium of recent work, see Reyna R. Reiter, ed., *Toward an Anthropology of Women* (New York: Monthly Review Press, 1975).

14. Cochran, "Social Role," p. 104. See also Robert Berkhofer, *A Behavioral Approach to Historical Analysis* (New York: Free Press, 1969), p. 91; Shirley S. Angrist, "The Study of Sex Roles," *Journal of Social Issues* 25 (1969):222.

15. While this may suffice as a structural logic, it would not do as a casual assumption. Historically, the definition of masculinity and femininity itself has often acted as a fetter on (or less frequently, a stimulus to) what men and women could do, and thus culture has become the active force in the formation and change of the division of labor. I proceed here on the assumption that to begin by examining the organization of sex-specific behavior provides a reasonable context for the evaluation of evidence about attitudes and feelings. By following this methodological convention, however, I do not wish to imply judgments about a specific genesis and development of the sexual division of labor to 1850, or judgments concerning the historical play of cultural and behavioral forces in the development of relations between the sexes in the century since. These are matters calling not for assumptions but for specific historical investigation.

For a historical and structural discussion of the origins of men's and women's work, I have found the following most helpful and influential: M. Kay Martin and Barbara Voorhies, *Female of the Species* (New York: Columbia University Press, 1975); Kathleen Gough, "The Origins of the Family," Gayle Rubin, "The Traffic in Women: Notes on the 'Political Economy' of Sex," and Karen Sacks, "Engels Revisited: Women, the Organization of Production, and Private Property," all in Reiter, ed., *Toward an Anthropology of Women*; and Judith K. Brown, "A Note on the Division of Labor by Sex," *American Anthropologist* 72 (1970):1073–78. Heidi Hartmann, "Capitalism, Patriarchy, and Job Segregation by Sex," *Signs* 1, no. 3, pt. 2 (1976): 137–69, is an excellent review and evaluation of the literature.

16. General sources for the following dis-

cussion of men's and women's work are Taylor, *Tarpleywick*, Sloane, *Seasons of America*, and Esarey, *Indiana Home*.

17. Calculated from figures in R. C. Buley, *The Old Northwest Pioneer Period, 1815–1840* (Indianapolis, 1950), I:182.

18. Men were responsible for cleaning the privy. Most farms had outhouses used by women and children but disdained by men as effeminate. Ibid., 1:223.

19. Ibid., 1:153, 319.

20. Ibid., 1:217–18; Marjorie Caroline Taylor, "Domestic Arts and Crafts in Illinois (1800–1860)," *Journal of the Illinois State Historical Society* 33 (1940):294. Jo Ann Carrigan, "Nineteenth Century Rural Self-sufficiency," *Arkansas Historical Quarterly* 21 (1962):132–45, reprints from an antebellum manuscript many kitchen, garden, washday, and medicinal formulas and recipes, most from women's experience.

21. Oliver, *Eight Months*, pp. 109–10; Hamilton, *In No Time*, p. 163.

22. M. G. Wadsworth, in *History of Sangamon County, Illinois* (Chicago: Inter-State Publishing Company, 1881), p. 176; Everett N. Dick, *The Dixie Frontier* (New York: Knopf, 1948), p. 104; Buley, *Old Northwest*, 1:216–17.

23. For American variations of this traditional English chant, see Chuck Perdue, "Come Butter Come: A Collection of Churning Chants from Georgia," *Foxfire* 3 (1966): 20–24, 65–72.

24. Buley, *Old Northwest*, 1:392.

25. Loehr, "Diaries," p. 296; Taylor, *Tarpleywick*, p. 15.

26. Howells, *Recollections*, pp. 156–57.

27. For this discussion of diet I have relied on Buley, *Old Northwest*, 1:218–21; Evadene A. Burris, "Frontier Food," *Minnesota History* 14 (1933):378–92; Burris, "Keeping House"; Edward Everett Dale, "The Food of the Frontier," *Journal of the Illinois State Historical Society* 40 (1947):38–61; Hamilton, *In No Time*, pp. 143–45.

28. Taylor, "Domestic Arts," p. 287; Charles Beneulyn Johnson, *Illinois in the Fifties* (Champaign, Ill.: Flanigan-Pearson, 1918), pp. 18 ff; Ocie Lybarger, "Every Day Life on the Southern Illinois Frontier" (Master's thesis, Southern Illinois University, 1951), pp. 47 ff.

29. Samuel Willard, "Personal Reminiscences of Life in Illinois, 1830–1850," *Transactions of the Illinois State Historical Society* 11 (1906):80; Evadene A. Burris, "Furnishing the Frontier Home," *Minnesota History* 15 (1934):192; Richard Lyle Power, *Planting*

Corn Belt Culture (Indianapolis: Indiana Historical Society, 1953), pp. 109–10; Charles Beneulyn Johnson, "Everyday Life in Illinois near the Middle of the Nineteenth Century," *Transactions of the Illinois State Historical Society* 13 (1914):51.

30. Buley, *Old Northwest*, 1:233–34; Hamilton, *In No Time*, p. 146.

31. Taylor, *Tarpleywick*, pp. 9, 13. For general studies, see Rolla Milton Tryon, *Household Manufactures in the United States, 1640–1860* (Chicago: University of Chicago Press, 1917); Luther Hooper, "The Loom and Spindle: Past, Present and Future," in Smithsonian Institution, *Annual Report* (Washington, D.C. 1914), pp. 629–78; Taylor, "Domestic Arts"; and Jared Van Wagenen, Jr., *The Golden Age of Homespun* (Ithaca: Cornell University Press, 1953).

32. Howells, *Recollections*, p. 123.

33. William Oliver, *Eight Months*, pp. 89–90. "Inventories of the property of estates all through the period mention wheels"; Hubert Schmidt, "Farming in Illinois . . . ," *Journal of the Illinois State Historical Society* 31 (1938):144.

34. Van Wagenen, *Golden Age of Homespun*, pp. 264–65; Sloane, *Seasons of America*, p. 118.

35. Johnson, *Illinois*, p. 16.

36. Van Wagenen, *Golden Age of Homespun*, pp. 264–65; Sloane, *Seasons of America*, p. 118; Buley, *Old Northwest*, 1:205.

37. The emigrants of 1846 were, according to Francis Parkman, "enveloped in brown homespun, evidently cut and adjusted by the hands of a domestic female tailor"; *The Oregon Trail* (New York: New American Library–Signet Classics, 1950), p. 50. See also Schmidt, "Farming in Illinois," p. 151; Taylor, *Tarpleywick*, p. 13.

38. Buley, *Old Northwest*, 1:201–10; Margaret Gilbert Mackey and Louise Pickney Sooy, *Early California Costumes, 1769–1847* (Stanford: Stanford University Press, 1932), pp. 101–10.

39. Wiley Britton, *Pioneer Life in Southwestern Missouri* (Kansas City: Smith-Grieves Company, 1929), p. 130.

40. Aunt Jane (of Kentucky), quoted in Elizabeth Wells Robertson, *American Quilts* (New York: Studio Publications, 1948), pp. 59–60.

41. Taylor, "Domestic Arts," p. 303; Patricia Mainardi, "Quilts: The Great American Art," *Radical America* 7 (1973):39–40; quote in Mainardi, "Quilts," p. 40.

42. Soapmaking, Buley reports, was the last domestic manufacture to pass from the

farm household; *Old Northwest*, 1:223. Soap-making was still a common activity among Kansas farm women in the 1920s; Edgar Schmiedler, *The Industrial Revolution and the Home: A Comparative Study of Family Life in Country, Town, and City* (Washington, D.C., 1927), pp. 4–6.

43. Hamilton, *In No Time*, pp. 35, 37.

44. Schmiedler, *Industrial Revolution and the Home*, p. 6.

45. Vance Randolph, *The Ozarks: An American Survival of Primitive Society* (New York: Vanguard Press, 1931), p. 59.

46. *Compendium of the Eleventh Census; 1890: Part I—Population* (Washington, D.C.: Government Printing Office, 1893), p. 866.

47. Grabill estimates an age-specific infant (0–5) mortality of 220 out of 1,000 live births for the nineteenth century as a whole; W. H. Grabill, C. V. Kiser, and P. K. Whelpton, *The Fertility of American Women* (New York: John Wiley, 1958), p. 379.

48. S. B. Nerlove, "Women's Workload and Infant Feeding Practices: A Relationship with Demographic Implications," *Ethnology* 13 (1974):207–14; establishes that in societies where women contribute significantly to the production of subsistence, mothers tend to introduce their babies to supplemental food earlier than mothers in other societies. This insight was the result of a quite logical reversal of standard assumptions: "Consider first how the energies of adult women are used for the acquisition of subsistence and for other economic tasks, and then, once these requirements have been established, to see how child-spacing and child tending are accommodated to the requirements of the woman's task"; Friedl, *Women and Men*, p. 8. This premise has been basic to my study.

49. Buley, *Old Northwest*, 1:310.

50. Lactation does indeed have the effect of prolonging postpartum amenorrhea and delaying ovulation. Lactation beyond a year, however, by which time the infant must be receiving its essential protein from supplemental sources, has little continued effect in delaying the menses. . . .

51. Using the scale employed by Nerlove, "Women's Workload," pp. 208–10. The several variables can be only approximated—the dependence of the midwestern economy on hunting, husbandry, and agriculture, respectively, and the determination of women's participation in the various subsistence activities

listed. Scaling at the lowest range for women (that is, giving high relative importance to hunting, or estimating women's participation at low levels) and at the maximum (giving husbandry relative importance; or estimating women's participation at high levels) provides the range of 32 to 46 percent.

52. Dr. W. W. Hall, "Health of Farmer's Families," in *Report of the Commissioner of Agriculture for the Year 1862* (Washington, D.C.: Government Printing Office, 1863), pp. 462–63. All subsequent quotations from ibid., pp. 462–70, passim.

53. The following all document the same situation for farm women in the first quarter of the twentieth century: Randolph, *The Ozarks*, pp. 41–43; Schmiedler, *Industrial Revolution and the Home*; Edward B. Mitchell, "The American Farm Woman As She Sees Herself," in U.S. Department of Agriculture, *Yearbook of Agriculture, 1914* (Washington, D.C.: Government Printing Office, 1915), pp. 311–18; U.S. Department of Agriculture, "The Needs of Farm Women," Reports nos. 103–106 (Washington, D.C.: Government Printing Office, 1905).

54. Daniel Drake, quoted in Harriet Martineau, *Retrospect of Western Travel* (London: Saunders and Otley, 1838), 3:224.

55. See Randolph, *The Ozarks*, pp. 41–43; Esarey, *Indiana Home*; Taylor, *Tarpleywick*; Sloane, *Seasons of America*.

56. Friedl, *Women and Men*, pp. 8, 135.

57. Of these, only whiskey was a male product. Buley, *Old Northwest*, 1:235; Taylor, *Tarpleywick*, p. 14; Hamilton, *In No Time*, pp. 46, 168.

58. Mitchell, "American Farm Women," p. 314.

59. Mary Meek Atkeson, *The Woman on the Farm* (New York: Century, 1924), pp. 4–5.

60. "The Wife Who Wouldn't Spin Tow," Vance Randolph, *Ozark Folksongs*, 4 vols. (Columbia: State Historical Society of Missouri, 1946–1950), 1:123–24.

61. "The Scolding Wife," Paul G. Brewster, "Some Folk Songs from Indiana," *Journal of American Folk Lore* 57 (1944):282–83; Mary O. Eddy, *Ballads and Songs from Ohio* (New York: J. J. Angustin, 1939), p. 214; last verse supplied in another version, "The Dumb Wife Cured," Randolph, *Ozark Folksongs*, 3:119.

62. Randolph, *The Ozarks*, p. 42.

63. Hamilton, *In No Time*, p. 73.

BARBARA MAYER WERTHEIMER
The Factory Bell

Traditional histories are apt to discuss industrialization in technical and economic terms, then pause for a colorful description of the Lowell mill girls. These views require refocusing. To put it simply, the textile factories of the first wave of industrialization might not have been built at all had their owners not believed they could count on a steady supply of cheap female labor. The history of industrialization as it affected both men and women needs to be understood in the context of the segmented labor market that women entered. Women formed the first new work force that was shaped into "modern" work patterns: long, uninterrupted hours of labor in a mechanized factory with little or no room for individual initiative. As the strikes at Lowell described in the following selection show, women were among the earliest workers to use modern forms of labor protest such as work stoppages, strikes, and unions.

Despite of toil we all agree
Or out of the mills, or in,
Dependent on others we ne'er will be
So long as we're able to spin.
—"Song of the Spinners," *The Lowell Offering*, 1842

THE BOARDINGHOUSES

The Merrimack River races through New Hampshire and Massachusetts and tumbles over six waterfalls on its way to the sea. Each of these falls provided a site for ambitious nineteenth-century industrialists to develop what soon became New England's leading industry: textiles.

Lowell, Massachusetts, was one such site, a sleepy village of 200 farm families in 1820. By 1826, just three years after the first cloth was produced there by the Mer-

rimack Manufacturing Company, it had mushroomed into a bustling town of 2,000. Its six textile mills employed 1,200 persons, 90 percent of them women.[1]

Who were these women and how were they recruited to millwork? Factory owners knew how angry agricultural interests would be if men were drawn away from farming, yet in the immediate vicinity of the mills the female labor supply was most inadequate. The young women they needed as workers would have to be recruited from miles away and housed "respectably" in town if family permission was to be obtained for their coming to work in the mills.

Thus it was that the boardinghouse plan, known later as the Waltham or Lowell system, evolved. Morally acceptable to farmers, since their daughters

Excerpted from "The Factory Bell, 1815–1860," Chap. 5 of *We Were There: The Story of Working Women in America* by Barbara Mayer Wertheimer (New York: Pantheon Books, 1977). Copyright © 1977 by Barbara Mayer Wertheimer. Condensed and reprinted by permission of the publisher. Notes have been renumbered.

would be supervised by matrons (often widows with children to bring up), it was socially enticing to young farm women. Relishing the chance to get out on their own, they flocked to the mills in response to company advertisements and recruiters. They met women with similar backgrounds from different New England towns, tasted independence, earned their own money, and enjoyed the excitement of what must have seemed "the big city." For unmarried women forced to live with relatives, millwork opened the door to self-support. Nor has anyone counted the numbers of brothers these mill women put through college, the farm mortgages they helped to pay off, or the sweethearts they supported while they built their new homes in the West.

This is only part of the story, however. Farm families could no longer count on the "putting out" system, the home weaving of yarn supplied by contractors, for extra income. Wives were still needed on the farms to raise the children and cook, but daughters could be spared for the mills, work that young women found vastly preferable to the other option open to most of them: domestic service. In any event, they viewed millwork as merely an interlude before marriage and family responsibilities. The farm was always there to come home to in case of illness, homesickness, job loss, or—as they would learn—blacklisting.

Each boardinghouse became a close-knit community, a sisterhood, for the mill women seldom were alone. They spent thirteen or more hours a day together at work, their evenings together in the boardinghouse sewing, talking, reading, and singing, and their Sundays together at church and walking by the river. This boardinghouse community became a surrogate family. If a woman did not fit into her particular rooming house, she felt the group pressure and moved. This same pressure, plus the ability to return home whenever they wished, gave these spirited young women the freedom to "turn out," or strike, against company wage cuts that threatened their livelihood and company rules that offended their dignity.

As prices skyrocketed during the 1830s, the matrons could no longer maintain the dormitory atmosphere of the boardinghouses. The $1.25 a week they received for board and room, deducted by the company from the pay of each millworker, proved most inadequate. The mill women soon found themselves crowded six and eight to a room, often three to a bed. The quality and quantity of their food declined; after a long day in the mill, bread and gravy might be their only supper. As their anger and militancy grew, the women came to regard the housemothers as spies who reported their activities and church attendance (or nonattendance) to the company, and evicted them, on company orders, when they went on strike. The regulations that surrounded their lives in and out of the mills rankled. These rules, from one of the earliest boardinghouses, that of the Poignaud and Plant mill at Lancaster, seem typical:

Rules and Regulations to be attended to and followed by the Young Persons who come to Board in this House:
Rule first: Each one to enter the house without unnecessary noise or confusion, and hang up their bonnet, shawl, coat, etc., etc., in the entry.
Rule second: Each one to have their place at the table during meals, the two which have worked the greatest length of time in the Factory to sit on each side of the head of the table, so that all new hands will of course take their seats lower down, according to the length of time they have been here. . . .
Rule seventh: As a lamp will be lighted every night upstairs and placed in a lanthorn, it is expected that no boarder will take a light into the chambers.
Rule eighth: The doors will be closed at ten o'clock at night, winter and summer, at which time each boarder will be expected to retire to bed.

Rule ninth: Sunday being appointed by our Creator as a Day of Rest and Religious Exercises, it is expected that all boarders will have sufficient discretion as to pay suitable attention to the day, and if they cannot attend to some place of Public Worship they will keep within doors and improve their time in reading, writing, and in other valuable and harmless employment.[2]

BEHIND THE FAÇADE

The New England mills of the 1820s and 1830s usually fronted on a river, tall, imposing buildings five, six, or even seven stories high. They were also low-ceilinged, poorly lit, and badly ventilated. Overseers insisted on closed windows, often nailing them shut to preserve the humidity they thought kept the threads from breaking. Weaving rooms, unbearably hot in summer, were even more unhealthy in winter, the "lighting up" season. Then workers started up their looms before daylight and worked until after dark, their only light from whale-oil "petticoat" lamps that hung on each loom, mingling their smoky fumes with the thick cotton dust in the air.

From Hannah Borden, reported to be the best weaver of her day, comes our first account of millwork, and we begin to sense the role of the factory bell in the lives of the women. Borden had learned handloom weaving at the age of eight and was quick to adapt her skill to the early power looms of Fall River, Massachusetts, when, in 1817, she became one of its first three weavers.

The factory bell woke her at 4:00 in the morning. Taking her breakfast along, she readied her looms by 5:00, when the bell signaled the start of work. At 7:30 it announced the breakfast break, and called workers back afterward. At noon it rang the half-hour lunch period, and at 12:30 summoned them back. It dismissed them at 7:30 each evening, unless they worked overtime. When they got back to their boardinghouses at night, they were often too tired to eat. At 10:00 the bell rang for bed and lights out. Sundays it called them to church.[3]

Early mill songs reflect the workers' resentment of the bells that ruled their lives.

> The factory bell begins to ring
> And we must all obey,
> And to our old employment go
> Or else be turned away.[4]

Later, another millworker would write:

> It was morning, and the factory bell
> Had sent forth its early call,
> And many a weary one was there,
> Within the dull factory wall.
>
> And amidst the clashing noise and din
> Of the ever beating loom,
> Stood a fair young girl with throbbing brow
> Working her way to the tomb.[5]

Poetry from mill women? Yes, indeed. Not only were the New England women from the farms literate, but many of them could trace their independent spirit directly to parents and grandparents who had fought in the Revolution. They read the protest journals of the day and followed accounts of strikes on the docks and in the cities, and of the political activities of working men's associations in their campaigns for the ten-hour day and for Andrew Jackson's election.

It was the mill women who made Lowell one of the cultural centers of its day. Many of these women, 80 to 85 percent of whom were under thirty, found the energy at the end of a long workday to organize and attend lectures, forums, and language classes, sewing groups, and literary "improvement circles." Out of one of these circles grew the *Lowell Offering*, the first journal ever written by and for mill women. From the start it seems to have been influenced by the considerable though quiet financial support it received from the owners, who saw in it a useful vehicle for counteracting community prejudice against millwork and for recruiting new workers. The women who wrote for the *Offering*, however, found it an outlet for their talents and a vindication of their role as millworkers; they portrayed themselves in a dignified light, and this gave status to their work.[6]

But mill life was changing. Tourists to Lowell saw only the bright red factories with their white cupolas, wide flowered lawns, and mill windows lit up prettily at night. They did not see the growing impersonality of industrialization. As absentee owners took over the mills, they left overseers in charge who had total power over their workers. Factory rules became increasingly severe. So little time was allowed for meals—one half-hour at noon for dinner—that the women raced from the hot, humid weaving rooms several blocks to their boardinghouses, gulped down their main meal of the day, and ran back to the mill in terror of being fined if they were late. In winter they dared not stop to button their coats and often ate without taking them off. This was pneumonia season; in summer, spoiled food and poor sanitation led to dysentery. Tuberculosis was with them in every season.

To combat the high turnover in the mills, overseers sought to stabilize the work force and limit worker protest. They fired women for the smallest offense, or for none at all, and imposed mill rules requiring two weeks' notice plus one year's employment at the mill to earn an honorable discharge. Workers who left without this discharge were blacklisted in every mill village. . . .

MILL WOMEN STRIKE

Inflation! Depression! No matter which, wages lagged behind prices, and factory owners sought to increase stockholder profits by cutting costs—in particular, the monthly paycheck. Throughout the late 1820s and 1830s workers struck in protest. Mill women took part in these "turnouts" from the start.

The first record we have of women turning out is that of the 202 women who joined the men in walking out of a Pawtucket, Rhode Island, mill in 1824, and held their own meetings. Women struck on their own for the first time, however, not in the New England mills, but in New York City, when the United Tailoresses formed their own union in 1825 and demanded higher wages.

Dover, New Hampshire, can lay claim to the first strike of mill women on their own. In 1828, several hundred young women shocked the community by parading with banners and flags, shooting off gunpowder, and protesting the company's attempt to enforce new factory rules. They objected to the company's locking the yard gate after the bell had rung and then charging a 12½-cent fine to open it for latecomers; forbidding any talking on the job; giving "disgraceful" discharges for undefined "debaucheries"; requiring church attendance; and specifying fourteen days' notice in order to leave the mill "honorably."[7] The fine for lateness and the threat of blacklisting for dishonorable discharge provoked the most bitterness.

Newspapers from Maine to Georgia carried the strike story. A Philadelphia journal reported that the walkout exhibited "the Yankee sex in a new and unexpected light."[8] Dover millowners advertised for several hundred "better behaved women" to replace the strikers, while some papers made sport of the women for objecting to the ban on talking during work. The strike was soon over, with nothing gained, and the women returned to the mill—minus their leaders, who undoubtedly received "disgraceful dismissals" and were blacklisted. . . .

. . . When a wage cut was announced at the Lowell mills in February 1834, the women met and laid careful plans. To avoid the blacklist, they gave the required two weeks' notice of intent to leave the mill, then trooped down to the Lowell banks en masse to withdraw their savings. The company-owned banks, unprepared for this "run," were embarrassed (as the women hoped they would be) and had to send to Boston for funds to pay the accounts. Meanwhile the company, not unexpectedly, called in the woman they spotted as the leader and fired her. As she left the mill office, she waved her calash in the air, a prearranged signal to the women watching from the windows, and out they poured, eight hundred strong, to march bravely around the town. One of the women "mounted a stump and made a flaming Mary Wollstonecraft speech on the rights of women and the iniquities of the 'monied aristocracy.'" The strikers vowed they would "have their own way, if they died for it."[9]

On Saturday, the second day of the strike, they issued a proclamation, their words such a touching mixture of ladylike dignity and revolutionary zeal that they are reprinted here in full:

Issued by the ladies who were lately employed in the factories at Lowell to their associates, they having left their former employment in consequence of the proposed reduction in their wages from 12 to 25 per cent, to take effect on the first of March.

UNION IS POWER.—Our present object is to have union and exertion, and we remain in possession of our own unquestionable rights. We circulate this paper, wishing to obtain the names of all who imbibe the spirit of our patriotic ancestors, who preferred privation to bondage and parted with all that renders life desirable—and even life itself—to produce independence for their children. The oppressing hand of avarice would enslave us, and to gain their object they very gravely tell us of the pressure of the times; this we are already sensible of and deplore it. If any are in want of assistance, the ladies will be compassionate

and assist them, but we prefer to have the disposing of our charities in our own hands, and, as we are free, we would remain in possession of what kind Providence has bestowed upon us, and remain daughters of freemen still.

All who patronize this effort we wish to have discontinue their labor until terms of reconciliation are made.

Resolved, That we will not go back into the mills to work unless our wages are continued to us as they have been.

Resolved, That none of us will go back unless they receive us all as one.

Resolved, That if any have not money enough to carry them home that they shall be supplied.

Let oppression shrug her shoulders,
    And a haughty tyrant frown,
And little upstart Ignorance
    In mockery look down.
Yet I value not the feeble threats
    Of Tories in disguise,
While the flag of Independence
    O'er our noble nation flies.[10]

Each woman pledged to forfeit five dollars (close to a month's pay) if she went back to work before they all went back together. But the company did not stand idly by. Sunday brought church sermons against the strike by company-supported ministers, and on Monday, at a meeting which it seems likely the company arranged, a Methodist preacher exhorted the women to return in gratitude that they had jobs at all. Meanwhile the company publicized its attempts to recruit women from nearby farms to fill the jobs of those who did not return to work. This threat, combined with criticism from the local press and clergy, brought the women back at reduced wages. Only strike leaders were refused entrance. . . .

. . . the Lowell women, wiser after the disastrous strike of 1834, organized the Factory Girls' Association. By the time dissatisfaction in the mills erupted again in 1836, it had 2,500 members. This time mill women struck over an increase in their board charges. Although rising prices certainly made the increase from $1.25 a week to $1.50 necessary, and only half the increase would have come from the paychecks of the women, still it amounted to a 12.5 percent pay cut for them.

Close to 1,500 women walked out in protest. Young Harriet Hanson, only eleven at the time, recalled years later her impressions of that strike:

I worked in a lower room where I had heard the proposed strike fully, if not vehemently, discussed; I had been an ardent listener to what was said against this attempt at "oppression" on the part of the corporation, and naturally I took sides with the strikers. When the day came on which the girls were to turn out, those in the upper rooms started first, and so many of them left that our mill was at once shut down. Then, when the girls in my room stood irresolute, uncertain what to do . . . I, who began to think they would not go out, after all their talk, became impatient, and started on ahead, saying, with childish bravado, "I don't care what you do, I am going to turn out, whether anyone else does or not;" and I marched out, and was followed by the others.

As I looked back at the long line that followed me, I was more proud than I have ever been since at any success I may have achieved, and more proud than I shall ever be again until my own beloved State gives to its women citizens the right of suffrage.[11]

The strikers, twice as strong in number as in the turnout two years earlier, marched through the Lowell streets singing parodies of popular songs of the day. The best known, to the tune of "I Won't Be a Nun," is:

Oh! Isn't it a pity that such a pretty girl as I
Should be sent to the factory to pine away and die?
Oh! I cannot be a slave,
I will not be a slave,
For I'm so fond of liberty
That I cannot be a slave.[12]

Resolving that millowners would have to communicate with them through the officers of the Factory Girls' Association, and that they would accept no discrimination against strike leaders, they stated:

As our fathers resisted unto blood the lordly avarice of the British ministry, so we, their daughters, never will wear the yoke which has been prepared for us.[13]

By the end of the month their money ran out. Evicted from their boardinghouses and with no funds, many straggled back to their jobs, although the 250 skilled weavers who went home instead caused considerable havoc to mill production for a while afterward. Strike leaders were fired, and revenge was taken even on young Harriet Hanson's mother, a widowed boardinghouse matron. "Mrs. Hanson," a factory agent told her, "you could not prevent the older girls from turning out, but your daughter is a child, and her you could control." Mrs. Hanson was removed from her post.[14]

Perhaps with more help the women might have held out. The National Trades' Union Convention* voted moral support, but more clearly revealed its attitude toward working women by passing resolutions that millwork was physically and morally injurious to women and that hiring them caused unnecessary competition for the men. When it proposed protective laws and equal pay for women, it declared that these would successfully restrict women's jobs, since employers would have to pay women equally and would therefore prefer to hire men. For women who remained in the work force, however, the National Trades' Union recommended that unions take them in and set up all-female locals.

Some unionists saw farther into the

* The National Trades' Union was a loose federation of local craft unions and city trades assemblies which met in 1834 and 1835. By 1837, it seems to have vanished.

future. Seth Luther, New England's leading labor organizer, urged unions to admit women. "It is quite certain," he stated, "that unless we have the female sex on our side, we cannot hope to accomplish any object we have in view."[15] Luther discovered and publicized the fact that mill women often were locked in during the day, with serious consequences when fires broke out, and that mill windows were nailed shut and ventilation nonexistent.

THE 1840s; THE FEMALE LABOR REFORM ASSOCIATION AND THE TEN-HOUR DAY

But, if I still must wend my way,
Uncheered by hope's sweet song,
God grant that, in the mills, a day
May be but "ten hours" long.[16]

All labor organization came to a standstill with the depression of 1837. The mills, particularly hard hit in the early 1840s, did not begin to recover until after 1843. At the same time the farm was no longer a refuge for the mill women. Mortgages were being foreclosed, and families depended on every penny the women could send home.

Millwork was different now. The premium system of production bonuses to the overseers added new pressures. Heavier, faster, noisier machines were installed and regularly speeded up, while workers were assigned extra looms to tend and piece rates were cut. Take-home pay for mill women remained at the same level as when the mills first opened in 1823, while the amount each worker was required to produce increased all the time. Some skilled workers had already won the ten-hour day, but mill women still worked a seventy-five-hour week. With jobs scarce, overseers easily forced workers into competing with each other for their favor. Women feared staying out even when they were ill because it affected production and angered the bonus-hungry overseer. Inde-

pendent, spirited mill women lost their jobs for reading publications the overseer thought radical, or for taking part in the ten-hour movement.

When the long recession shattered their unions, workers turned to organizing politically, focusing on the shorter workday. Although voteless, the mill women had as great a stake in the ten-hour day as the men and eagerly took part in the movement.

One of the most remarkable women of her day surfaced during this campaign. Agitator, labor organizer, journalist, public speaker, adult educator, abolitionist, and political activist, Sarah Bagley appeared on the scene about 1836, coming to Lowell from her native New Hampshire to work in the mills. We know little about her except during the period between that date and 1846, when she slips from view. She believed all women workers should belong to labor unions and was the first to pressure a state legislature into holding public hearings on working conditions, as well as the first to initiate a political campaign by women.

During the first four years of the 1840s, Bagley conducted free classes at night for her sister millworkers and was an early contributor to the *Lowell Offering*, until articles of hers pointing out flaws in the Lowell system were rejected for publication. Late in December 1844, she began meeting with eleven fellow workers to plan an organization to work for the ten-hour day. In January 1845, the Female Labor Reform Association was born. The idea caught on. Within six months 500 women had joined. Bagley was elected president and her friend and close associate, Huldah Stone, secretary.

A fiery, persuasive speaker, Bagley was as skilled and effective in a small committee meeting as she was addressing a crowd of two thousand, without the aid of microphones, at a Fourth of July rally. She also possessed boundless energy, and knew how to organize and what was important to women in the mill. She had watched the mills grow and change, and had seen overseers speed up the machines and post ever harsher rules, including the hated blacklist. She lived in a boarding-house and knew how it had deteriorated. After a full day in the mill, she devoted her evenings to the Female Labor Reform Association and to organizing the Industrial Reform Lyceum to give a platform to liberal lecturers not invited to Lowell's company-dominated forums. Somehow she found time to initiate fairs and socials to keep her organization together and raise money for its campaigns. Contributing regularly to *Voices of Industry*, the labor paper of the New England Workingmen's Association, she served also as one of its three-member publications committee.

Under her leadership, the Lowell Female Labor Reform Association adopted as its slogan "Try Again," and affiliated with the New England Workingmen's Association, where Bagley and her co-workers represented the mill women at numerous conventions. She knew the lonely path she would have to travel as she violated society's sanctions on women's proper place, but as she said in a speech to the first convention of the Workingmen's Association:

> For the last half a century, it has been deemed a violation of woman's sphere to appear before the public as a speaker; but when our rights are trampled upon and we appeal in vain to legislators, what shall we do but appeal to the people?[17]

By 1845, mill women were eager for a new kind of campaign. They had the Female Labor Reform Association, and a newspaper to publicize their views—the association bought *Voices of Industry* and moved it to Lowell. They had a goal: the ten-hour day; and they had allies in the New England Workingmen's Association. The campaign they evolved was political, and began with petitions to the Massachusetts legislature.

Launched in Fall River in 1842, the petition drives to the state legislature rapidly gathered momentum. In 1843, 1,600 signed a ten-hour-day petition in Lowell. In 1844, 1,000 signed another on hours and against wage cuts. They submitted still another with 2,000 names, until finally the legislature was forced to hold public hearings on working conditions in the mills—the first such investigation ever held by an American governmental body. Six mill women and two men were invited to testify before the legislative committee, and unladylike or not, all six women appeared, including Sarah Bagley.

Like experts, they documented their statements. Eliza Hemingway told of the poor ventilation in the room where she worked with 150 others, of the thick smoke that filled the air from 293 small and 61 large oil lamps that burned morning and night during the "lighting season." Judith Payne reported on her own illnesses due to millwork. Other witnesses told of low wages, rushed mealtimes, and long hours. The testimony brought out the fact that newly arrived immigrant workers, illiterate and uninformed, were paid 18 percent less than the New England mill women.[18]

So keen was the pressure on the legislative committee that it decided to visit Lowell to see conditions for itself. But, with ample warning, the company made sure the mills were clean and sparkling when the committee arrived. The committee's report echoed industry's concern about placing Massachusetts at a competitive disadvantage with textile mills elsewhere, and found nothing unhealthy about the long hours the women worked. It spoke of grassy lawns and fine flowers, and found "everything in and about the mills and boardinghouses . . . to have for its end, health and comfort. . . . Your committee returned fully satisfied that the order, decorum, and general appearance of things in and around the mills could not be improved by any suggestion of theirs or by any act of the legislature."[19] It was small comfort that the committee also stated that it would be nice if shorter hours prevailed, ventilation were improved, and mealtimes extended, for it disclaimed any responsibility for legislating to make these improvements possible.

"Shame, shame," cried the Female Labor Reform Association, and passed unanimously a resolution chastising the committee:

> . . . the Female Labor Reform Association deeply deplore the lack of independence, honesty, and humanity in the committee to whom were referred sundry petitions relative to the hours of labor, especially in the chairman of that committee; and as he is merely a corporation machine, or tool, we will use our best endeavors and influence to keep him in the "City of Spindles" where he belongs, and not trouble Boston folks with him.[20]

A political campaign began such as Lowell had never before witnessed, spearheaded by voteless females determined to punish Colonel William Schouler, chairman of the hearings committee and Lowell's representative to the state legislature. After his defeat, the Female Labor Reform Association publicly thanked the voters of Lowell for "consigning William Schouler to the obscurity he so justly deserves."[21]

Schouler, however, retaliated promptly, digging up damaging information, not about Bagley, but about one of the men with whom she had worked during the election campaign, and damning her by association. She and her beloved Female Labor Reform Association suffered, and not long afterward she withdrew from her leadership role. But not before she had helped organize a new petition for the ten-hour day and against the year-employment rule of the mills. This petition, 130 feet long, with 4,500 signatures, was submitted along with the names of 10,000 workers from other parts of the state who signed similar petitions. But the special legislative committee that resulted from this effort reported even less satisfactorily than the first. Nothing was changed, except that after 1846, the Lowell mills extended the dinner hour by fifteen minutes in the summer, while in 1847 the New Hampshire mills did the same.[22]

We see Bagley's spirit best in the constitution she drafted for the Female Labor Reform Association, the model for similar reform associations that she and her core of organizers helped to establish in Manchester, Nashua, and Dover, New Hampshire, as well as in Waltham and Fall River, Massachusetts. Article 8 states: "Any person signing this constitution shall literally pledge herself to labor actively for reform in the present system of labor." Article 9 continues:

> The members of this association disapprove of all hostile measures, strikes, and turn-outs until all pacific measures prove abortive, and then that it is the imperious duty of everyone to assert and maintain that independence which our brave ancestors bequeathed us and sealed with their blood.[23]

The preamble to the constitution reveals not only the influence of the Associationists and Utopians, reform groups allied with labor organizations at that time, but also the struggle, as leaders of the Female Labor Reform Association saw it, of worker against owner. Their need to maintain their dignity and self-esteem as factory workers is clear. . . .

At its convention in 1846, probably in recognition of the role of the mill women in the organization, the New England Workingmen's Association changed its name to the New England Labor Reform League. Three of its eight board members were women: Huldah Stone, recording secretary (with a man to assist her), Mary Emerson, and Mrs. C. N. M. Quimby. The Female Labor Reform Association held equal status with other affiliates in the League from the start.

Sadly, this first convention of the New England Labor Reform League in Nashua, New Hampshire, was also its last. . . .

In the late 1840s, the exodus of the militant New England farm women from the mills began. Some went home to marry, some to teach in other New England towns or in the West; some sought work as missionaries or in occupations that were opening to women in offices or stores. As they left—and strikes in 1848 and 1853 contributed to the exodus—their places were taken by increasing numbers of immigrants, particularly the Irish fleeing the potato famine in their homeland.

The steady flow of immigrants to America had become a flood. The fifty-year period between 1776 and 1825 had seen the arrival of 1 million immigrants. But in the single decade of 1840–1850, close to 2 million came, and in the ten years between 1850 and 1860, the number rose to over 2.5 million.[24] The Irish who arrived in America during the twenty years preceding the Civil War totaled 1.7 million, equal to almost one-quarter of the population of Ireland at the time the famine began in 1845.[25] They came in family groups, huddled into the poorest slum tenements in town, and accepted less pay than the New England mill women had received. They knew little about unions and did not contribute to organizing efforts at this point. By the 1860s, the permanent mill population of textile towns formerly on the Lowell plan could hardly be distinguished from those which from the start had operated on the family system and employed men, women, and children as workers.

NOTES

1. *Encyclopaedia Britannica*, 14th ed. (1929), vol. 14, p. 443; Edith Abbott, *Women in Industry* (New York, 1910), p. 90.

2. Abbott, *Women in Industry*, pp. 374–5.

3. Ibid., pp. 94–95, 125–7.

4. "The Lowell Factory Girl," *Southern Exposure*, vol. 2, no. 1 (spring-summer 1974), p. 42.

5. Helen L. Sumner, *History of Women in Industry in the United States* (Washington, D.C.: Government Printing Office, 1910), p. 102, from *Voice of Industry*, May 7, 1847.

6. Caroline F. Ware, *The Early New England Cotton Manufacture* (Boston: Houghton Mifflin Co., 1931), pp. 214, 221. The Hamilton Company's agent is quoted by Ware as having written in 1845: "I should have mentioned to you yesterday that the proprietors of the *Lowell Offering* have recently made a request to the agents of the mills here for some aid to relieve them from the embarrassment they find themselves in. . . . It has been thought advisable to aid them by purchasing a lot of the back numbers to the amount of a thousand dollars. . . . It was thought best that assistance should be rendered to them in the way proposed . . . so that it might not be said that the concern is at present supported by the corporations or under their influence" (p. 222, from the *Hamilton Company Papers*).

7. John B. Andrews and W. D. P. Bliss, *History of Women in Trade Unions*, Bureau of Labor Report on Conditions of Women and Child Wage-Earners in the United States, vol. 10 (Washington, D.C.: Government Printing Office, 1911), p. 24. Quoting *Mechanics Free Press*, Jan. 17, 1829.

8. Ibid., p. 23, quoting *National Gazette*, Jan. 7, 1829.

9. Ibid., p. 27, quoting *Lowell Journal* and *Essex Tribune*, Feb. 22, 1834.

10. Ibid., p. 28, quoting *The Man*, Feb. 22, 1834.

11. Harriet H. Robinson, *Loom and Spindle, or Life Among the Early Mill Girls* (New York: Thomas Y. Crowell & Co., 1898), pp. 84–5.

12. Ibid., p. 84.

13. Andrews and Bliss, *Women in Trade Unions*, p. 30, from *National Laborer*, Oct. 29, 1836.

14. Robinson, *Looms and Spindle*, p. 85.

15. Philip Sheldon Foner, *History of the Labor Movement in the U.S.* (New York, 1947), vol. 1, p. 110. Taken from "An Address on the Origin and Progress of Avarice, and its Deleterious Effects on Human Happiness" (Boston, 1834).

16. Published anonymously in *Voice of Industry*, Feb. 20, 1846; quoted in Sumner, *History of Women in Industry*, p. 69.

17. Andrews and Bliss, *Women in Trade Unions*, p. 71, from *Voice of Industry*, June 5, 1845.

18. Hannah Josephson, *The Golden Threads* (New York: Duell, Sloan & Pearce, 1949), p. 259.

19. Norman Ware, *The Industrial Worker, 1840–1860* (1924; reprint ed., Quadrangle Books, 1964), p. 137; quoting Massachusetts House Document no. 50 (1845).

20. Andrews and Bliss, *Women in Trade Unions*, p. 74, quoting *Voice of Industry*, Jan. 9, 1846.

21. Ibid., p. 74, quoting *Voice of Industry*, Nov. 28, 1846.

22. C. F. Ware, *New England Cotton Manufacture*, p. 280.

23. Andrews and Bliss, *Women in Trade Unions*, p. 72, from *Voice of Industry*, Feb. 27, 1846.

24. Foster Rhea Dulles, *Labor in America* (New York, 1960), p. 78. Also Ware, *Industrial Worker*, p. 10.

25. *Alistair Cook's America* (New York: Alfred A. Knopf, 1974), p. 275.

KATHRYN KISH SKLAR
Catharine Beecher: Transforming the Teaching Profession

In the following essay Kathryn Kish Sklar describes the merger of economic and ideological concerns in the career of Catharine Beecher. By publicizing the appropriateness of teaching as a career for women, Beecher facilitated the entry of many women into the profession. In the process she also developed her own career, traveling widely, speaking in public frequently, and publishing popular books. Beecher made use of the familiar ideology that stressed women's "natural" docile and nurturing qualities and has been called the "Cult of True Womanhood." It was said, for example, that women had a duty to be teachers because their natural role as mothers suited them to the care of young children.

Within a single generation women replaced men in the ranks of teachers and were entrusted with classes that included boys as well as girls. It has been estimated that approximately one out of five white women in antebellum Massachusetts was a schoolteacher at some time in her life. Once the profession of teaching was "feminized" it would remain so; in 1970 more than 85 percent of the nation's elementary school teachers were women.

Excerpted from "Education at the West, 1843–1847," Chap. 12 of *Catharine Beecher: A Study in American Domesticity* by Kathryn Kish Sklar (New Haven: Yale University Press, 1973). Copyright © 1973 by Yale University Press. Reprinted by permission of the author and the publisher. Notes have been renumbered.

For the next decade and a half Catharine Beecher maintained the pace of life that she began in the summer of 1843. She sought out people . . . who were either themselves wealthy or could open doors to the wealth of other evangelical individuals and groups. She toured constantly in both East and West, raising funds, seeking sites for schools and seminaries, and recruiting teachers to occupy them. Her *Treatise* [*on Domestic Economy*] made her nationally known, and her frequent speaking tours kept her immediately in the public view. By the end of the 1840s she was one of the most widely known women in America.

Over the course of the decade, as she met with greater and greater success in promoting the primacy of women in American education, Catharine's public and private lives converged. Finally she had found a role commensurate with her personal needs and desires, and much of her achievement during this decade may have arisen from that congruence. As she traveled about the country advocating a special role for her sex, she became the living embodiment of that role. This new consistency in Catharine's life lent conviction to her activities and greatly enhanced her powers of persuasion. . . .

Catharine returned to Cincinnati in the fall of 1843. . . . She spent the winter striving to create a national organization to promote "the cause of popular education, and as intimately connected with it, the elevation of my sex by the opening of a profession for them as educators of the young." All that winter and spring she corresponded with prominent individuals in the East and West, soliciting their endorsement of such an organization.[1] . . .

. . . in the winter of 1845 she visited almost every major city in the East, delivering a standard speech and organizing local groups of church women to collect and forward funds and proselytize her views.[2]

Catharine's addresses were subsequently published in three volumes by Harpers. The first was entitled *The Evils Suffered by American Women and American Children: The Causes and the Remedy*; it was followed by *The Duty of American Women to Their Country*; and lastly, by *An Address to the Protestant Clergy of the United States*. These addresses clarified the ideas Catharine had evolved over the course of the last two decades. Now however like a practiced evangelist she played expertly upon the feelings and fears of her audience and ultimately brought them to commit themselves to her vision of a nation redeemed by women. The full meaning of Catharine's exhortation was not revealed until halfway through her addresses. First she gained her audiences' sympathy for the sufferings of masses of American children under cruel teachers and in degenerate environments. She quoted from several reports to state legislatures that described "the comfortless and dilapidated buildings, the unhung doors, broken sashes, absent panes, stilted benches, gaping walls, yawning roofs, and muddy moldering floors," of contemporary schools and "the self-styled teachers, who lash and dogmatize in these miserable tenements of humanity." Many teachers were "low, vulgar, obscene, intemperate," according to one report to the New York State legislature, "and utterly incompetent to teach anything good."[3]

To remedy this situation Catharine then proposed a national benevolent movement, similar to the temperance movement or the missionary boards, to raise money for teachers and schoolrooms. Yet Catharine's plan went even beyond the contemporary benevolent models. Her chief goal was to "elevate and dignify" her sex, and this goal was inextricably bound to her vision of a more consolidated society. The united effort of women in the East, combined with the moral influence of women in the West, would create homogeneous national institutions, Catharine asserted. The family, the school, and the social morality upon which these institutions were based would everywhere be similar. Sectional and ethnic diversities would give way to national unity as the influence of women increased.

To make her image of a unified society more understandable to her audience, she explained that it was a Protestant parallel to the Catholic pattern of close interaction between social and religious forms. Protestant women should have the same social support for their religious and moral activities as Catholic nuns received from their society. She related the stories of many women she had known who were willing to sacrifice themselves to socially ameliorative efforts, but who had been rebuffed by public opinion and restricted to quiet domestic lives. "Had these ladies turned Catholic and offered their services to extend that church, they would instantly have found bishops, priests, Jesuits and all their subordinates at hand, to counsel and sustain; a strong *public sentiment* would have been created in their favor; while abundant funds would have been laid at their feet," she said.[4] Her plan envisioned a similar kind of cultural support for Protestant women. A web of interlocking social institutions, including the family, the school, and the church, would form a new cultural matrix within which women would assume a central role.

The ideological basis of Catharine's social theory was self-denial. The Catholic church's employment of self-denying women initially attracted Catharine to it as a model for her own plan. Yet Catharine emphasized that her notion of self-denial was different from the Catholic one. The Catholics had "a selfish and ascetic self-denial, aiming mainly to save *self* by inflictions and losses," Catharine said, whereas she advocated self-denial not as the means of personal salvation, but as the means of social cohesion.[5] . . . Self-denial was an inclusive virtue that could

be practiced by wealthy and poor, converted and unconverted, by persons of all ages and both sexes. As the ideological basis of a national morality it was especially congenial to Catharine since women could be both the embodiment and the chief instructors of self-denial. It made possible an expanded cultural role for women as the exemplars and the teachers of a national morality.

To support this cultural role for women Catharine advocated three corollary ideas, each of which pointed toward a more consolidated American society. First, she said, women should abolish class distinctions among themselves and form one united social group. Catharine Beecher had earlier defended class distinctions as a part of the natural order of God's universe, but such divisions were no longer endorsed in her public writings. This change in her views was prompted in part by a visit she made to Lowell, Massachusetts, where she went to look for teachers. Catharine did not believe the Lowell owners' claims that factory work was a means of self-improvement for the women operatives. She concluded that at Lowell and in New York City women were deliberately exploited. "Work of all kinds is got from poor women, at prices that will not keep soul and body together," Catharine wrote, "and then the articles thus made are sold for prices that give monstrous profits to the capitalist, who thus grows rich on the hard labors of our sex."[6] Rather than participate in this kind of class exploitation, Catharine suggested women should donate their services to the cause of education. Although they might still be poor, their economic sacrifice would transcend class lines and benefit the whole nation instead of a self-interested class of businessmen.

While economic factors oppressed working-class women, social custom suppressed upper-class women. "The customs and prejudices of society forbid" educated young women from engaging in socially useful employments. Their sufferings were just as keen as those of working-class women, Catharine said, the only difference being that their spirits were starved instead of their bodies. "A little working of muslin and worsted, a little light reading, a little calling and shopping, and a great deal of the high stimulus of fashionable amusement, are all the ailment their starving spirits find," Catharine wrote. "The influence and the principle of *caste*," she maintained, must cease to operate on both these groups. Her solution was to secure "a proper education for all classes, and make productive labor honorable, by having all classes engage in it."[7]

The specific labor Catharine endorsed for both groups was teaching. Working-class women should leave the factories and seize the opportunity to go to the West as missionary teachers. Their places in the factories should be taken by men. Upper-class women, Catharine said, should do whatever they could to contribute to the "proper education" of American children. Whether by teaching themselves, or by raising funds, or by supervising schools in their community, all well-to-do women could do some productive labor for education. By their efforts, moreover, the public attitude toward the teaching profession could be changed. Teaching is regarded "as the most wearying drudgery, and few resort to it except from necessity," Catharine said, but by elevating the teaching profession into a "true and noble" one, and by making it the special "profession of a woman," women would be freed from the caste principles that suppressed them and enter into a new casteless, but elevated condition.[8] In effect Catharine would eliminate the extremes of class identity and fortify a middle-class social order.

The second corollary to the new social role Catharine described for women was that of fostering the nation's social conscience. Young women teachers in the West would be in the vanguard of settle-ment, and from them the character of the place would take its shape. "Soon, in all parts of our country, in each neglected village, or new settlement, the Christian female teacher will quietly take her station, collecting the ignorant children around her, teaching them habits of neatness, order and thrift; opening the book of knowledge, inspiring the principles of morality, and awakening the hope of immortality," she said.[9] . . . Catharine cited several examples of western settlement where the female teacher preceded the minister. Thus she asserted that a woman could be chiefly responsible for setting the moral tone of the community. A community could coalesce around women rather than the church.

The promotion of national unity was a third aspect of the new social role Catharine was defining for women. The special esteem in which American women were held meant that their united actions would have a nationwide effect. "It is the pride and honour of our country," she said, "that woman holds a commanding influence in the domestic and social circle, which is accorded to the sex in no other nation, and such as will make her wishes and efforts, if united for a benevolent and patriotic object, almost omnipotent." Women thus had the power to shape the character of the whole nation, and that character, Catharine said, would be one of a united nation rather than a collection of sections.[10] . . .

At the end of each address Catharine presented to her audience her plan for practical action. A committee of clergymen led by [Calvin] Stowe would, as soon as sufficient funds were raised for a salary, "appoint one man who shall act as an agent," giving his full time to the organization. The committee would also appoint "a Board of Managers, consisting of men from each of the principal Protestant denominations from each of the different sections of the country." In addition, local committees of women would raise funds "to aid in educating and locating missionary teachers." In the West such committees could aid in providing schools for those sent out. In both places the committees could publicize the cause. Lastly Catharine revealed how "every woman who feels an interest in the effort can contribute at least a small sum to promote it" by immediately purchasing Catharine's *Treatise on Domestic Economy* and her *Domestic Receipt Book*, since half the profits from the sale of these books was to be given to the cause.[11]

Catharine Beecher apparently misled her audience when she claimed that "the copyright interest in these two works is held by a board of gentlemen appointed for the purpose." Her original contract with Harper & Brothers, still preserved by Harper & Row, gave Catharine full control of the profits and did not mention a "board of gentlemen." Catharine's contract gave her 50 percent of the net profits, so she was correct in representing to her audience the fact that only half the price went to the publisher. But when she said that "Half the profits (after paying a moderate compensation to the author for the time and labour of preparing them, the amount to be decided by the above gentlemen) will be devoted to this object," she misrepresented the flow of power and profit between herself and the "gentlemen." For neither Stowe nor any of the other named Cincinnati clergymen would have been capable of questioning Catharine's use of the money that came to her from Harpers. Catharine had a reputation in her family of being "clever" to deal with financially, and it was extremely unlikely that Calvin Stowe would have crossed swords with his sister-in-law on financial issues. Later, when a salaried agent was found for the organization, he received his funds from the money he himself raised, not from the profits of Catharine's books.

Catharine's tactics in presenting herself and her cause to the public made her an enormously successful publicist. She sent circulars signed by Calvin Stowe to county newspapers and small-town clergymen throughout the East and West, asking for the names of women who might be willing to serve as missionary teachers and for the names of towns and villages where such teachers would be welcomed. The Catholic analogy and the ideology of self-denial made her efforts newsworthy, and to make the work of county editors easier she dispatched articles, such as the one entitled "Education at the West—Sisters of Charity," for newspapers to print alongside Stowe's circular.[12] The primary targets for Catharine's fund-raising efforts were the local groups of church women she organized in every city and town she visited.[13] She asked each group to make at least a hundred-dollar donation, this being the amount necessary to train and locate one teacher.

Catharine's efforts gained the endorsement of the most prominent American educators. Horace Mann, Henry Barnard, Thomas Burrowes, Samuel Lewis, and Gorham Abbot lent their support, and with each new endorsement by a national figure, Catharine's local fund-raising became more successful.[14] Catharine's tactic in each city was to plead her cause with the town's most eminent personage and, having gained his or her endorsement, to use it to build a substantial and active local committee. In this way she even drew into her cause those who traditionally opposed evangelical projects and especially opposed the Beecher family. . . .

By the spring of 1846 Catharine had delivered her addresses in most of the major cities of the East. Everywhere she called upon women to "save" their country from ignorance and immorality, and everywhere women responded. In Boston the Ladies Society for Promoting Education at the West donated several thousand dollars over the course of the decade to Catharine Beecher and her cause, and in other cities similar groups of women were organized by her into active proponents of her ideas on women and education. She corresponded with these groups constantly, relating her recent advances in other cities and exhorting her followers on to greater efforts. In a typical five-week period early in 1846 Catharine spoke in Pittsburgh, Baltimore, Washington, D.C., Philadelphia, New York City, Troy, Albany, and Hartford. She retraced her steps often, sometimes staying only one night in a place—long enough to deliver a public speech, encourage her old supporters, and welcome new ones. She traveled like a candidate for political office, moving quickly from one city to another, thereby promoting a large amount of newspaper coverage of her arrivals and departures.[15] . . .

In Albany in the spring of 1847 and in Hartford in the fall Catharine collected two groups of thirty-five young women for one month's training before they were sent to locations . . . in the West. The local women's committees provided room and board for Catharine and her young women. Catharine lectured the prospective teachers on how to meet all the difficulties that were to face them in the West: how to overcome the lack of books and proper schoolrooms; how to train children to good moral habits "when all domestic and social influences tend to weaken such habits"; how to impart spiritual training "without giving occasion for sectarian jealousy and alarm"; and how to preserve their health "from the risks of climate and the dangers of overexertion and excessive care." Catharine also lectured on the ways in which they could influence the community outside the schoolroom. They learned how to teach "the laws of health by the aid of simple drawings on the blackboard so that the children could copy

them on slates to take home and explain to their parents," and how to teach certain branches of "domestic economy" so that parents would "be willing to adopt these improvements." Most of all they learned how to be moral examples that the rest of the community could imitate.[16]

Most of the seventy young women were New Englanders; only three came from New York and one from Pennsylvania. More than half of them went to Illinois and Indiana, seven crossed the Mississippi into Iowa, and a few went to Wisconsin, Michigan, Kentucky, and Tennessee. Each of them was expected to act as "a new source of moral power" in her community, and the reports they made at the end of the year revealed how seriously they took this charge.[17] . . .

The letters Catharine received from these teachers testified to the effectiveness of her training and to the tenacity of purpose she instilled. One woman went West to join a constituency that had migrated from North Carolina, Tennessee, and Germany and was met with a log cabin classroom holding forty-five pupils ranging in age from six to eighteen, and a community of hostile parents. "They seem desirous to have their children educated, but they differed so much about almost every thing, that they could not build a schoolhouse," she wrote Catharine.

> I was told, when I came, that they would not pay a teacher for more than three months in a year. At first, they were very suspicious, and watched me narrowly; but, through the blessing of my heavenly Father, I have gained their good will and confidence, so that they have provided me a good frame schoolhouse, with writing-desks and a blackboard, and they promise to support me all the year around.

Having proved herself in their eyes, she succeeded next in drawing both parents and children to a Sunday school. Then, because the nearest church was seven miles away and the people did not go to it, she persuaded them "to invite the nearest clergyman to preach" in her schoolhouse the next Sunday. This New England woman, though unused to frontier conditions, decided to stay on in the place even though she had to board "where there are eight children and the parents and only two rooms in the house," and she went without simple amenities such as candles and a place to bathe.[18] . . .

Developments shaping the teaching profession at this precise moment made the field especially receptive to Catharine Beecher's view that it properly belonged to women. Although female teachers began to replace men in some eastern states in the 1830s, the utility of that shift was not apparent to most state and local boards of education until 1840. What had begun as an improvised economy measure had by then proved to be a pedagogic as well as a fiscal improvement, and as these obvious benefits were discovered by state and local boards of education from 1840 to 1880, women gradually replaced their male predecessors in the teaching profession. By 1888 63 percent of American teachers were women, and in cities women constituted 90 percent of the teaching force.[19]

Although it is impossible to measure completely Catharine Beecher's impact on the profession, her publicizing in behalf of women did at least facilitate an otherwise confused transition period in the nation's schools. For the traditionally higher value attached to male labor blinded many communities to the advantages of female teachers, and as late as 1850 the state of Indiana viewed the female teacher as the exception rather than the rule.[20] The West was, on the whole, slower to employ women as teachers, perhaps because it attracted ample numbers of ambitious men who, typically, would teach for a brief period or even a few years before locating more lucrative commercial employment.[21]

These male teachers were usually paid twice as much as female teachers, and a male teacher frequently brought fewer pedagogic talents to the job than a woman. In New York, one of the earliest states to shift to women teachers, the state board of regents in 1838 still assumed that teachers should be male, and they failed to approve the governor's request that normal schools be attached to female academies because they concluded that men, rather than women, needed the normal training.[22] Therefore it was far from obvious to the American public that teaching was a woman's profession.

On the other hand the shift to women teachers was well enough along by 1843 to provide a solid factual basis for Catharine Beecher's claims on their behalf. In Massachusetts, the first state to promote the employment of women as teachers, women outnumbered men three to two in 1837 and two to one in 1842.[23] Many school districts had since the 1820s routinely employed women to teach the summer session, although they believed men were needed to "manage" the older boys present at the winter school session. Some New York districts learned in the 1820s that they could, with the state subsidy of half a teacher's salary, employ a woman to teach full-time and thus not have to bear any of the cost themselves.[24] As a leading educator pointed out later in the century, "the effective reason" women were employed in schools was that they were "cheaper than men." If they had not been cheaper, "they would not have replaced nine-tenths of the men in American public schools."[25]

The need for such educational economies became more critical in the 1830s and 1840s, when immigration and internal migration increased the population of many areas, but did not immediately increase the tax base. By reducing the school costs by hiring women, a district could accommodate its larger numbers of children without taxing itself at a higher rate.[26]

Three basic assumptions were used to justify these lower salaries for women: women, unlike men, did not have to support a family; women were only working temporarily until they married; and the free workings of the economic marketplace determined cheaper salaries for women. Women do not "expect to accumulate much property by this occupation; if it affords them a respectable support and a situation where they can be useful, it is as much as they demand," wrote the state superintendent of Ohio in 1839. He therefore urged "those counties who are in the habit of paying men for instructing little children" to hire women since "females would do it for less than half the sum and generally much better than men can."[27]

Catharine chose to exploit the short-term gains that these discriminatory practices brought to women, and her publicity on behalf of female teachers emphasized their willingness to work for less money. "To make education universal, it must be moderate in expense," Catherine wrote in a petition to Congress in 1853 for free normal schools for female teachers, "and women can afford to teach for one-half, or even less, the salary which men would ask, because the female teacher has only to sustain herself; she does not look forward to the duty of supporting a family, should she marry; nor has she the ambition to amass a fortune." Catharine also insisted that women's employment as teachers would not create a "celibate class" of women, but that their employment was only temporary, and would in fact prepare them to be better wives and mothers. By defining teaching as an extension of the duties of the home, Catharine presented her idea in a form most likely to gain widespread public support. "It is ordained by infinite wisdom, that, as in the family, so in the social state, the interests of young children and of women are one and the same," Catharine insisted.[28]

Since the profession had lower pay and status than most men qualified to teach could get elsewhere, since the economics of education called for even lower pay in the 1830s and 1840s, and since the schoolroom could be seen as functionally akin to the home, both public sentiment and economic facts supported Catharine Beecher's efforts to redefine the gender of the American teacher.

NOTES

1. Catharine Beecher, *Educational Reminiscences and Suggestions* (New York, 1874), p. 101. Hereafter cited as CB, *Reminiscences*. . . .

2. CB, "Memoranda," 3 October 1844 to 7 June 1845, Beecher-Stowe Collection, Radcliffe College, Cambridge, Massachusetts.

3. CB, *The Evils Suffered by American Women and American Children: The Causes and the Remedy* (New York, 1846), p. 29.

4. CB, *An Address to the Protestant Clergy of the United States* (New York, 1846), p. 29.

5. Ibid., pp. 22–23; CB, *The Evils Suffered*, p. 16.

6. CB, "Memoranda," 29 November to 4 December 1844; CB, *The Evils Suffered*, pp. 6–9.

7. CB, *The Evils Suffered*, pp. 11–14.

8. Ibid., p. 11.

9. Ibid., pp. 9–10.

10. Ibid., p. 11.

11. CB, *The Duty of American Women to Their Country* (New York, 1845), pp. 112–31.

12. CB to Judge Lane, 26 July 1845, Ebenezer Lane Papers, Rutherford B. Hayes Library, Fremont, Ohio. CB undoubtedly knew that Elizabeth Seton had founded the first American religious community for women called "The Sisters of Charity" in 1810 and had soon thereafter opened the first parochial school free to children of all classes. Edward James et al., *Notable American Women, 1607–1950: A Biographical Dictionary*, 3 vols. (Cambridge, Mass., 1971), 3: 265.

13. CB, *Reminiscences*, p. 115.

14. Samuel Lewis was the state superintendent of schools for Ohio; Gorham Abbot,

the brother of Jacob Abbot, was the director of a fashionable school for girls in New York City. CB also appealed to Rufus Choate, then the director of the Smithsonian Institution, and Mrs. James K. Polk, the nation's first lady, for their endorsements. See CB to The Hon. Rufus Choate, 29 August 1846, Harriet Beecher Stowe Collection, Clifton Waller Barrett Library, University of Virginia; CB to Mrs. James K. Polk [1847], Hillhouse Family Papers, box 27, Sterling Memorial Library.

15. CB, "Memoranda," 21 March to 27 April 1846. Charles H. Foster, *An Errand of Mercy, The Evangelical United Front, 1790–1837* (Chapel Hill, 1960), p. 136, describes the traditional support New England women gave to education. The first female organizations in the country were formed for such a purpose—specifically to support men studying for the ministry. Early in the nineteenth century these female "cent societies" maintained 20 per cent of the ministerial students in New England. CB therefore drew on an organizational structure and a charitable predisposition that had existed among New England women for at least a generation.

16. William Slade, "Circular to the Friends of Popular Education in the United States," 15 May 1847, Increase Lapham Papers, State Historical Society of Wisconsin, Madison.

17. *First Annual Report of the General Agent of the Board of National Popular Education* (Hartford, 1848), pp. 15, 22–26.

18. CB, *The True Remedy for the Wrongs of Women* (Boston, 1851), pp. 163, 167.

19. Thomas Woody, *A History of Women's Education in the United States* ((New York, 1929), 1:499.

20. Richard G. Boone, *A History of Education in Indiana* (New York, 1892), p. 142.

21. Michael Katz, *The Irony of Early School Reform: Innovation in Mid-Nineteenth Century Massachusetts* (Cambridge, Mass., 1968), pp. 57–58. Katz's evidence disproves the stereotype of the antebellum male teacher as a vacationing college student. His data suggests that teachers shifted to the ministry, commerce, and medicine. He concludes that "others may well have looked on teaching as a way both to stay alive and to establish a local reputation while waiting for the right business opportunity to appear." Paul Monroe, *Founding of the American Public School System* (New York, 1940), 1:487: "In the newer settled regions of the Middle West men still predominated in the teaching profession throughout this period."

22. Elsie Garland Hobson, "Educational Legislation and Administration in the State of New York from 1772 to 1850," *Supplementary Educational Monographs* 3, no. 1 (Chicago, 1918): 75.

23. Woody, *History of Women's Education*, 1:497.

24. Hobson, "Educational Legislation," p. 66.

25. A comparison of salary rates for a three- to four-month period near the end of the 1840s compiled from the above sources reveals these differentials:

State	Year	Men	Women
Michigan	1847	$12.87	$5.74
Indiana	1850	12.00	6.00
Massachusetts	1848	24.51	8.07
Maine	c. 1848	15.40	4.80
New York	c. 1848	15.95	6.99
Ohio	c. 1848	15.42	8.73

Henry Barnard was practically alone in protesting this discriminatory practice. See "Report to the Secretary of the Board," *Connecticut Common School Journal* 1, no. 13 (1839): 163–64. Charles William Eliot, "Wise and Unwise Economy in Schools," *Atlantic Monthly*, no. 35 (June 1875):715, quoted in Katz, *Irony of Early School Reform*, p. 58.

26. Katz, *Irony of Early School Reform*, pp. 56–58.

27. Woody, *History of Women's Education*, 1:491.

28. Petition appeared in *Godey's Lady's Book* (January 1853), pp. 176–77. CB wrote Horace Mann: "The great purpose of a woman's life—the happy superintendence of a family—is accomplished all the better and easier by preliminary teaching in school. All the power she may develop here will come in use there" (CB to Horace Mann, in *Common School Journal* 5 [Boston, 1843]: 353).

MARY E. YOUNG
Women, Civilization, and the Indian Question

There were many aspects of Amerindian culture that Euroamericans simply did not understand. One of these aspects was the role of women. Federal officials and missionaries disagreed on many things, but they agreed in thinking that *all* women should be what white, middle-class women seemed to be. As Mary E. Young's essay shows, politics and ideology were inextricably intertwined, and "civilization" was measured by conformity with the stereotype. Whites seemed particularly troubled by the "responsible and independent economic position of the traditional Cherokee woman." They also regarded the work of Indian women as unsuitable and the leisure behavior of Indian women as immoral. Those who sought to change Indians' way of life often addressed themselves directly to women. It may be that Indian women had particular reasons, rooted in their own culture, to welcome some aspects of modernization; as Young points out, modern devices made some of women's traditional work easier. The cultural relativism that Young describes—the belief that Euroamerican culture was "progressive" and Amerindian culture "backward"—would persist far into the twentieth century.

What specific aspects of Cherokee women's lives did missionaries and federal agents regard as particularly "backward?" How do you think a historian might assess these same practices?

Americans have achieved historical notoriety for their energetic efforts at self-reformation and their equally vigorous attempts to convert other societies to a (rather statically defined) "American Way." While nineteenth-century citizens strove by exhortation and organization to reform the home, the church, the school, and the community in the name of liberty, order, industry, and Christian principle, they also labored to convert native Ameri-can Indians to the emulation of an idealized model of "Christian civilization."

Part of America's mission to itself entailed the elaboration of a "cult of true womanhood," or female domesticity. The cult confined middle-class, or ideal, woman to the household or the school. In her separate sphere, she was enjoined to subordinate her will—to her father, her husband, or the nearest appropriate male surrogate—and to direct her energies to the efficient management of resources her men might bring from the marketplace, to the transmission of approved cultural disciplines and values to children, and to the exercise of selfless, gentle, benign, and humane moral influence over all.[1] Positively, the constriction of women's activity to the private sphere while men went public in work and politics implied an increasingly critical role for women in transmitting "civilization" to the rising generation.

One might therefore suppose that efforts to civilize the allegedly childlike savages would entail a similar emphasis on the role of women as transmitters of culture. For both practical and ideological reasons, however, the overwhelming emphasis of official prescriptions for "civilizing" the savage fell on the role of men in relation to work, property, and law. Such emphasis reveals, I believe, a general assumption that woman's place could be defined properly only in the context of a market society in which property-owning males dominated production and politics.[2] In addition, of course, federal officials believed that if Indian families could be confined to small farms and induced by private possession to work the land intensively, they could and would turn over millions of acres of "surplus" hunting ground for white farmers to use. Federal policy aimed at *that* conversion above all others.[3]

As early as 1789, Secretary of War Henry Knox suggested to President Washington that introducing the love of exclusive property was the best way to civilize Indians. Knox proposed to begin by presenting domestic animals to chiefs, or their wives, and by appointing missionaries to live among the tribes with tools and stock.[4] Subsequent secretaries elaborated the plan: Indians should receive plows and hoes to encourage them to farm; both academic and vocational education would make them better farmers; and their adoption of regular laws would protect their property. Eventually each family should be allotted a farm it could own exclusively. Various officials differed as to whether education, tools, and stock, or laws took precedence in the process. They nearly all agreed, however, on the centrality of private property as an inducement to laborious and cultivated living. T. Hartley Crawford, Van Buren's commissioner of Indian Affairs, argued that "at the foundation of the whole social system lies individual property. It is, perhaps nine times in ten, the stimulus that manhood first feels. It has produced the energy, industry, and enterprise that distinguish the civilized world. . . . With it come all the delights that the word home expresses. . . ."[5] . . .

Crawford, a Pennsylvania politician who had taken an active part in the legislative establishment of his state's school system, expatiated at length in two annual reports on the importance of educating at least as many Indian girls as Indian boys: "Unless the Indian female character is raised, and her relative position changed, such education as you can give the males will be a rope of sand. . . . Necessity may force the culture of a little ground, or the keeping of a few cattle, but the savage nature will break out at every temptation. If the women are made good industrious housewives, and taught what befits their condition, their husbands and sons will find comfortable homes and social enjoyments, which, in any state of society, are essential to morality and thrift. . . . [Educated women] will acquire influence and weight, and must form, in good degree, there as elsewhere, the characters of their children. . . ."[6]

Crawford's brief tenure of the Indian Office offers the sole example, in the antebellum period, of official adoption of the ideology of domestic feminism. But agents in the field, and especially Christian missionaries, paid closer attention to the education of females and to inducing change in family structure, family life, and the division of labor between the sexes. An outstanding illustration of their concern for modifying sex role definitions can be found in the work of U.S. agents and Presbyterian-Congregationalist missionaries among that exemplary "civilized tribe," the Cherokee.

Like most eastern tribes, the Cherokee of the southern Appalachian region had been so far drawn into the international trade in skins and furs that they had become dependent on that trade for weapons, tools, clothing, and cosmetics.[7] As the supply of game diminished, they sought other means to get the kettles, guns, cloth, and vermilion their deerskins had brought them. Cloth proved an especially significant item, for many Cherokee were fond of elegant dress. Moreover, their yearly "conciliation" ceremony entailed—among other activities—going into the river, letting their old clothes float downstream, and emerging to put on new clothes and a fresh outlook.[8] Consequently, when President Washington proposed to give them spinning wheels and looms, they welcomed the gift. Benjamin Hawkins, the first U.S. agent to the southern tribes, and his assistant Silas Dinsmoor, found many women eager to receive implements and instruction.[9] Although some hunters initially opposed gifts that might make their wives oppressively independent, the agents found Cherokee men easy to convert. One, Bold Hunter by name, returned from a disappointing winter in the woods to find that his wife and daughter had produced several dozen yards of cloth. According to legend, he remarked that "they had become better hunters than he —and took up the plow."[10]

Bold Hunter's was not the universal reaction. Rather, women generally took to cultivating cotton themselves, and they sent their town chiefs to the U.S. agency to demand increasing quantities of wheels, cards, and looms. By February 1805, Cherokee agent Return J. Meigs reported to Hawkins that raising cotton, spinning, and weaving were indeed carried on widely in Cherokee Nation, "but this is totally done by the females, who are not held in any degree of respectable estimation by the real Indian & therefore have no charms to tame the savage." The male savages had informed their agent that "they are favorites of the great Spirit & that he never intended they should live the laborious lives of whites."[11]

So impressed was Meigs by the "industriousness" of the female Cherokee that he actively encouraged their marriages to neighboring white men. He hoped such men in turn might set good examples for the "indolent" Indian males.[12] If we may judge from the Cherokee census of 1835, such men at least found imitators among their mixed-blood sons, hundreds of whom became managers of extensive farms and plantations.[13] The wealthiest also acquired over twelve hundred slaves as early as 1825.[14] . . .

Yet throughout Meigs's tenure as Cherokee agent (1801–1823), he continued to complain of Cherokee "indolence." Of course, he defined dancing all night as dissipation rather than effort. Moreover, he shared with all the officials of his generation the tacit assumption that societies in which males hunted and females farmed were "hunting" societies; and towns where women hoed corn during the day while men smoked, conferred, and slept, were "abodes of indolence."[15] In truth, Meigs did not need to promote agriculture as such among the Cherokee, whose women had cultivated corn, beans, squash, and pumpkins for centuries. But Meigs required a man behind a plow to define his tribe as a "nation of farmers." So he gave away plows. By 1811 he estimated that approximately five hundred of these critical implements had found their way among the tribe's farmers. This would amount to approximately one plow for every four or five (nuclear) families.[16]

In many parts of the world, the introduction of the plow has fostered a transition from female to male agriculture.[17] In the long run, the Cherokee proved no exception. No tradition proscribed male participation in agricultural work. William Bartram, writing in the 1770s, insists that men did most of the "hard labor" on Cherokee fields. Certainly they normally participated in preparing the ground and harvesting the crop; neither of these activities occurred during the principal hunting season. One may reasonably suppose a period of transition in which men prepared the fields by plowing that eliminated weeds and thus made subsequent cultivation less time-consuming for whoever happened to wield the hoe.[18]

Many material and technical innovations that whites introduced lightened the burden of female labor without greatly augmenting the amount of agricultural labor required of males. Cloth was easier to work into garments than skins; iron pots and kettles relieved the potter; gristmills saved women the labor of grinding corn into meal. At the same time, men came at least partially to substitute stock-raising for hunting as a source of meat. Their search for grazing land led them to disperse their settlements, and in the nineteenth century the Cherokee found no need to work in groups to protect themselves against military attack. By the mid-1820s, a town field worked collectively "at the mother's side" was a rarity.[19] Thus a variety of influences molded the Cherokee pattern of farming on the model of the white. Variations in individual taste for "leisure" time activity meant that some expanded their fields and improved the elegance of their households, while those who preferred playing ball, watching ball-games, gossiping, and all-night dancing combined with daytime rest maintained their reputations for "indolence."[20]

Intermarriage, the rise to social prominence and political power of a mixed-blood elite of planters, merchants, millers, and ferry-keepers, and the shift to male agriculture changed the status as well as the work of Cherokee women. Tradition-

ally, they attended village council meetings and exercised at least indirect influence upon their deliberations. Women held two important councils of their own during a critical controversy over the proposed removal of the tribe in 1817 and 1818. The first such council firmly admonished the males against selling land that belonged to women and children; it precipitated the formation of a constitutional law that for the first time carefully defined and restricted the agencies of tribal government who might negotiate for the sale of the tribe's land. Yet the more famous and more comprehensive Cherokee constitution of 1827 disfranchised women.[21]

Since Cherokee law awarded land to those who cultivated it, women who did not farm no longer "owned" the family homestead. The first recorded law of the tribe (1808) provided for the possibility of inheritance through the male line. Long-term shifts from matrilineal to patrilineal inheritance patterns and from lineal to generational definitions of "kin" are reflected in gradual changes in kinship terminology. As early as 1829, the Cherokee *Phoenix* reported that prohibitions against marrying members of the parents' clans could be disregarded with impunity.[22]

Despite far-reaching changes in women's political and economic status, and shifts in the direction of patrilineal and patriarchal family structures, Cherokee legislation continued to protect the economic status of women who farmed or directed slaves in farming. A woman's husband could not control her property; no one could levy on her property to pay his debts. Widowers, or widows, and children each enjoyed an equal claim on the property of an intestate parent.[23]

While U.S. agents and male Cherokee legislators focused their attention on matters of property and contract, missionaries who managed educational institutions in the Nation concerned themselves with the subtler nuances of the female role.[24] Their main object was to convert the heathen, but they believed that a common school English education and vocational training would reinforce Christian professions with the practical values of the Puritan ethic. Missionaries of the American Board of Commissioners of Foreign Missions proved especially active in establishing schools where both boys and girls boarded with missionary families. The girls learned to read, write, cypher, and reproduce Bible verses and responses to the catechism. They spun, wove, quilted, made clothing, and did household chores. Several young Cherokee women who studied grammar, geography, and fancy sewing became teachers. All the young women learned to set a proper table, and to display neatness, reserve, and modesty—or so their teachers hoped. Yet as Presbyterians viewed Cherokee culture, neatness, reserve, and modesty ran counter to the grain of common practice.

The responsible and independent economic position of the traditional Cherokee woman, together with the importance the society accorded to avoiding direct interpersonal conflict, produced marital and family relations different from those the missionaries found respectable. The Cherokee accorded little importance to premarital chastity. Their custom prescribed "joking" relationships among persons of similar age whose paternal or maternal grandfathers belonged to the same clan. Frequent social and ceremonial dances—which might last all night—provided appropriate occasions on which young people were expected to tease, tickle, and exchange clothing with members of the opposite sex and appropriate clan. . . .[25]

The young peoples' carefully prescribed behavior appeared to missionaries as merely promiscuous, and in truth obscene. They expelled students and suspended church communicants for sexual experi-

mentation, and even for attendance at ball-plays and all-night dances.[26] They explained to young women that only decorous behavior would attract cultivated young men—and bemoaned the attractiveness of their cultivated and well-dressed young women who left the mission's watchful supervision without having internalized the code of respectability.[27] They encouraged Christian marriage and deplored the traditional custom of divorce at the will of either partner. By keeping the young people unremittingly at work and beating them when they misbehaved, they set an example of the "family government" they hoped to substitute for the subtler disciplinary methods of the Cherokee. Though missionary correspondence reflects much heart-burning and discouragement, they frequently hoped to succeed.[28] The Cherokee National Council offered an appreciation of their efforts by outlawing polygamy, though the law carried no penalty. More seriously, the council provided severe penalties for abortion, a practice traditional society had left to the mother's discretion.[29]

Although they accepted children of the poor, and proved especially hospitable to orphans, the American Board schools self-consciously focused their efforts on training children of the tribal elite. As the board's corresponding secretary, Jeremiah Evarts, informed a member of the Cherokee mission in 1827, "It is of great consequence to have the females of the principal families well instructed. In this way only will education become popular & fashionable."[30] Certainly education became "popular and fashionable" among the Cherokee, who established their own public school system at a time when other states in the South had none. A law of 1851 also established seminaries—one for males, another for females. Just how much this concern for learning and female education attests to female domestication and influence remains conjectural. Certainly both female education and the values it sought to inculcate both reflected and reinforced the social class divisions that burgeoning wealth had created within the tribe.[31]

. . . the changes in female roles we can identify through archival sources perhaps raise as many questions as they resolve. Censuses and records of claims for lost property give an impressive measure of the diffusion of plows, spinning wheels, delft pottery, and teaspoons throughout the Cherokee Nation by the fourth decade of the nineteenth century.[32] They cannot tell us definitively the proportions of male and female participation in agriculture, or whether most families ate from delft or

merely exhibited it. Agency and missionary archives, Cherokee legal records, and the field reports of modern anthropologists indicate the directions of cultural changes. They do not tell us to what extent and with what results fathers replaced mothers' brothers as disciplinary authorities—though a change in kinship terminology to designate "mother's brothers" as "step-fathers" is suggestive.[33] Nor do the records indicate how far "family government" among the Cherokee approached the rigor of the missionary model. Did industrious and enlightened mothers commend "industry" to their sons? How? With what results? We cannot be sure. . . .

Notes

1. Barbara Welter, "The Cult of True Womanhood, 1820–1860," *American Quarterly* 18 (1966):151–74; Gerda Lerner, "The Lady and the Mill Girl: Changes in the Status of Women in the Age of Jackson," *Midcontinent American Studies Journal* 10 (1969); Glenda L. Riley, "The Subtle Subversion: Changes in the Traditionalist Image of American Woman," *Historian* 32 (1970): 210–27; William R. Taylor, *Cavalier and Yankee: The Old South and American National Character* (New York: George Braziller, 1961); Kathryn Kish Sklar, *Catharine Beecher: A Study in American Domesticity* (New Haven: Yale University Press, 1973).

2. Elizabeth Fox-Genovese, "The Paradoxical Paradigm: The Domestic Origins of Bourgeois Ideology," delivered before the Union of Radical Political Economists, New Brunswick, New Jersey, 22 March 1976.

3. Mary Elizabeth Young, *Redskins, Ruffleshirts, and Rednecks: Indian Allotments in Alabama and Mississippi, 1830–1860* (Norman: University of Oklahoma Press, 1961).

4. Knox to Washington, 17 July 1789, *American State Papers: Indian Affairs* 1: 53–54.

5. Crawford to Poinsett, 25 November 1838, *New American State Papers: Indian Affairs* 1:512 (hereafter cited as *NASPIA*).

6. Crawford to Poinsett, 5 November 1839, *NASPIA*, p. 594. For Crawford's background, see Ronald N. Satz, *American Indian Policy in the Jacksonian Era* (Lincoln: University of Nebraska Press, 1975), p. 259.

7. David H. Corkran, *The Cherokee Frontier: Conflict and Survival, 1740–62* (Norman: University of Oklahoma Press, 1962).

8. Fred O. Gearing, *Priests and Warriors: Social Structure for Cherokee Politics in the 18th Century*, Memoir of the American Anthropological Association 64, no. 5, pt. 2 (October 1962):3–4.

9. Benjamin Hawkins, *A Sketch of the Creek Country in the Years 1798 and 1799* (New York: Kraus Reprint Corp., 1971); Hawkins, "A Sketch of the Present State of the Objects under the Charge of the Principal Agent for Indian Affairs South of Ohio," 8 December 1801, *NASPIA*, 5:176.

10. John Ridge to Albert Gallatin, 27 February 1826, John Howard Payne Transcripts, 8:103, Newberry Library, Chicago, Illinois.

11. Meigs to Hawkins, 15 February 1805, Records of the Cherokee Indian Agency in Tennessee, vol. 3, Records of the Bureau of Indian Affairs, Record Group 75, National Archives Building, National Archives Microfilm Publication M208 (hereafter cited as RG __, NA __, M __). Compare Meigs, Journal of Occurrences in the Cherokee Nation, 1802, ibid., vol. 1, M208.

12. Meigs to Chulio, draft, 14 March 1808, vol. 4, RG 75, NA, M208.

13. Census Roll, 1835, of the Cherokee Indians East of the Mississippi and Index to the Roll, RG 75, NA, T496.

14. McKenney to Barbour, 13 December 1825, Letters Sent by the Office of Indian

Affairs, 1824–1881, vol. 2, p. 298, RG 75, NA, M21.

15. For example, Meigs to Dearborn, 3 June 1808, Records of the Cherokee Indian Agency in Tennessee, 1801–35, vol. 4, M208; Meigs to Eustis, 5 April 1811, ibid., vol. 5, M208.

16. Meigs to Eustis, 10 May 1811, ibid. I have computed the rough proportions by dividing the census figures for 1809 (Meigs to Lee, 11 March 1820, ibid., vol. 8) by the average family size reported in the census for 1835.

17. Esther Boserup, *Woman's Role in Economic Development* (New York: St. Martins Press, 1970), pp. 15–25.

18. Compare William Bartram, "Observations on the Creek and Cherokee Indians, 1789," *American Ethnological Society* 3, pt. 1 (1858):30–33; Gearing, *Priests and Warriors*, pp. 2, 3; Boserup, *Woman's Role in Economic Development*. Obviously the pace, extent, and manner by which the introduction of the plow leads to change in sex roles in agriculture will vary according to the social situation of the groups involved. On this point in general, see Claude Meillassoux, *Femmes, Greniers, & Capitaux* (Paris: Maspero, 1975), p. 64.

19. Ridge to Gallatin, John Howard Payne Transcripts; Ridge's observation is borne out by the various records of Cherokee claims for farm improvement in RG 75, NA. On the impact of stockraising, see Hawkins, *A Sketch of the Creek Country*.

20. On household matters, see Chamberlain to Greene, 21 February 1832, Records of the American Board of Commissioners for Foreign Missions, ABC 18.3.1, vol. 7, Houghton Library, Harvard University, Cambridge, Massachusetts.

21. On the women's councils, see "Address of Women at Amoiah Council," 2 May 1817, Andrew Jackson Papers, Library of Congress Microfilm, reel 22; and Journal of the Cherokee Mission, 30 June 1818, ABC 18.3.1. On changes in women's political role and legal status, see Rennard Strickland, *Fire and the Spirits: Cherokee Law from Clan to Court* (Norman: University of Oklahoma Press, 1975).

22. *Laws of the Cherokee Nation, Adopted by the Council at Various Periods* (Tahlequah: Cherokee Nation Press, 1852), pp. 3–4; Fred Eggan, *The American Indian: Perspectives for Study of Social Change* (Chicago: Aldine Publishing Co., 1966), pp. 31–39; Cherokee *Phoenix* 1 (February 1829):49. (Mi-

crofilm edition, Western Historical Collections, University of Oklahoma).

23. See, in general, Strickland, *Fire and the Spirits: Laws of the Cherokee Nation*, 6 May 1817, pp. 3–4; 2 November 1819, p. 10; 9 November 1826, p. 82; 2 November 1829, pp. 142–43.

24. On the missionary subculture and its special sensitivities, see Robert F. Berkhofer, Jr., *Salvation and the Savage: An Analysis of Protestant Missions and American Indian Response, 1789–1862* (Lexington: University of Kentucky Press, 1965).

25. W. H. Gilbert, Jr., "Eastern Cherokee Social Organization," in Fred Eggan, ed., *Social Anthropology of the North American Tribes* (Chicago: University of Chicago Press, 1955), pp. 285–340.

26. Mary Young, "Indian Removal and the Attack on Tribal Autonomy: The Cherokee Case," in John K. Mahon, ed., *Indians of the Lower South: Past and Present* (Gainesville: University of Florida Press, 1975), pp. 129–30.

27. Sawyer to Evarts, 21 August 1824, ABC 18.3.1, vol. 5; Sawyer to Greene, 6 July 1833, ibid., vol. 8.

28. Kingsbury, Hall, and Williams to Worcester, 25 November 1817, ibid., vol. 2; Journal of the Cherokee Mission, 21 January 1819, ibid., vol. 8; Chamberlain to Evarts, 30 July 1824, ibid., vol. 4; Chamberlain to Wisner, 4 June 1833, ibid., vol. 9.

29. *Laws of the Cherokee Nation*, 11 November 1825, p. 58; ibid., 16 October 1826, p. 79.

30. Evarts to Proctor, 3 January 1827, ABC 1.01. vol. 6:21.

31. Grace Steele Woodward, *The Cherokee* (Norman: University of Oklahoma Press, 1963); Althea Bass, *Cherokee Messenger* (Norman: University of Oklahoma Press, 1936).

32. For claims, see the records of the Board of Cherokee Commissioners, RG 75, NA; Cherokee Collection, Tennessee Department of Archives and History, Nashville; John Ross Papers, Gilcrease Institute, Tulsa, Oklahoma.

33. In addition to the works of Eggan and Gilbert, cited above, see Leonard Bloom, "The Cherokee Clan: A Study in Acculturation," *American Anthropologist* 41 (1939): 266–68; and John Gulick, "Language and Passive Resistance among the Eastern Cherokees," *Ethnohistory* 5 (1958):64; Eggan, *The American Indian*, p. 21.

CARROLL SMITH-ROSENBERG
The Female World of Love and Ritual: Relations between Women in Nineteenth-Century America

Women's associations with each other have traditionally been ignored by historians. One reason for this has been a fascination with public life; only women who were powerful in the same fashion as men or whose lives were intertwined with the lives of powerful men attracted the historical spotlight. The world of women was treated as wholly private or domestic, encompassing only family responsibilities. Women's diaries and letters were used primarily as a source of illustrative anecdote.

Carroll Smith-Rosenberg has read the letters and diaries of women in a strikingly original way. She evaluates nineteenth-century American society in much the same way an anthropologist might observe a distant culture. She describes relations between women as intellectually active, personally rewarding, mutually supportive, and socially creative. Smith-Rosenberg offers a radically new account of the relationship between the sexes in Victorian America. What revision does she suggest ought to be made in our traditional understanding of Victorian sexuality?

The female friendship of the nineteenth century, the long-lived, intimate, loving friendship between two women, is an excellent example of the type of historical phenomena which most historians know something about, which few have thought much about, and which virtually no one has written about.[1] It is one aspect of the female experience which consciously or unconsciously we have chosen to ignore. Yet an abundance of manuscript evidence suggests that eighteenth- and nineteenth-century women routinely formed emotional ties with other women. Such deeply felt, same-sex friendships were casually accepted in American society. Indeed, from at least the late eighteenth through the mid-nineteenth century, a female world of varied and yet highly structured relationships appears to have been an essential aspect of American society. These relationships ranged from the supportive love of sisters, through the enthusiasms of adolescent girls, to sensual avowals of love by mature women. It was a world in which men made but a shadowy appearance.[2]

Defining and analyzing same-sex relationships involves the historian in deeply problematical questions of method and interpretation. This is especially true since historians, influenced by Freud's libidinal theory, have discussed these relationships almost exclusively within the context of individual psychosexual developments or, to be more explicit, psychopathology.[3] Seeing same-sex relationships in terms of a dichotomy between normal and abnormal, they have sought the origins of such apparent deviance in childhood or adolescent trauma and detected the symptoms of "latent" homosexuality in the lives of both those who later became "overtly" homosexual and those who did not. Yet theories concerning the nature and origins of same-sex relationships are frequently contradictory or based on questionable or arbitrary data. In recent years such hypotheses have been subjected to criticism both from within and without the psychological professions. Historians who seek to work within a psychological framework, therefore, are faced with two hard questions: Do sound psychodynamic theories concerning the nature and origins of same-sex relationships exist? If so, does the historical datum exist which would permit the use of such dynamic models?

I would like to suggest an alternative approach to female friendships—one which would view them within a cultural and social setting rather than from an exclusively individual psychosexual perspective. Only by thus altering our approach will we be in the position to evaluate the appropriateness of particular dynamic interpretations. Intimate friendships between men and men and women and women existed in a larger world of social relations and social values. To interpret such friendships more fully they must be related to the structure of the American family and to the nature of sex-role divisions and of male-female relations both within the family and in society generally. The female friendship must not be seen in isolation; it must be analyzed as one aspect of women's overall relations with one another. The ties between mothers and daughters, sisters, female cousins and friends, at all stages of the female life cycle constitute the most suggestive framework for the historian to begin an analysis of intimacy and affection between women. Such an analysis would not only emphasize general cultural patterns rather than the internal dynamics of a particular family or childhood; it would shift the focus of the study from a concern with deviance to that of defining configurations of legitimate behavioral norms and options.[4]

This analysis will be based upon the correspondence and diaries of women and men in thirty-five families between the 1760s and the 1880s. These families, though limited in number, represented a broad range of the American middle class, from hard-pressed pioneer families and orphaned girls to daughters of the intellectual and social elite. It includes families from most geographic regions, rural and urban, and a spectrum of Protestant denominations ranging from Mormon to orthodox Quaker. Although scarcely a comprehensive sample of America's increasingly heterogeneous population, it does, I believe, reflect accurately the literate middle class to which the historian working with letters and diaries is necessarily bound. It has involved an analysis of many thousands of letters written to women friends, kin, husbands, brothers, and children at every period of life from adolescence to old age. Some collections encompass virtually entire life spans; one contains over 100,000 letters as well as diaries and account books. It is my contention that an analysis of women's private letters and diaries which were never intended to be published permits the historian to explore a very private world of emotional realities central both to women's lives and to the middle-class family in nineteenth-century America.[5]

The question of female friendships is peculiarly elusive; we know so little or perhaps have forgotten so much. An intriguing and almost alien form of human relationship, they flourished in a different social structure and amidst different sexual norms. Before attempting to reconstruct their social setting, therefore, it might be best first to describe two not atypical friendships. These two friendships, intense, loving, and openly avowed, began during the women's adolescence and, despite subsequent marriages and geographic separation, continued throughout their lives. For nearly half a century these women played a central emotional role in each other's lives, writing time and again of their love and of the pain of separation. Paradoxically to twentieth-century minds, their love appears to have been both sensual and platonic.

Sarah Butler Wister first met Jeannie Field Musgrove while vacationing with her family at Stockbridge, Massachusetts, in the summer of 1849.[6] Jeannie was then sixteen, Sarah fourteen. During two subsequent years spent together in boarding school, they formed a deep and intimate friendship. Sarah began to keep a bouquet of flowers before Jeannie's portrait and wrote complaining of the intensity and anguish of her affection.[7] Both young women assumed nom de plumes, Jeannie a female name, Sarah a male one; they would use these secret names into old age.[8] They frequently commented on the nature of their affection: "If the day should come," Sarah wrote Jeannie in the spring of 1861, "when you failed me either through your fault or my own, I would forswear all human friendship, thenceforth." A few months later Jeannie commented: "Gratitude is a word I should never use toward you. It is perhaps a misfortune of such intimacy and love that it makes one regard all kindness as a matter of course, as one has always found it, as natural as the embrace in meeting."[9]

Sarah's marriage altered neither the frequency of their correspondence nor their desire to be together. In 1864, when twenty-nine, married, and a mother, Sarah wrote to Jeannie: "I shall be entirely alone [this coming week]. I can give you no idea how desperately I shall want you. . . ." After one such visit Jeannie, then a spinster in New York, echoed Sarah's longing: "Dear darling Sarah! How I love you & how happy I have been! You are the joy of my life. . . . I cannot tell you how much happiness you gave me, nor how constantly it is all in my thoughts. . . . My darling how I long for the time when I shall see you. . . ." After another visit Jeannie wrote: "I want you to tell me in your next letter, to assure me, that I am your dearest. . . . I do not doubt you, & I am not jealous but I long to hear you say it once more & it seems already a long time since your voice fell on my ear. So just fill a quarter page with caresses & expressions of endearment. Your silly Angelina." Jeannie ended one letter: "Goodbye my dearest, dearest lover—ever your own Angelina." And another, "I will go to bed . . . [though] I could write all night—A thousand kisses— I love you with my whole soul—your Angelina."

When Jeannie finally married in 1870 at the age of thirty-seven, Sarah underwent a period of extreme anxiety. Two days before Jeannie's marriage Sarah, then in London, wrote desperately: "Dearest darling—How incessantly have I thought of you these eight days—all today—the entire uncertainty, the distance, the long silence—are all new features in my separation from you, grievous to be borne. . . . Oh Jeannie. I have thought & thought & yearned over you these two days. Are you married I wonder? My dearest love to you wherever and *who*ever you are."[10] Like many other women in this collection of thirty-five families, marriage brought Sarah and Jeannie physical separation; it did not cause emotional distance. Although at first they may have wondered how marriage would affect their relationship, their affection remained unabated throughout their lives, underscored by their loneliness and their desire to be together.[11]

During the same years that Jeannie and Sarah wrote of their love and need for each other, two slightly younger women began a similar odyssey of love, dependence and—ultimately—physical, though not emotional, separation. Molly and Helena met in 1868 while both attended the Cooper Institute School of Design for Women in New York City. For several years these young women studied and explored the city together, visited each other's families, and formed part of a social network of other artistic young women. Gradually, over the years, their initial friendship deepened into a close intimate bond which continued throughout their lives. The tone in the letters which Molly wrote to Helena changed over these years from "My dear Helena," and signed "your attached friend," to "My dearest Helena," "My Dearest," "My Beloved," and signed "Thine always" or "thine Molly."[12]

The letters they wrote to each other during these first five years permit us to reconstruct something of their relationship together. As Molly wrote in one early letter:

I have not said to you in so many or so few words that I was happy with you during those few so incredibly short weeks but surely you do not need words to tell you what you must know. Those two or three days so dark without, so bright with firelight and contentment within I shall always remember as proof that, for a time, at least—I fancy for quite a long time—we might be sufficient for each other. We know that we can amuse each other for many idle hours together and now we know that we can also work together. And that means much, don't you think so?

She ended: "I shall return in a few days. Imagine yourself kissed many times by one who loved you so dearly."

The intensity and even physical nature of Molly's love was echoed in many of the letters she wrote during the next few years, as, for instance in this short thank-you note for a small present: "Imagine yourself kissed a dozen times my darling. Perhaps it is well for you that we are far apart. You might find my thanks so expressed rather overpowering. I have that delightful feeling that it doesn't matter much what I say or how I say it, since we shall meet so soon and forget in that moment that we were ever separated. . . . I shall see you soon and be content."[13]

At the end of the fifth year, however, several crises occurred. The relationship, at least in its intense form, ended, though Molly and Helena continued an intimate and complex relationship for the next half-century. The exact nature of these crises is not completely clear, but it seems to have involved Molly's decision not to live with Helena, as they had originally planned, but to remain at home because of parental insistence. Molly was now in her late twenties. Helena responded with anger and Molly became frantic at the thought that Helena would break off their relationship. Though she wrote distraught letters and made despairing attempts to see Helena, the relationship never regained its former ardor—possibly because Molly had a male suitor.[14] Within six months Helena had decided to marry a man who was, coincidentally, Molly's friend and publisher. Two years later Molly herself finally married. The letters toward the end of this period discuss the transition both women made to having male lovers—Molly spending much time reassuring Helena, who seemed depressed about the end of their relationship and with her forthcoming marriage.[15]

It is clearly difficult from a distance of 100 years and from a post-Freudian cultural perspective to decipher the complexities of Molly and Helena's relationship. Certainly Molly and Helena were lovers—

emotionally if not physically. The emotional intensity and pathos of their love becomes apparent in several letters Molly wrote Helena during their crisis: "I wanted so to put my arms round my girl of all the girls in the world and tell her . . . I love her as wives do love their husbands, as *friends* who have taken each other for life—and believe in her as I believe in my God. . . . If I didn't love you do you suppose I'd care about anything or have ridiculous notions and panics and behave like an old fool who ought to know better. I'm going to hang on to your skirts. . . . You can't get away from [my] love." Or as she wrote after Helena's decision to marry: "You know dear Helena, I really was in love with you. It was a passion such as I had never known until I saw you. I don't think it was the noblest way to love you." The theme of intense female love was one Molly again expressed in a letter she wrote to the man Helena was to marry: "Do you know sir, that until you came along I believe that she loved me almost as girls love their lovers. *I know I loved her so.* Don't you wonder that I can stand the sight of you." This was in a letter congratulating them on their forthcoming marriage.[16]

The essential question is not whether these women had genital contact and can therefore be defined as heterosexual or homosexual. The twentieth-century tendency to view human love and sexuality within a dichotomized universe of deviance and normality, genitality and platonic love, is alien to the emotions and attitudes of the nineteenth century and fundamentally distorts the nature of these women's emotional interaction. These letters are significant because they force us to place such female love in a particular historical context. There is every indication that these four women, their husbands and families—all eminently respectable and socially conservative—considered such love both socially acceptable and fully compat-

ible with heterosexual marriage. Emotionally and cognitively, their heterosocial and their homosocial worlds were complementary.

One could argue, on the other hand, that these letters were but an example of the romantic rhetoric with which the nineteenth century surrounded the concept of friendship. Yet they possess an emotional intensity and a sensual and physical explicitness that is difficult to dismiss. Jeannie longed to hold Sarah in her arms; Molly mourned her physical isolation from Helena. Molly's love and devotion to Helena, the emotions that bound Jeannie and Sarah together, while perhaps a phenomenon of nineteenth-century society were not the less real for their Victorian origins. A survey of the correspondence and diaries of eighteenth- and nineteenth-century women indicates that Molly, Jeannie, and Sarah represented one very real behavioral and emotional option socially available to nineteenth-century women.

This is not to argue that individual needs, personalities, and family dynamics did not have a significant role in determining the nature of particular relationships. But the scholar must ask if it is historically possible and, if possible, important, to study the intensely individual aspects of psychosexual dynamics. Is it not the historian's first task to explore the social structure and the world view which made intense and sometimes sensual female love both a possible and an acceptable emotional option? From such a social perspective a new and quite different series of questions suggests itself. What emotional function did such female love serve? What was its place within the hetero- and homosocial worlds which women jointly inhabited? Did a spectrum of love-object choices exist in the nineteenth century across which some individuals, at least, were capable of moving? Without attempting to answer these questions it will be difficult to understand either nineteenth-century sexuality or the nineteenth-century family.

Several factors in American society between the mid-eighteenth and the mid-nineteenth centuries may well have permitted women to form a variety of close emotional relationships with other women. American society was characterized in large part by rigid gender-role differentiation within the family and within society as a whole, leading to the emotional segregation of women and men. The roles of daughter and mother shaded imperceptibly and ineluctably into each other, while the biological realities of frequent pregnancies, childbirth, nursing, and menopause bound women together in physical and emotional intimacy. It was within just such a social framework, I would argue, that a specifically female world did indeed develop, a world built around a generic and unself-conscious pattern of single-sex or homosocial networks. These supportive networks were institutionalized in social conventions or rituals which accompanied virtually every important event in a woman's life, from birth to death. Such female relationships were frequently supported and paralleled by severe social restrictions on intimacy between young men and women. Within such a world of emotional richness and complexity devotion to and love of other women became a plausible and socially accepted form of human interaction.

An abundance of printed and manuscript sources exists to support such a hypothesis. Etiquette books, advice books on child rearing, religious sermons, guides to young men and young women, medical texts, and school curricula all suggest that late eighteenth- and most nineteenth-century Americans assumed the existence of a world composed of distinctly male and female spheres, spheres determined by the immutable laws of God and nature.[17] The unpublished letters and diaries of Americans during this same period

concur, detailing the existence of sexually segregated worlds inhabited by human beings with different values, expectations, and personalities. Contacts between men and women frequently partook of a formality and stiffness quite alien to twentieth-century America and which today we tend to define as "Victorian." Women, however, did not form an isolated and oppressed subcategory in male society. Their letters and diaries indicate that women's sphere had an essential integrity and dignity that grew out of women's shared experiences and mutual affection and that, despite the profound changes which affected American social structure and institutions between the 1760s and the 1870s, retained a constancy and predictability. The ways in which women thought of and interacted with each other remained unchanged. Continuity, not discontinuity, characterized this female world. Molly Hallock's and Jeannie Fields's words, emotions, and experiences have direct parallels in the 1760s and the 1790s.[18] There are indications in contemporary sociological and psychological literature that female closeness and support networks have continued into the twentieth century—not only among ethnic and working-class groups but even among the middle class.[19]

Most eighteenth- and nineteenth-century women lived within a world bounded by home, church, and the institution of visiting—that endless trooping of women to each others' homes for social purposes. It was a world inhabited by children and by other women.[20] Women helped each other with domestic chores and in times of sickness, sorrow, or trouble. Entire days, even weeks, might be spent almost exclusively with other women.[21] Urban and town women could devote virtually every day to visits, teas, or shopping trips with other women. Rural women developed a pattern of more extended visits that lasted weeks and sometimes months, at times even dislodging husbands from their beds and bedrooms so that dear friends might spend every hour of every day together.[22] When husbands traveled, wives routinely moved in with other women, invited women friends to teas and suppers, sat together sharing and comparing the letters they had received from other close women friends. Secrets were exchanged and cherished, and the husband's return at times viewed with some ambivalence.[23]

Summer vacations were frequently organized to permit old friends to meet at water spas or share a country home. In 1848, for example, a young matron wrote cheerfully to her husband about the delightful time she was having with five close women friends whom she had invited to spend the summer with her; he remained at home alone to face the heat of Philadelphia and a cholera epidemic.[24] Some ninety years earlier, two young Quaker girls commented upon the vacation their aunt had taken alone with another woman; their remarks were openly envious and tell us something of the emotional quality of these friendships: "I hear Aunt is gone with the Friend and wont be back for two weeks, fine times indeed I think the old friends had, taking their pleasure about the country . . . and have the advantage of that fine woman's conversation and instruction, while we poor young girls must spend all spring at home. . . . What a disappointment that we are not together. . . ."[25]

Friends did not form isolated dyads but were normally part of highly integrated networks. Knowing each other, perhaps related to each other, they played a central role in holding communities and kin systems together. Especially when families became geographically mobile women's long visits to each other and their frequent letters filled with discussions of marriages and births, illness and deaths, descriptions of growing children, and reminiscences of times and people past provided an important sense of continuity in a rapidly changing society.[26]

Central to this female world was an inner core of kin. The ties between sisters, first cousins, aunts, and nieces provided the underlying structure upon which groups of friends and their network of female relatives clustered. Although most of the women within this sample would appear to be living within isolated nuclear families, the emotional ties between nonresidential kin were deep and binding and provided one of the fundamental existential realities of women's lives.[27] Twenty years after Parke Lewis Butler moved with her husband to Louisiana, she sent her two daughters back to Virginia to attend school, live with their grandmother and aunt, and be integrated back into Virginia society.[28] The constant letters between Maria Inskeep and Fanny Hampton, sisters separated in their early twenties when Maria moved with her husband from New Jersey to Louisiana, held their families together, making it possible for their daughters to feel a part of their cousins' network of friends and interests.[29] The Ripley daughters, growing up in western Massachusetts in the early 1800s, spent months each year with their mother's sister and her family in distant Boston; these female cousins and their network of friends exchanged gossip-filled letters and gradually formed deeply loving and dependent ties.[30]

Women frequently spent their days within the social confines of such extended families. Sisters-in-law visited each other and, in some families, seemed to spend more time with each other than with their husbands. First cousins cared for each other's babies—for weeks or even months in times of sickness or childbirth. Sisters helped each other with housework, shopped and sewed for each other. Geographic separation was borne with difficulty. A sister's absence for even a week or two could cause loneliness and depression and would be bridged by frequent letters. Sibling rivalry was hardly unknown, but with separation or illness the theme of deep affection and dependency reemerged.[31]

Sisterly bonds continued across a lifetime. In her old age a rural Quaker matron, Martha Jefferis, wrote to her daughter Anne concerning her own half-sister, Phoebe: "In sister Phoebe I have a real friend—she studies my comfort and waits on me like a child. . . . She is exceedingly kind and this to all other homes (set aside yours) I would prefer—it is next to being with a daughter." Phoebe's own letters confirmed Martha's evaluation of her feelings. "Thou knowest my dear sister," Phoebe wrote, "there is no one . . . that exactly feels [for] thee as I do, for I think without boasting I can truly say that my desire is for thee."[32]

Such women, whether friends or relatives, assumed an emotional centrality in each others' lives. In their diaries and letters they wrote of the joy and contentment they felt in each others' company, their sense of isolation and despair when apart. The regularity of their correspondence underlines the sincerity of their words. Women named their daughters after one another and sought to integrate dear friends into their lives after marriage.[33] As one young bride wrote to an old friend shortly after her marriage: "I want to see you and talk with you and feel that we are united by the same bonds of sympathy and congeniality as ever."[34] After years of friendship one aging woman wrote of another: "Time cannot destroy the fascination of her manner . . . her voice is music to the ear. . . ."[35] Women made elaborate presents for each other, ranging from the Quakers' frugal pies and breads to painted velvet bags and phantom bouquets.[36] When a friend died, their grief was deeply felt. Martha Jefferis was unable to write to her daughter for three weeks because of the sorrow she felt at the death of a dear friend. Such distress was not unusual. A generation earlier a young Massachusetts farm woman filled pages of her diary with her grief at the death of her "dearest friend" and transcribed the letters of condolence other women sent her. She marked the anniversary of Rachel's death each year in her diary, contrasting her faithfulness with that of Rachel's husband who had soon remarried.[37]

These female friendships served a number of emotional functions. Within this secure and empathetic world women could share sorrows, anxieties, and joys, confident that other women had experienced similar emotions. One mid-nineteenth-century rural matron in a letter to her daughter discussed this particular aspect of women's friendships: "To have such a friend as thyself to look to and sympathize with her—and enter into all her little needs and in whose bosom she could with freedom pour forth her joys and sorrows—such a friend would very much relieve the tedium of many a wearisome hour. . . ." A generation later Molly more informally underscored the importance of this same function in a letter to Helena: "Suppose I come down . . . [and] spend Sunday with you quietly," she wrote Helena ". . . that means talking all the time until you are relieved of all your latest troubles, and I of mine. . . ."[38] These were frequently troubles that apparently no man could understand. When Anne Jefferis Sheppard was first married, she and her older sister Edith (who then lived with Anne) wrote in detail to their mother of the severe depression and anxiety which they experienced. Moses Sheppard, Anne's husband, added cheerful postscripts to the sisters' letters—which he had clearly not read—remarking on Anne's and Edith's contentment. Theirs was an emotional world to which he had little access.[39]

This was, as well, a female world in which hostility and criticism of other women were discouraged, and thus a milieu in which women could develop a sense of inner security and self-esteem. As one young woman wrote to her mother's longtime friend: "I cannot sufficiently thank you for the kind unvaried affection & indulgence you have ever shown and expressed both by words and actions for me. . . . Happy would it be did all the world view me as you do, through the medium of kindness and forbearance."[40] They valued each other. Women, who had little status or power in the larger world of male concerns, possessed status and power in the lives and worlds of other women.[41]

An intimate mother-daughter relationship lay at the heart of this female world. The diaries and letters of both mothers and daughters attest to their closeness and mutual emotional dependency. Daughters routinely discussed their mother's health and activities with their own friends, expressed anxiety in cases of their mother's ill health and concern for her cares.[42] Expressions of hostility which we would today consider routine on the part of both mothers and daughters seem to have been uncommon indeed. On the contrary, this sample of families indicates that the normal relationship between mother and daughter was one of sympathy and understanding.[43] Only sickness or great geographic distance was allowed to cause extended separation. When marriage did result in such separation, both viewed the distance between them with distress.[44] Something of this sympathy and love between mothers and daughters is evident in a letter Sarah Alden Ripley, at age sixty-nine, wrote her youngest and recently married daughter: "You do not know how much I miss you, not only when I struggle in and out of my mortal envelop and pump my nightly potation and no longer pour into your sympathizing ear my senile gossip, but all the day I muse away, since the sound of your voice no longer rouses me to sympathy with your joys or sorrows. . . . You cannot know how much I miss your affectionate demonstrations."[45] A dozen aging moth-

ers in this sample of over thirty families echoed her sentiments.

Central to these mother-daughter relations is what might be described as an apprenticeship system. In those families where the daughter followed the mother into a life of traditional domesticity, mothers and other older women carefully trained daughters in the arts of housewifery and motherhood. Such training undoubtedly occurred throughout a girl's childhood but became more systematized, almost ritualistic, in the years following the end of her formal education and before her marriage. At this time a girl either returned home from boarding school or no longer divided her time between home and school. Rather, she devoted her energies on two tasks: mastering new domestic skills and participating in the visiting and social activities necessary to finding a husband. Under the careful supervision of their mothers and of older female relatives, such late-adolescent girls temporarily took over the household management from their mothers, tended their young nieces and nephews, and helped in childbirth, nursing, and weaning. Such experiences tied the generations together in shared skills and emotional interaction.[46]

Daughters were born into a female world. Their mother's life expectations and sympathetic network of friends and relations were among the first realities in the life of the developing child. As long as the mother's domestic role remained relatively stable and few viable alternatives competed with it, daughters tended to accept their mother's world and to turn automatically to other women for support and intimacy. It was within this closed and intimate female world that the young girl grew toward womanhood.

One could speculate at length concerning the absence of that mother-daughter hostility today considered almost inevitable to an adolescent's struggle for autonomy and self-identity. It is possible that taboos against female aggression and hostility were sufficiently strong to repress even that between mothers and their adolescent daughters. Yet these letters seem so alive and the interest of daughters in their mothers' affairs so vital and genuine that it is difficult to interpret their closeness exclusively in terms of repression and denial. The functional bonds that held mothers and daughters together in a world that permitted few alternatives to domesticity might well have created a source of mutuality and trust absent in societies where greater options were available for daughters than for mothers. Furthermore, the extended female network— a daughter's close ties with her own older sisters, cousins, and aunts—may well have permitted a diffusion and a relaxation of mother-daughter identification and so have aided a daughter in her struggle for identity and autonomy. None of these explanations are mutually exclusive; all may well have interacted to produce the degree of empathy evident in those letters and diaries.

At some point in adolescence, the young girl began to move outside the matrix of her mother's support group to develop a network of her own. Among the middle class, at least, this transition toward what was at the same time both a limited autonomy and a repetition of her mother's life seemed to have most frequently coincided with a girl's going to school. Indeed education appears to have played a crucial role in the lives of most of the families in this study. Attending school for a few months, for a year, or longer, was common even among daughters of relatively poor families, while middle-class girls routinely spent at least a year in boarding school.[47] These school years ordinarily marked a girl's first separation from home. They served to wean the daughter from her home, to train her in the essential social graces, and, ulti-

mately, to help introduce her into the marriage market. It was not infrequently a trying emotional experience for both mother and daughter.[48]

In this process of leaving one home and adjusting to another, the mother's friends and relatives played a key transitional role. Such older women routinely accepted the role of foster mother; they supervised the young girl's deportment, monitored her health and introduced her to their own network of female friends and kin.[49] Not infrequently women, friends from their own school years, arranged to send their daughters to the same school so that the girls might form bonds paralleling those their mothers had made. For years Molly and Helena wrote of their daughters' meeting and worried over each others' children. When Molly finally brought her daughter east to school, their first act on reaching New York was to meet Helena and her daughters. Elizabeth Bordley Gibson virtually adopted the daughters of her school chum, Eleanor Custis Lewis. The Lewis daughters soon began to write Elizabeth Gibson letters with the salutation "Dearest Mama." Eleuthera DuPont, attending boarding school in Philadelphia at roughly the same time as the Lewis girls, developed a parallel relationship with her mother's friend, Elizabeth McKie Smith. Eleuthera went to the same school and became a close friend of the Smith girls and eventually married their first cousin. During this period she routinely called Mrs. Smith "Mother." Indeed Eleuthera so internalized the sense of having two mothers that she casually wrote her sisters of her "Mamma's" visits at her "mother's" house—that is at Mrs. Smith's.[50]

Even more important to this process of maturation than their mother's friends were the female friends young women made at school. Young girls helped each other overcome homesickness and endure the crises of adolescence. They gossiped about beaux, incorporated each other into their own kinship systems, and attended and gave teas and balls together. Older girls in boarding school "adopted" younger ones, who called them "Mother."[51] Dear friends might indeed continue this pattern of adoption and mothering throughout their lives; one woman might routinely assume the nurturing role of pseudomother, the other the dependency role of daughter. The pseudomother performed for the other woman all the services which we normally associate with mothers; she went to absurd lengths to purchase items her "daughter" could have obtained from other sources, gave advice and functioned as an idealized figure in her "daughter's" imagination. Helena played such a role for Molly, as did Sarah for Jeannie. Elizabeth Bordley Gibson bought almost all Eleanor Parke Custis Lewis's necessities—from shoes and corset covers to bedding and harp strings—and sent them from Philadelphia to Virginia, a procedure that sometimes took months. Eleanor frequently asked Elizabeth to take back her purchases, have them redone, and argue with shopkeepers about prices. These were favors automatically asked and complied with. Anne Jefferis Sheppard made the analogy very explicitly in a letter to her own mother written shortly after Anne's marriage, when she was feeling depressed about their separation: "Mary Paulen is truly kind, almost acts the part of a mother and trys to aid and *comfort me,* and also to *lighten my new cares.*"[52]

A comparison of the references to men and women in these young women's letters is striking. Boys were obviously indispensable to the elaborate courtship ritual girls engaged in. In these teenage letters and diaries, however, boys appear distant and warded off—an effect produced both by the girl's sense of bonding and by a highly developed and deprecatory whimsy. Girls joked among themselves about the conceit, poor looks or af-

fectations of suitors. Rarely, especially in the eighteenth and early nineteenth centuries, were favorable remarks exchanged. Indeed, while hostility and criticism of other women were so rare as to seem almost tabooed, young women permitted themselves to express a great deal of hostility toward peer-group men.[53] When unacceptable suitors appeared, girls might even band together to harass them. When one such unfortunate came to court Sophie DuPont she hid in her room, first sending her sister Eleuthera to entertain him and then dispatching a number of urgent notes to her neighboring sister-in-law, cousins, and a visiting friend who all came to Sophie's support. A wild female romp ensued, ending only when Sophie banged into a door, lacerated her nose, and retired, with her female cohorts, to bed. Her brother and the presumably disconcerted suitor were left alone. These were not the antics of teenagers but of women in their early and mid-twenties.[54]

Even if young men were acceptable suitors, girls referred to them formally and obliquely: "The last week I received the unexpected intelligence of the arrival of a friend in Boston," Sarah Ripley wrote in her diary of the young man to whom she had been engaged for years and whom she would shortly marry. Harriet Manigault assiduously kept a lively and gossipy diary during the three years preceding her marriage, yet did not once comment upon her own engagement nor indeed make any personal references to her fiance—who was never identified as such but always referred to as Mr. Wilcox.[55] The point is not that these young women were hostile to young men. Far from it; they sought marriage and domesticity. Yet in these letters and diaries men appear as an other or out group, segregated into different schools, supported by their own male network of friends and kin, socialized to different behavior, and coached to a proper formality in courtship behavior. As a consequence, relations between young women and men frequently lacked the spontaneity and emotional intimacy that characterized the young girls' ties to each other.

Indeed, in sharp contrast to their distant relations with boys, young women's relations with each other were close, often frolicsome, and surprisingly long lasting and devoted. They wrote secret missives to each other, spent long solitary days with each other, curled up together in bed at night to whisper fantasies and secrets.[56] In 1862 one young woman in her early twenties described one such scene to an absent friend: "I have sat up to midnight listening to the confidences of Constance Kinney, whose heart was opened by that most charming of all situations, a seat on a bedside late at night, when all the household are asleep & only oneself & one's confidante survive in wakefulness. So she has told me all her loves and tried to get some confidences in return but being five or six years older than she, I know better. . . ."[57] Elizabeth Bordley and Nelly Parke Custis, teenagers in Philadelphia in the 1790s, routinely secreted themselves until late each night in Nelly's attic, where they each wrote a novel about the other.[58] Quite a few young women kept diaries, and it was a sign of special friendship to show their diaries to each other. The emotional quality of such exchanges emerges from the comments of one young girl who grew up along the Ohio frontier:

Sisters CW and RT keep diaries & allow me the inestimable pleasure of reading them and in turn they see mine—but O shame covers my face when I think of it; theirs is so much better than mine, that every time. Then I think well now I *will* burn mine but upon second thought it would deprive me the pleasure of reading theirs, for I esteem it a very great privilege indeed, as well as very improving, as we lay our hearts open to each other, it

heightens our love & helps to cherish & keep alive that sweet soothing friendship and endears us to each other by that soft attraction.[59]

Girls routinely slept together, kissed and hugged each other. Indeed, while waltzing with young men scandalized the otherwise flighty and highly fashionable Harriet Manigault, she considered waltzing with other young women not only acceptable but pleasant.[60]

Marriage followed adolescence. With increasing frequency in the nineteenth century, marriage involved a girl's traumatic removal from her mother and her mother's network. It involved, as well, adjustment to a husband, who, because he was male came to marriage with both a different world view and vastly different experiences. Not surprisingly, marriage was an event surrounded with supportive, almost ritualistic, practices. (Weddings are one of the last female rituals remaining in twentieth-century America.) Young women routinely spent the months preceding their marriage almost exclusively with other women—at neighborhood sewing bees and quilting parties or in a round of visits to geographically distant friends and relatives. Ostensibly they went to receive assistance in the practical preparations for their new home—sewing and quilting a trousseau and linen—but of equal importance, they appear to have gained emotional support and reassurance. Sarah Ripley spent over a month with friends and relatives in Boston and Hingham before her wedding; Parke Custis Lewis exchanged visits with her aunts and first cousins throughout Virginia.[61] Anne Jefferis, who married with some hesitation, spent virtually half a year in endless visiting with cousins, aunts, and friends. Despite their reassurance and support, however, she would not marry Moses Sheppard until her sister Edith and her cousin Rebecca moved into the groom's home, met his friends, and explored his personality.[62] The wedding did not take place until Edith wrote to Anne: "I can say in truth I am entirely willing thou shouldst follow him even away in the Jersey sands believing if thou are not happy in they future home it will not be any fault on his part. . . ."[63]

Sisters, cousins, and friends frequently accompanied newlyweds on their wedding night and wedding trip, which often involved additional family visiting. Such extensive visits presumably served to wean the daughter from her family of origin. As such they often contained a note of ambivalence. Nelly Custis, for example, reported homesickness and loneliness on her wedding trip. "I left my Beloved and revered Grandmamma with sincere regret," she wrote Elizabeth Bordley. "It was sometime before I could feel reconciled to traveling without her." Perhaps they also functioned to reassure the young woman herself, and her friends and kin, that though marriage might alter it would not destroy old bonds of intimacy and familiarity.[64]

Married life, too, was structured about a host of female rituals. Childbirth, especially the birth of the first child, became virtually a *rite de passage*, with a lengthy seclusion of the woman before and after delivery, severe restrictions on her activities, and finally a dramatic reemergence.[65] This seclusion was supervised by mothers, sisters, and loving friends. Nursing and weaning involved the advice and assistance of female friends and relatives. So did miscarriage.[66] Death, like birth, was structured around elaborate unisexed rituals. When Nelly Parke Custis Lewis rushed to nurse her daughter who was critically ill while away at school, Nelly received support, not from her husband, who remained on their plantation, but from her old school friend, Elizabeth Bordley. Elizabeth aided Nelly in caring for her dying daughter, cared for Nelly's other children, played a major role in the

elaborate funeral arrangements (which the father did not attend), and frequently visited the girl's grave at the mother's request. For years Elizabeth continued to be the confidante of Nelly's anguished recollections of her lost daughter. These memories, Nelly's letters make clear, were for Elizabeth alone. "Mr. L. knows nothing of this," was a frequent comment.[67] Virtually every collection of letters and diaries in my sample contained evidence of women turning to each other for comfort when facing the frequent and unavoidable deaths of the eighteenth and nineteenth centuries.[68] While mourning for her father's death, Sophie DuPont received elaborate letters and visits of condolence—all from women. No man wrote or visited Sophie to offer sympathy at her father's death.[69] Among rural Pennsylvania Quakers, death and mourning rituals assumed an even more extreme same-sex form, with men or women largely barred from the deathbeds of the other sex. Women relatives and friends slept with the dying woman, nursed her, and prepared her body for burial.[70]

Eighteenth- and nineteenth-century women thus lived in emotional proximity to each other. Friendships and intimacies followed the biological ebb and flow of women's lives. Marriage and pregnancy, childbirth and weaning, sickness and death involved physical and psychic trauma which comfort and sympathy made easier to bear. Intense bonds of love and intimacy bound together those women who, offering each other aid and sympathy, shared such stressful moments.

These bonds were often physical as well as emotional. An undeniably romantic and even sensual note frequently marked female relationships. This theme, significant throughout the stages of a woman's life, surfaced first during adolescence. As one teenager from a struggling pioneer family in the Ohio Valley wrote in her diary in 1808: "I laid with my dear R[ebecca] and a glorious good talk we had until about 4[A.M.]—O how hard I do *love* her. . . ."[71] Only a few years later Bostonian Eunice Callender carved her initials and Sarah Ripley's into a favorite tree, along with a pledge of eternal love, and then waited breathlessly for Sarah to discover and respond to her declaration of affection. The response appears to have been affirmative.[72] A half-century later urbane and sophisticated Katherine Wharton commented upon meeting an old school chum: "She was a great pet of mine at school & I thought as I watched her light figure how often I had held her in my arms—how dear she had once been to me." Katie maintained a long intimate friendship with another girl. When a young man began to court this friend seriously, Katie commented in her diary that she had never realized "how deeply I loved Eng and how fully." She wrote over and over again in that entry: "Indeed I love her!" and only with great reluctance left the city that summer since it meant also leaving Eng with Eng's new suitor.[73]

Peggy Emlen, a Quaker adolescent in Philadelphia in the 1760s, expressed similar feelings about her first cousin, Sally Logan. The girls sent love poems to each other (not unlike the ones Elizabeth Bordley wrote to Nellie Custis a generation later), took long solitary walks together, and even haunted the empty house of the other when one was out of town. Indeed Sally's absences from Philadelphia caused Peggy acute unhappiness. So strong were Peggy's feelings that her brothers began to tease about her affection for Sally and threatened to steal Sally's letters, much to both girls' alarm. In one letter that Peggy wrote the absent Sally she elaborately described the depth and nature of her feelings: "I have not words to express my impatience to see My Dear Cousin, what would I not give just now for an hours sweet conversation with her, it seems as if I had a thousand things to say to thee, yet when I see thee, everything will be forgot

thro' joy. . . . I have a very great friendship for several Girls yet it dont give me so much uneasiness at being absent from them as from thee. . . . [Let us] go and spend a day down at our place together and there unmolested enjoy each others company."[74]

Sarah Alden Ripley, a young, highly educated woman, formed a similar intense relationship, in this instance with a woman somewhat older than herself. The immediate bond of friendship rested on their atypically intense scholarly interests, but it soon involved strong emotions, at least on Sarah's part. "Friendship," she wrote Mary Emerson, "is fast twining about her willing captive the silken hands of dependence, a dependence so sweet who would renounce it for the apathy of self-sufficiency?" Subsequent letters became far more emotional, almost conspiratorial. Mary visited Sarah secretly in her room, or the two women crept away from family and friends to meet in a nearby woods. Sarah became jealous of Mary's other young friends. Mary's trips away from Boston also thrust Sarah into periods of anguished depression. Interestingly, the letters detailing their love were not destroyed but were preserved and even reprinted in a eulogistic biography of Sarah Alden Ripley.[75]

Tender letters between adolescent women, confessions of loneliness and emotional dependency, were not peculiar to Sarah Alden, Peggy Emlen, or Katie Wharton. They are found throughout the letters of the thirty-five families studied. They have, of course, their parallel today in the musings of many female adolescents. Yet these eighteenth- and nineteenth-century friendships lasted with undiminished, indeed often increased, intensity throughout the women's lives. Sarah Alden Ripley's first child was named after Mary Emerson. Nelly Custis Lewis's love for and dependence on Elizabeth Bordley Gibson only increased after her marriage. Eunice Callender remained enamored of her cousin Sarah Ripley for years and rejected as impossible the suggestion by another woman that their love might some day fade away.[76] Sophie DuPont and her childhood friend, Clementina Smith, exchanged letters filled with love and dependency for forty years while another dear friend, Mary Black Couper, wrote of dreaming that she, Sophie, and her husband were all united in one marriage. Mary's letters to Sophie are filled with avowals of love and indications of ambivalence toward her own husband. Eliza Schlatter, another of Sophie's intimate friends, wrote to her at a time of crisis: "I wish I could be with you present in the body as well as the mind & heart— I would turn your *good husband out of bed*—and snuggle into you and we would have a long talk like old times in Pine St.—I want to tell you so many things that are not *writable*. . . ."[77]

Such mutual dependency and deep affection is a central existential reality coloring the world of supportive networks and rituals. In the case of Katie, Sophie, or Eunice—as with Molly, Jeannie, and Sarah— their need for closeness and support merged with more intense demands for a love which was at the same time both emotional and sensual. Perhaps the most explicit statement concerning women's lifelong friendships appeared in the letter abolitionist and reformer Mary Grew wrote about the same time, referring to her own love for her dear friend and lifelong companion, Margaret Burleigh. Grew wrote, in response to a letter of condolence from another woman on Burleigh's death: "Your words respecting my beloved friend touch me deeply. Evidently . . . you comprehend and appreciate, as few persons do . . . the nature of the relation which existed, which exists, between her and myself. Her only surviving niece . . . also does. To me it seems to have been a closer union than that of most marriages. We know there have been other such between two men and also between two

women. And why should there not be. Love is spiritual, only passion is sexual."[78]

How then can we ultimately interpret these long-lived intimate female relationships and integrate them into our understanding of Victorian sexuality? Their ambivalent and romantic rhetoric presents us with an ultimate puzzle: the relationship along the spectrum of human emotions between love, sensuality, and sexuality.

One is tempted, as I have remarked, to compare Molly, Peggy, or Sophie's relationships with the friendships adolescent girls in the twentieth century routinely form—close friendships of great emotional intensity. Helene Deutsch and Clara Thompson have both described these friendships as emotionally necessary to a girl's psychosexual development. But, they warn, such friendships might shade into adolescent and postadolescent homosexuality.[79]

It is possible to speculate that in the twentieth century a number of cultural taboos evolved to cut short the homosocial ties of girlhood and to impel the emerging women of thirteen or fourteen toward heterosexual relationships. In contrast, nineteenth-century American society did not taboo close female relationships but rather recognized them as a socially viable form of human contact—and, as such, acceptable throughout a woman's life. Indeed it was not these homosocial ties that were inhibited but rather heterosexual leanings. While closenesss, freedom of emotional expression, and uninhibited physical contact characterized women's relationships with each other, the opposite was frequently true of male-female relationships. One could thus argue that within such a world of female support, intimacy, and ritual it was only to be expected that adult women would turn trustingly and lovingly to each other. It was a behavior they had observed and learned since childhood. A different type of emotional landscape existed in the nineteenth century, one in which Molly and Helena's love became a natural development.

Of perhaps equal significance are the implications we can garner from this framework for the understanding of heterosexual marriages in the nineteenth century. If men and women grew up as they did in relatively homogeneous and segregated sexual groups, then marriage represented a major problem in adjustment. From this perspective we could interpret much of the emotional stiffness and distance that we associate with Victorian marriage as a structural consequence of contemporary sex-role differentiation and gender-role socialization. With marriage both women and men had to adjust to life with a person who was, in essence, a member of an alien group.

I have thus far substituted a cultural or psychosocial for a psychosexual interpretation of women's emotional bonding. But there are psychosexual implications in this model which I think it only fair to make more explicit. Despite Sigmund Freud's insistence on the bisexuality of us all or the recent American Psychiatric Association decision on homosexuality, many psychiatrists today tend explicitly or implicitly to view homosexuality as a totally alien or pathological behavior—as totally unlike heterosexuality. I suspect that in essence they may have adopted an explanatory model similar to the one used in discussing schizophrenia. As a psychiatrist can speak of schizophrenia and of a borderline schizophrenic personality as both ultimately and fundamentally different from a normal or neurotic personality, so they also think of both homosexuality and latent homosexuality as states totally different from heterosexuality. With this rapidly dichotomous model of assumption, "latent homosexuality" becomes the indication of a disease in progress—seeds of a pathology which belie the reality of an individual's heterosexuality.

Yet at the same time we are well aware that cultural values can effect choices in the gender of a person's sexual partner. We, for instance, do not necessarily consider homosexual-object choice among men in prison, on shipboard or in boarding schools a necessary indication of pathology. I would urge that we expand this relativistic model and hypothesize that a number of cultures might well tolerate or even encourage diversity in sexual and nonsexual relations. Based on my research into this nineteenth-century world of female intimacy, I would further suggest that rather than seeing a gulf between the normal and the abnormal we view sexual and emotional impulses as part of a continuum or spectrum of affect gradations strongly affected by cultural norms and arrangements, a continuum influenced in part by observed and thus learned behavior. At one end of the continuum lies committed heterosexuality, at the other uncompromising homosexuality; between, a wide latitude of emotions and sexual feelings. Certain cultures and environments permit individuals a great deal of freedom in moving across this spectrum. I would like to suggest that the nineteenth century was such a cultural environment. That is, the supposedly repressive and destructive Victorian sexual ethos may have been more flexible and responsive to the needs of particular individuals than those of mid-twentieth century.

Notes

1. The most notable exception to this rule is now eleven years old: William R. Taylor and Christopher Lasch, "Two 'Kindred Spirits': Sorority and Family in New England, 1839–1846," *New England Quarterly* 36 (1963):25–41. Taylor has made a valuable contribution to the history of women and the history of the family with his concept of

"sororial" relations. I do not, however, accept the Taylor-Lasch thesis that female friendships developed in the mid-nineteenth century because of geographic mobility and the breakup of the colonial family. I have found these friendships as frequently in the eighteenth century as in the nineteenth and would hypothesize that the geographic mobility of the mid-nineteenth century eroded them as it did so many other traditional social institutions. Helen Vendler (*Review of Notable American Women, 1607–1950*, ed. Edward James and Janet James, *New York Times*, [November 5, 1972]: sec. 7) points out the significance of these friendships.

2. I do not wish to deny the importance of women's relations with particular men. Obviously, women were close to brothers, husbands, fathers, and sons. However, there is evidence that despite such closeness relationships between men and women differed in both emotional texture and frequency from those between women. Women's relations with each other, although they played a central role in the American family and American society, have been so seldom examined either by general social historians or by historians of the family that I wish in this article simply to examine their nature and analyze their implications for our understanding of social relations and social structure. I have discussed some aspects of male-female relationships in two articles: "Puberty to Menopause: The Cycle of Femininity in Nineteenth-Century America," *Feminist Studies* 1 (1973): 58–72, and, with Charles Rosenberg, "The Female Animal: Medical and Biological Views of Women in 19th Century America," *Journal of American History* 59 (1973): 331–56.

3. See Freud's classic paper on homosexuality, "Three Essays on the Theory of Sexuality," in *The Standard Edition of the Complete Psychological Works of Sigmund Freud*, trans. James Strachey (London: Hogarth Press, 1953), 7:135–72. The essays originally appeared in 1905. Prof. Roy Shafer, Department of Psychiatry, Yale University, has pointed out that Freud's view of sexual behavior was strongly influenced by nineteenth-century evolutionary thought. Within Freud's schema, genital heterosexuality marked the height of human development (Schafer, "Problems in Freud's Psychology of Women," *Journal of the American Psychoanalytic Association* 22 [1974]: 459–85).

4. For a novel and most important exposition of one theory of behavioral norms and options and its application to the study of human sexuality, see Charles Rosenberg,

"Sexuality, Class and Role," *American Quarterly* 25 (1973): 131–53.

5. See, e.g., the letters of Peggy Emlen to Sally Logan, 1768–72, Wells Morris Collection, Box 1, Historical Society of Pennsylvania; and the Eleanor Parke Custis Lewis Letters, Historical Society of Pennsylvania, Philadelphia.

6. Sarah Butler Wister was the daughter of Fanny Kemble and Pierce Butler. In 1859 she married a Philadelphia physician, Owen Wister. The novelist Owen Wister is her son. Jeannie Field Musgrove was the half-orphaned daughter of constitutional lawyer and New York Republican politician David Dudley Field. Their correspondence (1855–98) is in the Sarah Butler Wister Papers, Wister Family Papers, Historical Society of Pennsylvania.

7. Sarah Butler, Butler Place, S.C., to Jeannie Field, New York, September 14, 1855.

8. See, e.g., Sarah Butler Wister, Germantown, Pa., to Jeannie Field, New York, September 25, 1862, October 21, 1863; or Jeannie Field, New York, to Sarah Butler Wister, Germantown, July 3, 1861, January 23 and July 12, 1863.

9. Sarah Butler Wister, Germantown, to Jeannie Field, New York, June 5, 1861, February 29, 1864; Jeannie Field to Sarah Butler Wister, November 22, 1861, January 4 and June 14, 1863.

10. Sarah Butler Wister, London, to Jeannie Field Musgrove, New York, June 18 and August 3, 1870.

11. See, e.g., two of Sarah's letters to Jeannie: December 21, 1873, July 16, 1878.

12. This is the 1868–1920 correspondence between Mary Hallock Foote and Helena, a New York friend (the Mary Hallock Foote Papers are in the Manuscript Division, Stanford University). Wallace E. Stegner has written a fictionalized biography of Mary Hallock Foote (*Angle of Repose* [Garden City, N.Y.: Doubleday & Co., 1971]). See, as well, her autobiography: Mary Hallock Foote, *A Victorian Gentlewoman in the Far West: The Reminiscences of Mary Hallock Foote*, ed. Rodman W. Paul (San Marino, Calif.: Huntington Library, 1972). In many ways these letters are typical of those women wrote to other women. Women frequently began letters to each other with salutations such as "Dearest," "My Most Beloved," "You Darling Girl," and signed them "tenderly" or "to my dear dear sweet friend, good-bye." Without the least self-consciousness, one woman in her frequent letters to a female friend referred to her husband as "my other

love." She was by no means unique. See, e.g., Annie to Charlene Van Vleck Anderson, Appleton, Wis., June 10, 1871, Anderson Family Papers, Manuscript Division, Stanford University; Maggie to Emily Howland, Philadelphia, July 12, 1851, Howland Family Papers, Phoebe King Collection, Friends Historical Library, Swarthmore College; Mary Jane Burleigh to Emily Howland, Sherwood, N.Y., March 27, 1872, Howland Family Papers, Sophia Smith Collection, Smith College; Mary Black Couper to Sophia Madeleine DuPont, Wilmington, Del.: n.d. [1834] (two letters), Samuel Francis DuPont Papers, Eleutherian Mills Foundation, Wilmington, Del.; Phoebe Middleton, Concordville, Pa., to Martha Jefferis, Chester County, Pa., February 22, 1848; and see in general the correspondence (1838–49) between Rebecca Biddle of Philadelphia and Martha Jefferis, Chester County, Pa., Jefferis Family Correspondence, Chester County Historical Society, West Chester, Pa.; Phoebe Bradford Diary, June 7 and July 13, 1832, Historical Society of Pennsylvania; Sarah Alden Ripley, to Abba Allyn, Boston, n.d. [1818–20], and Sarah Alden Ripley to Sophia Bradford, November 30, 1854, in the Sarah Alden Ripley Correspondence, Schlesinger Library, Radcliffe College; Fanny Canby Ferris to Anne Biddle, Philadelphia, October 11 and November 19, 1811, December 26, 1813, Fanny Canby to Mary Canby, May 27, 1801, Mary R. Garrigues to Mary Canby, five letters n.d. [1802–8], Anne Biddle to Mary Canby, two letters n.d., May 16, July 13, and November 24, 1806, June 14, 1807, June 5, 1808, Anne Sterling Biddle Family Papers, Friends Historical Society, Swarthmore College; Harriet Manigault Wilcox Diary, August 7, 1814, Historical Society of Pennsylvania. See as well the correspondence between Harriet Manigault Wilcox's mother, Mrs. Gabriel Manigault, Philadelphia, and Mrs. Henry Middleton, Charleston, S.C., between 1810 and 1830, Cadwalader Collection, J. Francis Fisher Section, Historical Society of Pennsylvania. The basis and nature of such friendships can be seen in the comments of Sarah Alden Ripley to her sister-in-law and longtime friend, Sophia Bradford: "Hearing that you are not well reminds me of what it would be to lose your loving society. We have kept step together through a long piece of road in the weary journey of life. We have loved the same beings and wept together over their graves" (Mrs. O. J. Wister and Miss Agnes Irwin, eds., *Worthy Women of Our First Century* [Philadelphia: J. B. Lippincott & Co., 1877] p. 195).

13. Mary Hallock [Foote] to Helena, n.d. [1869–70], n.d. [1871–72], Folder 1, Mary Hallock Foote Letters, Manuscript Division, Stanford University.

14. Mary Hallock [Foote] to Helena, September 15 and 23, 1873, n.d. [October 1873], October 12, 1873.

15. Mary Hallock [Foote] to Helena, n.d. [January 1874], n.d. [Spring 1874].

16. Mary Hallock [Foote] to Helena, September 23, 1873; Mary Hallock [Foote] to Richard, December 13, 1873. Molly's and Helena's relationship continued for the rest of their lives. Molly's letters are filled with tender and intimate references, as when she wrote, twenty years later and from 2,000 miles away: "It isn't because you are good that I love you—but for the essence of you which is like perfume" (n.d. [1890s?]).

17. I am in the midst of a larger study of adult gender-roles and gender-role socialization in America, 1785–1895. For a discussion of social attitudes toward appropriate male and female roles, see Barbara Welter, "The Cult of True Womanhood: 1820–1860," *American Quarterly* 18 (Summer 1966):151–74; Anne Firor Scott, *The Southern Lady: From Pedestal to Politics, 1830–1930* (Chicago: University of Chicago Press, 1970), chaps. 1–2; Smith-Rosenberg and Rosenberg.

18. See, e.g., the letters of Peggy Emlen to Sally Logan, 1768–72, Wells Morris Collection, Box 1, Historical Society of Pennsylvania; and the Eleanor Parke Custis Lewis Letters, Historical Society of Pennsylvania.

19. See esp. Elizabeth Botts, *Family and Social Network* (London: Tavistock Publications, 1957); Michael Young and Peter Willmott, *Family and Kinship in East London*, rev. ed. (Baltimore: Penguin Books, 1964).

20. This pattern seemed to cross class barriers. A letter that an Irish domestic wrote in the 1830s contains seventeen separate references to women and but only seven to men, most of whom were relatives and two of whom were infant brothers living with her mother and mentioned in relation to her mother (Ann McGrann, Philadelphia, to Sophie M. DuPont, Philadelphia, July 3, 1834, Sophie Madeleine DuPont Letters, Eleutherian Mills Foundation).

21. Harriet Manigault Diary, June 28, 1814, and passim; Jeannie Field, New York, to Sarah Butler Wister, Germantown, April 19, 1863; Phoebe Bradford Diary, January 30, February 19, March 4, August 11, and October 14, 1832, Historical Society of Pennsylvania; Sophie M. DuPont, Brandywine, to

Henry DuPont, Germantown, July 9, 1827, Eleutherian Mills Foundation.

22. Martha Jefferis to Anne Jefferis Sheppard, July 9, 1843; Anne Jefferis Sheppard to Martha Jefferis, June 28, 1846; Ann Sterling Biddle Papers, passim, Biddle Family Papers, Friends Historical Society, Swarthmore College; Eleanor Parke Custis Lewis, Virginia, to Elizabeth Bordley Gibson, Philadelphia, November 24 and December 4, 1820, November 6, 1821.

23. Phoebe Bradford Diary, January 13, November 16–19, 1832, April 26 and May 7, 1833; Abigail Brackett Lyman to Mrs. Catling, Litchfield, Conn., May 3, 1801, collection in private hands; Martha Jefferis to Anne Jefferis Sheppard, August 28, 1845.

24. Lisa Mitchell Diary, 1860s, passim, Manuscript Division, Tulane University; Eleanor Parke Custis Lewis to Elizabeth Bordley [Gibson] February 5, 1822; Jeannie McCall, Cedar Park, to Peter McCall, Philadelphia, June 30, 1849, McCall Section, Cadwalader Collection, Historical Society of Pennsylvania.

25. Peggy Emlen to Sally Logan, May 3, 1769.

26. For a prime example of this type of letter, see Eleanor Parke Custis Lewis to Elizabeth Bordley Gibson, passim, or Fanny Canby to Mary Canby, Philadelphia, May 27, 1801; or Sophie M. DuPont, Brandywine, to Henry DuPont, Germantown, February 4, 1832.

27. Place of residence is not the only variable significance in characterizing family structure. Strong emotional ties and frequent visiting and correspondence can unite families that do not live under one roof. Demographic studies based on household structure alone fail to reflect such emotional and even economic ties between families.

28. Eleanor Parke Custis Lewis to Elizabeth Bordley Gibson, April 20 and September 25, 1848.

29. Maria Inskeep to Fanny Hampton Correspondence, 1823–60, Inskeep Collection, Tulane University Library.

30. Eunice Callender, Boston, to Sarah Ripley [Stearns], September 24 and October 29, 1803, February 16, 1805, April 29 and October 9, 1806, May 26, 1810.

31. Sophie DuPont filled her letters to her younger brother Henry (with whom she had been assigned to correspond while he was at boarding school) with accounts of family visiting (see, e.g., December 13, 1827, January 10 and March 9, 1828, February 4 and March 10, 1832; also Sophie M. DuPont to Victorine Du-

Pont Bauday, September 26 and December 4, 1827, February 22, 1828; Sophie M. DuPont, Brandywine, to Clementina B. Smith, Philadelphia, January 15, 1830; Eleuthera DuPont, Brandywine, to Victorine DuPont Bauday, Philadelphia, April 17, 1821, October 20, 1826; Evelina DuPont [Biderman] to Victorine DuPont Bauday, October 18, 1816). Other examples, from the Historical Society of Pennsylvania, are Harriet Manigault [Wilcox] Diary, August 17, September 8, October 19 and 22, December 22, 1814; Jane Zook, Westtown School, Chester County, Pa., to Mary Zook, November 13, December 7 and 11, 1870, February 26, 1871; Eleanor Parke Custis [Lewis] to Elizabeth Bordley [Gibson], March 30, 1796, February 7 and March 20, 1798; Jeannie McCall to Peter McCall, Philadelphia, November 12, 1847; Mary B. Ashew Diary, July 11 and 13, August 17, Summer and October 1858, and, from a private collection, Edith Jefferis to Anne Jefferis Sheppard, November 1841, April 5, 1842; Abigail Brackett Lyman, Northampton, Mass., to Mrs. Catling, Litchfield, Conn., May 13, 1801; Abigail Brackett Lyman, Northampton, to Mary Lord, August 11, 1800. Mary Hallock Foote vacationed with her sister, her sister's children, her aunt, and a female cousin in the summer of 1874; cousins frequently visited the Hallock farm in Milton, N.Y. In later years Molly and her sister Bessie set up a joint household in Boise, Idaho (Mary Hallock Foote to Helena, July [1874?] and passim). Jeannie Field, after initially disliking her sister-in-law, Laura, became very close to her, calling her "my little sister" and at times spending virtually every day with her (Jeannie Field [Musgrove] New York, to Sarah Butler Wister, Germantown, March 1, 8, and 15, and May 9, 1863).

32. Martha Jefferis to Anne Jefferis Sheppard, January 12, 1845; Phoebe Middleton to Martha Jefferis, February 22, 1848. A number of other women remained close to sisters and sisters-in-law across a long lifetime (Phoebe Bradford Diary, June 7, 1832, and Sarah Alden Ripley to Sophia Bradford, cited in Wister and Irwin, p. 195).

33. Rebecca Biddle to Martha Jefferis, 1838–49, passim; Martha Jefferis to Anne Jefferis Sheppard, July 6, 1846; Anne Jefferis Sheppard to Rachael Jefferis, January 16, 1865; Sarah Foulke Farquhar [Emlen] Diary, September 22, 1813, Friends Historical Library, Swarthmore College; Mary Garrigues to Mary Canby [Biddle], 1802–8, passim; Anne Biddle to Mary Canby [Biddle], May 16, July 13, and November 24, 1806, June 14, 1807, June 5, 1808.

34. Sarah Alden Ripley to Abba Allyn, n.d., Schlesinger Library.

35. Phoebe Bradford Diary, July 13, 1832.

36. Mary Hallock [Foote] to Helena, December 23 [1868 or 1869]; Phoebe Bradford Diary, December 8, 1832; Martha Jefferis and Anne Jefferis Sheppard letters, passim.

37. Martha Jefferis to Anne Jefferis Sheppard, August 3, 1849; Sarah Ripley [Stearns] Diary, November 12, 1808, January 8, 1811. An interesting note of hostility or rivalry is present in Sarah Ripley's diary entry. Sarah evidently deeply resented the husband's rapid remarriage.

38. Martha Jefferis to Edith Jefferis, March 15, 1841; Mary Hallock Foote to Helena, n.d. [1874–75?]; see also Jeannie Field, New York, to Sarah Butler Wister, Germantown, May 5, 1863, Emily Howland Diary, December 1879, Howland Family Papers.

39. Anne Jefferis Sheppard to Martha Jefferis, September 29, 1841.

40. Frances Parke Lewis to Elizabeth Bordley Gibson, April 29, 1821.

41. Mary Jane Burleigh, Mount Pleasant, S.C., to Emily Howland, Sherwood N.Y., March 27, 1872, Howland Family Papers; Emily Howland Diary, September 16, 1879, January 21 and 23, 1880; Mary Black Couper, New Castle, Del., to Sophie M. DuPont, Brandywine, April 7, 1834.

42. Harriet Manigault Diary, August 15, 21, and 23, 1814, Historical Society of Pennsylvania; Polly [Simmons] to Sophie Madeleine DuPont, February 1822; Sophie Madeleine DuPont to Victorine Bauday, December 4, 1827; Sophie Madeleine DuPont to Clementina Beach Smith, July 24, 1828, August 19, 1829; Clementina Beach Smith to Sophie Madeleine DuPont, April 29, 1831; Mary Black Couper to Sophie Madeleine DuPont, December 24, 1828, July 21, 1834. This pattern appears to have crossed class lines. When a former Sunday school student of Sophie DuPont's (and the daughter of a worker in her father's factory) wrote to Sophie she discussed her mother's health and activities quite naturally (Ann· McGrann to Sophie Madeleine DuPont, August 25, 1832; see also Elizabeth Bordley to Martha, n.d. [1797], Eleanor Parke Custis [Lewis] to Elizabeth Bordley [Gibson], May 13, 1796, July 1, 1798; Peggy Emlen to Sally Logan, January 8, 1786. All but the Emlen/Logan letters are in the Eleanor Parke Custis Lewis Correspondence, Historical Society of Pennsylvania).

43. Mrs. S. S. Dalton, "Autobiography," (Circle Valley, Utah, 1876), pp. 21–22, Bancroft Library, University of California, Berkeley; Sarah Foulke Emlen Diary, April 1809; Louisa G. Van Vleck, Appleton, Wis., to Charlena Van Vleck Anderson, Göttingen, n.d. [1875], Harriet Manigault Diary, August 16, 1814, July 14, 1815; Sarah Alden Ripley to Sophy Fisher [early 1860s], quoted in Wister and Irwin (n. 12 above), p. 212. The Jefferis family papers are filled with empathetic letters between Martha and her daughters, Anne and Edith. See, e.g., Martha Jefferis to Edith Jefferis, December 26, 1836, March 11, 1837, March 15, 1841; Anne Jefferis Sheppard to Martha Jefferis, March 17, 1841, January 17, 1847; Martha Jefferis to Anne Jefferis Sheppard, April 17, 1848, April 30, 1849. A representative letter is this of March 9, 1837 from Edith to Martha: "My heart can fully respond to the language of my own precious Mother, the absence has not diminished our affection for each other, but has, if possible, strengthened the bonds that have united us together & I have had to remark how we had been permitted to mingle in sweet fellowship and have been strengthened to bear one another's burdens. . . ."

44. Abigail Brackett Lyman, Boston, to Mrs. Abigail Brackett (daughter to mother), n.d. [1797], June 3, 1800; Sarah Alden Ripley wrote weekly to her daughter, Sophy Ripley Fisher, after the latter's marriage (Sarah Alden Ripley Correspondence, passim); Phoebe Bradford Diary, February 25, 1833, passim, 1832–33; Louisa G. Van Vleck to Charlena Van Vleck Anderson, December 15, 1873, July 4, August 15 and 29, September 19, and November 9, 1875. Eleanor Parke Custis Lewis's long correspondence with Elizabeth Bordley Gibson contains evidence of her anxiety at leaving her foster mother's home at various times during her adolescence and at her marriage, and her own longing for her daughters, both of whom had married and moved to Louisiana (Eleanor Parke Custis [Lewis] to Elizabeth Bordley [Gibson], October 13, 1795, November 4, 1799, passim, 1820s and 1830s). Anne Jefferis Sheppard experienced a great deal of anxiety on moving two days' journey from her mother at the time of her marriage. This loneliness and sense of isolation persisted through her marriage until, finally a widow, she returned to live with her mother (Anne Jefferis Sheppard to Martha Jefferis, April 1841, October 16, 1842, April 2, May 22, and October 12, 1844, September 3, 1845, January 17, 1847, May 16, June 3, and October 31, 1849; Anne Jefferis Sheppard to Susanna Lightfoot, March 23, 1845, and to Joshua Jefferis, May 14, 1854). Daughters evidently frequently slept with

their mothers—into adulthood (Harriet Manigault [Wilcox] Diary, February 19, 1815; Eleanor Parke Custis Lewis to Elizabeth Bordley Gibson, October 10, 1832). Daughters also frequently asked mothers to live with them and professed delight when they did so. See, e.g., Sarah Alden Ripley's comments to George Simmons, October 6, 1844, in Wister and Irwin, p. 185: "It is no longer 'Mother and Charles came out one day and returned the next,' for mother is one of us: she has entered the penetratice, been initiated into the mystery of the household gods, . . . Her divertissement is to mend the stockings . . . whiten sheets and napkins, . . . and take a stroll at evening with me to talk of our children, to compare our experiences, what we have learned and what we have suffered, and, last of all, to complete with pears and melons the cheerful circle about the solar lamp. . . ." We did find a few exceptions to this mother-daughter felicity (M.B. Ashew Diary, November 19, 1857, April 10 and May 17, 1858). Sarah Foulke Emlen was at first very hostile to her stepmother (Sarah Foulke Emlen Diary, August 9, 1807), but they later developed a warm supportive relationship.

45. Sarah Alden Ripley to Sophy Thayer, n.d. [1861].

46. Mary Hallock Foote to Helena [winter 1873] (no. 52); Jossie, Stevens Point, Wis., to Charlena Van Vleck [Anderson], Appleton, Wis., October 24, 1870; Pollie Chandler, Green Bay, Wis., to Charlena Van Vleck [Anderson], Appleton, n.d. [1870]; Eleuthera DuPont to Sophie DuPont, September 5, 1829; Sophie DuPont to Eleuthera DuPont, December 1827; Sophie DuPont to Victorine Bauday, December 4, 1827; Mary Gilpin to Sophie DuPont, September 26, 1827; Sarah Ripley Stearns Diary, April 2, 1809; Jeannie McCall to Peter McCall, October 27 [late 1840s]. Eleanor Parke Custis Lewis's correspondence with Elizabeth Bordley Gibson describes such an apprenticeship system over two generations—that of her childhood and that of her daughters. Indeed Eleanor Lewis's own apprenticeship was quite formal. She was deliberately separated from her foster mother in order to spend a winter of domesticity with her married sisters and her remarried mother. It was clearly felt that her foster mother's (Martha Washington) home at the nation's capital was not an appropriate place to develop domestic talents (October 13, 1795, March 30, May 13, and [summer] 1796, March 18 and April 27, 1797, October 1827).

47. Education was not limited to the daughters of the well-to-do. Sarah Foulke Emlen, the daughter of an Ohio Valley frontier farmer, for instance, attended day school for several years during the early 1800s. Sarah Ripley Stearns, the daughter of a shopkeeper in Greenfield, Mass., attended a boarding school for but three months, yet the experience seemed very important to her. Mrs. S. S. Dalton, a Mormon woman from Utah, attended a series of poor country schools and greatly valued her opportunity, though she also expressed a great deal of guilt for the sacrifices her mother made to make her education possible (Sarah Foulke Emlen Journal, Sarah Ripley Stearns Diary, Mrs. S. S. Dalton, "Autobiography").

48. Maria Revere to her mother [Mrs. Paul Revere], June 13, 1801, Paul Revere Papers, Massachusetts Historical Society. In a letter to Elizabeth Bordley Gibson, March 28, 1847, Eleanor Parke Custis Lewis from Virginia discussed the anxiety her daughter felt when her granddaughters left home to go to boarding school. Eleuthera DuPont was very homesick when away at school in Philadelphia in the early 1820s (Eleuthera DuPont, Philadelphia, to Victorine Bauday, Wilmington, Del., April 7, 1821; Eleuthera DuPont to Sophie Madeleine DuPont, Wilmington, Del., February and April 3, 1821).

49. Elizabeth Bordley Gibson, a Philadelphia matron, played such a role for the daughters and nieces of her lifelong friend, Eleanor Parke Custis Lewis, a Virginia planter's wife (Eleanor Parke Custis Lewis to Elizabeth Bordley Gibson, January 29, 1833, March 19, 1826, and passim through the collection). The wife of Thomas Gurney Smith played a similar role for Sophie and Eleuthera DuPont (see, e.g., Eleuthera DuPont to Sophie Madeleine DuPont, May 22, 1825; Rest Cope to Philema P. Swayne [niece] West Town School, Chester County, Pa., April 8, 1829, Friends Historical Library, Swarthmore College). For a view of such a social pattern over three generations, see the letters and diaries of three generations of Manigault women in Philadelphia: Mrs. Gabrielle Manigault, her daughter, Harriet Manigault Wilcox, and granddaughter, Charlotte Wilcox McCall. Unfortunately the papers of the three women are not in one family collection (Mrs. Henry Middleton, Charleston, S.C., to Mrs. Gabrielle Manigault, n.d. [mid 1800s]; Harriet Manigault Diary, vol. 1; December 1, 1813, June 28, 1814; Charlotte Wilcox McCall Diary, vol. 1, 1842, passim. All in Historical Society of Philadelphia).

50. Frances Parke Lewis, Woodlawn, Va., to Elizabeth Bordley Gibson, Philadelphia,

April 11, 1821, Lewis Correspondence; Eleuthera DuPont, Philadelphia, to Victorine DuPont Bauday, Brandywine, December 8, 1821, January 31, 1822; Eleuthera DuPont, Brandywine, to Margaretta Lammont [DuPont], Philadelphia, May 1823.

51. Sarah Ripley Stearns Diary, March 9 and 25, 1810; Peggy Emlen to Sally Logan, March and July 4, 1769; Harriet Manigault [Wilcox] Diary, vol. 1, December 1, 1813, June 28 and September 18, 1814, August 10, 1815; Charlotte Wilcox McCall Diary, 1842, passim; Fanny Canby to Mary Canby, May 27, 1801, March 17, 1804; Deborah Cope, West Town School, to Rest Cope, Philadelphia, July 9, 1828, Chester County Historical Society, West Chester, Pa.; Anne Zook, West Town School, to Mary Zook, Philadelphia, January 30, 1866, Chester County Historical Society, West Chester, Pa.; Mary Gilpin to Sophie Madeleine DuPont, February 25, 1829; Eleanor Parke Custis [Lewis] to Elizabeth Bordley [Gibson], April 27, July 2, and September 8, 1797, June 30, 1799, December 29, 1820; Frances Parke Lewis to Elizabeth Bordley Gibson, December 20, 1820.

52. Anne Jefferis Sheppard to Martha Jefferis, March 17, 1841.

53. Peggy Emlen to Sally Logan, March 1769, Mount Vernon, Va.; Eleanor Parke Custis [Lewis] to Elizabeth Bordley [Gibson], Philadelphia, April 27, 1797, June 30, 1799; Jeannie Field, New York, to Sarah Butler Wister, Germantown, July 3, 1861, January 16, 1863, Harriet Manigault Diary, August 3 and 11–13, 1814; Eunice Callender, Boston, to Sarah Ripley [Stearns], Greenfield, May 4, 1809. I found one exception to this inhibition of female hostility. This was the diary of Charlotte Wilcox McCall, Philadelphia (see, e.g., her March 23, 1842 entry).

54. Sophie M. DuPont and Eleuthera DuPont, Brandywine, to Victorine DuPont Bauday, Philadelphia, January 25, 1832.

55. Sarah Ripley [Stearns] Diary and Harriet Manigault Diary, passim.

56. Sophie Madeleine DuPont to Eleuthera DuPont, December 1827; Clementina Beach Smith to Sophie Madeleine DuPont, December 26, 1828; Sarah Faulke Emlen Diary, July 21, 1808, March 30, 1809; Annie Hethroe, Ellington, Wis., to Charlena Van Vleck [Anderson], Appleton, Wis., April 23, 1865; Frances Parke Lewis, Woodlawn, Va., to Elizabeth Bordley [Gibson], Philadelphia, December 20, 1820; Fanny Ferris to Debby Ferris, West Town School, Chester County, Pa., May 29, 1826. An excellent example of the warmth of women's comments about each other and

the reserved nature of their references to men are seen in two entries in Sarah Ripley Stearn's diary. On January 8, 1811 she commented about a young woman friend: "The amiable Mrs. White of Princeton . . . one of the loveliest most interesting creatures I ever knew, young fair and blooming . . . beloved by everyone . . . formed to please & to charm. . . ." She referred to the man she ultimately married always as "my friend" or "a friend" (February 2 or April 23, 1810).

57. Jeannie Field, New York, to Sarah Butler Wister, Germantown, April 6, 1862.

58. Elizabeth Bordley Gibson, introductory statement to the Eleanor Parke Custis Lewis Letters [1850s], Historical Society of Pennsylvania.

59. Sarah Foulke [Emlen] Diary, March 30, 1809.

60. Harriet Manigault Diary, May 26, 1815.

61. Sarah Ripley [Stearns] Diary, May 17 and October 2, 1812; Eleanor Parke Custis Lewis to Elizabeth Bordley Gibson, April 23, 1826; Rebecca Ralston, Philadelphia, to Victorine DuPont [Bauday], Brandywine, September 27, 1813.

62. Anne Jefferis to Martha Jefferis, November 22 and 27, 1840, January 13 and March 17, 1841; Edith Jefferis, Greenwich, N.J., to Anne Jefferis, Philadelphia, January 31, February 6 and February 1841.

63. Edith Jefferis to Anne Jefferis, January 31, 1841.

64. Eleanor Parke Custis Lewis to Elizabeth Bordley, November 4, 1799. Eleanor and her daughter Parke experienced similar sorrow and anxiety when Parke married and moved to Cincinnati (Eleanor Parke Custis Lewis to Elizabeth Bordley Gibson, April 23, 1826). Helena DeKay visited Mary Hallock the month before her marriage; Mary Hallock was an attendant at the wedding; Helena again visited Molly about three weeks after her marriage; and then Molly went with Helena and spent a week with Helena and Richard in their new apartment (Mary Hallock [Foote] to Helena DeKay Gilder [Spring 1874] (no. 61), May 10, 1874 [May 1874], June 14, 1874 [Summer 1874]. See also Anne Biddle, Philadelphia, to Clement Biddle (brother), Wilmington, March 12 and May 27, 1827; Eunice Callender, Boston, to Sarah Ripley [Stearns], Greenfield, Mass., August 3, 1807, January 26, 1808; Victorine DuPont Bauday, Philadelphia, to Evelina DuPont [Biderman], Brandywine, November 25 and 26, December 1, 1813; Peggy Emlen to Sally Logan, n.d. [1769–70?]; Jeannie Field, New

York, to Sarah Butler Wister, Germantown, July 3, 1861).

65. Mary Hallock to Helena DeKay Gilder [1876] (no. 81); n.d. (no. 83), March 3, 1884; Mary Ashew Diary, vol. 2, September-January, 1860; Louisa Van Vleck to Charlena Van Vleck Anderson, n.d. [1875]; Sophie DuPont to Henry DuPont, July 24, 1827; Benjamin Ferris to William Canby, February 13, 1805; Benjamin Ferris to Mary Canby Biddle, December 20, 1825; Anne Jefferis Sheppard to Martha Jefferis, September 15, 1884; Martha Jefferis to Anne Jefferis Sheppard, July 4, 1843, May 5, 1844, May 3, 1847, July 17, 1849; Jeannie McCall to Peter McCall, November 26, 1847, n.d. [late 1840s]. A graphic description of the ritual surrounding a first birth is found in Abigail Lyman's letter to her husband Erastus Lyman, October 18, 1810.

66. Fanny Ferris to Anne Biddle, November 19, 1811; Eleanor Parke Custis Lewis to Elizabeth Bordley Gibson, November 4, 1799, April 27, 1827; Martha Jefferis to Anne Jefferis Sheppard, January 31, 1843, April 4, 1844; Martha Jefferis to Phoebe Sharpless Middleton, June 4, 1846; Anne Jefferis Sheppard to Martha Jefferis, August 20, 1843, February 12, 1844; Maria Inskeep, New Orleans, to Mrs. Fanny G. Hampton, Bridgeton, N.J., September 22, 1848; Benjamin Ferris to Mary Canby, February 14, 1805; Fanny Ferris to Mary Canby [Biddle], December 2, 1816.

67. Eleanor Parke Custis Lewis to Elizabeth Bordley Gibson. October-November 1820, passim.

68. Emily Howland to Hannah, September 30, 1866; Emily Howland Diary, February 8, 11, and 27, 1880; Phoebe Bradford Diary, April 12 and 13, and August 4, 1833; Eunice Callender, Boston, to Sarah Ripley [Stearns], Greenwich, Mass., September 11, 1802, August 26, 1810; Mrs. H. Middleton, Charleston, to Mrs. Gabrielle Manigault, Philadelphia, n.d. [mid 1800s]; Mrs. H. C. Paul to Mrs. Jeannie McCall, Philadelphia, n.d. [1840s]; Sarah Butler Wister, Germantown, to Jeannie Field [Musgrove], New York, April 22, 1864; Jeannie Field [Musgrove] to Sarah Butler Wister, August 25, 1861, July 6, 1862; S. B. Raudolph to Elizabeth Bordley [Gibson], n.d. [1790s]. For an example of similar letters between men, see Henry Wright to Peter McCall, December 10, 1852; Charles McCall to Peter McCall, January 4, 1860, March 22, 1864; R. Mercer to Peter McCall, November 29, 1872.

69. Mary Black [Couper] to Sophie Madeleine DuPont, February 1827, [November 1, 1834], November 12, 1834, two letters [late

November 1834]; Eliza Schlatter to Sophie Madeleine DuPont, November 2, 1834.

70. For a few of the references to death rituals in the Jefferis papers see: Martha Jefferis to Anne Jefferis Sheppard, September 28, 1843, August 21 and September 25, 1844, January 11, 1846, summer 1848, passim; Anne Jefferis Sheppard to Martha Jefferis, August 20, 1843; Anne Jefferis Sheppard to Rachel Jefferis, March 17, 1863, February 9, 1868. For other Quaker families, see Rachel Biddle to Anne Biddle, July 23, 1854; Sarah Foulke Farquhar [Emlen] Diary, April 30, 1811, February 14, 1812; Fanny Ferris to Mary Canby, August 31, 1810. This is not to argue that men and women did not mourn together. Yet in many families women aided and comforted women and men, men. The same-sex death ritual was one emotional option available to nineteenth-century Americans.

71. Sarah Foulke [Emlen] Diary, December 29, 1808.

72. Eunice Callender, Boston, to Sarah Ripley [Stearns] Greenfield, Mass., May 24, 1803.

73. Katherine Johnstone Brinley [Wharton] Journal, April 26, May 30, and May 29, 1856, Historical Society of Pennsylvania.

74. A series of roughly fourteen letters written by Peggy Emlen to Sally Logan (1768–71) has been preserved in the Wells Morris Collection, Box 1, Historical Society of Pennsylvania (see esp. May 3 and July 4, 1769, January 8, 1768).

75. The Sarah Alden Ripley Collection, the Arthur M. Schlesinger, Sr., Library, Radcliffe College, contains a number of Sarah Alden Ripley's letters to Mary Emerson. Most of these are undated, but they extend over a number of years and contain letters written both before and after Sarah's marriage. The eulogistic biographical sketch appeared in Wister and Irwin (n. 12 above). It should be noted that Sarah Butler Wister was one of the editors who sensitively selected Sarah's letters.

76. See Sarah Alden Ripley to Mary Emerson, November 19, 1823. Sarah Alden Ripley routinely, and one must assume ritualistically, read Mary Emerson's letters to her infant daughter, Mary. Eleanor Parke Custis Lewis reported doing the same with Elizabeth Bordley Gibson's letters, passim. Eunice Callender, Boston, to Sarah Ripley [Stearns], October 19, 1808.

77. Mary Black Couper to Sophie M. DuPont, March 5, 1832. The Clementina Smith–Sophie DuPont correspondence of 1,678 letters is in the Sophie DuPont Correspondence.

The quotation is from Eliza Schlatter, Mount Holly, N.J., to Sophie DuPont, Brandywine, August 24, 1834. I am indebted to Anthony Wallace for informing me about this collection.

78. Mary Grew, Providence, R.I., to Isabel Howland, Sherwood, N.Y., April 27, 1892,

Howland Correspondence, Sophia Smith Collection, Smith College.

79. Helena Deutsch, *Psychology of Women* (New York: Grune & Stratton, 1944), vol. 1, chaps. 1–3; Clara Thompson, *On Women*, ed. Maurice Green (New York: New American Library, 1971).

JAMES C. MOHR
Abortion in America

If we observe nineteenth-century society through women's eyes, surely no statistic was as significant as the one that marked the decline in the average number of children borne by each woman. Childbirth was a time of terror; as James C. Mohr shows, many women sought actively to control the number of times they faced it. When unsuccessful in avoiding pregnancies, they attempted to abort them. The methods of the times were dangerous, but until the 1840s the women were rarely censured by the community if fetal movement had not been felt. The vigorous attack on abortion after 1840 may well have been a response to the growing willingness of married women to attempt it. After 1840 an act that had been dealt with in a biological context was given ideological overtones. What does the debate on abortion policy reveal about public attitudes toward women and their place in the family and in society?

ABORTION IN AMERICA, 1800–1825

In the absence of any legislation whatsoever on the subject of abortion in the United States in 1800, the legal status of the practice was governed by the traditional British common law as interpreted by the local courts of the new American states. For centuries prior to 1800 the key to the common law's attitude toward

abortion had been a phenomenon associated with normal gestation known as quickening. Quickening was the first perception of fetal movement by the pregnant woman herself. Quickening generally occurred near the midpoint of gestation, late in the fourth or early in the fifth month, though it could and still does vary a good deal from one woman to another. The common law did not formally recognize the existence of a fetus in criminal cases until it had quickened. After quickening, the expulsion and destruction of a fetus without due cause was considered a crime, because the fetus itself had manifested some semblance of a separate existence: the ability to move. The crime was qualitatively different from the destruction of a human being, however, and punished less harshly. Before quickening, actions that had the effect of terminating what turned out to have been an early pregnancy were not considered criminal under the common law in effect in England and the United States in 1800.[1]

Both practical and moral arguments lay behind the quickening distinction. Practically, because no reliable tests for pregnancy existed in the early nineteenth century, quickening alone could confirm with absolute certainty that a woman really was pregnant. Prior to quickening, each of the telltale signs of pregnancy could, at least in theory, be explained in alternative ways by physicians of the day. Hence, either a doctor or a woman herself could take actions designed to restore menstrual flow after one or more missed periods on the assumption that something might be unnaturally "blocking" or "obstructing" her normal cycles, and if left untreated the obstruction would wreak real harm upon the woman. Medically, the procedures for removing a blockage were the same as those for inducing an early abortion. Not until the obstruction moved could either a physician or a woman, regardless of their suspicions, be completely certain that it was a "natural" blockage—a pregnancy—rather than a potentially dangerous situation. Morally, the question of whether or not a fetus was "alive" had been the subject of philosophical and religious debate among honest people for at least 5000 years. The quickening doctrine itself appears to have entered the British common law tradition by way of the tangled disputes of medieval theologians over whether or not an impregnated ovum possessed a soul.[2] The

upshot was that American women in 1800 were legally free to attempt to terminate a condition that might turn out to have been a pregnancy until the existence of that pregnancy was incontrovertibly confirmed by the perception of fetal movement.

An ability to suspend one's modern preconceptions and to accept the early nineteenth century on its own terms regarding the distinction between quick and unquick is absolutely crucial to an understanding of the evolution of abortion policy in the United States. However doubtful the notion appears to modern readers, the distinction was virtually universal in America during the early decades of the nineteenth century and accepted in good faith. Perhaps the strongest evidence of the tenacity and universality of the doctrine in the United States was the fact that American courts pointedly sustained the most lenient implications of the quickening doctrine even after the British themselves had abandoned them. . . .

Because women believed themselves to be carrying inert non-beings prior to quickening, a potential for life rather than life itself, and because the common law permitted them to attempt to rid themselves of suspected and unwanted pregnancies up to the point when the potential for life gave a sure sign that it was developing into something actually alive, some American women did practice abortion in the early decades of the nineteenth century. One piece of evidence for this conclusion was the ready access American women had to abortifacient information from 1800 onward. A chief source of such information was the home medical literature of the era.

Home medical manuals characteristically contained abortifacient information in two different sections. One listed in explicit detail a number of procedures that might release "obstructed menses" and the other identified a number of specific things to be avoided in a suspected pregnancy because they were thought to bring on abortion. Americans probably consulted William Buchan's *Domestic Medicine* more frequently than any other home medical guide during the first decades of the nineteenth century.[3] Buchan suggested several courses of action designed to restore menstrual flow if a period was missed. These included bloodletting, bathing, iron and quinine concoctions, and if those failed, "a tea-spoonful of the tincture of black hellebore [a violent purgative] . . . twice a day in a cup of warm water." Four pages later he listed among "the common causes" of abortion "great evacuations [and] vomiting," exactly as would be produced by the treatment he urged for suppressed menses. Later in pregnancy a venturesome, or desperate, woman could try some of the other abortion inducers he ticked off: "violent exercise; raising great weights; reaching too high; jumping, or stepping from an eminence; strokes [strong blows] on the belly; [and] falls."[4] . . .

Like most early abortion material, Buchan's . . . advice harked back to almost primordial or instinctual methods of ending a pregnancy. Bloodletting, for example, was evidently thought to serve as a surrogate period; it was hoped that bleeding from any part of the body might have the same flushing effect upon the womb that menstrual bleeding was known to have. This primitive folk belief lingered long into the nineteenth century, well after bleeding was abandoned as medical therapy in other kinds of cases, and it was common for abortionists as late as the 1870s to pull a tooth as part of their routine.[5] . . .

In addition to home medical guides and health manuals addressed to women, abortions and abortifacient information were also available in the United States from midwives and midwifery texts.[6] . . .

Herbal healers, the so-called Indian doctors, and various other irregular practitioners also helped spread abortifacient information in the United States during the early decades of the nineteenth century. Their surviving pamphlets, of which Peter Smith's 1813 brochure entitled "The Indian Doctor's Dispensary" is an example, contained abortifacient recipes that typically combined the better-known cathartics with native North American ingredients thought to have emmenagogic properties. For "obstructed menses" Smith recommended a concoction he called "Dr. Reeder's chalybeate." The key ingredients were myrrh and aloes, combined with liquor, sugar, vinegar, iron dust, ivy, and Virginia or seneca snakeroot.[7] A sweet-and-sour cocktail like that may or may not have induced abortion, but must certainly have jolted the system of any woman who tried one. . . .

Finally, and most importantly, America's regular physicians, those who had formal medical training either in the United States or in Great Britain or had been apprenticed under a regular doctor, clearly possessed the physiological knowledge and the surgical techniques necessary to terminate a pregnancy by mechanical means. They knew that dilation of the cervix at virtually any stage of gestation would generally bring on uterine contractions that would in turn lead to the expulsion of the contents of the uterus. They knew that any irritation introduced into the uterus would have the same effect. They knew that rupturing the amniotic sac, especially in the middle and later months of pregnancy, would usually also induce contractions and expulsion, regardless of whether the fetus was viable. Indeed, they were taught in their lecture courses and in their textbooks various procedures much more complex than a simple abortion, such as in utero decapitation and fetal pulverization, processes they were instructed to employ in lieu of the even more horribly dangerous Caesarean section. Like the general public, they knew the drugs and herbs most commonly used as abortifacients and emmenagogues, and also like the general public, they believed such preparations to have been frequently effective.[8] . . .

This placed great pressure on physicians to provide what amounted to abortion services early in pregnancy. An unmarried girl who feared herself pregnant, for example, could approach her family doctor and ask to be treated for menstrual blockage. If he hoped to retain the girl and her family as future patients, the physician would have little choice but to accept the girl's assessment of the situation, even if he suspected otherwise. He realized that every member of his profession would testify to the fact that he had no totally reliable means of distinguishing between an early pregnancy, on the one hand, and the amenorrhea that the girl claimed, on the other. Consequently, he treated for obstruction, which involved exactly the same procedures he would have used to induce an early abortion, and wittingly or unwittingly terminated the pregnancy. Regular physicians were also asked to bring to a safe conclusion abortions that irregulars or women themselves had initiated. . . . And through all of this the physician might bear in mind that he could never be held legally guilty of wrongdoing. No statutes existed anywhere in the United States on the subject of abortion, and the common law . . . considered abortion actionable only after a pregnancy had quickened. No wonder then that Heber C. Kimball, recalling his courtship with a woman he married in 1822, claimed that she had been "taught . . . in our young days, when she got into the family way, to send for a doctor and get rid of the child"; a course that she followed.[9]

In summary, then, the practice of aborting unwanted pregnancies was, if not common, almost certainly not rare in the United States during the first decades of the nineteenth century. A knowledge of various drugs, potions, and techniques was available from home medical guides, from health books for women, from midwives and irregular practitioners, and from trained physicians. Substantial evidence suggests that many American women sought abortions, tried the standard techniques of the day, and no doubt succeeded some proportion of the time in terminating unwanted pregnancies. Moreover, this practice was neither morally nor legally wrong in the eyes of the vast majority of Americans, provided it was accomplished before quickening.

The actual number of abortions in the United States prior to the advent of any statutes regulating its practice simply cannot be known. But an equally significant piece of information about those abortions can be gleaned from the historical record. It concerns the women who were having them. Virtually every observer through the middle of the 1830s believed that an overwhelming percentage of the American women who sought and succeeded in having abortions did so because they feared the social consequences of an illegitimate pregnancy, not because they wanted to limit their fertility per se. The doctor who uncovered the use of snakeroot as an abortifacient, for example, related that in all of the many instances he heard about "it was taken by women who had indulged in illegitimate love."[10]

In short, abortion was not thought to be a means of family limitation in the United States, at least on any significant scale, through the first third of the nineteenth century. This was hardly surprising in a largely rural and essentially preindustrial society, whose birthrates were exceeding any ever recorded in a European nation.[11] One could, along with medical student [Thomas] Massie, be less than enthusiastic about such an "unnatural" practice as abortion, yet tolerate it as the "recourse . . . of the victim of passion . . . the child of nature" who was driven by "an unrelenting world" unable to forgive any "deviation from what they have termed virtue."[12] Consequently, Americans in the early nineteenth century could and did look the other way when they encountered abortion. Nothing in their medical knowledge or in the rulings of their courts compelled them to do otherwise, and, as Massie indicated, there was considerable compassion for the women involved. It would be nearly midcentury before the perception of who was having abortions for what reasons would begin to shift in the United States, and that shift would prove to be one of the critical developments in the evolution of American abortion policy.

A final point remains to be made about abortion in the United States during the first decades of the nineteenth century. Most observers appeared to consider it relatively safe, at least by the medical standards of the day, rather than extremely dangerous. . . . This too must have reassured women who decided to risk an abortion before quickening. According to the lecture notes of one of his best students, Walter Channing told his Harvard classes that abortion could be troublesome when produced by external blows, because severe internal hemorrhage would be likely, but that generally considered, "abortion [was] not so dangerous as commonly supposed."[13]

The significance of these opinions lay less in whether or not they were accurate than in the fact that writers on abortion, including physicians, saw no reason to stress the dangers attendant to the process. Far from it. They were skeptical about poisons and purgatives, but appear to have assessed physically induced abortions as medically acceptable risks by the standards of the day, especially if brought on during the period of pregnancy when both popular belief and the public courts condoned them anyhow. Here again was a significant early perception that would later change. That change, like the shift in the perception of who was having abortions for what purposes, would also have an impact on the evolution of American abortion policy. . . .

THE SOCIAL CHARACTER OF ABORTION IN AMERICA, 1840–1880

Before 1840 abortion was perceived in the United States primarily as a recourse of the desperate, especially of the young woman in trouble who feared the wrath of an overexacting society. After 1840, however, evidence began to accumulate that the social character of the practice had changed. A high proportion of the women whose abortions contributed to the soaring incidence of that practice in the United States between 1840 and 1880 appeared to be married, native-born, Protestant women, frequently of middle- or upper-class status. The data came from disparate sources, some biased and some not, but in the end proved compelling.

Even before the availability of reliable evidence confirmed that the nation's birthrates were starting to plummet, observers noticed that abortion more and more frequently involved married women rather than single women in trouble. Professor Hugh L. Hodge of the University of Pennsylvania, one of the first physicians in the United States to speak out about abortion in anything approaching a public forum, lectured his introductory obstetrics students in 1839 that abortion was fast becoming a prominent feature of American life. Hodge still considered women trying "to destroy the fruit of illicit pleaure" to be the ones most often seeking abortions, but he alerted his students to the fact that "married women, also, from the fear of labor, from indisposition to have the care, the expense, or the trouble of children, or some other motive" were more and more frequently requesting "that the embryo be destroyed by their medical attendant." Hodge attributed a good deal of this activity to the quickening doctrine, which allowed "women whose moral character is, in other respects, without reproach; mothers who are devoted, with an ardent and self-denying affection, to the children who already constitute[d] their family [to be] perfectly indifferent respecting the foetus in the utero."[14] . . .

Opinion was divided regarding the social status of the women who accounted for the great upsurge of abortion during the middle period of the nineteenth century. While most observers agreed "all classes of society, rich and poor" were involved to some extent, many thought that the middle and upper classes practiced abortion more extensively than the lower classes.[15] The Michigan State Medical Society in 1859 declared that abortion "pervade[d] all ranks" in that state.[16] The Medical Society of Buffalo pointed out that same year "now we have ladies, yes, *educated and refined ladies*" involved as well.[17] On the other hand, court cases revealed at least a sprinkling of lower-class women, servant girls, and the like. . . .

Although the going price for an abortion varied tremendously according to place, time, practitioner, and patient, abortions appear to have been generally quite expensive. Regular physicians testified repeatedly throughout the period that the abortion business was enormously lucrative. Those doctors pledged not to perform abortions bitterly resented men like the Boston botanic indicted for manslaughter in an abortion case in 1851, who posted $8000 bond and returned to his offices, at a time when the average university professor in the United States earned under $2000 per year.[18] . . .

When women turned from regulars to the commercial abortionists, the prices were still not cheap. Itinerants and irregulars generally tried to charge whatever they judged the traffic would bear, which could vary anywhere from $5 to $500. During the 1840s, for example, Madame Restell charged $5 for an initial visit and diagnosis, then negotiated the price of the operation "according to the wealth and liberality of the parties." In a case for which she was indicted in 1846 she asked a young woman about "her beau's circumstances" before quoting a figure, and then tried to get $100 when she found out the man was a reasonably successful manufacturer's representative. The man thought that was too costly, and only after extensive haggling among go-betweens was a $75 fee agreed upon.[19] . . .

Despite the apparent gradual leveling of prices, however, the abortion business remained a profitable commercial venture well into the 1870s. Anthony Comstock, the single-minded leader of a massive anti-obscenity campaign launched in the United States during the 1870s, kept meticulous and extensive records of all of the people he helped arrest while operating as a special agent of the Post Office Department. Between 1872 and 1880 Comstock and his associates aided in the indictment of 55 persons whom Comstock identified as abortionists. The vast majority were very wealthy and posted large bonds with ease. . . .

. . . abortion entered the mainstream of American life during the middle decades of the nineteenth century. While the unmarried and the socially desperate continued to have recourse to it as they had earlier in the century, abortion also became highly visible, much more frequently practiced, and quite common as a means of family limitation among white, Protestant, native-born wives of middle- and upper-class standing. These dramatic changes, in turn, evoked sharp comment from two ideologically opposed groups in American society, each of which either directly or indirectly blamed the other for the shift in abortion patterns. On one side of the debate were the antifeminists, led by regular physicians, and on the other side were the nation's feminists. Both groups agreed that abortion had become a large-scale and socially significant phenomenon in American life, but they disagreed over the reasons why.

Before examining the two chief explanations put forward by contemporaries for the striking shifts in the incidence and the character of abortion in the United States after 1840, two observations may be worth making. First, it is never easy to understand why people do what they do even in the most straightforward of situations; it is nearly impossible to know with certainty the different reasons, rational and irrational, why people in the past might have taken such a psychologically loaded action as the termination of a suspected pregnancy. Second, most participants on both sides of the contemporary debate over why so many American women began to practice abortion after 1840 actually devoted most of their attention to the question of why American women wanted to limit their fertility. This confirmed that abortion was important between 1840 and 1880 primarily as a means of family limitation, but such discussions offer only marginal help in understanding why so many American women turned to abortion itself as a means toward that end.

Cultural anthropologists argue that abortion has been practiced widely and frequently in pre-industrial societies at least in part because "it is a woman's method [of limiting fertility] and can be practiced without the man's knowledge."[20] This implies a sort of women's conspiracy to limit population, which would be difficult to demonstrate in the context of nineteenth-century America. Nonetheless, there is some evidence, though it must be considered carefully, to suggest that an American variant of this proposition may have been at least one of the reasons why abortion became such a common form of family limitation in the United States during the period. A number of physicians, as will become evident, certainly believed that one of the keys to the upsurge of abortion was the fact that it was a uniquely female practice, which men could neither control nor prevent. . . .

Earlier in the century observers had alleged that the tract literature and lecturers of the women's rights movement advocated family planning and disseminated abortifacient information.[21] In 1859 Harvard professor Walter Channing reported the opinion that "women for whom this office of foeticide, unborn-child-killing, is committed, are *strong-minded*," and no later writer ever accused them of being weak-minded.[22] . . .

The most common variant of the view that abortion was a manifestation of the women's rights movement hinged upon the word "fashion." Over and over men claimed that women who aborted did so because they cared more about scratching for a better perch in society than they did about raising children. They dared not waste time on the latter lest they fall behind in the former. Women, in short, were accused of being aggressively self-indulgent. Some women, for example, had "the effrontery to say boldly, that they have neither the time nor inclination to nurse babies"; others exhibited "self-indulgence in most disgusting forms"; and many of the women practicing abortion were described as more interested in "selfish and personal ends" or "fast living" than in the maternity for which God had supposedly created them.[23] . . . For this reason, some doctors urged that feticide be made a legal ground for divorce.[24] A substantial number of writers between 1840 and 1880, in other words, were willing to portray women who had abortions as domestic subversives. . . .

Notwithstanding the possibility that recourse to abortion sometimes reflected the rising consciousness of the women who had them, and notwithstanding the fact that some males, especially regular physicians, were distinctly uneasy about the practice because of what its ultimate effects upon the social position of women might be, the relationship between abortion and feminism in the nineteenth century nevertheless remained indirect and ironical. This becomes evident when the arguments of the feminists themselves are analyzed. One of the most forceful early statements of what subsequently became the feminist position on abortion was made in the 1850s in a volume entitled *The Unwelcome Child*.[25] The author, Henry C. Wright, asserted that women alone had the right to say when they would become pregnant and blamed the tremendous outburst of abortion in America on selfishly sensual husbands. Wright's volume was more interesting than other similar tracts, however, because he published a large number of letters from women detailing the circumstances under which they had sought abortions.

One of Wright's letters was from a woman who had her first abortion in 1841, because her one-year-old first born was sick and her husband was earning almost nothing. She "consulted a lady friend, and by her persuasion and assistance, killed" the fetus she was carrying. When she found herself pregnant again shortly thereafter she "consulted a physician. . . . He was ready with his logic, his medicines and instruments, and told me how to destroy it. After experimenting on myself three months, I was successful. I killed my child about five months after conception." She steeled herself to go full term with her next pregnancy and to "endure" an addition to her impoverished and unhappy household. When pregnant again she "employed a doctor, to kill my child, and in the destruction of it . . . ended my power to be a mother." The woman's point throughout, however, was that abortion "was most repulsive" to her and her recourse to it "rendered [her] an object of loathing to [her]self." Abortion was not a purposeful female conspiracy, but an undesirable necessity forced by thoughtless men. As this woman put it: "I was the veriest slave alive."[26] . . .

The attitudes expressed by Wright's correspondents in the 1840s and 1850s became the basis of the official position of American feminists toward abortion after the Civil War. As Elizabeth Cady Stanton phrased it, the practice was one more result of "the degradation of woman" in the nineteenth century, not of woman's rising consciousness or expanding opportunities outside the home.[27] . . . The remedy to the problem of abortion in the United States, in their view, was not legalized abortion open to all but *"the education and enfranchisement of women"* which would make abortion unnecessary in a future world of egalitarian respect and sexual discretion.[28] In short, most feminists, though they agreed completely with other observers that abortion was endemic in America by midcentury, did not blame the increase on the rising ambitions of women but asserted with Matilda E. J. Gage "that this crime of 'child murder,' 'abortion,' 'infanticide,' lies at the door of the male sex."[29] The *Woman's Advocate* of Dayton, Ohio, put it even more forcefully in 1869: "Till men learn to check their sensualism, and leave their wives free to choose their periods of maternity, let us hear no more invectives against women for the destruction of prospective unwelcome children, whose dispositions, made miserable by unhappy ante-natal conditions, would only make their lives a curse to themselves and others."[30] . . .

Despite the blame and recrimination evoked by the great upsurge of abortion in the United States in the nineteenth century, some of which was directed at women and some at men, it appears likely that most decisions to use abortion probably involved couples conferring together, not just men imposing their wills or women acting unilaterally, and that abortion was the result of diffuse pressures, not merely the rising consciousness of women or the tyrannical aggressions of men. American men and women wanted to express their sexuality and mutual affections, on the one hand, and to limit their fertility, on the other. Abortion was neither desirable nor undesirable in itself, but rather one of the few available means of reconciling and realizing those two higher priorities. And it seems likely that the man and woman agreed to both of those higher priorities in most instances, thus somewhat mooting in advance the question of which one was more responsible for the decisions that made abortion a common phenomenon in mid-nineteenth-century America.[31]

Court records provide one source of evidence for the mutuality of most abortion decisions. Almost every nineteenth-century abortion case that was written up, whether in the popular press, in medical journals, or in the official proceedings of state supreme courts, involved the agreement of both the man and the woman. There is no record of any man's ever having sued any woman for aborting his child. . . .

Perhaps the best evidence for the likely mutuality of most abortion decisions is contained in the diary that Lester Frank Ward, who later became one of America's most famous sociologists, kept as a newly-wed in the 1860s. Though Ward was unique in writing down the intimate decisions that he and his wife had to make, the couple seemed otherwise typical young Americans, almost as Tocqueville might have described them, anxious for further education and ambitious to get ahead quickly. Both Ward and his wife understood that a child would overburden their limited resources and reduce the probability of ever realizing either their individual goals of self-improvement or their mutual goals as a couple. They avoided pregnancy in pre-marital intercourse, then continued to avoid it after their marriage in August 1862. Not until early in 1864 did Lizzie Ward become pregnant. In March, without consulting her husband, she obtained "an effective remedy" from a local woman, which made her very sick for two days but helped her to terminate

her pregnancy. She probably took this action after missing three or four periods; it was still early enough in gestation that her husband did not realize she was pregnant but late enough that lactation had begun. Ward noted in his diary that "the proof" she had been pregnant was "the milk" that appeared after the abortion.[32]

Anti-feminists might have portrayed Lizzie Ward's action as diabolical, a betrayal of duty. Feminists might have viewed it as the only recourse open to a female who wanted both to further her own education and to remain on good terms with an ambitious spouse who would certainly have sacrificed his wife's goals to child-rearing, while he pursued his own. But the decision was really the result of a pre-existing consensus between the two of them. Though Ward had not been party to the process in a legal or direct sense, which may go some distance toward confirming the role of abortion as a more uniquely female method of family limitation than contraception, he was clearly delighted that his wife was "out of danger" and would not be having a child. After this brush with family responsibility, the Wards tried a number of new methods of contraception, which they presumably hoped would be more effective than whatever they had been using to avoid pregnancy before Lizzie had to resort to abortion. These included both "pills" and "instruments." Not until the summer of 1865, after Ward had obtained a decent job in Washington, did the couple have a baby.[33]

Abortion had been for the Wards what it apparently also was for many other American couples: an acceptable means toward a mutually desirable end, one of the only ways they had to allow themselves both to express their sexuality and affection toward each other with some degree of frequency and to postpone family responsibilities until they thought they were better prepared to raise children. The line of acceptability for most

Americans trying to reconcile these twin priorities ran just about where Lizzie Ward had drawn it. Infanticide, the destruction of a baby after its birth, was clearly unacceptable, and so was abortion after quickening, though that was a much grayer area than infanticide. But abortion before quickening, like contraception itself, was an appropriate and legally permissible method of avoiding unwanted children. And it had one great advantage, as the Wards learned, over contraception: it worked. As more and more women began to practice abortion, however, and as the practice changed from being invisible to being visible, from being quantitatively insignificant to being a systematic practice that terminated a substantial number of pregnancies after 1840, and from being almost entirely a recourse of the desperate and the socially marginal to being a commonly employed procedure among the middle and upper classes of American society, state legislators decided to reassess their policies toward the practice. Between 1840 and 1860 law-makers in several states began to respond to the increase of abortion in American life.

NOTES

1. The quickening doctrine went back to the thirteenth century in England and was well established by the time Coke wrote his famous commentaries in the first half of the seventeenth century. On quickening in the common law see Cyril C. Means, Jr., "The Law of New York concerning Abortion and the Status of the Foetus, 1664–1968: A Case of Cessation of Constitutionality," *New York Law Forum*, XIV, No. 3 (Fall 1968), 419–426.

2. Ibid. 411–419, and John T. Noonan, Jr., "An Almost Absolute Value in History," in John T. Noonan, Jr., ed., *The Morality of Abortion* (Cambridge, Mass., 1970), 1–59, represent two learned summaries, from different perspectives, on the long philosophical debate over the legal status of abortion in the Western world since the time of the Greeks.

3. The full title was *Domestic Medicine, or a Treatise on the Prevention and Cure of Diseases by Regimen and Simple Medicines.* Buchan's volume was published in Philadelphia as early as 1782, where it went through many editions. The 1816 edition, published in New Haven, Connecticut, carried the subtitle: *With an Appendix, Containing a Dispensatory for the Use of Private Practitioners.* This remarkably successful book continued to be reprinted in America through 1850.

4. Buchan, *Domestic Medicine*, 400, 403–404.

5. See, for example, Frederick Hollick, *Diseases of Women, Their Causes and Cure Familiarly Explained: With Practical Hints for Their Prevention, and for the Preservation of Female Health: For Every Female's Private Use* (New York, 1849), 150; Edward H. Dixon, *Woman and Her Diseases, from the Cradle to the Grave: Adapted Exclusively to Her Instruction in the Physiology of Her System, and All the Diseases of Her Critical Periods* (New York, 1847), 254–255. . . .

6. For the continued reputation of midwives as abortionists in nineteenth-century America see George Ellington, *The Women of New York, or the Under-World of the Great City* (New York, 1869), 399–400.

7. Peter Smith, "The Indian Doctor's Dispensary, Being Father Peter Smith's Advice Respecting Diseases and Their Cure; Consisting of Prescriptions for Many Complaints: And a Description of Medicines, Simple and Compound, Showing Their Virtues and How to Apply Them," [1813] reproduced in J. U. Lloyd, ed., *Bulletin of the Lloyd Library of Botany, Pharmacy and Materia Medica* (1901), Bull. #2, Reproduction Series #2, 46–47.

8. John Burns, *Observations on Abortion: Containing an Account of the Manner in Which It Takes Place, the Causes Which Produce It, and the Method of Preventing or Treating It* (Troy, New York, 1808), 73–81. . . .

9. Heber C. Kimball in the *Journal of Discourses*, 26 vols. (Liverpool, 1857), V, 91–92. Kimball, it should be pointed out, was not an unbiased observer, which was probably why he would testify so straightforwardly about abortion. He was a leader of the Mormon church in Utah in 1857 when he made the statement quoted, and the Mormons, who were under attack on the polygamy issue, frequently counterattacked by pointing out how common abortion was in the East. I am greatly indebted to Dr. Lester Bush for this and other references to abortion in the *Journal of Discourses.*

10. Thomas Massie, "An Experimental In-

quiry into the Properties of the Polygala Senega," in Charles Caldwell, ed., *Medical Theses, Selected from among the Inaugural Dissertations, Published and Defended by the Graduates in Medicine, of the University of Pennsylvania, and of Other Medical Schools in the United States* (Philadelphia, 1806), 203.

11. Between 1800 and 1830 the population profile of the United States corresponded closely to an ideal type identified and recognized by many different historical demographers, though the different scholars call the type by different names. William Petersen's widely used *Population* (New York, 3rd ed., 1975), 15, labels it the "underdeveloped" type and identifies its characteristics as a mixed economy, high fertility rates, falling mortality rates, and very high rates of population growth.

12. Massie, "Polygala Senega," 204.

13. John G. Metcalf, student notebooks written while attending Dr. Walter Channing's lectures of midwifery at Harvard Medical School, 1825–1826 (Countway Library, Harvard Medical School), entry for December 27, 1825. There had been cases of abortion induced by blows to the belly tried in British courts in the eighteenth century.

14. Hugh L. Hodge in Francis Wharton and Moreton Stillé, *Treatise on Medical Jurisprudence* (Philadelphia, 1855), 270. Hodge did not publish the lecture he gave in 1839 until 1854.

15. "Report On Criminal Abortion," *Transactions of the American Medical Association*, XII (1859), 75.

16. E. P. Christian, "Report to the State Medical Society on Criminal Abortions," *Peninsular & Independent Medical Journal*, II, 135.

17. "Criminal Abortions," *Buffalo Medical Journal and Monthly Review*, XIV (1859), 249.

18. *Boston Medical and Surgical Journal*, XLIV, No. 14 (May 7, 1851), 288. For an excellent example of this bitterness and jealousy see Worthington Hooker, *Physician and Patient* . . . (New York, 1849), passim, and especially 405–408. The estimate on income is from Colin B. Burke, "The Quiet Influence" (Ph.D. dissertation, Washington University of St. Louis, 1973), 69, Table 2.19.

19. A Physician of New-York, *Trial of Madame Restell, For Producing Abortion on the Person of Maria Bodine, to which is added, a Full Account of her Life & Horrible Practices: Together with Prostitution in New-York; Its Extent—Causes—and Effects upon Society* (New York, 1847), 3–4, 10.

20. Kingsley Davis and Judith Blake, "Social Structure and Fertility: An Analytical Framework," *Economic Development and Cultural Change*, IV, No. 3 (April 1956), 230.

21. Hooker, *Physician and Patient*, 93; James Reed, *From Private Vice to Public Virtue: The Birth Control Movement and American Society since 1830* (New York, 1978), chaps. 1–5.

22. Walter Channing, "Effects of Criminal Abortion," *Boston Medical and Surgical Journal*, LX (March 17, 1859), 135.

23. E. M. Buckingham, "Criminal Abortion," *Cincinnati Lancet & Observer*, X (March 1867), 141; Channing, "Effects of Criminal Abortion," 135; J. C. Stone, "Report on the Subject of Criminal Abortion," *Transactions of the Iowa State Medical Society*, I (1867), 29; J. Miller, "Criminal Abortion," *The Kansas City Medical Record*, I (Aug. 1884), 296.

24. H. Gibbons, Sr., "On Feticide," *Pacific Medical and Surgical Journal* (San Francisco), XXI, No. 3 (Aug. 1879), 97–111; H. C. Markham, "Foeticide and Its Prevention," *Journal of the American Medical Association*, XI, No. 23 (Dec. 8, 1888), 805–806.

25. Henry C. Wright, *The Unwelcome Child; or, the Crime of an Undesigned and Undesired Maternity* (Boston, 1860). The volume was copyrighted in 1858.

26. Ibid., 65–69.

27. E[lizabeth] C[ady] S[tanton]", "Infanticide and Prostitution," *Revolution*, I, No. 5 (Feb. 5, 1868), 65.

28. Ibid. For the same point reiterated see "Child Murder," in ibid. I, No. 10 (March 12, 1868), 146–147 and ibid. I, No. 18 (May 1868), 279.

29. Ibid., I, No. 14 (April 9, 1868), 215–216.

30. E. V. B., "Restellism, and the N.Y. Medical Gazette," *Woman's Advocate* (Dayton, Ohio), I, No. 20 (April 8, 1869), 16. Note the reference to the belief in antenatal character formation that was used, as here implied, as another rationale for abortion during the nineteenth century.

31. Carl N. Degler is one of those who has argued persuasively that nineteenth-century American women were very much aware of their own sexuality and desirous, morality books notwithstanding, of expressing it: "What Ought To Be and What Was: Women's Sexuality in the Nineteenth Century," *American Historical Review*, LXXIX, No. 5 (Dec. 1974), 1467–1490.

32. Lester Ward, *Young Ward's Diary*, Bernhard J. Stern, ed. (New York, 1935), 140.

33. Ibid. 150, 152–153, 174.

LOIS W. BANNER
Elizabeth Cady Stanton:
Early Marriage and Feminist Rebellion

No issue is so useful a warning against applying to women generalizations about men than is the matter of citizenship. Women were citizens (if they were born or naturalized in the United States, and if they were not slaves), but they could not vote. "I am tired of explaining this charming system of equality and independence," sneers a fictional woman created by the first American novelist, Charles Brockden Brown. Real abolitionists asked plaintively, "Are we aliens because we are women?"*

Most histories leap to the conclusion that since women did not vote they were not part of the political community. Yet throughout the nineteenth century non-voting citizens tried to influence public policy. Individual women sent private petitions to legislatures; philanthropic groups established charities when public pensions failed. Women turned the temperance movement into their own; they joined the abolitionist movement and shaped its campaigns. In 1839–40, in fact, the national abolitionist movement splintered over the issue of whether women could be full members of the association, hold office, and speak in public. When in 1848 Elizabeth Cady Stanton formulated the Declaration of Sentiments (document 2 in Essential Documents) as an echo of the Declaration of Independence, she was attempting to bring the status of women into belated congruence with the changes made for men by the founders' generation.

Stanton was particularly sensitive to the interrelationship of public and private life. The defense of women's rights that she developed and her attention to married women's property rights demonstrate her recognition of the interrelationship of economics and politics. As Lois W. Banner shows, Stanton's political career emerged out of issues with which she began to wrestle in her private life. Throughout her long career she would have important things to say about the major issues that confronted American society.

* Charles Brockden Brown, *Alcuin: A Dialogue* (1798), ed. Lee R. Edwards (New York: Grossman Publishers, 1971), p. 33.

Excerpted from "Early Marriage and Feminist Rebellion: From London to Seneca Falls," chap. 2 of *Elizabeth Cady Stanton: A Radical for Woman's Rights* by Lois W. Banner (Boston: Little, Brown, 1980). Copyright © 1980 by Lois W. Banner. Reprinted by permission of Little, Brown and Company.

The Stantons traveled to London in 1840 for the antislavery cause. But Cady Stanton returned six months later affected not so much by the plight of the slaves as by the situation of women.

The London Anti-Slavery Convention welcomed Henry Stanton as a leading American abolitionist and named him its secretary. Antislavery societies throughout the British Isles invited him to speak. Influential reformers entertained them, and Cady Stanton could hardly believe that she actually met people she "had so long worshipped from afar." The Stantons toured London, journeyed through Ireland and Scotland, and spent time in Paris.

Meetings and discussions with the American women delegates at the convention, however, impressed Cady Stanton more profoundly than the sights or the antislavery issue. The American Anti-Slavery Society, founded in 1833, had divided in 1839 over allowing women to participate in its affairs. New York members, fearing that any association with feminism would undermine abolitionism, wanted women's societies kept separate from the organizations of men. In 1840 they would take leading roles in moving abolitionism boldly into the male world of politics by founding the Liberty party. The Boston and Philadelphia supporters of William Lloyd Garrison, who retained control of the American society, held that both sexes should participate equally in the same societies. In support of their positions, both groups sent delegates to the London convention. But only among the Garrisonians were women to be found.

Before she arrived in London, Cady Stanton's sympathies lay with the New Yorkers. Her husband, active in forming the Liberty party, sided with his New York colleagues, as did Gerrit Smith and the Welds. . . .

Her attitude changed when they reached London. The Stantons were lodged in the same boarding house as the women delegates, and they had meals together. Cady Stanton sat next to Lucretia Mott, a renowned Philadelphia Quaker preacher, twenty years her senior, who was the acknowledged leader of the American women representatives. The first night at dinner, despite Birney's frowns and her husband's nudgings under the table, Cady Stanton supported Mott's arguments for woman's equal participation in the antislavery societies. Cady Stanton had always been fascinated by Quaker women, who were allowed to speak in public and to become ministers and who, like Mott and the Grimké sisters, often took on public roles as reformers. Indeed, Mott was different from the women Cady Stanton knew. She was gentle, serene, and good humored, although she questioned all creeds; she was at peace with herself in defying society's dogmas about women's behavior; and she had the self-confidence to challenge men directly. During the weeks in London, Cady Stanton continually sought Mott out and solicited her views on social and theological issues. Spellbound, she witnessed Mott preach in a London Unitarian church. It was the first time she had heard a woman speak in public before an audience which included men.

At the convention, too, Cady Stanton became Mott's confederate. The question of whether the women should even be accepted as delegates preempted the first days of the meeting. The conservatives were in control. The women were not permitted to speak on their own behalf nor to sit on the convention floor. Instead, they were relegated to a curtained gallery at one end of the hall. Henry Stanton was sufficiently sensitive to his wife's feelings that he, alone among the New Yorkers, spoke in favor of seating the women. Yet, in contrast to William Lloyd Garrison, who was also present, he did not leave his seat on the convention floor to join the women in the gallery. Nor did his advocacy of the women approach the fervor of Wendell Phillips, a patrician Boston Garrisonian whose new wife had been largely responsible for his conversion to antislavery. Wendell and Ann Phillips were also on their wedding trip; the comparison was not lost on Cady Stanton.

The acrimonious debates canvassed all possible arguments for woman's subordination. Cady Stanton found the exchanges "such refined torture as I had never before experienced." The only relief was "the placid comments and smiles of derision that passed around the distinguished circle of women." Barred from speaking at the convention, the women engaged in long debates with the men at their boarding house. . . . Cady Stanton resolved her anger by a decision to act. She proposed to Lucretia Mott that they hold a woman's rights convention as soon as they returned to the United States, and Mott agreed.

That gathering was not to take place until 1848. Time and other concerns intervened. . . .

During the first eight years of her marriage, domesticity dominated Cady Stanton's life. . . .

. . . Decorating, cleaning, and gardening fascinated her, especially after the Stantons moved into their own home in Boston. Cooking became a passion: "I spent half my time preserving, pickling, and experimenting with new dishes." While still in Johnstown, her first son, Daniel, was born, followed by two more sons, Henry and Gerrit, born during the Boston years. Motherhood added another absorbing interest.

Caring for her children engaged her intellect as well as her emotions. From the birth of her first child, she questioned accepted procedures. The local Johnstown woman she hired as a nurse for Daniel swaddled the infant, tightly wrapping him in strips of cloth which prevented the

movement of arms and legs, in the belief that new limbs needed support during the first year of life. She closed the windows to keep out supposed evil substances from the air outside. She counseled Cady Stanton to feed the baby continuously, in the belief that an unfilled stomach caused colic and rickets. She kept on hand an arsenal of herbal concoctions and soothing syrups, many of which contained laudanum, an opium derivative. Despite these attentions, the child cried constantly. Distraught, Cady Stanton "wept, prayed, and philosophized by turns."

She then turned to the available literature on child rearing. Rejecting most treatises as useless, she found validation of both homeopathic medical advice and her common sense in an 1840 work on infant care by Andrew Combe, a Scottish physician and the younger brother of the phrenologist George Combe. Defying her husband, her parents, and her male doctor, she threw off the swaddling clothes, opened the windows to let in fresh air, threw away the medicines, and nursed the baby on a regular schedule during the day and not at night. The results were striking. Although the new schedule monopolized her time as much as the nurse's procedures, the baby stopped crying. And there were other, more personal benefits. She claimed through this experience to have learned "another lesson in self-reliance." Moreover, her involvement in infant care had important ramifications for her later feminist thought, in which she would identify maternity as a key factor in human development.

In neither Johnstown nor Boston did Cady Stanton entirely forego activities outside the home or forget her earlier interest in woman's rights. In both places she found time to study theology, law, and history—particularly as they pertained to women. Before she left Johnstown she took an interest in the Married Women's Property Act, introduced in the New York

State legislature in 1836 and designed to give married women control over their property. The bill had garnered considerable public support, particularly from the wealthy, whose daughters' dowries and inheritances were prey to the debts of bankrupt and improvident sons-in-law. The bill, however, dealt only with property rights; it did not address any of the other legal inequalities of women. . . .

In 1842 she made her first public speech in Johnstown, not on woman's rights or the property bill for married women, but on the respectable subject of temperance. Her insecurity was evidenced by the fact that she did no more than mention the inflammatory issue of woman's rights in the speech. Nor was she any bolder in private conversation. Defensively, she wrote to Lucretia Mott that she did her best to interject the issue into social discourse. But Cady Stanton did not yet have the courage and self-confidence that speaking out for woman's rights required.

The Stantons' move to Boston in 1843 placed her in the intellectual and reform center of the nation. Margaret Fuller, the transcendentalist intellectual and feminist ideologue whose conversational gatherings with Boston women were renowned, had already left the city. But Cady Stanton seized every opportunity to go to concerts, lectures, plays, and church services. She faithfully attended temperance, peace, prison, and antislavery reform conventions. She met Emerson and Hawthorne and visited Brook Farm, the transcendentalist commune near Boston—an experience which almost converted her to communitarianism. She remained for the most part a private person, however. Although she collected signatures on antislavery petitions, she did not become a leader in any of the reform organizations. On separate occasions she discussed holding a woman's rights convention with both Lucretia Mott and black abolitionist Frederick

Douglass, a recent escapee from slavery whom she converted to woman's rights advocacy, but again she did nothing further actually to implement the project.

Yet too public an association with the Garrisonian leaders of Boston reform might have undermined Henry Stanton's political career. Besides, Cady Stanton still found housekeeping fulfilling, and religious exploration doubly absorbing in the national center of religious liberalism. . . .

So wary did Boston make her of reform activities that she continued her woman's rights activity instead in New York, not in Massachusetts, where, in fact, woman's rights petitions were not circulated until 1848 and a married woman's property bill not drafted until 1854. During long visits to her family, both in Johnstown and in Albany, she continued to circulate petitions on behalf of the Married Women's Property Act, still pending before the legislature. In Albany, she lobbied on behalf of the bill among the legislators, many of whom she encountered in local society. Again her efforts were modest. But the experience gave Cady Stanton useful training in politics and in defending her position before male opponents.

In 1847, after four year in Boston, the Stantons moved to Seneca Falls, New York. Stanton suffered from chronic lung congestion in Boston's damp climate; he had failed to win elective office despite several attempts; and he was dissatisfied with the shady ethics of his law partner. . . . Seneca Falls was a growing town, holding out professional possibilities, and it was near the reform centers of Rochester and Buffalo. Down the road in Auburn lived Lucretia Mott's sister, Martha Wright, as well as William Henry Seward, reform governor and antislavery politician. In the nearby town of Waterloo was a large community of reform Quakers.

Yet the situation did not work out as

expected. Before the move Cady Stanton worried that Henry would be unhappy in a small town. But the reverse proved to be the case. The years in Johnstown and Boston had been fulfilling for her; the initial months in Seneca Falls were not. Life in her new community revealed years of accumulated grievances, often only dimly perceived at the time. To cope with her discontent and to legitimate her own desire for a broader sphere of action, she began seriously to consider the timeliness of a woman's rights convention. Once again she successfully overcame depression through action; this time her movement toward what, in Emersonian terms, she often called "self-reliance" was almost complete.

More than anything else, Cady Stanton traced her discontent in Seneca Falls to the burden of increased housework. In Johnstown the Stantons had lived with her parents, and in Boston she had always found capable servants. But in provincial Seneca Falls such help seemed unavailable. Her house was only a block away from the town's most imposing avenue, along which the wealthy factory owners and merchants lived. But her street was not paved; it was dusty; and the business district of town, containing shops and churches and meeting places, was a good mile or two away.

Domestic tasks that had charmed her in Johnstown and Boston now bored her. Her three children, boys of eight, six, and three, were difficult to manage, and their activities left the house in an uproar. From a nearby community of Irish laborers came regular complaints that her boys threw rocks. The lakes of the area were fertile breeding grounds for mosquitoes, and respiratory ailments were common. Her children, it seemed, were constantly sick. For the first time in many years, Cady Stanton felt directly and personally oppressed as a woman.

Yet other, deeper reasons lay behind her discontent. In later years dusty streets and minor illnesses did not bother her, and she regained her pleasure in domestic tasks. She would then find substitutes for Boston's cultural life by organizing a town discussion group, advising neighbors, and bringing friends to Seneca Falls. But at the moment, all the grievances of her life in a small town converged with one other mounting problem: her marriage to Henry Stanton.

Strong-willed and opinionated, Stanton was not easy to live with. Ten years Cady Stanton's senior, married for the first time at thirty-five, he was set in his ways. His kindly but nonetheless patronizing control is evident in an 1843 letter in which he addressed her as "My Dearest Daughter." Two women abolitionist friends who had traveled with the Stantons for a brief time in 1840 privately commented on Stanton's overbearing treatment of his wife.

Moreover, as a lawyer and politician Stanton simply did not meet the promise of his early career. Although he devoted enormous time and energy to volunteer party activism, his attempts at elective office, except for two terms in the New York Senate, failed. . . .

Increasingly he left home for long periods on business trips and political assignments. He was absent at the birth of at least two of his children. Whenever possible, he journeyed to Washington to witness the debates in Congress and mingle informally with the politicians. Eventually he became the Washington reporter for the *New York Tribune*. His enthusiasm for politics went beyond the desire to effect social change. He was equally drawn to its masculine nature and the easy camaraderie of men whose careers were based on pleasing others and who usually left their families at home. On the way to Washington, he invariably detoured to Albany to exchange gossip with the state's master politician, Thurlow Weed, on whose newspaper, the *Rochester Telegraph*, he had worked as a reporter in his prereform days. In 1857 Susan B. Anthony noted that Stanton had spent his usual seven months in Washington, pursuing, as she sarcastically put it, "Political Air Castles." Increasingly Cady Stanton resented his absences and, even more, his freedom to do what he wanted. In 1848 she wrote to a friend of her great love for Henry; in 1858 she poured out her discontent to Anthony. "How rebellious it makes me feel when I see Henry going about where and how he pleases," she wrote. "He can walk at will through the whole wide world or shut himself up alone. As I contrast his freedom with my bondage I feel that, because of the false position of women I have been compelled to hold all my noblest aspirations in abeyance in order to be a wife, a mother, a nurse, a cook, a household drudge."

Stanton's behavior at home also bothered her. The derisive descriptions of American husbands in her writings were clearly modeled after him. The once doting lover had become staid and indifferent, absorbed in his career and his interests outside the home. His pipe and his evening newspapers were irritants that symbolized all the rest. Buried behind his ritual reading, he answered his wife's questions with a vacant stare, while the children were carefully schooled not to disturb "his devotions to his God, his evening paper."

Henry Stanton was not entirely to blame for Cady Stanton's discontent. Both husband and wife liked to live well, but Stanton's income was never large. Daniel Cady gave them their houses in both Boston and Seneca Falls in addition to other financial aid. Nor was Cady Stanton, increasingly strong-willed and opinionated, easy to live with. As early as 1840, on her postwedding visit, the Welds were concerned about Cady Stanton's fashionable ways, and they worried that Henry Stanton was not, in fact, strong enough to guide her in the direction of self-denial and reform. Her son

Gerrit contended that his father often went on trips because his mother regularly filled the house with so many visitors that there was hardly room to move. Moreover, after 1848, Cady Stanton's well-known feminism was an obstacle to Stanton's political career, for her reform involvement challenged entrenched cultural conventions about the proper role of women. During Stanton's 1850 campaign for the state senate, a furor was raised because Cady Stanton was wearing the bloomer reform dress, which substituted short skirts and trousers for women's regular long, restrictive dress. Cady Stanton and several other feminists, notably Seneca Falls' editor and Assistant Postmaster Amelia Bloomer, had designed it, and Bloomer's name had quickly been attached to it. Cady Stanton's feminism almost cost Stanton his one elective office.

The Stantons' sexual relationship also was probably a source of frustration. In contrast to many of her contemporaries, Cady Stanton was aware of woman's sexuality, and she agreed with an 1853 phrenological analysis of herself as "able to enjoy the connubial relationship in a high degree." But in her public writings she consistently rated mental and spiritual relationships as more fulfilling than sexual ones and criticized the unregulated sexual drives of men. Her ambivalence about sex probably derived partly from her ambivalence about her own fertility. The Stantons did not practice birth control. Historians now think that knowledge of birth control was widespread in nineteenth-century America. But in her later life Cady Stanton implied that during her childbearing years she was ignorant of such techniques. The many children she bore indicates that she rejected abstinence, although she later stated that at some point after the birth of her third son, Gerrit, in 1845, she began to practice her own eugenic theories about conceiving children only when husband and wife were in optimal condition. The lack of power over her reproductive life increased Cady Stanton's sense of subordination and eventually contributed to the centrality of the birth control message in her feminist theory and activism. In the Seneca Falls years it added to the frustration of an already strained marital relationship.

Despite their difficulties, Cady Stanton never considered divorcing Henry Stanton. She vigorously denied contemporary attacks that her liberal ideas about divorce grew out of her negative experiences with men and insisted that they derived from observations of the experiences of other women, particularly of a childhood friend who discovered shortly after her wedding that her husband had married her only for her dowry. . . .

Cady Stanton expected an enormous amount from marriage: an intense emotional and intellectual relationship, a sense of total union with a soul mate whom she could "reverence and worship as a God." Her writings extolled this kind of union and contrasted it to the usual marriage held together by emotional need, legal entanglement, or the tyranny of husband over wife. Occasionally, however, she described other kinds of imperfect, but workable unions. One such relationship involved two opposite personalities both powerfully attracted to one another and in constant conflict, reflecting her own situation.

Merry and carefree Elizabeth Cady had married strong and sensible Henry Stanton; the romantic idealist and feminist was linked to the pragmatic politician. Yet by and large Henry Stanton did not interfere in her reform activities, no small gesture from a man of his era. He acquiesced to her changes in their marriage ceremony, and did not refuse to be seen with her in bloomer dress, although Susan Anthony claimed that he finally opposed it. As a New York state senator he introduced several woman's rights petitions

into the legislature, and he helped her draft the resolutions for the Seneca Falls convention. Although she complained in 1855 that he opposed her advocacy of woman's rights, he rarely interfered with her later career, even when for many months of the year she abandoned her domestic role for nationwide lecture tours and left him at home with responsibility for the family. In 1862 he was the catalyst behind the Woman's Loyal National League, designed to mount a petition campaign to end slavery. At the 1869 organizing meeting of the National Woman Suffrage Association he supported his wife's proposal that membership be limited to women, stating that "he had been drilled for twenty years privately, and he was convinced that women could do it better alone."

Yet there were tensions during all these years. Infuriated, Stanton refused to attend the 1848 woman's rights convention when his wife introduced a resolution for woman suffrage. He was a spokesman for political antislavery; she became a Garrisonian. He supported the Republican stand on Reconstruction, while Cady Stanton mounted a campaign against the antifeminist Fourteenth and Fifteenth Amendments. Returning to his Democratic identification, he supported Horace Greeley for president in 1872, despite his wife's support of Ulysses S. Grant and her bitter controversy over woman's rights with Greeley, a former friend and early supporter of the woman's movement.

Cady Stanton often mused about the unhappy marriages of great men. But it was a self-indulgent half-truth when she implied to her son in 1898 that the function of work in her life had been to "heal her sorrows." Her drive for work, for regular and stimulating occupation, was intense. On some level she discerned that competition with her husband had caused a basic friction in their marriage. Writing after Stanton's death, she recalled how her young son Theodore had praised a speech he heard his father deliver while criticizing one of hers. Rather than accepting the judgment, she traced her son's preference to society's belief in men's superiority. She was perturbed at losing even so minor a competition to Stanton.

Yet the Stantons ultimately worked out some mutually satisfactory arrangement. When the news of Stanton's death reached her while she was visiting her daughter in England in 1887, she felt a deep loss and regretted "every unkind, ungracious word, every act of coldness and neglect." In his autobiography, largely a catalogue of his career, Stanton mentioned his wife only once, referring to her formally, along with Susan B. Anthony, as the leader of the American woman's movement. "We lived together, without more than the usual matrimonial friction, for nearly half a century" was the judgment of her marriage in Cady Stanton's autobiography.

That Cady Stanton became a reformer had little to do with any sense of status discontent, of having lost her social position as the daughter of a wealthy judge and the granddaughter of the patrician Livingstons—whether because of her reform activities or because the rise of new commercial elites in economically expanding America had challenged the holders of old wealth for social predominance. Rather than feeling displaced as a daughter of the old elite, she was in sympathy with the new economic order. A committed individualist, she liked laissez faire economics. The egalitarian rhetoric of the Democratic party appealed to her. She chose to make her friends among reformers and individuals outside of the social elite. She liked elegance, but her style of life was informal, not patrician. If anything, her privileged background gave her the motivation and the assurance to reject her past, as many reformers and radicals have often

done, such as Gerrit Smith, Wendell Phillips, and the Grimké sisters in her own day, all of whom traced their origins to the elite.

Cady Stanton's decision to become a reformer was an outgrowth of her upbringing, her experiences, her intelligence, her reading, her maternal instincts, and her sensitivity to others. Had she been completely satisfied with her marriage, she might have been content to remain in the background. But once she had made her personal discontent public, the course of events and her considerable ability propelled her into a position of leadership.

In July 1848, after the Stantons had lived in Seneca Falls for nearly a year, Martha Wright, Lucretia Mott's sister, informed Cady Stanton that Mott was due to visit and invited her to spend July 13 with Quaker friends in Waterloo. Present on that occasion were Jane Hunt and Mary McClintock, in addition to Wright, Mott, and Cady Stanton. In the course of conversation, Cady Stanton so eloquently expressed her discontent that she and the others, deeply moved, agreed to convene a woman's rights convention and issue a statement of grievances.

The decision was not as precipitous as it seems at first glance. In April 1848, the New York State legislature had finally passed the Married Women's Property Act. Other states, too, had begun to modify their statutes. Cady Stanton knew that Lucretia Mott regularly visited her sister each year at the time of the regional Quaker meeting. After years of antislavery work, Mott had considerable expertise in the planning of such conventions. The intention of the women at Waterloo was to mobilize reform sentiment only in the immediate Seneca Falls area; they announced the meeting only in the local newspaper and, since it was harvest season, expected a small attendance.

They called the convention for July 19 and 20 and spent a day drawing up an agenda and a declaration of grievances. Developing the latter document occupied most of their time. Again Cady Stanton was the guiding force. She chose the 1776 Declaration of Independence as the model and did most of the actual writing, keeping close to the original phraseology of the eighteenth-century document but substituting the word "male" for the name of "King George." Finding that the Declaration of Independence included eighteen grievances, the women in Waterloo spent most of one day combing law books and other documents to find eighteen injustices of their own. The unexpected difficulty of the task was both frustrating and exhilarating and, drawing on Cady Stanton's particular love of fun, they teased each other about the actuality of their individual oppression. But they felt the gravity of their position as pioneers in a new and radical reform, and laughter relieved their tension.

A half century of feminist thought and writing lay behind their endeavors. They were all familiar with Mary Wollstonecraft's *Vindication of the Rights of Woman* (1792), the first modern feminist treatise; with Sarah Grimké's *Letters on the Equality of the Sexes* (1838); and with Margaret Fuller's *Woman in the Nineteenth Century* (1845). In contrast to these longer works, they intended to present a short and compelling list of grievances on the order of the lawyer's briefs which had been an important part of Cady Stanton's education.

In the end they did not have far to search to discover woman's wrongs. Although married women in some states had secured the right to their own property, they still had no legal right to their earnings or to their children. They could not testify against their husbands in court. Single women could own property, but they paid taxes on it without enjoying the right to vote—the very issue of "taxation without representation" that had triggered

the American Revolution. In all occupations women were paid much less than men. The double standard of morality required women to remain virgins until married and then faithful to their husbands, while male indiscretions were condoned. No liberal arts college, with the exception of Oberlin, admitted women. With the exception of writing and schoolteaching the professions were closed to them. Not until 1869 would an Iowa woman be licensed to practice law, and the graduation of Elizabeth Blackwell from Geneva Medical College in nearby Geneva, New York, only a month before the convention was the first episode in a long struggle to secure the regular training and licensing of women in medicine. To Cady Stanton and the others the list of grievances justified the charge of tyranny. In this document they held man to blame for woman's state. "He has endeavored, in every way that he could, to destroy her confidence in her own powers, to lessen her self-respect, and to make her willing to lead a dependent and abject life." In a lengthy series of resolutions, Cady Stanton and the others called for an end to all discrimination based on sex.

Cady Stanton's appropriation of the Declaration of Independence was a brilliant propagandistic stroke. She thereby connected her cause to a powerful American symbol of liberty. She adopted the celebrated felicity of expression of Thomas Jefferson, the author of the original document, who was, in his own time, a proponent of human rights—at least for white men. As did many radicals after her, using the 1776 declaration as the basis of their creeds and manifestoes, she astutely placed her movement within the mainstream of the American tradition and reiterated her own loyalty to the revolutionary generation, whom she often identified as "fathers" of the feminists, at least in revolutionary temper. Moreover, her manifesto was in tune with the popular, democratic revolutions against monarchical rule which were sweeping European states in 1848.

Despite the boldness of their action in calling the convention, Cady Stanton and her confederates were seized by insecurity when the convention opened in a local Methodist chapel. On the spot, none of them had sufficient self-possession to chair the meeting. They pressed James Mott, Lucretia Mott's husband, into service, even though the women had previously agreed that men should not take part in the event. But their audience of 300 was much larger than they had expected, and it included forty men. The Waterloo Quakers were there in full force, as were representatives from the Rochester reform community, including black abolitionist Frederick Douglass. In Seneca Falls the meeting was a major event, and it attracted many townspeople, including aggrieved women factory workers, committed reformers, and the curious.

The first day of the convention was devoted to speeches by Mott, McClintock, and Cady Stanton, among others. When Cady Stanton took the podium, the prospect was so threatening, she later recalled, that she felt like "suddenly abandoning all her principles and running away." Amelia Bloomer, who along with her husband managed the Seneca Falls post office, contended that Cady Stanton spoke so softly it was impossible to hear her. Yet by the second day, which was devoted to reading the Declaration of Sentiments and voting on its resolutions, Cady Stanton was sufficiently bold to electrify the meeting with a new and controversial resolution. She proposed that the Declaration of Sentiments demand suffrage for women. All other resolutions passed unanimously. But only a bare majority voted in favor of suffrage and only after an eloquent speech by Frederick Douglass.

The Quakers at the convention opposed the demand for suffrage because, as pacifists, they abjured any participation in a polity that condoned war as national policy. But there was much more to the opposition than that. Henry Stanton, the reformer, helped his wife draft the resolutions for the convention. But Stanton, the politician, refused to attend when his wife decided to introduce the suffrage resolution. Even Lucretia Mott contended that the demand would make them appear ridiculous.

The exclusive right to vote, Stanton and Mott knew, was central to male political hegemony. Early in the century state legislatures had disenfranchised women in the states where colonial voting rights were still theirs, just as they had disenfranchised free blacks in the 1820s and 1830s when they eliminated property qualifications for voting and instituted universal male suffrage. The democratization of American politics coincided with an increasing conservatism with regard to the position of women and an increasing tendency to define their proper role as domestic. Democracy and the free enterprise economy created a volatile social order in which neither status nor income was entirely secure. In compensation, the society reinforced traditional definitions of separate masculine and feminine spheres of behavior, particularly after the woman's rights movement challenged it. Republican ideology, which was a legacy of the Revolution, and the religious revivals of the 1820s and 1830s, in which most converts were women, both centered on purifying the nation; and both regarded woman's natural virtue and influence in the home as primary agents of national regeneration. The rough worlds of business and politics were for men; women provided a secure haven in the home and through it attempted to institute moral reformation.

The average politician, patterning himself after Andrew Jackson, strove to be forceful and aggressive. Martin Van Buren was ridiculed for his elegant manners: the age's worst epithet, "man-milliner," with its pejorative reference to effete male hatmakers, dogged him throughout his career. William Henry Harrison underscored his identity by adopting as his symbols the coonskin cap and the whiskey barrel—potent symbols of masculinity. The political world was masculine, its competitiveness symbolized by party battles and ritualized by tempestuous elections, in which heavy drinking and fist fights were the order of the day at the saloons and barber shops where many polls were set up. When Lucretia Mott described the demand for suffrage as "ridiculous," she meant that the culture would view the entry of women into the political world as so outlandish as to seem comical.

To Cady Stanton, the daughter of a statesman and the wife of a politician, the political world was neither strange nor impregnable. For years her husband had argued that politics was the key to abolitionist success; it was a primary source of power in the democratic polity. It was no less the key to feminist success, Cady Stanton came to understand, and the vote was the first step. Nor was suffrage potentially as culturally explosive as other radical ideas, like divorce reform or birth control, which were becoming crucial to Cady Stanton's emerging ideology, and which she avoided at Seneca Falls. In her personal experience and her own ideology, the demand for suffrage was pragmatic, not radical.

Furthermore, for years Cady Stanton had resented her husband's preoccupation with politics. It is not surprising that she chose the issue of woman's access to politics as her first significant act of feminist rebellion. As early as the spring before the convention she had approached New York legislator Ansel Bascom, a former classmate at Johnstown Academy and a Seneca Falls neighbor, to suggest that he introduce a woman suffrage bill before the legislature. In addition, in August 1848, just a few weeks after the Seneca Falls convention, political abolitionists, among whom Henry Stanton was prominent, were to meet to form a new Free-Soil party that would appeal as much to the economic ambitions of Northerners as to their antislavery sentiment. Henry Stanton stormed out of Seneca Falls; any connection with the controversial issue of woman suffrage might seriously damage the future of the new party, as well as his own career within it.

In advocating a position that varied from that of other feminists, Cady Stanton established her mature reform style. Within the context of reform politics and prevailing social attitudes, the emphasis on enfranchisement was radical. It was calculated to shock woman's rights advocates into a stand that would directly confront social prejudices and prove that they lacked neither courage nor commitment. . . . Cady Stanton gave a number of explanations for introducing the suffrage resolutions in the 1848 convention. . . .

[Her primary model in this behavior was] William Lloyd Garrison. She had criticized his militant style during the London Anti-Slavery Convention and in 1841 declared her support for her husband's advocacy of political action. But even then she was wavering, writing of her partial conversion to Garrison's ideas. His early support of woman's rights always impressed her. Nor did she forget his willingness to choose principle over politics; his role in the abolitionist movement as prophet and moralist deeply appealed to her. Garrisonian strategy recognized that the number of dedicated abolitionists was too small ever to be more than a pressure group and that the very nature of politics inevitably compromised their goals. The key to antislavery success lay therefore in changing public opinion and not in party action. . . .

Throughout her career Cady Stanton was pulled toward the opposite poles of politics and morality and of partisan maneuver and direct confrontation. That she usually chose confrontation and a high moral stance over indirect political methods had much to do with her emotional makeup. Politics was not really congenial to her. Independent by nature, with a childlike love of surprises, impatient of partial solutions and unable to tolerate delay, the political mode of moderation, compromise, and slow progress did not fit her. Rather she preferred to shock her colleagues, to stir them out of complacency, to arouse their passions through introducing issues they had not considered. Furthermore, emotionally volatile, powerful in personality, and liking extravagant praise, the platform and the lecture hall, not the assembly chamber, appealed to her. She loved the theater and often suggested that acting was an exciting career for women. She became a brilliant interpreter of feminist ethics as a writer and orator and not as a political strategist. She attributed her successful effort for suffrage at Seneca Falls to arguments delivered from the public podium and not in private conversation.

Had the Seneca Falls convention not occurred, the woman's rights movement would nonetheless have shortly come into being. Groups in Ohio and Massachusetts were contemplating action, and the Seneca Falls declaration called for similar meetings throughout the nation. Indeed, Boston reform women, former associates of Cady Stanton, in 1850 organized the first woman's rights convention purposefully designed to be national in scope in the reform center of Worcester, Massachusetts. Nonetheless the legend of the primacy of Seneca Falls was quickly established. No other meeting produced such a powerful document as its Declaration of Sentiments, and the immediate and nationwide reaction of the press quickly gained it public notoriety. The telegraph

and the newly formed Associated Press quickly disseminated the news of the meeting. Until then, newspapers had paid little attention to woman's rights activities; all those present at Seneca Falls were amazed at the ferocity of the medium's response.

Somewhere they had touched a raw nerve. Whether out of fear or disdain, whether because all editors were men and most newspapers were quasi-official organs for political parties, the press was vituperative in denouncing the meeting. They advanced charges that would become characteristic of the opposition to feminism throughout the century: the leaders were frustrated old maids; the demands were unnecessary because most American women, pampered by husbands and fathers, were satisfied with their lots; and abandonment of the domestic sphere threatened marriage, the family, and the entire social order.

Cady Stanton later asserted that, had she realized the furor the convention would rouse, she would never have called it. Indeed, she opposed having a woman chair a convention held two weeks later in Rochester to continue the discussions. Of the 100 men and women who signed the declaration, many retracted their signatures under pressure from relatives. When Daniel Cady heard about the meeting, he hurried to Seneca Falls, along with his son-in-law, Daniel Eaton, whose wife Harriet had been visiting Cady Stanton and had signed the declaration. Under pressure from her father and her husband, Harriet retracted her signature and returned home. But despite the entreaties of her father, Cady Stanton refused to withdraw her name. She would not recant. In calling the Seneca Falls convention, in writing the declaration, in holding firm for suffrage, she had taken her stand. In the process, she had found herself.

DOCUMENTS: Political Oratory

SOJOURNER TRUTH
"And a'n't I a Woman?"

Our only account of impassioned oratory by this black abolitionist comes from the pen of Frances D. Gage, who chaired a large women's rights meeting in Akron, Ohio, in May 1851. Sojourner Truth had already achieved renown as an effective abolitionist speaker, although it is clear from Gage's account that the people at the Akron meeting regarded her as a pariah. In the 1850s and 1860s she toured the upper Midwest, speaking on behalf of antislavery and women's rights. Her presence at a meeting of white women, however, was exceptional. Black abolitionists split from the white movement in the 1850s, and few black women seem to have been welcomed at white women's rights meetings.

May 29, 1851

There were very few women in those days who dared to "speak in meeting"; and the august teachers of the people were seemingly getting the better of us, while the boys in the galleries, and the sneerers among the pews, were hugely enjoying the discomfiture, as they supposed, of the "strong-minded." Some of the tender-skinned friends were on the point of losing dignity, and the atmosphere betokened a storm. When, slowly from her seat in the corner rose Sojourner Truth, who, till now, had scarcely lifted her head. "Don't let her speak!" gasped half a dozen in my ear. She moved slowly and solemnly to the front, laid her old bonnet at her feet, and turned her great speaking eyes to me. There was a hissing sound of disapprobation above and below. I rose and announced "Sojourner Truth," and begged the audience to keep silence for a few moments.

The tumult subsided at once, and every eye was fixed on this almost Amazon form, which stood nearly six feet high, head erect, and eyes piercing the upper air like one in a dream. At her first word there was a profound hush. She spoke in deep tones, which, though not loud, reached every ear in the house, and away through the throng at the doors and windows.

"Wall, chilern, whar dar is so much racket dar must be somethin' out o' kilter. I tink dat 'twixt de niggers of de Souf and de womin at de Norf, all talkin' 'bout rights, de white men will be in a fix pretty soon. But what's all dis here talkin' 'bout?

"Dat man ober dar say dat womin

Excerpted from Frances D. Gage, Reminiscences of Sojourner Truth in *History of Woman Suffrage*, edited by Elizabeth Cady Stanton, Susan B. Anthony, and Matilda Joslyn Gage, vol. 1 (New York: Fowler & Wells, 1881), pp. 115–17.

needs to be helped into carriages, and lifted ober ditches, and to hab de best place everywhar. Nobody eber helps me into carriages, or ober mud-puddles, or gibs me any best place!" And raising herself to her full height, and her voice to a pitch like rolling thunder, she asked. "And a'n't I a woman? Look at me! Look at my arm! (and she bared her right arm to the shoulder, showing her tremendous muscular power). I have ploughed, and planted, and gathered into barns, and no man could head me! And a'n't I a woman? I could work as much and eat as much as a man—when I could get it—and bear de lash as well! And a'n't I a woman? I have borne thirteen chilern, and seen 'em mos' all sold off to slavery, and when I cried out with my mother's grief, none but Jesus heard me! And a'n't I a woman?

"Den dey talks 'bout dis ting in de head; what dis dey call it?" ("Intellect," whispered some one near.) "Dat's it, honey. What's dat got to do wid womin's rights or nigger's rights? If my cup won't hold but a pint, and yourn holds a quart, wouldn't ye be mean not to let me have my little half-measure full?" And she pointed her significant finger, and sent a keen glance at the minister who had made the argument. The cheering was long and loud.

"Den dat little man in black dar, he say women can't have as much rights as men, 'cause Christ wan't a woman! Whar did your Christ come from?" Rolling thunder couldn't have stilled that crowd, as did those deep, wonderful tones, as she stood there with outstretched arms and eyes of fire. Raising her voice still louder, she repeated, "Whar did your Christ come from? From God and a woman! Man had nothin' to do with Him." Oh, what a rebuke that was to that little man.

Turning again to another objector, she took up the defense of Mother Eve. I can not follow her through it all. It was pointed, and witty, and solemn; eliciting at almost every sentence deafening applause; and she ended by asserting: "If de fust woman God ever made was strong enough to turn de world upside down all alone, dese women togedder (and she glanced her eye over the platform) ought to be able to turn it back, and get it right side up again! And now dey is asking to do it, de men better let 'em." Long-continued cheering greeted this. " 'Bleeged to ye for hearin' on me, and now ole Sojourner hasn't got nothin' more to say."

Amid roars of applause, she returned to her corner, leaving more than one of us with streaming eyes, and hearts beating with gratitude. She had taken us up in her strong arms and carried us safely over the slough of difficulty turning the whole tide in our favor.

MARY C. VAUGHAN
"We would act as well as endure"

Temperance was a more popular reform movement among women than abolition and probably accounted for more recruits to the women's rights cause. Mary C. Vaughan's speech at an Albany, New York, temperance meeting suggests some of the issues to which women responded that led them from a concern over alcoholism to one for women's rights. Which sex does Vaughan think is most likely to abuse alcohol? Who does she think most requires protection? Note that, at the end, Vaughan mentions "the true woman"; what does Vaughan imply are the characteristics of a "true woman"?

January 28, 1852

We have met to consider what we, as women, can do and may do, to forward the temperance reform. We have met, because, as members of the human family, we share in all the sufferings which error and crime bring upon the race, and because we are learning that our part in the drama of life is something beside inactive suffering and passive endurance. We would act as well as endure; and we meet here to-day because many of us have been trying to act, and we would combine our individual experiences, and together devise plans for the future, out of which shall arise well-based hopes of good results to humanity. We are aware that this proceeding of ours, this calling together of a body of women to deliberate publicly upon plans to carry out a specified reform, will rub rather harshly upon the mould of prejudice, which has gathered thick upon the common mind.

. . . There are plenty of women, as well as men, who can labor for reforms without neglecting business or duty. It is an error that clings most tenaciously to the public mind, that because a part of the sex are wives and mothers and have absorbing duties, that all the sex should be denied any other sphere of effort. To deprive every unmarried woman, spinster, or widow, or every childless wife, of the power of exercising her warm sympathies for the good of others, is to deprive her of the greatest happiness of which she is capable; to rob her highest faculties of their legitimate operation and reward; to belittle and narrow her mind; to dwarf her affections; to turn the harmonies of her nature to discord; and, as the human mind must be active, to compel her to employ hers with low and grovelling thoughts, which lead to contemptible actions.

There is no reform in which woman can act better or more appropriately than temperance. I know not how she can resist or turn aside from the duty of acting in this; its effects fall so crushingly upon

Excerpted from Mary C. Vaughan, Address, Daughters of Temperance Assembly, in *History of Woman Suffrage*, edited by Elizabeth Cady Stanton, Susan B. Anthony, and Matilda Joslyn Gage, vol. 1 (New York: Fowler & Wells, 1881), pp. 476–78.

her and those whose interests are identical with her own; she has so often seen its slow, insidious, but not the less surely fatal advances, gaining upon its victim; she has seen the intellect which was her dearest pride, debased; the affections which were her life-giving springs of action, estranged; the children once loved, abused, disgraced and impoverished; the home once an earthly paradise, rendered a fit abode for lost spirits; has felt in her own person all the misery, degradation, and woe of the drunkard's wife; has shrunk from revilings and cowered beneath blows; has labored and toiled to have her poor earnings transferred to the rum-seller's ill-gotten hoard; while her children, ragged, fireless, poor, starving, gathered shivering about her, and with hollow eyes, from which all smiles had fled, begged vainly for the bread she had not to bestow. Oh! the misery, the utter, hopeless misery of the drunkard's wife! . . . We account it no reason why we should desist, when conscience, an awakened sense of duty, and aroused heart-sympathies, would lead us to show ourselves something different than an impersonation of the vague ideal which has been named, Woman, and with which woman has long striven to identify herself. A creature all softness and sensibility, who must necessarily enjoy and suffer in the extreme, while sharing with man the pleasures and the ills of life; bearing happiness meekly, and sorrow with fortitude; gentle, mild, submissive, forbearing under all circumstances; a softened reflex of the opinions and ideas of the masculines who, by relationship, hold mastery over her; without individualism, a mere adjunct of man, the chief object of whose creation was to adorn and beautify his existence, or to minister to some form of his selfishness. This is nearly the masculine idea of womanhood, and poor womanhood strives to personify it. But not all women. This is an age of iconoclasms; and daring hands are raised to sweep from its pedestal, and dash to fragments, this false image of woman. We care not how soon, if the true woman but takes its place.

SUSAN B. ANTHONY
"Guaranteed to us and our daughters forever"

The capstone of the celebration of the Centennial was a public reading of the Declaration of Independence in Independence Square, Philadelphia, by a descendant of a signer, Richard Henry Lee. Elizabeth Cady Stanton, who was then president of the National Woman Suffrage Association, asked permission to present silently a women's protest and a written Declaration of Rights. The re-

Excerpted from Susan B. Anthony, Declaration of Rights for Women by the National Woman Suffrage Association, in *History of Woman Suffrage*, edited by Elizabeth Cady Stanton, Susan B. Anthony, and Matilda Joslyn Gage, vol. 3 (Rochester, N.Y.: Susan B. Anthony, 1886), pp. 31–34.

quest was denied. "Tomorrow we propose to celebrate what we have done the last hundred years," replied the president of the official ceremonies, "not what we have failed to do."

Led by suffragist Susan B. Anthony, five women appeared at the official reading, distributing copies of their declaration. After this mildly disruptive gesture they withdrew to the other side of Independence Hall, where they staged a counter-Centennial and Anthony read the following address. Compare it to the Declaration of Sentiments (document 2 in Essential Documents) of twenty-eight years before. Note the splendid oratorical flourish of the final paragraph.

July 4, 1876

While the nation is buoyant with patriotism, and all hearts are attuned to praise, it is with sorrow we come to strike the one discordant note, on this one-hundredth anniversary of our country's birth. When subjects of kings, emperors, and czars, from the old world join in our national jubilee, shall the women of the republic refuse to lay their hands with benedictions on the nation's head? Surveying America's exposition, surpassing in magnificence those of London, Paris, and Vienna, shall we not rejoice at the success of the youngest rival among the nations of the earth? May not our hearts, in unison with all, swell with pride at our great achievements as a people; our free speech, free press, free schools, free church, and the rapid progress we have made in material wealth, trade, commerce and the inventive arts? And we do rejoice in the success, thus far, of our experiment of self-government. Our faith is firm and unwavering in the broad principles of human rights proclaimed in 1776, not only as abstract truths, but as the corner stones of a republic. Yet we cannot forget, even in this glad hour, that while all men of every race, and clime, and condition, have been invested with the full rights of citizenship under our hospitable flag, all women still suffer the degradation of disfranchisement.

The history of our country the past hundred years has been a series of assumptions and usurpations of power over woman, in direct opposition to the principles of just government, acknowledged by the United States as its foundation. . . .

And for the violation of these fundamental principles of our government, we arraign our rulers on this Fourth day of July, 1876,—and these are our articles of impeachment:

Bills of attainder have been passed by the introduction of the word "male" into all the State constitutions, denying to women the right of suffrage, and thereby making sex a crime—an exercise of power clearly forbidden in article 1, sections 9, 10, of the United States constitution. . . .

The right of trial by a jury of one's peers was so jealously guarded that States refused to ratify the original constitution until it was guaranteed by the sixth amendment. And yet the women of this nation have never been allowed a jury of their peers—being tried in all cases by men, native and foreign, educated and ignorant, virtuous and vicious. Young girls have been arraigned in our courts for the crime of infanticide; tried, convicted, hanged—victims, perchance, of judge, jurors, advocates—while no woman's voice could be heard in their defense. . . .

Taxation without representation, the immediate cause of the rebellion of the colonies against Great Britain, is one of the grievous wrongs the women of this country have suffered during the century. Deploring war, with all the demoralization that follows in its train, we have been taxed to support standing armies, with their waste of life and wealth. Believing in temperance, we have been taxed to support the vice, crime and pauperism of the liquor traffic. While we suffer its wrongs and abuses infinitely more than man, we have no power to protect our sons against this giant evil. . . .

Unequal codes for men and women. Held by law a perpetual minor, deemed incapable of self-protection, even in the industries of the world, woman is denied equality of rights. The fact of sex, not the quantity or quality of work, in most cases, decides the pay and position; and because of this injustice thousands of fatherless girls are compelled to choose between a life of shame and starvation. Laws catering to man's vices have created two codes of morals in which penalties are graded according to the political status of the offender. Under such laws, women are fined and imprisoned if found alone in the streets, or in public places of resort, at certain hours. Under the pretense of regulating public morals, police officers seizing the occupants of disreputable houses, march the women in platoons to prison, while the men, partners in their guilt, go free. . . .

Representation of woman has had no place in the nation's thought. Since the incorporation of the thirteen original States, twenty-four have been admitted to the Union, not one of which has recognized woman's right of self-government. On this birthday of our national liberties, July Fourth, 1876, Colorado, like all her elder sisters, comes into the Union with the invidious word "male" in her constitution. . . .

The judiciary above the nation has proved itself but the echo of the party in power, by upholding and enforcing laws that are opposed to the spirit and letter of the constitution. When the slave power was dominant, the Supreme Court decided that a black man was not a citizen, because he had not the right to vote; and when the constitution was so amended as to make all persons citizens, the same high tribunal decided that a woman, though a citizen, had not the right to vote. Such vacillating interpretations of constitutional law unsettle our faith in judicial authority, and undermine the liberties of the whole people.

These articles of impeachment against our rulers we now submit to the impartial judgment of the people. To all these wrongs and oppressions woman has not submitted in silence and resignation. From the beginning of the century, when Abigail Adams, the wife of one president and mother of another, said, "We will not hold ourselves bound to obey laws in which we have no voice or representation," until now, woman's discontent has been steadily increasing, culminating nearly thirty years ago in a simultaneous movement among the women of the nation, demanding the right of suffrage. In making our just demands, a higher motive than the pride of sex inspires us; we feel that national safety and stability depend on the complete recognition of the broad principles of our government. Woman's degraded, helpless position is the weak point in our institutions today; a disturbing force everywhere, severing family ties, filling our asylums with the deaf, the dumb, the blind; our prisons with criminals, our cities with drunkenness and prostitution; our homes with disease and death. It was the boast of the founders of the republic, that the rights for which they contended were the rights of human nature. If these rights are ignored in the case of one-half the people, the nation is surely preparing for its downfall. Governments try themselves. The recognition of a governing and a governed class is incompatible with the first principles of freedom. Woman has not been a heedless spectator of the events of this century, nor a dull listener to the grand arguments for the equal rights of humanity. From the earliest history of our country woman has shown equal devotion with man to the cause of freedom, and has stood firmly by his side in its defense. Together, they have made this country what it is. Woman's wealth, thought and labor have cemented the stones of every monument man has reared to liberty.

And now, at the close of a hundred

years, as the hour-hand of the great clock that marks the centuries points to 1876, we declare our faith in the principles of self-government; our full equality with man in natural rights; that woman was made first for her own happiness, with the absolute right to herself—to all the opportunities and advantages life affords for her complete development; and we deny that dogma of the centuries, incorporated in the codes of all nations—that woman was made for man—her best interests, in all cases, to be sacrificed to his will. We ask of our rulers, at this hour, no special privileges, no special legislation. We ask justice, we ask equality, we ask that all the civil and political rights that belong to citizens of the United States, be guaranteed to us and our daughters forever.

II_B

Industrializing America

1880–1920

Americans triumphantly celebrated the end of the nineteenth century. They had secured sectional unity between North and South and the benefits of continental expansion. The industrial revolution, dominated by the vision and organizational genius of a few hard-driving, ruthless entrepreneurs, had transformed a wilderness into a new landscape, crisscrossed by railroads and telegraph and telephone lines and dotted with foundries, factories, and mills. Sprawling cities and industrial centers lured native and immigrant alike with the promise of a new job and a fresh start. As the urban population increased from 15 million in 1880 to 45 million in 1910, America's farmers expanded their output not only to feed this nation's teeming cities but those of Europe as well. American technology provided its own "miracles." The Brooklyn Bridge, upon completion in 1883, was the longest suspension bridge in the world. Serving thousands of daily commuters between Brooklyn and Manhattan, it stood as a symbol not only of the technological achievements of the American people but of the emergence of a new nation—industrial, urban, and ethnically diverse.

Maturing as an economic power in an age of imperialism, America was fast becoming an international power as well. Competing with Europe in a worldwide quest for new trade outlets, the United States picked up new territories along with new markets. Acquisition of Alaska (1867) was followed by involvement in —and ultimately annexation of—Samoa (1872) and Hawaii (1898). After a "splendid little war" with Spain, this nation was left with Puerto Rico, Guam, and the Philippines. Eager to protect strategic interests in the Pacific, the United States acquired the right to construct an interoceanic canal to be owned by the new country of Panama but under American control. The Panama Canal, another triumph of American engineering, was one of many developments portending this nation's willingness to intervene in the affairs of other nations to the south in order to establish hemispheric dominance and protect American investments.

The economic expansion that had enabled, and indeed encouraged, this former British colony to create its own imperial system did not occur painlessly. The populist movement of the 1890s, for example, expressed the anger of agrarians who attacked the injustices of an economic system that victimized farmers while benefiting industrial, railroad, and banking interests. The growing socialist movement was but one expression of workers' discontent with an industrial order in which 5 percent of the population owned nearly half the nation's property while more than a third of its 76 million people in 1910 lived below the poverty line. Living conditions were no better than working conditions for the millions trapped in the poverty and misery of teeming urban ghettos. Cities, ill prepared to cope with rapid population growth, were governed inadequately and often dishonestly by politicians whose base of support lay in wards populated by immigrants inexperienced with American politics and grateful for services provided by the "machine."

Attempting to steer a middle course between radicalism and reaction, many Americans at the turn of the century turned to progressivism, participating in a multifaceted coalition of reformers that included insurgent intellectuals and university professors, Christian "social gospelers," women activists, investigative reporters, business and professional men, farmers, and laborers. A diverse lot dedicated to a variety of goals, progressives generally agreed on certain basic propositions. Government, particularly at the local and state level, must be made more democratic, honest, and efficient; monopolies must be controlled and big business made more responsive to the public interest; natural resources must be used more rationally; social conditions must be made more just and humane and the environment in which people lived and worked made safer. Extending to international affairs this same concern for order and reform, they agreed that in the wake of World War I the postwar world created must be progressive as well. Although their efforts to meet the needs of this new urban, industrial society were sometimes contradictory and not always successful, progressives laid the foundations of the modern welfare state.

Technology, industrialization, immigration, urbanization, domestic reform, and international involvement: these were the developments shaping American life between 1880 and 1920, and they involved women as well as men. Women, many from southern and eastern Europe, moved to cities, seeking there some measure of economic survival and family stability. Women worked on farms and in factories, some emerging as populist agitators, socialist activists, and labor organizers. Women also became progressives and pacifists, serving in the vanguard of those struggling for economic and social justice and international peace.

Historians have customarily acknowledged these women with little more than a cursory nod toward such figures as Mary Elizabeth Lease, the populist orator who urged farmers "to raise less corn and more hell"; Mary Harris ("Mother") Jones, the fiery labor agitator who became a symbol of defiance wherever strikers gathered; and, of course, Jane Addams, the humanitarian reformer whose settlement house work made her a relentless foe of political corruption and economic exploitation. Although historians usually include women's winning the vote among progressive achievements, they have been reluctant to examine the ways in which men and women differed in their experiences of industrial work and technological change. Even in studying reform most historians of progressivism have focused on males, whether as business, professional, or political elites or as working-class voters. Suppose, however, we reverse this emphasis, exploring progressivism as one example of the way in which the inclusion of women's experience prompts a refocusing of what we know about this much studied era in American reform.

We should begin by reversing the relation of women reformers to progressivism. Instead of focusing on them as part of a reform coalition, let us, for the moment, view progressivism as part of women's history, looking especially at the way in which women steadily moved from the domestic into the public sphere, in the process changing both. The first stage of that process we can locate in the early years of the republic when women as "Republican Mothers" assumed a role that made their domestic domain of education and nurture into a schoolroom for the next generation of virtuous citizens. This acknowledgment of the mother's private domain as a public trust helped to establish women—in the ideal, at least—as public persons with public responsibilities, even if exercised within the privacy of the family. At an ever-accelerating pace between 1820 and 1880—the dates are approximations—women expanded that role into what might be called "Reformist Motherhood." Instead of influencing the public domain indirectly through the lives of their sons, women began to extend their role as nurturer and teacher of morals from the domestic sphere into the public sphere through church, missionary, and moral reform groups. Women sought to make the world conform more strictly to values taught in the home—sexual responsibility and restraint for men as well as women, self-discipline for those who used strong drink, charity and rehabilitation for those who were entrapped by poverty and crime, sympathy and justice for Afro-Americans.

Between 1880 and 1920 a new role developed that might be called "Political Motherhood." Increasing numbers of women joined the Woman's Christian Temperance Union (WCTU), the Young Women's Christian Association (YWCA), the settlement house movement, the General Federation of Women's Clubs, the National Association of Colored Women, the Children's Aid Society, the National Child Labor Committee, the National Consumers' League, the Pure Food Association, and a host of others. (By 1920, for example, the WCTU had

800,000 members, the General Federation of Women's Clubs nearly one million.) Through these organizations and related activities, women enlarged still further their sphere in public life where once only men had acted. They worked to protect industrial workers, especially women and children, to clean up local politics as well as unsanitary slaughterhouses and polluted water supplies, to promote health, education, social welfare, and mental hygiene. Even big business was no longer "off limits" to women as Ida Tarbell proved when she exposed the corrupt practices used by John D. Rockefeller to create his oil empire. In their rejection of an individualism that, in the hands of such men, had become exploitative, and in their willingness to use government at all levels to create a more humane, caring community, women were thinking and acting in ways that were quintessentially progressive.

In transforming women's sphere from the private, family-oriented world of domesticity into the formerly male world of politics and public policy, a major change was occurring. The "womanhood" identified with "mothering" was becoming less a biological fact—giving birth to children—and more a political role with new ideological dimensions. The traditional word *motherhood* was being reshaped so as to justify women's assuming new, ever-more-public responsibilities. Women now clearly meant to transform the domestic housekeeping responsibilities of their grandmothers into an attack on the worst abuses of an urban, industrial society. The household now included marketplace and city hall.

Viewed in this context, prohibition, a progressive reform often regarded as a political aberration, can be seen as the logical extension of women's traditional concern for those women and children who were so often the victims of alcohol-related abuse. Indeed, such protection seemed as necessary and as logical as legislation abolishing child labor or limiting the hours of working women whose health as potential mothers would affect the health of the next generation. In this context, too, suffrage marks the final step in the movement out of the domestic sphere into the political sphere. That women should justify the need to vote in terms of their domestic responsibilities, a justification criticized by some historians, becomes quite consistent. That, too, must be viewed as part of a long process in which the drive to enlarge women's sphere came through gradual transformation of ideals identified with an older domesticity into a new and broader sense of responsibility appropriate for a public sphere itself changing under the impact of industrialization, immigration, and urbanization.

What, then, have we accomplished through this exercise of taking women out of the progressive coalition and putting progressivism into women's history? We discover first of all that female reformers were not merely one group among many in the progressive coalition. Women's perspective quite as much as their participation gave progressivism much of its ideological direction as well as its momentum. Indeed, we can even say that the progressive perspective was, in large part, the appropriation by male reformers of those ideas most intimately associated with the social perspective of women, almost literally the application to society of moral issues nurtured in women's domain. The significance of this achievement is understood, however, only when we include women's experience as basic, *not incidental*, to how we view the past. Refocusing history is, to be sure, a complicated task, but this one example—women and progressivism— suggests how we may begin to view afresh the first two decades of the twentieth century.

DAVID M. KATZMAN
Seven Days a Week: Domestic Work

For women who needed to work outside the home, domestic service has always been one of the limited job options available. Housekeeping was, after all presumed to be "women's work." By 1900 over one-third of the wage-earning women in this country were employed as domestics or waitresses. Many were either immigrants or the daughters of immigrants from Europe; others were Afro-Americans. The lot of such women was not easy, especially in the years before the invention of the labor-saving appliances that became common fixtures in middle-class households by 1920. Note the number of tasks expected of a domestic in a single-servant household, the long hours, the low pay, the necessity of always being at the "beck-and-call" of the mistress, and the lack of time of one's own. Because of these factors, many women of European background left domestic service for jobs in factories or shops, leaving black women—victims of even greater discrimination—to form a larger proportion of domestic workers.

The best way of illustrating the daily and weekly cycles is to follow a general household worker through a part of her week's work. Inez Godman recorded her activities on a typical workday in 1901. She worked in a Northern home, doing all the work except the wash. She had negotiated a 75¢-a-week reduction in wages to $2.75 in return for her mistress hiring the wash out. Godman began work on a Wednesday afternoon and immediately prepared the dinner. Apparently no time was allotted for her to adjust to her new work and living environment. Wearing the apron and cap provided her, she served the meal. After cleaning up the kitchen and dining room, she prepared bread dough; her mistress had become "weary of baker's stuff." At 9:00 P.M. she was through for the day.[1]

On Thursday she rose at 6:00 A.M. and served breakfast an hour later. By 9:30 A.M. the kitchen and dining room had been cleaned, and her weekly chores began. She spent two hours cleaning the sitting room. "Everything had to be carried into the adjoining room, and there was much china and bric-a-brac," she wrote. The carpet had to be moved, and each slat of the Venetian blinds wiped

Excerpted from "Household Work," chap. 3 of *Seven Days a Week: Women and Domestic Service in Industrializing America* by David M. Katzman (New York: Oxford University Press, 1978). Copyright © 1978 by Oxford University Press. Reprinted by permission. Notes have been renumbered.

clean. Twice she had to go to the kitchen to check the bread she was baking (it had risen overnight), and five times she had to answer the doorbell. Lunch required an hour of preparation, and she served her mistress at one. Already she had worked seven hours: "I was thankful for a chance to sit, and dawdled over my lunch for half an hour." By 2:30 P.M. the kitchen and dining room were clean again, and her mistress suggested Godman clean the kitchen floor. Afterwards, she rested in her room from 3:20 to 4:00 P.M.. At 4:00 she had to go downstairs to heat the oven and begin the evening meal. "Dinner was a complex meal," she explained, "and coming at night when I was tired was always something of a worry. To have the different courses ready at just the right moment, to be sure that nothing burned or curdled while I was waiting on the table, to think quickly and act calmly; all this meant weariness."[2]

The alternation of the daily and weekly chores continued during each day. On Friday after breakfast she cleaned the halls, stairs, vestibule, and bathroom: "It was heavy work, for the halls were carpeted with moquette, but I sat on the stairs as I swept them with a whisk broom, thus saving my feet." Before lunch she had gone to the market, then returned and made the midday meal. After cleaning the kitchen and dining room and doing the weekly cleaning of the refrigerator, she wearily climbed to her room. She passed her mistress, who "sat with a flushed face still sewing." She offered to help, and her mistress responded: "I don't know how to rush sewing but I wish to wear this skirt to-morrow, and if you *would* do it I would like to rest." Godman finished it in half an hour. She still had another hour of rest, since she was cooking fish for dinner and would not have to light the oven. She could rest until 4:30. She was rewarded for doing the skirt; her employer gave her Saturday evening off, since she was going out to dinner.[3]

Sunday was filled with daily chores, but Godman was pressed for time because she had to help her mistress dress for church. She rushed and managed to finish by 2:00 P.M. so she could attend a Sunday school class. That night she served a light supper and managed to retire at 8:00 P.M. On Monday morning she cleaned the dining room, polished silver, did the marketing, and baked bread. Since guests were invited to dinner that evening she worked straight through her afternoon break, and did not finish cleaning up until 10:00 P.M. Monday had turned into a sixteen-hour workday, including time for meals. The laundress came on Tuesday, and Godman spent all afternoon plus all day Wednesday and part of Thursday between her daily chores and ironing. But Thursday began a new weekly cycle. Wisely her mistress went out for lunch that first week so Godman could complete the ironing and clean the sitting room without having to make lunch and clean up. She finished the ironing at 11:00 A.M. Thursday and then went to the sitting room. She simply rested there for an hour, then cleaned the room in just twenty minutes. Though she thought it looked clean, she knew it was not thoroughly done. Each week she failed to complete the ironing on Wednesday; it was physically impossible for her. The result was that Thursday was "a hard day, for my lady did not go out to luncheon after that first week, and with her in the house I could not slight the work nor stop to rest. Every Thursday night I was ready to collapse.[4]

Inez Godman's full workdays are typical. Daily chores for the maid-of-all-work included lighting fires (in stoves, for hot water, in winter fireplaces or furnaces), preparing and serving meals and cleaning up, making beds, doing light dusting, sweeping or scrubbing front steps and porch, answering the doorbell, and running errands. The weekly cycle, dominated by washing, ironing, and heavy cleaning, was more physically demanding.

A typical week would begin with washing on Monday, ironing on Tuesday, and mending on Wednesday. On Thursday the dining room would be thoroughly cleaned, including the polishing of silver and glass. On Friday the house would be swept and the windows cleaned. Saturday would entail major housecleaning—the kitchen, cellar, and rooms not cleaned thoroughly on other days—and then perhaps breadbaking. Repetition of tasks made the work monotonous, but the complaint heard most seemed to be that of physical fatigue and tiredness. Over and over again women mentioned how they often collapsed in bed at the end of the day, too tired to read or even take a bath. "If one of the twelve labors of Hercules had been to solve the servant girl problem," one servant wrote, "he never would have had the reputation he has."[5]

NOTES

1. Inez A. Godman, "Ten Weeks in a Kitchen," *Independent* LIII (October 17, 1901), 2459.

2. Ibid., p. 2460.
3. Ibid.
4. Ibid., p. 2461.

5. Catherine Owen, *Progressive Housekeeping: Keeping House Without Knowing How*, and *Knowing How to Keep House Well* (Boston and New York, 1896), p. 14; "A Servant Girl's Letter," *Independent* LIV (January 2, 1902), 37.

ELIZABETH BEARDSLEY BUTLER
Women and the Trades

In 1907 a team of writers and social workers descended on the city of Pittsburgh. The new Russell Sage Foundation had decided to make its first major project an effort to put social work and philanthropy on a new footing. The young men and women who worked on the project intended to report social conditions dispassionately and help Pittsburgh's own charity workers to develop a rational set of priorities for improving life in a heavily industrialized city. It was clear that baskets of food at Christmas were not enough.

Their survey of conditions resulted in six significant volumes of description and analysis. Entitled *The Pittsburgh Survey*, these volumes became a classic document in the history of American social work.

The project was directed by Paul U. Kellogg, only twenty-eight years old but

Excerpted from "Workers and Workrooms" and "The Metal Trades," chaps. 1 and 13 of *Women and the Trades: Pittsburgh, 1907–1908* by Elizabeth Beardsley Butler (New York: Charities Publication Committee, 1909). Copyright © 1909 by the Russell Sage Foundation. Tables have been omitted.

already an experienced social worker and journalist. He hired Louis Hine, then an unknown amateur photographer, to accompany the investigators. Hine's photographs are important documents in the history of photojournalism. Among the authors of the individual volumes were Margaret Byington, whose sensitive book *Homestead* documented "the sense of powerlessness that pervaded everything the [immigrant] families thought and did"; Crystal Eastman, who would proceed from her book on *Work Accidents and the Law* to a significant career on the New York State Industrial Commission; and Elizabeth Beardsley Butler, who wrote the first book in the series, *Women and the Trades*. Occupational segregation in Pittsburgh was particularly severe, since women did not work in the steel mills.

Women and the Trades was startling. It attacked many assumptions middle-class Americans made about women's work. Most women did not work for pin money. Working conditions were not reasonable or safe. Evidence like that collected by Butler would provide important support for those who wished to establish protective legislation for working women (see, e.g., *Muller* v. *Oregon*, document 8 in Essential Documents).

WORKERS AND WORKROOMS

Pittsburgh as a workshop for women seems a contradiction in terms. Workshop this city is, but a workshop which calls for the labor of men. To dig crude ores, to fuse and forge them, are not among the lighter handicrafts at which women can readily be employed. Look down from Mount Washington at the merging of the two dull brown rivers, at the irregular succession of bridges, at scows and small river craft slowly finding way from wharf to wharf; and on either shore, at the black enclosures, gleaming now with leaping flames, now with the steady white-hot glow of Bessemer converters, but everywhere swarthy from the rising columns of black smoke. The cry of the dwarfs under the earth, the first metal smiths, rings again in the blows of the miners' tools and in the shouts of gangs of furnacemen and engine crews in the recesses of the mills.

Nevertheless, in this city whose prosperity is founded in steel, iron and coal, there has come into being beside the men a group of co-laborers. If we listen closely enough, we hear the cry of the dwarfs not only from gangs of furnacemen, but from the girl thread makers at the screw and bolt works, and from the strong-armed women who fashion sand cores in foundries planned like Alberich's smithy in the underworld. And if we listen still more closely, we shall hear answering voices in many other workrooms, in the hum of machines in a garment factory, in the steady turn of metal rolls in a laundry, and even in the clip of the stogy roller's knife in a tenement loft. For Pittsburgh is not only a great workshop, it is many workshops; and in these workshops women stand beside the men. Forced by individual and group necessities, they have found a place in industry in the steel district of the Alleghenies.

Various selective forces have played a part in recruiting these women, in the teeth of the tonnage industries that shut them out. The influence of climate, the commercial wants of a rich producing district and the demands of a great laboring force as consumers, can readily be seen in tracing the development of the trades which employ them. As the shopping center of a nest of mill towns, Pittsburgh gives employment to over 6,000 saleswomen. The city is also an office center for plants and mines; and the printing trades, alive in every city, have taken on character, and with almost no edition work, turn out the ledgers and office paper of the big companies. In walking through the business streets, you are impressed by the number and size of the commercial stationers. They fairly flourish on every corner, and the function of Pittsburgh's pressrooms and binderies is to supply them. Pittsburgh's location and its knot of railroad lines have made it a distributing point within a radius of 200 miles for articles of use and wear. Scattered industrial plants make brooms and brushes, caskets, trunks and suit-cases, and cork. The manufactories of foodstuffs (canned goods, crackers and candy) were first called into being by the demands of neighboring counties in Ohio, West Virginia and Pennsylvania, but now they supply national markets. The success of the stogy industry is traceable in large measure to the demand for cheap tobacco of workingmen who for forty miles along the rivers are busy at metals or coal or steel. Similarly, garment trades came into being to supply cheap jeans and railroad jumpers by the hundred thousands. Moreover, no making of fine garments, no textile manufacture, could persist in this region of smoke-clouds. The city sets its seal upon fabrics. They survive by their wearing qualities and by their ability to withstand smoke and grime and fog. Although the growth of the city and of neighboring towns developed a market for a greater variety of goods, workmen's overalls are still the staple article of trade.

All of these Pittsburgh industries have recruited women as wage-earners. . . .

Altogether, 22,185 women wage-earners, excluding agricultural and pro-

fessional workers and domestic servants, are employed in Pittsburgh. These figures are based on a careful census of the women-employing trades, made during the winter of 1907–8. This working force is distributed in 449 factories and shops and stores. . . .

Surveying the city, then, we see English-speaking girls holding the positions for which a few months' training and some intelligence are needed, a knowledge of English, or of reading and writing. The Italian girl, hindered by tradition, scarcely figures, but within a limited circle of industries, immigrant Jewesses hold positions beside girls of native birth. We see much inferior and unpleasant work yielded to Slavic immigrants, and we see these newcomers, sometimes by sheer physical strength, sometimes by personal indifference and a low standard, competing on the basis of lower wages for men's work which otherwise would never have been given to girls to do. Workrooms that would not long be tolerated for American women have been regarded with indifference for the Slavs, perhaps because of our inability to share the sensations of a foreigner. The place of the Slav, scrubbing floors and sorting onions for canners, packing crackers, stripping tobacco for stogy makers, and trimming bolts for the metal workers, is lowest industrially among the women workers of Pittsburgh. It is the place of the woman who is fighting her way, but has not yet thought where she is going. Marriage is not suffered to act as a hindrance. A determination to work and to earn is uppermost.

Our survey of the city shows us more than this. We see that since the days of settlement and mill town, Pittsburgh has become an industrial center whose workrooms give hire to more than 22,000 wage-earning women. These women have left household work and home industry for the field of collective service. From doing the whole of a thing and from knowing the user, the younger generation has gradually found its work more and more minutely subdivided; the individual worker makes not even a whole hinge, but a tenth part of it, and knows neither the use nor the destination of the finished product. She does not know the relation of her fraction of the work to the other fractions nor to the product as a whole,—and she works with a speed unknown to the houseworker. These younger women have pushed past the traditional activities of cleaning and cooking and sewing. Relatively few are occupied even by the congregate form of these industries, such as the laundries and garment factories. They have not only gone into pressrooms and binderies, into cork factories, and workrooms where candies are made and fruit is preserved, but they help to finish the glass tumblers that the men in the next room blow, they make the cores for the foundrymen, they are among the shapers of metals for lamps and for hinges and bolts and screws. In a district that is pre-eminent for the making of steel and iron and the products of steel and iron, women have gained a foothold in industries that seemed wholly in the hands of men. If mere numbers were the criterion, in the discussion of occupations which follows the Pittsburgh saleswomen should demand our first attention; but it has been the task of this investigation to consider primarily these factory trades where women are extending the boundaries of their industrial activity.

Pittsburgh as a city of wage-earning women is seen in all this to be not a contradiction in terms, but an actuality. From river to river, women have rapidly come to share in the modern industrial life of the city. It is a movement 22,000 strong. An industrial movement which makes for cheapness, or for efficiency, or for the utilization of a hitherto only partially utilized labor force, cannot be turned back by any theory as to its inappropriateness. But our survey shows us still other and more fundamental issues to be reckoned with

in this situation. Many of these women are put to work at wages below the cost of subsistence, for hours longer than the measure of their strength, in buildings and at ill-constructed machines which cannot but injure their health, and at processes which must handicap heavily the development of both body and mind. Industrial movements and practices which lead to such consequences may not easily be stayed, yet they may be directed and controlled by law and by public opinion grounded on considerations of the social welfare. To this end the investigation has sought more thorough knowledge of conditions under which women work in the industries than has hitherto been available to the public, to the progressive individual employer, or to the women themselves. The study has thrown light on how the occupations of women and of men are related, how far women have reached the point of self-support, and what the social effect of their work seems to be.

The numbers of women workers in competitive industry are greater, not less, than they were fifty years ago, or twenty-five years ago, or ten years ago. There is every indication that these numbers will continue actually and proportionately to increase. We have no reason to think that the problems presented by the industrial employment of women will be solved by a cessation of that employment. But there is reasonable prospect that through change in the conditions of their labor much that seems evil in it may be done away, and the participation of women in industry may become a force of permanent value.

THE METAL TRADES

Men in the Pittsburgh metal trades, in the steel mills, the foundries, the machine shops, are doing work that is both heavy and difficult. They are carrying loads of crude ore, they are running engines, mixing metals in crucibles or operating the levers which move huge, sensitive electric cranes. The product at which they work is measured in tons of metal or reduced to threads and mechanical parts accurate to the thousandth part of an inch. It is shaped into rails and carwheels and tubes, into electric motors and delicate and intricate machinery. Women also have found work to do in these plants, but their product is of a different order. Instead of the brass parts of an engine, they make the sand cores for the molds in which the brass takes form. Instead of electric motors, they make the simplest and smallest of the coils of which the motor is built. Instead of steel rails, they trim the bolts with which the rails are fastened down. They split mica for the insulators which are built by men; they assemble the parts of small metal novelties; they feed light hinges into a machine, or solder tin, or dip pieces of tinware into enamel. They have nothing to do with the great ingots or with the fashioning or assembling of involved machinery; rather they handle the small pieces of brass or aluminum or steel which are needed in such quantities that the process of making them can be turned into a mere series of repetitions, or they tend machines which they do not control or understand. Their product is used either in preparation for the final metal shaping, as in the case of sand cores, or it is finishing work, as japanning, after the metal has been shaped.

Light as the product is, subsidiary as the process often is, the work done by women is a significant part of the metal trades of Pittsburgh. The number of women [1,954], too, is significant. Only two other factory trades, stogy making and laundry work, exceed metal work in the number of women employed. . . .

FOUNDRIES

Fifty core makers work in the largest foundry core room which employs women in Pittsburgh. All are women. Through the narrow entrance you can see them moving about among wreaths of coal smoke and black dust, working on molds at their benches, or carrying trays to the ovens. Some are Polish girls, round featured, with high foreheads and fair hair; others are peasant women of the Hungarian type, strong and mature, their dark hair roughly combed back, their waists half open and their sleeves rolled high. Muscular and dark of skin, they strike you as an incarnation of the activities of smoking ovens, boiling crucibles and iron soft with fierce heat. The dim light through windows encrusted with black dust hardly reaches to the rows of ovens in the centre of the room, and even the glare of an electric bulb cannot dispel the impression of unreality and remoteness.

The benches of the core makers are on either side of the ovens, ranged through seventy feet of drifting dust. Each girl has her little heaps of different kinds of sand, her mold and shaping tools. She makes the sand cores and carries them, a trayful at a time, weighing sometimes ten pounds, sometimes twenty, sometimes fifty, to the ovens to be baked hard. Her work may be on cores with vents and spikes, or on simple finger-shaped cores which pay the makers $.10 a 1000. Quick girls can make three a minute or 10,000 a day. The large intricate cores which fit into big machines are not made by girls, but by men in another room.

Altogether the seven core rooms which make use of women core makers employed 159 women in 1907. Some are with brass foundries, some are operated in connection with malleable iron companies, while others are adjuncts to machine shops. In some foundries two or three women supplement the work of men and in others women make all the cores. They are employed irrespective of the kind of foundry so long as the work is not too heavy or too intricate for them to handle. The cores which they make of sand are set in the molds into which the hot metal is poured. In this way a hollow metal shape is produced, lighter and easier to handle than would be the solid metal.

The core room is, of course, but an adjunct to the foundry; core making a subsidiary process; and the convenience of other departments is consulted first in the laying out of the plant. Sometimes part of the foundry itself is used as a core room. Sometimes a space is set apart between machines, or a narrow bit of a room is partitioned off on the floor above. For example, in one case twelve girls work in a loft above a brass foundry. The fumes from the brass find their way up the narrow stairway leading to the loft and out through the one window at the end of the room. The girls stand at their benches in the midst of the dust and fumes. In every core room but one the ovens are either in the room or close beside it. This one plant provides a workplace apart from machinery and dust, in a clean, freshly painted room lighted by side windows and a skylight. High stools are placed at the tables and girls can sit at their work.

The influence of the machinists' union has closed some of the core rooms at 5:30 P.M. Others close at five, but all the foundries save one obtain a ten-hour day by cutting short the rest time at noon. . . .

Unlike men core makers, women are paid by the piece. As trades go, the returns are not high, if we take into consideration the length of time spent in learning. It is two years before a girl is considered expert. In some places, the girls do not earn more than $1.00 a day after they have learned, but $1.25 is more usual, and in two foundries the core makers regularly draw a day's pay of $1.40. An American girl who had worked for five years, said that she usually made from $7.00 to $8.00 a week, although in poor weeks she had fallen as low as $6.00. Once she had made $10.50, and

sometimes at long intervals she had made $9.00, but such wages as these were by no means to be regarded as regular earnings. Much of the time her work was on finger-shaped cores with vents, that paid $.07 a 100, and very often on "round liners" for Kelso couplers. These round liners are finger-shaped with vent and spike. They pay $.12 a 100, and an experienced girl can turn out from 1,200 to 1,500 a day. These cores are the lightest in weight and are set 13 on a tray, a total weight of not over 10 pounds; but other kinds of cores are set 58 on a tray and weigh from 20 to 25 pounds, if not more. There is a tradition in the core room of this foundry that a girl once made $2.00 a day at a new kind of work and that when the firm found it out, the rate was cut so that no girl thereafter should be able to make more than $1.50, or a maximum, rarely reached, of $1.85. Another foundry has a fixed maximum of $1.75, but 20 out of the 30 women whom it employs do not exceed $1.00 or at most $1.20 a day.

One dollar and twenty-five cents may be regarded as the mean wage of the women core makers in Pittsburgh. For unorganized men, employed on the small work at which girls are otherwise used, the minimum day's pay is $2.50. I am told by men in the trade that there are 500 core makers in Pittsburgh and the North Side, and that 75 per cent of them are organized. The union rate of wages is $3.50 a day up. That nearly a fourth of all the core makers should be women, would seem at first sight to indicate that this, too, is a trade for which men and women are competing, and that the greater cheapness of women workers is winning them ground. They get $1.25 less a day than the unorganized men; $2.25 less than the union scale. The union, to combat this tendency, admits no women to its membership and prohibits the employment of women in core rooms with union men; its aim is to force women out of the occupation as it increases the number of union shops.

Yet it is only in part true that women in this trade are actively competing with men. A line of cleavage separates the kinds of work at which they are severally employed. The heavy work, the cores of intricate design that require for their making long training and the skill of a craftsman—these cores are made by men. It is the men in the trade who know what kinds of sand to use and how to combine several cores in one. Women are used for the simpler, more obvious things, for the stock shapes of cores which can be learned in a few weeks. The core maker's trade, as men know it, is not by any means in women's hands. No women are apprenticed to learn the work in all its ramifications.

In the more difficult branches of the trade, therefore, there is no active competition between men and women. Yet potentially there is real competition. The small work, as well as the large, was at one time in the hands of men. Except where the union has been strong enough to force a shop to employ only men in the core room, the small work has been given over to women. The proportion of women in the trade is great enough to be menacing, in that they are doing the work at half the price of unorganized, and at a third the price of organized, men. Within a few years they have crept into shops that the public and even people in the trade still suppose to be employing men. They are doing the men's work. They are themselves carrying the trays and handling the tools. Except for the natural limitations to their work on heavy cores and the artificial limitations to their trade apprenticeship, these women core makers are in a fair way to become not only numerically important in the core rooms of machine shops, but economically effective in depressing the wages of the men.

PAULINE NEWMAN
The Triangle Shirtwaist Factory

One of the earliest industries in which women found employment was the garment industry. Based in New York City—the port of entry for millions of immigrants—the industry provided countless married women with piecework to take back to dimly lit tenements where they often enlisted the help of grandmothers and children. By the end of the nineteenth century much of the work had been transferred to sweatshops notorious for their low wages and squalid working conditions. Later the work was done in small factories such as the Triangle Shirtwaist Factory. This building became the scene of one of the great industrial

Adapted from "Pauline Newman," in *American Mosaic: The Immigrant Experience in the Words of Those Who Lived It*, edited by Joan Morrison and Charlotte Fox Zabusky (New York: E. P. Dutton, 1980), pp. 9–14. Copyright © 1980 by Joan Morrison and Charlotte Fox Zabusky. Reprinted by permission of the publisher.

tragedies in New York City's history. Although the factory contained several elevators and two staircases, the eight-story wooden building had no sprinkler system; the doors to the fire escapes were locked to prevent outdoor relaxation. When fire broke out in 1911, five hundred employees—many of them young Jewish and Italian women—were trapped behind locked doors. Some jumped to their death; others burned or asphyxiated inside. Altogether the fire claimed the lives of 146 women. Viewing their charred bodies on the street, one reporter recalled that some of these same women had gone on strike only the year before to demand decent wages, more sanitary working conditions, and safety precautions.

One of the strikers was Pauline Newman, who had worked at the Triangle Factory until she became an organizer for the International Ladies Garment Workers Union (ILGWU). Its educational director at the age of eighty-six, Newman conveys in this brief account a sense of what it was like to be a garment worker in the early twentieth century. She also expresses the indomitable spirit of these early women organizers who carried on a tradition established by their predecessors in the Lowell mills.

A cousin of mine worked for the Triangle Shirtwaist Company and she got me on there in October of 1901. It was probably the largest shirtwaist factory in the city of New York then. They had more than two hundred operators, cutters, examiners, finishers. Altogether more than four hundred people on two floors. The fire took place on one floor, the floor where we worked. You've probably heard about that. But that was years later.

We started work at seven-thirty in the morning, and during the busy season we worked until nine in the evening. They didn't pay you any overtime and they didn't give you anything for supper money. Sometimes they'd give you a little apple pie if you had to work very late. That was all. Very generous.

What I had to do was not really very difficult. It was just monotonous. When the shirtwaists were finished at the machine there were some threads that were left, and all the youngsters—we had a corner on the floor that resembled a kindergarten—we were given little scissors to cut the threads off. It wasn't heavy work, but it was monotonous, because

you did the same thing from seven-thirty in the morning till nine at night.

Well, of course, there were [child labor] laws on the books, but no one bothered to enforce them. The employers were always tipped off if there was going to be an inspection. "Quick," they'd say, "into the boxes!" And we children would climb into the big boxes the finished shirts were stored in. Then some shirts were piled on top of us, and when the inspector came—no children. The factory always got an okay from the inspector, and I suppose someone at City Hall got a little something, too.

The employers didn't recognize anyone working for them as a human being. You were not allowed to sing. Operators would have liked to have sung, because they, too, had the same thing to do and weren't allowed to sing. We weren't allowed to talk to each other. Oh, no, they would sneak up behind if you were found talking to your next colleague. You were admonished: "If you keep on you'll be fired." If you went to the toilet and you were there longer than the floor lady thought you should be, you would be laid off for half a day and sent home. And, of course, that meant no pay. You were not allowed to have your lunch on the fire escape in the summertime. The door was locked to keep us in. That's why so many people were trapped when the fire broke out.

My pay was $1.50 a week no matter how many hours I worked. My sisters made $6.00 a week; and the cutters, they were the skilled workers, they might get as much as $12.00. The employers had a sign in the elevator that said: "If you don't come in on Sunday, don't come in on Monday." You were expected to work every day if they needed you and the pay was the same whether you worked extra or not. You had to be there at seven-thirty, so you got up at five-thirty, took the horse car, then the electric trolley to Greene Street, to be there on time. . . .

I stopped working at the Triangle Factory during the strike in 1909 and I didn't go back. The union sent me out to raise money for the strikers. I apparently was able to articulate my feelings and opinions about the criminal conditions, and they didn't have anyone else who could do better, so they assigned me. And I was successful getting money. After my first speech before the Central Trade and Labor Council I got front-page publicity, including my picture. I was only about fifteen then. Everybody saw it. Wealthy women were curious and they asked me if I would speak to them in their homes. I said I would if they would contribute to the strike, and they agreed. So I spent my time from November to the end of March upstate in New York, speaking to the ladies of the Four Hundred [the elite of New York's society] and sending money back. . . .

We didn't gain very much at the end of the strike. I think the hours were reduced to fifty-six a week or something like that. We got a 10 percent increase in wages. I think that the best thing that the strike did was to lay a foundation on which to build a union. There was so much feeling against unions then. The judge, when one of our girls came before him, said to her: "You're not striking against your employer, you know, young lady. You're striking against God," and sentenced her to two weeks on Blackwell's Island, which is now Welfare Island. And a lot of them got a taste of the club. . . .

After the 1909 strike I worked with the union, organizing in Philadelphia and Cleveland and other places, so I wasn't at the Triangle Shirtwaist Factory when the fire broke out, but a lot of my friends were. I was in Philadelphia for the union and, of course, someone from here called me immediately and I came back. It's very difficult to describe the feeling because I knew the place and I knew so many of the girls. The thing that bothered me was the employers got a lawyer. How anyone could have *defended* them!—because I'm quite sure that the fire was planned for insurance purposes. And no one is going to convince me otherwise. And when they testified that the door to the fire escape was open, it was a lie! It was never open. Locked all the time. One hundred and forty-six people were sacrificed, and the judge fined Blank and Harris seventy-five dollars!

Conditions were dreadful in those days. But there was something that is lacking today and I think it was the devotion and the belief. We *believed* in what we were doing. We fought and we bled and we died. Today they don't have to.

You sit down at the table, you negotiate with the employers, you ask for 20 percent, they say 15, but the girls are working. People are working. They're not disturbed, and when the negotiations are over they get the increases. They don't really have to fight. Of course, they'll belong to the union and they'll go on strike if you tell them to, but it's the inner faith that people had in those days that I don't see today. It was a terrible time, but it was interesting. I'm glad I lived then.

Even when things were terrible, I always had that faith . . . Only now, I'm a little discouraged sometimes when I see the workers spending their free hours watching television—trash. We fought so hard for those hours and they waste them. We used to read Tolstoy, Dickens, Shelley, by candlelight, and they watch the "Hollywood Squares." Well, they're free to do what they want. That's what we fought for.

ALICE KESSLER-HARRIS
Where Are the Organized Women Workers?

Because so many wage-earning women in the early twentieth century were young, single women who regarded their work as a temporary necessity until rescued by marriage, male labor leaders—and historians—usually assumed that women workers had little interest in joining unions. Alice Kessler-Harris explores this assumption and other barriers to the organization of women workers. She demonstrates with particular effectiveness how unionization was inhibited by fears of job competition on the part of male workers and the conviction of male trade unionists and employers alike that women's proper place of work was in the home. The result, Kessler-Harris points out, was not only the division of the working class on the basis of gender but the perpetuation of an underclass of workers whose experience with wage work is still characterized by "sex-typing" that limits job options, by low pay whatever the job involved, and by the absence of significant union membership.

"The Organization of Women," wrote Fannia Cohn, an officer of the International Ladies Garment Workers Union to William Green, newly elected president of the American Federation of Labor, "is not merely a moral question, but also an economic one. Men will never be certain with their conditions unless the conditions of the millions of women are improved."[1] Her letter touched a home truth and yet in 1925, the year in which Cohn's letter was written, the A. F. of L., after nearly forty years of organizing, remained profoundly ambivalent about the fate of more than eight million wage-earning women.

During these four decades of industrial growth, the women who worked in

"Where Are the Organized Women Workers?" by Alice Kessler-Harris, in *Feminist Studies* 3, no. 1/2 (Fall 1975):92–110. Copyright © 1975 by Feminist Studies, Inc. Reprinted by permission of the publisher, Feminist Studies, Inc., c/o Women's Studies Program, University of Maryland, College Park, Maryland 20742.

the industrial labor force had not passively waited to be organized. Yet their best efforts had been tinged with failure. Figures for union members are notoriously unreliable, and estimates fluctuate widely. But something like 3.3 percent of the women who were engaged in industrial occupations in 1900 were organized into trade unions. As low as that figure was, it was to decline even further. Around 1902 and 1903 trade union membership among women began to decrease, reaching a low of 1.5 percent in 1910. Then, a surge of organization among garment workers lifted it upwards. A reasonable estimate might put 6.6 percent of wage-earning women into trade unions by 1920. In a decade that saw little change in the relative proportion of female and male workers, the proportion of women who were trade union members quadrupled, increasing at more than twice the rate for trade union members in general. Even so, the relative numbers of wage-earning women who were trade union members remained tiny. One in every five men in the industrial workforce belonged to a union, compared to one in every fifteen women. Although more than 20 percent of the labor force was female, less than 8 percent of organized workers were women. And five years later, when Fannia Cohn was urging William Green to pay attention to female workers, these startling gains had already been eroded.[2]

Figures like these have led historians of the working class to join turn-of-the-century labor organizers in lamenting the difficulty of unionizing female workers. Typically, historians argue that the traditional place of women in families, as well as their position in the workforce, inhibited trade unionism. Statistical overviews suggest that these arguments have much to be said for them. At the turn of the century, most wage-earning women were young temporary workers who looked to marriage as a way to escape the shop or factory. Eighty-five percent of these women were unmarried and nearly half were under twenty-five years old. Most women worked at traditionally hard-to-organize unskilled jobs: a third were domestic servants and almost one quarter worked in the garment and textile industries. The remainder were scattered in a variety of industrial and service jobs, including the tobacco and boot and shoe industries, department stores, and laundries. Wage-earning women often came from groups without a union tradition: about one-half of all working women were immigrants or their daughters who shared rural backgrounds. In the cities, that figure sometimes climbed to 90 percent.[3]

For all these reasons, women in the labor force unionized with difficulty. Yet the dramatic fluctuations in the proportions of organized working women testify to their potential for organization. And the large numbers of unions in which the proportion of women enrolled exceeded their numbers in the industry urge us to seek further explanations for the small proportions of women who actually became union members.[4]

No apparent change either in the type of women who worked or in the structure of jobs explains the post-1902 decline in the proportion of unionized women. On the contrary, several trends would suggest the potential for a rise in their numbers. The decline began just at the point when union membership was increasing dramatically after the devastating depression of 1893–1897. The proportion of first-generation immigrant women who were working dropped after the turn of the century only to be matched by an increase in the proportion of their Americanized daughters who worked. Married women entered the labor force in larger numbers suggesting at once a more permanent commitment to jobs and greater need for the security unions could provide. Large declines in the proportion of domestic workers reduced the numbers of women in these isolated, low-paying, and traditionally hard-to-organize jobs. At the same time, increases in office and clerical workers, department store clerks, and factory operatives, offered fertile areas for promoting unionization among women. Strenuous organizing campaigns by and among women in all these areas achieved few results.

Although cultural background, traditional roles, and social expectations hindered some unionizing efforts, they were clearly not insurmountable barriers. Given a chance, women were devoted and successful union members, convinced that unionism would serve them as it seemed to be serving their brothers. In the words of a seventeen-year-old textile worker, "We all work hard for a mean living. Our boys belong to the miners' union so their wages are better than ours. So I figured that girls must have a union. Women must act like men, ain't?"[5] In the garment workers union where women were the majority of members, they often served as shop "chairladies" and reached positions of minor importance in the union structure. Faige Shapiro recalled how her union activity began at the insistence of a business agent but quickly became an absorbing interest. In these unions, women arrested on picket lines thought highly enough of the union to try to save it bail money by offering to spend the night in jail before they returned to the line in the morning.[6]

In mixed unions, women often led men in militant actions. Iowa cigar makers reported in 1899 that some striking men had resumed work, while the women were standing pat.[7] Boot and shoe workers in Massachusetts were reported in 1905 to be tough bargainers. "It is harder to induce women to compromise," said their president, "they are more likely to hold out to the bitter end . . . to obtain exactly what they want."[8] The great uprising of 1909 in which 20,000 women walked out of New York's garment shops occurred over the objections of the male leadership, striking terror into the hearts of Jewish men afraid "of the security of their jobs."[9] Polish "spool girls" protesting a rate cut in the textile mills of Chicopee, Massachusetts, refused their union's suggestion that they arbitrate and won a resounding victory. Swedish women enrolled in a Chicago Custom Clothing Makers local, lost a battle against their bosses' attempts to subdivide and speed up the sewing process when the United Garment Workers union, largely male, agreed to the bosses' conditions. The bosses promptly locked out the women forcing many to come to terms and others to seek new jobs.[10] At the turn of the century, female garment workers in San Francisco and tobacco strippers, overall and sheepskin workers, and telephone operators in Boston ran highly successful sex-segregated unions.[11]

If traditional explanation for women's failure to organize extensively in this period are not satisfying, they nevertheless offer clues to understanding the unionization process among women. They reveal the superficiality of the question frequently asked by male organizers and historians alike: "Why don't women organize?" And they encourage us to adopt economist Theresa Wolfson's more sensitive formulation: "Where are the organized women workers?"[12] For when we stop asking why women have not organized themselves, we are led to ask how women were, and are, kept out of unions.

The key to this question lies, I think, in looking at the function that wage-earning women have historically played in the capitalist mode of production. Most women entered the labor force out of economic necessity. They were encouraged by expanding technology and the continuing division of labor which in the last half of the nineteenth century reduced the need for skilled workers and increased the demand for cheap labor. Like immigrant men, and blacks today, women formed a large reservoir of unskilled workers. But they offered employers additional advantages. They were often at the mercy of whatever jobs happened to be available in the towns where their husbands or fathers worked, and they willingly took jobs that offered no access to upward mobility. Their extraordinarily low pay and exploitative working conditions enabled employers to speed up the process of capital accumulation. Their labor was critical to industrial expansion, yet they were expected to have few job-related aspirations and to look forward instead to eventual marriage. Under these circumstances, employers had a special incentive to resist unionization among women. As John Andrews, writing in the 1911 Report on the Condition of Women and Child Wage Earners, put it: ". . . the moment she organizes a union and seeks by organization to secure better wages she diminishes or destroys what is to the employer her chief value."[13]

If the rising numbers of working women are any gauge, women for the most part nicely filled the expectations of employers. Traditional social roles and the submissive behavior expected of women with primary attachments to home and family precisely complemented the needs of their bosses. To those women whose old world or American family norms encouraged more aggressive and worldly behavior—Russian Jews, for example—unionization came easier. Yet, for the most part, women fought on two fronts: against the weight of tradition and expectation, and against employers. If that were not enough, there was yet a third battlefront.

Unionists, if they thought about it at all, were well aware of women's special economic role. Samuel Gompers, head of the American Federation of Labor, editorialized in 1911 that some companies had "taken on women not so much to give them work as to make dividends fatter."[14] In a competitive labor market unionists tended to be suspicious of women who worked for wages and to regard them as potentially threatening to men's jobs. "Every woman employed," wrote an editor in the A. F. of L. journal, American Federationist, "displaces a man and adds one more to the idle contingent that are fixing wages at the lowest limit."[15]

Since employers clearly had important economic incentives for hiring women, male trade unionists felt they had either to eliminate that incentive, or to offer noneconomic reasons for restricting women's labor-force participation. In the early 1900s they tried to do both. In order to reduce the economic threat, organized labor repeatedly affirmed a commitment to unionize women wage earners and to extract equal pay for them. Yet trade unionists simultaneously argued that women's contributions to the home and their duties as mothers were so valuable that women ought not to be in the labor force at all. Their use of the home-and-motherhood argument had two negative effects: it sustained the self-image on which the particular exploitation of women rested, and it provided employers with a weapon to turn against the working class as a whole.

Buttressed by the grim realities of exploitative working conditions and the difficulties of caring for children while working ten or more hours a day, and supported by well-intentioned social reformers, the argument to eliminate women from the work force, in the end, held sway. It was, of course, impossible to achieve, so the A. F. of L. continued to organize women and to demand equal pay for equal work. But genuine ambivalence tempered its efforts. The end result was to divide the working-class firmly along gender lines and to confirm women's position as a permanently threatening underclass of workers who finally resorted to the protection of middle-class reformers and legislators to ameliorate intolerable working conditions. The pattern offers us some lessons about what happens to the work force when one part of it attacks another.

The published sources of the A. F. of L. reveal some of the attitudes underlying A. F. of L. actions, and I have focused attention on these because I want to illustrate not only how open and prevalent the argument was, but because the A. F. of L.'s affiliated unions together constituted the largest body of collective working-class opinion. We have amassed enough evidence by now to know that the A. F. of L. was a conservative force whose relatively privileged members sacrificed the larger issues of working-class solidarity for a piece of the capitalist pie. In the creation of what labor economist Selig Perlman called "a joint partnership of organized labor and organized capital," the Federation cooperated extensively with corporation-dominated government agencies, sought to exclude immigrants, and supported an imperialist foreign policy.[16] Its mechanisms for dealing with the huge numbers of women entering the labor force are still unclear. Yet they are an integral part of the puzzle surrounding the interaction of ideological and economic forces in regulating labor market participation.

In the period from 1897 to 1920, the A. F. of L. underwent dramatic expansion. It consolidated and confirmed its leadership over a number of independent unions, including the dying Knights of Labor. Membership increased from about 265,000 members in 1897 to more than four million by 1920, and included four-fifths of all organized workers. In the same period, the proportion of women working in the industrial labor force climbed rapidly. Rapid and heady expansion offered a golden opportunity for organizers. That they didn't take advantage of it is one of the most important facts in the history of labor organizing in America.

Union leaders were sure that women did not belong in the workforce. Anxious about losing jobs to these low-paid workers, they tried instead to drive women out of the labor force. "It is the so-called competition of the unorganized defenseless woman worker, the girl and the wife, that often tends to reduce the wages of the father and husband," proclaimed Samuel Gompers.[17] And the *American Federationist* was filled with tales of men displaced by women and children. "One house in St. Louis now pays $4 per week to women where men got $16," snapped the journal in 1896. "A local typewriter company has placed 200 women to take the place of unorganized men," announced an organizer in 1903.[18]

The Federation's fears had some basis. In the late nineteenth and early twentieth century, new technology and techniques of efficiency pioneered by Frederick Taylor eroded the control and the jobs of skilled workmen, replacing them with managerial experts and the unskilled and semiskilled. Skilled members of the A. F. of L. who might appropriately have directed their anger at the way technology was being manipulated, lashed out instead at women who dared to work. Gompers offers a good example. In an article published in 1904, he declared, "The ingenuity of man to produce the world's wealth easier than ever before, is utilized as a means to pauperize the worker, to supplant the man by the woman and the woman by the child. . . ."[19] Some of the least appropriate bitterness was expressed by Thomas O'Donnell, secretary of the National Spinners Union whose constituency, once largely female, had been replaced by men after the Civil War. The advent of simple electric-powered machinery caused him to complain that "the manufacturers have been trying for years to discourage us by dispensing with the spinning mule and substituting female and child labor for that of the old time skilled spinners. . . ."[20]

Real anxieties about competition from women stimulated and supported rationalizations about woman's role as wife and mother. Working men had argued belonged at home, and both the harsh conditions of labor and the demands of rearing a family supported their contention. But the women who worked for wages in the early 1900s were overwhelmingly single, and often supported widowed mothers and younger siblings with their meagre pay. An argument that could have been used to improve conditions for all workers was directed at eliminating women from the work force entirely. By the early 1900s it had become an irrepressible chorus. "The great principle for which we fight," said the A. F. of L.'s treasurer in 1905, "is opposed to taking . . . the women from their homes to put them in the factory and the sweatshop."[21] "We stand for the principle," said another A. F. of L. member, "that it is wrong to permit any of the female sex of our country to be forced to work, as we believe that the man should be provided with a fair wage in order to keep his female relatives from going to work. The man is the provider and should receive enough for his labor to give his family a respectable living."[22] And yet a third proclaimed, "Respect for women is apt to decrease when they are compelled to work in the factory or the store. . . . More respect for women brings less degeneration and more marriages . . . if women labor in factories and similar institutions they bring forth weak children who are not educated to become strong and good citizens."[23] No language was too forceful or too dramatic. "The demand for female labor," wrote an official of the Boston Central Labor Union in 1897, is "an insidious assault upon the home . . . it is the knife of the assassin, aimed at the family circle."[24] The *American Federationist* romanticized the role of women's jobs at home, extolling the virtues of refined and moral mothers, of good cooking and even of beautiful needlework and embroidery.[25]

These sentiments did not entirely prevent the A. F. of L. from attempting to unionize women. Gompers editorialized on the subject in 1904: "We . . . shall bend every energy for our fellow workmen to organize and unite in trade unions; to federate their effort without regard to . . . sex."[26] Yet the limited commitment implied by the wish that women would get out of the work force altogether was tinged with the conviction and perhaps the hope that women would in the end, fail. The Federation's first female organizer, Mary Kenny, had been appointed as early as 1892. But the Federation had supported her only half-heartedly and allowed her position to expire when she gave up the job to marry. It was 1908 before the organization appointed another woman, Annie Fitzgerald, as full-time organizer. While Gompers and others conceded the "full and free opportunity for women to work whenever and wherever necessity requires," Gompers did not address himself to the problem of how to determine which women were admissible by these standards, and his actions revealed that he thought their numbers relatively few.[27] The A. F. of L. repeatedly called for an end to discriminatory pay for women and men: "Equal compensation for equal service performed."[28] The demand was a double-edged sword. While it presumably protected all workers from cheap labor, in the context of the early 1900s labor market it often functioned to deprive women of jobs. The Boston Typographical Union, noted one observer, saw "its only safety in maintaining the principle of equal pay for men and women. . . ."[29] Officials must have been aware that equal compensation for women often meant that employers would as soon replace them with men. It was no anomaly, then, to find an A. F. of L. organizer say of his daughters in 1919 that though he had "two girls at work [he] . . . wouldn't think of having them belong to a labor organization."[30]

When the A. F. of L. did organize women, its major incentive was often the need to protect the earning power of men. Women were admitted to unions after men recognized them as competitors better controlled from within than allowed to compete from without. "It has been the policy of my associates and myself," wrote Gompers in 1906, "to throw open wide the doors of our organization and invite the working girls and working women to membership for their and our common protection."[31] *American Federationist* articles that began with pleas that women stay out of the work force concluded with equally impassioned pleas to organize those who were already in it. Alice Woodbridge, writing in 1894, concluded an argument that women who worked for wages were neglecting their duties to their "fellow creatures" with the following statement: "It is to the interest of both sexes that women should organize . . . until we are well organized there is little hope of success among organizations of men."[32] The A. F. of L. officially acknowledged competition as a primary motivation for organizing women in 1923. "Unorganized they constitute a menace to standards established through collective action. Not only for their protection, but for the protection of men . . . there should be organization of all women. . . ."[33]

These were not of course the only circumstances of which men suspended their hostility toward women's unions. Occasionally in small towns female and male unions in different industries supported each other against the hostile attacks of employers. Minersville, Pennsylvania miners, for example, physically ousted railroad detectives who tried to break up a meeting of female textile workers.[34] The women in this case were the daughters, sisters and sweethearts of miners. Far from competing with men for jobs, women were helping to support the same families as the miners. Similarly, women and men in newly established industries could cooperate more effectively in unionizing to-but equally effective organization among gether. The garment industry saw parallel

its various branches. Though female organizers complained bitterly of the way they were treated, male leadership depended on the numerical majority of female workers to bargain successfully with employers and did not deny women admission. Yet, even here, union leadership successfully eliminated "home work" without offering to the grossly underpaid and often needy female workers who did it a way of recouping their financial losses.

Occasional exceptions notwithstanding, the general consequence of union attitudes toward women was to isolate them from the male work force. Repeatedly women who organized themselves into unions applied for entry to the appropriate parent body only to be turned down or simply ignored. Pauline Newman, who had organized and collected dues from a group of candy makers in Philadelphia, in 1910 offered to continue to work with them if the International Bakery and Confectionery Workers union would issue a charter. The International stalled and put them off until the employers began to discharge the leaders and the group disintegrated.[35] Waitresses in Norfolk, Virginia, suffered a similar fate. Mildred Rankin, who requested a charter for a group of fifteen, was assured by the local A. F. of L. organizer that she was wasting her time. "The girls were all getting too much money to be interested," was his comment on denying the request.[36] New York's International Typographical Union refused to issue female copyholders a charter on the grounds that they were insufficiently skilled. When the group applied to the parent A. F. of L. for recognition, they were refused on the grounds that they were within the ITU's jurisdiction. The Women's Trade Union League got little satisfaction when it raised this issue with the A. F. of L.'s executive council the following year. Though the Federation had agreed to issue charters to black workers excluded from all-white unions, it refused to accord the same privilege to women.

The parent body agreed only to "take up the subject with the trade unions and to endeavor to reach an understanding" as far as women were concerned.[37]

A strong union could simply cut women out of the kinds of jobs held by unionized men. This form of segmenting the labor market ran parallel to, and sometimes contradicted the interests of employers who would have preferred cheap labor. A Binghamton, New York printing establishment, for example, could not hire women linotype operators because "the men's union would not allow it."[38] The technique was as useful for excluding racial minorities as it was for restricting women.[39] Like appeals to racist beliefs, arguments based on the natural weakness of women worked well as a rationale, as the following examples will indicate. Mary Dreier, then President of the New York Chapter of the Women's Trade Union League, recalled a union of tobacco workers whose leaders refused to admit women because "they could only do poor sort of work . . . , because women had no colour discrimination."[40] A Boston metal polishers union refused to admit women. "We don't want them," an official told a Women's Bureau interviewer. "Women can only do one kind of work while men can polish anything from iron to gold and frame the smallest part to the largest," and besides, he added, "metal polishing is bad for the health."[41]

Women were often excluded from unions in less direct but equally effective ways. The International Retail Clerks Union charged an initiation fee of $3, and dues of 50¢ a month. Hilda Svenson, a local organizer in 1914, complained that she had been unable to negotiate a compromise with the International. "We want to be affiliated with them," she commented, "but on account of the dues and initiation fee we feel it is too high at the present time for the salaries that the girls in New York are getting."[42] Sometimes union pay scales were set so high that the employer would not pay the appropriate wage to women. Joining the union could mean that a female printer would lose her job, so women simply refused to join.

Though the A. F. of L. supported its few female organizers only half-heartedly, male organizers complained of the difficulty of organizing women. Social propriety hindered them from talking to women in private or about moral or sanitary issues. Women felt keenly the absence of aid. When the Pennsylvania State Federation of Labor offered to finance the Philadelphia Women's Trade Union League's program for organizing women, its secretary pleaded with Rose Schneiderman to take the job. "We have never had a wise head to advise, or an experienced worker," she wrote.[43]

But even membership in a union led by men guaranteed little to women. Such well-known tactics as locating meetings in saloons, scheduling them at late hours, and ridiculing women who dared to speak deprived women of full participation. And unions often deliberately sabotaged their female members. Fifteen hundred female street railway conductors and ticket agents, dues-paying members of New York City's Amalgamated Street Workers Union, complained in 1919 that their brother union members had supported a reformers' bill to deprive them of their jobs. When the women discovered they had been betrayed they resigned from the union and formed their own organization sending women throughout the state to Albany "to show them that they . . . were able to take care of their own health and morals." To no avail. Eight hundred of the 1500 women lost their jobs and the remaining 700 continued to work only at reduced hours.[44] Supporting union men was not likely to benefit women either. Mary Anderson, newly appointed head of the Women's Bureau, got a frantic telegram from a WTUL organizer in Joliet, Illinois, early in 1919. The women in a Joliet steel plant who, in return for the promise of protection, had supported unionized men in a recent strike, were fighting desperately for jobs that the union now insisted they give up. The company wanted to retain the women, but union men argued the work was too heavy for them.[45]

As the idea of home-and-motherhood was used to exclude women from unions, so it enabled unionized workers to join legislatures and middle-class reformers in restricting women's hours and regulating their working condition through protective labor legislation. The issue for the Federation's skilled and elite corps of male workers was clearly competition. Their wives did not work for wages, and most could afford to keep their daughters outside the marketplace. In an effort to preserve limited opportunity, they attacked fellow workers who were women, attempting to deny them access to certain kinds of jobs. Abused by employers who valued women primarily for their "cheap labor," women were isolated by male workers who were afraid their wages and their jobs would fall victim to the competition. Arguments used by male workers may have undercut their own positions, confirming the existence of a permanent underclass of workers and locking men psychologically and economically into positions of sole economic responsibility for their families. Appeals to morality and to the duties of motherhood obscured the economic issues involved, encouraging women and men alike to see women as impermanent workers whose major commitment would be to families and not to wage earning. Women would, therefore, require the special protection of the state for their presumably limited wage-earning lives.

The argument reached back at least as far as the 1880s and it was firmly rooted in the idea that the well-being of the state depended on the health of future mothers. But the line between the interests of the state and those of working men was finely drawn, and occasionally a protagonist

demonstrated confusion about the issue. A few examples will illustrate the point. The cigar maker, Adolph Strasser, testifying before a Congressional Committee in 1882, concluded a diatribe against the number of women entering the trade with a plea to restrict them. "Why?" asked his questioner. "Because," replied Strasser, "I claim that it is the duty of the government to protect the weak and the females are considered among the weak in society."[46] Nearly forty years later, a Women's Bureau investigator reported that the Secretary of the Amalgamated Clothing Workers Union, fearful that women were taking jobs from men, had argued that women were "going into industry so fast that home life is very much in danger, not to mention the propagation of the race."[47] As the idea spread, it took on new forms, leading a Boston streetcar union secretary to acknowledge that "he would not care to see [women] employed as conductors. . . . It coarsened [them] to handle rough crowds on cars."[48] But in more sophisticated form, the argument for protective legislation appeared as a patriotic appeal to enlightened national self-interest. "Women may be adults," argued one A. F. of L. columnist in 1900, "and why should we class them as children? Because it is to the interest of all of us that female labor should be limited so as not to injure the motherhood and family life of a nation."[49] Sometimes pleas were more dramatic. In a piece entitled, "The Kingdom of God and Modern Industry," Ira Howerth, a sociologist writing for the *American Federationist*, asserted:

The highest courts in some of our states declare that a law limiting the hours of labor for these women is unconstitutional. It may be so, but if it is so, so much the worse for the state. The state or nation that permits its women to stunt their bodies and dwarf their minds by overexertion in insanitary [sic] stores and mills and factories is thereby signing its own death warrant. For the degeneracy of women is the degeneracy of the race. A people can never be any better than its mothers.[50]

Gompers, as well as other Federation officials, at first opposed the idea of legislation. But in the period following World War I, their attitudes changed, perhaps as a result of what seemed like an enormous increase in the number of women in the industrial labor force. The A. F. of L. encouraged the Department of Labor to set up a Women's Bureau to defend the interests of wage earning women.[51] The Bureau, on investigation, found that many union officials viewed unionization and protective legislation as alternate means to the same goal: better working conditions. Sara Conboy, United Textile Workers' official and a WTUL activist, told a Women's Bureau interviewer that she believed in "legislation to limit long hours of work for women where and when the union [was] not strong enough to limit hours."[52] Some unionized workers thought legislation surer and faster or remarked that it was more dependable than possibly untrustworthy union leaders. A. J. Muste, then secretary of the Amalgamated Textile Workers Union of America, preferred unionization, but was said to have believed that legislation did not hinder organization and might be essential in industries with many women and minors.[53] But some women union leaders were not so sanguine. Fannia Cohn of the International Garment Workers Union only reluctantly acquiesced to the need for protective legislation. "I did not think the problem of working women could be solved in any other way than the problem of working men and that is through trade union organization," she wrote in 1927, "but considering that very few women are as yet organized into trade unions, it would be folly to agitate against protective legislation."[54] Cohn laid the problems of female workers on the absence of organization.

In any event, exclusion from unions merely confirmed the discomfort many women felt about participating in meetings. Italian and Southern families disliked their daughters going out in the evenings. Married and self-supporting women and widows had household duties at which they spent after-work hours. Women who attended meetings often participated reluctantly. They found the long discussions dull and were often intimidated by the preponderance of men. Men, for their part, resented the indifference of the women and further excluded them from leadership roles, thereby discouraging more women from attending. Even fines failed to spark attendance. Some women preferred to pay them rather than to go to the meetings.[55]

Self-images that derived from a paternalistic society joined ethnic ties in hindering unionization. Wage-earning women, anxious to marry, were sometimes reluctant to join unions for what they felt would be a temporary period. Occasionally, another role conflict was expressed: "No nice girl would belong to one," said one young woman.[56] An ILG organizer commented that most women who did not want to join a union claimed that "the boss is good to us and we have nothing to complain about and we don't want to join the union."[57] A woman who resisted unionization told an organizer that she knew "that $6 a week is not enough pay but the Lord helps me out. He always provides . . . I won't ever join a union. The Lord doesn't want me to."[58] A recent convert to unionism apologized for her former reticence. She had always scabbed because church people disapproved of unions. Moreover she and her sister had only with difficulty, she told an organizer, overcome their fear of the Italian men who were organizing their factory.[59]

Exceptions to this pattern occurred most often among women whose ethnic backgrounds encouraged both wage labor and a high level of social consciousness, as in the American Jewish community for example. Young Jewish women constituted the bulk of the membership of the International Ladies Garment Workers Union in the period from 1910 to 1920. Their rapid organization and faithful tenure is responsible for at least one quarter of the increased number of unionized women in the second decade of the twentieth century. And yet, they were unskilled and semiskilled workers, employed in small, scattered shops, and theoretically among the least organizable workers. These women, unionized at their own initiative, formed the backbone of the ILGWU, which had originally been directed toward organizing the skilled, male, cutters in the trade.

As it became clear to many laboring women that unionists would offer them little help, many women turned to such middle-class allies as the Women's Trade Union League. Established in 1905, the WTUL, an organization founded by female unionists and upper-middle-class reformers, offered needed financial and moral support for militant activity. Its paternalistic and benevolent style was not unfamiliar to women and those who came from immigrant families seemed particularly impressed with its Americanizing aspects. Young immigrant girls spoke with awe of the "fine ladies" of the WTUL and did not object to the folk-dancing classes that were part of the Chicago League's program.[60] But help from these nonwage-earning women came at a price. Working women who became involved in the WTUL moved quickly from working-class militance to the search for individual social mobility through vocational training, legislation, and the social refinements that provided access to better paying and rapidly increasing clerical and secretarial jobs. Rose Schneiderman illustrates this syndrome well. Beginning as a fiery organizer of the hat and cap makers, she moved through the WTUL to become Secretary of the New York State Department of Labor. Like the WTUL, which had begun by organizing women into

trade unions, she began in the 1920s to devote herself to attaining protective legislation, even borrowing some of the arguments used by men who did not wish women to compete with them.

By this time many working women were themselves moving in the direction of legislative solutions to exploitative working conditions. It seemed to be the most accessible solution to the problems of exploitation. Female workers interviewed by the Women's Bureau at first felt that both women and men should be included in any legislation. Later, they asked that office workers be exempted.[61] Other women acquiesced reluctantly. "I have always been afraid," wrote a supervisor in a Virginia silk mill, "that if laws were made discriminating for women, it would work a hardship upon them." By 1923 she had changed her mind: ". . . it would in time raise the entire standard rather than make it hard for women."[62] As women came to accept the necessity for legislation, they, like men, saw it as an alternative to unionization and rationalized its function in terms of their female "roles." A Women's Bureau agent noted of the reactions to a 48-hour law passed in Massachusetts that "the girls felt that legislation establishing a 48-hour week was more 'dignified' and permanent than one obtained through the union as it was not so likely to be taken away."[63] By the mid-1920s only business and professional women remained staunchly opposed to protective legislation.

Within this framework of trade-union ambivalence and the real need of wage-earning women for some form of protection employers who were particularly anxious that women not unionize pressed their advantage. Using crude techniques, rationalized by the home-and-motherhood argument, they contributed more than their share toward keeping women out of unions. In the small businesses in which women most often worked, employers used a variety of techniques to discourage organization, some of them familiar to men. Department store employees whose union membership became known were commonly fired. Many stores had spy systems so that employees could not trust their coworkers. Blacklists were common. A representative of the year-old retail clerks union testifying before a Congressional Committee in 1914 was afraid even to reveal the number of members in her union. Owners of New York's garment shops, fighting a losing battle by 1910, nevertheless frequently discharged employees who were thought to be active organizers or union members.[64]

Other tactics were no more subtle. Employers often played on ethnic and racial tensions in order to prevent women from unionizing. Rose Schneiderman, who formed the Hat and Cap Makers Union in 1903, fought against bosses who urged immigrant workers to stick to the "American shop"—a euphemism for an antiunion shop. Jewish owners sometimes hired only Italian workers who were thought to be less prone to unionization than Jews.[65] Others hired "landsmen" from the same old country community, hoping that fraternal instincts might keep them from striking. Blacks were played off against whites. Waitresses picketing Knab's restaurant in Chicago were met with counterpickets paid by the employers. A representative of the waitresses union reported indignantly that the employer "placed colored pickets on the street, colored women who wore signs like this 'Gee, I ain't mad at nobody and nobody ain't mad at Knab.'" When the nonunion pickets attracted a crowd, police moved in and arrested the union members. The women were further discouraged by trials engineered by employers who had previously given "every policeman a turkey free."[66]

Police routinely broke up picket lines and outdoor union meetings. Women who were accused of obstructing traffic or were incited into slapping provocateurs were arrested. More importantly, women who might have been interested in unionization were intimidated by police who surrounded open air meetings or by department store detectives who mingled obtrusively with potential recruits. Department store owners diverted workers from street meetings by locking all but one set of doors or sending trucks, horns honking full blast, to parade up and down the street in which a meeting was scheduled.[67]

Small employers formed mutual assistance associations to help them resist their employees' attempts to unionize. The Chicago Restaurant Keepers Association, for example, denied membership to any "person, firm or corporation . . . having signed agreements with any labor organization."[68] Garment manufacturers in both New York and Chicago created protective associations to combat what they called "the spreading evil of unionism."[69] In small towns, the power of town officials was called into play. Ann Washington Craton, organizing textile workers in Minersville, Pennsylvania, was warned by the town burgess: "You are to let our girls alone . . . Mr. Demsky will shut the factory down rather than have a union. . . . The town council brought this factory here to provide work for worthy widows and poor girls. We don't intend to have any trouble about it."[70]

Employers justified continued refusal to promote women or to offer them access to good jobs on the grounds that women's major contribution was to home and family. When they were challenged with the argument that bad working conditions were detrimental to that end, they responded slowly with paternalistic amelioration of the worst conditions and finally by acquiescing to protective labor legislation. Often concessions to workers were an effort to undercut mounting union strength, as for example when department store owners voluntarily closed their shops one evening a week. Some employers introduced welfare work in their factories, providing social workers, or other women, to help smooth relationships between them and their female employees. Mutual benefit associations, sometimes resembling company unions, were a more familiar tactic. Though they were presumably cooperative and designed to incorporate input from workers, membership in them was compulsory and dues of ten to twenty-five cents per month were deducted from wages. In return employees got sickness and health benefits of varying amounts but only after several months of continuous employment. A 1925 investigation of one widely publicized cooperative association operated by Filene's department store in Boston revealed that in all its twelve years, only store executives had ever served on its board of directors.[71]

Manufacturers seemed to prefer legislation regulating the hours and conditions of women's work to seeing their workers join unions. One, for example, told the Women's Bureau of the Department of Labor that a uniform 48-hour week for women would equalize competition and would, in any event, only confirm existing conditions in some shops. Some went even further hoping for federal legislation that would provide uniform standards nationwide.[72]

When occasionally employers found it in their interests to encourage unionism they did so in return for certain very specific advantages. One of these was the union label. In the garment industry the label on overalls in certain parts of the country assured higher sales. To acquire the right to use it, some employers rushed into contracts with the United Garment Workers and quite deliberately urged their workers into the union.[73] New York

garment manufacturers negotiated a preferential union shop, higher wages, and shorter hours with the ILGWU in return for which the union agreed to discipline its members and to protect employers against strikes. The garment manufacturers' protective association urged employers to "make every effort to increase the membership in the union so that its officers may have complete control of the workers and be enabled to discipline them when necessary."[74] Southern textile mill owners, otherwise violently opposed to unions, were similarly interested in the disciplinary functions of unionism. They would, an observer reported, modify their opposition "if the purposes of the union were to improve the educational, moral and social conditions of the workers."[75]

In general, however, employers made valiant attempts to keep women out of unions. The paternalism, benevolence, and welfare they offered in compensation were supported by other sectors of their society, including the trade unions. Middle-class reformers and government investigators had long viewed the harsh conditions under which women worked as detrimental to the preservation of home and family, and government regulation or voluntary employer programs seemed to many an adequate alternative. Unions played into this competitive structure adopting the home-and-motherhood argument to restrict women's labor-force participation. In the process they encouraged women to see their interests apart from those of male workers.

Limited labor-force opportunities, protective labor legislation and virtual exclusion from labor unions institutionalized women's isolation from the mainstream of labor. Not accidentally, these tendencies confirmed traditional women's roles, already nurtured by many ethnic groups and sustained by prevailing American norms. Together they translated into special behavior on the part of female workers that isolated them still further from male workers and added up to special treatment as members of the labor force.

In acquiescing, women perhaps bowed to the inevitable, seeking for themselves the goals of employers who preferred not to see them in unions, of male workers who hoped thereby both to limit competition and to share in the advantages gained, and of middle-class reformers who felt they were helping to preserve home and motherhood. Echoing labor union arguments of twenty years earlier, Women's Bureau head Mary Anderson defended protective legislation in 1925 on the grounds that such laws were necessary to conserve the health of the nation's women.[76]

A final consequence for women was to lead them to search for jobs in non-sex-stereotyped sectors of the labor market. Employers' needs in the rapidly expanding white-collar sector led women increasingly toward secretarial and clerical work. Vocational education to train women for office jobs, teaching, and social work expanded rapidly in the early twentieth century. Working women rationalized these jobs as steps up the occupational ladder; state and local governments and employers provided financial aid; and middle-class women launched a campaign to encourage women to accept vocational training.[77] It took an astute

union woman like Fannia Cohn to see what was happening. She drew a sharp line between her own function as educational director of the International Ladies Garment Workers Union and the functions of the new schools. Her hope was to train women to be better union members, not to get them out of the working class.

The parallel development of protective legislation and vocational education confirmed for many working women their marginal positions in the labor force, positions they continued to rationalize with obeisance to marriage and the family. As Alice Henry said of an earlier group of female wage-earners, "They did not realize that women were within the scope of the labor movement."[78] Fannia Cohn understood what that meant. That hard-headed and clear-sighted official of the ILGWU prefaced a call for a revolution in society's view of women with a plea for an end to competition between working women and men. Because it was destructive for all workers, she argued, "this competition must be abolished once and for all, not because it is immoral, yes inhuman, but because it is impractical, it does not pay."[79] But in the first two decades of the twentieth century, the moral arguments prevailed—releasing some women from some of the misery of toil, but simultaneously confirming their place in those jobs most conducive to exploitation.

Notes

Abbreviations: WB/NA: Women's Bureau collection, Record Group no. 86, National Archives; CIR: Final Report and Testimony of the Commission on Industrial Relations, Senate Documents, vol. 21, 64th Congress, 1st session, vol. 3, 1914; AF: American Federationist.

1. Fannia Cohn to William Green, March 6, 1925. Fannia Cohn collection, New York Public Library, Box 4.

2. Figures are derived from John Andrews

and W. D. P. Bliss, History of Women in Trade Unions, Report on the Condition of Women and Child Wage Earners in the U.S. (Washington, D.C.: G.P.O., 1911), vol. 10, pp. 136–39; Leo Wolman, Ebb and Flow in Trade Unionism (New York: National Bureau of Economic Research, 1936), pp. 74, 116; Leo Wolman, The Growth of American Trade Unions, 1880–1923 (New York: National Bureau of Economic Research, 1923), chapter 5. Wolman estimates that about 40 percent of organized women were in the three garment industry unions: ILGWU, Amalgamated Clothing Workers, and United Garment Workers, unions that had been either literally or virtually nonexistent before 1910. See Wolman, and Alice Henry, *Women and the Labor Movement* (New York: George Doran, 1923), chapter 4, for discussions of the difficulty of collecting trade union figures. Henry illustrates the numbers of women in specific unions.

3. The proportion of foreign-born and native-born and native-born daughters of foreign-born women declined slightly in this period and women continued to shift from manual sectors to low-level clerical sectors of the work force. See U.S. Census, *14th Census of Populations* (Washington, D.C.: G.P.O.: 1920), vol. 3, p. 15. Such occupations as taking in boarders, homework, and working on husbands' farms or in family businesses are not counted by census takers. Including these legitimate forms of labor would create drastic upward revisions in the proportion of working women, but we have no way of knowing by how much. The figures include black women, more than 40 percent of whom worked for wages, compared to about 20 percent of white women. However, about 32 percent of married black women worked, compared to less than 6 percent of married white women. Black wage-earning women are far more heavily concentrated in agricultural and domestic service jobs than their white counterparts. Figures are from Joseph Hill, *Women in Gainful Occupations: 1870–1920*, Census Monographs, no. 9 (Washington, D.C.: G.P.O., 1929), chapters 5 and 9; Janet Hooks, *Women's Occupations Through Seven Decades*, Women's Bureau Bulletin, no. 218 (Washington, D.C.: G.P.O., 1947), pp. 37, 39.

4. Andrews and Bliss, *History of Women in Trade Unions*, pp. 138–39. Even before the great uprising of 1909–1910, women, who made up 63 percent of the workers in the garment trades, represented 70 percent of the trade union members. This is all the more remarkable because their skill levels did not, by and large, match those of men. 32.5 percent of hat and cap makers were women, and 54 percent of union members were women. Women made up 50 percent of bookbinders, and 40 percent of the trade union members in that industry.

5. Ann Blankenhorn, miscellaneous notes, chapter 2, p. 12, file no. 23, box no. 1, Ann Craton Blankenhorn collection, Archives of Labor History, Wayne State University. For another example, see interview with Netti Chandler, Virginia Home visits, Bulletin no. 10, accession no. 51A101, WB/NA.

6. Interview with Faigele Shapiro, August 6, 1964. Amerikaner Yiddishe Geshichte Bel-pe, YIVO, pp. 2, 7.

7. AF 6 (November 1899):228.

8. Quoted in Andrews and Bliss, *History of Women in Trade Unions*, p. 173.

9. New York Women's Trade Union League, *Report of the Proceedings*, 4th Annual Conference of Trade Union Women, October 9, 10, 1926, p. 18.

10. Vera Shlakman, *Economic History of a Factory Town: A Study of Chicopee, Massachusetts*, Smith College Studies in History, vol. 20, no. 1–4 (October 1934–July 1935), p. 216; Andrews and Bliss, *History of Women in Trade Unions*, p. 166.

11. Andrews and Bliss, *History of Women in Trade Unions*, p. 168; Massachusetts Women's Trade Union League, *The History of Trade Unionism among Women in Boston* (Boston: WTUL, n.d., but c. 1907) pp. 22, 23.

12. Theresa Wolfson, "Where Are the Organized Women Workers?" AF 32 (June 1925):455–57.

13. Andrews and Bliss, *History of Women in Trade Unions*, p. 151.

14. AF 17 (November 1911), p. 896. James Kenneally, "Women and Trade Unions," *Labor History* 14 (Winter 1973), describes, but does not explain, the A. F. of L.'s mixed feelings.

15. Eva McDonald Valesh, "Women and Labor," AF 3 (February 1896):222.

16. Selig Perlman, *A History of Trade Unionism in the U.S.* (New York: Macmillan, 1923), p. 166. For illustrations of A. F. of L. policies see James Weinstein, *The Corporate Ideal in the Liberal State: 1900–1918* (Boston: Beacon Press, 1968), especially chapters 1 and 2; Ronald Radosh, *American Labor and United States Foreign Policy* (New York: Vintage, 1970); Stanley Aronowitz, *False Promises* (New York; McGraw-Hill, 1973).

17. Samuel Gompers, "Should the Wife Help Support the Family?" AF 13 (January 1906):36. See also Stuart Reid, "The Joy of Labor? Plutocracy's Hypocritical Sermonizing Exposed—A Satire," AF 11 (November 1904): 977–78.

18. "Mainly Progressive," AF 3 (March 1896):16, "What Our Organizers Are Doing," AF 10 (April 1903):370.

19. Editorial, AF 11 (July 1904):584.

20. "Trade Union History," *AF* 9 (November 1902):871.

21. John Safford, "The Good That Trade Unions Do," part I, *AF* 9 (July 1902):353, 358; "Talks on Labor," *AF* 12 (November 1905):846.

22. William Gilthorpe, "Advancement," *AF* 17 (October 1910): 847.

23. Safford, "The Good That Trade Unions Do," part 2, *AF* 9 (August 1902):423.

24. Edward O'Donnell, "Women as Breadwinners: The Error of the Age," *AF* 4 (October 1897): 186. The article continued: "The wholesale employment of women in the various handicrafts must gradually unsex them as it most assuredly is demoralizing them, or stripping them of that modest demeanor that lends a charm to their kind, while it numerically strengthens the multitudinous army of loafers, paupers, tramps and policemen."

25. Safford, "The Good That Trade Unions Do," part 1, pp. 357–58.

26. Gompers, "Should the Wife Help Support the Family?" p. 36.

27. Ibid. See also Louis Vigoreux, "Social Results of the Labor Movement in America," *AF* 6 (April 1899):25.

28. Women's Labor Resolution, *AF* 5 (January 1899):220; "Talks on Labor," *AF* 10 (June 1903):477.

29. Massachusetts, WTUL, *History of Trade Unionism Among Women in Boston*, p. 13; Elizabeth Baker, *Technology and Women's Work* (New York: Columbia University Press, 1964), p. 33.

30. Mildred Rankin to Mrs. Raymond Robins, March 30, 1919, Margaret Dreier Robins Collection, University of Florida, Gainesville, Florida. In 1918, two women members of the federation offered a resolution to the national convention urging the addition of two women to the all-male executive board. It was quietly suppressed.

31. Gompers, "Should the Wife Help Support the Family?" p. 36.

32. Alice Woodbridge, "Women's Labor," *AF* 1 (April 1894):66–67; Valesh, "Women and Labor," p. 222; and Massachusetts WTUL, *History*, p. 32. 2.

33. WTUL Action of Policies, pp. 3, 8, box 4, accession no. 55A556, WB/NA: Proceedings of the A. F. of L. convention, 1923. See also Massachusetts WTUL, *History of Trade Unionism Among Women in Boston*, p. 32.

34. Blankenhorn manuscript notes, chapter 4, p. 17, box 1, file no. 24. Such examples of family unity are not unusual in the mine/mill towns of Western Pennsylvania and the Appalachian mountains. Women helped to picket during strikes, provided essential support services, and sometimes spearheaded attacks against mine management.

35. Pauline Newman, interview, undated, Amerikaner Yiddisher Geschichte Bel-pe, p. 21, YIVO. Gladys Boone, *The Women's Trade Union League in Great Britain and the U.S.A.* (New York: Columbia University Press, 1942), p. 166, recounts a similar incident as having taken place in 1918. I suspect that it might be the same one and that her date is incorrect. Andrews and Bliss, *History of Women in Trade Unions*, p. 149, notes that women practically disappeared from this union between 1905 and 1910—a period in which master bakers were rapidly being eliminated by machinery.

36. Mildred Rankin to Mrs. Raymond Robins, March 30, 1919, Robins papers.

37. Boone, *The Women's Trade Union League*, p. 167; Alice Henry, *Women in the Labor Movement* (New York: Doran, 1923): 102.

38. Interview with Vail Ballou Press, Effects of Legislation: Night Work Schedule, New York, NA/WB.

39. See for example Rankin to Robins, March 30, 1919; and M. E. Jackson, "The Colored Woman in Industry," *Crisis* 17 (November 1918):14.

40. New York Women's Trade Union League, *Report of the Proceedings*, 4th Conference, p. 14.

41. Undated interviews, unions, for Bulletin no. 65, NA/WB.

42. Testimony of Hilda Svenson, C.I.R., p. 2307; the testimony was taken in June 1914.

43. Florence Sanville to Rose Schneiderman, November 28, 1917, Rose Scheiderman collection. Tamiment Institute library, box A 94. For examples of union discrimination see Massachusetts WTUL, *History of Trade Unionism Among Women in Boston*, p. 13; Andrews and Bliss, *History of Women in Trade Unions*, pp. 156, 157; Alice Henry, *The Trade Union Woman* (New York: Burt Franklin, 1973), p. 150.

44. Testimonies, box 15, accession no. 51A101, WB/NA. The women had been hired when the war broke out.

45. Emma Steghagen to Mary Anderson, January 15, 1919, WTUL Action on Policies, accession no. 55A556, WB/NA.

46. United States Education and Labor Committee, *Report Upon the Relations Between Capital and Labor* (Washington, D.C., G.P.O., 1882), vol. 1, p. 453. See

Andrews and Bliss, *History of Women in Trade Unions*, p. 94, for Strasser's often-quoted "We cannot drive the females out of the trade but we can restrict their daily quota of labor through factory laws," and p. 155 of the same volume for Samuel Gompers' fears of female competition as expressed in 1887.

47. Interview with Mr. Salerno, Amalgamated Clothing Workers, interviews, unions, accession no. 51A101, WB/NA.

48. Interview with Mr. Hurley, July 1919, Women Street Car Conductors, accession no. 51A101, WB/NA.

49. Sir Lyon Playfair, "Children and Female Labor," *AF* 7 (April 1900):103. See also Martha Moore Avery, "Boston Kitchen Help Organize," *AF* 10 (April 1903):259, 260.

50. Ira Howerth, "The Kingdom of God in Modern Industry," *AF* 14 (August 1907): 544.

51. Mary Anderson, "The Federal Government Recognizes Problems of Women in Industry," *AF* 32 (June 1925):453.

52. Individual interviews, Massachusetts, April 12, 1920, accession no. 51A101, WB/NA. Her preference rested on the union's ability to ask for wage raises to compensate for the reduction in hours.

53. Individual interviews, Massachusetts and New Jersey, accession no. 51A101, WB/NA. See especially interviews with A. J. Muste, Mr. Sims, Secretary of the Weavers union, and Amalgamated meeting of workers at Princeton Worsted Mills. These are undated but must have occurred in early 1921.

54. Fannia Cohn to Dr. Marion Phillips, September 13, 1827, Fannia Cohn Collection, box 4.

55. Interviews with Tony Salerno, Amalgamated Clothing Workers Union and Hat and Cap Makers Local 7, Boston, individual interviews, unions, accession no. 51A101, BW/NA. Massachusetts WTUL, *History of Trade Unionism among Women in Boston*, p. 11.

56. Lizzie Swank Holmes, "Women Workers of Chicago," *AF* 12 (August 1905): 507–10; Eva McDonald Valesh, "Women in Welfare Work," *AF* 15 (April 1908):282–84; "Mainly Progressive," *AF* 3 (March 1896): 16.

57. Shapiro, p. 25.

58. *Justice* (April 19, 1919):2.

59. Blankenhorn manuscript notes, chapter 13, p. 4, box 1, file 25.

60. For example, see Mary Dreier, address to New York WTUL in *Report of the Pro-ceedings*, 4th conference, 1926, p. 14. Dreier refers in this speech to the difficulty the WTUL had getting female workers to serve on the executive board at first. See Nancy Schrom Dye, "Creating a Feminist Alliance: Sisterhood and Class Conflict in the New York WTUL, 1903–1914," *Feminist Studies* 2 (1975):24–38. Kenneally, "Women and Trade Unions," treats the WTUL's relations with the A. F. of L. at length.

61. Individual interviews, California, effects of legislation, accession no. 51A101, WB/NA.

62. Quoted in a letter from Mary Van Kleech to Mary Anderson, February 2, 1923, Mary Van Kleech collection, Smith College, unsorted.

63. Breman and O'Brien, individual interviews, Massachusetts, accession no. 51A101, WB/NA. Such sentiments must, however, be treated cautiously. We know, for example, that the National Consumers' League in Philadelphia orchestrated an anti-E.R.A. letter-writing campaign by wage-earning women in 1922. The league urged women to write letters arguing that the E.R.A. would limit or eliminate protective labor legislation. See Barbara Klazcynska, "Working Women in Philadelphia: 1900–1930," (Ph.D. dissertation, Temple University, 1975). Janice Hedges and Stephen Bemis point out that most "protective" legislation has now been invalidated by EEOC decisions. "Sex Stereotyping: Its Decline in Skilled Trades," *Monthly Labor Review* 97 (May 1974):18.

64. Sylvia Shulman, testimony, CIR, pp. 2285, 2292; Hilda Svenson, testimony, CIR, pp. 2311, 2317; Elizabeth Dutcher, testimony, CIR, p. 2392. Exceptions sometimes occurred in small western towns where workers would not patronize nonunion stores. Dutcher testified that 75 employees of Macy's were discharged in 1907 after they attended a union ball. Svenson, CIR, p. 2307; Lillian Mallach to David Dubinsky, December 18, 1964, YIVO. See also minutes of the Waistmakers Conference, January 10, 1911, ILGWU, Ladies Waist and Dress Makers Union file, Rose Schneiderman collection, Tamiment, box A 95.

65. Rose Schneiderman with Lucy Goldthwaite, *All for One* (New York: Paul Erickson, 1967):59, Shapiro, p. 9.

66. Elizabeth Maloney testimony, CIR, pp. 3246–47. See also M. E. Jackson, "The Colored Woman in Industry," pp. 12–17.

67. Agnes Nestor, testimony, CIR, p. 3389; Elizabeth Dutcher testimony, CIR, p. 2405.

68. Elizabeth Maloney testimony, CIR, p. 3245.

69. Leon Stein, *The Triangle Fire* (Philadelphia: J. B. Lippincott, 1952), Nestor, CIR, p. 3382.

70. Blankenhorn, manuscript notes, chapter 4, p. 17, file 24, box 1.

71. Nestor, CIR, p. 3382; Svenson, CIR, p. 3382 and Svenson, CIR, p. 2308, reveal the degree to which this was an attempt to undercut union strength; see also an unsigned typescript entitled "Personnel and Management in a Retail Store: A Study of the Personnel Policies and Practices of William Filene's Sons Co., Boston, Mass.," p. 14, in the Mary Van Kleeck collection, unsorted, Smith College; and Marie Obenauer and Charles Verrill, *Wage Earning Women in Stores and Factories*, Report on the Condition of Women and Child Wage Earners (Washington, D.C.: G.P.O., 1911), vol. 5, p. 48; Svenson, CIR, p. 2309.

72. See Cambridge Paper Box Company,

Long Hour Day Schedule, accession no. 51A101, WB/NA.

73. Andrews and Bliss, *History of Women in Trade Unions*, p. 169.

74. U.S. Department of Labor, Bureau of Labor Statistics, Bulletin no. 145, 1914, p. 37.

75. *The Cotton Textile Industry*, Report on the Condition of Women and Child Wage Earners (Washington, D.C.: G.P.O., 1910), vol. 1, p. 608.

76. Mary Anderson, "Industrial Standards for Women," *AF* 32 (July 1925):21.

77. See Massachusetts WTUL, *History of Trade Unionism among Women in Boston*, pp. 7, 32; New York WTUL, *Report of the Proceedings*, 4th Conference, p. 21.

78. Henry, *Woman and the Labor Movement*, p. 108.

79. Typescript of "Complete Equality Between Men and Women," from the December 1917 issue of the *Ladies Garment Worker*, Fannia Cohn collection, box 7.

MAXINE SELLER
The Education of the Immigrant Woman, 1900–35

The way Americans have viewed intellectual activity among women tells us a great deal about what they believed to be women's proper roles. By the late nineteenth and early twentieth centuries a slightly higher proportion of girls than boys were attending school and girls were increasing their lead over boys in the upper age group. This achievement was, to some traditionalists, a threat; they believed that too much education would leave women unfit for their primary role as wife and mother. In the following essay Maxine Seller explores how the familiar ideology that women were naturally destined for domesticity was fused with stereotyped notions about the intellectual inferiority of the new immigrants from southern and eastern Europe to produce educational programs for immigrant women that were vocational rather than academic. Note how the educational material used in some of these programs made even the learning of

"The Education of the Immigrant Woman, 1900–1935" by Maxine Seller, in *Journal of Urban History* 4, no. 3 (May 1978): 307–30. Copyright © 1978 by Sage Publications, Inc. Reprinted by permission of the author and the publisher, Sage Publications, Inc.

the English language a lesson in traditional sex role expectations. Note, too, Seller's sensitivity to differences among various ethnic groups and to the conflicting views among immigrant families themselves as to the kind of education best for their wives and daughters. In her judgment, why were efforts on the part of immigrant communities to educate their women more successful in meeting their needs than progressive programs?

In the late nineteenth and early twentieth centuries, millions of southern and eastern European immigrants made their way from Europe to the growing cities of a rapidly industrializing United States. Their arrival coincided with and contributed to a ferment of educational reform, as Progressive educators set to work developing new programs to meet the needs of new urban populations.[1] This article will examine the encounter between Progressive educational reform and the immigrant woman. It will explore three interrelated questions. First, what programs did educators develop to meet the needs of urban immigrant women and their American-born daughters? Second, how did immigrant women react to these programs? And finally, what kinds of educational programs did immigrant women participate in within their own community?

An examination of the education of immigrant women adds an important dimension to the current controversy over the intent and result of early twentieth-century educational reform. In recent years scholars have challenged the traditional view that public schools gave the poor, including the immigrant, a chance to get ahead in American society.[2] The educational experience of immigrant women lends support to a moderate revisionist view. School superintendents, social workers, home missionaries, and other educational professionals were usually earnest and well-intended, but their programs were shaped by preconceived, socially conservative ideas about the limited interests and abilities of immigrant women. Therefore, these programs were not so varied, not so intellectually challenging, and not so effective in reaching their intended audience as programs developed within the immigrant communities, often by the immigrant women themselves.

Progressive educators believed that educational programs should be adapted to meet the needs and capabilities of different populations.[3] Consequently, the programs they designed for immigrant women reflected their judgment of the needs and capabilities of immigrants in general, of women in general, and of immigrant women in particular. Most old stock Americans, including educators, saw the new southern and eastern European immigrants as a morally, culturally, and intellectually inferior species which, if left un-Americanized, would destroy the American city and menace the middle class Anglo-Saxon way of life. Appropriate education for immigrants in general, then, was thought to be social and vocational rather than academic—schools should teach immigrants the English language and acceptable American-style behavior, help them adjust to the demands of life in the urban slums, and prepare them for their proper place in the lower ranks of the labor force of a growing industrial nation.[4]

Sexism as well as nativism influenced the thinking of many educators during the Progressive era. G. Stanley Hall, prominent leader of the child study movement, advised educators to concentrate on development of intuition rather than intellect in female adolescents, warning that "bookishness is probably a bad sign in girls."[5] Edward Thorndike, the leading educational psychologist of the day, believed the intellectual training of women to be socially wasteful, since women had mediocre abilities.[6] Physicians as well as educators worried that too much mental effort injured women's health, making them less efficient for their primary purpose, the production of the next generation.[7]

Immigrant women had the double disadvantage of being both female and foreign-born; hence, it was considered doubly appropriate that their education be social and vocational rather than academic or intellectual. "The wives of the new immigration are far more backward than the men," wrote Peter Roberts, expressing a widely held point of view that immigrant women were unintelligent, uninformed, and "dirty in the home."[8]

After the passing of the Nineteenth Amendment, educators and organizations such as the League of Women Voters pleaded the necessity of training immigrant women for intelligent voting (a plea which became more plausible after the Cable Act of 1922 gave immigrant women the right to apply for citizenship separately from their husbands).[9] A few insightful social workers—women like Jane Addams, Sophonisba Breckinridge, and Grace Abbott—were concerned about improving the quality of life for the urban immigrant women, who had much to teach America as well as much to learn from America.

Far more frequently, however, education for the immigrant woman was seen not as a means of aiding the development of the individual, but rather as a means of enhancing her performance of her roles as housewife and mother. Proper (from the educator's point of view) performance of these roles was seen not only as beneficial to the immigrant woman's family, but more importantly, as vital to the health and safety of American society as a whole. Public school systems, settlement houses, and churches sought to give the immigrant woman a smatter-

ing of English and an understanding of American manners and mores, so that she would reinforce rather than undermine their efforts to Americanize the rest of the family. Educators took great pains to teach the immigrant women the fundamentals of housecleaning and hygiene not only to protect the immigrant family from disease, but more importantly to prevent immigrant quarter contagions from spreading to their own more affluent neighborhoods. Finally, the literature of the period stressed the need to educate the immigrant mother, so that she could maintain authority over her American-born children and thereby control one of the most troubling of the urban social problems, juvenile delinquency among the second generation.[10]

The education of young girls as well as mature women focused on their roles as housewives and mothers, albeit in the future. Sociologist Robert Woods assured his readers that:

> it is not the acquisition of facts, but cultivation that the foreign girls need for their future happiness and usefulness— correct ideas of life and freedom from superstition rather than definite knowledge about trade winds and syntax. . . . The daughters of Russian and Italian immigrants do not look upon teaching, book-keeping, stenography, or shoptending as aims in life. They simply and openly desire a sound mind . . . within a sound body, that they may make good wives and present their husbands with healthy sons.[11]

The most widely acclaimed program instituted for immigrant women in the public schools, therefore, was home economics, which included cooking, sewing, laundering, housecleaning, nutrition, childcare, hygiene, and a timid but persistent approach to sex education. "At the present day, when everyone concedes that, for older girls, the household arts are the most valuable subject in the curriculum, we look back with amazement to the time when . . . the training of girls differed in no whit from that given to boys," wrote Superintendent Henry Emerson of Buffalo, New York.[12] Home economics was considered appropriate for all girls, but especially for "the average girl of foreign parentage," who spent many hours in it as early as fifth or even third grade, in summer school and in extracurricular activities such as "little mothers" leagues.[13] Progressive educational reformers favored home economics because it was suited to the laboratory or project method which they strongly favored, because it related to the "real" life of family and community,[14] and because it saved money. For example, the school girls of Buffalo made great quantities of linens for the city's public bathhouses, hospital, and orphanages.[15]

For immigrants, home economics instruction was a means of Americanization and social control. This is explicitly stated in Pearl Ellis's *Americanization through Homemaking*,[16] a handbook written for the education of Mexican American girls but applicable to other immigrant groups as well. Emphasizing health and hygiene education, Ellis recommended that immigrant girls be taught "the importance of durable and clean underwear. They are apt to be lax in this respect."[17] Ellis advocated the use of homemaking classes to Americanize the life style of Mexican immigrants, suggesting, for example, substitution of American-style salad for the more nutritious bean dishes.[18] She warned that Americanization through the use of American consumer products was to be encouraged with caution, however, lest immigrant girls aspire to a lifestyle beyond their station.[19]

Home economics programs could be used as a means of keeping immigrant women and their families "in their place," that is, in the lower socioeconomic classes. For example, Ellis recommended that immigrant girls be taught to cook with inexpensive ingredients ("conservation cook-

ing") and to budget carefully so that "when the supply of cheap labor exceeds the demand" and immigrant men became jobless, the housewife would somehow manage to keep food on the table. Thus, the wife would save her husband from a life of crime, or, even worse, labor activism. Ellis warns:

> The pangs of hunger are accelerators of criminal tendencies. . . . Forgery or stealing follows. The head of the family lands in jail. The rest of the family . . . become county charges. Property owners pay the taxes for their maintenance. If we can teach the girls food values and a careful system of budgeting, how to plan in prosperity for the day of no income and adversity, we shall avoid much of the trouble. . . . Employers maintain that a man with home and family is more dependable and less revolutionary in his tendencies. Thus, the influence of the home extends to labor problems.[20]

Finally, home economics was seen as the perfect vocational training for immigrant girls and women. Instruction in laundering, cooking, serving, housecleaning, sewing, and childcare prepared girls not only for housewifery but also for the appropriate low status, low paying jobs as domestic servants, kitchen workers, waitresses, laundresses, nursemaids, and commercial seamstresses. Home economics programs in the high schools prepared girls for better paying positions in millinery, fancy embroidery, dietetics, and the like, but immigrant girls rarely got to high school.[21]

Home economics dominated education for immigrant women of all ages in settlement house and church programs, home teacher programs, and vocational programs, as well as in the public schools. Men's programs in these agencies included classes in various trades, citizenship, and English, and a wide range of clubs, debating societies, and athletics; women's programs concentrated on cooking and sewing, with the occasional addition of singing, dramatics, and typewriting.[22] The commitment of most religious settlement houses to programs reflecting narrowly defined traditional sex roles is expressed in the aim of the Presbyterian Neighborhood House in Chicago, "To give to strong men more strength, to graceful women more grace."[23]

Some secular settlements defined women's interests more broadly, offering serious instruction in music, drama, and literature, consumer education, and political action. Jewish mothers' clubs discussed political and economic issues, education, books, and music.[24] Hull House in Chicago sponsored exhibits of women's crafts. In New York City, the Social Centers of the Political Equality Association gave classes in public speaking, civics, city history, and current events and held weekly discussions of women's suffrage.[25] In Chicago, a Bohemian settlement house women's group fulfilled the Progressive educator's ideal of learning by doing: the women learned about American government by participating in a campaign first to rid the neighborhood of garbage, and finally to rid the city of a corrupt administration.[26]

The late nineteenth and early twentieth centuries saw the rise of vocational education, but immigrant women, like native-born women, did not participate fully in the benefits of this movement. In 1910 only 26 out of 193 special trade schools were for women.[27] An officer of the National Women's Trade Union League complained that in a coeducational agricultural school in an eastern city "the boy learns chemistry of the soil . . . but the girl is taught cooking and sewing."[28] The public school system did offer two important vocational opportunities to the relatively small number of immigrant girls who were academically and financially able to go beyond elementary education— office work and teaching.[29]

Immigrant women too old for public school could attend night school classes in many cities where they were offered courses in cooking, sewing, typewriting, and the English language. English classes for immigrant adults used special materials focusing almost exclusively on women's roles as wives, mothers, and homemakers.[30] A typical manual for night school English teachers suggested the following exercise for male students:

> I wash my hands. I sharpen my pencil. I read a book. I come into the room. I go out of the room.

The parallel exercise for the women's classes:

> I wash my hands. I wash the dishes. I set the table. I sweep the floor. I dust the furniture.

Men were taught to name the president of the United States and to locate the city hall; women were taught to name kitchen utensils. Men learned to read signs such as "Exit" and "Fire Alarm"; women learned to read signs such as "Bargain Sale" and "Reduced." Men practiced telling how to send a telegram, file a complaint, apply for a job. Women practiced telling how to make an apron and put up a lunch for a man.[31]

California, Massachusetts, Pennsylvania, and other states experimented with home teacher programs to reach immigrant women kept at home by family responsibilities. Home teachers gave parties for immigrant women, took them to clinics, and advised them about personal problems, housekeeping, and child-care. An early home teacher in California who reported that her English language class had doubled was equally enthusiastic over the progress of a housecleaning campagin.[32] The home teacher's first duty was to investigate the background of the truant school child; her interest in the immigrant mother was secondary.[33]

When time was devoted to the education of the mother, it was a narrowly conceived education indeed. An English lesson manual for the California home teachers program offered instructions in bedmaking ("I take off the dirty sheets . . . I put on the clean sheets"), in hygiene ("We must bathe often . . . Stale garbage is dangerous . . . A clean house is a good doctor"), and in consumerism ("I am happy . . . I have money . . . I go to the store"). A model dialogue suggests the job aspirations considered appropriate for the pupils:

First pupil: I want to work.
Second pupil: What can you do?
First pupil: I can wash and iron.
Second pupil: What else?
First pupil: I can wash windows and clean house.
Second pupil: Will you come to my house Monday to wash?
First pupil: Gladly.[34]

The reaction of immigrant women to the programs planned for them by American-born "Progressive" educators varied widely. Some first- and second-generation immigrant girls had no reaction at all to the new educational programs because they were not exposed to them. Public schools in major cities were often so crowded that there were not enough seats for all the potential students.[35] Inundated by the size of the attendance problem, truant officers and social workers concentrated on keeping immigrant boys in school (and off the streets), allowing immigrant girls to drop out early or, in some cases, never to attend at all.[36] Immigrant parents sometimes kept school age girls at home to help with housework, to care for younger children, to earn money in unskilled domestic or industrial work, or to prepare for marriage. Many parents doubted that schooling beyond the elementary level would increase the earning powers of their daughter,[37] doubts not without foundation. Scarce resources were more likely to be invested in continuing the education of sons than of daughters.[38]

Many foreign-born girls were overage for their classes because of linguistic and cultural differences, and their drop-out rate was high. Children from urban areas with high literacy rates and well-developed educational systems similar in style, content, and values to that of the United States did better than children from rural areas with low literacy rates and vastly different learning systems.[39] Additional factors came into play for women, such as the roles women had played in the home society. In Finland, for example, women were enfranchised in 1905, and in the Russian Pale, young, secularized Jewish women took active roles in Socialist and Zionist movements. For these reasons Japanese, Bohemian, Finnish and Jewish women seemed particularly successful in using existing American educational opportunities and in creating new opportunities within their own communities. Generalizations based on ethnic origin must be approached with caution, however, since there were wide variations within each group based on age, class, length of time in the United States, and religious and political background.

Immigrant girls who did attend school were more likely than boys to find facilities inadequate. Money spent on girls' vocational programs in public schools was less than that spent on similar programs for boys. The problem of inadequate facilities was even more acute for the adult woman. At their post–World War I peak, night schools throughout the nation enrolled only a quarter of a million out of a possible thirteen and three quarters million immigrants; but, for a variety of reasons, women constituted less than a third of this already small number.[40] In 1920 Chicago had a nonnaturalized immigrant population of over 300,000 men and women, yet mothers' classes in the Chicago schools showed a meager registration of 400, of whom 240 actually attended regularly.[41] In smaller communities the situation was even worse. Private agencies that talked a great deal about the necessity of education for immigrant women balked at committing their resources. Industrialists lauded the benefits of factory schools for immigrant workers but were unwilling to pay teachers or to allow publicly funded instruction on company time.[42] In 1919 the industrial metropolis of Chicago provided factory schools for 1,678 men and only 178 women.[43]

Evidence about the response of the many girls and women who did participate in the special programs designed for them is mixed. According to Superintendent Emerson, immigrant parents "hailed with approbation" the introduction of home economics instruction for their daughters, and "domestic science" was the most popular course in Buffalo's vocation and evening schools.[44] While the originator of a program may be less than objective in evaluating it, undoubtedly many girls found cooking and sewing instruction a welcome relief from uninspiring academic classes, especially when language problems made those classes unintelligible. Because they had acquired domestic skills at home, many girls had successful and pleasant experiences in home economics programs, and second-generation girls usually welcomed opportunities to learn American methods of cooking and housekeeping. Some of the more traditional immigrant parents agreed with the Progressive educators that domestic science was more appropriate than Latin or mathematics for their daughters. There were practical benefits as well; most immigrants were poor, and food and clothing prepared in class could be used at home.

Immigrant parents and daughters were far from unanimous, however, in their support of education that was social and vocational rather than academic. When educational reformers tried to introduce the Gary Plan—with its emphasis upon laboratories, workshops, and "learning by doing"—into the New York public schools, immigrant parents rioted in the streets for ten days and elected a mayor who voiced their determination that "our boys and *girls* shall have an opportunity to become doctors, lawyers, clergymen, musicians, artists, orators, poets . . . notwithstanding the views of the Rockefeller Board of Education."[45] While a large proportion of the irate parents who blocked the Gary Plan in New York City were Jewish, other ethnic groups had similar ambitions for their children. Early Polish parochial high schools for girls, supported at great sacrifice by a poor community, were rigorously academic, training girls to be teachers, not housewives.

Classes in night schools, settlement houses, and churches got mixed reactions. Some women found those programs valuable and deeply satisfying. This is illustrated by the story, probably apocryphal, of the family who, on opening the safe box of their immigrant mother, found along with her citizenship papers a tattered membership card to the Educational Alliance (a Jewish-sponsored settlement house in New York).[46]

Consistently low registrations and high drop-out rates, however, indicate that many women, perhaps the majority, reacted negatively. Directors of night schools complained that it was difficult to get and keep immigrant pupils, especially women.[47] Most night school students were native-born. The much-praised pioneer California home teachers program for immigrant women had a drop-out rate of 80 percent.[48] Settlement houses and "Y" programs had loyal followings, yet the majority of women who participated in their clubs and other educational activities were native-born or had been in the United States since childhood and spoke English fluently—not the population the educators hoped most to reach. Moreover, the number of settlements was so small and the number of people they affected so few that, according to one community leader, "if they were to disappear overnight, the life, growth, and development of my people and their assimilation into American life would go on just the same."[49]

Obviously, many women worked so hard earning a living, rearing children, or both, that they had no time or energy left for schooling. Traditional attitudes toward women's roles kept others from participating. For example, Italian women dropped out of English classes in Buffalo because their husbands felt they belonged at home.[50] Though Italian and Asian communities tended to be more conservative than the Polish and Jewish, immigrant women of every ethnic group faced this problem. A young Jewish woman complained to the editor of the *Forward* that her husband, "an intelligent man . . . in favor of the emancipation of women," refused to let her into the apartment when she returned from night school![51]

The structure and the content of the programs themselves caused difficulties. Classes usually met four nights a week; women with family responsibilities had trouble attending this often. Many women were discouraged by teachers who spoke only English, and, in some cases, by male teachers in coeducational classrooms. Catholic and Jewish women were suspicious of programs sponsored by the YWCAs or by Protestant settlement houses, fearing (sometimes rightly and sometimes wrongly) that efforts would be made to convert them to an alien faith.

Emphasis upon Americanization at the expense of ethnic traditions alienated women who cherished their distinctive lifestyles. The problem was aggravated by the ignorance and insensitivity many educators demonstrated toward immigrant culture. Traditional South Italian women withdrew in shock when social workers came to their homes to discuss personal hygiene and sex education, subjects about which their community displayed great reticence. For centuries South Italian mores had been strict in demanding the

virginity of unmarried girls and the respectful subordination of children to parents; Italian women must, therefore, have been amused, if not outraged, by a YWCA pamphlet urging them to caution their daughters against impurity and to be "chums" to their sons.[52]

Often immigrant women dropped out simply because programs did not meet their needs. When women requested instruction in "plain cooking" and received lessons on pie-baking instead, the class dwindled. Proud homemakers were insulted by efforts to get them to substitute cheap ingredients for butter, milk, and eggs in their treasured recipes. Many immigrant women were frustrated by educators' insistence on giving them domestic science to the exclusion of everything else. When Lithuanian women came to the Immigration Protective League for lessons in English and were treated to the project's method of instruction—English lessons through biscuit-making—they refused to come back.[53]

Confusing lack of past educational opportunity with lack of intelligence, educators often treated immigrant women with condescension. Home teachers in California were advised that in dealing with immigrant women they must "appeal to the dramatic spirit of a play folk."[54] Teachers were told not to expect much from immigrant women, whose minds supposedly had been stagnating for years. Even when educators approached women with good will, their "progressive" methods were often inappropriate for their traditionally minded clients. As late as the mid 1930s, a training manual for home teachers in Pennsylvania advised teachers to come to class with crayons, paste, and paper clips and to plan the lesson around simple household objects—"pan, pot, kettle, broom." Ironically, the same manual warned teachers that their pupils would refuse to begin any lesson until they had paper, pen, something to copy, and a book.[55] Clearly the educators and the population to be educated had different ideas of the nature of the task at hand.

Vocational education, too, often failed to meet the needs of immigrant women, especially younger women who avoided the service roles often taken by their mothers. In 1910 a million and a half foreign-born women were employed in a wide range of industrial as well as domestic activities. A few practiced professions, managed businesses, edited newspapers, wrote novels, produced plays, and organized unions. Obviously, vocational education that focused exclusively on domestic skills was not appropriate for these women.[56]

The failure of American educators to plan challenging academic programs for the intellectually oriented immigrant woman—and the frustration that resulted from this failure—are vividly portrayed in a short story by Anzia Yezierska. In the story, a young woman, "crazy to learn," comes to an institution called "The Immigrant School for Girls." Here the gracious but cool Mrs. Olney encourages her to enroll in something useful—a course in sewing machine operation or in cooking:

> "Ain't thoughts useful?" (protests the would-be student in dismay). "Does America only want the work from my body. . . . Us immigrants wants to be people . . . and it's the chance to think out thoughts that makes people . . . I got grand things in me, and American won't let me give nothing."
>
> "I'm afraid you have come to the wrong place," (responds Mrs. Olney). "We only teach trades here."[57]

Despite the inadequacies of the programs designed for them by American educators, immigrant women learned English, and many acquired a broad, general education as well as becoming literate, perhaps for the first time, in both their native language and English. Most adults achieved this on their own initiative

through a variety of formal and informal institutions usually within their own ethnic communities. The self-education of immigrant women differed from that provided by American educators in several significant ways. First, it was often carried out in the native language. Second, it incorporated rather than conflicted with the cultural heritage of the old country. Finally, it grew out of a realistic rather than a stereotyped view of immigrant women; thus, it embraced not only household and language skills, but also a wide range of political, economic, and cultural interests.

Many immigrant women attended educational institutions created by religious, cultural, or political elements within their ethnic communities. German, Irish, Polish, and other Slavic girls often attended bilingual and bicultural parochial schools supported by their religious communities. Adults attended a variety of institutions similar to the nineteenth-century American lyceums. The bilingual Hungarian Free Lyceum in New York City gave lectures on Hungarian and American culture, such as "Modern Hungarian Poets" and "The American Revolution," and on subjects of current interest, such as "Industrial Hazards" and "The Influence of the Press." The socialist-sponsored Polish University of Chicago gave lectures in Polish about "the theory of evolution, primitive man, and the development of language" and took students to visit civic agencies all over the city. Its public lectures drew as many as a thousand men and women at a time.[58]

Ethnic parishes provide education experiences in a familiar setting. Catholic churches in ethnic neighborhoods fostered knowledge of traditional immigrant languages and cultures as a means of strengthening religious loyalty, but before World War I were often hesitant about venturing into Americanization education. During and after the war, the Church launched a nationwide Americanization campaign, preparing textbooks and holding classes in farming and mining communities as well as in cities. In San Francisco in 1921, a church-sponsored civics program was taught by Italian speaking lawyers to an enrollment of 787 Italian immigrant men and women.[59] Many Protestant parishes also provided a variety of educational opportunities, both formal and informal. In Finnish Luthern churches, for example, women wrote parish newspapers, chaired fund-raising campaigns, and traveled to church conventions around the country.[60]

Labor organizations, many actually ethnic organizations, played an important role in the education of immigrant working women. Radical Finnish women attended Marxist reading groups and social gatherings, organized campaigns in support of strikers, and participated in plays to educate themselves and others about the political and economic plight of the Finns.[61] In 1915 the Ladies Waist Makers Union of New York sponsored a series of lectures and concerts attended by 1,500 people, mostly Jewish working women.[62] The International Ladies Garment Workers Union carried out a massive educational program for its members, mostly Jewish working women, including classes, movies, tours of museums, theater performances (the opera *Aida* was performed for an audience of 20,000), reading rooms, and libraries.[63] Italian, Polish, Irish, and other working women were involved in similar activities. When labor organizer Arturo Caroti injected eight lectures on trade unionism into the program of a social club for Italian working women in 1912, the women fled,[64] but two decades later the predominantly Italian International Ladies Garment Workers Union Local in Newark, New Jersey, had over 1,000 members, most of them women, participating in classes on labor problems, current events, history of unions, parliamentary procedure, citizenship, dramatics, Italian, and choral work.[65]

Working women with an interest in the labor movement studied at radical coeducational labor schools such as the Finnish Work People's College in Duluth (sponsored by the Industrial Workers of the World) and Brookwood Labor College in Katonah, New York.[66] Labor groups cooperated with academic institutions to set up summer programs for working women, the best known of which was the Bryn Mawr Summer School. Its stated purpose was "to offer young women of character and ability a fuller education in order that they may widen their influence in the industrial world, help in the coming social reconstruction, and increase the happiness and usefulness of their own lives." This was a striking departure from the traditional view that young women should be educated primarily for the fulfillment of their roles as wives and mothers. At Bryn Mawr, as in other labor sponsored programs, the instruction was broadly cultural, including English, literature, art, and drama, as well as the social sciences and labor theory. "Whatever the teachers and administrators may decide," wrote Hilda Smith, "the workers themselves are not willing to be confined to any program less broad than life itself."[67]

Participation in workers' education of a broad and liberal nature was not surprising among women who had developed working-class consciousness before immigration—Finnish socialists and members of the Jewish Socialist Bund in eastern Europe. In the United States, however, it spread from this nucleus of leaders to women of many different ethnic groups who came to the labor force from traditional, agrarian backgrounds. Knowledge about American politics and the American economy and about organizational techniques spread from the women in the garment factories to the women in the tenements. Young Jewish, Italian, and Irish women used what they had learned in unionizing their shops to organize tenant associations and rent strikes in the lower East Side of New York City in the decades just before and after World War I. Membership in these tenant organizations became, in turn, an educational experience for other immigrant women who were recruited into them.[68]

Ethnic women's organizations provided important educational opportunities for members of their own communities, with women who had been in the United States longer (or who had been born here) serving as teachers and counselors to more recent arrivals. Some women's clubs operated as auxiliaries to men's lodges, benevolent societies, or cultural or nationalist associations. Others were independent, with their own staff, publications, and national as well as local activities. The Polish Women's Alliance separated from the men's organization in order to provide leadership opportunities for women. Among the better known were groups such as the Union of Czech Women, the Ladies of Kalova (Finnish), the Council of Jewish Women, the Lithuanian Women's Alliance, the Polish Women's Alliance of America, Zivena (Slovak), and the Ukrainian Women's Alliance.

Many of the leaders of these organizations were American-born or Americanized ethnic women who shared the interest of other "Americanizers" in making newer arrivals socially acceptable to the general American population. Their attitude, like that of nonethnic social workers, could be condescending. Still, they usually understood the language and religion of the women with whom they worked, they often recruited immigrant women not only as clients but also as leaders, and they offered Americanization mixed with sociability and other benefits. The Lithuanian Women's Alliance refused to enroll women in its popular mutual benefit society unless they enrolled in its educational programs as well.[69]

Though ethnic women's organizations concentrated on teaching English and the traditional homemaking skills, some had other interests, too. The Ukrainian Women's Alliance published a newspaper with articles on women's suffrage as well as hygiene, nutrition, and childcare.[70] Many women's organizations conducted successful fund-raising drives, provided scholarships, camps, and other educational services to children, informed themselves about social and political issues, and acted on those issues.

The immigrant woman who spoke no English, or who was illiterate in her own language as well as English, found opportunities for self-education in her own community. Immigrant autobiographies tell of women of all ages attending innumerable poetry readings, plays, concerts, and lectures (on anything from Darwin to anarchism to the history of Ancient Greece) sponsored by a broad spectrum of social, political, cultural, and nationalist societies.[71] Marie Syrkin tells of being taken to political lectures in New York at a very early age because "babysitters were an unheard of institution. . . . Besides, I believe my parents felt that a bright ten-year-old should be able to appreciate political discourse at any hour."[72] Labor leader Elizabeth Gurley Flynn not only attended but was a featured speaker at such gatherings by the time she was sixteen.[73]

Large numbers of women participated in singing societies, drama clubs, and literary circles. Here they immersed themselves in the culture of the traditional homeland, the well-educated few introducing others to its musical and literary treasures often for the first time. In major cities women attended commercial ethnic theater, where, in addition to melodrama and burlesque, they could often see the best of classical and modern theater from their homelands and, in translation, from the world—Shakespeare, Molière, Dumas, Goethe, Molnar, and Ibsen. Working women went without lunch to buy tickets to the theater.[74]

Millions of urban immigrant women

educated themselves through the ethnic press, which had a daily circulation in 1920 conservatively estimated at seven and one-half million.[75] Some moved from semiliteracy to literacy by studying first the advertisements and headlines with their large print and simple words, and then the articles which provided information on life in the United States as well as the homeland. The women's pages of commercial papers and of the papers put out by the churches and lodges presented information on food, clothing, hygiene, and child care in a form that the immigrant woman was able to use, as well as material on the United States designed to stimulate patriotism. A different kind of political education was offered by the radical press. The Finnish *Toveritar*, printed in Astoria, Oregon, offered a radical critique of American society and recruited women into the Industrial Workers of the World by warning them that "capitalism crushes even young workers' lives and uses the best youth of the land like cattle in their bloody sport."[76] A Chicago-based Bohemian feminist paper, *Zemske Listy*, edited and printed entirely by women, campaigned militantly for women's suffrage and for "the uplifting of the mental attitude of working women."[77] It had a circulation of more than 6,000. Many women were less interested in the political propaganda of the Right and the Left than in the lively advertisements which gave information (both accurate and inaccurate) on the material aspects of the new American lifestyle.

Immigrant women of all ages educated themselves through books. Some ethnic institutions had their own libraries, and the better public libraries in urban areas ordered books in the major immigrant languages as well as English. Jewish school girls on the Lower East Side of New York read voraciously, vied for the honor of helping reshelve books, and wrote passionate love notes to their favorite librarians.[78] "Reading was our sole indoor pastime," reminisced Elizabeth Gurley Flynn, whose mother, born in Ireland, was an avid reader. "We read everything we could understand, and some we did not."[79] Librarians noted the popularity of sophisticated works by William James, Henri Bergson, Charles Dickens, George Bernard Shaw, Leo Tolstoy, and other Russian authors; and while there is no information on the sex of borrowers, it is safe to assume that many of them were women.

Immigrant literature is filled with poignant evidence of how desperately some of the most isolated and uneducated immigrant women wanted to broaden their mental horizons. "I go wild for want of something which I cannot get," wrote a Japanese woman, who could not read the election placard in the window.[80] Abraham Cahan's classic novel of immigrant Jewish life, *The Rise of David Levinsky*, describes the uneducated Dora, who will not let her American-born daughter out of the house after school until the whimpering child goes over the day's reading lesson with her mother. Monica Krawczyk's story, "For Nickels and Dimes," tells of the Polish Antosia, who works as a domestic to earn money for an encyclopedia, supposedly for her husband and children. The encyclopedia becomes the focus of her own life.

> Each morning after the family left, Antosia was down on her knees in the front room, looking over the books, studying the pictures, giving sound to the words. Sometimes she stayed with them so long that the bread dough was running out of the pan or her lunch was late, or beds had gone unmade.[81]

In sum, the evidence from immigrant novels, short stories, and memoirs, as well as the records of immigrant organizations and the observations of knowledgeable contemporary observers, indicates that the educational interests of immigrant women in American cities at the turn of the century were more intense and more diverse than most American educators believed. The evidence also indicates that the educational facilities in the ethnic communities were more varied and, except for the compulsory public school, more widely used than those provided by outside experts. American educators were correct in assuming that most immigrant women wanted to improve their homemaking skills and their English. They were incorrect in assuming that immigrant women would not or could not learn anything else. Supplementing the limited fare offered them by the American educational community, many immigrant women took up the task of educating themselves with ingenuity, determination, and much success.

Notes

1. See Lawrence Cremin, *The Transformation of the School: Progressivism in American Education 1876–1957* (New York, 1961), and David Tyack, *The One Best System* (Cambridge: Harvard University Press, 1974).

2. See Joel Spring, *Education and the Rise of the Corporate State* (Boston: Beacon Press, 1972); Michael Katz, *The Irony of Early School Reform: Educational Innovation in Mid-Nineteenth Century Massachusetts* (Cambridge: Harvard University Press, 1968) and *Class, Bureaucracy, and Schools: The Illusion of Educational Change in America* (New York: Praeger, 1971); Clarence Karier, *Shaping the American Educational State: 1900 to the Present* (New York: Free Press, 1975); and Colin Greer, *The Great School Legend: A Revisionist Interpretation of American Public Education* (New York: Basic Books, 1972).

3. Cremin, viii–ix.

4. Ibid., 66–69. See also Tyack, 188–191.

5. G. Stanley Hall, *Adolescents*, Vol. 2 (New York: D. Appleton, 1903), 640; cited Anne F. Scott, ed., *The American Woman Who Was She?* (Englewood Cliffs, N.J.: Prentice-Hall, 1971), 74.

6. Edward Thorndike, "Sex in Education," *The Bookman* XXIII (April, 1906), 213; cited in Willystine Goodsell, *The Education of Women: Its Social Background and Its Problem* (New York: Macmillan, 1925), 73.

7. Goodsell, ibid., 84–91.

8. Peter Roberts, *The New Immigration: A Study of the Industrial and Social Life of Southern and Eastern Europeans in America* (New York: Macmillan, 1912), 286.

9. William Sharlip and Albert A. Owens, *Adult Immigrant Education* (New York: Macmillan, 1928), 192. See also *Work of the Public Schools with the Division of Citizenship Training*—5th Annual Report, Raymond Crest, Director (Washington, D.C.: Government Printing Office, 1921).

10. Ibid., 192–197. See also *Second Annual Report of the Commission of Immigration and Housing of California* (San Francisco: California State Printing Office, 1916), 139; and Lester K. Ade, *Home Classes for Foreign Born Mothers* (Harrisburg: Commonwealth of Pennsylvania Department of Public Instruction Bulletin 295, 1939), 10–13; L. R. Alderman, *Helps for Teachers of Adult Immigrants and Native Illiterates*, Department of Interior, U.S. Bureau of Education, Bulletin No. 27 (Washington, DC: Government Printing Office, 1928), 35–36.

11. Robert A. Woods, *Americans in Progress: A Settlement Study of Residents and Associations of the South End House* (New York: Riverside Press, 1903), 303–304.

12. Henry Emerson, *Annual Report of the Superintendent of Education of the City of Buffalo, 1914–1915* (Buffalo, 1915), 37.

13. Ibid., 37–38, 51; *Examination of the Public School System of the City of Buffalo* (Albany: University of the State of New York, 1916), 197.

14. *Second Annual Report of the Commission of Immigration and Housing of California*, 117–118.

15. Emerson, 38.

16. Pearl Idelia Ellis, *Americanization through Homemaking* (Los Angeles: Wetzel Publishing Company, 1929), throughout.

17. Ibid., 14.

18. Ibid., 29.

19. Ibid., 14–15.

20. Ibid., 30–31.

21. Ibid., 25. See also Emerson, 39.

22. Albert Kennedy and Robert Woods, *Handbook of Settlements* (New York: Russell Sage Foundation, 1911), throughout.

23. P. Mathew Titus, "A Study of Protestant Charities in Chicago, History, Develop-

ment, Philosophy" (Ph.D. dissertation, University of Chicago, 1939).

24. John Daniels, *America Via the Neighborhood* (New York: Harper Brothers, 1920), 185, 282.

25. Kennedy and Woods. See also Allen F. Davis, *Spearheads for Reform: The Social Settlements and the Progressive Movement 1890–1914* (New York: Oxford University Press, 1967).

26. Daniels, 189–191.

27. *Report of the Commissioner of Education*, 1915–1916, Vol. I: 1970, cited in Goodsell, 178.

28. "Industrial Education for Women," *Proceedings of the National Society for the Promotion of Industrial Education*, Bulletin 10, 78; cited in Goodsell, 209.

29. John Horace Mariano, *The Italian Contribution to American Democracy* (Boston, 1922; New York: Arno, 1975), 46. For a fictitious account of the struggles of a Jewish immigrant girl to become a teacher, see Anzia Yezierska, *Bread Givers* (New York: Doubleday, 1925; Venture Books, 1975).

30. For a bibliography of these materials, see *Teaching English to the Foreign Born* (New York: Common Council for American Unity, Foreign Language Information Service, 1924).

31. Frederick Houghton, *Immigrant Education: A Handbook Prepared for the Board of Education* (New York, 1927), 7–13.

32. *Second Annual Report of the Commission of Immigration and Housing of California*, 142–143.

33. Ibid., 151.

34. Ibid., 155–157.

35. Diana Ravitch, *The Great School Wars, New York City 1805–1973* (New York: Basic Books, 1974), 171–172.

36. Emerson, 61. Leonard Covello cites case histories of Italian-American girls, some born in the United States, who attended school for a short time or not at all. Leonard Covello, *The Social Background of the Italo-American School Child* (Leiden, 1967), 285, 273, 294.

37. Covello, ibid., 294.

38. Mariano, 294.

39. David Cohen, "Immigrants and the Schools," *Review of Educational Research* 40 (February, 1970), 13–78. Maxine Seller, "Ethnicity As a Factor in the School Performance of Immigrant Children 1890–1930," *Foundational Studies*, Vol. III, 2 (Spring 1976), 3–26, 42–53.

40. Margaret D. Moore, *Citizenship Training of Adult Immigrants in the United States: Its Status in Relation to the Census of 1920* (Washington, DC: Government Printing Office, 1925), 304.

41. Grace Abbott, *The Immigrant and the Community* (New York: Century Publishing Company, 1917), reprinted in Winthrop Talbot, *Americanization* (Handbook Series; New York: H. W. Wilson Company, 1917), 225–232; and Frank D. Loonis, *Americanization in Chicago* (pamphlet; Chicago: The Chicago Community Trust, 1920), 22–24.

42. *Proceedings of the National Conference on Americanization in Industry*, Nantucket Beach, Massachusetts, June 22–24, 1919.

43. *The Educational Needs of Immigrants in Illinois* (by Grace Abbott), Bulletin of the Immigration Commission 1 (Springfield, Ill., 1920), 25.

44. Emerson, 38–39.

45. Ravitch, 223–228 (emphasis added).

46. Morris Isaiah Berger, "The Settlement, the Immigrant, and the Public School: A Study of the Influence of the Settlement Movement upon Public Education, 1890–1924" (Ph.D. dissertation, Columbia University, 1956), 117.

47. Ibid., 112.

48. Dr. Albert Shiels, *Americanization* (District of Los Angeles Public Schools, 1919), 29.

49. Daniels, 222–223.

50. Virginia McLaughlin, "Like the Fingers of the Hand: The Family and Community Life of First Generation Italian-Americans in Buffalo, New York, 1880–1930" (Ph.D. dissertation, University of Buffalo, 1970), 230–231.

51. Issac Metzker, ed., *A Bintel Brief: Sixty Years of Letters from the Lower East Side to the Jewish Daily Forward* (New York: Ballantine Books, 1971), 106.

52. McLaughlin, 234–235, and Cecile L. Griel, "I Problemi Della Madre in un Paese Nuovo" ("The Problems of the Mother in a New Country"; Italian text, New York, 1919), National Board of the Young Women's Christian Associations, New York City, 1919. Reprinted in *Italians in the United States: A Repository of Rare Tracts and Miscellanea* (New York: Arno Press, 1975).

53. Sophonsiba Breckinridge, *New Homes for Old* (New York: Harper & Bros., 1921), 243.

54. *Second Annual Report of the Commission of Immigration and Housing of California*, 154.

55. Ade, 39.

56. Elizabeth Beardsley Butler, *Women*

and the Trades, Pittsburgh, 1907–1908 (New York: Russell Sage Foundation, 1909); Caroline Manning, The Immigrant Woman and Her Job (Washington, DC: Government Printing Office, 1930); and Maxine S. Seller, "Beyond the Stereotype: A New Look at the Immigrant Woman 1880–1924," Journal of Ethnic Studies, 3 (Spring, 1975), 59–70.

57. Anzia Yezierska, "How I Found America," Hungry Hearts (Cambridge: Houghton Mifflin Company, 1920; reprinted by Arno Press, 1975), 279–282.

58. Daniel, 136–139.

59. Richard M. Linkh, American Catholicism and European Immigrants 1900–1924 (Staten Island: Center for Migration Studies, 1975), 147–156.

60. Patricia A. Book, "Red and White: Sex Roles and Politics in a North American Finnish Community," paper presented at the 73rd Annual Meeting of the American Anthropology Association, 13.

61. Ibid., 13–14.

62. Irving Howe, World of Our Fathers (New York: Harcourt, Brace, Jovanovich, 1976), 238.

63. Fannia Cohn, "Educational and Social Activities of the International Ladies Garment Workers Union," American Federationist, 36 (1929), 1446–1452, and "Twelve Years of Educational Activities of the International Ladies Garment Workers Union," American Federationist, 36 (1929), 105–111.

64. Edwin Fenton, "Immigrants and Unions: A Case Study: Italians and American Labor 1870–1920" (Ph.D. dissertation, Harvard University, 1957; New York: Arno Press, 1975), 502.

65. Charles W. Churchill, "The Italians of Newark, A Community Study" (Ph.D. dissertation, New York University, 1942; New York: Arno Press, 1975), 72.

66. "The Work People's College: Where Industrial Unionists Are Efficiently Educated," The Industrial Pioneer, II (February, 1925), 47–48. See Charles Beard, "An American Adventure in Workers' Education," Workers Education, XIII (October, 1936), 16–17 for a description of Brookwood College.

67. Florence Schneider, Patterns of Work-

ers Education: The Story of the Bryn Mawr Summer School (Washington, DC: American Council of Public Affairs, 1951), 67, 21. Also Hilda Smith, Proceedings of the 8th Annual Conference of Teachers in Workers Education (Brookwood College, 21 February 1931), 101. Cited in Schneider, 21.

68. John J. McLaughlin, "History of Tenant Education in New York City 1890–1970," paper presented at annual meeting of the American Education Research Association, New York City, April 7, 1977.

69. Daniels, 211–212.

70. Ibid., 61.

71. Golda Meir, My Life (New York: G. P. Putnam's Sons, 1975); Elizabeth Gurley Flynn, The Rebel Girl: An Autobiography (New York: International Publishers, 1973); Emma Goldman, Living My Life (New York: Dover Publications, Inc., 1931, 1970); Sydelle Kramer and Jenny Masur, ed., Jewish Grandmothers (oral histories; Boston: Beacon Press, 1976).

72. Howe, 242.

73. Flynn, 53–60.

74. Book, 13–14; Hutchins Hapgood, The Spirit of the Ghetto (Funk & Wagnalls Co., 1902; New York: Schocken, 1966); Lawrence Estavan, The Italian Theater in San Francisco (San Francisco: United States Works Progress Administration, North California District, 1939).

75. Robert Park, The Immigrant Press and Its Control (New York: Harper and Brothers, 1922), 245.

76. Ibid.

77. Emily Balch, Our Slavic Fellow Citizens (New York: Charities Publications Committee, 1910), 383–384.

78. New York Evening Post (October 3, 1903), "Jew Babes at the Library," cited in Allen Schoener, The Lower East Side 1870–1925 (New York: Holt, Rinehart and Winston, 1967), 133–134.

79. Flynn, 40.

80. Park, 160.

81. Monica Krawczyk, "For Nickels and Dimes," in If the Branch Blossoms and Other Stories (Minneapolis: Polanie Publishing Company, 1950), 94.

DOCUMENTS: Creating Colleges

M. CAREY THOMAS

"The passionate desire of women . . .

for higher education"

The struggle of immigrant women to learn more than homemaking skills and basic English was paralleled in the affluent households of old-stock Americans. At a time when medical experts warned that too much exposure to the "impedimenta of libraries" could leave young female graduates incapable of performing their normal reproductive function, girls born into families that sent sons to college as a matter of course had to be especially persuasive if they also wanted a liberal education. M. Carey Thomas conveys with particular effectiveness the yearnings of the young college-bound women of her generation. When she later became president of Bryn Mawr College, one of several elite women's colleges founded in the latter half of the nineteenth century, she strongly disagreed with those who argued that the primary purpose of a woman's education was to prepare her for marriage and motherhood. Insisting that the Bryn Mawr student enter college with the same qualifications in Greek, Latin, and mathematics required of her male counterpart at Harvard or Yale, Thomas expected Bryn Mawr graduates to lead lives as productive, economically independent women, finding, as did men, "their greatest happiness in congenial work."* Note her insistence on the importance of having women scholars who could serve as role models for their students.

The passionate desire of women of my generation for higher education was accompanied thruout its course by the awful doubt, felt by women themselves as well as by men, as to whether women as a sex were physically and mentally fit for it. I think I can best make this clear to you if I refer briefly to my own experience. I cannot remember the time when I was not sure that studying and going to college were the things above all others which I wished to do. I was always wondering

* M. Carey Thomas, "The Future of Women's Higher Education," in *Mount Holyoke College: The Seventy-Fifth Anniversary* (South Hadley, Mass., 1913), p. 104.

Excerpted from "Present Tendencies in Women's College and University Education" by M. Carey Thomas, in *Educational Review* 30 (1908): 64–85.

whether it could be really true, as every one thought, that boys were cleverer than girls. Indeed, I cared so much that I never dared to ask any grown-up person the direct question, not even my father or mother, because I feared to hear the reply. I remember often praying about it, and begging God that if it were true that because I was a girl I could not successfully master Greek and go to college and understand things to kill me at once, as I could not bear to live in such an unjust world. When I was a little older I read the Bible entirely thru with passionate eagerness because I had heard it said that it proved that women were inferior to men. Those were not the days of the higher criticism. I can remember weeping over the account of Adam and Eve because it seemed to me that the curse pronounced on Eve might imperil girls' going to college; and to this day I can never read many parts of the Pauline epistles without feeling again the sinking of the heart with which I used to hurry over the verses referring to women's keeping silence in the churches and asking their husbands at home. . . .

It was not to be wondered at that we were uncertain in those old days as to the ultimate result of women's education. Before I myself went to college I had never seen but one college woman. I had heard that such a woman was staying at the house of an acquaintance. I went to see her with fear. Even if she had appeared in hoofs and horns I was determined to go to college all the same. But it was a relief to find this Vassar graduate tall and handsome and dressed like other women. When, five years later, I went to Leipzig to study after I had been graduated from Cornell, my mother used to write me that my name was never mentioned to her by the women of her acquaintance. I was thought by them to be as much of a disgrace to my family as if I had eloped with the coachman. Now, women who have been to college are as plentiful as black-berries on summer hedges. Even my native city of Baltimore is full of them, and women who have in addition studied in Germany are regarded with becoming deference by the very Baltimore women who disapproved of me.

During the quarter of the century of the existence of the Association of Collegiate Alumnae [now American Association of University Women] two generations of college women have reached mature life, and the older generation is now just passing off the stage. We are therefore better prepared than ever before to give an account of what has been definitely accomplished, and to predict what will be the tendencies of women's college and university education in the future.

The curriculum of our women's colleges has steadily stiffened. Women, both in separate, and in coeducational colleges, seem to prefer the old-fashioned, so-called disciplinary studies. They disregard the so-called accomplishments. I believe that to-day more women than men are receiving a thoro college education, even altho in most cases they are receiving it sitting side by side with men in the same college lecture rooms.

The old type of untrained woman teacher has practically disappeared from women's colleges. Her place is being taken by ardent young women scholars who have qualified themselves by long years of graduate study for advanced teaching. Even the old-fashioned untrained matron, or house-mother, is swiftly being replaced in girls' schools, as well as in women's colleges, by the college-bred warden or director.

We did not know when we began whether women's health could stand the strain of college education. We were haunted in those early days by the changing chains of that gloomy little specter, Dr. Edward H. Clarke's *Sex in Education.* With trepidation of spirit I made my mother read it, and was much cheered by her remark that, as neither she, nor any of the women she knew, had ever seen girls or women of the kind described in Dr. Clarke's book, we might as well act as if they did not exist. Still, we did not *know* whether colleges might not produce a crop of just such invalids. Doctors insisted that they would. We women could not be sure until we had tried the experiment. Now we have tried it, and tried it for more than a generation, and we know that college women are not only not invalids, but that they are better physically than other women in their own class of life. We know that girls are growing stronger and more athletic. Girls enter college each year in better physical condition. For the past four years I have myself questioned closely all our entering classes, and often their mothers as well. I find that an average of sixty per cent. enter college absolutely and in every respect well, and that less than thirty per cent. make, or need to make, any periodic difference whatever in exercise, or study, from year's end to year's end. This result is very different from that obtained by physicians and others writing in recent magazines and medical journals. These alarmists give grewsome statistics from high schools and women's colleges, which they are very careful not to name. Probably they are investigating girls whose general hygienic conditions are bad. . . .

We are now living in the midst of great and, I believe on the whole beneficent, social changes which are preparing the way for the coming economic independence of women. Like the closely allied diminishing birth rate, but unlike the higher education of women, this great change in opinion and practise seems to have come about almost without our knowledge, certainly without our conscious coöperation. The passionate desire of the women of my generation for a college education seems, as we study it now in the light of coming events, to have been a part of this greater movement.

In order to prepare for this economic independence, we should expect to see what is now taking place. Colleges for women and college departments of coeducational universities are attended by ever-increasing numbers of women students. In seven of the largest western universities women already outnumber men in the college departments.

A liberal college course prepares women for their great profession of teaching. College women have proved to be such admirably efficient teachers that they are driving other women out of the field. Until other means of self-support are as easy for women as teaching, more and more women who intend to teach will go to college. Such women will elect first of all the subjects taught by women in the high schools, such as Latin, history, and the languages. They will avoid chemistry, physics, and other sciences which are usually taught by men. Until all women become self-supporting, more women than men will go to college for culture, especially in the west, and such women will tend to elect the great disciplinary studies which men neglect because they are intrinsically more difficult and seem at first sight less practical. For these obvious reasons certain college courses are therefore already crowded by women and almost deserted by men in many of the coeducational universities.

And just because women have shown such an aptitude for a true college education and such delight in it, we must be careful to maintain it for them in its integrity. We must see to it that its disciplinary quality is not lowered by the insertion of so-called practical courses which are falsely supposed to prepare for life. Women are rapidly coming to control women's college education. It rests with us to decide whether we shall barter for a mess of pottage the inheritance of the girls of this generation which the girls of my generation agonized to obtain for themselves and for other girls. . . .

I believe also that every women's college ought to maintain . . . a graduate school of philosophy of the highest grade. . . .

. . . The highest service which colleges can render to their time is to discover and foster imaginative and constructive genius. Such genius unquestionably needs opportunity for its highest development. This is peculiarly the case with women students. As I watch their gallant struggles I sometimes think that the very stars in their courses are conspiring against them. Women scholars can assist women students, as men can not, to tide over the first discouragements of a life of intellectual renunciation. Ability of the kind I am speaking of is, of course, very rare, but for this reason it is precious beyond all other human products. . . .

The time has now come for those of us who are in control of women's education to bend ourselves to the task of creating academic conditions favorable for the development of this kind of creative ability. We should at once begin to found research chairs for women at all our women's colleges, with three or four hours a week research teaching and the rest of the time free for independent investigation. We should reserve all the traveling fellowships in our gift for women who have given evidence, however slight, of power to do research work. We should bring pressure on our state universities to give such women opportunities to compete for professors' chairs. In the four woman suffrage states this can be accomplished in the twinkling of an eye: it will only be necessary for women's organizations to vote for university regents with proper opinions. The Johns Hopkins University situated in conservative Baltimore has two women on its academic staff who are lecturing to men. Why can not all chairs in the arts departments of universities, that is, in the college and school of philosophy, be thrown open to the competition of women? This is the next advance to be made in women's education—the last and greatest battle to be won.

MARY McLEOD BETHUNE
"How the Bethune-Cookman college campus started"

Mary McLeod Bethune was one of the most distinguished educators of her generation. The daughter of slaves, she received her early education from missionary teachers. Like others of her race who saw education as a key to racial advancement at a time when the white South was indifferent if not hostile to the aspirations of Afro-Americans, Bethune faced extraordinary obstacles. When she began a little school at Daytona Beach, Florida, in 1904, America was entering

Excerpted from "Faith That Moved a Dump Heap" by Mary McLeod Bethune, in *Who, The Magazine about People* 1, no. 3 (June 1941): 31–35, 54.

an era of reform. Yet even most northern progressives—with the notable exception of women such as Mary White Ovington, one of the founders of the National Association for the Advancement of Colored People—shared the racist assumptions of that era, believing that the future of black women, like immigrant women, lay in domestic service. Bethune had larger dreams. Because of her courage, energy, and vision she was able to keep her little school afloat with her intrepid fund raising, guiding its growth from grammar school to high school and to what finally became an accredited four-year college. President of the institution from its founding until her resignation in 1942, she remained a trustee of Bethune-Cookman College until her death in 1955. She was an activist and held many important posts within the black community, founding such organizations as the National Association of Colored Women's Clubs and the National Council of Negro Women. A national figure as well, she served in the Roosevelt administration during the 1930s, advising the president on minority affairs. She was also involved in early efforts on behalf of the United Nations. Her many offices and honors, however, never diverted her from her primary purpose—the pursuit of full citizenship rights for all black Americans.

On October 3, 1904, I opened the doors of my school, with an enrollment of five little girls, aged from eight to twelve, whose parents paid me fifty cents' weekly tuition. My own child was the only boy in the school. Though I hadn't a penny left, I considered cash money as the smallest part of my resources. I had faith in a living God, faith in myself, and a desire to serve. . . .

We burned logs and used the charred splinters as pencils, and mashed elderberries for ink. I begged strangers for a broom, a lamp, a bit of cretonne to put around the packing case which served as my desk. I haunted the city dump and the trash piles behind hotels, retrieving discarded linen and kitchenware, cracked dishes, broken chairs, pieces of old lumber. Everything was scoured and mended. This was part of the training to salvage, to reconstruct, to make bricks without straw. As parents began gradually to leave their children overnight, I had to provide sleeping accommodations. I took corn sacks for mattresses. Then I picked Spanish moss from trees, dried and cured it, and used it as a substitute for mattress hair.

The school expanded fast. In less than two years I had 250 pupils. In desperation I hired a large hall next to my original little cottage, and used it as a combined dormitory and classroom. I concentrated more and more on girls, as I felt that they especially were hampered by lack of educational opportunities. . . .

I had many volunteer workers and a few regular teachers, who were paid from fifteen to twenty-five dollars a month and board. I was supposed to keep the balance of the funds for my own pocket, but there was never any balance—only a yawning hole. I wore old clothes sent me by mission boards, recut and redesigned for me in our dress-making classes. At last I saw that our only solution was to stop renting space, and to buy and build our own college.

Near by was a field, popularly called Hell's Hole, which was used as a dumping ground. I approached the owner, determined to buy it. The price was $250. In a daze, he finally agreed to take five dollars down, and the balance in two years. I promised to be back in a few days with the initial payment. He never knew it, but I didn't have five dollars. I raised this sum selling ice cream and sweet-potato pies to the workmen on construction jobs, and I took the owner his money in small change wrapped in my handkerchief.

That's how the Bethune-Cookman college campus started. . . .

As the school expanded, whenever I saw a need for some training or service we did not supply, I schemed to add it to our curriculum. Sometimes that took years. When I came to Florida, there were no hospitals where a Negro could go. A student became critically ill with appendicitis, so I went to a local hospital and begged a white physician to take her in and operate. My pleas were so desperate he finally agreed. A few days after the operation, I visited my pupil.

When I appeared at the front door of the hospital, the nurse ordered me around to the back way. I thrust her aside—and found my little girl segregated in a corner of the porch behind the kitchen. Even my toes clenched with rage.

That decided me. I called on three of my faithful friends, asking them to buy a little cottage behind our school as a hospital. They agreed, and we started with two beds.

From this humble start grew a fully equipped twenty-bed hospital—our college infirmary and a refuge for the needy throughout the state. It was staffed by white and black physicians and by our own student nurses. We ran this hospital for twenty years as part of our contribution to community life; but a short time ago, to ease our financial burden, the city took it over.

Gradually, as educational facilities expanded and there were other places where small children could go, we put the emphasis on high-school and junior-college training. In 1922, Cookman College, a men's school, the first in the state for the higher education of Negroes, amalgamated with us. The combined coeducational college, now run under the auspices of the Methodist Episcopal Church, is called Bethune-Cookman College. We have fourteen modern buildings, a beautiful campus of thirty-two acres, an enrollment in regular and summer sessions of 600 students, a faculty and staff of thirty-two, and 1,800 graduates. The college property, now valued at more than $800,000, is entirely unencumbered.

When I walk through the campus, with its stately palms and well-kept lawns, and think back to the dump-heap foundation, I rub my eyes and pinch myself. And I remember my childish visions in the cotton fields.

But values cannot be calculated in ledger figures and property. More than all else the college has fulfilled my ideals of distinctive training and service. Extending far beyond the immediate sphere of its graduates and students, it has already enriched the lives of 100,000 Negroes.

In 1934, President Franklin D. Roosevelt appointed me director of the division of Negro affairs of the National Youth Administration. My main task now is to supervise the training provided for 600,000 Negro children, and I have to run the college by remote control. Every few weeks, however, I snatch a day or so and return to my beloved home.

This is a strenuous program. The doctor shakes his head and says, "Mrs. Bethune, slow down a little. Relax! Take it just a little easier." I promise to reform, but in an hour the promise is forgotten.

For I am my mother's daughter, and the drums of Africa still beat in my heart. They will not let me rest while there is a single Negro boy or girl without a chance to prove his worth.

RAY GINGER
The Women at Hull–House

Hull House was a pioneering social settlement, established in Chicago in 1889 by twenty-nine-year-old Jane Addams. In the years to come it would be the model for settlement houses in cities all across America, staffed by women and men who shared Addams's vision and were caught up in the excitement of developing the new field of professional social service. They represented, as we have suggested in our introduction to this section, a distinctive female component in American progressivism.

In the following selection, first published in 1958, Ray Ginger seeks to account for this development by describing the early experiences of some of the women who formed the core group at Hull House. What influences did Addams, Lathrop, Kelley, and Hamilton have in common? How does Ginger explain their invention of this novel institution? In what ways did their public role serve their private needs?

To most children of the nineteenth century, morality was a drab discipline, a tiresomely reiterated list of simple and foolish maxims. But Florence Kelley found real vitality in the preachments and practices that she observed in her Grandaunt Sarah's tranquil home in Philadelphia.

Aunt Sarah was a Quaker. She was also an abolitionist who had refused to use sugar in her tea and had substituted linen underwear for cotton, because, as she explained to her niece Florence, "these things were the products of slave labor." . . . She thought that evil could best be fought by recruiting the young to battle against it, and she found the frail, somewhat sickly Florence receptive to crusades. After all, the foster-great-grandparents of Florence Kelley had made the crossing to America with Joseph Priestley, the chemist and Unitarian minister who had to flee England after a mob wrecked his house, library, and scientific equipment because of his defense of the French Revolution.

Florence Kelley grew up four miles from Independence Hall. Her home was serene, even though her mother had lost five children. Florence's father, William Darrah Kelley, encouraged her lively curiosity, and together they explored many fields of knowledge. He was a self-made man who started in the printer's trade when only eleven years old, studied law at night, was admitted to the bar and then elected to the bench, where he served for nine years. In 1856 Judge Kelley was one of those premature Republicans, running unsuccessfully for Congress on the Free

Soil ticket with Frémont, and in 1860 he was among the frenzied, cheering delegates who nominated Lincoln at the Chicago Wigwam. His political foresight then was rewarded with a seat in Congress, where he remained for twenty-eight years and (contrary to the free-trade teachings of Aunt Sarah) came to be known as "Pig Iron" Kelley through his championship of a high tariff for that booming Pennsylvania industry. Emblazoned on his political record was the inscription, "I knew Abraham Lincoln." For the daughter, as for a multitude of other Americans, this was akin to having touched the garment of the divine.

The uncertain health of the girl often interrupted her formal schooling, but her father's library provided a voluminous substitute, and she absorbed the English and American classics. One winter in Washington, D.C., she spent long hours in the Library of Congress. William Kelley, a supporter of equal suffrage for women, approved his daughter's enrolment at sixteen at Cornell, one of the few colleges which then offered equal education for women. Florence Kelley recalled those years: "Little did we care that there was no music, no theatre, almost no library; that the stairs to the lecture halls were wooden, and the classrooms heated with coal stoves. No one, so far as I know, read a daily paper, or subscribed for a monthly or quarterly. Our current gossip was Froude's life of Carlyle." A degree and a highly commended thesis on common and statute law dealing with children was followed, however, by frustration. She was denied permission to enter the graduate school of law at the University of Pennsylvania and turned instead to establishing an evening school for girls in Philadelphia.

The continuing desire for study led to a trip abroad with her elder brother. Again frustration. After a year of study at Leipzig she was denied a degree. Next she took a walking vacation in England in the summer of 1883, and saw the Black Country

of the coal miners and the cottages of the sweated nailmakers and chainmakers. Going then to Zurich because she had heard that its university did not exclude women, she became acquainted with social revolutionaries, refugees from Russia, Germany, and Austria.

She already knew a little about their doctrines. In Philadelphia, a lace importer and friend of Karl Marx had brought Judge Kelley some red-bound agitational pamphlets, and the girl had found them "startling." Now in Zurich she attended socialist meetings, participated in debates, translated *The Condition of the Working-Class in England in 1844*, by Friedrich Engels, into English, and married a revolutionist, Lazare Wischnewetsky, a young Polish-Russian physician. They had three children, a son born abroad and a son and daughter born in New York, where the family settled in 1886. Florence Kelley's interest in socialism continued in the United States, although her membership in the Socialist Labor party was an uneasy one. After a year she was expelled because the German and Russian "impossibilists" were suspicious of her "too fluent" English. And her marriage broke up. Dr. Wischnewetsky had virtually no medical practice. Debts were heavy and oppressive. Five years after her wedding Florence Kelley moved to Illinois where, on the grounds of nonsupport, she obtained a divorce, the custody of her children, and resumption of her maiden name.

A new way of life had to be constructed, and her attention came to focus on the problem of child labor. Deploring this exploitation had little effect. She developed the better weapon of research. Soon she was reading a paper at a convention of commissioners of labor statistics, publishing a paper on "Our Toiling Children." But this was mere guerilla assault; she wanted the efficiency of a regular battalion of reform. Hopefully, she approached the Woman's Christian Temperance Union, but it was concerned only with the demon rum. Then, shortly after Christmas of 1891, Florence Kelley enlisted in Chicago's new settlement, Hull-House.

There she met Julia Lathrop, whose ancestors had been in America even longer than her own. In 1634 the Reverend John Lathropp, an English noncomformist sent to prison for his beliefs, successfully petitioned for "liberty in exile," and emigrated to Boston, where he gained a reputation as "a sound scholar and a lively preacher." Julia heard the story many times from her father, and in adulthood she liked to claim that her kinsman "would have come over on the Mayflower but for the unfortunate circumstance that he was in jail at the moment that doughty vessel set sail."

Among John Lathropp's descendants, some drifted westward; William Lathrop, out of Genessee County, New York, settled in Rockford, Illinois, where by 1857 he was well established in the practice of law, and had a wife, and home, and $10,000 in the bank. The next year Julia Clifford was born, one of five children.

The girl was shy. In school she was reported a "good child" and a "smart scholar," but she felt an absence of understanding on the part of her teachers. What the school lacked, however, the parents supplied. At home the children were encouraged to express their opinions and, without interference from the adults, to develop their particular interests. William Lathrop held a tight purse but it opened readily when the proposal was for books or education. His accomplishments in politics and the law were instruction by example. In 1854 he helped found the Republican party in northern Illinois, and this activity brought about his election to the legislature where a former member of that body, Abraham Lincoln, once helped him in his search for a book at the library. The event was casual; the recollection permanent.

This was the period when Susan B. Anthony appeared before the Illinois legislature to advocate equal rights for women, when Dorothea Dix rode by wagon to Springfield from Chicago to plead for the humane treatment of the insane, when the author of the best-selling novel was a woman abolitionist, Harriet Beecher Stowe. The legal practice of the Rockford legislator reflected his exposure to these ideas. When a Mrs. Dixon shot her husband because she believed he intended to steal her baby from her, William Lathrop successfully offered emotional insanity as the defense, the first such plea in the history of Illinois jurisprudence. (Thus early are the origins of the type of legal argument that Clarence Darrow, a friend of Julia Lathrop, would use in dozens of murder trials.) He set another precedent in welcoming Alta M. Hulett to prepare for the law in his office while he drew up the bill permitting women to practice. She was the first woman admitted to the bar in Illinois.

William Lathrop . . . was concerned with his wife's school, Rockford Seminary (now Rockford College), and served it diligently as a trustee.

The daughter Julia, slender, sallow, and dark-eyed, enrolled at Rockford for a year completing high school, with the intent of qualifying for Vassar. Her father was pleased at her ambition and employed German and mathematics tutors when it grew obvious that the girl was not adequately prepared for the eastern school. In 1880, after hard work and little fun, Julia Lathrop was graduated from Vassar. The college apparently did not inspire her for a particular vocation. Teaching held no appeal. She went into her father's law office as secretary, read a good deal of law with keen understanding, and displayed a head for business by becoming secretary for two different companies in which she had invested and profited. Manufacturing was growing rapidly in Rockford; the town was turning into a city.

In the winter of 1888–1889, the Lathrops were invited to a meeting at Rockford College where Jane Addams and Ellen Gates Starr, graduates of the school, were appealing for support of a new kind of project, a social settlement to be opened the coming fall in Chicago. There were many friendly questions about the enterprise that was intended "to make social intercourse express the growing sense of economic unity of society and to add the social function to democracy." To William Lathrop this was as vaporous as most of the missionary enterprises hatched at the college, idealistic, but not very practical. Nevertheless, he interposed no objection when Julia Lathrop decided to join the settlement.

She had been at Hull-House six years when Dr. Alice Hamilton came. The newcomer was also a native of a small midwestern city, Fort Wayne, Indiana, where the streets were shaded by elms and maples, the sidewalks paved with red brick, the shops austere except for the drugstore with its flasks of colored water. . . .

Montgomery Hamilton, Alice's father, had run away from Princeton to enlist in the Union Army at nineteen, but in later years he never mentioned the war except . . . to proclaim the foolishness of his enlistment through a boyish desire for adventure. . . . Theology, primarily, and literature, secondarily, were his interests. . . .

. . . The mother, Gertrude Pond Hamilton, . . . neglected the fine points of theology, but she could speak with authority on such taboo subjects as pregnancy, childbirth, and sex. Virtue to her was not the same as fear of public opinion, and she brushed aside contemporary prudery. Interwoven with her beliefs was the capacity for indignation: against the lynching of Negroes, child labor, police brutality, and a system that permitted such injustices. Alice Hamilton frequently heard from her mother: "There are two kinds of people, the ones who say, 'Somebody ought to do something about it, but why should it be I?' and those who say, 'Somebody must do something about it, then why not I?' " The choice was obvious to the daughter.

Miss Porter's School in Farmington, Connecticut, a requirement for all the Hamilton girls, was Alice Hamilton's preliminary to the study of medicine at the University of Michigan. She chose this field of study, not because she was scientifically minded, but because she thought that as a doctor she would secure freedom from the restraints on women. At Ann Arbor the training was advanced, German-influenced, and included courses in biochemistry, bacteriology, physiology, and pharmacology. Above all, Ann Arbor offered emancipation. No one fretted about Alice Hamilton's hours; no one stood at the doorstep worrying about her safety. . . .

Bacteriology and pathology appeared more attractive to Alice Hamilton than a general medical practice. From Ann Arbor she went for two brief unhappy months to the Hospital for Women and Children in Minneapolis. There she was left on her own to cope with typhoid fever and obstetrical cases, of which she knew little. Then came an opening at the New England Hospital for Women and Children on the outskirts of Boston. This, at last, was the big city. On the first evening she was called to a case some distance away in a poverty-ridden neighborhood. The patient lived above a saloon, and it was not until midnight that Alice Hamilton was ready to leave. She immediately lost her way. Fearful of asking any man for assistance, she approached a pert little woman, a chorus girl, who laughingly gave her directions and added, "Just walk along fast with your bag in your hand, not looking at anybody, and nobody will speak to you. Men don't want to be snubbed; they are looking for a woman who is willing." The advice was sound, for the young Doctor Hamilton, going by night into sordid tenements and houses of prostitution, was never molested.

Visiting back in Fort Wayne, Alice Hamilton, now acquainted with the city slum, discussed socialism and settlements with sister Norah and cousin Agnes Hamilton. Agnes was an enthusiast for Richard Ely's Christian socialism and promptly converted Alice. One day Norah burst into the house with the breathless news that Jane Addams of Hull-House was to speak at the Methodist Church. Hull-House was about six years old, with a fame that had spread quickly. Both Agnes and Alice, absorbing every word spoken by Jane Addams, decided that some day they must become a part of settlement life. . . .

The cluster of hills around the village of Cedarville broke the flat sweep of the prairie in northern Illinois, and on one of these elevations pine trees flourished, grown from seeds planted by John H. Addams in 1844. Through the village a stream flowed, with caves eroded into its banks. In the summer the purple anemones were a daytime delight and at twilight the whippoorwill introduced an appropriate solemnity. In this setting the girl Jane Addams, born in 1860, found places for play and dreaming. She was slightly stooped, pigeon-toed, and bashful, perhaps because of a spinal curvature. In the crude surgery of the day her spine was seared with a red hot iron but the result, if not actually harmful, was without benefit.

The mother of Jane Addams had died when the daughter was a baby, too soon for even a vague memory to take root, and her father did not remarry for eight years. In that interval, however, there was no neglect or shunting aside of the questioning child. . . .

John H. Addams began work as a miller, but he went into politics because of his concern with the abolitionist movement, the formation of the Republican party, and the Civil War. It was politics in the highest sense. In his long service in the Illinois Senate, 1854 to 1870, he earned the distinction of never having been offered a bribe. Senator Addams brought his politics home. Jane Addams was not yet four when she entered her father's room one morning to find him in whispered conversation with a Negro. The fugitive was on his way to freedom in Canada and, young as she was, Jane Addams abided by her childish pledge not to talk about the slave's visit. . . .

Rockford Seminary, where her father along with William Lathrop served as a trustee, was a logical choice for Jane Addams in 1877. But the choice was made by the parent. Jane preferred Smith College. However, three sisters had attended Rockford, and John Addams believed that education should be near home followed by travel abroad. And Rockford was gaining a reputation. It was a school where intense effort was the norm. The education was a combination of classical reading and evangelical appeals. . . . Of mathematics there was a dash, of economics nothing, of oratory an abundance. In the last subject she had some skill, being selected to represent the school in a state-wide oratorical contest. She placed fifth or "exactly in the middle," not a bad showing for the only woman entrant who was pitted against such wonders as William Jennings Bryan, who won second prize.

John Addams' promise of a European tour was fulfilled. In 1883 Jane Addams embarked on a journey that took her through England, France, Germany, Austria, and Italy and lasted two years. She was an indefatigable tourist, exploring the misery of East London, interviewing a Saxe-Coburg brewery owner who exploited women, spending a considerable sum for an engraving by Dürer, whose work was "surcharged with pity for the downtrodden." She prowled through the slums of Naples, strolled across the sunny

Campagna into Rome. It was a nervous, maladjusted, intellectually confused Jane Addams who returned home to Cedarville. She shuttled between there and Baltimore, where she received treatment of her spine (during her lifetime it required four major operations) and heard comforting lectures on Mazzini's philosophy. But she was shaken by mankind's resistance to the dictates of morality, and at the advanced age of twenty-five she joined the Presbyterian Church at Cedarville. She was seeking, not respectability, but "an outward symbol of fellowship, some bond of peace, some blessed spot where unity of spirit might claim right of way over all differences."

After another two years, Jane Addams sailed again for Europe. Some cities were revisited, others added to her itinerary. In a vague way she was thinking about renting a house in a poor city area back home where young women of comfortable circumstances might engage in social activity to overcome the one-sidedness of viewing life through books and foreign travel. The dream became clearer in Spain where she was traveling with her Rockford classmate, Ellen Gates Starr. Then in London the two young women saw the first settlement house in the world. Toynbee Hall was the conception of a young clergyman, Samuel A. Barnett, who wanted to remedy the undermining of the old parish system by the industrial revolution. Here at Toynbee in 1884 a colony of young men became a part of the community of the poor, organized clubs, lectures, and concerts, identified themselves with the aspirations and struggles of the dispossessed. Mutuality was to bring about class rapprochement. Practicality from below was to replace preaching from on top. Jane Addams had found the device she had been seeking.

Back in the United States, she and Ellen Gates Starr began looking in Chicago for a suitable building for their settlement house. On the first day of their search they stumbled upon the former country home of Charles J. Hull. This house on South Halsted Street was surrounded by tenements and factories, the area populated by immigrant Russian and Polish Jews, Italians, Irish, Germans, and Bohemians. Nine churches had 250 saloons as competitors. Life in the Nineteenth Ward was, for the most part, dominated by disease, poverty, vice, premature death, foul housing, blighted childhood, and crushing labor.

The old home, occupied on September 18, 1890, "responded kindly to repairs." Jane Addams had an income of her own, and this combined with contributions paid for restoration of the residence. It had been constructed in 1846 when builders believed in ample room. The lofty ceilings had elaborate cornices. The long drawing room had French windows and carved white mantelpieces. New furniture was brought in, other pieces were donated, and the house was decorated with knickknacks and pictures collected on European travels. The dining room was long and paneled, with chandeliers of Spanish wrought iron.

There was no perplexity over where to begin. The streets of the ward, crowded with children, suggested a kindergarten and clubs; in the first few weeks Ellen Starr organized a reading party for young women with George Eliot's *Romola* as the first selection. As time went on, a penny savings bank was established, a day nursery, an employment bureau, an orchestra, quarters for the organization of women's trade unions. Parties were frequent, although Jane Addams was taken aback by the refusal of a number of little girls to accept gifts of candy at Christmas. (They had been working in candy factories from seven in the morning until nine at night and "could not bear the sight of it.")

Julia Lathrop organized a Plato Club and soon had men like John Dewey coming on Sunday afternoons to lead uneducated immigrants in sessions about Greek philosophy. The discussions often wandered beyond that topic to embrace the whole of culture, and the allotted two hours stretched to five. Courses in arts and crafts resulted in an invitation to Frank Lloyd Wright in 1895 to lecture at Hull-House. . . .

Hull-House thus tried not only to relieve the physical want that stifled most residents of the Nineteenth Ward; it also aimed at ending their spiritual deprivation. And it did so with no hint of self-consciousness or uplift, because it rejected the distinction between intellectuals and workers. Greek philosophy and modern architecture were part of the common heritage of the human race, and one man had as much right as another to share in them. Nor were the women of Hull-House tainted with the earnest solemnity that made many reformers intolerable. "When men and women, boys and girls, work all day in sweatshops, they want to have fun," Jane Addams insisted. This sort of realism was repellent to the evangelists and romanticists who wandered into Hull-House, and for most of them a single visit was enough.

Wisely Jane Addams avoided a denominational or even a religious subscription from those who participated in the activity of Hull-House. She was wary of anything divisive. Religious spokesmen were welcome, although the reception they met was not always to their satisfaction. The Women's Club had as one of its first speakers a Christian Scientist who at the close of a lengthy address said: "Now here in this neighborhood, when you are out at night, just as the sun is setting and you go down to the river and notice the odors which arise from it, you must think of the pine trees and how they smell and say to yourself, 'Oh! what a lovely evening; how sweet everything smells!'" An elderly German woman, well acquainted with the slimy stream, arose and remarked: "Vell, all I can say is if dot woman say dot river smell good den dere must be something de matter with dot woman's nose." The club members roared with approval.

But Hull-House welcomed the noncon-formist and the eccentric. An elderly anarchist, who probably shuddered at slapping a fly, preached violent revolution and assassination. But a self-styled Hindu Mahatma converted him to another way of life. The anarchist was instructed to lift his face to Heaven, to say, "I am divine," and to restrict his diet to garlic and popcorn.

Some anarchists were more dedicated. Marie Sukloff had attempted to kill the governor of Kiev with a bomb, been sentenced to life imprisonment in Siberia, and escaped via Japan to America and Hull-House. With Alice Hamilton she visited the penitentiary at Joliet and was horrified. "It is worse than any thing in Russia or Siberia," she said. "Russian prisons are dirty and the guards are often cruel, but they are human—they may hit you one minute but the next minute they talk to you as if you were their sister. In Joliet it is all whitewashed and still, it works like a machine, it is terrifying."

Sometimes the numerous crises of the poor caused Jane Addams to wonder if the higher purposes of the settlement were being lost. Once she and Julia Lathrop were called to help a young woman who was about to give birth unattended in a tenement. Neighboring women refused to help the girl because she was unmarried and because anyone calling a doctor might be held responsible financially. The two women from Hull-House hurried to the tenement and were initiated as midwives. As they walked back slowly to the settlement, Jane Addams exclaimed, "This doing things that we don't know how to do is going too far. Why did we let ourselves be rushed into midwifery?" Julia Lathrop's answer was never forgotten: "If we have to begin to hew down to the line of our ignorance, for goodness' sake don't let us begin at the humanitarian end. To refuse to respond to a poor girl in the throes of childbirth would be a disgrace to us forever. If Hull-House does not have its roots in human kindness, it is no good at all."

Under the impact of life in the Nineteenth Ward, the Toynbee Hall objective of class reconciliation, although never formally abandoned, dwindled to lesser importance than the host of problems tossed on the doorstep of Hull-House. And Jane Addams was learning, too, that there were various practitioners of class harmony. Alderman Johnny Powers, for instance, manipulated the workingman's vote for the service of the employer. Powers demonstrated to Jane Addams the reality of municipal government, the political science of making and manipulating friends. Jane Addams "soon discovered that approximately one out of every five voters in the Nineteenth Ward held a job dependent on the good will of the alderman." At the outset she did not grasp why there were so many streetcar and telephone company employees in the ward; then she found out how franchises were secured.

On election day, Powers would drive to all the polling places, including the one at Hull-House, his big bandwagon playing "Nearer, My God, to Thee"; nickels would be tossed to the kids, cigars to the men. He would see Jane Addams and call out, "Miss Addams, if you ever want any little favor from me, just tell me and I'll see to it." She would thank him, but if ever a favor was needed, a legitimate request for a city permit, she asked some other resident of Hull-House to run the errand. Powers never failed to respond favorably. "How is she?" he would ask and, when told "Pretty well," would say witsfully, "Did she ask you to come?" Informed, "Oh, no, she just told me she wanted it," Powers would sigh and comment, "Well, Miss Addams is always O.K. with me, but I wish just once she'd ask me and not fight me all the time."

Fight him she did, and in the third campaign against the alderman, serious inroads were made into his majority. . . . To a close friend she gave the impression of "always being very sad, as if the sorrows of the neighborhood were pressed upon her."

To relieve those sorrows took money, and she had to get money from people who had it. She was a regular visitor at Bar Harbor, Maine, in spite of its wealthy snobbery and its marked bias against women, because she found she could get nearly as much in contributions in a summer there as she could during the rest of the year elsewhere. But when employers offered money to Hull-House in the expectation that she would temper her program, she refused them, while wondering why she was offered bribes when her father never had been. It was one of the few subjects on which she was sensitive enough to lose her temper. Once when she was telling an audience of workingmen about the aims of Hull-House, a heckler interrupted to call out: "You won't talk like that when the millionaires begin to subsidize you." Stung deeply, she retorted: "I don't intend to be subsidized by millionaires or bullied by labor unionists."

It probably was in one of her periods of despondency that she investigated socialism. The outcome was that she recoiled from the contention that men's ideas originated in their class position. Nor could she accept class consciousness as desirable in an America where individuals could still rise out of one class into another. Hull-House, she came to resolve, must be built on the "solidarity of the human race" and on the premise that "without the advance and improvement of the whole, no man can hope for any lasting improvement in his own moral or material individual conditions." Based on this genuinely catholic acceptance of mankind, Hull-House was open to the most diverse viewpoints. What bound it together was the personality of Jane Addams.

From other states, from Europe and

Asia, visitors came to examine this Chicago on Lake Michigan. For many, there were three attractions: the stockyards, the new university, and Hull-House. In 1893 Sidney and Beatrice Webb and Governor Altgeld were the guests of Clarence Darrow at Hull-House, where the visiting Englishwoman persuaded Jane Addams to try a cigarette for the first and last time. . . . But that year marked more than the mushrooming growth of a settlement with a reputation. Following the recommendation of Henry Demarest Lloyd, who was completing his *Wealth against Commonwealth*, Governor Altgeld appointed Florence Kelley as chief factory inspector of Illinois, a post created by a new law. Now the activity of the women of Hull-House was to spread into a far wider field. The core of this remarkable work was concern for the family: the unschooled child, the working mother, the exploited father. Within a few years the women of Hull-House recorded accomplishments that had never before been achieved by any group of American women—or equaled since.

A year after Hull-House opened, Florence Kelley and her children arrived on a snowy December morning. Already standing at the door ringing the bell was Henry Standing Bear, a Kickapoo Indian. The door was opened by Jane Addams. She had the cook's fat baby on her left arm while the right restrained a little Italian girl, whose mother was at a sweatshop, from dashing out into the snow. The next day a place was found for the Kelley children at the Winnetka home of Henry Lloyd, within easy reach of Hull-House.

At the time the sweating system of Chicago was being attacked by the Chicago Trades and Labor Assembly. Mrs. Thomas J. Morgan, wife of a socialist leader in the labor movement, had begun to expose the conditions in the garment industry, and a suggestion was made to the Illinois state bureau of labor that accurate statistical information be compiled on the industry. Florence Kelley was appointed to conduct the inquiry. So effective was her report that a special legislative committee was named to study the sweatshops. Then, with the women of Hull-House, the labor unions, and Governor Altgeld as the chief promoters, the legislature enacted the first meaningful factory law of Illinois. Although a weak measure, the law did prohibit the employment of children in factories, fixed an eight-hour day for women, and, most important, provided for factory inspectors.

Florence Kelley as chief inspector was provided with a staff of twelve, several of whom were residents of Hull-House. Now the settlement gained a reputation for reckless radicalism. Businessmen associated its leaders with Altgeld, the pardoner of the Haymarket anarchists, with the Trades and Labor Assembly and socialists, with agitation for and enactment of the bothersome law. If this was to be a step in erasing class antagonisms, the manufacturing interests of Illinois wanted no part of it.

The opposition of manufacturers, city authorities, and courts was formidable. Florence Kelley brought before the state's attorney of Cook County the case of an eleven-year-old boy illegally employed at gilding picture frames with a poisonous fluid. The youngster had lost the use of his right arm and Mrs. Kelley sought the prosecution of the employer, who could be fined $20 but otherwise not held responsible.

"Are you calculating on *my* taking the case?" the state's attorney asked with astonishment.

"I thought you were the district attorney," Mrs. Kelley said.

"Well, suppose I am. You bring me this evidence this week against some two-by-six cheap picture-frame maker, and how do I know you won't bring me a suit against Marshall Field next week? Don't count on me. I'm overloaded. I wouldn't reach this case inside of two years. . . ."

Indignation drove Florence Kelley to enroll the next day at Northwestern University and by June, 1894, she had her law degree. . . .

Julia Lathrop, not inclined to charge headlong into battle like Florence Kelley, preferring the flanking attack instead, was appointed early in the Altgeld administration to the state board of charities. She astounded a stodgy officialdom by visiting each of the 102 county farms or almshouses. In one institution she abandoned her usual reserve and slid down a new fire escape to test its effectiveness. In her conservative dress, usually a blue tailored suit, Julia Lathrop made the dreary rounds of the poor, the epileptic, the insane, the unwanted. Most distressing to her was the treatment of delinquent children; those over ten years of age were handled in the same fashion as the adult criminal. . . .

Out of these experiences of neighborhood needs, welfare institutions, factory conditions, law and courts, the women of Hull-House wrought their change in social work. That change was to transform the social worker from an amateur to a professional and to shift projects, once public confidence had been won, from private to government hands. With Sophonisba Breckinridge, Julia Lathrop persuaded Edith Abbot to leave Wellesley College and help them establish a department of social research in the School of Civics and Philanthropy at the University of Chicago. The objective was to relate social research to the professional concerns of social workers and to educate a group scientifically trained in the public services. One of the first courses at the new school was given by Dr. William Healy, who introduced social psychiatry to the school of social work.

Jane Addams now was pushing the transfer of private charity to public bodies. Hull-House took on the function of an experimental pilot. If an enterprise proved its worth, the next step was to convince the city or state to enter the field. The playground, the public bath, the kindergarten—such projects instituted by Hull-House were year by year taken over by the city. The work was not always done as well by the municipality. Political appointees did not match the volunteers of Hull-House, but the weakness, Jane Addams insisted, was incidental to the greater step forward of public acceptance. In 1889, for example, the state had been persuaded to enact a law regulating private employment agencies. A poor, loopholed measure, it was policed by Grace Abbott, sister of Edith and superintendent of the League for the Protection of Immigrants.

John P. Altgeld was an ex-governor on the day Alice Hamilton arrived at Hull-House. That evening he was the guest of honor at a dinner where Jane Addams, Florence Kelley, and Julia Lathrop expressed their appreciation of his administration. It was not an occasion of jubilation. Florence Kelley had been dismissed from her post and replaced by an employee of the Illinois Glass Company, one of the most flagrant exploiters of child labor. Altgeld himself was under the heaviest attack of his career. But there was no air of defeat either.

Alice Hamilton was promptly put to work establishing a baby clinic. She had learned from books that babies should have nothing but milk until their teeth came, and she was startled when foreign-born women ignored her dietary teaching. An Italian-born woman explained how she had fed her robust three-year-old son, who had been difficult as a baby. "I gave him the breast and there was plenty of milk, but he cried all the time. Then one day I was frying eggs and just to make him stop I gave him one and it went fine. The next day I was making cup cakes and as soon as they were cool I gave him one, and after that I gave him whatever we had and he got fat and didn't cry any more."

Intimate association with ordinary people taught Alice Hamilton that "education and culture have little to do with real wisdom, the wisdom that comes from life experience," and that "the banal, the bromide and the cliché" can be used with complete sincerity. She came to know a widow who preferred to be a scrubwoman at night rather than turn her child over to an orphanage; a young eight-dollar-a-week Irish girl who shunned an offer of well-paid prostitution because "It would be selling my soul"; a woman who frankly said, "My sister's got it good. Her old man's dead."; a young Italian mother who paced the floor night after night with a sick baby until exhaustion warred with her love, and she exclaimed: "My God, if you're going to die, why don't you die?"

She learned, too, that her scientific knowledge could not always be applied when confronted with a person's sense of right and wrong. When she remonstrated with a woman who had taken a year-old baby into a room where a child was sick in bed with diphtheria, the shocked mother replied, "Do you think that God would punish me for going in to help Maria with her sick child? No, he would rather punish me if I did not." The baby did not catch diphtheria. "They never did when I said they would," Alice Hamilton remarked.

Life at Hull-House aroused an interest in industrial ailments, and Alice Hamilton acquired the background that enabled her to become a pioneer in industrial disease. She wrote a paper which held flies responsible for a serious typhoid epidemic in Chicago. The paper was a success; it provoked a public investigation and the complete reorganization of the city health department. Later she was to learn that her flies had little to do with the case.

"The cause was simpler but so much more discreditable that the Board of Health had not dared reveal it. It seems that in our local pumping station . . . a break had occurred which resulted in an escape of sewage into the water pipes and for three days our neighborhood drank that water before the leak was discovered and stopped."

In these trial-and-error days for the young doctor, she escaped the narrowness which so commonly curses the specialist. She found time to listen to Bill Haywood expound his one-big-union philosophy, to hear Emma Goldman denounce government, law, police, religion, and moral codes, to chat with the young Upton Sinclair who was writing *The Jungle*. Much of what she found stimulating was far from respectable. Hull-House itself was under constant attack from those who dominated Chicago's affairs; the settlement was especially wary of reporters because any event there was likely to be twisted into a sensation. When an anarchist shot the chief of police, Hull-House was pictured as a "nest of anarchists" by reporters who learned that Jane Addams and her associates did not apply a political loyalty test to participants in its activities. Police, assigned to watch mass meetings at Hull-House, brought a sense of fear and possible violence. When a group of immigrants engaged in a loud discussion of political theory, a club-twirling policeman lectured Alice Hamilton: "Lady, you people oughtn't to let bums like these come here. If I had my way they'd all be lined up against a wall at sunrise and shot."

Hull-House, more and more, was offering adventure that was both practical and exhilarating, a combination that helped to reconcile so many brilliant women to an unmarried, childless, career-cloistered life.

In the nineteenth century, Jane Addams observed, women could not combine a career, if that rare opportunity opened, with marriage. Men rejected the career woman as a matrimonial prospect, public opinion was hostile to the dual role, and the labors of homemaking took all of a woman's time. A professional woman usually had to have some independent income or financial patronage. But a career, for most of the women of Hull-House, possessed an attraction as powerful as the distant horizon that had lured restless Daniel Boone. In a new frontier, the city slum, these women found endless fascination.

BLANCHE WIESEN COOK
Female Support Networks and Political Activism: Lillian Wald, Crystal Eastman, Emma Goldman

In his evaluation of "the women at Hull House" Ray Ginger strongly suggested that exciting, useful, and important as their work might be, it was ultimately best understood as a compromise "that helped to reconcile so many brilliant women to an unmarried, childless, career-cloistered life." This last phrase may, however, tell us more about the assumptions of its author and popular attitudes of the 1950s than it does of the way Jane Addams viewed her own life. Did *she* think her career was a compromise, valuable primarily as consolation for a marriage and children she could not have?

The sensitive essay that follows reflects a very different interpretation of the choices Addams and her friends made. It is a particularly good example of the way in which historians' interpretations may be shaped by the cultural climate in which they write; virtually all of the material Blanche Wiesen Cook uses was available to Ray Ginger.

What does Cook mean by the phrase "female support networks"? To what extent does her interpretation extend the suggestion made in the last paragraph of Carroll Smith-Rosenberg's essay "The Female World of Love and Ritual" (part IIA)? How does Cook evoke private lives in order to point toward a more precise understanding of the ways in which these women built public careers?

Excerpted from "Female Support Networks and Political Activism: Lillian Wald, Crystal Eastman, Emma Goldman" by Blanche Wiesen Cook, in *Chrysalis* 3 (1977): 43–61. Copyright © 1977 by Blanche Wiesen Cook. Reprinted by permission of the author. Notes have been renumbered.

In Vera Brittain's *Testament of Friendship*, the biography of her beloved friend Winifred Holtby, the British activist and author wrote that

> From the days of Homer the friendships of men have enjoyed glory and acclamation, but the friendships of women, in spite of Ruth and Naomi, have usually been not merely unsung, but mocked, belittled and falsely interpreted. . . .[1]

Part of the problem is general in scope and involves a distorted vision of the historian's craft that is no longer operable. Historians of my generation were trained to believe that the proper study of our past should be limited to the activities of great men—the wars of kings, the hero's quest for power. We were taught that the personal was separate from the political and that emotions were irrelevant to history.

Recent history and the movements of the sixties, the decade of our professional maturing, have revealed the absurdity of that tradition. It has become clear that in history, no less than in life, our personal choices and the nature of our human relationships were and remain inseparable from our political, our public efforts. Once the personal impact of such confined historical perspective emerged, the need for revision became clear.

In my own work, ten years of work on the historical peace movement—studies that included such significant women as Lillian Wald, Jane Addams, Crystal Eastman, and Emma Goldman—I had focused entirely on women's political contributions. I wrote about their programs for social justice and their opposition to international war. Nothing else. Whenever I came across a love letter by Lillian Wald, for example, I would note "love letter," and move on.

This paper is the result of a long overdue recognition that the personal is the political: that networks of love and support are crucial to our ability as women to work in a hostile world where we are not in fact expected to survive. And it comes out of a recognition that frequently the networks of love and support that enable politically and professionally active women to function independently and intensively consist largely of other women.

LILLIAN WALD, CRYSTAL EASTMAN, EMMA GOLDMAN

Beyond their commitment to economic and social change and their opposition to America's entrance into World War I, Lillian Wald, Crystal Eastman, Emma Goldman, and Jane Addams had very little in common. They are of different generations, represent contrary political solutions, and in private lives reflect a broad range of choice. Yet all four women expanded the narrow contours of women's role and all four left a legacy of struggle against poverty and discrimination.

Jane Addams and Lillian Wald were progressive social reformers. The most famous of the settlement-house crusaders, Wald created the Henry Street Settlement and Visiting Nurse Service in New York while Addams founded Hull-House in Chicago.

Crystal Eastman, a generation younger than Addams and Wald, was an attorney and journalist who investigated labor conditions and work accidents. In 1907 she authored New York State's first workman's compensation law, which became the model for most such laws in the United States. One of the three founders of Alice Paul's Congressional Union for suffrage, Eastman was a socialist and radical feminist who believed in "free love."

More outspoken and less respectful of authority than Addams and Wald, Eastman nevertheless worked closely with them in the peace movement. Wald was president of the American Union Against

Militarism, the parent organization of the American Civil Liberties Union, and Eastman was its executive secretary. Addams was president of the Woman's Peace Party (renamed the Women's International League for Peace and Freedom), and Eastman, also one of its founders, was president of the New York branch. Their differences of temperament and tactics tell us much about the nature of the women's movement during the rapidly changing era of World War I.[2]

Emma Goldman was outside their company, but always in the vanguard of their activity. Addams, Wald, and Eastman worked to improve immigrant and labor conditions. Goldman, an anarchist immigrant worker, sought to recreate society. They worked within the law to modify it. Goldman worked without the law to replace it with anarchist principles of voluntary communism.

Goldman frequently visited the Nurses' Settlement on Henry Street and liked Lillian Wald and her co-workers, particularly Lavinia Dock, well enough. She thought them "women of ideals, capable of fine, generous deeds." But she disapproved of their work and feared that their activities created "snobbery among the very people they were trying to help." Although Jane Addams was influenced by anarchist writings, Goldman regarded her even more critically. She thought Addams an elitist snob.[3]

Emma Goldman's work with Crystal Eastman on behalf of birth control, the legalization of prostitution, and free speech in wartime was also dissatisfying. They agreed on more issues: but when Eastman and her circle were on the same picket line or in the same park distributing birth-control literature with Goldman and her allies, only Goldman's group would be arrested. That was the nature of class in America.

Wald, Eastman, and Addams worked to keep America out of war through the American Union Against Militarism (AUAM). They dined at the White House with Wilson and his advisors. They hired professional lobbyists to influence Congress. Goldman worked through the Antimilitarist League and spoke throughout the United States on the capitalist nature of war and the cruelties of the class system. When she was arrested, the Civil Liberties Bureau of the AUAM defended her; but the members of the AUAM were not themselves arrested. Goldman's wartime activities resulted in her deportation. Wald and Addams received commendations from the government because, in addition to their anti-war work, they allowed their settlement houses to be used as conscription centers.[4]

As different as their political visions and choice of strategies were, Addams and Wald, Eastman and Goldman were dedicated to a future society that guaranteed economic security and the full development of individual potential for women and men on the basis of absolute equality. Reformists, socialist, anarchist, all four women made contributions toward progressive change that are today being dismantled. The playgrounds, parks, and school lunch facilities they built are falling apart all over America because of lack of funding and a callous disregard for the needs of our country's children. The free-speech and human-rights issues they heralded are today facing a reawakened backlash that features the needs of "national security" and a fundamentalist Christianity that seems more appropriate to the seventeenth century.

THE HISTORICAL DENIAL OF LESBIANISM
The vigor and strength of these four women, born daughters in a society that reared daughters to be dependent and servile, cannot be explained without an understanding of their support networks and the nature of their private lives. Their lifestyles varied as dramatically as did their public activities from the prescribed norm of "wife-mother in obedient service

to husband-father" that their culture and their era valued above all.

Of the four women, only Emma Goldman relied predominantly on men for emotional sustenance and political support. Although she was close to many anarchist and radical women, there were few with whom she had intimate and lasting relations. The kind of communal and noncompetitive intimacy of the settlement houses or the younger feminist movement Crystal Eastman was associated with was never a feature of Goldman's life.

Yet throughout her life, Goldman wrote, she "longed for a friend of my own sex, a kindred spirit with whom I could share the innermost thoughts and feelings I could not express to men. . . . Instead of friendship from women I had met with much antagonism, petty envy and jealousy because men liked me." There were exceptions, and Goldman listed them in her autobiography. But basically, she concluded, "there was no personal, intimate point of contact."[5]

Like Goldman, Crystal Eastman was also surrounded by men who shared her work, her vision, and her commitment to social change. Unlike Goldman, she had a feminist support group as well. Her allies consisted of her husband (particularly her second husband, Walter Fuller), her brother Max, and the women who were her friends, many of them from childhood and Vassar until her early death in 1928. Eastman's comrades were the "new women" of Greenwich Village. Radical feminists and socialists, they considered men splendid lovers and friends, but they believed that women needed the more egalitarian support of other women. For Crystal Eastman and her associates this was not only an emotional choice, it was a political necessity.

Jane Addams and Lillian Wald were involved almost exclusively with women who remained throughout their lives a nurturing source of love and support. Henry Street and Hull House were staffed by their closest friends, who, night and day, made possible their unrelenting schedules.

In the past, historians tended to ignore the crucial role played by the networks of love and support that have been the very sources of strength that enabled political women to function. Women's friendships were obscured and trivialized. Whether heterosexual or homosexual, the private lives of political women were declared beyond the acceptable boundaries of historical inquiry. As a result, much of our history and the facts that define our heritage have been removed from our consciousness. Homophobia, a bigotry that declares woman-loving women an evil before God or a mental disease or both, has served to erase the very aspects of our history that would have enabled us to deal healthfully with what has been for most lesbians an isolating and cruel experience. Homophobia has also erased a variety of role-models whose existence would tend to obliterate crude and dehumanizing stereotypes. . . .

This denial has persisted over time. The figures that serve as the frontispiece for Dolores Klaich's book Woman + Woman symbolize the problem. We see a sculpture, dated c. 200 B.C., of two women in a tender and erotic embrace. It has been called by the curators of the British Museum, "Women Gossiping."

Similarly, companionate women who have lived together all their adult lives have been branded "lonely spinsters." When their letters might reveal their love, their papers have often been rendered unavailable.* Interpreting Freud through a Victorian prism and thinking it enlight-

---

* See Dolores Klaich, Woman + Woman: Attitudes Toward Lesbianism (Morrow, 1974). The recently successful pressure to open the Mary E. Woolley Papers at Mt. Holyoke is a case in point. The famous college president lived with the chairwoman of the English Department, Jeannette Marks, for many years. They were lovers. When that fact was discovered their papers were closed.

ened, male historians have concluded that the settlement-house reformers were asexual women who sublimated their passionate energies into their work. Since they were not recognizably "dykes" on the order of Radclyffe Hall or Gertrude Stein, and they always functioned too successfully to be called "sick," the historical evidence was juggled to deny the meaning of their lifestyles altogether.

So, for example, William O'Neill can refer to the 40-year relationship between Mary Rozet Smith and Jane Addams as that of "spouse-surrogates" and then conclude: "Finally, one suspects, the very qualities that led [Addams] to reject the family claim prevented her from experiencing the human reality that she celebrated in her writings and defied convention to encounter. She gave her time, money, and talents entirely to the interests of the poor. . . . In a sense she rejected the personal claims upon her, . . . and remained largely untouched by the passionate currents that swirled around her. The crowning irony of Jane Addam's life, therefore, was that she compromised her intellect for the sake of human experiences which her nature prevented her from having. Life, as she meant the term, forever eluded her."[6]

Allen Davis observes a different phenomenon. "It would be easy to misunderstand," Davis writes, the friendship and affection between Jane Addams and her early companion Ellen Gates Starr. Quoting Gordon Haight, Davis concludes: " 'The Victorian conception of love between those of the same sex cannot be fairly understood by an age steeped in Freud—where they say only beautiful friendship, the modern reader suspects perversion.' "[7]

It is important to understand the language here. We are being told that, since Jane Addams was a conventional lady with pearls, her intense "romantic attachments" to other women could not possibly be suspected of "perversion." As a result, the perfectly ordinary nature of women's differing sexual preferences has been denied expression. Without information and history, we have become ignorant of the range of our choices. Repression and conformity have been fostered and an entire generation of activist and passionate women branded by historians, on no evidence whatsoever, as "asexual."

Our prejudices are such that it has been considered less critical—kinder, even— to label a woman "asexual" rather than "lesbian." . . .

More sensitive than most male historians, Allen Davis notes that although the romantic words and the love letters "can be easily misinterpreted," what is important is "that many unmarried women drew warmth and strength from their supportive relationships with other women." But he concludes that "whether or not these women were actually lesbians is essentially irrelevant."[8]

If we lived in a society where individual choice and the diversity of our human rhythms were honored, the actuality of lesbianism would in fact be irrelevant. But we live in a society where children are taken away from lesbian mothers, where teachers are fired for bedroom activities, where in June 1976 the Supreme Court endorsed the imprisonment of consenting adults for homosexual relations, and where as I sit typing this paper—in June 1977—the radio announces that Dade County, Florida, by a vote of 2:1, has supported Anita Bryant's hate campaign against homosexuals.

Such legal and social manifestations of bigotry and repression have been reinforced and are validated by the historical rejection and denial of diversity in general and of independent and alternative lifestyles among women in particular. It is the very conventionality of women like Jane Addams and Lillian Wald that is significant. Not until our society fully accepts as moral and ordinary the wide range of personal choice will differences be "essentially irrelevant."

As I think about Anita Bryant's campaign to "Save Our Children" from homosexuality, my thoughts turn to Lillian Wald, who insisted that every New York City public school should have a trained nurse in residence and who established free lunch programs for the city's school children. My thoughts then turn to Jane Addams, who, in an essay called, "Women, War and Babies," wrote:

As women we are the custodians of the life of the ages and we will not longer consent to its reckless destruction. We are particularly charged with the future of childhood, the care of the helpless and the unfortunate, and we will not longer endure without protest that added burden of maimed and invalid men and poverty-stricken women and orphans which war places on us.

We have built by the patient drudgery of the past the basic foundations of the home and of peaceful industry; we will not longer endure that hoary evil which in an hour destroys or tolerate that denial of the sovereignty of reason and justice by which war and all that makes for war today render impotent the idealism of the race.[9]

And in the wake of the first mid-twentieth-century American vote to discriminate against an entire group of people,[10] my thoughts turn again to Lillian Wald and Jane Addams, who campaigned for the creation of the United States Children's Bureau. That bureau set up programs throughout the United States to care for battered wives and battered children; it crusaded against child labor and for humane child care.[11] Yet Anita Bryant would demand that we save our children from Jane Addams if Anita Bryant knew that Jane Addams slept in the same house, in the same room, in the same bed with Mary Rozet Smith for 40 years. (And when they travelled, Addams even wired ahead to order a large double bed for their hotel room.)

Because difference arouses fear and condemnation, there are serious methodological problems involved in writing about women who, for political and economic reasons, kept their private lives as secret as possible. The advent of the homosexual "closet" at the end of the nineteenth century was not accidental. Oscar Wilde had, after all, been released from prison on 19 May 1897. In addition to the criminal stigma now attached to homosexuality, a sudden explosion of "scientific" publications on "sexual disorders" and "perversions" appeared at the turn of the century. Nancy Sahli, historian and archivist, reports that in the first series of 16 volumes of the *Index Catalogue of the Library of the Surgeon General's Office, U.S. Army*, covering the years 1740 to 1895, only one article ("A Case of Man-Impersonation") dealt specifically with lesbians. In the second series, published between 1896 and 1916, there were over 90 books and 566 articles listed that related to women's "perversions," "inversions," and "disorders."[12]

Secrecy is not a surprising response to this psychoanalytic assault. How then, male historians continually ask, do you know these women were lesbians? Even if we were to assume that Addams and Smith never in 40 years in the same bed touched each other, we can still argue that they were lesbians because they chose each other. Women who love women, who choose women to nurture and support and to create a living environment in which to work creatively and independently, are lesbians.

It may seem elementary to state here that lesbians cannot be defined simply as women who practice certain physical rites together. Unfortunately, the heterosexist image—and sometimes even the feminist image—of the lesbian is defined by sexual behavior alone, and sexual in the most limited sense. It therefore seems important to reiterate that physical love between women is one expression of a whole range of emotions and responses to each other that involves all the mysteries of our human nature. Women-related women feel attraction, yearning, and excitement with women. Nobody and no theory has yet explained why for some women, despite all cultural conditioning and societal penalties, both intellectual and emotional excitement are aroused in response to women.

LILLIAN WALD

Besides, there *is* evidence of these women's lesbianism. Although Lillian Wald's two volumes of memoirs are about as personal as her entry in *Who's Who among American Women*, her letters underscore the absurdity of a taxi conversation that Mabel Hyde Kittredge reported to Wald after a meeting at Henry Street:

1st man:	*Those women are really lonely.*
Second man:	*Why under the sun are they lonely?*
1st man:	*Any woman is lonely without a man.*

Unlike Jane Addams, Lillian Wald seems not to have had one particular "great friend," and the chronology of the women in her life, with their comings and goings, is impossible to follow. There are gaps and surprises throughout over 150 boxes of correspondence. But all of Lillian Wald's companions appear to have been friends for life.

Wald's basic support group consisted of the long-term residents of Henry Street, Ysabella Waters, Anne Goodrich, Florence Kelley, Helene MacDowell, and Lavinia L. Dock. They worked together on all projects, lived and vacationed together for over 50 years, and, often in company with the women of Hull House, travelled

together to Europe, Japan, Mexico, and the West Indies.

But the letters are insufficient to tell us the specifics of her life. There are turmoils that we will probably never know anything about—upheavals that result, for example, in a 10-year hiatus in Wald's correspondence with Lavinia Dock. This hiatus, combined with the fact that in November 1915, after 20 years, "Docky" moved out of the Henry Street Settlement and, in an icy and formal note of March 1916, even resigned from the Henry Street Corporation, remains unexplained. There is also the puzzling fact that Dock, the ardent suffragist, feminist and socialist, a pioneer of American nusing education and organization, appears to be R. L. Duffus' major source of information—beyond Wald herself—for his 1938 biography, *Lillian Wald: Neighbor and Crusader*. The first letter to appear in the collection after Dock's 1916 resignation is dated 1925 and implies that the two women have not had a long-term falling out at all:

> why-dear-I was imagining you radiating around the town telling about Mexico and here you are in the hospital just like any commonplace person—oh dear oh dear! . . . Dearest I would scrape up some money if you need—you have often done the same for me . . . and I am not telling anyone that you are ill and in the hospital for I know how you would dislike being thought just a mere mortal. . . .[13]

It is clear from another letter that Dock went to New York to be with Wald during her first operation. She wrote Wald's nurse that she was so relieved the tumor turned out to be benign that "for the first time my knees wobbled as I went down the steps to go to the train. . . ." The next week Dock wrote to Wald: "Dearest—I'm not sure whether to give you letters yet so I haven't written before and just send this line to tell you that you do your illnesses and recoveries in the same dazzling form and with the same vivacity and originality as all your other deeds! With Love/Ever yours/Docky."

Why then did Dock leave? Was there a personal reason? A new lover? An old anger? Or was it connected with the political differences that emerged between them in 1915 when Wald became more absorbed by antimilitarist activities and Dock, also a pacifist, joined the radical suffragist movement of Alice Paul's Congressional Union? All the evidence indicates that the only significant differences between these women at this time were political. Their lives were dedicated to work each regarded as just and right. When they disagreed so intensively that they could no longer support and nurture each other's activities, they temporarily parted. . . .

During the war, while Wald was meeting with President Wilson and being as conciliatory as possible on behalf of the peace movement, Dock and the militant suffragists were infuriating official Washington, getting themselves arrested, and generally aggravating the very people Wald was attempting to persuade—and for a different purpose.

Dock considered Paul's Congressional Union "fresh-young-glorious." She wrote to Paul in June 1915: "Pay no attention to criticism. Go right ahead with your splendid daring and resourcefulness of youth." Dock reacted furiously to criticism that the Congressional Union's confrontational tactics not only harmed the suffrage movement but threatened the peace movement. And Lillian Wald was one of the leading critics of such tactics. On this issue they disagreed utterly. Dock was adamant: "And what is this terrible burden of responsibility and anxiety now resting on the American Men's President? Is it arising from anything women have done or are going to do? Not at all. . . . I can't see it—surely there could be no

more appropriate moment for women to press forward with their demand for a voice—women—who are at this moment going on errands of peace—and who are being called a national menace for doing so—followed wherever he goes, by the demand which, so long as it remains unanswered shows a painful insincerity in those rounded and sonorous paragraphs on American ideals and American freedom that he utters so eloquently. . . .[14]

Five months after this exchange, Lavinia Dock moved permanently out of her Henry Street home of 20 years. I have not yet found one correspondence between her and Wald that deals with the event. And all Wald says about Dock in *Windows on Henry Street* is that "Everyone admired her, none feared her, though she was sometimes very fierce in her denunciations. Reputed a man-hater, we knew her as a lover of mankind."

WALD'S OTHER SUPPORT NETWORK

There were two other categories of women close to Wald and the settlement. The first consisted of affluent women such as Irene and Alice Lewisohn and Rita Morgenthau. Younger than Wald, they admired her and regarded her as a maternal figure. She in turn nurtured their spirits, supported their ambitions, and provided them with sustaining and secure friendship. They, together with Wald's "friend of friends" Jacob Schiff, contributed tirelessly and abundantly to Henry Street. The Lewisohns founded the Neighborhood Play House and supported the famous music and dance education projects that continue to this day. They were also coworkers in the Woman's Peace Party and the American Union Against Militarism. On occasion they travelled with Wald. And they wrote numerous letters of affection and devotion to their dear "Lady Light." Alice Lewisohn frequently signed her letters

"Your Baby Alice." One letter from Irene, conveying love and gratitude after a trip the Lewisohn sisters took with Ysabella Waters and Wald, is replicated in the collection by scores of others:

> Why attempt to tell a clairvoyant all that is in one's mind? You know even better than I what those months of companionship with you and Sister Waters have meant. For way and beyond even the joys of our wanderings I have some memories that are holier by far than temples or graves or blossoms. A fireside romance and a moonlight night are among the treasures carefully guarded. . . . As an offering for such inspirations, I am making a special vow to be and to do. . . . Much of my heart to you!

Wald's closest friend among the younger nonresidents appears to have been Rita Wallach Morgenthau, who generally signed her letters with love from "Your Daughter," "Your Foolish Daughter," or "Your Spoiled Child." However much Wald may have spoiled her "adoptive daughters," the very fact of her nurturing presence helped establish the nature of their life's work; and their work focused on social change and the education, dance, and theatre programs they created.[15] . . .

All of Wald's friends and correspondents wrote of how she inspired them, fired their imaginations, and directed their lives to greater heights of consciousness and activity. Lavinia Dock referred to this quality in a letter to Duffus for his biography of Wald: "She believed absolutely in human nature and as a result the best of it was shown to her. People just naturally turned their best natures to her scrutiny and developed what she perceived in them, when it had been dormant and unseen in them before. I remember often being greatly impressed by this inner vision that she had. . . ."[16]

The last group of women involved with Wald and the settlement differed basically from the other two. Although they also served as residents or volunteered their time to Henry Street, they were "society women" perhaps more interested in Wald than in social change. Such long-term residents as Dock, Waters, and MacDowell, and Wald's younger friends, Morgenthau and the Lewisohns, supported Wald emotionally and politically and shared collectively in all her interests. The society women, however, attempted to possess or monopolize Wald, lamented that her activities kept her from them, and were finally rebuffed in what must have been thoroughly specific terms. Generally they fell into that trap that Margaret Anderson defined so well: "In real love you want the other person's good. In romantic love you want the other person."[17]

Lillian Wald had structured her life to avoid becoming anybody's possession. While she did get involved in emotional enthusiasms, as soon as the woman involved sought to redirect her priorities Wald's enthusiasm evaporated.

The clearest representatives of the society group were Mabel Hyde Kittredge and Helen Arthur. Both women were rich "uptowners" who spent many years "downtown." Both were highly educated, hardworking, and demanding. Both devoted their time to good works, in large part because their friendship with Wald encouraged them to think politically, and not because social change was their life's commitment. But they were loyal. Kittredge, for example, evidently left Henry Street because Wald encouraged her to do so. Yet she continued to be involved in settlement activities, helped organize the free lunch program in public schools in 1908, and founded the Association of Practical Housekeeping Centers that operated as a subsidiary organization for many years.

To understand Lillian Wald fully, it is necessary to deal with her relationship with Mabel Hyde Kittredge. Kittredge's demands seem on occasion outrageous, and her biases are transparent. Yet it is clear that for a time Wald was not only smitten by this lady, but relied upon her for comfort and trusted her deeply.

A Park Avenue socialite who frequently played bridge whist all night after she had played in a golf tournament all day, Kittredge was the daughter of Reverend Abbott E. Kittredge of the prominent Madison Avenue Church. After she had lived at Henry Street for several years, she wrote to Wald on 28 April 1904 that she understood Wald's objections to what appears to have been a moment of flagrant ethnic bigotry: "I believe that I will never again say 'my people and *your* people.' It may be that even though I have no prejudice I have used words and expressions that have done something to keep the lines drawn between the two peoples. . . ."

Whatever her views, it appears that when Wald was troubled she turned for a time to Kittredge. In a long letter of tender assurance and sensible advice to Wald concerning a bereaved friend, Kittredge wrote:

> . . . I seemed to hold you in my arms and whisper all this. . . . If you want me to stay all night tomorrow night just say so when you see me. . . . Please dont feel that I keep before me the signs of sorrow that you trusted me enough to let me see —of the things of Thursday evening that are consciously with me are first the fact that in a slight degree I can share with you the pain that you suffer. Then I can hear you say "I love you"—and again and again I can see in your eyes the strength, and the power and the truth that I love but the confidence in yourself not there. All this I have before me— never a thought of weakness because you dared to be human. Why dear I knew that you were human before Thursday night— I think though that our love never seemed quite so real a thing before then. Good night.

But after 1904 most of Kittredge's letters became competitive—Kittredge *vs.* humanity in their claims on Wald's attentions. Wald evidently reserved one night in the week for Kittredge and then occasionally cancelled their date, infuriating her friend:

> Just because you have reformed on Tuesday night—I havent got to give you entirely to humanity. I am human too and tonight I'd keep you up until—well later than Miss MacDowell would approve of —if I had you. . . .

On a similar evening Kittredge wrote that she had just done two very sensible things, not telephoned to say good night and torn up a whiny letter:

> But what business has a great grown woman like myself to sit up in her nightclothes and write nothings. . . . I am getting altogether too close to you Lady Wald—or is it . . . all those doors that you have pushed open for me? Half open-dear-just half open. And then I come up here and grow hungry for more knowledge. . . . And I feel that my strength ends and love you so. . . . I can feel your arms around me as you say I really must go.

When Wald cancelled a visit to Kittredge at Monmouth Beach, she wrote: "And so the verdict has gone forth—I cant have you. . . . But even you must want the ocean at times instead of Henry Street. . . ."

Wald did want the ocean at times. More than that, she sought the relaxation and comfort of Kittredge's friendship. During a business trip that was evidently particularly hectic, Wald wrote to Kittredge from Chattanooga that she looked forward to long, quiet, cosy evenings on the back porch. Kittredge replied that Wald's letter "was a real life-giving thing." But she no longer believed that Wald would actually make such free time possible and wrote: "When Lady Lillian is that cosy time to be? Miss MacDowell says not after midnight and your humanity world would not let me have you before. 'Long evenings on the back porch'—it sounds fine—and improbable. . . ."

Eventually Kittredge's jealousy extended from humanity in general to the residents of Henry Street in particular:

> If you think that I wasnt damned mad today it is simply that I have inherited so much self-control and sweetness from my minister parent that the fact was hidden. . . .
>
> There are times when to know that Miss Clark is standing behind one curtain, Miss MacDowell behind another and to feel an endless lot of people forever pressing the door or presenting unsigned papers makes me lack that perfect sympathy with "work for others" as exemplified by a settlement. No wonder I am called "one of your crushes." . . . It is kiss and run or run without kissing—there really isnt time for anything else. . . .

After what appears to have been for Kittredge a particularly difficult Christmas season, she gave up entirely the competition for Wald's affections:

> These may be "Merry" days but they starve one to death as far as any satisfaction in calm, every day loving and talking goes. . . . I would very much like to meet you on a desert island or a farm where the people cease from coming and the weary are at rest—will the day ever come? Or is that white ring, those long, lazy drives, the quiet and the yellow trees only a lost dream? And yet you love me —the plant on my table tells me so. The new coffee tray tells me so . . . and a look that I see in your eyes makes me sure. . . .

Refusing to participate, evidently for the first time, in Henry Street's Christmas festivities, Kittredge wrote that she was

> . . . not loveless nor lonely. I am free and strong and alive and awfully happy—But someway as I think back over this year, I believe that I needed you—it may be as much as the others— . . . I know that it would be a loss out of my life if my thoughts of you, my love for you and my confidence in you were taken away—I don't believe they ever could be less than they are tonight. . . .[18]

Judging from the letters, whatever gap the loss of Mabel Hyde Kittredge's friendship may have opened Wald seems to have filled by that summer. Wald vacationed through August and September 1906 with another society woman, Helen Arthur, an attorney and director of the research department of the Woman's Municipal League. Helen Arthur seems to have been more spontaneous and less complaining than Kittredge; and she had a sense of humor. . . .

Arthur was also more dependent on Wald, and in this relationship Wald's maternal aspects were more evident. She coaxed Arthur out of repeated depressions, encouraged her law practice, managed her finances, and kept her bankbook so that she would not overspend. This last made Arthur pout, especially during one Christmas season when she wrote to Wald that she tried to buy "exactly 28 presents for $10 worth of currency without visiting the 5 and 10 cent store which is, I regret to say, not on the Consumer's League list! If you were at 265 Henry Street—I should hold you up for my bankbook—What's vacation money compared to Christmas toys—Surely it is more blessed to give than to receive interest on deposits! Couldn't you be an old dear and let me rob it for a month? Please, mommy."

When Wald travelled, Arthur wrote long newsy letters about her law cases and activities; but they all concluded or began with a note of despair that her good mother had left her sad or naughty "son" all alone: "Such a strange feeling —no one to telephone me no 'Hello-de-e-ar' to listen for—Rainy horrid day outside and a lonesome atmosphere within. . . ." At another time she wrote "I am as near blue tonight as green can ever get and if I just had my nicest mommy to snuggle up to and talk it out straight for her son, I'd feel less like a disbarred judge. . . . Couldnt you write me a note and tell me—something?"

Eventually, Wald's busy schedule resulted in disappointments, cancelled dates, loneliness for Arthur, and what must have been for Wald familiar letters of discontent:

> Dearest, nothing could have relieved the gloom of this day except the presence of the one person her secretary notified me not to expect. . . . Now that I am being severely left alone—I have much time to spend in my own room—the walls of which formerly saw . . . me only from 2 until 7 a.m. . . . I've put you—the dear old you in your silver frame on my desk and close to me when I write and I shoved my decanter and cigarette case to the other side—if I had you, the real you instead of one-ten-thousandth part of you I might shove the unworthy things way off—Summertime has spoiled the judge who longs to get back to your comfortable lap and the delights of kicking her pajammaed legs in peace and comfort instead of being solicitously hustled from your room at 10 o'clock. . . .

In another letter, Arthur, like so many others, expressed her desire to live up to Wald's expectations of her: "If only I could pull out of my easy ways—the pleasant vices which hinder me so. . . ." But her physical longing for Wald was equally powerful. The two combined to explain Wald's magnetism: "If only August and September, 1906 were all the year round for me, but their memories stay by and perhaps some day you'll be proud of your small judge. . . . I think so often of the hundreds who remember you with affection and of the tens who openly adore you and I appreciate a little what it all means and I'm grateful to think that your arms have been close around me and that you did once upon a time, kiss me goodnight and even good morning, and I am your lonesome little/Judge."

Arthur, more than many others, was genuinely mindful of Wald's time and her emotional needs. On 30 January 1907, she wrote that "Little by little there is being brought in upon me, the presumption of my love for you—the selfishness of its demands, the triviality of its complaints—and more slowly still, is coming the realization of what it ought to bring to you and what I mean it shall. . . ."[19]

Whatever special friend came or went in Lillian Wald's life, the women of Henry Street, the residents who called themselves her "steadies," were the mainstay of her support. The women in Wald's communal family served each other as well as society. There was nothing self-sacrificing about that community: It was a positive choice. For Wald it was the essential key to her life—and the only aspect of her personal life about which she wrote clearly. On the 40th anniversary of the settlement, Wald wrote: "I came with very little program of what could or should be done. I was perhaps conscious only of a passionate desire to have people, who had been separated and who for various causes were not likely to come together, know each other that they might sympathize and understand the problems and difficulties of each other. I made no sacrifices. My friend Mary Brewster [the first coworker at Henry Street] and I were engrossed in the edifice which was taking form and in which my friends and I might dwell together."[20]

Wald and her friends lived together for over 50 years. At the end, during long years of pain and poor health, she was surrounded by love and support. After her first operation, Mabel Hyde Kittredge wrote to Wald that "at least you must feel that this is a world full of friends and love and sympathy. I hope all the bread you ever cast upon any waters has come back fresh and lovely and so much as to be a surprise. . . ." On the morning of her death, Lillian Wald turned to her nurse and said, "I'm a very happy woman . . . because I've had so many people to love, and so many to love me."[21]

The letters in the Wald collections

document only a fragment of her life, and they raise as many questions as they answer. Because we can never know the intimate details of people's lives if they are censored, withheld, or destroyed, we are confined to the details we have. But the details we have make it abundantly clear that Lillian Wald lived in a homosocial world that was also erotic. Her primary emotional needs and desires were fulfilled by women. She was woman-supported, woman-allied. Once that has been established, it becomes entirely unnecessary to pursue evidence of a specific variety of genital contact. Beyond a certain point, we get into fairly small-minded questions of technique. Since society's presumption of heterosexuality stops short of any inquiry as to what the husband and wife do atop their conjugal bed, it is only to indulge our prejudices that we demand "evidence" of lesbianism from conventional or famous women. Insistence on genital evidence of proof for a lesbian identity derives from a male model that has very little to do with the love, support, and sensuality that exist among women.

EMMA GOLDMAN

Emma Goldman wrote vividly about the difficulties faced by people who attempt to express themselves in harmony with their own nature. In a 1906 essay, "The Child and Its Enemies," she wrote that society employs all its forces to mould out of all our human differences a thing of dehumanized, patterned regularity: "Every institution . . . , the family, the state, our moral codes, sees in every strong, beautiful uncompromising personality a deadly enemy." Every effort is made, from earliest infancy, "to cramp human emotion and originality of thought" in order to create "a patient work slave, professional automaton, taxpaying citizen, or righteous moralist." To that end, all the child's questions "are met with narrow, conventional, ridiculous replies mostly based on false-

hoods." Thus uniformity and order, rather than "eternal change, thousandfold variation, continual innovation," have become the hallmarks of our culture.

The full implications of our brutally deforming institutions were clear to Goldman: "Since every effort in our educational life seems to be directed toward making of the child a being foreign to itself, it must of necessity produce individuals foreign to one another. . . ."[22]

Urged to deny the secrets within our natures and to reject the differences of others, we are taught to be fearful of ourselves and contemptuous of others. Separated from ourselves and isolated from each other, we are encouraged to huddle together for comfort under the socially acceptable banners of racism, sexism, classism, and homophobia. While people are called "human resources" in advanced industrial societies, we are discouraged from seeing the ways in which we are all connected. We are thus rendered powerless and immobilized by our prejudices. This is not an accident.

Ardent feminists and fiercely independent, Emma Goldman and Crystal Eastman depended on men for the comradeship and pleasure Lillian Wald and Jane Addams sought from women. Far more specific about their sexual orientation, Eastman and Goldman wrote about their private lives and their commitment to free love. They made it clear that they refused to be trapped by conventional or legal arrangements such as marriage.

Both were, in the larger sense, maternal women. Crystal Eastman considered the status of the unmarried mother and decided to get married largely for the sake of the two children she would have. Emma Goldman nurtured all her friends and associates. According to Kate Richards O'Hare, Emma Goldman while in prison was, above all, "the tender cosmic mother."

Contrary to popular notions of "free love" as promiscuous and amoral, Goldman's long-term relations with the men she loved—Sasha Berkman, Ed Brady, Ben Reitman, Max Baginsky, and Hippolyte Havel—were nurturing and tender on her part and devoted and supportive on theirs. They worked for her and cared for her. Ed Brady enabled her to go to Europe to study. Ben Reitman, her manager, served as her "advance man"; he raised money for *Mother Earth* and arranged her speaking tours. These men did not possess her, control her, dominate her, or expect from her more than she would give freely because she loved them as a free woman.

Free love, for Emma Goldman and Crystal Eastman meant simply love given freely to the lover of one's choice. Both rejected the notion that love was a limited commodity. They believed that it was an undefinable sentiment that expanded in proportion to the number of people who evoked it. Possession and jealousy were anathema to them. They rejected the notion that women were love objects to be married into the service and control of men.

Despite the clarity of their writings, their views were frequently misunderstood. The refusal of Eastman and Goldman to separate the personal from the political, their contempt for sham and hypocrisy, and their unfaltering opennness about the most intimate subjects horrified their contemporaries. Among the social reformers with whom Crystal Eastman worked, she acquired a reputation as a reckless revolutionary. Her attitudes on free love and her frank affirmation of women's right to physical sexuality appeared hedonistic and horrible. A frequent contributor to feminist journals, her attitudes and behavior—notably her "affairs," divorce, and remarriage were perceived as scandalous. After years of leadership in the peace movement, as founder and president of the Woman's Peace Party of New York and as executive director of the American Union Against Militarism, she was blocked from attending the second meeting at the Hague in 1919 by a com-

mittee chaired by Jane Addams, specifically because of Eastman's radical socialism and her espousal of free love.[23]

The reaction of the older social-reform women such as Jane Addams to Crystal Eastman's lifestyle is not explained by the simple fact that the sword of bigotry is many-edged. The failure of Jane Addams and most social-reform women to analyze traditional assumptions about marriage and sexuality is another byproduct of the societal pressure that kept alternative lifestyles of any kind in the closet for so many years. The settlement-house women were supplicants to the rich on behalf of the poor. Steadfast about their priorities, they frequently made political decisions which were not in harmony with their lives and which locked them into a conservative public position regarding such issues as sexuality.

CRYSTAL EASTMAN'S VISION

Emma Goldman was adamant in her opposition to marriage, which she considered an economic arrangement. Since a wife's body is "capital to be exploited and manipulated, she came to look on success as the size of her husband's income." For Goldman marriage was the very antithesis of love. Why, she asked, should two people who love each other get married? Marriage is an arbitrary, mercenary, legal tie; while it does not bind, it fetters. Only love is free. Love for Emma was "the strongest and deepest element in all life; . . . . love, the freest, the most powerful moulder of human destiny; how can such an all-compelling force be synonymous with that poor State-and-Church begotten weed, marriage?"[24]

Although Crystal Eastman shared Goldman's views on marriage, she married twice. But she was not limited or stifled in these marriages and arranged them to suit both her work and her emotional needs. According to one of her closest friends, Jeannette Lowe, Crystal Eastman was free

—"You would not believe how free she was."[25] Vigorous and bold, Crystal Eastman discarded her first marriage with alacrity and then sought to revolutionize the institution. In her own life she extended the contours of marriage beyond recognition. During the first years of her second marriage, she and her husband, her brother Max, and several of their friends lived communally.

After the war she, her two children, and her husband, Walter Fuller, lived in England "under two roofs" as ordinary lovers. "He keeps a change of clothes and all the essentials for night and morning comfort at my house, as might a favorite and frequent guest." They phoned each other daily and often met for the theatre or dinner or at a friend's house. After the evening's entertainment they decided, "like married lovers," whether to part on the street or go home together. "Marriage under two roofs makes room for moods." As for the children, "without a scowling father around for breakfast, the entire day began cheerfully. . . ."

Crystal Eastman was, above all, a feminist. She considered the true feminist the most radical member of society. The true feminist, Eastman wrote, begins with the knowledge "that the vast majority of women as well as men are without property, and are of necessity bread and butter slaves under a system which allows the very sources of life to be privately owned by a few, and she counts herself a loyal soldier in the working-class army that is marching to overthrow that system." But she had no illusions about where men in that army placed women. "If we should graduate into communism tomorrow . . . man's attitude to his wife would not be changed." For Eastman, the creation of a communistic society based on sex equality was the task of the organized feminist movement.[26]

Unlike Emma Goldman, who lived almost exclusively among men, Crystal Eastman always had a feminist support group of considerable importance to her life. She was supported by women with whom she had deep and lasting relations: many of the ardent suffragists of the Congressional Union, her friends from Vassar who worked with her in the Woman's Peace Party of New York and who were part of her communal family in Greenwich Village. On several occasions she lived with one or more of these friends, and her experiences enabled her to write in "Now We Can Begin":

> Two business women can "make a home" together without either one being over-burdened or over-bored. It is because they both know how and both feel responsible.
>
> But it is a rare man who can marry one of them and continue the home-making partnership. Yet if there are no children, there is nothing essentially different in the combination. Two self-supporting adults decide to make a home together: if both are women it is a pleasant partnership, more fun than work; if one is a man, it is almost never a partnership—the woman simply adds running the home to her regular outside job. Unless she is very strong, it is too much for her, she gets tired and bitter over it, and finally perhaps gives up her outside work and condemns herself to the tiresome half-job of housekeeping for two.

Crystal Eastman evidently solved that problem for herself by spending her summers in the south of France with Jeannette Lowe and their children, leaving her husband under his separate roof and in his separate country.

Throughout the postwar years Eastman had planned to write a book about women. But in 1928, one year after returning to New York to look for new work, she died of a kidney ailment. She was 47 years old, and her death came as a shock to her friends. Claude McKay wrote: "Crystal Eastman was a great-hearted woman whose life was big with primitive and exceptional gestures. She never wrote that Book of Woman which was imprinted on her mind. She was poor, and fettered with a family. She had a grand idea for a group of us to go off to write in some quiet corner of the world, where living was cheap and easy. But it couldn't be realized. And so life was cheated of one contribution about women that no other woman could write."[27]

EMMA GOLDMAN AND WOMEN

Emma Goldman's lack of a feminist support group did not affect her adversely until the postwar years. Before and during the war she was surrounded by her anarchist comrades and Ben Reitman. But even then her friends found Reitman distasteful and tended to admonish Goldman for her choice of lovers. Sasha Berkman in particular hated Reitman because he was not dedicated to the revolution, anarchism, or even social change. Margaret Anderson thought that the "fantastic" Dr. Reitman was not "so bad if you could hastily drop all your ideas as to how human beings should look and act. . . ." But Emma loved him and wrote that he "gave without measure or restraint. His best years, his tremendous zest for work, he had devoted to me. It is not unusual for a woman to do as much for the man she loves. Thousands of my sex had sacrificed their own talents and ambitions for the sake of the man. But few men had done so for women. Ben was one of the few; he had dedicated himself completely to my interests."[28] . . .

. . . Before the war Goldman idealized heterosexual relations. In many of her writings she scorned the bourgeois American feminists whose "narrow puritanical vision banished man as a disturber and doubtful character out of their emotional life. . . ." In a March 1906 essay, "The Tragedy of Woman's Emancipation," she argued that the "greatest shortcoming" of the feminist movement was "its narrow respectabilities which produce an emptiness in woman's soul that will not let her drink from the fountain of life." In September 1915 she published a similar editorial in *Mother Earth* by one "R.A.P.," who argued that "American feminists are the exponents of a new slavery," which denied sexual activity, encouraged inhibition, and crusaded against the "sexual victimization of virtuous females by some low, vulgar male." R.A.P. judged the bourgeois feminist movement classist and hypocritical and of "no interest except as an amusing and typical instance of feminine intellectual homosexuality."[29]

This is not to imply that Emma Goldman was homophobic in any intellectual or traditional sense. On the contrary, she was the only woman in America who defended homosexuality in general and the [rights] of Oscar Wilde in particular. Although she was absolute about a person's right to sexual choice, she felt a profound ambivalence about lesbianism as a lifestyle. She believed that "the body, in all its splendid sensuality, had to be reclaimed from the repressive hands of the prudes and the philistines." When she was criticized by her comrades for dealing with such "unnatural themes as homosexuality," thereby increasing the difficulties of the already misunderstood anarchist movement, she persisted. "I minded the censors of my own ranks as little as I did those in the enemy's camp." Censorship from her comrades had, she wrote, "the same effect on me as police persecution; it made me . . . more determined to plead for every victim, be it of social wrong or of moral prejudice."[30]

There is even some evidence that Goldman may have experimented with a woman herself. The 1912 letters of an anarchist worker, Almeda Sperry, to Goldman are very one-sided. They consist in part of affirmations of passionate love by Sperry and apparent rebuffs by Goldman. These do not deter Sperry, who evidently luxuriated for a time in a state of unrequited yearning: "God how I dream of you! You say that you would like to have me near you always if you were a man, or if you felt as I do. I would not if I could. . . ." In response to Goldman's queries about Sperry's feelings toward men, she replies: "If you mean have I ever loved a man I will frankly say that I never *saw* a man. No, I have never deeply loved any man." Sperry was, however, married, and several letters refer to her affection for her husband.

Then, in the summer of 1912, the letters take a different turn. Sperry thanks Goldman for addressing her with terms of endearment, and . . . she tells Goldman to know, just before she sleeps, that "I kiss your body with biting kisses—I inhale the sweet pungent odor of you and you plead with me for relief." A month later Sperry refers to the week they spent together after all in the country:

> Dearest, I have been flitting about from one thing to another . . . to quell my terrible longing for you . . . I am . . . seized with a fire that races over my body in recurrent waves. My last thoughts at night are of you . . . and that hellish alarm clock is losing some of its terrors for me for my first waking thoughts are of you.
>
> Dear, that day you were so kind to me and afterwards took me in your arms, your beautiful throat, that I kissed with a reverent tenderness. . . .
>
> Do you know, sweet cherry-blossom, that my week with you has filled me with such an energy, such an eagerness to become worthy of your friendship, that I feel that I must either use my intensity towards living up to my best self or ending it all quickly in one last, grand debauch. . . .
>
> How I wish I [were] with you on the farm! You are so sweet in the mornings —your eyes are like violets and you seem to forget, for a time, the sorrows of the world. And your bosom—ah, your sweet bosom, unconfined.[31]

There is nothing simple about Goldman's attitude toward lesbianism. She never refers to Almeda Sperry, and it is impossible to know the significance of this correspondence in her life. Her absolute commitment to personal liberty and her total respect for individual choice prompted Magnus Hirschfeld, a leading homosexual rights advocate in Germany and the founder of the Humanitarian Committee, organized in 1897, to write that Goldman was the "only human being of importance in America to carry the issue of homosexual love to the broadest layers of the public."[32]

But in a long article in the 1923 Yearbook of Hirschfeld's committee, Goldman criticizes an earlier article on Louise Michel in puzzling terms. Goldman reaffirms her political commitment to free sexual choice and affirms her disinterest in "protecting" Louise Michel from the charge of lesbianism. "Louise Michel's service to humanity and her great work of social liberation are such that they can be neither enlarged nor reduced, whatever her sexual habits were." Then follows a long tirade against minorities who claim for themselves all the earth's significant people, and a longer analysis of why it would be "nonsensical" to assume that Louise Michel was a lesbian. In an ultimately vague and paradoxical paragraph, Goldman concludes: "In short, Louise Michel was a complete woman, free of all the prejudices and traditions which for centuries held women in chains and degraded them to household slaves and objects of sexual lust. The new woman celebrated her resurrection in the figure of Louise, the woman capable of heroic deeds but one who remains a woman in her passion and in her love."[33]

It appears that, in Goldman's mind, to be a lesbian was an absolute right, and nothing nasty about it. But it was also to be rendered somehow less a woman.

EMMA GOLDMAN IN EXILE

In the long years of Emma Goldman's exile, years made lonelier by her political isolation, she wrote a series of letters that explored the difficulties and the pain of being a free and independent woman without a support group that provided emotional nurturance as well as a shared vision of the work to be done. After two years of disappointment in Soviet Russia, Goldman travelled back and forth between England, France, and Germany, seeking to rebuild her shattered life and attempting to convince her friends on the left that her critical analysis of the Soviet experiment was correct. In these letters she revealed the toll on her spirit taken by her personal loneliness and her political isolation. Also revealed is the brutal double standard to which even advanced women in progressive anarchist circles are subjected if their friendships are limited to men. On 28 May 1925 she wrote to Berkman:

> I agree with you that both men and women need some person who really cares. The women needs it more and finds it impossible to meet anyone when she has reached a certain age. That is her tragedy. . . . I think in the case of one who gave out so much in her life, it is doubly tragic not to have anyone, to really be quite alone. . . . I am consumed by longing for love and affection for some human being of my own.[34] . . .

As Goldman looked back over her life while in exile, even the good times seemed bitter. In a heartbreaking letter to Sasha she deals with the sexist double standard of her closest comrades:

> Where did you ever get the idea that I suspected you of being jealous of Ben in any sexual sense. . . . What I did suspect—more than that what I knew—was that you are a prig who constantly worries about what the comrades will say and how it will affect the movement when you yourself lived your life to suit yourself, I mean as far as women are concerned. It was painful to me, at the time, as it has been on many other occasions, to see you fly the movement in the face a hundred times and then condemn me

for doing the same. . . . Do I mean to deny Ben's faults? Of course not, my dear. . . . I knew Ben inside and out two weeks after we went on tour; I not only knew but loathed his sensational ways, his bombast, his braggadocio, and his promiscuity, which lacked the least sense of selection. But above all that there was something large, primitive, unpremeditated, and simple about Ben which had terrific charm. Had you and the other friends concerned in my salvation recognized this . . . instead of writing to the university to find out about his medical degree (which the boy never could forget). . . . Ben would not have become a renegade. . . . The trouble with you was . . . as with all our comrades, you are a puritan at heart. . . .

> I have been too long in the movement not to know how narrow and moral it is, how unforgiving and lacking in understanding toward everyone different from them. . . . You will repeat your objections to Ben were because . . . "he did not belong in our ranks." All right, but what were your objections to Arthur Swenson? He never was in our ranks. Why did you treat him like a dog after he came to Berlin? Why did you fail to understand the terrific turmoil the boy created in my being? . . . Of course it is nonsense to say that the attitude of men and women in their love to younger people is the same. . . . It is nothing of the kind. . . . Hundreds of men marry women much younger than themselves; they have circles of friends; they are accepted by the world. Everybody objects, resents, in fact dislikes a woman who lives with a younger man; they think her a god-damned fool; no doubt she is that, but it is not the business or concern of friends to make her look and feel like a fool. . . .

In another letter Emma tried to console Sasha after the sudden departure of his former lover Fitzie. Secretary of the Provincetown Players, Eleanor Fitzgerald had been Sasha's companion until his arrest during World War I. In 1928 she arrived in St. Tropez to be with Djuna Barnes and to visit Berkman. Although the events are unclear, Goldman's letters of explanation for Fitzie's behavior over several years formulate her own reflections on the struggle of women to be liberated: "Here we have been worrying about who should meet Fitzie, then that crazy Djuna kidnaps her. Damned fool. . . . Really, the Lesbians are a crazy lot. Their antagonism to the male is almost a disease with them. I simply cant bear such narrowness. . . ."

By implication, Goldman denied that Fitzie's affair with Barnes might have been a positive choice. To understand Fitzie, Goldman wrote, it was necessary to understand that all her relations with men had been disastrous. Her tragedy "is the tragedy of all emancipated women, myself included. We are still rooted in the old soil, though our visions are of the future and our desire is to be free and independent. . . . It is a longing for fulfillment which very few modern women find because most men too are rooted in the old tradition. They too want the woman as wife and mother in the old sense, and the new medium has not yet been devised, I mean the way of being wife, mother, friend and yet retain one's complete freedom. Will it ever? . . ."[35]

Emma Goldman doubted it. Ultimately she even doubted that women could enjoy real satisfaction even physically with men. After a lifetime of celebrating woman's absolute right to full sexual pleasure, there is something intensively poignant about a letter to Dr. Samuel D. Schmalhausen in which she implied that all through the years the pleasure she received from the men she loved had been inadequate. Schmalhausen had written *Woman's Coming of Age,* and on 26 January 1935 Goldman wrote that ever since her "intellectual awakening" she had had the same thought. Namely,

that the sex act of the man lasts from the moment of its dominant motivation to its climax. After that the brute has done of his share. The brute can go to sleep. Not so the woman. The climax of the embrace, far from leaving her relaxed or stupefied as it does the man, raises all her sensibilities to the highest pitch. All her yearning for love, affection, tenderness becomes more vibrant and carries her to ecstatic heights. At that moment she needs the understanding of and communion with her mate perhaps more than the physical. But the brute is asleep and she remains in her own world far removed from him. I know this from my personal experience and experiences of scores of women who have talked freely with me. I am certain that the cause for the conflict between the sexes which continues to exist regardless of woman's emancipation is due to the differences in quality of the sex embrace. Perhaps it will always be that way. Certainly I find very few men who have the same need, or who know how to minister that of the woman's. Naturally, I felt elated to read your analysis . . . which actually expresses what I have felt and voiced for well nigh 45 years. . . .[36]

Despite anger, isolation, and disappointment, Emma Goldman remained active and enthusiastic to the end of her life. After her despondent years in London, several friends presented her with a cottage on St. Tropez: "Georgette LeBlanc, Margaret Anderson, Peggy Guggenheim, Lawrence Vail and many others came for an hour or a day to discuss serious matters or in jolly company." Life in St. Tropez, Goldman wrote, restored her health and her "fighting spirit." It was there that she decided to write her memoirs, tour Canada, and cable friends in the United States for loans to continue her important work, now focused mainly in Spain.[37] But she never found the one great friend who could understand her empty places, and she never acknowledged the value of feminist alliances for active women whose very activity, depths of passion, and committed independence alienated them from the men with whom they worked and struggled.

Lillian Wald, Jane Addams, Crystal Eastman, and Emma Goldman all had visions of social change and economic justice that, 60 years later, we have yet to see fulfilled. They lived as they did at a time when, as Vera Brittain noted, women were programmed to monopolize their husbands, dominate their sons, possess their daughters, and make fetishes of their kitchens and shrines of their homes. These four women present a range of choices and affinities that were charged with courage, experiment, fulfillment, and intensity. In viewing women of the past it has been a common practice to assume that feminists, spinsters, woman-related women, and most women engaged in social reform were asexual, self-denying, and puritanical, sublimating their sexual passions in their work. Even today the myth persists that women unattached to men are lonely, bitter, and without community; that women who are political activists working with men can function effectively without a support network of women. In the lives of Wald, Addams, and Eastman, we see clearly the energy and strength they received from feminist networks. Crystal Eastman's feminism drew upon and allowed her to appreciate the woman-identification of her lesbian friends. On the other hand, despite Emma Goldman's intellectual and political identification with the oppressed, including women and homosexuals, she never did understand or identify with the feminist movement, and she never did find a friend of her own sex, "a kindred spirit with whom she could share her innermost thoughts and feelings."

For Jane Addams and Lillian Wald, service to humanity and leadership in public life were constantly refueled by their female support communities and by personal relationships with women who gave them passionate loyalty and love. The power of communities of independent women, and of the love between individual women, expressed not only sensually but in a range of ways, is part of the history that has been taken from us by heterosexist culture. To recognize this history is to recognize our own personal forces of energy and courage and the power to change.

NOTES

1. See Vera Brittain, *Testament of Friendship: The Story of Winifred Holtby* (London: Macmillan, 1947), p. 2: "Within the framework of this biography I have tried to tell . . . the story of a friendship which continued unbroken and unspoilt for sixteen incomparable years. . . ."

2. See Blanche Wiesen Cook, "Democracy in Wartime: Antimilitarism in England and the United States, 1914–1918," *American Studies* (Spring 1972), reprinted in Charles Chatfield, ed., *Peace Movements in America* (Schocken Books, 1973), pp. 39–57; Cook, "Woodrow Wilson and the Antimilitarists, 1914–1918" (unpublished Ph.D. dissertation, The Johns Hopkins University, 1970); and Cook, ed., *Toward the Great Change: Crystal and Max Eastman on Feminism, Antimilitarism and Revolution* (Garland Publishing, 1976).

3. Emma Goldman, *Living My Life*, Vol. I (Dover Reprint, 1970), pp. 160, 375, passim.

4. Blanche Wiesen Cook, "The Woman's Peace Party: Collaboration and Non-Cooperation," *Peace and Change* (Fall 1972), pp. 36 ff.

5. Goldman, op. cit., pp. 157–160.

6. William O'Neill, *Everyone Was Brave: Feminism in America* (Quadrangle, 1969), p. 120.

7. Allen Davis, *American Heroine: The Life and Legend of Jane Addams* (Oxford University Press, 1973), p. 46.

8. Davis, op. cit., p. 91.

9. Jane Addams, "Women, War and Babies" (31 July 1915), reprinted in Allen Davis, ed., *Jane Addams on Peace, War and International Understanding, 1895–1932* (Garland Publishing, 1976).

10. George Will, "How Far Out of the Closet?" *Newsweek*, 3 May 1977, p. 92.

11. For information about the U.S. Children's Bureau, see Nancy P. Weiss, "The Children's Bureau: A Case Study of Women's

Voluntary Networks," an unpublished paper presented at the Berkshire Conference on the History of Women, 10 June 1976, Bryn Mawr.

12. See Nancy Sahli's unpublished paper, "Changing Patterns of Sexuality and Female Interaction in Nineteenth-Century America," presented at the Berkshire Conference, 11 June 1976, pp. 12–13.

13. Lillian Wald's correspondence is divided between the New York Public Library and Columbia University. See Dock to Wald, 27 April 1925; 10 May 1925; 10 March 1916, Columbia University.

14. Lavinia Dock's correspondence with the Congressional Union is in the Woman's Party Papers, Library of Congress. See especially Dock to Paul, 8 September 1914, tray 1, box 6; 28 June 1915, New York, tray 1, box 6; Dock to C.U., 22 May 1915, tray 1, box 5.

15. Irene Lewisohn to Dear Lady Light, n.d., Wald Papers, Columbia. This probably refers to a round-the-world trip that lasted six months (1910). See R. L. Duffus, *Lillian Wald* (Macmillan, 1938), pp. 123 ff.; Rita Morgenthau to Wald, 1 January 1905, box 14, . . . Wald Papers, Columbia.

16. Dock to Duffus, 28 May 1936, in Duffus, op. cit., pp. 346–347.

17. Margaret Anderson, *The Fiery Fountains* (Horizon Press, 1969 [1951]), p. 84.

18. Mabel Hyde Kittredge to Wald, 28 April 1904; all Kittredge letters, Wald Papers, Columbia.

19. Helen Arthur's correspondence with Wald is generally undated between 1906 and 1908. Ibid.

20. Wald quoted in Duffus, op. cit., p. 55.

21. Kittredge to Wald, 11 May 1925, Wald Papers, Columbia; George V. Alger, Oral History, Columbia, pp. 251–252; Allen Reznick, "Lillian Wald: The Years at Henry Street" (unpublished Ph.D. dissertation, University of Wisconsin, 1973), p. ii.

22. Emma Goldman, "The Child and Its Enemies," *Mother Earth* (April 1906), pp. 107–109.

23. A long correspondence to block Eastman's participation at the Hague may be found in the Balch and Addams Papers at the Swarthmore College Peace Collection; see especially Lucia Ames Mead to Emily Green Balch, Balch Papers. See also Nan Bauer

Maglin, "Early Feminist Fiction: The Dilemma of Personal Life," *Prospects* (1976), pp. 167 ff., for an overview of the reformists' unwillingness to deal with changing social and sexual mores.

24. See Richard Drinnon, *Rebel in Paradise: A Biography of Emma Goldman* (University of Chicago Press, 1961), pp. 149–151; and Goldman, "Marriage and Love," in Alix Shulman, ed., *Red Emma Speaks* (Vintage, 1972), pp. 158 ff. See also Shulman, *To the Barricades: The Anarchist Life of Emma Goldman* (Crowell, 1971).

25. Jeannette Lowe to author, 27 March 1973.

26. Crystal Eastman, "Marriage under Two Roofs" (1923); "Feminists Must Fight" (1924); and "Now We Can Begin" (1920)—all reprinted in Blanche Wiesen Cook, *Toward the Great Change*.

27. Claude McKay, *A Long Way from Home* (Harcourt, 1970 [1935]), pp. 154–155.

28. Margaret Anderson, *My Thirty Years' War* (Corici, Friede, 1930), pp. 54–55; Goldman, *Living My Life*, Vol. II, p. 694.

29. Goldman, "The Tragedy of Woman's Emancipation," *Mother Earth* (No. 3, 1906), pp. 9–18 (reprinted in *Red Emma Speaks*); R.A.P., "Feminism in America," *Mother Earth* (February 1915), pp. 392–394.

30. Goldman, *Living My Life*, Vol. I, p. 555.

31. See Sperry to Goldman in Jonathan Katz, *Gay American History* (Crowell, 1976), pp. 523–530.

32. John Lauritsen and David Thorstad, *The Early Homosexual Rights Movement, 1864–1935* (Times Change Press, 1974), pp. 36–37.

33. Katz, op. cit., pp. 376–380.

34. Richard and Anna Maria Drinnon, eds., *Nowhere At Home: Letters From Exile of Emma Goldman and Alexander Berkman* (Schocken Books, 1975), p. 128.

35. Ibid., pp. 132–133, p. 86.

36. Goldman to Dr. Samuel Schmulhausen, 26 January 1935, Goldman Papers, Labadie Collection, University of Michigan.

37. Goldman, *Living My Life*, Vol. II, pp. 985–986; see also Goldman to Margaret Anderson, ed., *The Little Review Anthology* (Horizon Press, 1953), p. 363.

ANNE F. SCOTT and ANDREW M. SCOTT
One Half the People:
The Fight for Woman Suffrage

Enfranchisement of women is part of many histories: the history of suffrage, of democracy, of social reform, of popular movements, and of women. It is a story bound up with defense of privilege and fear of reform. Yet despite conservative attacks on woman's suffrage as a major innovation that would undermine the sexual-social division of labor by permitting women to invade the male world of politics, some historians have accused suffragists of diverting attention from feminism and women's "real" problems to the ritual of casting the ballot. This view, however, ignores the historic role of suffrage as symbolic of the rights of citizens to participate in shaping the future of the republic for their own benefit as well as that of others. It also ignores the sharp challenge to tradition that occurred when women broke out of the domestic sphere into the traditionally male public sphere. If women could do little about their subordinate status within the family in the nineteenth century, they could, as the historian Ellen Du Bois has pointed out, *bypass* the family or private sphere and focus on the public sphere, demanding as citizens and as voters the right to participate directly as individuals, not indirectly as an extension of their positions as wives and mothers.

The following selection shows how in the first two decades of the twentieth century politically adept and energetic suffragists were able to establish the public role of women as a legitimate, constitutional right. Although later generations would have to develop the full meaning of this achievement, winning the vote was essential to establishing the principle that women's rights were "public" and that citizenship was not limited by sex.

Excerpted from "Turning the Corner: 1896–1916" and "Victory: 1917–1920," chaps. 3 and 4 of *One Half the People: The Fight for Woman Suffrage* by Anne F. Scott and Andrew M. Scott (Philadelphia: J. B. Lippincott, 1975). Copyright © 1975 by J. B. Lippincott Company. Reprinted by permission of Harper & Row, Publishers, Inc. Notes have been renumbered and cross-references adjusted.

TURNING THE CORNER,
1896–1916

NEW ORGANIZATIONAL FERVOR

"Progressivism" brought a change in the atmosphere of politics, and of the suffrage movement. Young people were attracted to social and political action, and enthusiasm was joined with willingness to cross class lines, study economic questions, and engage in public demonstrations. This energy was evident in the growth of local suffrage groups, and in the formation of new kinds of groups alongside the traditional ones. While NAWSA's [National American Woman Suffrage Association] National Board did not immediately reflect the change, an increase in membership and the emergence of new leaders took place in many communities. After years of slow growth the suffrage movement was in the process of developing a mass base.

In Massachusetts a group of young women in 1901 had created two important new organizations: the Boston Equal Suffrage Association for Good Government and the College Equal Suffrage League, both aimed at reaching members of the community who had hitherto been indifferent to suffrage. Maud Wood Park, just out of Radcliffe, formed the College Equal Suffrage League. The idea proved so timely that she was soon being asked to help with similar groups in other states.

Meantime the Boston Equal Suffrage Association was experimenting with bold new kinds of campaigning: going door-to-door in Boston in every kind of neighborhood, or sending groups of women on a trolley tour of the state, to make suffrage speeches at every stop along the interurban line. Outdoor meetings, set up spontaneously wherever a crowd could be found, brought the message to people who would never have gone to a suffrage meeting on their own. Timid at first, the women took courage from experience and were soon enjoying themselves as well as recruiting new supporters.[1]

Young American women were increasingly aware of the rise of a militant wing in the English suffrage movement. In 1903 Emmeline and Christabel Pankhurst, members of the Labour Party, had launched the Women's Social and Political Union, and by 1905 they were experimenting with dramatic tactics. After they had heckled candidates for Parliament by demanding that they state a position on woman suffrage, members of the union, when they spit upon policemen attempting to quiet them and organized a protest meeting outside the hall, were arrested and sent to jail. For the first time the English press began to pay considerable attention to the suffrage movement. The lesson was not lost on impatient young Americans, who were themselves engaged in developing new and more colorful tactics.

Harriot Stanton Blatch, daughter of Elizabeth Cady Stanton, had come back to New York after years in England during which she had moved in radical circles. Shocked by the inertia of the traditional suffrage groups, she set about organizing the Equality League of Self-Supporting Women, drawing from a new source (women employed in factories, laundries and garment shops) and using such tactics as open air meetings, silent pickets, women poll watchers, and suffrage parades. She brought Mrs. Pankhurst and other English militants to speak in New York, and was adroit in gaining publicity. In a comparatively short time the Equality League recruited nineteen thousand members.

Inez Milholland exemplified one new style of leader. She had organized two-thirds of the Vassar student body in a college suffrage league before her graduation in 1909. Turned down at a number of law schools, she finally got a law degree from New York University, joined Mrs. Blatch's Equality League of Self-Supporting Women, and divided her time between legislative hearings and suffrage parades on the one hand, and picket lines in the interest of the shirtwaist and laundry worker's strikes on the other. She became a Socialist, and edited a "Department for Women" in *McClure's Magazine*. She was only the most flamboyant of a number of college women who came on the scene in the first decade of the century and added a new dimension to suffrage leadership.

In July 1911 the Philadelphia *Public Ledger* carried a notice that a wagon load of women speakers had appeared on a street corner, adding: "The spectacle of a woman with a wagon for a platform pleading for the use of the ballot was so novel that the audience was quick to respond, . . ." Nor was the new wave confined to the eastern seaboard or to big cities. In Boone, Iowa, the state's annual suffrage convention in 1908 was addressed by two English militants. A spontaneous parade followed, and even Anna Howard Shaw, there to represent NAWSA, was carried along by the spirit of the affair and gave an open air speech at the end.[2]

Between 1910 and 1913 campaigns in three states showed what new energy and careful organization could do. The first was in the state of Washington, where Mrs. Emma DeVoe (who had learned her political methods under Mrs. Catt's tutelage) ran a quiet campaign based on carefully planned district-by-district organization. Suffrage won almost two to one, and a wave of enthusiasm spread through the movement.

Even more encouraging was the California campaign which began in the spring of 1911. There women combined every new technique they knew of, making use of automobiles (still something of a novelty), contests, billboards and detailed organization aimed at getting out the vote and insuring a fair election. Money and help came from suffragists all over the country. The key to success, Eleanor Flexner concluded, was close attention to small town and village meetings, parlor talks, and "small groups organized where previously there had been no visible signs of interest in woman suffrage."[3] The California victory, though narrow, was enough. Women could now vote in six western states.

The third major breakthrough came in Illinois where the Equal Suffrage Association, with the help of Progressives in the legislature, put through a bill granting women the right to vote in presidential elections, a measure which did not require a constitutional amendment. There, too, the organization for the legislative campaign was impressively thorough. For the first time in a state east of the Mississippi (and a large populous state at that), women would be able to vote in presidential elections. Morale rose again.

INTERNAL CHANGES IN THE MOVEMENT

Members of NAWSA, including some on the National Board, were beginning to demand that a clear-cut political strategy be found to take advantage of what was clearly a new opportunity. Between 1910 and 1916 the board was in turmoil, and experienced considerable turnover. For a time it seemed that the organization might destroy itself through internal conflict.

Two young women who had lived in England and taken part in the militant movement there became a focal point of conflict and eventually precipitated a significant reorganization. Alice Paul and Lucy Burns came back to the United States in 1910, helped initiate the use of new methods in Pennsylvania, and in 1912 offered their services to NAWSA for the purpose of organizing a new drive for a national amendment. The board welcomed them, and dispatched them to Washington as its Congressional Committee. It was not long before they made auguration on March 3, 1913 and finding their presence felt.

Woodrow Wilson, arriving for his in-no crowd at the station, was told the people were all watching a suffrage parade. Alice Paul could not have planned it better: crowds in town for the inauguration, rowdies undeterred by the police, troops from Fort Belvoir to the rescue, and indignant congressmen demanding an investigation of the police department for its failure to protect a lawful demonstration, dramatized the suffrage cause.

It was not long, however, before members of the NAWSA board began to recognize some important differences between their own philosophy and that of Paul and Burns. Not only had the two young women organized and raised money for a separate lobbying group which they called the Congressional Union, but they were also ready to operate on a different set of political assumptions. Their English experience led them to believe that effective political action required holding the party in power responsible for policy decisions. Since the Democratic party controlled both houses of Congress and the presidency, they reasoned that all Democrats, those who had supported suffrage as well as those who had opposed it, should be held responsible if no action was taken on the suffrage amendment. They proposed to organize women to oppose Democrats in all the suffrage states.

NAWSA had always held to the view that in the American Congress men of both parties would be needed to make up two-thirds in each house, and had therefore insisted on a nonpartisan policy. Suffragists who had worked actively for the Progressive party had been criticized on just this ground.

Paul and Burns failed to understand the essential difference between the English parliamentary system and the United States system. In England the executive had a working majority in Parliament, party discipline was strong, and Parliament could grant the vote to women by a simple legislative act. In the United States the achievement of woman suffrage required that both houses of Congress pass a proposed amendment by a two-thirds vote and that the legislatures or special conventions in three-quarters of the states approve it. Furthermore, party discipline is notoriously weak in this system, and when most measures pass legislatures they are approved by coalitions comprised of members from both of the major parties. Suffrage needed every legislative friend it could find, and it made little sense to oppose supporters in the name of a principle—party responsibility—which was not understood in American politics.

At the 1913 convention, after much discussion, the NAWSA board withdrew its support from Paul and Burns who went their own way thereafter, first in the Congressional Union, then in the National Woman's Party. For the second time the suffrage movement was divided. Few long-lived reform movements escape factionalism, and when splits occur they are apt to separate the radical from the relatively conservative, the venturesome from the cautious, and are likely to revolve around questions of strategy and tactics. This new division was reminiscent of the earlier cleavage between the National and the American associations. Then Lucy Stone and the Bostonians had emphasized moderation, and had tried to avoid extreme actions that might antagonize friends and neutrals. Stanton and Anthony had been prepared to press ahead, letting the chips fall where they might. Now the NAWSA had fallen into comfortable and conservative ways, and was flanked on the left by the more militant Congressional Union.

Events had outrun the leaders of the NAWSA. While new life was stirring in many states, and the Congressional Union was generating excitement in Washington, the board appeared to be plodding along with no clear political strategy. Discontent within the organization was exacerbated by controversy over the board's decision to support a new constitutional amendment, the so-called Shafroth-Palmer amendment, which would have thrown the suffrage issue once again back to the states. On March 19, 1914, for the first time in the twentieth century, the federal amendment was brought to a vote in the Senate, and overwhelmingly defeated. Of the sixty-nine members voting, thirty-four opposed. A roll call in the House on January 12, 1915 was similarly discouraging: yeas 174, nays 204. Discontent came to a head in 1915 after the defeat, despite excellent and imaginative campaigns, of constitutional amendments in four crucial eastern states. Many members of NAWSA called for Carrie Chapman Catt to take the presidency.

In 1887, as a talented young widow with some legal training and experience in education and journalism already behind her, Carrie Chapman had joined the Iowa Woman Suffrage Association. Within two years she was organizing all over the state, and in 1890 Iowa had sent her to the national convention. Her marriage the following year to George Catt had taken her first to Seattle and then to New York, but not out of suffrage activity. She campaigned in South Dakota, Colorado and Idaho, winning in the latter two states. In Idaho she first experimented with an organization based on election districts. She next headed the Organization Committee of NAWSA, and then was president for four years. During the period immediately after her husband's death she had spent a good deal of time organizing the International Suffrage Alliance, and then had returned to New York where she organized the Woman Suffrage party, and began preparing for the referendum which finally came in 1915. In the meantime, methods she had helped to develop contributed to the victories in Washington, California, and Illinois. When the 1915 campaign in New York got forty-two percent of the vote, she had at once launched the next campaign aimed at 1917.

It was this record which led the dis-contented members of NAWSA to fix their hopes on Mrs. Catt. At the 1915 convention she was persuaded to take the presidency, on the condition that she could choose her own board. She went to work at once to turn NAWSA into a tightly organized, effective force. Now both suffrage organizations were ready to campaign seriously for a national amendment.

MOVING TOWARDS A NATIONAL AMENDMENT: THE ELECTION OF 1916

The two groups approached the task with different philosophies, and as time went by the divergence would grow. Under Mrs. Catt's leadership, NAWSA would depend upon a high degree of organizational coherence; a close relationship between local, state and national workers, a mass base, careful, low-key lobbying, and ladylike behavior. The Congressional Union also believed in organization, and it tried to develop a base in the country, especially in the suffrage states. But, in addition, Alice Paul believed in dramatic action, the symbolic gesture, headlines, and in a small, disciplined group of activists. As the union moved further in this direction, NAWSA would take pains to separate itself from its flamboyant activities, and especially to keep the distinction clear in the minds of congressmen.

It is hard now to avoid concluding that the existence of the militant group was important. The temper of the times called for a vigorous pursuit of the goal. Once again, as in the 1868 division, the two groups stimulated each other. Indeed, the challenge from the Congressional Union was part of the stimulus which led to Mrs. Catt's election, and for that reason NAWSA owed the union an unacknowledged debt.

With the Congressional Union and NAWSA both at work the militants could press ahead with shock tactics, while the more conservative group could develop its careful organization based on congressional districts. It was a good one-two punch, as events in 1916 would demonstrate.

That was an important year for woman suffrage. In June NAWSA organized a giant parade to the Republican National Convention being held in Chicago. On a cold, windy, rainy day ten thousand women marched to the convention hall and the *New York Times* reported that some politicians felt this was "the pluckiest thing they ever knew women to do." The Republicans came out for suffrage but in a disappointing states' rights plank. They "recognized the right of each state to settle this question for itself." When the Democrats met in St. Louis, delegates walked to the convention hall through streets lined with women wearing yellow sashes and carrying yellow parasols to remind them of the suffrage issue. After an acrimonious floor debate the Democrats, too, came out for suffrage "state, by state, on the same terms as men."

Carrie Chapman Catt responded by calling an emergency convention to meet in September to which she invited both presidential candidates. Wilson came and, using notes supplied to him by Alice Stone Blackwell, declared his support for suffrage but added ambiguously "we will not quarrel in the long run as to the method of it." Charles Evans Hughes, the Republican candidate, did not accept the invitation but had already endorsed suffrage by federal amendment. Both parties were beginning to contend for the suffrage votes that had gone to the Progressive party in 1912.

During this convention state presidents and officers of the national association met in secret to hear what would come to be called Mrs. Catt's "Winning Plan." The essence of the plan was that suffragists should move forward on *all* fronts, and each state was given responsibilities depending on its particular status. The eleven full suffrage states and Illinois were to get resolutions from their

legislatures memorializing the Congress to submit the federal amendment. In others, referendum campaigns were the task at hand; in some states, campaigns for presidential suffrage, and in the South campaigns for primary suffrage—all aimed at increasing the number of electoral votes which women could influence. Representatives of thirty-six state associations signed a compact to carry out these plans and to keep them secret until they revealed themselves in action. Insofar as possible, the opposition was to be caught napping.

As for the federal amendment, work in Washington was to be organized at a new level of intensity. Just before the Atlantic City convention Mrs. Catt had written to Maud Wood Park:

> I do feel keenly that the turn of the road has come. . . . I really believe that we might pull off a campaign which would mean the vote within the next six years if we could secure a Board of officers who would have sufficient momentum, confidence and working power in them. . . .
>
> Come! My dear Mrs. Park, gird on your armor once more. . . .[4]

That Atlantic City convention gave the National Board—Carrie Chapman Catt's board—authority to direct all the activities of the organization. A million dollar budget was authorized and Mrs. Park and quite a few others did "gird on their armor" and move to Washington for the duration of the struggle.

When Woodrow Wilson surveyed his prospects for reelection in 1916 it was clear that his best hope lay in attracting the votes of many citizens who in 1912 had cast their ballots for Theodore Roosevelt. Accordingly, under his aggressive leadership, the Congress that summer had adopted a number of measures which progressives considered a test of his commitment to their position, especially the Keating-Owen Child Labor Bill. Accordingly, too, he had gone to the NAWSA convention and made his tantalizing statement, opening the door to his eventual support of the federal amendment.

As in 1914, the Congressional Union took the position that since the Democrats had controlled the government for four years *all* Democrats must be opposed. NAWSA held to its careful bipartisanship, supporting its friends in either party. With war going on in Europe, peace was a major issue, and on a platform of peace and progressivism Wilson went to the country, polling nearly three million votes beyond what he had received in 1912.

The *New York Times* postelection analysis indicated that women voters had helped to swell this number and had contributed significantly to his victory in California, Idaho, Utah and Arizona. The Woman's Party effort to persuade women to vote against all Democrats had not, apparently, hurt the president very much except in Illinois.[5]

The immediate tactics of the two suffrage organizations had pulled in opposite directions. The failure of the Woman's Party tactic was not surprising since it was based on an erroneous conception of the American political process. Even though its objective was Quixotic, however, the campaign contributed to the growing momentum of the suffrage movement. While the Congressional Union in *The Suffragist* of November 11, 1916 asserted that "the Democratic campaign in the West consisted almost entirely of an attempt to combat the Woman's Party attack," other suffragists were content to give women credit for helping Wilson win, and to let all politicians draw the obvious lesson. Women now voted in states totalling nearly a hundred electoral votes. Candidates had to take notice.

If the *New York Times* is any test, the press, too, was taking increasing notice. From December 1915 to March 1916, only six suffrage stories appeared on the first five pages of the *Times,* and many that did appear were printed along with engagement, marriage, birth and death notices. By July coverage began to pick up, and two and three column articles replaced the earlier brief paragraphs. By late summer editorials and letters to the editor appeared in considerable numbers, including a protracted argument over the right of the federal government to impose woman suffrage on states which had previously defeated state constitutional amendments.[6]

The Sixty-fourth Congress met on December 4, 1916 to hear President Wilson read his message to Congress. Now safely reelected, he did not mention woman suffrage. While he spoke representatives of the Congressional Union seated in the gallery quietly unfurled a large banner: "Mr. President, What Will You Do For Woman Suffrage?" The press reported that after a moment's pause he continued reading, but it was a question that neither Wilson nor the American nation could sidestep much longer.[7]

Four more years of hard work lay ahead for suffragists, but by the end of 1916 the corner had been turned. The ideological and political spectrum had shifted to the left, and in the process woman suffrage had been legitimized in the minds of many Americans. It was rapidly picking up support among women and men in all parts of the country.

After a period of stagnation, new energies and new tactical ideas emerged within the movement and precipitated a division. The new organization, modelled to some extent on that of the English militants, had found its way to new and dramatic tactics.[8] Its emergence, its vigor, and its tactics all served to challenge the National American Woman Suffrage Association and led to its reinvigoration. Though neither organization had much use for the other, they supplemented one another very well. In the atmosphere of progressivism the question was no longer whether women would have the vote in the United States, but only when.

VICTORY: 1917–1920

WINNING PLANS

For suffragists, scattering from the NAWSA emergency convention to pick up their assigned tasks or gathering in intense conference around Alice Paul at the "Little White House" on LaFayette Square, the fall of 1916 was an exciting time to be alive. Suffrage was suddenly a major issue; newspapers and magazines were full of it, the environment was more accepting than it had ever been, four million women in eleven states could now vote, and members of both organizations were in fine fettle. Women were increasingly exhilarated by the experience of concentrated, demanding work for a high cause, one which was at last making visible progress. An English militant could have been speaking for them all when she wrote: "All the time, watching, attacking, defending, moving and counter-moving! . . . how glorious those . . . days were! To lose the personal in the great impersonal is to live!"[9] For many women the suffrage movement gave a meaning and force to life that would be remembered with keen nostalgia in later years.

The essence of Mrs. Catt's "Winning Plan" was careful coordination of work in the states with lobbying in Washington. In order for women in the congressional districts to do their job, they were supplied with a steady flow of precise information, along with constant reminders to send letters of appreciation to every member of Congress who did anything to help the cause. They were responsible for building every kind of pressure from home: resolutions of all sorts, letters from politically active men, news of mass meetings—whatever they could drum up. The flow of information from Washington required a major effort at that end. Mrs. Park described what she saw when she arrived to join the Congressional Committee:

. . . file cases holding . . . 531 portfolios, 96 for the Senate and 435 for the House . . . provided . . . all the known data about a senator or representative. There were printed sketches of his life; there were facts supplied by our members in the state about his personal, political, business and religious affiliations; there were reports of interviews . . . there was everything that could be discovered about his stand on woman suffrage and more or less about his views on other public questions. . . .[10]

From time to time groups of women from individual states would journey to Washington at their own expense to add their efforts to those of the regular members of the NAWSA Congressional Committee. In January 1917, for example, twenty-nine women arrived from sixteen states. Mrs. Catt's later judgment was that no group ever came to know the inside of Congress as suffragists did.

The Congressional Union deployed smaller numbers in its lobbying effort, but these members were equally diligent—walking the corridors of the House and Senate office buildings by day, and gathering in the evening to exchange information and plot the next step. The Congressional Union also kept full and careful files and sought to use its information in much the same way as did NAWSA.

Although the two groups made similar organizational preparations for lobbying they had different self-images. This was reflected to some extent in the manner in which they conducted their congressional activities. Mrs. Park was concerned with finding just the right woman to make a favorable impression on the member being interviewed. She always sent a woman from a man's own region if possible, recognizing the difficulty a New England woman might have, for example, with a congressman from Georgia. She thought on balance her most successful lobbyists were women from the Middle-West, middle-aged, and "rather too dressy," but "possessed of much common sense and understanding of politics in general, as well as of the men from their districts." They impressed the members, she thought, as substantial citizens of the type who had great weight with office holders.[11]

Congressional Union women did not pride themselves on diplomacy; rather the contrary:

> Here was an army of young Amazons who looked them [congressmen] straight in the eye, who were absolutely informed, who knew their rights, who were not to be frightened by bluster, put off by rudeness, or thwarted either by delay or political trickery. They never lost their tempers and they never gave up. . . . They were young and they believed they could do the impossible. . . .[12]

There was a measure of fantasy in this description, and doubtless the constant emphasis upon the youth and vigor of Congressional Union women contributed to the friction between the two groups. Neither Mrs. Park in her late thirties nor Mrs. Catt in her fifties felt themselves ready to be put out to pasture.

NAWSA was by now the largest voluntary organization in the country. Two million women, slowly being organized along lines of political jurisdictions, learning the ways of politics, were beginning to make their weight felt. A conference set up to train local people for more effective work in their congressional districts gave evidence of a sense of growing confidence when it adopted a resolution to the effect that if the Sixty-fifth Congress should fail to submit the federal suffrage amendment before the 1918 election, the association would "select a sufficient number of Senators and Representatives for replacement" to assure passage by the Sixty-sixth.[13]

The Texas congressional chairman was an example of the new breed NAWSA was developing: she arrived in Washington well acquainted with the situation in most Texas districts, and went off at once for interviews on Capitol Hill. Coming back to Suffrage House at night she remarked of one Texas member, "There is nothing we can do but retire him. That is what we will have to do."[14]

Every new achievement in the states added to the stock of "good news" the congressional committee found so helpful in Washington. In one eight-month period in 1917 the number of electoral votes dependent in part on women jumped from 91 to 172. Good news indeed.[15]

With the help of Wilson's close friend Helen Hamilton Gardener ("a woman of genius," Maud Wood Park wrote, "who was to teach me almost everything of value I came to know during those years in Washington") NAWSA kept up a steady pressure on the president. Mrs. Gardener was infinitely polite and diplomatic.

Not so the Congressional Union. Convinced that Wilson could and should do more to push the Congress, on January 10, 1917, pickets appeared at the White House bearing banners with such slogans as MR. PRESIDENT! HOW LONG MUST WOMEN WAIT FOR LIBERTY? As Wilson went out for his afternoon drive, fine words from his own writings on democracy were waved before him. On inauguration day a thousand women walked slowly round and round the executive mansion.

The president whom they were trying to recruit to their cause was, by this time, almost wholly preoccupied with the implications of the European War for the United States. In January he had laid before the Congress his "Peace without Victory" message describing the kind of settlement he hoped would be reached among the warring powers. His grand hope was that the United States, from a position of strict neutrality, would be able to bring both sides to the peace table, and lead them to a new era in international relations. In the end, he got not peace but war. By the end of February the Germans had made it clear that they were determined to sink every ship in the war zones they could, neutral and belligerent alike. This, Wilson felt, the United States could not tolerate. This new Congress was summoned into special session to receive the president's war message, and on April 6 it declared war on the Central Powers. There were many pacifists among suffrage workers, and these watched with pride as Jeannette Rankin of Montana, the first woman to be elected to the Congress, cast one of the fifty votes against the war resolution. There was also some dismay as other suffrage leaders counted the possible cost of being identified with Miss Rankin's presumed lack of patriotism.

The war changed the situation in which the suffrage campaign was conducted. Mrs. Catt had foreseen the possibility that war would come, and in February the Executive Council of NAWSA, after long debate, had decided to pledge service to the government if war should come, but decided also that it would continue the suffrage effort without relaxation. The National Woman's Party, which now encompassed the Congressional Union, decided in convention that while individual members could do as their consciences dictated, the organization as such would take no part in war work. It would continue to work for woman suffrage and for that alone, believing that in so doing it would "serve the highest interest of the country."[16]

MILITANT AND EFFECTIVE TACTICS

Picketing of the White House by the Woman's Party had proceeded peacefully at first, but in the summer of 1917 the placards became more provocative. The president was called "Kaiser Wilson" and Russian envoys from the Kerensky government arriving at the White House were greeted with signs warning them

that there was no real democracy in the United States. Onlookers were provoked, skirmishes broke out, and in time arrests began. More than two hundred women were arrested, and ninety-seven sentenced to jail for "obstructing the sidewalk." The newspapers reported every incident, usually on the front pages. In jail the women protested their miserable conditions and rough handling, demanded to be treated as the political prisoners they felt themselves to be, and finally went on a hunger strike. Embarrassed and outmaneuvered, the administration dropped the charges and released the prisoners.

The women of NAWSA and many of their friends in Congress were sure these militant tactics hurt the movement and slowed the progress of the amendment. The Woman's Party insisted that the reverse was true, and took credit for the favorable report which came from the Senate Committee on Woman Suffrage on September 15, and for the long-delayed appointment of a House Committee on Woman Suffrage on September 24, accomplishments which NAWSA thought "we came very near losing because of their activities."[17]

Probably the militant tactics did more good than harm. Nervousness about what the radical women might do next encouraged both Congress and the president to make concessions and to embrace the more conservative suffragists as the lesser evil. The sequence here, as elsewhere, illustrates the usefulness of a radical faction in a reform movement. But for the rivalry and complementarity of the two, the federal amendment might have been delayed for years, though neither faction was prepared, then or later, to recognize the contribution of the other.

While the country slowly geared itself to fight a war, suffragists in New York were busier and better organized than ever before. In November the suffrage referendum there carried by an impressive margin of one hundred thousand votes. This was dramatic progress, especially at a time when much energy of activist women was going to war work. When the Sixty-fifth Congress met for its regular session in December, women in Washington could tell the difference the New York referendum result had made in their reception on the Hill.

Almost immediately the House adopted the prohibition amendment, which removed another obstacle. The liquor interests had long feared that women voters would enact prohibition; if prohibition was coming anyway there was no reason to waste time and effort fighting woman suffrage. Maud Wood Park noted that "Many wet opponents . . . felt their chief reason for objection was gone."[18]

President Wilson was coming to believe that both party necessity and his own position as an international leader required him to support a federal suffrage amendment. On January 4, 1918 the *New York Times* reported that Theodore Roosevelt had written the Republican National Committee urging that everything possible be done to persuade Republican congressmen to vote for the amendment, and suggesting that a woman from each suffrage state be added to the National Committee itself. Five days later Wilson advised a delegation of Democrats to vote for the amendment "as an act of right and justice to the women of the country and of the world." On the same day in a private letter he said that though he hesitated to volunteer advice to congressmen, when anyone asked he advised them to vote for the amendment.[19]

In the first issue of *The Revolution* in 1868 Elizabeth Cady Stanton had foreseen a time when party necessity would force men to vote for woman suffrage. That time had finally arrived. As each additional state adopted suffrage, national party leaders became more respectful. The women's vote had become a factor in many election calculations.

On January 10, 1918 the House of Representatives witnessed one of those dramas of which myths are made: galleries packed with tense, waiting women; sick men brought from their beds to vote; a New York congressman leaving the deathbed of his suffragist wife to cast his ballot. Only six members failed to vote (or to be paired)—itself an indication of how important the amendment had become since 1915 when forty-one had failed to be recorded. When the roll call ended there were 274 yeas and 136 nay votes—the necessary two-thirds had finally been achieved.

Thirty-three New Yorkers had voted yes, twenty-two more than in 1915. Eighteen percent of the southern representatives now voted for the bill; two percent had voted yes in 1915. And while ninety percent of the men from suffrage states had voted yes, so had half those from nonsuffrage states, a gain from the thirty-six percent in 1915. While the increase in the number of suffrage states was the most vital factor in victory, the increase in suffrage sentiment in nonsuffrage states was also very helpful.

As women poured out of the galleries a Woman's Party member from Massachusetts struck up the doxology. The marble halls reverberated to the sound of "Praise God from which all blessings flow . . ." and for a few minutes NAWSA and Woman's Party members sang in harmony.

BATTLE FOR THE SENATE

God's blessing did not flow all at once, however, for there was still the Senate to be conquered, and that body proved itself capable of resistance to both popular and presidential pressure. Six-year terms protected senators from the immediate impact of public opinion, and though direct election had been in effect since 1913, one-third of the members still held their seats courtesy of a state legislature. Ten prosuffrage senators had died during the Sixty-fifth congress. And then there was the South. Southern senators from one-party states had less to fear from competition at election time, and more dread of the possible consequences of a federal amendment. Southern women were flocking to the cause: Senator Simmons from North Carolina, for one, heard often from his daughters on the subject, but his vote was not changed. Many southern women came, bearing petitions and other evidence of the change of opinion back home. A petition signed by one thousand of the country's "best known" men added to the pressure on the Senate.

Still NAWSA's careful check list indicated that two additional votes were needed for the required two-thirds. The women praised the courage of Louisiana Senator Ransdell who supported suffrage as a matter of justice, while admitting that many of his constituents did not agree, and gave grudging admiration to McCumber of North Dakota who said he would vote for the amendment despite his own convictions, because his state had granted women the vote.

During the winter and spring of 1918 both suffrage organizations tried to recruit two more senators. On May 22 Wilson said ruefully that he had done everything he could think of, to no avail. Mass meetings were organized throughout the country, and on July 13 a massive demonstration was mounted on Boston Common. Conventions of the American Federation of Labor and the National Education Association among others called for action.

By July 17, in response to Mrs. Park's urgent plea, 554 resolutions had come in from a variety of organizations. Indiana alone supplied 120, and only Delaware and Georgia failed to send any.[20] The Democratic National Committee voted unanimously to support the amendment; the Republicans had already done so.

In August the Woman's Party once again took to the streets, and a new round of arrests began. In September the pickets added a new twist—burning Wilson's speeches before the White House gate,

once again accusing him of hypocrisy, despite his by now vigorous efforts on behalf of the amendment. (Between June and August he made personal pleas to eight antisuffrage senators.) Twice the Senate had seemed ready to vote; twice the chairman of the Woman Suffrage Committee, Senator A. A. Jones, had withdrawn the amendment rather than risk defeat. Then, on September 26, he moved to take it up.

After five days of debate in which all the old arguments were once again rehearsed, the president took the extraordinary step of appearing in person to plead for a favorable vote. He argued that the suffrage amendment was vital to "the winning of the war and to the energies alike of preparation and of battle." It was also, he said, ". . . vital to the right solution of the great problems we must settle . . . when the war is over."[21] Other members of his party were saying, not so publicly, that the fall elections might well turn upon the passage of the amendment. Neither the president nor the prosuffrage Democrats prevailed; the roll call was taken and still two votes were needed for a two-thirds majority.

The New York Tribune reported that Republicans expected to gain Progressive votes in November as a result of the intransigence on the part of southern Democrats, and suggested that both houses of Congress might change hands as a result. It thought the voters would rebuke senators who had voted "no," since the United States "will not long support a Senate that insists upon being more reactionary and less progressive than the British House of Lords." The New York World could "find no evidence of consistency or principle," saying that the adverse vote "represented personal prejudice rather than adherence to any known theory of government." David Lawrence writing in the Evening Post reported that northern and western Democrats were indeed worried about the election. "It is truly an extraordinary situation," he said with some wonder, "and woman is at the bottom of it all."[22]

On October 25 Wilson again took an unusual step when he asked the voters to return a Democratic Congress to help him end the war and win the peace. When the dust settled after the election the Republicans had gained twenty-five seats in the House, and six in the Senate. This election has sometimes been interpreted as a sharp rebuke to the president, but one of the country's leading political scientists assessed the change, at the time, as about normal for off year elections.

Republicans gained six seats in Ohio, four each in Indiana and Kansas, three each in New York, Pennsylvania, Missouri and Nebraska, two in Colorado, and one each in California, and West Virginia. All but five of these were suffrage states. However, Democrats also defeated Republicans for particular seats in New York, New Jersey, Pennsylvania, California, Nevada, and Oklahoma, so generalization is impossible. The chances are that local situations were as important in many races as national issues.[23]

NAWSA had lived up to its threat to select recalcitrant senators for defeat, and had chosen four, two from each party, as objects of special campaign efforts. Somewhat to their own amazement, by excellent organization of women in both states, Republican Senator Weeks in Massachusetts and Democratic Senator Saulsbury in Delaware were defeated. The other two, Moses of New Hampshire and Baird of New Jersey were returned, but with diminished majorities. Unless death once again took off prosuffrage senators, the precious two votes were now assured.

But the women were taking no chances. After yet another failure to get a favorable vote in the lameduck session of the Sixty-fifth Congress, they turned all their energy toward making sure of the Sixty-sixth. Resolutions again poured in: twenty-four state legislatures asked the Congress to submit the amendment.

Wilson, in Paris for the peace talks, continued to urge support upon hesitant Democrats. The fall elections had added three more full suffrage states and six more presidential suffrage states, as well as bringing primary suffrage in Arkansas and Texas. Women could now vote for presidential electors in thirty states for a total of 339 electoral votes. The "Winning Plan" was working. The House, with 117 new members, passed the amendment for a second time, this time by a vote of 304 to 89. Of all the new men voting, only six voted no! Two hundred and twenty-four of those voting yes came from suffrage states, and eighty from nonsuffrage ones. Thirty percent of the southerners were now voting yes, a significant change in sentiment since the first roll call in 1915. All six Arkansas congressmen, three of four from Florida, and ten of seventeen from Texas swelled the southern contribution. Only Mississippi and South Carolina remained solidly "no."

Then, at long last, came June 4 when the Senate was to vote once again. This time it bowed to the inevitable, but just barely. Even now, when the amendment was certain to pass, there was no rush to get on the bandwagon: thirty senators still voted no. Of the thirteen new men, however, eleven voted for the amendment. The women took no time for rejoicing: they were already busy with the drive for ratification.

RATIFICATION: THE FINAL STEP

A constitutional amendment must be approved by legislatures (or special conventions) in three-fourths of the states. The federal system had presented American suffragists with difficult political and legal problems from the beginning and the difficulties were to continue to the very end. The magic number was thirty-six, and eleven ratifications came in the first month. The next five months brought eleven more ratifications. While the proponents of suffrage needed the support of thirty-six states, opponents had to hold only *thirteen* states to block ratification, and the opposition was never more active.

With an eye on the electoral votes already affected by woman suffrage, the national committees of both parties urged speedy ratification As is usual with state legislators, however, local conditions were more important than the preferences of national leaders. Weary, but by now experienced, local suffrage organizations went to work. Armed with well-researched lists of governors and legislators they began again the process of persuasion. Mrs. Catt travelled where ever she was needed and the Woman's Party deployed its organizers.

By August 1920 thirty-five states had ratified and only one state remained in which ratification was deemed feasible before the presidential election. A special session of the Tennessee legislature was scheduled to begin on August 9 and suffragists and opponents poured into Nashville. It was a wild ten days. The liquor interests, railroad lobby and manufacturers lobby were all active. Opponents of suffrage set up shop on the 8th floor of the Hermitage Hotel and "dispensed Old Bourbon and moonshine whisky with lav-

ish insistence."[24] There was considerable intoxication and on one dismal night, reports circulated that the entire legislature was drunk. In any case by August 13 state senators were sober enough to ratify the amendment by a vote of twenty-five to four.

The contest now swirled around the lower House. There were rumors of deals and bribes and offers of loans on attractive terms. Supporters the suffragists had counted on mysteriously defected, and it was alleged that an attempt was made to kidnap a suffrage member. The vote was so close that it turned on the decision of twenty-four year old Harry Burn, the youngest member of the legislature. In the end he supported suffrage because, so legend has it, his mother urged him to "help Mrs. Catt." The amendment carried by forty-nine to forty-seven.

In the early morning hours of August 26, 1920 the United States secretary of state issued a formal proclamation, and the struggle was over. Seventy-two years had passed since the women at Seneca Falls resolved to "seek their sacred right to the elective franchise." Everywhere in the United States women had the legal right to vote.

NOTES

1. See Sharon Hartman Strom, "Leadership and Tactics in the American Woman Suffrage Movement: A New Perspective from Massachusetts," *Journal of American History* 62 (Sept. 1975), pp. 262–82.

2. See Harriot Stanton Blatch, *Challenging Years* (New York: G.P. Putnum's Sons, 1940), pp. 91–242. Caroline Katzenstein, *Lifting the Curtain* (Philadelphia: Dorrance and Company, 1955), pp. 46–47. Louise Noun, *Strong Minded Women* (Ames: The Iowa State University Press, 1969), pp. 246–247, and the *Woman's Journal*, 1905–1910 for evidence of the growing influence of English militant methods in the American suffrage movement. Enthusiastic crowds turned out to hear Mrs. Pankhurst, the leader of the English militants, in New York in 1909 and in Boston in 1910.

3. Eleanor Flexner, *Century of Struggle*

(Cambridge: Harvard University Press, 1958), p. 256.

4. Carrie Chapman Catt to Maud Wood Park, August 30, 1916, Maud Wood Park Papers, Schlesinger Library, Radcliffe College, Cambridge, Massachusetts.

5. See *New York Times*, Nov. 12, 1916. The analysis is based on observations of local politicians and correspondents; no survey data of the kind which we might have now was available. The only place where women's vote could be accurately measured was Illinois (since women there could vote only for president). In that state women voted more heavily for Charles Evans Hughes, the Republican candidate, than did the men.

6. We are indebted to an unpublished paper by Myla Taylor, Duke University student, for this information.

7. Inez Haynes Irwin, *The Story of the Woman's Party* (New York: Harcourt-Brace, 1921), pp. 185–86.

8. It is important to note that woman suffrage as an international movement had spread widely since New Zealand enfranchised its women in 1893. Australia, Austria, Canada, Czechoslovakia, Denmark, England, Finland, Germany, Hungary, Ireland, Mexico, Norway, Poland, Russia, and Scotland all had woman suffrage before 1919. See Ross Evans Paulson, *Women's Suffrage and Temperance* (Glenview, Illinois: Scott-Foresman, 1973) for . . . discussion of the international suffrage movement.

9. Christabel Pankhurst, *Unshackled: The Story of How We Won the Vote* (London: Hutchinson, 1959), p. 83. Such a spirit supplies great energy to a social movement; it pervades the personal documents of the women who did the work in NAWSA and in the Woman's Party. By the time of the first House victory in January 1918 many members of Congress had come to share the sense of a great cause, and some went to extraordinary lengths to insure the success of the amendment on that occasion. The feeling of solidarity in a good cause is powerful.

10. Maud Wood Park, *Front Door Lobby* (Boston: Beacon Press, 1960. Copyright © 1960 by Edna Lamprey Stantial. Reprinted by permission of Beacon Press), p. 19.

11. Park, *Front Door Lobby*, p. 44.

12. Irwin, *Story of the Woman's Party*, p. 334.

13. Carrie Chapman Catt and Nettie R. Shuler, *Woman Suffrage and Politics* (New York: Charles Scribner's Sons, 1923), p. 318. The figure of two million is based on Aileen Kraditor's careful estimates. See *Ideas of the Woman Suffrage Movement* (New York: Columbia University Press, 1965), p. 45.

14. Ethel Smith to Maud Wood Park, October 10, 1917, Maud Wood Park Papers, Schlesinger Library, Cambridge, Massachusetts.

15. Park, *Front Door Lobby*, p. 71.

16. Doris Stevens, *Jailed for Freedom* (New York: Boni and Liveright, 1920), p. 82.

17. Loretta Zimmerman, Alice Paul and the National Woman's Party" (PH.D. dissertation, Tulane University, 1964), p. 241.

18. Report of the National Congressional Committee, December 1, 1917–January 11, 1918, Maud Wood Park Papers, Schlesinger Library, Cambridge, Massachusetts.

19. Ray Stannard Baker, *Woodrow Wilson: Life and Letters* (New York: Doubleday Page and Co., 1927), vol. VII, p. 460.

20. Memo in Maud Wood Park Papers, Schlesinger Library, Cambridge, Massachusetts. These papers are filled with information concerning the effort to turn the Senate around.

21. U.S., Congress, Senate, Document 284, 65th Cong. 1st sess.

22. These comments were reported in *The Literary Digest* 59 (October 12, 1918), pp. 12–13.

23. P. Orman Ray, "American Government and Politics," *American Political Science Review* 12, no. 1 (Feb. 1910), pp. 80–84.

24. Catt and Shuler, *Woman Suffrage*, p. 442. See also A. Elizabeth Taylor, *The Woman Suffrage Movement in Tennessee* (New York: Bookman Associates, 1957), chapter 7.

DOCUMENT: Controlling Reproduction

MARGARET SANGER
My Fight for Birth Control

Nowhere does gender matter more than in the area of reproduction. The contrast between the high fertility of newly arriving immigrants and the low birth rate among old-stock Americans around the turn of the century prompted such leaders as Theodore Roosevelt to lament "race suicide" and to exhort women of the "proper sort" to perform their maternal functions in the selfless fashion dictated by time and tradition. Viewed through women's eyes, however, these population trends looked different, as this selection on the beginnings of the birth control movement dramatically illustrates. While a few radicals such as Emma Goldman saw contraception as a means of liberating women by restoring to them control over their own bodies and thereby lessening their economic dependence on men, it was Margaret Higgins Sanger whose name would become most closely linked with the crusade for birth control.

The factors that propelled Sanger—always a complex personality—to leadership were many. One of eleven children, she helped bury her mother, who died of tuberculosis. Young Margaret, however, was convinced that it was the passion of her father who lived to be eighty which was the real cause of her mother's death. A nursing career also shaped Sanger's thinking, as the following account suggests. Arrested under the Comstock Law (document 6 in Essential Documents) for publication of a newspaper advocating contraception, she fled in 1914 to England with her husband and three children. There she met the famous British psychologist and sex expert, Havelock Ellis, who further convinced her that sexual experience should be separated from reproduction, enabling couples to enhance the quality of their sexual relationship. Returning to New York, the Sangers continued their activities on behalf of birth control. The opening of the Brownsville clinic in 1916, recounted here, resulted in still further confrontation with authorities. The hunger strike of Sanger's sister, Ethel Byrne, a nurse at the

Excerpted from "Awakening and Revolt," "A 'Public Nuisance,' " and "Hunger Strike," chaps. 3, 12, and 13 of *My Fight for Birth Control* by Margaret Sanger (New York: Farrar & Reinhart, 1931). Copyright © 1931 by Margaret Sanger. Reprinted by permission of Grant Sanger. Cross-references have been adjusted.

clinic, was followed by Sanger's own trial. Convicted of "maintaining a public nuisance," she was sentenced to thirty days in the workhouse. Ever the iconoclast and rebel, she gave talks to other inmates on sex hygiene when the matrons were out of sight. Divorcing William Sanger, she subsequently married a wealthy oil man who contributed liberally to the American Birth Control League, which she founded in 1921.

Important financial aid would also come in later years from the wealthy feminist, Katherine McCormick, who shared Sanger's commitment to research in contraception. In the early 1950s McCormick provided funds for experiments in endocrinology that led to the development of the birth control pill. At a time when few scientists thought an oral contraceptive was possible, the insistence of Sanger and McCormick that every woman had the right to control her own body helped bring about a major breakthrough in medical technology. In 1960 "the pill" became available to the public. The timing was propitious, for it coincided with a period of sexual liberation that, while proving in some respects to be a mixed blessing for women, also coincided with new recognition of the intensity of their sexual drive and capacity for sexual pleasure.

Although Sanger saw the development of an oral contraceptive as another victory in a long and difficult struggle for reproductive freedom, others viewed the birth control movement differently. Arguments that limiting family size could not only free women's energies for social reform but prevent the world's poor from producing children they were unable to care for met with opposition from women themselves in the early years of Sanger's crusade. Some feared that birth control would contribute to promiscuity; others feared it would deny women the dignity that was theirs by virtue of motherhood. The Roman Catholic Church was unrelenting in its opposition, maintaining that the use of contraceptives is a sin. Among groups in the self-styled profamily movement of the 1980s Sanger is still being angrily attacked. Her contribution to the lives of modern American women remains a matter of political debate. Birth control is not only a technical way of spacing and limiting children so as to benefit both mother and child but is part of a larger debate about the extent to which women should be able to control their own reproductive lives.

AWAKENING AND REVOLT

Early in the year 1912 I came to a sudden realization that my work as a nurse and my activities in social service were entirely palliative and consequently futile and useless to relieve the misery I saw all about me. . . .

It is among the mothers here that the most difficult problems arise—the outcasts of society with theft, filth, perjury, cruelty, brutality oozing from beneath.

Ignorance and neglect go on day by day; children born to breathe but a few hours and pass out of life; pregnant women toiling early and late to give food to four or five children, always hungry; boarders taken into homes where there is not sufficient room for the family; little girls eight and ten years of age sleeping in the same room with dirty, foul smelling, loathsome men; women whose weary, pregnant, shapeless bodies refuse to accommodate themselves to the husbands' desires find husbands looking with lustful eyes upon other women, sometimes upon their own little daughters, six and seven years of age.

In this atmosphere abortions and birth become the main theme of conversation. On Saturday nights I have seen groups of fifty to one hundred women going into questionable offices well known in the community for cheap abortions. I asked several women what took place there, and they all gave the same reply: a quick examination, a probe inserted into the uterus and turned a few times to disturb the fertilized ovum, and then the woman was sent home. Usually the flow began the next day and often continued four or five weeks. Sometimes an ambulance carried the victim to the hospital for a curetage, and if she returned home at all she was looked upon as a lucky woman.

This state of things became a nightmare with me. There seemed no sense to it all, no reason for such waste of mother life, no right to exhaust women's vitality and to throw them on the scrap-heap before the age of thirty-five.

Everywhere I looked, misery and fear stalked—men fearful of losing their jobs, women fearful that even worse conditions might come upon them. The menace of another pregnancy hung like a sword over the head of every poor woman I came in contact with that year. The question which met me was always the same: What can I do to keep from it? or, What can I do to get out of this? Sometimes they talked among themselves bitterly.

"It's the rich that know the tricks," they'd say, "while we have all the kids." Then, if the women were Roman Catholics, they talked about "Yankee tricks," and asked me if I knew what the Protes-

tants did to keep their families down. When I said that I didn't believe that the rich knew much more than they did I was laughed at and suspected of holding back information for money. They would nudge each other and say something about paying me before I left the case if I would reveal the "secret." . . .

I heard over and over again of their desperate efforts at bringing themselves "around"—drinking various herb-teas, taking drops of turpentine on sugar, steaming over a chamber of boiling coffee or of turpentine water, rolling down stairs, and finally inserting slippery-elm sticks, or knitting needles, or shoe hooks into the uterus I used to shudder with horror as I heard the details and, worse yet, learned of the conditions *behind the reason* for such desperate actions. . . .

. . . Each time I returned it was to hear that Mrs. Cohen had been carried to a hospital but had never come back, that Mrs. Kelly had sent the children to a neighbor's and had put her head into the gas oven to end her misery. Many of the women had consulted midwives, social workers and doctors at the dispensary and asked a way to limit their families, but they were denied this help, sometimes indignantly or gruffly, sometimes jokingly; but always knowledge was denied them. Life for them had but one choice: either to abandon themselves to incessant childbearing, or to terminate their pregnancies through abortions. Is it any wonder they resigned themselves hopelessly, as the Jewish and Italian mothers, or fell into drunkenness, as the Irish and Scotch? The latter were often beaten by husbands, as well as by their sons and daughters. They were driven and cowed, and only as beasts of burden were allowed to exist. . . .

They claimed my thoughts night and day. One by one these women, with their worried, sad, pensive and ageing faces would marshal themselves before me in my dreams, sometimes appealingly, sometimes accusingly. I could not escape from the facts of their misery, neither was I able to see the way out of their problems and their troubles. . . .

Finally the thing began to shape itself, to become accumulative during the three weeks I spent in the home of a desperately sick woman living on Grand Street, a lower section of New York's East Side.

Mrs. Sacks was only twenty-eight years old; her husband, an unskilled worker, thirty-two. Three children, aged five, three and one, were none too strong nor sturdy, and it took all the earnings of the father and the ingenuity of the mother to keep them clean, provide them with air and proper food, and give them a chance to grow into decent manhood and womanhood.

Both parents were devoted to these children and to each other. The woman had become pregnant and had taken various drugs and purgatives, as advised by her neighbors. Then, in desperation, she had used some instrument lent to her by a friend. She was found prostrate on the floor amidst the crying children when her husband returned from work. Neighbors advised against the ambulance, and a friendly doctor was called. The husband would not hear of her going to a hospital, and as a little money had been saved in the bank a nurse was called and the battle for that precious life began.

. . . The three-room apartment was turned into a hospital for the dying patient. Never had I worked so fast, so concentratedly as I did to keep alive that little mother. . . .

. . . July's sultry days and nights were melted into a torpid inferno. Day after day, night after night, I slept only in brief snatches, ever too anxious about the condition of that feeble heart bravely carrying on, to stay long from the bedside of the patient. With but one toilet for the building and that on the floor below, everything had to be carried down for disposal, while ice, food and other necessities had to be carried three flights up. It was one of those old airshaft buildings of which there were several thousands then standing in New York City.

At the end of two weeks recovery was in sight, and at the end of three weeks I was preparing to leave the fragile patient to take up the ordinary duties of her life, including those of wifehood and motherhood. . . .

But as the hour for my departure came nearer, her anxiety increased, and finally with trembling voice she said: "Another baby will finish me, I suppose."

"It's too early to talk about that," I said, and resolved that I would turn the question over to the doctor for his advice. When he came I said: "Mrs. Sacks is worried about having another baby."

"She well might be," replied the doctor, and then he stood before her and said: "Any more such capers, young woman, and there will be no need to call me."

"Yes, yes—I know, Doctor," said the patient with trembling voice, "but," and she hesitated as if it took all of her courage to say it, "*what* can I do to prevent getting that way again?"

"Oh ho!" laughed the doctor good naturedly, "You want your cake while you eat it too, do you? Well, it can't be done." Then, familiarly slapping her on the back and picking up his hat and bag to depart, he said: "I'll tell you the only sure thing to do. Tell Jake to sleep on the roof!"

With those words he closed the door and went down the stairs, leaving us both petrified and stunned.

Tears sprang to my eyes, and a lump came in my throat as I looked at that face before me. It was stamped with sheer horror. I thought for a moment she might have gone insane, but she conquered her feelings, whatever they may have been, and turning to me in desperation said: "He can't understand, can he?—he's a man after all—but you do, don't you? You're a woman and you'll tell me the secret and I'll never tell it to a soul."

She clasped her hands as if in prayer, she leaned over and looked straight into my eyes and beseechingly implored me to tell her something—something *I really did not know.* . . .

I had to turn away from that imploring face. I could not answer her then. I quieted her as best I could. She saw that I was moved by the tears in my eyes. I promised that I would come back in a few days and tell her what she wanted to know. The few simple means of limiting the family like *coitus interruptus* or the condom were laughed at by the neighboring women when told these were the means used by men in the well-to-do families. That was not believed, and I knew such an answer would be swept aside as useless were I to tell her this at such a time. . . .

The intelligent reasoning of the young mother—how to *prevent* getting that way again—how sensible, how just she had been—yes, I promised myself I'd go back and have a long talk with her and tell her more, and perhaps she would not laugh but would believe that those methods were all that were really known.

But time flew past, and weeks rolled into months. . . . I was about to retire one night three months later when the telephone rang and an agitated man's voice begged me to come at once to help his wife who was sick again. It was the husband of Mrs. Sacks, and I intuitively knew before I left the telephone that it was almost useless to go.

. . . I arrived a few minutes after the doctor, the same one who had given her such noble advice. The woman was dying. She was unconscious. She died within ten minutes after my arrival. It was the same result, the same story told a thousand times before—death from abortion. She had become pregnant, had used drugs, had then consulted a five-dollar professional abortionist, and death followed.

The doctor shook his head as he rose from listening for the heart beat. . . .

The gentle woman, the devoted mother, the loving wife had passed on leaving behind her a frantic husband, helpless in his loneliness, bewildered in his helplessness as he paced up and down the room, hands clenching his head, moaning "My God! My God! My God!"

The Revolution came—but not as it has been pictured nor as history relates that revolutions have come. . . .

After I left that desolate house I walked and walked and walked; for hours and hours I kept on, bag in hand, thinking, regretting, dreading to stop; fearful of my conscience, dreading to face my own accusing soul. At three in the morning I arrived home still clutching a heavy load the weight of which I was quite unconscious.

. . . As I stood at the window and looked out, the miseries and problems of that sleeping city arose before me in a clear vision like a panorama: crowded homes, too many children; babies dying in infancy; mothers overworked; baby nurseries; children neglected and hungry —mothers so nervously wrought they could not give the little things the comfort nor care they needed; mothers half sick most of their lives—"always ailing, never failing"; women made into drudges; children working in cellars; children aged six and seven pushed into the labor market to help earn a living; another baby on the way; still another; yet another; a baby born dead—great relief; an older child dies —sorrow, but nevertheless relief—insurance helps; a mother's death—children scattered into institutions; the father, desperate, drunken; he slinks away to become an outcast in a society which has trapped him.

. . . There was only one thing to be done: call out, start the alarm, set the heather on fire! Awaken the womanhood of America to free the motherhood of the world! I released from my almost paralyzed hand the nursing bag which unconsciously I had clutched, threw it across the room, tore the uniform from my body, flung it into a corner, and renounced all palliative work forever.

I would never go back again to nurse women's ailing bodies while their miseries were as vast as the stars. I was now finished with superficial cures, with doctors and nurses and social workers who were brought face to face with this overwhelming truth of women's needs and yet turned to pass on the other side. They must be made to see these facts. I resolved that women should have knowledge of contraception. They have every right to know about their own bodies. I would strike out —I would scream from the housetops. I would tell the world what was going on in the lives of these poor women. I *would* be heard. No matter what it should cost. *I would be heard.* . . .

I announced to my family the following day that I had finished nursing, that I would never go on another case—and I never have.

I asked doctors what one could do and was told I'd better keep off that subject or Anthony Comstock would get me. I was told that there were laws against that sort of thing. This was the reply from every medical man and woman I approached. . . .

A "PUBLIC NUISANCE"

The selection of a place for the first birth control clinic was of the greatest importance. No one could actually tell how it would be received in any neighborhood. I thought of all the possible difficulties: The indifference of women's organizations, the ignorance of the workers themselves, the resentment of social agencies, the opposition of the medical profession. Then there was the law—the law of New York State.

Section 1142 was definite. It stated that *no one* could give information to prevent conception to *anyone* for any reason.

There was, however, Section 1145, which distinctly stated that physicians (*only*) could give advice to prevent conception for the cure or prevention of disease. I inquired about the section, and was told by two attorneys and several physicians that this clause was an exception to 1142 referring only to venereal disease. But anyway, as I was not a physician, it could not protect me. Dared I risk it?

I began to think of the doctors I knew. Several who had previously promised now refused. I wrote, telephoned, asked friends to ask other friends to help me find a woman doctor to help me demonstrate the need of a birth control clinic in New York. None could be found. No one wanted to go to jail. No one cared to test out the law. Perhaps it would have to be done without a doctor. But it had to be done; that I knew.

Fania Mindell, an enthusiastic young worker in the cause, had come on from Chicago to help me. Together we tramped the streets on that dreary day in early October, through a driving rainstorm, to find the best location at the cheapest terms possible . . .

Finally at 46 Amboy Street, in the Brownsville section of Brooklyn, we found a friendly landlord with a good place vacant at fifty dollars a month rental; and Brownsville was settled on. It was one of the most thickly populated sections. It had a large population of working class Jews, always interested in health measures, always tolerant of new ideas, willing to listen and to accept advice whenever the health of mother or children was involved. I knew that here there would at least be no breaking of windows, no hurling of insults into our teeth; but I was scarcely prepared for the popular support, the sympathy and friendly help given us in that neighborhood from that day to this. . . .

With a small bundle of handbills and a large amount of zeal, we fared forth each morning in a house-to-house canvass of the district in which the clinic was located. Every family in that great district received a "dodger" printed in English, Yiddish and Italian. . . .

Women of every race and creed flocked to the clinic with the determination not to have any more children than their health could stand or their husbands could support. Jews and Christians, Protestants and Roman Catholics alike made their confessions to us, whatever they may have professed at home or in the church. Some did not dare talk this over with their husbands; and some came urged on by their husbands. Men themselves came after work; and some brought timid, embarrassed wives, apologetically dragging a string of little children. . . .

When I asked a bright little Roman Catholic woman what she would say to the priest when he learned that she had been to the Clinic, she answered indignantly: "It's none of his business. My husband has a weak heart and works only four days a week. He gets twelve dollars, and we can barely live on it now. We have enough children."

Her friend, sitting by, nodded a vigorous approval. "When I was married," she broke in, "the priest told us to have lots of children, and we listened to him. I had fifteen. Six are living. Nine baby funerals in our house. I am thirty-six years old now. Look at me! I look sixty."

As I walked home that night, I made a mental calculation of fifteen baptismal fees, nine funeral expenses, masses and candles for the repose of nine little souls, the physical suffering of the mother, and the emotional suffering of both parents; and I asked myself, "Was it fair? Is this the price of Christianity?" . . .

Ethel Byrne, who is my sister and a trained nurse, assisted me in advising, explaining, and demonstrating to the women how to prevent conception. As all of our 488 records were confiscated by the detectives who later arrested us for

violation of the New York State law, it is difficult to tell exactly how many more women came in those days to seek advice; but we estimate that it was far more than five hundred. As in any new enterprise, false reports were maliciously spread about the clinic; weird stories without the slightest foundation of truth. We talked plain talk and gave plain facts to the women who came there. We kept a record of every applicant. All were mothers; most of them had large families.

It was whispered about that the police were to raid the place for abortions. We had no fear of that accusation. We were trying to spare mothers the necessity of that ordeal by giving them proper contraceptive information. . . .

The arrest and raid on the Brooklyn clinic was spectacular. There was no need of a large force of plain clothes men to drag off a trio of decent, serious women who were testing out a law on a fundamental principle. My federal arrest, on the contrary, had been assigned to intelligent men. One had to respect the dignity of their mission; but the New York city officials seem to use tactics suitable only for crooks, bandits and burglars. We were not surprised at being arrested, but the shock and horror of it was that a *woman*, with a squad of five plain clothes men, conducted the raid and made the arrest. A woman—the irony of it!

I refused to close down the clinic, hoping that a court decision would allow us to continue such necessary work. I was to be disappointed. Pressure was brought upon the landlord, and we were dispossessed by the law as a "public nuisance." In Holland the clinics were called "public utilities."

When the policewoman entered the clinic with her squad of plain clothes men and announced the arrest of Miss Mindell and myself (Mrs. Byrne was not present at the time and her arrest followed later), the room was crowded to suffocation with women waiting in the outer room. The police began bullying these mothers, asking them questions, writing down their names in order to subpoena them to testify against us at the trial. These women, always afraid of trouble which the very presence of a policeman signifies, screamed and cried aloud. The children on their laps screamed, too. It was like a panic for a few minutes until I walked into the room where they were stampeding and begged them to be quiet and not to get excited. I assured them that nothing could happen to them, that I was under arrest but they would be allowed to return home in a few minutes. That quieted them. The men were blocking the door to prevent anyone from leaving, but I finally persuaded them to allow these women to return to their homes, unmolested though terribly frightened by it all.

. . . The patrol wagon came rattling through the streets to our door, and at length Miss Mindell and I took our seats within and were taken to the police station. . . .

HUNGER STRIKE

Out of that spectacular raid, which resulted in an avalanche of nation-wide publicity in the daily press, four separate and distinct cases resulted:

Mrs. Ethel Byrne, my sister, was charged with violating Section 1142 of the Penal Code, designed to prevent dissemination of birth control information.

Miss Fania Mindell was charged with having sold an allegedly indecent book entitled "What Every Girl Should Know" written by Margaret Sanger.

I was charged with having conducted a clinic at 46 Amboy Street, Brooklyn, in violation of the same section of the Penal Code.

Having re-opened the clinic, I was arrested on a charge of "maintaining a public nuisance," in violation of Section 1530 of the Penal Code.

The three of us were held for trial in the Court of Special Sessions, with bail fixed at $500 each. This meant that our cases would be decided by three judges appointed by the Mayor and not by a jury. . . .

My sister was found guilty, and on January 22 she was sentenced to thirty days in the Workhouse. A writ of habeas corpus as a means of suspending sentence during appeal was refused by Supreme Court Justice Callahan. She spent the night in jail.

Ethel Byrne promptly declared a hunger strike. I knew that she would not flinch. Quiet, taciturn, with a will of steel hidden by a diffident air, schooled by her long training as a professional nurse, she announced briefly that she would neither eat, drink, nor work until her release. Commissioner of Correction Burdette G. Lewis promptly announced that she would be permitted to see no one but her attorney.

While the newspapers were reporting —always on the front page—the condition of the hunger striker, plans were hastened for a monster mass meeting of protest, to be held in Carnegie Hall. Helen Todd acted as chairman, and Dr. Mary Halton was an additional speaker. The hall was crowded by a huge audience of all classes. The women patients of the Brownsville clinic were given places of honor on the platform. The salvos of applause which greeted me showed that intelligent opinion was strongly behind us, and did much to give me the courage to fight with renewed strength for the immediate release of Ethel Byrne.

This meeting was acclaimed by the press as a "triumph of women, for women, by women." The meeting was said to have struck the right note—that of being instructive and persuasive, instead of agitational.

In the meantime, Ethel Byrne's refusal to eat and drink was crowding all other news off the front pages of the New York papers. Her defiance was sharpening the issue between self-respecting citizens and the existing law, which was denounced on every street corner as hypocritical. In the subway crowds, on street-corners, everywhere people gathered, the case was discussed. "They are imprisoning a woman for teaching physiological facts!" I heard one man exclaim. . . .

"It makes little difference whether I starve or not," she replied, through her attorney, "so long as this outrageous arrest calls attention to the archaic laws which would prevent our telling the truth about the facts of life. With eight thousand deaths a year in New York State from illegal operations on women, one more death won't make much difference."

All this served to convince the now panic-stricken Mr. Lewis [Commissioner of Correction in charge of Blackwell's Island] that Mrs. Byrne was different, after all, from the alcoholics and drug addicts who had given him his previous experience, and with whom he had gallantly compared her. When she had gone 103 hours without food, he established a precedent in American prison annals. He ordered her forcibly fed. She was the first woman so treated in this country. . . .

The truth was that Mrs. Byrne was in a critical condition after being rolled in a blanket and having milk, eggs and a stimulant forced into her stomach through a rubber tube. I realized this as soon as I heard that she was "passive under the feeding." Nothing but loss of strength could have lessened the power of her resistance to such authority. Nothing but brutality could have reduced her fiery spirit to acquiescence. I was desperate; torn between admiration for what she was doing and misery over what I feared might be the result.

On January 31st, a committee headed by Mrs. Amos Pinchot, Jessie Ashley and myself went to Albany for the purpose of asking Governor Whitman to appoint a commission to investigate birth control and make a report to the state legislature. Governor Whitman, a wise, fair, intelligent executive and statesman, received us, and listened to our exposition of the economic and moral necessity for birth control; the medical theory behind its justification. He promised to consider appointing the commission. During the interview Miss Jessie Ashley introduced the subject of Mrs. Byrne's treatment on Blackwell's Island and the anxiety we felt about her condition. We tried to make him see the outrage committed by the state in making anyone suffer for so just a cause. The Governor offered Mrs. Byrne a pardon on condition that she would not continue to disseminate birth control information. . . .

When we left Albany that day, I had the promise of a provisional pardon for Mrs. Byrne, but best of all I had in my purse a letter from the Governor to the authorities at Blackwell's Island authorizing me to see her. I was shocked and horrified when, in the late afternoon of February 1st, I saw my sister. She was lying semi-conscious on a cot in a dark corner of the prison cell. . . .

There was not time to inform her of the conditions of her pardon, and moreover she was too ill to face the question. I still believe that I was right in accepting the conditions which the Governor imposed. There was no other course. I saw that she was dangerously ill, that nothing further was to be gained by her keeping on, and that her death would have been a terrible calamity. Her life was what mattered to me, regardless of her future activities. . . .

At any rate, by the time she was released the subject was a burning issue. Newspapers which previously had ignored the case, had to mention a matter important enough to bring the Governor of the State from Albany to New York.

III

Modern America

1920–80

The years between 1920 and 1980 have, in the main, been years of crisis. Domestically, innovations in technology, management, and marketing transformed an industrial nation into a consumer society. But consumption did not automatically bring the good life that advertisers promised. In the early years after World War I Americans were plagued by tensions that erupted into strikes, attacks upon radicals, and indiscriminate accusations of communism. The climate of suspicion and anxiety brought out the uglier aspects of American society— the Ku Klux Klan enjoyed a brief rebirth. Conflict between generations underscored anxiety over the continuing erosion of Victorian moral standards. Although elements of progressivism persisted, successive Republican administrations pursued policies designed primarily to benefit American corporations on the assumption that the prosperity of the few would bring prosperity to the many. Whether the assumption was true or not, the collapse of corporate America brought collapse to all after the stock market crash of 1929.

The resulting depression crippled industry and left 20 percent of the labor force unemployed. In 1932, after the Hoover administration had failed to produce recovery, voters turned to Franklin Delano Roosevelt and the Democrats. Promising a "new deal" at a time when people were homeless and starving, Roosevelt launched a program of economic recovery and reform, much of it improvised, not all of it successful, and some of it far less radical and extensive than many critics had wished. The result, however, was that in its efforts to cope with economic disaster, the Roosevelt administration redefined the responsibility of the federal government to its citizens. Relief and work programs were provided, unemployment compensation and minimum wages and hours legislation passed, old-age pensions introduced, individual savings accounts insured, farm prices supported, farm ownership encouraged, farm and home mortgages guaranteed, rural houses electrified, and regional development and soil conservation promoted. The welfare state had arrived. Presidents of both parties would subsequently expand it, designing their own programs to benefit the American people. In the process other changes accelerated by international crises occurred: growth in the power of the presidency, in the size of the federal bureaucracy, and in the level of government spending.

If domestic events had occupied the attention of most Americans in previous years, Nazi aggression and Japan's attack upon Pearl Harbor in 1941 thrust their country into a new international role. Mobilized for total war along conventional lines, Americans were psychologically unprepared for their entry into the new atomic age as citizens of the strongest industrial and military power in world history. The implications of these new developments were scarcely understood when tensions between the United States and its former ally, the USSR, escalated into a "cold" war. The expansion of Russian hegemony in eastern Europe and the victory of Chinese communists in a bloody civil war convinced key policy makers that this nation would have to pursue a vigorous policy to "contain" communism throughout the world. If historians cannot agree on the process that led to cold war, they can agree that the persistent confrontations between East and West during the 1950s profoundly affected American life. Viewing North Korea's invasion of South Korea as proof of Russia's drive for world domination and convinced that the credibility of "containment" was at stake, the Truman administration sent troops to check communist aggression. In the United States there was another kind of warfare. Fearing domestic subversion, anticommunists during the McCarthy era purged government, organized labor, the entertainment industry, and schools and universities of communists—real and alleged. Dissent had become tantamount to disloyalty. By the mid-1950s it was axiomatic to some Americans that any critique of American foreign policy or American society—even if justified—was communist inspired. It was not surprising, therefore, that in the 1960s and 1970s blacks and women who wished to improve their social position should be accused of leftist and un-American sympathies. Many Americans, however, weary of conflict and crisis, had long since sought refuge in suburban privatism and the affluent consumerism of the postwar years.

The election of John Fitzgerald Kennedy in 1960 promised energy and optimism. The succeeding years exemplified both, but not in the manner anticipated. Blacks refused to be intimidated any longer by appeals to "gradualism" or threats of violence. They forced white America to address domestic problems too long deferred; they also provided insight, tactics, rhetoric, and impetus to a resurgent feminist movement. Through the vivid images conveyed to them by television, Americans faced a new and disorderly world. Blacks, Chicanos, Indians, students, women, and protesters against the Vietnam War—all confronted the nation in its living rooms. America seemed to be disintegrating. Convinced that protest had become anarchy, middle America elected Richard M. Nixon in 1968 and again in 1972. But the candidate of "law and order" became the president who put himself above the law. His successors tried to repair the damage done the nation's highest office. In some measure, they succeeded. However, they also faced overwhelming economic problems. These became so grave that the American people would elect a conservative to the presidency in 1980—one whose "old-fashioned values" kept him from supporting an amendment to give women equal rights under the Constitution. The time of social reform was over. The expansive mood of the 1960s disintegrated in the face of anxiety over the unemployment, inflation, rising energy costs, and declining productivity. Foreign relations were no consolation. There was the embarrassment of Vietnam and the danger of Soviet aggression, the weakening ties with our allies, and a greater interdependence of the industrial nations and the Third World. Looking ahead to the remaining years of the century, a distinguished historian observed that this nation's vaunted capacity for self-renewal would be "sorely tested." Few would disagree.[1]

Recounting these successive decades in traditional fashion suggests the difficulty of specifying the impact of women's experience. During an era when international developments assumed increasing importance, women were simply not part of the inner councils that debated issues of national security. Women were, of course, included in other aspects of historical experience. As shoppers in the 1920s, they purchased new consumer goods. As unemployed laborers and as wives and daughters of unemployed laborers and dispossessed farmers, they shared the economic problems of the Depression; as members of the Roosevelt administration, they shared in the search for solutions. As industrial workers and as members of the armed forces during World War II, women filled critical jobs in a time of labor shortages and contributed to an allied victory. We can even incorporate women into the Washington drama of the McCarthy era, recognizing Margaret Chase Smith as one of the first senators to denounce the " 'know-nothing suspect everything' attitudes" that had transformed the Senate into a "forum of hate and character assassination."[2]

Including women, even in this cursory fashion, requires recognition of differing experiences that are gender related. Two examples come immediately to mind. The first concerns the differing experience of male and female industrial workers employed during World War II. For working-class men wartime jobs provided a foundation on which to build a secure future in a postwar era of full employment. For working-class women the jobs were only a temporary bonus that they forfeited to returning veterans. Although no long-term study exists to support firm conclusions, Sheila Tobias and Lisa Anderson point out that many of the women who lost their jobs were heads of households. Some may have found low-paying jobs as clerical workers, beauticians, waitresses, or domestics, but in 1947 the increases in the number of women listed as unemployed—as actively seeking work—may have "foreshadow[ed] the great shift among poor women onto unemployment and later welfare rolls." One need not push that hypothesis further to conclude that wartime industrial employment could constitute economically a new beginning—or an end—depending on gender.

A second example concerns participation in the protest movements that shattered the complacency of the affluent society, transforming the 1960s into a decade of self-criticism and turmoil. Two groups in the vanguard of the struggle were the Student Nonviolent Coordinating Committee (SNCC), part of the militant wing of the civil rights movement, and the Students for a Democratic Society (SDS), an organization of the new left. Both attracted young white women who shared with their male counterparts a commitment to equality. But while men in these organizations often assumed leadership roles, women found themselves functioning in traditional fashion as housekeepers and sexual partners. That this should be so in movements dedicated to radical change, and above all to equality, seemed an inconsistency of such magnitude that women began to organize on their own behalf.

Including women's experience, even as it differed significantly from that of men, does not in itself refocus history, although it does remind us that attention only to public events and international relations can divert us from understanding how most people lived. The process of refocusing history can occur successfully only when we have a fuller understanding of the way gender has affected *all* aspects of human life. We know, for example, that technological developments have been basic to the development of a modern economy. Yet we have only begun to probe the way in which gender has affected technological development. In the garment industry, women have long been employed as seamstresses, sewing being work women have traditionally done and therefore not a skill to command high wages. Men have been employed at higher pay as cutters and pressers. In part because of gender-related wage differentials, little technological change has occurred in sewing since the invention of the sewing machine, according to Ruth Schwartz Cowan.[3] Yet substantial change has occurred in the ancillary process of cutting and pressing. If the relationship between gender, the price of labor, and technological innovation has eluded us in the past, it need not do so in the future. The situation of women sewing-machine operators is but one area in which scholarship informed by the insights of contemporary feminism has begun to capture a larger portion of historical reality. As feminist scholars—male as well as female—restore women to history, comparing both the differences and similiarities in the experiences of both sexes and valuing the experience of both, we can begin to refocus history. We must search then for a new paradigm that will enable us to find a past in which, as Gerda Lerner suggests, both *men and women are the measure of significance.*[4]

NOTES

1. William E. Leuchtenburg, *A Troubled Feast: American Society since 1945* (New York, 1973), p. 270.
2. *Congressional Record,* 96 (June 1, 1950):7894–95.
3. Ruth Schwartz Cowan, "From Virginia Dare to Virginia Slims: Women and Technology in American Life," *Technology and Culture* 20 (1979):51–63.
4. Gerda Lerner, *The Majority Finds Its Past: Placing Women in History* (New York, 1979), p. 180.

RUTH SCHWARTZ COWAN

The "Industrial Revolution" in the Home: Household Technology and Social Change in the Twentieth Century

The industrial technology that changed factory work also changed housework; the washing machine replaced the washtub just as the power loom replaced the handloom. Yet the impact of changing household technology on household workers has been little explored. In the following essay Ruth Schwartz Cowan examines how housework changed with the introduction of a variety of labor-saving appliances and the aggressive use of advertising designed to promote their sale. What emerges is a job that has changed in structure. Less burdensome physically, housework became no less time consuming as new duties were added and the work itself invested with new expectations and greater emotional content. What Cowan describes, in part, is the transition from the nineteenth-century mistress of the household who directed a servant's work to the twentieth-century middle-class housewife who, as jane-of-all-trades—laundress, scrub woman, gardener, nursemaid, chauffeur, and cook—was expected to find self-fulfillment in housework. What does this assumption suggest about the role of ideology as well as technology in defining work?

When we think about the interaction between technology and society, we tend to think in fairly grandiose terms: massive computers invading the workplace, railroad tracks cutting through vast wildernesses, armies of women and children toiling in the mills. These grand visions have blinded us to an important and rather peculiar technological revolution which has been going on right under our noses: the technological revolution in the home. This revolution has transformed the conduct of our daily lives, but in somewhat unexpected ways. The indus-trialization of the home was a process very different from the industrialization of other means of production, and the impact of that process was neither what we have been led to believe it was nor what students of the other industrial revolutions would have been led to predict.

Some years ago sociologists of the functionalist school formulated an explanation of the impact of industrial technology on the modern family. Although that explanation was not empirically verified, it has become almost universally accepted.[1]

Despite some differences in emphasis, the basic tenets of the traditional interpretation can be roughly summarized as follows:

Before industrialization the family was the basic social unit. Most families were rural, large, and self-sustaining; they produced and processed almost everything that was needed for their own support and for trading in the marketplace, while at the same time performing a host of other functions ranging from mutual protection to entertainment. In these preindustrial families women (adult women, that is) had a lot to do, and their time was almost entirely absorbed by household tasks. Under industrialization the family is much less important. The household is no longer the focus of production; production for the marketplace and production for sustenance have been removed to other locations. Families are smaller and they are urban rather than rural. The number of social functions they perform is much reduced, until almost all that remains is consumption, socialization of small children, and tension management. As their functions diminished, families became atomized; the social bonds that had held them together were loosened. In these postindustrial families women have very little to do, and the tasks with which they fill their time have lost the social utility that they once possessed. Modern women are in trouble, the analysis goes, because modern families are in trouble; and modern families are in trouble because industrial technology has either eliminated or eased almost all their former functions, but modern ideologies have not kept pace with the change. The results of this time lag are several: some women suffer from role anxiety, others land in the divorce courts, some enter the labor market, and others take to burning their brassieres and demanding liberation.

This sociological analysis is a cultural artifact of vast importance. Many Americans believe that it is true and act upon that belief in various ways: some hope to reestablish family solidarity by relearning lost productive crafts—baking bread, tending a vegetable garden—others dismiss the women's liberation movement as "simply a bunch of affluent housewives who have nothing better to do with their time." As disparate as they may seem, these reactions have a common ideological source—the standard sociological analysis of the impact of technological change on family life.

As a theory this functionalist approach has much to recommend it, but at present we have very little evidence to back it up. Family history is an infant discipline, and what evidence it has produced in recent years does not lend credence to the standard view.[2] Phillippe Ariès has shown, for example, that in France the ideal of the small nuclear family predates industrialization by more than a century.[3] Historical demographers working on data from English and French families have been surprised to find that most families were quite small and that several generations did not ordinarily reside together; the extended family, which is supposed to have been the rule in preindustrial societies, did not occur in colonial New England either.[4] Rural English families routinely employed domestic servants, and even very small English villages had their butchers and bakers and candlestick makers; all these persons must have eased some of the chores that would otherwise have been the housewife's burden.[5] Preindustrial housewives no doubt had much with which to occupy their time, but we may have reason to wonder whether there was quite as much pressure on them as sociological orthodoxy has led us to suppose. The large rural family that was sufficient unto itself back there on the prairies may have been limited to the prairies—or it may never have existed at all (except, that is, in the reveries of sociologists).

Even if all the empirical evidence were

to mesh with the functionalist theory, the theory would still have problems, because its logical structure is rather weak. Comparing the average farm family in 1750 (assuming that you knew what that family was like) with the average urban family in 1950 in order to discover the significant social changes that had occurred is an exercise rather like comparing apples with oranges; the differences between the fruits may have nothing to do with the differences in their evolution. Transferring the analogy to the case at hand, what we really need to know is the difference, say, between an urban laboring family of 1750 and an urban laboring family 100 and then 200 years later, or the difference between the rural nonfarm middle classes in all three centuries, or the difference between the urban rich yesterday and today. Surely in each of these cases the analyses will look very different from what we have been led to expect. As a guess we might find that for the urban laboring families the changes have been precisely the opposite of what the model predicted; that is, that their family structure is much firmer today than it was in centuries past. Similarly, for the rural nonfarm middle class the results might be equally surprising; we might find that married women of that class rarely did any housework at all in 1890 because they had farm girls as servants, whereas in 1950 they bore the full brunt of the work themselves. I could go on, but the point is, I hope, clear: in order to verify or falsify the functionalist theory, it will be necessary to know more than we presently do about the impact of industrialization on families of similar classes and geographical locations.

With this problem in mind I have, for the purposes of this initial study, deliberately limited myself to one kind of technological change affecting one aspect of family life in only one of the many social classes

of families that might have been considered. What happened, I asked, to middle-class American women when the implements with which they did their everyday household work changed? Did the technological change in household appliances have any effect upon the structure of American households, or upon the ideologies that governed the behavior of American women, or upon the functions that families needed to perform? Middle-class American women were defined as actual or potential readers of the better-quality women's magazines, such as the *Ladies' Home Journal, American Home, Parents' Magazine, Good Housekeeping,* and *McCall's.*[6] Nonfictional material (articles and advertisements) in those magazines was used as a partial indicator of some of the technological and social changes that were occurring.

The *Ladies' Home Journal* has been in continuous publication since 1886. A casual survey of the nonfiction in the *Journal* yields the immediate impression that that decade between the end of World War I and the beginning of the depression witnessed the most drastic changes in patterns of household work. Statistical data bear out this impression. Before 1918, for example, illustrations of homes lit by gaslight could still be found in the *Journal;* by 1928 gaslight had disappeared. In 1917 only one-quarter (24.3 percent) of the dwellings in the United States had been electrified, but by 1920 this figure had doubled (47.4 percent—for rural nonfarm and urban dwellings), and by 1930 four-fifths of all households had been electrified.[7] If electrification had meant simply the change from gas or oil lamps to electric lights, the changes in the housewife's routines might not have been very great (except for eliminating the chore of cleaning and filling oil lamps); but changes in lighting were the least of the changes that electrification implied. Small electric appliances followed quickly on the heels of the electric light, and some of those augured much more profound changes in the housewife's routine.

Ironing, for example, had traditionally been one of the most dreadful household chores, especially in warm weather when the kitchen stove had to be kept hot for the better part of the day; irons were heavy and they had to be returned to the stove frequently to be reheated. Electric irons eased a good part of this burden.[8] They were relatively inexpensive and very quickly replaced their predecessors; advertisements for electric irons first began to appear in the ladies' magazines after the war, and by the end of the decade the old flatiron had disappeared; by 1929 a survey of 100 Ford employees revealed that ninety-eight of them had the new electric irons in their homes.[9]

Data on the diffusion of electric washing machines are somewhat harder to come by; but it is clear from the advertisements in the magazines, particularly advertisements for laundry soap, that by the middle of the 1920s those machines could be found in a significant number of homes. The washing machine is depicted just about as frequently as the laundry tub by the middle of the 1920s; in 1929, forty-nine out of those 100 Ford workers had the machines in their homes. The washing machines did not drastically reduce the time that had to be spent on household laundry, as they did not go through their cycles automatically and did not spin dry; the housewife had to stand guard, stopping and starting the machine at appropriate times, adding soap, sometimes attaching the drain pipes, and putting the clothes through the wringer manually. The machines did, however, reduce a good part of the drudgery that once had been associated with washday, and this was a matter of no small consequence.[10] Soap powders appeared on the market in the early 1920s, thus eliminating the need to scrape and

boil bars of laundry soap.[11] By the end of the 1920s Blue Monday must have been considerably less blue for some housewives—and probably considerably less "Monday," for with an electric iron, a washing machine, and a hot water heater, there was no reason to limit the washing to just one day of the week.

Like the routines of washing the laundry, the routines of personal hygiene must have been transformed for many households during the 1920s—the years of the bathroom mania.[12] More and more bathrooms were built in older homes, and new homes began to include them as a matter of course. Before the war most bathroom fixtures (tubs, sinks, and toilets) were made out of porcelain by hand; each bathroom was custom-made for the house in which it was installed. After the war industrialization descended upon the bathroom industry; cast iron enamelware went into mass production and fittings were standardized. In 1921 the dollar value of the production of enameled sanitary fixtures was $2.4 million, the same as it had been in 1915. By 1923, just two years later, that figure had doubled to $4.8 million; it rose again, to $5.1 million, in 1925.[13] The first recessed, double-shell cast iron enameled bathtub was put on the market in the early 1920s. A decade later the standard American bathroom had achieved its standard American form: the recessed tub, plus tiled floors and walls, brass plumbing, a single-unit toilet, an enameled sink, and a medicine chest, all set into a small room which was very often 5 feet square.[14] The bathroom evolved more quickly than any other room of the house; its standardized form was accomplished in just over a decade.

Along with bathrooms came modernized systems for heating hot water: 61 percent of the homes in Zanesville, Ohio, had indoor plumbing with centrally heated water by 1926, and 83 percent of the homes valued over $2,000 in Muncie, In-

diana, had hot and cold running water by
1935.[15] These figures may not be typical
of small American cities (or even large
American cities) at those times, but they
do jibe with the impression that one gets
from the magazines: after 1918 references
to hot water heated on the kitchen range,
either for laundering or for bathing, become increasingly difficult to find.

Similarly, during the 1920s many
homes were outfitted with central heating; in Muncie most of the homes of the
business class had basement heating in
1924; by 1935 Federal Emergency Relief
Administration data for the city indicated
that only 22.4 percent of the dwellings
valued over $2,000 were still heated by a
kitchen stove.[16] What all these changes
meant in terms of new habits for the
average housewife is somewhat hard to
calculate; changes there must have been,
but it is difficult to know whether those
changes produced an overall saving of labor and/or time. Some chores were eliminated—hauling water, heating water on
the stove, maintaining the kitchen fire—
but other chores were added—most notably the chore of keeping yet another
room scrupulously clean.

It is not, however, difficult to be certain about the changing habits that
were associated with the new American
kitchen—a kitchen from which the coal
stove had disappeared. In Muncie in
1924, cooking with gas was done in two
out of three homes; in 1935 only 5 percent of the homes valued over $2,000 still
had coal or wood stoves for cooking.[17]
After 1918 advertisements for coal and
wood stoves disappeared from the Ladies'
Home Journal; stove manufacturers pur-
veyed only their gas, oil, or electric models. Articles giving advice to homemakers
on how to deal with the trials and tribula-
tions of starting, stoking, and maintaining
a coal or a wood fire also disappeared.
Thus it seems a safe assumption that
most middle-class homes had switched to
the new method of cooking by the time

the depression began. The change in routine that was predicated on the change
from coal or wood to gas or oil was profound; aside from the elimination of such
chores as loading the fuel and removing
the ashes, the new stoves were much
easier to light, maintain, and regulate
(even when they did not have thermostats,
as the earliest models did not).[18] Kitchens
were, in addition, much easier to clean
when they did not have coal dust regularly tracked through them; one writer in
the Ladies' Home Journal estimated that
kitchen cleaning was reduced by one-half
when coal stoves were eliminated.[19]

Along with new stoves came new foodstuffs and new dietary habits. Canned
foods had been on the market since the
middle of the nineteenth century, but they
did not become an appreciable part of
the standard middle-class diet until the
1920s—if the recipes given in cookbooks
and in women's magazines are a reliable
guide. By 1918 the variety of foods available in cans had been considerably expanded from the peas, corn, and succotash
of the nineteenth century; an American
housewife with sufficient means could
have purchased almost any fruit or vegetable and quite a surprising array of
ready-made meals in a can—from Heinz's
spaghetti in meat sauce to Purity Cross's
lobster à la Newburg. By the middle of
the 1920s home canning was becoming a
lost art. Canning recipes were relegated to
the back pages of the women's magazines;
the business-class wives of Muncie reported that, while their mothers had once
spent the better part of the summer and
fall canning, they themselves rarely put
up anything, except an occasional jelly or
batch of tomatoes.[20] In part this was also
due to changes in the technology of marketing food; increased use of refrigerated
railroad cars during this period meant that
fresh fruits and vegetables were in the
markets all year round at reasonable
prices.[21] By the early 1920s convenience
foods were also appearing on American

tables: cold breakfast cereals, pancake mixes, bouillon cubes, and packaged desserts could be found. Wartime shortages accustomed Americans to eating much lighter meals than they had previously been wont to do; and as fewer family members were taking all their meals at home (businessmen started to eat lunch in restaurants downtown, and factories and schools began installing cafeterias), there was simply less cooking to be done, and what there was of it was easier to do.[22]

Many of the changes just described— from hand power to electric power, from coal and wood to gas and oil as fuels for cooking, from one-room heating to central heating, from pumping water to running water—are enormous technological changes. Changes of a similar dimension, either in the fundamental technology of an industry, in the diffusion of that technology, or in the routines of workers, would have long since been labeled an "industrial revolution." The change from the laundry tub to the washing machine is no less profound than the change from the hand loom to the power loom; the change from pumping water to turning on a water faucet is no less destructive of traditional habits than the change from manual to electric calculating. It seems odd to speak of an "industrial revolution" connected with housework, odd because we are talking about the technology of such homely things, and odd because we are not accustomed to thinking of housewives as a labor force or of housework as an economic commodity—but despite this oddity, I think the term is altogether appropriate.

In this case other questions come immediately to mind, questions that we do not hesitate to ask, say, about textile workers in Britain in the early nineteenth century, but we have never thought to ask about housewives in America in the twentieth century. What happened to this particular work force when the technology of its work was revolutionized? Did structural changes occur? Were new jobs created for which new skills were required? Can we discern new ideologies that influenced the behavior of the workers?

The answer to all of these questions, surprisingly enough, seems to be yes. There were marked structural changes in the work force, changes that increased the work load and the job description of the workers that remained. New jobs were created for which new skills were required; these jobs were not physically burdensome, but they may have taken up as much time as the jobs they had replaced. New ideologies were also created, ideologies which reinforced new behavioral patterns, patterns that we might not have been led to expect if we had followed the sociologists' model to the letter. Middle-class housewives, the women who must have first felt the impact of the new household technology, were not flocking into the divorce courts or the labor market or the forums of political protest in the years immediately after the revolution in their work. What they were doing was sterilizing baby bottles, shepherding their children to dancing classes and music lessons, planning nutritious meals, shopping for new clothes, studying child psychology, and hand stitching color-coordinated curtains—all of which chores (and others like them) the standard sociological model has apparently not provided for.

The significant change in the structure of the household labor force was the disappearance of paid and unpaid servants (unmarried daughters, maiden aunts, and grandparents fall in the latter category) as household workers—and the imposition of the entire job on the housewife herself. Leaving aside for a moment the question of which was cause and which effect (did the disappearance of the servant create a demand for the new technology, or did the new technology make the servant obsolete?), the phenomenon itself is relatively easy to document. Before World War I, when illustrators in the women's magazines depicted women doing housework, the women were very often servants. When the lady of the house was drawn, she was often the person being served, or she was supervising the serving, or she was adding an elegant finishing touch to the work. Nursemaids diapered babies, seamstresses pinned up hems, waitresses served meals, laundresses did the wash, and cooks did the cooking. By the end of the 1920s the servants had disappeared from those illustrations; all those jobs were being done by housewives—elegantly manicured and coiffed, to be sure, but housewives nonetheless.

If we are tempted to suppose that illustrations in advertisements are not a reliable indicator of structural changes of this sort, we can corroborate the changes in other ways. Apparently, the illustrators really did know whereof they drew. Statistically the number of persons throughout the country employed in household service dropped from 1,851,000 in 1910 to 1,411,000 in 1920, while the number of households enumerated in the census rose from 20.3 million to 24.4 million.[23] In Indiana the ratio of households to servants increased from 13.5/1 in 1890 to 30.5/1 in 1920, and in the country as a whole the number of paid domestic servants per 1,000 population dropped from 98.9 in 1900 to 58.0 in 1920.[24] The business-class housewives of Muncie reported that they employed approximately one-half as many woman-hours of domestic service as their mothers had done.[25]

In case we are tempted to doubt these statistics (and indeed statistics about household labor are particularly unreliable, as the labor is often transient, part-time, or simply unreported), we can turn to articles on the servant problem, the disappearance of unpaid family workers, the design of kitchens, or to architectural drawings for houses. All of this evidence reiterates the same point: qualified servants were difficult to find; their wages

had risen and their numbers fallen; houses were being designed without maid's rooms; daughters and unmarried aunts were finding jobs downtown; kitchens were being designed for housewives, not for servants.[26] The first home with a kitchen that was not an entirely separate room was designed by Frank Lloyd Wright in 1934.[27] In 1937 Emily Post invented a new character for her etiquette books: Mrs. Three-in-One, the woman who is her own cook, waitress, and hostess.[28] There must have been many new Mrs. Three-in-Ones abroad in the land during the 1920s.

As the number of household assistants declined, the number of household tasks increased. The middle-class housewife was expected to demonstrate competence at several tasks that previously had not existed at all. Child care is the most obvious example. The average housewife had fewer children than her mother had had, but she was expected to do things for her children that her mother would never have dreamed of doing; to prepare their special infant formulas, sterilize their bottles, weigh them every day, see to it that they ate nutritionally balanced meals, keep them isolated and confined when they had even the slightest illness, consult with their teachers frequently, and chauffeur them to dancing lessons, music lessons, and evening parties.[29] There was very little Freudianism in this new attitude toward child care: mothers were not spending more time and effort on their children because they feared the psychological trauma of separation, but because competent nursemaids could not be found, and the new theories of child care required constant attention from well-informed persons—persons who were willing and able to read about the latest discoveries in nutrition, in the control of contagious diseases, or in the techniques of behavioral psychology. These persons simply had to be their mothers.

Consumption of economic goods provides another example of the housewife's expanded job description; like child care, the new tasks associated with consumption were not necessarily physically burdensome, but they were time consuming, and they required the acquisition of new skills.[30] Home economists and the editors of women's magazines tried to teach housewives to spend their money wisely. The present generation of housewives, it was argued, had been reared by mothers who did not ordinarily shop for things like clothing, bed linens, or towels; consequently modern housewives did not know how to shop and would have to be taught. Furthermore, their mothers had not been accustomed to the wide variety of goods that were now available in the modern marketplace; the new housewives had to be taught not just to be consumers, but to be informed consumers.[31] Several contemporary observers believed that shopping and shopping wisely were occupying increasing amounts of housewives' time.[32]

Several of these contemporary observers also believed that standards of household care changed during the decade of the 1920s.[33] The discovery of the "household germ" led to almost fetishistic concern about the cleanliness of the home. The amount and frequency of laundering probably increased, as bed linen and underwear were changed more often, children's clothes were made increasingly out of washable fabrics, and men's shirts no longer had replaceable collars and cuffs.[34] Unfortunately all these changes in standards are difficult to document, being changes in the things that people regard as so insignificant as to be unworthy of comment; the improvement in standards seems a likely possibility, but not something that can be proved.

In any event we do have various time studies which demonstrate somewhat surprisingly that housewives with conveniences were spending just as much time on household duties as were housewives

without them—or, to put it another way, housework, like so many other types of work, expands to fill the time available. A study comparing the time spent per week in housework by 288 farm families and 154 town families in Oregon in 1928 revealed 61 hours spent by farm wives and 63.4 hours by town wives; in 1929 a U.S. Department of Agriculture study of families in various states produced almost identical results.[35] Surely if the standard sociological model were valid, housewives in towns, where presumably the benefits of specialization and electrification were most likely to be available, should have been spending far less time at their work than their rural sisters. However, just after World War II economists at Bryn Mawr College reported the same phenomenon: 60.55 hours spent by farm housewives, 78.35 hours by women in small cities, 80.57 hours by women in large ones—precisely the reverse of the results that were expected.[36] A recent survey of time studies conducted between 1920 and 1970 concludes that the time spent on housework by nonemployed housewives has remained remarkably constant throughout the period.[37] All these results point in the same direction: mechanization of the household meant that time expended on some jobs decreased, but also that new jobs were substituted, and in some cases—notably laundering—time expenditures for old jobs increased because of higher standards. The advantages of mechanization may be somewhat more dubious than they seem at first glance.

As the job of the housewife changed, the connected ideologies also changed; there was a clearly perceptible difference in the attitudes that women brought to housework before and after World War I.[38] Before the war the trials of doing housework in a servantless home were discussed and they were regarded as just that—trials, necessary chores that had to be got through until a qualified servant could be found. After the war, housework changed: it was no longer a trial and a chore, but something quite different—an emotional "trip." Laundering was not just laundering, but an expression of love; the housewife who truly loved her family would protect them from the embarrassment of tattletale gray. Feeding the family was not just feeding the family, but a way to express the housewife's artistic inclinations and a way to encourage feelings of family loyalty and affection. Diapering the baby was not just diapering, but a time to build the baby's sense of security and love for the mother. Cleaning the bathroom sink was not just cleaning, but an exercise of protective maternal instincts, providing a way for the housewife to keep her family safe from disease. Tasks of this emotional magnitude could not possibly be delegated to servants, even assuming that qualified servants could be found.

Women who failed at these new household tasks were bound to feel guilt about their failure. If I had to choose one word to characterize the temper of the women's magazines during the 1920s, it would be "guilt." Readers of the better-quality women's magazines are portrayed as feeling guilty a good lot of the time, and when they are not guilty they are embarrassed: guilty if their infants have not gained enough weight, embarrassed if their drains are clogged, guilty if their children go to school in soiled clothes, guilty if all the germs behind the bathroom sink are not eradicated, guilty if they fail to notice the first signs of an oncoming cold, embarrassed if accused of having body odor, guilty if their sons go to school without good breakfasts, guilty if their daughters are unpopular because of old-fashioned, or unironed, or—heaven forbid—dirty dresses. In earlier times women were made to feel guilty if they abandoned their children or were too free with their affections. In the years after

World War I, American women were made to feel guilty about sending their children to school in scuffed shoes. Between the two kinds of guilt there is a world of difference.

Let us return for a moment to the sociological model with which this essay began. The model predicts that changing patterns of household work will be correlated with at least two striking indicators of social change: the divorce rate and the rate of married women's labor force participation. That correlation may indeed exist, but it certainly is not reflected in the women's magazines of the 1920s and 1930s; divorce and full-time paid employment were not part of the life-style or the life pattern of the middle-class housewife as she was idealized in her magazines.

There were social changes attendant upon the introduction of modern technology into the home, but they were not the changes that the traditional functionalist model predicts; on this point a close analysis of the statistical data corroborates the impression conveyed in the magazines. The divorce rate was indeed rising during the years between the wars, but it was not rising nearly so fast for the middle and upper classes (who had, presumably, easier access to the new technology) as it was for the lower classes. By almost every gauge of socioeconomic status—income, prestige of husband's work, education—the divorce rate is higher for persons lower on the socioeconomic scale—and this is a phenomenon that has been constant over time.[39]

The supposed connection between improved household technology and married women's labor force participation seems just as dubious, and on the same grounds. The single socioeconomic factor which correlates most strongly (in cross-sectional studies) with married women's employment is husband's income, and the correlation is strongly negative; the higher his income, the less likely it will be that she is working.[40] Women's labor force participation increased during the 1920s but this increase was due to the influx of single women into the force. Married women's participation increased slightly during those years, but that increase was largely in factory labor—precisely the kind of work that middle-class women (who were, again, much more likely to have labor-saving devices at home) were least likely to do.[41] If there were a necessary connection between the improvement of household technology and either of these two social indicators, we would expect the data to be precisely the reverse of what in fact has occurred: women in the higher social classes should have fewer functions at home and should therefore be more (rather than less) likely to seek paid employment or divorce.

Thus for middle-class American housewives between the wars, the social changes that we can document are not the social changes that the functionalist model predicts; rather than changes in divorce or patterns of paid employment, we find changes in the structure of the work force, in its skills, and in its ideology. These social changes were concomitant with a series of technological changes in the equipment that was used to do the work. What is the relationship between these two series of phenomena? Is it possible to demonstrate causality or the direction of that causality? Was the decline in the number of households employing servants a cause or an effect of the mechanization of those households? Both are, after all, equally possible. The declining supply of household servants, as well as their rising wages, may have stimulated a demand for new appliances at the same time that the acquisition of new appliances may have made householders less inclined to employ the laborers who were on the market. Are there any techniques available to the historian to help us answer these questions?

In order to establish causality, we need to find a connecting link between the two sets of phenomena, a mechanism that, in real life, could have made the causality work. In this case a connecting link, and intervening agent between the social and the technological changes, comes immediately to mind: the advertiser—by which term I mean a combination of the manufacturer of the new goods, the advertising agent who promoted the goods, and the periodical that published the promotion. All the new devices and new foodstuffs that were being offered to American households were being manufactured and marketed by large companies which had considerable amounts of capital invested in their production: General Electric, Procter & Gamble, General Foods, Lever Brothers, Frigidaire, Campbell's, Del Monte, American Can, Atlantic & Pacific Tea—these were all well-established firms by the time the household revolution began, and they were all in a position to pay for national advertising campaigns to promote their new products and services. And pay they did; one reason for the expanding size and number of women's magazines in the 1920s was no doubt, the expansion in revenues from available advertisers.[42]

Those national advertising campaigns were likely to have been powerful stimulators of the social changes that occurred in the household labor force; the advertisers probably did not initiate the changes, but they certainly encouraged them. Most of the advertising campaigns manifestly worked, so they must have touched upon areas of real concern for American housewives. Appliance ads specifically suggested that the acquisition of one gadget or another would make it possible to fire the maid, spend more time with the children, or have the afternoon free for shopping.[43] Similarly, many advertisements played upon the embarrassment and guilt which were now associated with household work. Ralston, Cream of

Wheat, and Ovaltine were not themselves responsible for the compulsive practice of weighing infants and children repeatedly (after every meal for newborns, every day in infancy, every week later on), but the manufacturers certainly did not stint on capitalizing upon the guilt that women apparently felt if their offspring did not gain the required amounts of weight.[44] And yet again, many of the earliest attempts to spread "wise" consumer practices were undertaken by large corporations and the magazines that desired their advertising: mail-order shopping guides, "product-testing" services, pseudoinformative pamphlets, and other such promotional devices were all techniques for urging the housewife to buy new things under the guise of training her in her role as skilled consumer.[45]

Thus the advertisers could well be called the "ideologues" of the 1920s, encouraging certain very specific social changes—as ideologues are wont to do. Not surprisingly, the changes that occurred were precisely the ones that would gladden the hearts and fatten the purses of the advertisers; fewer household servants meant a greater demand for labor- and time-saving devices; more household tasks for women meant more and more specialized products that they would need to buy; more guilt and embarrassment about their failure to succeed at their work meant a greater likelihood that they would buy the products that were intended to minimize that failure. Happy, full-time housewives in intact families spend a lot of money to maintain their households; divorced women and working women do not. The advertisers may not have created the image of the ideal American housewife that dominated the 1920s—the woman who cheerfully and skillfully set about making everyone in her family perfectly happy and perfectly healthy—but they certainly helped to perpetuate it.

The role of the advertiser as connecting link between social change and technological change is at this juncture simply a hypothesis, with nothing much more to recommend it than an argument from plausibility. Further research may serve to test the hypothesis, but testing it may not settle the question of which was cause and which effect—if that question can ever be settled definitively in historical work. What seems most likely in this case, as in so many others, is that cause and effect are not separable, that there is a dynamic interaction between the social changes that married women were experiencing and the technological changes that were occurring in their homes. Viewed this way, the disappearance of competent servants becomes one of the factors that stimulated the mechanization of homes, and this mechanization of homes becomes a factor (though by no means the only one) in the disappearance of servants. Similarly, the emotionalization of housework becomes both cause and effect of the mechanization of that work; and the expansion of time spent on new tasks becomes both cause and effect of the introduction of time-saving devices. For example the social pressure to spend more time in child care may have led to a decision to purchase the devices; once purchased, the devices could indeed have been used to save time—although often they were not.

If one holds the question of causality in abeyance, the example of household work still has some useful lessons to teach about the general problem of technology and social change. The standard sociological model for the impact of modern technology on family life clearly needs some revision: at least for middle-class nonrural American families in the twentieth century, the social changes were not the ones that the standard model predicts. In these families the functions of at least one member, the housewife, have increased rather than decreased and the dissolution of family life has not in fact occurred.

Our standard notions about what happens to a work force under the pressure of technological change may also need revision. When industries become mechanized and rationalized, we expect certain general changes in the work force to occur: its structure becomes more highly differentiated, individual workers become more specialized, managerial functions increase, and the emotional context of the work disappears. On all four counts our expectations are reversed with regard to household work. The work force became less rather than more differentiated as domestic servants, unmarried daughters, maiden aunts, and grandparents left the household and as chores which had once been performed by commercial agencies (laundries, delivery services, milkmen) were delegated to the housewife. The individual workers also became less specialized; the new housewife was now responsible for every aspect of life in her household, from scrubbing the bathroom floor to keeping abreast of the latest literature in child psychology.

The housewife is just about the only unspecialized worker left in America—a veritable jane-of-all-trades at a time when the jacks-of-all-trades have disappeared. As her work became generalized the housewife was also proletarianized: formerly she was ideally the manager of several other subordinate workers; now she was idealized as the manager and the worker combined. Her managerial functions have not entirely disappeared, but

they have certainly diminished and have been replaced by simple manual labor; the middle-class, fairly well educated housewife ceased to be a personnel manager and became, instead, a chauffeur, charwoman, and short-order cook. The implications of this phenomenon, the proletarianization of a work force that had previously seen itself as predominantly managerial, deserve to be explored at greater length than is possible here, because I suspect that they will explain certain aspects of the women's liberation movement of the 1960s and 1970s which have previously eluded explanation: why, for example, the movement's greatest strength lies in social and economic groups who seem, on the surface at least, to need it least—women who are white, well-educated, and middle-class.

Finally, instead of desensitizing the emotions that were connected with household work, the industrial revolution in the home seems to have heightened the emotional context of the work, until a woman's sense of self-worth became a function of her success at arranging bits of fruit to form a clown's face in a gelatin salad. That pervasive social illness, which Betty Friedan characterized as "the problem that has no name," arose not among workers who found that their labor brought no emotional satisfaction, but among workers who found that their work was invested with emotional weight far out of proportion to its own inherent value: "How long," a friend of mine is fond of asking, "can we continue to believe that we will have orgasms while waxing the kitchen floor?"

Notes

1. For some classic statements of the standard view, see W. F. Ogburn and M. F. Nimkoff, *Technology and the Changing Family* (Cambridge, Mass., 1955); Robert F. Winch, *The Modern Family* (New York,

1952); and William J. Goode, *The Family* (Englewood Cliffs, N.J., 1964).

2. This point is made by Peter Laslett in "The Comparative History of Household and Family," in *The American Family in Social*

Historical Perspective, ed. Michael Gordon (New York, 1973), pp. 28–29.

3. Phillippe Ariès, *Centuries of Childhood: A Social History of Family Life* (New York, 1960).

4. See Laslett, pp. 20–24; and Philip J. Greven, "Family Structure in Seventeenth Century Andover, Massachusetts," *William and Mary Quarterly* 23 (1966):234–56.

5. Peter Laslett, *The World We Have Lost* (New York, 1965), passim.

6. For purposes of historical inquiry, this definition of middle-class status corresponds to a sociological reality, although it is not, admittedly, very rigorous. Our contemporary experience confirms that there are class differences reflected in magazines, and this situation seems to have existed in the past as well. On this issue see Robert S. Lynd and Helen M. Lynd, *Middletown: A Study in Contemporary American Culture* (New York, 1929), pp. 240–44, where the marked difference in magazines subscribed to by the business-class wives as opposed to the working-class wives is discussed; Salme Steinberg, "Reformer in the Marketplace: E. W. Bok and *The Ladies' Home Journal*" (Ph.D. diss., Johns Hopkins University, 1973), where the conscious attempt of the publisher to attract a middle-class audience is discussed; and Lee Rainwater et al., *Workingman's Wife* (New York, 1959), which was commissioned by the publisher of working-class women's magazines in an attempt to understand the attitudinal differences between working-class and middle-class women.

7. *Historical Statistics of the United States, Colonial Times to 1957* (Washington, D.C., 1960), p. 510.

8. The gas iron, which was available to women whose homes were supplied with natural gas, was an earlier improvement on the old-fashioned flatiron, but this kind of iron is so rarely mentioned in the sources that I used for this survey that I am unable to determine the extent of its diffusion.

9. Hazel Kyrk, *Economic Problems of the Family* (New York, 1933), p. 368, reporting a study in *Monthly Labor Review* 30 (1930): 1209–52.

10. Although this point seems intuitively obvious, there is some evidence that it may not be true. Studies of energy expenditure during housework have indicated that by far the greatest effort is expended in hauling and lifting the wet wash, tasks which were not eliminated by the introduction of washing machines. In addition, if the introduction of the machines served to increase the total amount of wash that was done by the housewife, this would tend to cancel the energy-saving effects of the machines themselves.

11. Rinso was the first granulated soap; it came on the market in 1918. Lux Flakes had been available since 1906; however it was not intended to be a general laundry product but rather one for laundering delicate fabrics. "Lever Brothers," *Fortune* 26 (November 1940): 95.

12. I take this account, and the term, from Lynd and Lynd, p. 97. Obviously, there were many American homes that had bathrooms before the 1920s, particularly urban row houses, and I have found no way of determining whether the increases of the 1920s were more marked than in previous decades. The rural situation was quite different from the urban; the President's Conference on Home Building and Home Ownership reported that in the late 1920s, 71 percent of the urban families surveyed had bathrooms, but only 33 percent of the rural families did (John M. Gries and James Ford, eds., *Homemaking, Home Furnishing and Information Services*, President's Conference on Home Building and Home Ownership, vol. 10 [Washington, D.C., 1932], p. 13).

13. The data above come from Siegfried Giedion, *Mechanization Takes Command* (New York, 1948), pp. 685–703.

14. For a description of the standard bathroom see Helen Sprackling, "The Modern Bathroom," *Parents' Magazine* 8 (February 1933): 25.

15. *Zanesville, Ohio and Thirty-six Other American Cities* (New York, 1927), p. 65. Also see Robert S. Lynd and Helen M. Lynd, *Middletown in Transition* (New York, 1936), p. 537. Middletown is Muncie, Indiana.

16. Lynd and Lynd, *Middletown*, p. 96, and *Middletown in Transition*, p. 539.

17. Lynd and Lynd, *Middletown*, p. 98, and *Middletown in Transition*, p. 562.

18. On the advantages of the new stoves, see *Boston Cooking School Cookbook* (Boston, 1916), pp. 15–20; and Russell Lynes, *The Domesticated Americans* (New York, 1957), pp. 119–20.

19. "How To Save Coal While Cooking," *Ladies' Home Journal* 25 (January 1908):44.

20. Lynd and Lynd, *Middletown*, p. 156.

21. Ibid.; see also "Safeway Stores," *Fortune* 26 (October 1940):60.

22. Lynd and Lynd, *Middletown*, pp. 134–35 and 153–54.

23. *Historical Statistics*, pp. 16 and 77.

24. For Indiana data, see Lynd and Lynd, *Middletown*, p. 169. For national data, see D. L. Kaplan and M. Claire Casey, *Occupational Trends in the United States, 1900–1950*, U.S. Bureau of the Census Working Paper no. 5 (Washington, D.C., 1958), table 6. The extreme drop in numbers of servants between 1910 and 1920 also lends credence to the notion that this demographic factor stimulated the industrial revolution in housework.

25. Lynd and Lynd, *Middletown*, p. 169.

26. On the disappearance of maiden aunts, unmarried daughters, and grandparents, see Lynd and Lynd, *Middletown*, pp. 25, 99, and 110; Edward Bok, "Editorial," *American Home* 1 (October 1928):15; "How to Buy Life Insurance," *Ladies' Home Journal* 45 (March 1928):35. The house plans appeared every month in *American Home*, which began publication in 1928. On kitchen design, see Giedion, pp. 603–21; "Editorial," *Ladies' Home Journal* 45 (April 1928):36; advertisement for Hoosier kitchen cabinets, *Ladies' Home Journal* 45 (April 1928):117. Articles on servant problems include "The Vanishing Servant Girl," *Ladies' Home Journal* 35 (May 1918):48; "Housework, Then and Now," *American Home* 8 (June 1932): 128; "The Servant Problem," *Fortune* 24 (March 1938):80–84; and *Report of the YWCA Commission on Domestic Service* (Los Angeles, 1915).

27. Giedion, p. 619. Wright's new kitchen was installed in the Malcolm Willey House, Minneapolis.

26. Emily Post, *Etiquette: The Blue Book of Social Usage*, 5th ed. rev. (New York, 1937), p. 823.

29. This analysis is based upon various child-care articles that appeared during the period in the *Ladies' Home Journal*, *American Home*, and *Parents' Magazine*. See also Lynd and Lynd, *Middletown*, chap. 11.

30. John Kenneth Galbraith has remarked upon the advent of woman as consumer in *Economics and the Public Purpose* (Boston, 1973), pp. 29–37.

31. There was a sharp reduction in the number of patterns for home sewing offered by the women's magazines during the 1920s; the patterns were replaced by articles on "what is available in the shops this season." On consumer education see, for example, "How to Buy Towels," *Ladies' Home Journal* 45 (February 1928):134; "Buying Table Linen," *Ladies' Home Journal* 45 (March 1928):43; and "When the Bride Goes Shopping," *American Home* 1 (January 1928):370.

32. See, for example, Lynd and Lynd, *Middletown*, pp. 176 and 196; and Margaret G. Reid, *Economics of Household Production* (New York, 1934), chap. 13.

33. See Reid, pp. 64–68; and Kyrk, p. 98.

34. See advertisement for Cleanliness Institute—"Self-respect thrives on soap and water," *Ladies' Home Journal* 45 (February 1928): 107. On changing bed linen, see "When the Bride Goes Shopping," *American Home* 1 (January 1928): 370. On laundering children's clothes, see, "Making a Layette," *Ladies' Home Journal* 45 (January 1928):20; and Josephine Baker, "The Youngest Generation," *Ladies' Home Journal* 45 (March 1928): 185.

35. As reported in Kyrk, p. 51.

36. Bryn Mawr College Department of Social Economy, *Women During the War and After* (Philadelphia, 1945); and Ethel Goldwater, "Woman's Place," *Commentary* 4 (December 1947):578–85.

37. JoAnn Vanek, "Keeping Busy: Time Spent in Housework, United States, 1920–1970" (Ph.D. diss., University of Michigan, 1973). Vanek reports an average of 53 hours per week over the whole period. This figure is significantly lower than the figures reported above, because each time study of housework has been done on a different basis, including different activities under the aegis of housework, and using different methods of reporting time expenditures; the Bryn Mawr and Oregon studies are useful for the comparative figures that they report internally, but they cannot easily be compared with each other.

38. This analysis is based upon my reading of the middle-class women's magazines between 1918 and 1930. For detailed documentation see my paper "Two Washes in the Morning and a Bridge Party at Night: The American Housewife between the Wars," *Women's Studies* 3 (1976):147–72. It is quite possible that the appearance of guilt as a strong element in advertising is more the result of new techniques developed by the advertising industry than the result of attitudinal changes in the audience—a possibility that I had not considered when doing the initial research for this paper. See A. Michael McMahon, "An American Courtship: Psychologists and Advertising Theory in the Progressive Era," *American Studies* 13 (1972): 5–18.

39. For a summary of the literature on differential divorce rates, see Winch, p. 706; and William J. Goode, *After Divorce* (New

York, 1956), p. 44. The earliest papers demonstrating this differential rate appeared in 1927, 1935, and 1939.

40. For a summary of the literature on married women's labor force participation, see Juanita Kreps, *Sex in the Marketplace: American Women at Work* (Baltimore, 1971), pp. 19–24.

41. Valerie Kincaid Oppenheimer, *The Female Labor Force in the United States*, Population Monograph Series, no. 5 (Berkeley, 1970), pp. 1–15; and Lynd and Lynd, *Middletown*, pp. 124–27.

42. On the expanding size, number, and influence of women's magazines during the 1920s, see Lynd and Lynd, *Middletown*, pp. 150 and 240–44.

43. See, for example, the advertising campaigns of General Electric and Hotpoint from 1918 through the rest of the decade of the 1920s; both campaigns stressed the likelihood

that electric appliances would become a thrifty replacement for domestic servants.

44. The practice of carefully observing children's weight was initiated by medical authorities, national and local governments, and social welfare agencies, as part of the campaign to improve child health which began about the time of World War I.

45. These practices were ubiquitous. *American Home*, for example, which was published by Doubleday, assisted its advertisers by publishing a list of informative pamphlets that readers could obtain; devoting half a page to an index of its advertisers; specifically naming manufacturer's and list prices in articles about products and services; allotting almost one-quarter of the magazine to a mail-order shopping guide which was not (at least ostensibly) paid advertisement; and as part of its editorial policy, urging its readers to buy new goods.

MARGARET JARMAN HAGOOD
Of the Tenant Child as Mother to the Woman

In the midst of the Great Depression, President Franklin D. Roosevelt identified the South as the nation's number one "problem." Farm tenancy, sharecropping, eroding land, grinding poverty, and persistent illiteracy plagued the region; it also had the lowest rate of urbanization and the highest birth rate in the nation. These problems were human as well as economic, and they attracted the attention of a remarkable nucleus of scholars at the University of North Carolina at Chapel Hill who were interested not only in documentation but also in solutions. One of this small group was Margaret Jarman Hagood, who visited 254 carefully selected tenant houses in Piedmont North Carolina, Georgia, and Alabama to study "mothers of the South," as her book would be entitled when published in 1939. She brought to her task a fine blending of attributes that lent credibility to her work. As a professional sociologist, she used scientific methods of inquiry.

Excerpted from "Of the Tenant Child as Mother to the Woman," chap. 13 of *Mothers of the South: Portraiture of the White Tenant Farm Woman* by Margaret Jarman Hagood (Chapel Hill: University of North Carolina Press, 1939). Copyright © 1939 by the University of North Carolina Press. Reprinted by permission of the publisher.

As a wife and mother, she used the experience she shared with other women to overcome barriers of class and education so that she might enter the "distinctly feminine culture . . . centered around mating, child care and home-making" that she believed existed among these tenant farm women. (Note the woman's world that Carroll Smith-Rosenberg found among women of a different class and generation, part IIA.) The portraits resulting from Hagood's study provide a glimpse into the lives of women who bore their poverty and powerlessness with stoic courage and strength. Hagood's study shows how cotton, tobacco, and children—the economic production of society and the physical *re*production of society—were intertwined in the lives of rural southern women.

The story of the tenant child begins more than a quarter of a century ago. On Monday ten-year-old Mollie woke up when her mother lifted the stove lid and began making the fire. She slipped from underneath the cover easily, so as not to disturb her little brother, and took down her last year's red dress, which had been fleecy and warm, but now was slick and thin. Their bed was in the log kitchen of the Goodwin's two-room cabin, which would be warm enough in a half hour for the sickly knee-baby, who slept with Mollie, to face the December morning. . . .

Mollie's plump arms stretched tight the seams of her outgrown dress, and as she leaned over to pick up fresh wood for the fire, she felt her dress split at the shoulder. She wondered what she would do the washing in if she couldn't get into the old dress next Monday or the one after that. Her father's rule was that her two new dresses of the same cotton fleece lined material, one red and one blue, must never be worn except for school or Sunday School. She had no sisters to hand down clothes to her, for the other four children were boys. Some girls she knew wore overalls for working, but her father would not allow that either. A wicked thought came to her mind—maybe if she had nothing to wear to wash in next Monday, she wouldn't have to wash and instead could go to school with her brothers. She could iron on Tuesday inside the house in her underwear—then a vision of her mother bending over the wash tubs, moaning with the pain in her back, made her put aside the daydream of a washless Monday.

After breakfast Mollie's older brother cut wood and started a fire under the wash pot while she and the brother next younger drew and carried water from the well. Then the boys left for the mile walk to the one-teacher school and Mollie started back for the house to get up the clothes. She lingered on the way, debating whether her father's overalls, stiff with a week's accumulation of winter mud and stable stains, were harder to wash than the baby's soiled diapers. They *were* harder, but the odor from the diapers made you feel you couldn't go on. It was a sensory symbol of babies, of her sick mother, of crying, little brothers, and now was vaguely mixed with her distaste for what two girl friends had told her at recess last week about how babies come. Mollie tried not to think about this and hoped she never had any babies.

The school bell's ringing interrupted her musing and reminded Mollie of how much she wanted to be there. Her dress was as new as any in school and its color still bright. The teacher had smiled approvingly at Mollie last week when the visiting preacher pinched her dimpled cheek and said, "Miss Grace, you have a fine looking bunch of little girls." Mollie thought now of having, when she was grown, a dress like Miss Grace's Sunday one. The bell stopped ringing and Mollie resolved to stop thinking and to work very hard and fast. Once before she had finished all the washing in time to go back with the boys after dinner. And so she scrubbed with all her force against the washboard and paid no attention to the pain from her knuckles scraped raw.

By dinner time all the clothes were on the line and the first ones out already frozen stiff. Mollie, numbed by cold and fatigue, ate peas, fat pork, and cornbread without joining in the family talk. When she got up from the table, her back ached —she wondered how many years of washing it would take to make it as bent over as her mother's. She changed to her new dress in time to set off for the afternoon session of school. She pulled herself together to respond to the teacher's beaming look of approval for having come to school that afternoon, and then relaxed into a lethargy from weariness and missed words she knew in the Third Reader and was spelled down quickly. . . .

One stormy winter night three months before Mollie was twelve, she was put to bed early. Her father moved the trundle bed from the main room and all the children went to sleep in the kitchen—all but Mollie. She had a terrible feeling of impending disaster to her mother and herself. When she had asked her mother about babies not long before, her mother had told her she was going to have another and that something would happen to Mollie soon, too. From the front room Mollie heard groans and knew her mother was suffering. Her own body began to ache. Her mother's sounds grew louder and each time an anguished scream reached Mollie's ears, a shooting pain went through her. Hardly daring, Mollie reached down under the cover and felt that her legs were wet. All the boys were asleep and so she drew back the cover and in the moonlight saw black stains which had come from her body. Suddenly she thought she was having a baby. She tried to scream like her mother, but the terror of the realization paralyzed her. Fright overwhelmed her until she was no longer conscious of pain. She remained motionless for a long time, knowing and feeling nothing but a horrible fear of disgrace and dread. Then she became aware that the moaning in the next room had stopped and that someone had unlatched the kitchen door. Trembling, she eased out of bed and crept into her mother's room. There was a new baby lying on one side, but she slipped into the other side of the bed and nestled against her mother. The relaxing warmth and comfort of another's body released the inner tensions and Mollie melted into tears and weak, low sobs. Her mother stroked her but said nothing. She lay there for some minutes until the Negro "granny" said she must leave her mother and led her back to bed. Early in the morning she hid the soiled bedclothes in a corner until she could wash them secretly in the creek and found some cloths in her mother's drawer which she asked for without giving any reason. Not for two years, when a girl friend told her, did she have any instruction about how to fix and wear sanitary pads.

The summer Mollie was fourteen her mother persuaded Ben to buy her a silk dress. Mollie had worked so well that year that her father, in an appreciative mood, took her to town and let her select the material, which was a glamorous, changeable, rose and green taffeta. Mrs. Bynum helped her make it, and when her father consented to take the whole family to a Fourth of July celebration ten miles away, Mollie's cup overflowed with joy. She rolled up her hair in rags the night before. She helped bathe and dress the younger children two hours before leaving time so that she might extract the full delight from dressing leisurely in her new clothes for the first time. By eight o'clock in the morning, the family, now nine, piled into the wagon and set off. To keep from going through the county seat, they cut through a shorter, back road, which was rocky and went over steep hills. The boys got out and pushed on the worst places, but Mollie sat on the bench with her mother and father—accorded special privileges because of her new dress. The jolting and hot sun bearing down were unnoticed for the joy anticipated in being the most beautifully dressed girl at the celebration. Mollie was scarcely aware of her family in the wagon as she rode along with her head in the clouds.

They reached the tabernacle, where there were to be political speeches interspersed with hymn singing contests between churches. Mollie hopped down lightly and was about to run over to join a group of girls she knew when her mother, climbing over the edge of the wagon more slowly, called her back and took her a few steps away from the wagon.

"Your dress is ruined behind," she whispered to Mollie, "you'll have to set still over here by this tree all day." Excitement and the jolting had brought on her menstrual period early and the realization of this brought about a flush of hot shame which obliterated the festive scene of picnic tables and merry people. Mollie's heart seemed to close up and with it her capacity to perceive or respond. Passively she allowed herself to be led to a sheltered spot under an oak with protruding roots which afforded a seat. The loss of her life's triumph and the indescribable embarrassment kept her from comprehending meanings. She felt that she was dead and after awhile she leaned against the tree and slept. No one approached, for there seemed to be a tacit understanding of her plight. Late in the afternoon she rode home without speaking to her family. The next day she and her mother were unable to remove the stain from her dress and the beautiful taffeta was never worn.

Her father never bought her another silk dress.

Two years later, Mollie finished the seventh grade at sixteen. The other girls were now having boys drop by their houses, but Ben Goodwin was known for his sternness and none came to see Mollie. . . .

That summer one of Mrs. Bynum's many nieces went to a town in another county to work in a tobacco factory and her sister reveled in telling Mollie about the money she made and spent. They planned what sort of things Mollie could buy if she were to go to work in town. After weeks of whispered plans, the sister in town arranged for Mollie to have a job weighing and wrapping cigarettes. Without telling even her mother, Mollie bundled up her clothes and left early one morning, just as the cotton picking season was beginning. A neighbor boy drove her to town and she went to a relative of Ben's to board.

For four months Mollie worked in the tobacco factory and exulted in making $20 a week. This was during the postwar boom period and labor was scarce. As fast as the money came in, she spent $15 for a coat, $11 for hightop shoes, $8 for a hat, and smaller amounts for slippers, dresses, beads, and brooches. There were five other women boarding in the same house and Mollie's greatest delight was in the just-before-bedtime lunches they shared. Each one chipped in a nickel every night for cheese, crackers, and fancy canned things. Mollie had never before eaten "store bought" food and had never had even one cent to spend on self-indulgence. After she had bought an entire outfit of new clothes, she went to a county fair with the women. A boy who worked in the cigarette factory asked her to go with him, but she thought she would have a better time with the other women. This boy always hung around Mollie in the factory and said things she thought were fresh, but the landlady wouldn't allow her to go out with him. Once in December he asked Mollie to marry him but she laughed and said, "Why should I marry and keep house and have babies when I've got such a good job and can buy myself such fine clothes?"

Just before Christmas Ben Goodwin got someone to write a letter to Mollie for him. He told her she had to come back home, but that he would make arrangements for her to live during the week with an aunt in the county seat so that she could go to high school in town. Mollie cried and at first said she wouldn't go, but in the end she knew she had to mind her father. She spent her last week's wages buying presents for all the family and went home on Christmas Eve. The next day her mother took flu and one by one the children came down with it. The weakly brother's flu went into pneumonia and finally into tuberculosis, which required so much waiting on that Mollie didn't get to start to school after all.

The following summer Mollie's mother gave birth to her ninth child. It was in the daytime and the baby came in a hurry. No one was in the house except Mollie and the sick brother in the back room. Ben had gone for a doctor but not soon enough and the doctor did not get there in time. The suffering woman begged for help but Mollie did not know what to do. She even pled with Mollie to kill her and put an end to her tortures. Finally the baby was born, but with the covers pulled up so that Mollie could not see. The mother wrapped the baby up and let it lie there until the doctor came and cut the cord.

With a sick brother, a sickly mother, and a new baby in the house, Mollie had a busy summer. About the only times she had off from household duties were when she spent the night with her cousins or with Mrs. Bynum's nieces. On one such night the young people all went to watch a Negro revival meeting. While they were standing on the outside listening to the shouting through the windows, a man who knew some of the boys came up and joined them. His name was Jim and he was ten years older than Mollie, but he "took a shine" to her from their first meeting. For the rest of the summer he rode his mule for nine miles to come to see her whenever she could spend a night away from home, as Ben was still adamant about no sports coming to his house.

In the fall the brother was better and the original plan for Mollie to go to school in town was feasible. Because Ben had no buggy of his own, and because he wished so much to have his favorite daughter at home on week-ends, he finally consented for Jim to drive her out on Fridays and back to town on Sundays. His mule was the fastest one for miles around, but walked very slowly when Jim was taking Mollie home. This was when they did their courting, for Jim was never permitted to linger after delivering Mollie to her parents. He pressed his suit with urgency, for he was nearly thirty and felt it was time for him to be getting married. Mollie wasn't enjoying going back to school after being out for a year, since she was older than the town girls in her grade and felt awkward with them. She liked Jim although she never felt gay or excited with him the way she did with younger boys. She still did not want to think of marrying and settling down to repeat her mother's life—ruining her health and looks with overwork and childbearing. She made one last appeal to her father to let her go back to work in the cigarette factory, for her one-time job has remained to this day a symbol of money for clothes and luxuries. Ben would not consent, however; he said that factories were no place for his womenfolks and that she could never go back. And so Mollie gave Jim a lukewarm "yes" and they planned to marry on Christmas Day. . . .

Five years later Mollie was pregnant for the third time. She felt very hopeful because this was "the kickingest baby you ever felt." Her first child had been a girl, but a terrible disappointment to Mollie in looks. At four she was big, cumbersome, awkward, and slow moving, resembling her two-hundred-pound father so much that he was frequently told, "You couldn't deny that child if you wanted to!" The second baby was a boy, weakly and always crying just like the little brother Mollie used to sleep with and take care of. The alertness of the child she was now carrying promised better success.

Mollie showed more interest in everything that spring and summer. Jim's family had left them to go live and work in a cotton mill town and for the first time they were "tending" a farm and living in a house alone. Their family of four was the smallest she had ever cooked, cleaned, and washed for, and their tobacco crop looked good in July. She was glad Jim was raising tobacco instead of cotton because it meant more money in the fall. He was still kind about buying her one Sunday dress every year with the first tobacco money he got. Mollie was still pretty at twenty-three and during her nine months of pregnancy she often daydreamed of the child, who was to be a pert, attractive daughter whom she could dress daintily.

In midsummer when her time was nearing, the baby suddenly stopped moving one night, "right short like." Mollie knew that minute the baby was dead and alarmed she woke up Jim and told him about it. He reassured her, but on her insistence the next morning went to town and told the doctor about it. The doctor said there was nothing to do but wait, although it was eleven days before labor set in. The delivery was difficult for the dead fetus had begun disintegrating. The body was too much in pieces to be dressed for burial but they showed Mollie the face of her little girl and she thought it was the prettiest she had ever seen. Blood poison, complications, and a long illness afterwards made Mollie temporarily infertile and she had no more children for ten years.

At thirty-seven Mollie is again pregnant. She is not bitter about it, although she wishes doctors would tell you what to do when they say, "Now you shouldn't have any more children." She was quite surprised when she found she was "that way" four years ago, but she made up her mind she wouldn't hope or imagine anything because, "it's like counting your chickens before they're hatched." Then, too, Mollie has had many lessons in disappointment since her baby died. Several years there was not enough money even to "pay out," much less to buy the annual Sunday dress. Jim can't understand why he hasn't been able to buy a team. Of course, his labor force is small, but Mollie and the oldest daughter do almost full-time work in the summer. He has moved from one place to another in several counties trying to change his luck, but it has done no good. Mollie's greatest disappointment, next to the death of her pretty baby, was the year when they were living in a county where the land is supposed to be the best in the State for tobacco. Jim decided his luck had changed at last, for a week before time to begin priming, his tobacco was looking the finest of any crop he'd ever raised. He was so confident over the proceeds it would bring that he promised to give Mollie not only a finer dress than usual, but a permanent wave as soon as they sold the first load of tobacco. Mollie's straight hair had always been a source of dissatisfaction to her and she felt an almost girlish glow of anticipation over the thought of curls. Then hail came and tore the leaves, battered down the stalks, and ruined their tobacco crop. They had to sell their cow that year to pay up what they owed their landlord for furnishing.

And so Mollie, hoping no longer, was none the less delighted when her fourth child was again a pretty girl—not so pretty as the dead one, and a little plump, but much more nearly a replica of herself. Mollie began selling eggs to bring in a little money all during the year so she could buy cloth to make her daughter pretty clothes. At three now the little girl, always clean and dainty with a hair ribbon, seems incongruous with the meagerly furnished, not too well kept, three-room log cabin in which the family live. Mollie has already laid down the law that this child shall never have to do field work or heavy household tasks. She must go to school regularly and get an education so she can get a job early—"maybe a beauty parlor job"—and get away from farming with its hardships. . . .

Mollie doesn't worry too much about the child yet to be born. She is sorry about the trouble it will be, but she accepts the "Lord's will" here as she does when they have a bad crop year. She no longer expects to realize the goals of life herself, but has transferred her efforts to achieving them for her daughter. Last year she even chose to forego the Sunday dress in order to buy a fur-trimmed coat for her baby. And yet Mollie is cheerful, except when impatient with her two older children, and works routinely at her farm and housework without complaint.

WILLIAM H. CHAFE
Eleanor Roosevelt

Eleanor Roosevelt's limitless energy, humanitarian zeal, and compassion made her the most active First Lady in the nation's history. A complex woman with a difficult childhood and great inner doubts, she created a public life for herself that both preceded and extended well beyond the White House years. This process is skillfully and sensitively traced in this brief biography. Note the importance that women played in Eleanor Roosevelt's intellectual and political development: the impact of school mistress Marie Souvestre, the influence and support provided by a female reform network that included women who had come to prominence in the progressive era—Rose Schneiderman, Maud Swartz, and Mary Dreier of the Women's Trade Union League and Mary Dewson of the Consumers' League. Included, too, were female activists in the Democratic party such as Marion Dickerman and Nancy Cook as well as women in the

Expanded version of "Eleanor Roosevelt" by William H. Chafe, in *Notable American Women: The Modern Period,* edited by Barbara Sicherman and Carol Hurd Green (Cambridge, Mass.: Belknap Press of Harvard University Press, 1980), pp. 595–601. Copyright © 1980 by Radcliffe College. Reprinted by permission of the publisher.

Roosevelt administration such as Lorena Hickok. (That women can be at odds with each other over the appropriate roles they should play is exemplified in Eleanor Roosevelt's conflict with her husband's mother.) In what sense can Eleanor Roosevelt be said to have encompassed within her own life the long pilgrimage of millions of women over more than one life span during the nineteenth and twentieth centuries? Note how she moved from dependency to influence to power, from anonymity to repute to leadership, from reliance on a male-dominated structure to female "networks" to public activity to political influence, from the private world of her father's house to the United Nations. Is it easy to make a distinction between Eleanor Roosevelt the person and Eleanor Roosevelt the symbol?

Anna Eleanor Roosevelt was born in New York City [on October 11, 1884], the first child of Elliott and Anna (Hall) Roosevelt. Descended on both sides from distinguished colonial families active in commerce, banking, and politics, Eleanor seemed destined to enjoy all the benefits of class and privilege. By the time she was ten, both her parents had died, as had a younger brother, leaving Eleanor and her second brother, Hall, as the only survivors.

From that point forward, Eleanor Roosevelt's life was characterized by paradox. A woman of remarkable self-control, she yet reached out to touch the world in profoundly emotional ways. Although committed to the traditional idea of women as primarily responsible to husband and family, she personified the strength of the independent woman. Both by fate and by will, she became the most important public woman of the twentieth century.

Eleanor Roosevelt remembered herself as "a solemn child, without beauty. I seemed like a little old woman entirely lacking in the spontaneous joy and mirth of youth." She experienced emotional rejection early: her mother called her "granny" and, at least in Eleanor's memory, warmly embraced her son while being only "kindly and indifferent" to her little girl. From most of her family young Eleanor received the message that she was "very plain," almost ugly, and certainly "old-fashioned." When her parents died,

she went to live with her maternal grandmother, who was equally without warmth. As a cousin later remarked: "It was the grimmest childhood I had ever known. Who did she have? Nobody."

In fact, she had one person—her father. "He was the one great love of my life as a child," she later wrote, "and . . . like many children, I have lived a dream life with him." Described by his friends as "charming, impetuous . . . generous, [and] friendly," Elliott Roosevelt developed with Eleanor an intimacy that seemed almost magical. "As soon as I could talk," she recalled, "I went into his dressing room every morning and chattered to him . . . I even danced with him." She dreamed of the time when she and her father "would have a life of our own together."

But Elliott Roosevelt's capacity for ebullient play and love also contained the seeds of self-destruction. He was never able to provide stability for himself and his family, and his emotional imbalance caused his banishment from the household. He nourished the relationship with Eleanor through letters to "father's own little Nell," writing of "the wonderful long rides" that he wanted them to enjoy together. But when his long-awaited visits occurred, they often ended in disaster, as when he left Eleanor with the doorman at his club, promising to return but going off on a drunken spree. The pain of betrayal was exceeded only by a depth of love for the man who she believed to be "the only person who really cared."

The emotional void caused by her father's death persisted until, at the age of fifteen, she enrolled at Allenswood, a girls' school outside of London presided over by Marie Souvestre. The daughter of the French philosopher and radical Emil Souvestre, she passionately embraced unpopular causes, staunchly defending Dreyfus in France and the cause of the Boers in South Africa. Souvestre provided for Eleanor a deeply needed emotional bond, confiding in her as they toured the continent together, and expressing the affection that made it possible for the younger woman to flower. Roosevelt remembered the years at Allenswood as "the happiest years" of her life: "Whatever I have become since had its seeds in those three years of contact with a liberal mind and strong personality."

Souvestre's imprint was not lost when Eleanor Roosevelt returned to New York City at seventeen to come out in society. Even in the rush of parties and dances, she kept her eye on the more serious world of ideas and social service. Mlle. Souvestre had written her in 1901: "even when success comes, as I'm sure it will, bear in mind that there are more quiet and enviable joys than to be among the most sought after women at a ball." Heeding the injunction, Eleanor Roosevelt plunged into settlement house work and social activities.

Much of Eleanor Roosevelt's subsequent political life can be traced to this early involvement with social reform. At the age of eighteen she joined the National Consumers' League. Headed by Florence Kelley, the League was committed to securing health and safety for workers—especially women—in clothing factories and sweat shops. Visiting these workplaces, Eleanor learned firsthand the misery of the working poor and developed a lifelong commitment to their needs. At the same

time, she joined the Junior League and commenced work at the Rivington Street Settlement House where she taught calisthenics and dancing and witnessed both the deprivation of the poor and the courage of slum dwellers who sought to improve their lot. Eleanor Roosevelt discovered that she preferred social work to debutant parties. More and more, she came to be recognized as a key member of the social reform network in New York City.

At the same time, Eleanor Roosevelt was secretly planning to marry her cousin Franklin Roosevelt. Like Elliott Roosevelt, his godfather, Franklin was spontaneous, warm, and gregarious. But Franklin Roosevelt also possessed good sense and singleness of purpose. Eleanor Roosevelt saw in him the spark of life that she remembered from her father; he, in turn, saw in her the discipline that would curb his own instincts toward excess.

After their marriage on March 17, 1905, the young Roosevelts settled in New York City while Franklin finished his law studies at Columbia University. For the next fifteen years Eleanor Roosevelt's public activities gave way to other concerns. Sara Roosevelt, Franklin's mother, objected to her work at the settlement house because she might bring home diseases. The Roosevelts' first child, Anna, was born within a year (1906), James the next year, and two years later Franklin. Eleanor Roosevelt cherished her children, but it was not a happy time. Her mother-in-law dominated the household, and she came to feel that "Franklin's children were more my mother-in-law's children than they were mine." Fearing that she would hurt her husband and lose his affection, Eleanor Roosevelt did not rebel; but she did experience a profound sense of inadequacy about her abilities as a wife and mother which continued throughout her life. The death of her third child, seven months after his birth, only reinforced her pain and unhappiness. Three additional children were born in the next six years, Elliott in 1910, Franklin in 1914, and John in 1916. Eleanor Roosevelt was devoted to each of her children, yet motherhood could not be fulfilling in a household ruled by a grandmother who referred to the children as "my children . . . your mother only bore you."

Between 1910 and the beginning of World War I, Eleanor Roosevelt's activities revolved increasingly around her husband's growing political career. Elected as the Democratic assemblyman from Dutchess County, N.Y., in 1910, Franklin Roosevelt rapidly became a leader of insurgent anti-Tammany forces in Albany and Eleanor Roosevelt found herself organizing frequent social-political gatherings. In 1913 he was appointed assistant secretary of the navy and she became expert at hosting multiple social events while managing a large household and moving everyone to Campobello in New Brunswick during the summer, then to Hyde Park, and back to Washington.

The entry of the United States into World War I in 1917 provided Eleanor Roosevelt, as her biographer Joseph Lash has noted, with "a reason acceptable to her conscience to free herself of the social duties that she hated, to concentrate less on her household, and plunge into work that fitted her aptitude." She rose at 5:00 A.M. to coordinate activities at Washington's Union Station canteen for soldiers on their way to training camps, took charge of Red Cross activities, supervised the knitting rooms at the navy department, and spoke at patriotic rallies. Her interest in social welfare led to her drive to improve conditions at St. Elizabeth's Hospital for the mentally ill, while her sensitivity to suffering came forth in the visits she paid to wounded soldiers. "[My son] always loved to see you come in," one mother wrote. "You always brought a ray of sunshine."

The war served as a transition for Eleanor Roosevelt's reemergence as a public personality during the 1920s. After Franklin Roosevelt's unsuccessful campaign for the vice-presidency on James Cox's ticket in 1920, the family returned to New York where Eleanor became active in the League of Women Voters. At the time of her marriage, she had opposed suffrage, thinking it inconsistent with women's proper role; now she coordinated the League's legislative program, keeping track of bills that came before the Albany legislature, drafting laws providing for equal representation for men and women, and working with Esther Lape and Elizabeth Reid on the League's lobbying activities. In 1922 she also joined the Women's Trade Union League—then viewed as "left-leaning"—and found friends as well as political allies within the organization. In addition to working for programs such as maximum hours and minimum wages for women, she helped raise funds for WTUL headquarters in New York City. Her warm ties to first- and second-generation immigrants like Rose Schneiderman and Maud Swartz highlighted how far she had moved from the upper-class provincialism of her early years.

When her husband was paralyzed by polio in 1921, Eleanor Roosevelt's public life expanded still further as she became his personal representative in the political arena. With the aid of Louis Howe, Franklin Roosevelt's political mentor who had become her own close friend, she first mobilized Dutchess County women, then moved on to the state Democratic party, organizing all but five counties by 1924. "Organization," she noted, "is something to which [the men] are always ready to take off their hats." No one did the job better. Leading a delegation to the Democratic National Convention in 1924, she fought for equal pay legislation, the child labor amendment, and other planks endorsed by women reformers.

By 1928, Eleanor Roosevelt had become a political leader in her own right. Once just a political wife, she gradually extended that role into a vehicle for asserting her own personality and goals. She headed up the national women's campaign for the Democratic party in 1928, making sure that the party appealed to independent voters, to minorities, and to women. After Franklin Roosevelt's election as governor of New York, she was instrumental in securing Frances Perkins's appointment as the state's industrial commissioner. She dictated as many as a hundred letters a day, spoke to countless groups, and acted as an advocate of social reform and women's issues.

Eleanor Roosevelt's talent for combining partisan political activity with devotion to social welfare causes made her the center of an ever-growing female reform network. Her associates included Marion Dickerman and Nancy Cook, former suffragists and Democratic party loyalists; Mary Dewson, who was president of the New York Consumers' League from 1925 to 1931; and Mary Dreier of the WTUL. She walked on picket lines with Rose Schneiderman, edited the *Women's Democratic News*, and advised the League of Women Voters on political tactics. Not only did her political sophistication grow, but she also learned to uphold her beliefs even if she caused "disagreement or unpleasant feelings." By standing up for women in politics, she provided a model for others to follow.

During the 1932 campaign which led to her husband's election to the presidency, Eleanor Roosevelt coordinated the activities of the Women's Division of the Democratic National Committee, working with Mary Dewson to mobilize thousands of women precinct workers. After the election, Dewson took over direction of the Women's Division. She corresponded daily with Eleanor Roosevelt both about appointing women to office and about securing action on issues that would appeal to minorities, women, and such professional groups as educators and social workers. Together they brought to Wash-

ington an unprecedented number of dynamic women activists. Ellen Woodward, Hilda Worthington Smith and Florence Kerr all held executive offices in the Works Progress Administration, while Lorena Hickok acted as eyes and ears for WPA director Harry Hopkins as she traveled across the country to observe the impact of the New Deal's relief program. Mary Anderson, Director of the Women's Bureau, recalled that women government officials had formerly dined together in a small university club. "Now," she said, "there are so many of them that we need a hall."

Eleanor Roosevelt also provided a national forum for transmitting the views and concerns of these women. At regular press conferences for women reporters, she introduced Mary McLeod Bethune and other women leaders to talk about their work with the administration. These sessions provided new status and prestige for the female press corps; they also underlined the importance to Eleanor Roosevelt of women's issues and created a community of women reporters and government workers.

As a result of Eleanor Roosevelt's activities, women achieved a strong voice in the New Deal. The percentage of women appointed as post masters, for example, shot up from 17.6 percent in 1930 to 26 percent between 1932 and 1938. Eleanor Roosevelt's own political role was best seen in the 1936 reelection drive when she used the educational approach developed by the Women's Division in 1932 as a primary campaign weapon. More than 60,000 women precinct workers canvassed the electorate and for the first time women received equal representation on the Democratic platform committee, an event described by the *New York Times* as "the biggest coup for women in years."

Eleanor Roosevelt's fear that there would be no active role available to her as first lady had been unfounded. She toured the country repeatedly, surveying conditions in the coal mines, visiting relief projects, and speaking out for the human rights of the disadvantaged. Through her syndicated newspaper column "My Day," which first appeared in January 1936, and through radio programs and lectures, she reached millions and communicated to the country her deep compassion for those who suffered. At the White House, in turn, she acted as advocate of the poor and disenfranchised. "No one who ever saw Eleanor Roosevelt sit down facing her husband, and holding his eyes firmly, say to him 'Franklin, I think you should . . . or, Franklin surely you will not' . . . will ever forget the experience," Rexford Tugwell wrote. She had become, as columnist Raymond Clapper noted a "Cabinet Minister without portfolio—the most influential woman of our times."

But if Eleanor Roosevelt had achieved an unparalleled measure of political influence, it was in place of, rather than because of, an intimate personal relationship with her husband. Probably at no time after their first few years together did Franklin and Eleanor Roosevelt achieve the degree of intimacy that she once described as caring so much that a look and the sound of a voice would tell all. Not only did Sara Roosevelt remain a dominant presence, but Franklin had embarked on his own interests and enthusiasms, often different from those of his wife. The dissimilarities in their temperaments became a permanent barrier. While he loved to party, she held back, telling her daughter Anna in a letter from Warm Springs, Ga., in 1934, that she "always felt like a spoil-sport and policeman here . . . I'm an idiotic puritan and I wish I had the right kind of sense of humor and could enjoy certain things. At least, thank God, none of you children have inherited that streak in me."

During his years as assistant secretary of the navy, Franklin Roosevelt had often indulged his fun-loving instinct, causing a lasting breach in the marriage. When his wife was away, his frequent companion had been Lucy Mercer, Eleanor's social secretary. Over time, their relationship became intimate. Eleanor Roosevelt learned of the affair in 1918 and offered to divorce him. Although Franklin refused her offer, and Sara Roosevelt engineered an agreement for them to stay together if her son stopped seeing Lucy Mercer, Eleanor Roosevelt's marriage would never again achieve the magical possibility of being "for life, for death."

Some observers have connected Eleanor Roosevelt's reemergence as a public figure with her profound anger at her husband's betrayal. Yet her activism predated her discovery of the Mercer affair, going back to World War I and the settlement house years, and was rooted ultimately in her relationship with Mlle. Souvestre. The Lucy Mercer affair, like Franklin's polio, reinforced her move toward public self-assertion, but did not in itself cause a transformation. What it did cause was a gradual reallocation of emotional energy away from her husband. Throughout the 1920s a warmth of tone and feeling continued in her letters to and about him. Yet gradually their lives became more separate. She might be jealous of his secretary, Missy LeHand, or even of her daughter Anna, for the ease with which they supplied Franklin Roosevelt with fun and enjoyment. But part of her also accepted the idea that others must provide what she could not give. In a poignant piece entitled "On Being Forty-five," written for *Vogue* in 1930, Eleanor Roosevelt wrote that by middle-age a woman must recognize that the romantic dreams of youth are over. "We should know that happiness does not come from the seeking, that it is never ours by right, but we earn it through giving of ourselves." Above all, she concluded, the forty-five-year-old woman "must keep an open and speculative mind . . . [to] be ready to go out and try new adventures, create new work for others as well as herself, and strike deep roots in some community where her presence will make a difference to the lives of others."

Taking her own advice, Eleanor Roosevelt transferred her emotional attachments to others. Women reformers provided intimate friendship as well as political camaraderie. In 1926 she had moved with Nancy Cook and Marion Dickerman into Val-Kill, a newly constructed cottage at Hyde Park. The event accurately symbolized her growing detachment from Franklin and his mother. Although she returned to "the big house" at Hyde Park when her husband was present, it was always with a sense of resentment and regret. She and Dickerman purchased Todhunter, a private school in New York City where Eleanor Roosevelt taught three days a week even after Franklin was elected governor of New York. The three women also jointly managed a furniture crafts factory at Val-Kill. After 1920, she and Louis Howe developed profound bonds of affection and support, each carrying the other loyally through crises with Franklin and the vicissitudes of party politics. Harry Hopkins, director of the WPA, also became an intimate. But her most carefree relationship was probably that with Earl Miller, a former state trooper and subsequently a bodyguard for the Roosevelt family who became a close companion. Miller encouraged her to drive her own car, take up horseback riding again, and develop confidence in her personality.

With these and others, Eleanor Roosevelt developed a rich emotional life. Although she frequently appeared cold and distant, she passionately cared for her children and friends. Writing to her daughter Anna on Christmas Eve in 1935, she noted: "It was hard to decorate the tree or get things distributed without you . . . and if anyone says much I shall weep." She expressed similar affection in daily letters to Lorena Hickok, the former journalist and assistant to Harry Hopkins,

who moved to Hyde Park after a falling-out occurred between Eleanor Roosevelt and Marion Dickerman and Nancy Cook in the late 1930s. Most surprising of all, perhaps, she poured out her feelings to distant correspondents, answering the many pleas for help which came to her with either a sensitive letter, an admonition to a federal agency to take action, or even a personal check. The poor wrote to her because they knew she cared, and in caring, she found an outlet for her powerful emotional needs.

The same compassion was manifested in Eleanor Roosevelt's advocacy of the oppressed. Hearing about the struggle of Appalachian farmers to reclaim their land, she became a champion of the Arthurdale (W. Va.) Resettlement Administration project and devoted her lecture fees as well as her influence to help the community. She invited to the White House representatives of poor southern textile workers and northern garment workers, seating them next to the president at dinner so that he might hear of their plight. She and Franklin Roosevelt had worked out a tacit understanding which permitted her to bring the cause of the oppressed to his attention, and allowed him, in turn, to use her activism as a means of building alliances with groups to his left. Although the president frequently refused to act as she wished, the dispossessed at least had an advocate.

Largely because of Eleanor Roosevelt, the issue of civil rights for black Americans received a hearing at the White House. Although like most white Americans she had grown up in an environment suffused with racism and nativism, she was one of the few voices in the administration insisting that racial discrimination had no place in American life. As always, she led by example. At a 1939 Birmingham meeting inaugurating the Southern Conference on Human Welfare, she placed her chair so that it straddled the black and white sides of the aisle, thereby confounding local authorities who insisted on segregation. She resigned in the same year from the Daughters of the American Revolution after they denied the black artist Marian Anderson permission to perform at Constitution Hall. Instead, and in part through Eleanor Roosevelt's intervention, Anderson sang to 75,000 people from the Lincoln Memorial.

Eleanor Roosevelt also acted as behind-the-scenes lobbyist for civil rights legislation. With alacrity she accepted the suggestion of Walter White, executive secretary of the NAACP, that she act as an intermediary with the president in the association's attempt to secure legislation defining lynching as a federal crime. She also agreed to be a patron of an NAACP-sponsored exhibit in New York City of paintings and drawings dealing with lynching, and attended the showing. Although she lost out in her campaign for the president's strong endorsement of an antilynching bill, she had communicated to him her anger that "one could get nothing done." Continuing to speak forthrightly for the cause of civil rights, she addressed the NAACP's annual meeting in June 1939 and joined the biracial protest organization a few weeks later. As the threat of war increased, Eleanor Roosevelt joined her Negro friends in arguing vigorously for administration action to eliminate discrimination in the armed services and in defense employment. Although civil rights forces were not satisfied with the administration's response, the positive changes that did occur were due in large part to their alliance with Eleanor Roosevelt.

She brought the same fervor to her identification with young people. Fearing that a whole generation might be lost to democracy because of the depression, she reached out to make contact with them. Despite warnings from White House aides, between 1936 and 1940 Eleanor Roosevelt became deeply involved in the activities of the American Student Union and the American Youth Congress, groups committed to a democratic socialist program of massively expanded social welfare programs. She advanced their point of view in White House circles, and invited them to meet the president. Although she was later betrayed by some of her young allies who followed the Communist party line and denounced the European war as imperialistic after the Nazi-Soviet Non-Aggression Pact of 1939, she continued to believe in the importance of remaining open to dissent. "I have never said anywhere that I would rather see young people sympathetic with communism," Eleanor Roosevelt wrote. "But I have said I would rather see the young people actively at work, even if I considered they were doing things that were a mistake."

With the onset of World War II, Roosevelt persisted in her efforts for the disadvantaged. She insisted that administration officials consult women activists and incorporate roles for women as a major part of their planning for wartime operations, and she intervened repeatedly with war production agencies as well as the military to advocate fairer treatment for black Americans. When it seemed that many New Deal social welfare programs would be threatened by war, Eleanor Roosevelt became their defender. Increasingly she devoted herself to the dream of international cooperation, aware more than most of the revolution rising in Africa and Asia, and of the dangers posed by the threats of postwar conflict.

But her energies in the war were directed primarily to human needs. When Jewish refugees seeking a haven from Nazi persecution received less than an enthusiastic response from the State Department, Eleanor Roosevelt served as their advocate. Families separated by war always found an ally when they sought her help, and wounded veterans in army hospitals far from home received from her visits the cherished message that someone cared.

As the war proceeded, the worlds of

Franklin and Eleanor Roosevelt became still more separate. They were frequently adversaries and the president was less able to tolerate her advocacy of unpopular causes. In search of release from the unbearable pressures of the war, he had come to rely on the gaiety and laughter of his daughter Anna, and other women companions, including Lucy Mercer Rutherford, who, unknown to Eleanor, was with Franklin Roosevelt in Warm Springs when he died of a cerebral hemorrhage in April 1945.

With great discipline and dignity, Eleanor Roosevelt bore both the pain of Franklin's death and the circumstances surrounding it. Her first concern was with carrying forward the policies in which they had both believed despite their disagreements. Writing later about their relationship, she commented: "He might have been happier with a wife who had been completey uncritical. That I was never able to be and he had to find it in some other people. Nevertheless, I think that I sometimes acted as a spur . . . I was one of those who served his purposes." What she did not say was that Franklin Roosevelt had served her purposes as well. Though they never retrieved their early intimacy, they had created an unparalleled partnership to respond to the needs of a nation in crisis.

Not long after her husband's death, Eleanor Roosevelt told a reporter: "The story is over." But no one who cared so much for so many causes, and was so effective a leader, could long remain on the sidelines. Over the next decade and a half, she continued to be the most effective woman in American politics. In long letters to President Harry S Truman, she implored the administration to push forward with civil rights, maintain the Fair Employment Practices Commission, develop a foreign policy able to cope with the needs of other nations, and work toward a world system where atom bombs would cease to be a negotiating chip in international relations.

Appropriately, President Truman nominated Eleanor Roosevelt as a United States delegate to the United Nations. There she argued, debated, and lobbied for the creation of a document on human rights that would embody standards which civilized humankind would accept as sacred and inalienable. Finally on Dec. 10, 1948, the Universal Declaration of Human Rights, fundamentally shaped by her, passed the General Assembly. Delegates rose in a standing ovation to the woman who more than anyone else had come to symbolize the cause of human rights. Even those in the United States who had most opposed her applauded: "I want to say that I take back everything I ever said about her," Michigan Senator Arthur Vandenberg commented, "and believe me, it's been plenty." At times during the New Deal a figure of scorn among some conservatives, Eleanor Roosevelt was fast becoming a national heroine.

The cause of world peace and the desire to help the victims of war quickly became central to Roosevelt's efforts. In moving speeches that vividly portrayed the suffering wrought by war, she sought to educate the United States to its postwar responsibilities. She had traveled through England noting the names of all the young men who had died during the war, she told an audience. "There is a feeling that spreads over the land," she said, "the feel of civilization that of itself might have a hard time coming back." If the United States wished to avoid such a world, it must help those who had suffered, and avoid isolationism.

Although Eleanor Roosevelt disagreed profoundly with some of the military aspects of United States foreign policy, she supported the broad outlines of its response to the Soviet Union in the developing cold war. In debates at the UN she learned quickly that Soviet delegates could be hypocritical, and on more than one occasion she responded to their charges of injustice in America by proposing that each country submit to investigation of its social conditions—a suggestion the Soviets refused. She refused in 1947 to support the newly formed Progressive party with its platform of accommodation toward the Soviet Union, and instead spearheaded the drive to build Americans for Democratic Action, a group which espoused social reforms at home and support of Truman's foreign policy.

Throughout the 1950s Eleanor Roosevelt remained a singular public figure, able to galvanize the attention of millions by her statements. She became one of the staunchest advocates of Israel, argued vigorously for civil rights, and spoke forcefully against the witch hunts of McCarthyism. When Dwight D. Eisenhower became president in 1953 she resigned her UN post, but she continued to work tirelessly through the American Association for the United Nations to mobilize public support for international cooperation. She also gave unstintingly of her time to the election campaigns in 1952 and 1956 of her friend Adlai Stevenson, who brought to politics a wit and sophistication that she admired.

The private sphere, however, remained most precious. "The people I love," Eleanor Roosevelt wrote her friend and physician David Gurewitsch, "mean more to me than all the public things. I only do the public things because there are a few close people whom I love dearly and who matter to me above everything else." The Roosevelt children remained as much a trial as a comfort. After Franklin Roosevelt's death, she lived at Val-Kill with her secretary, Malvina Thompson (1893–1953), and her son Elliott and his family. More often than not, family gatherings degenerated into bitter arguments. But her grandchildren brought joy as did friends, old and new.

As she entered her seventies, Eleanor Roosevelt had become the first lady of the world. Traveling to India, Japan, and the Soviet Union, she spoke for the best that was in America. Although she did not initially approve of John F. Kennedy and would have much preferred to see Adlai Stevenson nominated again in 1960, she lived to see the spirit of impatience and reform return to Washington. In 1962 she sponsored hearings in Washington, D.C., where young civil rights workers testified about the judicial and police harassment of black protesters in the south.

It was fitting that Eleanor Roosevelt's last major official position was to chair President Kennedy's Commission on the Status of Women, to which she was appointed in December 1961. More than anyone else of her generation she had exemplified the political independence and personal autonomy that were abiding themes of the women's movement. Eleanor Roosevelt had not been a militant feminist and, like most social reformers, she had opposed the Equal Rights Amendment (ERA) until the mid-1940s, believing that it would jeopardize protective labor legislation for women. During the depression she accepted the popular view that, at least temporarily, some married women should leave the labor force to improve the chances of the unemployed. On occasion, she also adopted male-oriented definitions of fulfillment. "You are successful," she wrote in a 1931 article, "when your husband feels that he has been a success and that life has been worthwhile."

But on the issue of women's equality as in so many other areas, Roosevelt most often affirmed the inalienable right of the human spirit to grow and seek fulfillment. Brought up amidst anti-Semitic and anti-Negro attitudes, she had transcended her past to become one of the strongest champions of minority rights. Once opposed to suffrage, she had grown to exemplify women's aspirations for a full life in politics.

There was, in fact, a direct line from Mlle. Souvestre's advocacy of intellectual independence to Eleanor Roosevelt's involvement in the settlement house to her subsequent embrace of women's political activism in the 1920s and 1930s, and her final role as leader of the Commission on the Status of Women. She had personified not only the right of women to act as equals with men in the political sphere, but the passion of social activists to ease pain, alleviate suffering, and affirm solidarity with the unequal and disenfranchised of the world.

Eleanor Roosevelt participated in the activities of the Women's Commission until August 1962, testifying on behalf of equal pay laws at a congressional hearing in April of that year. She died at her home in New York City [on November 7, 1962] from a rare form of tuberculosis. Twenty years earlier she had written: "You can never really live anyone else's life, not even your child's. The influence you exert is through your own life and what you've become yourself."

Despite disappointment and tragedy, Eleanor Roosevelt had followed her own advice. "What other single human being," Adlai Stevenson asked at her memorial service, "has touched and transformed the existence of so many? . . . She walked in the slums . . . of the world, not on a tour of inspection . . . but as one who could not feel contentment when others were hungry." Because of her life, millions of others may have experienced a new sense of possibility. She would have wished for nothing more.

SHEILA TOBIAS and LISA ANDERSON
What Really Happened to Rosie the Riveter? Demobilization and the Female Labor Force, 1944–47

As a nation struggling with depression began fighting its second world war, unemployment lines quickly vanished. Manpower shortages meant that women and blacks would once again move into jobs in industry traditionally held by white males. Once the war was over, these women exchanged industrial tools for broom and mop, happily returning to domesticity in the rapidly growing suburbs—at least, so goes the story. Sheila Tobias and Lisa Anderson challenge

Excerpted from "What Really Happened to Rosie the Riveter? Demobilization and the Female Labor Force, 1944–47" by Sheila Tobias and Lisa Anderson, MSS Modular Publications, Module 9 (1974): 1–36. Copyright © 1973 by Sheila Tobias and Lisa Anderson. Reprinted by permission of the authors. Notes have been renumbered, tables omitted, and cross-references adjusted.

that assumption in this pioneering study of demobilization. Note not only the percentage of wage-earning women who wished to continue working but also the increasing percentage of *married* women in that group. To what extent have union attitudes to working women described earlier by Alice Kessler-Harris (part IIB) changed? How are we to account for the lack of resentment about dismissal on the part of those who lost their jobs? How did job classification work against women? Why do the authors regard job classification as "the inevitable corollary of protective legislation?"

INTRODUCTION

The generation of women war workers, symbolized by Rosie the Riveter, has not been seriously analyzed by historians. Perhaps it is because the women disappeared as a recognizable group after the war in pursuit, according to popular mythology, of the "best years of their lives" (the title of a popular postwar film) that the war had postponed; or, as Betty Friedan suggested fifteen years later in her book, *The Feminine Mystique*, they were hoodwinked by returning magazine editors selling a new product called "suburbia." In either case, the conventional view of Rosie's co-workers is that they were temporary workers: they had entered the work force for patriotic reasons only, donning unfamiliar working-class aprons and riveter masks; and they departed from factory work altogether as soon after the war as they could manage.

Although there was at least one "Back to Mamma" club founded in the late years of the war with the express purpose of persuading women to quit, most experts—among them Frances Perkins, Roosevelt's female Secretary of Labor—predicted that American women would go on preferring domesticity to factory work. Others—and among these were union leaders, anxious to avoid competition between war workers and returning veterans—hoped that women would retire voluntarily. But what the contemporaries failed to notice and what history has not yet set right is the degree to which the

women were forcibly laid off their jobs in the postwar period.

In our view, the conventional story of Rosie's wartime career not only ends incorrectly, but it is an inaccurate description of who was working and why. Aggregate statistics, for instance, indicate that of the 19.5 million women employed at the wartime peak (excluding women engaged in Red Cross work and the armed services), 15.9 million had been employed before the war, though not necessarily in factory work. The women who were working in the week prior to Pearl Harbor represented 25.3 percent of the female population over the age of 14, and though the increase to 19.5 million, or 36.1 percent of the female population, was substantial, it was but an increase in an already significant proportion of women working.

What was different about the woman working during the war was her age, her marital status, her participation in manufacturing, as against service and domestic work, and, above all, her rate of pay. For the second time in the twentieth century, due to the absence of men and the insatiable appetite of a war machine, women were needed badly enough to be offered highly paid jobs in manufacturing. In fact, one of the differences between the situation caused by the first World War and the second, was the presence in the 1940s of industrial unions which would, as we shall see, make the laying off of temporary workers a more complicated matter.

Still, the unions notwithstanding, three million fewer women were employed in 1946 than at the peak of the war. The critical questions are whether women were laid off against their will or merely accommodated in their wish to go home; and, if they were laid off, where they landed in the economy. Our guess is that Rosie did not run to the suburbs so much as fall into a lower-paying, more traditional female job after the war.[1] Since we know that by 1950 the percentage of employed women was almost back to the wartime peak, our suspicion is that Rosie stopped riveting, but she did not stop working. Further research will be needed to substantiate this view.

Mythology dies hard. Although it is beyond the scope of this paper to speculate on Friedan's allegation that the feminine mystique was revived to keep women from maintaining the economic gains they had won during the war, the issues of equal pay, desegregation of job categories, and government-supported child care, which were much discussed during the war, did not surface again until the 1960s. The quiescence of women in the fifties may well be the result not of Rosie's choice but of Rosie's frustration, which is another good reason for laying the myths surrounding Rosie the Riveter to rest.

SOURCES AND SCOPE

A full and comprehensive survey of women war workers will have to await disaggregated data and in-depth interviews of women who were working during the war. What we have attempted to do in this preliminary survey is to determine with some degree of accuracy answers to the following kinds of questions: What type of woman actually joined the labor force during the war? What was the impact on the female labor force of the opportunities opened up by war work? What was the real motivation of the women who worked and what were their postwar plans? In addition, we examined some of the issues that aroused women workers most. We looked at how equity was achieved, particularly in industries that had long segregated women and Negroes into separate job classifications and onto separate seniority lists; at how the federal surveillance of industry, made necessary by the war, tended to improve conditions and to set precedents that even the end of hostilities could not alter; and, finally, at the extent to which the marginal innovations which permitted some women to work, such as child-care arrangements, were meaningful.

We hypothesized that possibly there were two Rosies: one, a working-class girl who had been a waitress or laundress before the war and who expected to work for her living most of her life. This Rosie would have gravitated toward better-paying work in 1942 to the point of moving into one of the areas most affected by wartime contracts, even to an isolated, especially built bomber plant like Willow Run in the Detroit area. This Rosie, to carry the supposition further, had to join the union and may even have become an active member. After being "bumped" in 1945, she would have complained when her perceived seniority was overlooked in rehiring, resented the privileges afforded veterans, and, since she had to work to live, she would have moved grudgingly downward to a lower-paying, clerical or service job. The other Rosie would be the woman who initially fitted the stereotype; she was at home or still in school, when the war began. Having joined the labor force because of the war without previous intention to work, she then decided to stay employed. When the surveys taken at the end of the war showed that as many as 85 percent of the women working wanted to stay on the job after the war, that figure must include this Rosie, the erstwhile homemaker.

The myths about Rosie are probably

linked to middle-class notions that women who work do so for pin money, that few married women need to work, and that factory work is not the kind of work that women will enjoy doing in any case. The fact, however, that by 1940, 15 million American women (not of the middle class) out of a total female population of 50.1 million were working full time, despite discrimination, lower rates of pay, and segregated job classifications, indicates that these are indeed myths.

In the absence of many secondary sources on the subject, it seemed appropriate to focus on one industry in one of the ten most affected areas. The selection of Detroit and the auto and aircraft industries had many bases: Detroit had been known before the war as a "man-employing, one-industry city"; of the ten industrial areas studied by the Women's Bureau in 1944, Detroit was the largest, having a population of 1,917,724 of whom 917,447 were employed during the war; the increase of women workers in the Detroit area between 1940 and 1945 was reported to be 112 percent.

Further, the United Auto Workers, a CIO union, had between 300,000 and 350,000 women members by the end of the war and, in response to their interests and needs, developed a number of services for women workers, including the formation of the UAW Women's Bureau in 1944 and a regularly appearing column in the union newspaper, *Ammunition*, entitled "Sister Sue." The Women's Bureau (later renamed the Women's Department), together with the union's education and research departments, issued an array of special reports and pamphlets, most of which convey the impression that the union favored equal pay and equal rights for women. On paper the UAW was advanced. Private and at this point confidential sources suggest that this was only a paper commitment for many of the men in charge, but so far we have been unable to follow up resolutions to see whether they were forcibly administered. . . .

One of the most dramatic examples of a massive, war-related expansion was the construction almost overnight of the $100 million Ford Motor Company Willow Run Plant outside Detroit. The plant, designed to assemble B–24 Liberator bombers, is worth describing in some detail to give a sense of the dimension of war work and of the problem of reconversion. Built on a hitherto inaccessible site out of town, it had a capacity for 40,000 workers, although we have not found evidence as yet that more than 32,000 were employed at one time. The federal government built both the facility itself and public housing and community services for the workers. Figures reported in the press indicated that the factory cost $100 million, the public housing $25 million, and an approach highway $25 million more.

Even before the end of hostilities, Willow Run began to lay off workers. At the close of business, May 18, 1945, a union official noted a total of 9,814 workers had been laid off from Willow Run.[2] The UAW analyzed the layoff statistics and found that 52.6 percent of the persons laid off were women; that 44.7 percent of these women had not been employed before (but 55.3 percent had been); and that 58 percent of the women wished to continue working (66 percent of those under 30), and especially to continue in *factory work*.[3]

More significant for our understanding of the woman worker is that the average wage earned by all workers at the point of layoff in 1945 was $1.23 per hour, a good earning even for war work in 1945, and that the Ford Motor Car Company, owners of Willow Run, had never before employed women except in its administrative staff (clerical). Perhaps, in view of this background, it is not altogether surprising that 41 percent of the male workers laid off were offered a referral, at an average wage decrease of 8.5

cents an hour, but that less than 3 percent of the women were offered other jobs and that these jobs were at wage decreases averaging better than 48 percent.[4] It should be further noted that when the Willow Run plant was reconverted to suit the peacetime economy, women were not rehired.

The material that follows suggests that Willow Run is reasonably typical: in the period of reconversion, beginning in the summer of 1944, women were the first to be laid off; job referrals were not as available to them; the rehiring that took place as early as 1946 in some reconverted industries ignored the "seniority" of women; and even unemployment compensation was denied if the women appeared too "choosy" about maintaining their wage rates in the new job.[5]

LABOR MARKET DEVELOPMENTS DURING AND AFTER THE WAR

. . . In the spring of 1940 there were 46 million persons in civilian jobs, of whom 34 million were male and 12 million female, and 500,000 in the armed forces. Five years later, civilian employment had risen to 53.5 million, of whom 34.3 million were male and 19.3 million female, and the net strength of the armed forces was over 12 million men and women. In 1947, after reconversion to a peacetime economy was substantially completed, total employment was 56.7 million, of whom 40 million were male and 15.8 million female. . . .

The entry of women into industries and occupations previously reserved almost exclusively for men was the most striking labor-market development of the war period. Women also moved into clerical and sales occupations, again replacing men. Domestic service was the only field to show a large decline in employment of women between 1940 and 1945, and hundreds of laundries closed, as laundresses found jobs elsewhere. Even some teachers left their professional jobs (usually the most stable of occupational groups) to go into manufacturing.

Within two years after the war, about 14 million service men and women returned to civilian work and other millions were transferred. Any analysis of postwar employment patterns of males must distinguish between returning veterans and nonveterans. For veterans, the return to employment was made easier by concerted placement efforts by the United States Employment Service and educational benefits provided by federal laws. Pool and Pearlman report that probably well over half the ex-servicemen returned to work for their former employers, thanks to reemployment expectations and preference for hiring veterans. Fewer returned to farm work than had been on farms before the war, but that was part of a larger trend away from the farm. Of the nonveterans, however, one out of eight employed in civilian jobs both in August 1945 and in August 1946 had changed his occupational group in the course of the year.

Of the women employed both in August 1945 and in August 1947, the number working as operatives and craftsmen dropped by over one million. Women, however, still retained a somewhat greater proportion of industrial jobs than in prewar years (13 percent in 1947 compared to 8 percent in 1940).[6] . . .

As a result of the switch to manufacturing, union membership among females increased. In 1919 total female union membership was 250,000; in 1937, 500,000; and in 1944, 3,500,000. Industrial unions appeared quicker to open their doors to women than did crafts unions, which remained closer or gave temporary membership which expired with the end of the war-time emergency.

Factory work may have represented upward mobility for many in terms of increased pay and job security, but for some it required a readjustment of a young woman's image of herself. A young war worker is quoted in a "Sister Sue" column in *Ammunition*, the UAW newspaper, as saying, "When I first started to work in the shop, I was sort of ashamed of it. My mother had always wanted me to do office work."[7] Nonetheless, as we have already noted, the bulk of the women who worked in the factory during the war wanted to stay in factory work later on.

In addition to the shift to industrial employment, a marked shift in the marital status of the typical female worker occurred during the war, and it is one which has continued into the present day. Many more married women entered the labor market during the war than normally would have done so. In 1940, according to the census, single women constituted 48.5 percent of the female work force, married women 36.4 percent, and widows and divorcees 15.1 percent. During the war, however, 40.9 percent of the females working were single, 45.7 percent were married, and 13.4 percent were widowed or divorced. Of the married women, 11 percent had husbands in service. When asked if they expected to continue working, 87 percent of the single women, 94 percent of the divorced and widowed, and 57 percent of the married women said yes.[8]

Possibly the most dramatic shift in type of employment was registered by Negro women during the war. In 1940, two out of every five Negro women (compared to two out of every eight white women) worked. Few were in industry in upgraded jobs. Of the 1.5 million Negro women working in 1940, more than half were in service occupations, agriculture, domestic help, cooking, waiting, or were seeking work (i.e., unemployed). In 1945, however, more than two million Negro women were working. Their number as craftsmen, foremen, and factory workers quadrupled, and they even entered the armed services. There was a noticeable and what turned out to be a permanent decrease of Negro women in domestic service. Negro women's employment increased not only in the munitions factories but in food, clothing, textiles, leathers, and other manufacturing. The greatest increase was in metals, chemicals, and rubber.[9]

In 1942, when women mechanics were hired for the first time at the Brooklyn Navy Yard, a Negro woman got a grade of 99, the highest among the 6,000 women who applied.[10] The event was heralded among working Negro women as a sign of changing times. Yet the same issues as would determine white women's status would determine whether Negro women kept the gains, particularly in earning power, made during the war. In this respect, Negro men, Negro women, and white women were similarly affected by the war and disappointed by its aftermath.

Wages were highest in manufacturing and especially high in the airplane and associated industries. Next in order of rates of pay were other defense-related industries and nondefense manufacturing and, at the lowest end of the wage scale, were nonmanufacturing jobs. The nationwide female average for forty hours worked was $44.21 during this period.[11] The reasons for high wages were both wartime boom conditions and the fact that some women entering formerly males-only job classifications were permitted to earn men's wages. The peace was to end both the boom and the progress towards equal pay for equal work.

WOMEN'S COMMITMENT TO WORK

In the course of the war there were numerous assertions that wartime women workers would not stay on the job after the war was over. For the most part, these statements were based not on systematic surveys but rather on assumptions about woman's nature. To be sure, the turnover and absenteeism rates for women during the war were higher than those reported for men. Since "female workers changed jobs twice as often as men and stayed home twice as much," their motivation was often called into question.[12] Many viewed this employment behavior as a sign of women's dissatisfaction with war work. *The Detroit News*, for example, headlined an article, "Women Fade from Jobs, Prefer Homemaking to New Employment."[13] A far more likely cause of poor attendance was the lack of community services available to women to aid them in their dual role as worker and homemaker. Seventy-five percent of the new female workers were, as we have seen, married, and responsibilities in the home inevitably conflicted with performance on the job. A 1943 survey, conducted by the National Industrial Conference Board, reported that after illness, family needs were listed most often by females as the cause of absenteeism.[14]

Far more powerful than the facts, however, were the assumptions about woman's place. Typical was the statement that Betty Allie, state workmen's compensation official in Michigan, made.

> . . . women are working only to win the war and will return willingly to their home duties after the war is won. They will look on this period as an interlude, just as their men who have been called to service will consider military duties as interlude. The women are like Cincinnatus, who left his plow to save Rome and then returned to his plow. Women will always be women.[15]

Others, like Frederick Crawford, president of the National Association of Manufacturers, were not so sure women would willingly return to the home, but thought they ought to. He called it a "perplexing war's-end problem." He was convinced that women wanted to work, but re-minded his hearers that the "home is the basic American unit" and that "home-makers are essential to the morale and well-being of male workers and as a first line prevention [note the war metaphor] against juvenile delinquency." He also was aware that women with college educations might be better suited to careers than to domesticity, and concluded that single women, widows, and the well-educated might go on working without tearing the fabric of the American system.[16]

More ironic was the conviction, uttered often in this period by Frances Perkins, that at the close of the war women would "return to the homes they left for patriotic reasons." Many newspaper women predicted a mass exodus of women workers, assuming as did Secretary Perkins that nothing but the urgency of war had generated the increase in female labor force participation.[17]

The survey conducted by the Women's Bureau in 1944 obtained the following results when inquiring about postwar plans: 51 percent of the women who planned to continue working after the war were single; 34 percent were married; 15 percent were widowed or divorced. The highest percentage of prospective postwar workers came from the group of women who had been employed before Pearl Harbor rather than from those who had been in school or engaged in housework. On the average, 80 percent of the women who had been employed before Pearl Harbor intended to keep on working. . . .[18]

The crux of the problem was this: even if only one-half of the former housewives were converted to work by the war, it would not significantly reduce the postwar pressure for good jobs, since the bulk of the females working in 1944 wanted to go right on working. Thus, Frances Perkins and Frederick Crawford might be right about the magnet of the American home for former housewives, but they were wrong about the power of the home to attract those whose working lives had antedated Pearl Harbor and those who had gone directly from school to work.

This explanation is the only way we can make sense of other survey data having to do with women workers' postwar plans. The UAW, for example, reported that a survey done of their own membership indicated that fully 85 percent of the women then working wanted to continue to work after the war. The report predicted that of the 350,000 female UAW members, 300,000 would want to go on working. In answer to the question, "If a job is available, will you continue to work outside your home after the war?" 98.5 percent of the single women and 100 percent of the widows answered, "Yes." Among the married women 68.7 percent (this is the highest proportion of married women responding positively in any of the surveys taken) said yes. In reporting the figures, R. J. Thomas, president of the UAW, said the results of the study would "shatter the preconceived ideas of certain industrialists and 'experts' who think the majority of women workers will want to leave the labor market."[19] The union president might have released these figures because, at the time, the union was pressing for a national commitment to full employment, or the guarantee of 60 million postwar jobs through a public works program.[20]

Data from other sectors of the manufacturing economy confirm the results of the UAW survey. A survey done in Cleveland, Ohio, by the Emergency Day Care office found that 60 percent of the women working wanted to continue working after the war. In Dayton, Ohio, women in manufacturing indicated they wanted to keep working in the same industry, though laundresses and waitresses wanted to change jobs.[21] In a poll taken in 1944, by the Northwestern Life Insurance Company at seven scattered war plants, 66 percent of the women employed reported that they wanted to remain at work.

That Rosie the Riveter was not middle class became obvious when studies were done of the financial responsibilities borne by working women during the war. One such survey, undertaken by the Division of Industrial Relations in New York state in March 1946, concluded:

> Women, like men, work because their earnings are needed to support themselves and their families and to meet home expenses . . . single women support themselves and aged parents . . . married women support themselves and dependents.[22]

Of the 1,114 women workers surveyed in cooperation with the United Electrical, Radio and Machine Workers of America from 1944 to 1946, one-fifth were the only contributing wage earners to their families and one-half were the main source of income for relatives living elsewhere. More than 80 percent of this group planned to continue working, 93 percent of these for financial reasons.

LAYOFFS

In 1919, after World War I, a reaction against women war workers had set in, due largely to the fear that lower-paid women would be competing with men for scarce jobs. The AFL trade unions at the time received the backing of the War Labor Board in demanding that women workers give up their jobs. A strike of male employees against the street railways in Cleveland, Ohio, forced the War Labor Board to order the company to dismiss all its women workers. By 1920, as a result of such pressure, the percentage of women employed was no larger than if there had been no abnormal increase in the preceding war years.[23]

Towards the end of World War II, in anticipation of a recurrence of the problems of converting from a war to a peacetime economy, a number of conferences were held around the country. Organizations, ranging in type from the YWCA and ad-hoc committees to unions and management leagues, focused on the fears and needs of the postwar world.[24] A conference sponsored by the Women's Department of the UAW and held December 4–6, 1944, was typical. Frieda Miller, recently appointed director of the Women's Bureau, attended, as did Eleanor Roosevelt and Helen Gahagan Douglas, Congresswoman from California.[25]

Four issues were isolated as crucial in protecting female employees from postwar dislocation and discrimination: equal pay for equal work; postwar reemployment; wages; and seniority. In addition, the conference concerned itself with child care, maternity leaves, and the question of greater female participation in union activities. The equal rights amendment was still mostly condemned. The longest discussion turned on the issues relating to seniority, to which we have devoted an entire section in this paper. The resolution which was finally adopted called for strict application of seniority and the elimination of all discriminatory practices and clauses in contracts, and for the elimination of all separate seniority lists for men and women. (The resolution was adopted by the UAW in 1946.) Mrs. Roosevelt summed up the spirit of the meeting when she said she hoped women would not become "expendable home-front soldiers."[26]

Fundamental to the thinking of the union was the commitment to "full employment" which was to be an obligation of industry as compensation for its high profit margin during the war. One advantage of the total employment concept was that it relieved the union of having to take sides in a male/female or even a Negro/white competition for scarce jobs. Indeed, the final resolution passed at the meeting stated that "women do not want special consideration or privilege" in the postwar readjustment.[27] . . .

The conferences prevented nothing. Already in August 1944, early cutbacks,

monitored by the UAW, revealed that a disproportionate number of female employees were being laid off. In aircraft parts plants for example, although women amounted to 42.2 percent of the total working population, they constituted 60.2 percent of the workers laid off. In the aircraft engine plants, while women were 39.2 percent of the workers employed, they were 86 percent of the layoffs. In the truck and agricultural implements industry, women were 13.1 percent of the work force, but 51.6 percent of the layoffs. In ordinance, at 25.6 percent of the work force, they were 61 percent of the total layoffs.[28] Nothing in the women's contracts or performance, it appeared, was going to protect them from selective layoffs.

One reason was the conviction on the part of most that women did not want to work.[29] Since female attitudes toward layoffs were individual and idiosyncratic, no data has been accumulated systematically; however, our impression from reading selectively in grievances on file at the Labor and Urban Affairs Archives at Wayne State is that for the most part women war workers *expected* and *did not especially resent* being laid off as cutbacks marked the end of the war. What they did resent and what several filed grievances against was that *they were not rehired in accordance with their perceived seniority* when the plant was reconverted to postwar production, sometimes as early as one or two years later.[30] . . .

. . . In 1945 and 1946 . . . layoffs came suddenly and without much explanation. By February 1946, as a *New York Times* reporter wrote, "the courtship of women workers has ended." Four million fewer women were working than had worked at the peak employment period. In New York State alone women were down from a high of 33 percent of the work force to the prewar level of 27 percent. Unemployment figures for women had doubled. At Ford, where, as we have seen, women had not had factory jobs before the war, women were down to 4 percent of the work force from a peak of 22 percent.[31]

From union monitoring we get figures like the following: at Hoover Company, September 28, 1944—of 65 workers laid off, 55 were women; at Metal Stamping Job Shop, 98 percent of layoffs were women; at Aluminum Company of Ames, 50 percent of the layoffs were women; at American Brake and Block, 90 percent of the layoffs were women; at American Leather Products, 100 percent of the layoffs were women; at Asbestos Manufacturing Company, 100 percent of the layoffs were women; at Baker Roulang Company, 100 percent of the layoffs were women.[32]

Rationalizations flew thick and fast. Lucy Greenbaum, in the *New York Times* article cited above, quoted a Ford spokesman as saying that the wartime light assembly work that women could do was being replaced by the heavy, tiring assembly work of cars that women could not "handle." From the Oliver Company in Springfield, Ohio, that had manufactured 40mm antiaircraft shells came a report to UAW headquarters that of the male employees who were taken off war work, 50 percent had been placed in other jobs in the plant.

> There are jobs in this plant at the present time, but they are not suitable for female workers. The work is too heavy. The girls may find work in this area, but naturally it will have to be at lower wages as most plants seem to be asking for male workers.[33] . . .

SENIORITY

It is our impression, after this preliminary survey, that the bulk of the women war workers were not surprised or upset at being laid off at war's end, but did expect that seniority would be honored in rehiring. They did not want "special treatment," as the December 1944 conference said explicitly, but they wanted equal access to jobs. The issue of seniority, then, was a central one, made complicated by the fact that one cannot generalize about seniority arrangements, since they varied by union contract and by industry.

The war presented such an abnormal situation that ordinary expectations and ordinary standards could not be set or met. As demand for certain war products ended, for example, whole departments of plants closed down. Seniority, then, to be meaningful, had to be (1) "plant-wide" so that employees relocated from one to another department could retain their accumulated seniority wherever they went and (2) not "separate" for females and Negroes, as had so often been the case in seniority listing before the war.

A closer look at some union contracts reveals the stickiness of the issue of seniority. One contract, signed between the UAW and Ford Motor Company and which covered workers in most Ford-operated plants during much of the war, was dated November 4, 1942, that is, shortly after the demands of the wartime economy were beginning to be felt. Management was to provide broad protection for workers on a number of important points, and the union in return promised not to strike during the war emergency.[34] Although the document was supplemented by additional agreements reached on May 10, 1943, and on June 6, 1943, the salient paragraphs regarding seniority and rehiring rights are in the original version.

Seniority was defined in the contract as the right to employment after a six-month probationary period in order of the date of original hire. Whether seniority was to be by interchangeable occupational groups or plant-wide was to be determined locally. Thus far, the contract is not unusual. But there was to be a distinction made between employees who were working on or before June 20, 1941, and those who came to work later (presumably after Pearl Harbor). For the first group, seniority was to be cumulative from the first day of employment and would obtain even if there had been a "break" in employment not exceeding four years. Thus, long before the war's outcome or its duration could have been known, the contract promised preferential treatment to persons on the payroll in early 1941 and arranged to protect the seniority of persons, presumably male, who would be leaving their employ for a "break" in the armed forces. . . .

. . . This all but guaranteed the former worker who had been drafted a job. . . .

Another mode of differentiating seniority, found in other union contracts, was to retain separate seniority listings even when women and Negroes were assigned, because of the emergency, to formerly males-only or by tradition whites-only jobs. A typical clause, taken from the Federal Mogul Corporation's contract with Local 202, reads:

> . . . all female employees hired subsequent to July 1, 1942, shall be placed on a special seniority list and shall be considered as male replacements and as having been hired solely because of the shortage of male labor, and their tenure of employment shall be limited to the duration of the war, or as soon thereafter as they can be replaced by former male employees or other male applicants.[35]

In another contract between H. A. Douglas and Local 822, the clause read:

> In cases where women are presently employed on jobs which are defined as a man's job . . . it is agreed that as soon as the labor supply becomes adequate, men will be placed on these jobs without regard to seniority and women will continue to maintain their seniority separate and apart from men.

Separate was by no means equal, as the following excerpt from a Lamson and Sessions contract with Local 217 reveals:

> The Company shall have the right to transfer or place men temporarily on jobs

normally performed by women and to pay men's wages for such work without establishing males' rates for females when females are later returned to the job.

Finally, and most explicit, was a clause in a contract between United Steel & Wire and Local 704 which read:

> When a man is the youngest employee in a classification involved in a reduction of force . . . he shall be permitted to bump any woman filling a job designated as a man's job by job evaluation. . . .
>
> In case of plant-wide layoff, women employees holding duly designated men's jobs will be laid off before any man employee. . . . A woman employee is not permitted to bump a man employee off a man's job.

Job classification, then, as revealed by these agreements, was to be the loophole in the entire seniority system as regards women. A woman working in a "man's job" during the war could be bumped off that job at the end of the war, her seniority rights notwithstanding, simply because it was in a separate classification of "men's only jobs." If, at the same plant, no "women's jobs" remained available, she could legitimately be laid off altogether. The only protection a woman worker had against such discriminatory laying off was (1) where no men's or women's job classifications existed, or (2) where there were nondiscrimination clauses incorporated into the union contracts, along with general seniority provisions.

How seniority was to be honored after the war was over, however, was an even stickier matter. On the one hand, the unions had used seniority as a selling point to women workers. As one union brochure stated:

> History must not be allowed to repeat itself. . . . Join a union. Secure equal seniority with men. Seniority forms the basis of your right to a job in the plant. It should not depend on sex or race.[36] . . .

Wherever one stood on the issue of veterans' rights, it was clear to everyone that "postwar employment would weaken the entire seniority structure." Returning servicemen, women who wanted to stay in the industry, upgraded workers who refused to go back to assembly or common laborers' jobs, these all constituted pressure groups interested in breaking seniority rules. In some plants, as we have seen in our review of the UAW contract with Ford, the union interpreted the Selective Service Act of 1940 to mean that a worker's seniority accumulated on his old job while he was in the armed service and that upon his discharge he would be entitled to reemployment in order of relative senior standing. In other plants an even stronger position was taken on returning servicemen's rights, and it was assumed that "the Selective Service Act requires the reemployment of *all* servicemen regardless of their relative seniority standing in the plant."[37]

The problems going into the postwar period, then, were these: First, the position of the Selective Service was simply unenforceable since the federal government was not able to guarantee jobs in private industry to anyone; second, no "guarantee" could apply to the needs of those servicemen who had not worked prior to entering the service; and third, except if there were full employment, all such accommodation would be at the expense of the seniority rights of women and other minority workers.

Union leadership was aware of all the dangers. Victor Reuther, assistant director of the War Policy Division of the UAW, wrote to his brother Walter on March 16, 1944:

> It seems most employers are generally agreed that a line should be drawn probably at the date of Pearl Harbor, and that all veterans with no previous work experience should be given priority in employment as against those hired in war industries since Pearl Harbor. . . . I think

this is a very dangerous approach for the union to take, particularly in Pontiac, where large numbers of Negroes have been upgraded or integrated into plants, the bulk of whom, as well as many women, will be thrown out of work as the result of such an agreement.[38] . . .

That individual women workers resisted these developments is illustrated by the protests and picketing that went on at the Ford Highland Park plant in December 1945, for example, when 200 women picketed and demanded an end to alleged discriminatory practices by the company.[39] General Motors workers in Pontiac, Michigan, held regular meetings on the subject of women's seniority rights. A regional conference of UAW women workers met in November and December 1945 on the same subject. One victory is reported on behalf of women against General Motors in May 1947. The company had laid women off in 1945 and then rehired them in the late spring and early fall of 1946. By November 1946 the corporation's recruitment campaign to attract (male) workers from other parts of Michigan and from out of state had borne fruit and the women were fired, allegedly because they had become a "distracting influence." The order bypassed women with seniority and also ignored employees on guaranteed probation. Local 653 filed a grievance and 150 General Motors women were rehired.[40] Elsewhere, however, the union did not always press claims brought by women against their companies.

The Equal Rights Amendment, of course, would have rendered job classifications unconstitutional had it been passed before or during the war. But the controversy that surrounded the proposed amendment reveals again the ambivalence on the part of women and of labor unions when the question of women's rights was in conflict with women's protection. Separate job classifications were in our view the inevitable corollary of protective legislation. Although numerous protective requirements were suspended during the war to permit women to do "men's jobs" temporarily, states needed only to revive these requirements after the war in order to take men's jobs away from women.

Thus were seniority rights, layoffs, and women's protective laws enmeshed.

PROTECTIVE LEGISLATION

During the first two years of the war, provision was made in twenty states and in the District of Columbia, through enactment of laws or grants of emergency powers to executive officers, for extension of maximum daily or weekly working hours for women. Night work laws were modified in eight states, and in four states various occupations, previously covered by work-hour limitations, were exempted. Two states reduced the number of occupations denied women.[41] In most cases, the exemption granted was a special exemption and not a general modification. In her 1943 annual report, Secretary of Labor Frances Perkins recommended postwar revocation of all permits granted in the war period for more than eight-hour days or "grave-yard" shifts.[42] An example of the protections for women required by the State of Michigan in 1942 is:

Provisions Governing Employment of Women in the State of Michigan

1. Women shall not be required to remain standing constantly, and seats shall be provided.

2. Women shall not be required to lift more than 35 pounds in the course of their regular work, provided that women shall not be required to lift more than 20 pounds when ascending stairs.

3. Women shall be prohibited from doing any type of overhead lifting or stacking.

4. Women shall be prohibited from employment in foundries (except in core rooms).

5. Employment of women shall be prohibited in the handling of any of the following harmful substances or in the following operations, unless ventilation and working conditions are approved by the Department of Labor and Industry: a. Lead; b. Benzene; c. Carbon disulphide; d. Mercury; e. Arc welding; f. Dry grinding wheels.

6. Women's dressing rooms and first aid stations shall be furnished with a bed or cot.

7. Women shall not be employed in any other type of employment disproportionate to their strength or in any way detrimental to their morals, health, or potential capacity for motherhood.

8. No employer shall discriminate in any way in the payment of wages as between male and female employees in the manufacture or production of any article of like value either on piece work or time basis.

9. No women employed in manufacturing shall be required to work longer than 54 hours per week, not more than an average of 9 hours per day, and not over 10 hours in any one day.

Recommended Employment Practice

1. Female employees should be required to wear proper safety clothing.

2. Definite rest periods of fifteen minutes in morning and afternoon should be established.

3. Where possible, sanitary lunch room facilities should be made available.[43]

One of the functions of the UAW Women's Bureau was to act in an advisory capacity to management in regard to male and female job classifications. Although the Women's Bureau at the time stood in favor of protective laws and separate job classifications, the women found, when forced to apply their judgment to specific jobs, that they could "always think of *one* woman who could do any man's job."[44] Adjustments were made, however, to expand the jobs that women could do. One large filling-station chain, for instance, devised a tilting cradle to lift big jugs of distilled water for filling battery kits. Leverage tools were made to get tires out of rims without strain, and a new gadget on grease guns simplified the job of filling them. All these innovations, according to the *Wall Street Journal,* were going to be retained in peacetime.[45] Thus, the net effect of women taking over men's jobs, given the protective restrictions, was to improve the working and safety conditions which would eventually benefit men as well.

However, in the initial stages there was an incremental cost attached to putting women onto men's jobs. The new or improved equipment, the cost of lunch and rest periods, the transportation provided for night shift work, and the proportion of child-care cost, if any, provided by the corporation, all could be used to justify paying women lower rates for the same work done. Thus, protective legislation became in time an issue in regard to equal pay for equal work.

EQUAL PAY FOR EQUAL WORK

The "double standard" in industrial wage rates dates back to the beginning of the Industrial Revolution when the status of women as the "weaker sex" was accepted even by women themselves. The first significant revolt against wage differentials based on sex came during the first World War, when women found themselves able to do men's work and carry men's responsibilities. In 1917 the War Labor Board issued a policy supporting the principle of equal pay for equal work. When during World War II the National War Labor Board, the arbiter of price, wage, and

profit controls for the entire economy, finally adopted the principle of equal pay for equal work and heard specific cases on the subject, a precedent was set which eighteen years later would find its way into congressional legislation and become a goal of American industrial equity.

The problem of equal pay for equal work was and still remains complicated by standard hiring rate differentials, the widespread practice of designating certain job classifications as female and others as male in union contracts with management, and the rest periods, lunch periods, additional supervision, and occasional help needed by women which are or are thought to be unnecessary when men are employed. The reason the National War Labor Board got involved in the issue at all was through its control over wage rates. As women found themselves doing jobs identical to those done by men and protested their lower wage rates, permission had to be obtained from the board in order to raise their wages. Thus, when in November 1942 the board issued General Order 16, accepting the principle of equal pay for equal work, it was careful to *permit* wage increases to accommodate achievement of equity but not to *require* them. Some states did require equal pay at the time, however. They were Illinois, Michigan, Montana, New York, and Washington.[46]

Numerous cases came up before the board for the purpose of defining the principle of equal pay for equal work. One of the earliest was the Norman-Hoffman Bearing Corporation case. The judgment reached in this case was that women replacing men were entitled to the same wages for the same work, but that differentials based on a "proper time study" should be established for operations in which women required male assistance.[47]

Management could, of course, avoid paying women equal rates by slightly altering the job classifications to make them "different" and "unequal." Such practice, however, was explicitly outlawed by the board on September 26, 1942, when it ruled that "there should be no discrimination between employees whose production is substantially the same on comparable jobs."[48] The board continued by stating that the quantity and quality of production should be considered and not simply the physical characteristics of the operations. Still the board allowed proportionate adjustment in women's wages to be made if lower production or decreased performance were noticeable. There were some eighty cases that came before the national board and its regional units during the period of the war which bear witness to the fact that the principle of equal pay was difficult to apply.

The dynamics of the situation are not hard to recreate: the War Labor Board, committed to an anti-inflation policy, did not want to raise rates; the union did not want men's rates to be *lowered* to achieve equity with women. Indeed, one way to account for union pressure on behalf of women's equal pay is that the equal pay clauses in contracts were designed to protect the wage-earning potential of men when they returned from the war and were prompted by a fear that employers would try to reduce pay scales during the war because women were then holding jobs previously held by men. That the union was slow to see women as equal to men in their own ranks can be inferred from the fact that it was not until 1968 that a woman was elected to the UAW Board. . . .

We do not know the total number of equal pay cases brought by women during the war, but a few may give the flavor of the issues involved. One against Brown-Lipe Chapin, a General Motors plant in Syracuse, New York, netted an average of $500 per woman worker as pay was increased retroactively from $0.78 to $0.93 per hour.[49] Twelve hundred women at Hudson Car Company, for-

merly being paid $0.88 to $0.91 per hour for work for which men were getting $1.20 or more, filed a claim against the company. They, too, were awarded back pay and the case resulted in Hudson's promise to establish a single seniority list as well. The story does not end happily, however, as the women had to return to "women's jobs" after the war and in the fall of 1946 were again earning only $0.90 an hour.[50]

After the war, the equal pay decisions of the National War Labor Board were, of course, no longer binding. In any case, clerical workers and others had never been covered by the favorable rulings. To compensate, Congressmen Pepper of Florida and Morse of Oregon introduced the Equal Pay Act in 1945 and again in 1946 and 1947. The law was designed to eliminate discrimination in wage practices based on sex. Had it been approved, the Equal Pay Act would have:

1. Prohibited paying female employees at a lower rate than males for work of comparable quality or quantity;

2. prohibited discharging female employees and replacing them with males except to protect the reemployment rights of returned veterans.

The bill, of course, covered only industries engaged in interstate commerce, but in any case it was defeated on the floor when Senator Taft of Ohio argued for its postponement on the grounds that it would put another federal bureau into the executive office of every business in the country.[51]

Unions were not favorable to the Equal Pay Act, as George Meany revealed, on the grounds that equal pay should be a problem of collective bargaining and not one of federal legislation. Yet a Women's Bureau survey of collective bargaining agreements, undertaken in 1948, showed that only 17 percent had equal pay clauses.[52]

UNEMPLOYMENT COMPENSATION

As part of the myth that women workers were happy to be laid off, the newspapers after the war began to assert that women were looking forward to their unemployment compensation. The Wall Street Journal, on May 4, 1945, headlined an article: "Laid-Off Willow Run Workers 'Choosy' about New Jobs. Some Loafing. They Count on Unemployment Pay. Half the Women through with War Work." The article quoted many individual men and women talking of being laid off and concluded:

> Besides the workers who had had all the war plant work they wanted and the others who feel the urge for a little vacation before they take on a new job, there are a good many of those signifying a desire for immediate employment who have been turning up their noses at jobs offered them.[53]

The article never mentioned that pay differentials might have been the reason that the Willow Run employees were being "choosy," nor that Willow Run was not making equal efforts to place its female workers.

The other side of the story emerges out of a union report on the successful outcome of a struggle with the Michigan Unemployment Compensation Commission. The issue involved the requirement by the Unemployment Commission that to qualify for unemployment women seeking work must be willing to work all three shifts. Those women refusing (or not allowed under state law) to work the third shift, for example, were disqualified from unemployment compensation against their will.[54] Some women, though we do not yet have documentation on individual cases, were denied unemployment compensation when they refused jobs at lower rates of pay than they had been earning. Thus was the Unemployment Commission implicated in the more general attempt to force women to go back to "women's work."

CHILD CARE

About half of the war-employed women living with children of their own under 14 years of age arranged for the care of the children by relatives in the household. Other arrangements for caring for children varied widely.[55]

. . . Nursery schools contributed little to the child-care picture.

With 75 percent of the new workers married women and the official recognition that the lack of child-care centers could affect war production through high absenteeism, it was agreed during the war that child care ought to be provided. As Chafe suggests, the only issue was whether the government or the local community could provide the care. The first federal contribution was by Roosevelt in 1942 when $400,000 was allotted to assist local communities in funding child care. In 1943 the Lanham Act authorized the building of day-care centers with federal money. (Lanham had intended his bill to appropriate money for wartime "facilities," meaning factories, and the bill was interpreted to fund child care.)[56]

In 1945 another Lanham Bill, H.R. 3187, was introduced asking for $30 million to continue federal day-care centers after the war. Congressmen, in arguing against the bill, said "women should be driven back to their homes," and for this and other reasons the bill failed.[57] Instead, the Senate voted $20 million on July 15, 1945, to continue child-care centers through 1946, providing operating expenses but no money for expansion. After March 1, 1946, all federal support for child-care facilities ceased.

The UAW-CIO supported child-care appropriations by the federal government throughout. But increase in juvenile delinquency during the war years and the fear of psychological damage to children separated from the mother all militated against any permanent alteration in child-care patterns emerging from the war emergency. . . .

CONCLUSIONS

On February 21, 1946, the Women's Bureau called a conference to prepare suggested standards for union contract provisions affecting women. Of the six subjects covered—lunch periods, maternity leaves, discrimination, wages, seniority, and rest periods—only two would qualify under "protective legislation," as previously defined (lunch and rest periods); all the rest were meant to guarantee *equal* treatment. The maternity leave provision, for example, began with the sentence:

> Pregnancy shall not be grounds for dismissal of any women employee . . . and any woman absent from work for maternity purposes shall continue to accumulate seniority and shall retain full seniority until the expiration of one year from date of leaving . . . and shall upon returning to work be returned to her former job at a rate of pay not less than currently paid on the job at which she was formerly employed. . . .

Other recommendations were for clauses requiring that wage rates established under this contract shall be set by the job and not by the sex of the worker.

> Wage rates and job classifications [should be] based on job content. Jobs or departments shall not be designated by sex. All previously existing sex classifications shall be eliminated.

In terms of prevention of layoffs, the document stated explicitly that "no new employees shall be hired as long as women currently employed are available for upgrading" and recommended a general clause reading, "It is mutually agreed between the company and the union that no discrimination based on sex or marital status shall be practiced or permitted."[58]

What is interesting about this document is first that the Women's Bureau, which had emphasized *protective legislation* and not *equal rights* through most of the period up to the war, appears to have been educated by the union women during the war to the subtleties of factory discrimination. The second aspect of the document worth noting is that it assumes that there will be postwar compensation for wartime inequities, which of course never happens. At the very moment that the Women's Bureau Conference was formulating these standard clauses, corporations were, as we have seen, laying off women and not rehiring them or honoring their seniority.

The reasons that the Women's Bureau seems so peculiarly out of phase is a subject for a later paper. We have some evidence that there was real alienation between the UAW Women's Bureau, for example, and the National Women's Bureau. Perhaps the reason was the class difference dividing the women in Detroit from the women in Washington. But the Women's Bureau's ambivalence on the subject of women's rights is theoretical as well. After the war, the Bureau argued in a classic *non sequitur* that since women proved themselves during the war, they "therefore" could be expected to do competent work in very traditional, sex-stereotyped occupations. The pamphlet, written in January 1945 by the Director of the Bureau, discussed how the "skills" women had developed during the war could be turned to peacetime uses. She listed as "skills" their nimble fingers, their dexterity, and their perserverance; and she saw opportunities for women in the electrical industry, in radio parts and small metal products, in clocks, and in the new plastics.[59]

Another temptation was to reiterate after the war the familiar panegyric to the homemaker:

Though the. homemaker is not listed in the census as "gainfully employed," it is important to recognize her activities as an occupation. . . . She earns her living in services to home, family, community, society.[60]

For all the consciousness-raising, then, the Women's Bureau was still not willing to reconsider Mary Anderson's characterization of the Equal Rights Amendment as "vicious" or to support any view of the world which saw men and women in competition.

But if Frieda Miller, the economist who replaced Mary Anderson as Director of the Women's Bureau in 1944, was not yet willing to fight for equal rights, she was, as was the Bureau, committed to equal pay and equal right to work. The Bureau did show itself to be aware of postwar employment problems as well as gains when it reported in the January 12, 1947, issue of the *Balance Sheet* the facts that one million fewer women were working in 1947 than had been working in November 1945, and that many had left shipyard jobs at $60 per week to go into department store selling at lower wages and longer hours.[61] The report also noted that of the one million fewer women working, 500,000 were listed as unemployed (that is, actively seeking work) in 1947. This was to foreshadow the great shift among poor women onto unemployment and later welfare rolls.

Indeed, if as we have argued, Rosie the Riveter was probably a working woman before the war, the gains made during the war may have been such to make unacceptable a return to her *status quo ante*. Or, with technological and other shifts in the economy her kind of service job may have been permanently eliminated. Further research is needed to determine whether the women who worked in well paying jobs during the war found service jobs, became unemployed, or drifted into poverty during the fifties. We do not know what happened to every Rosie. What we do know is that by 1953 one million women were listed nationally as job seekers and that of these, the largest percentage were Negro women. Moreover, of the additional 37 million women reported as nonworkers (housewives), there is no way of knowing how many would have been working if they could.[62]

Regional shifts in employment and the increasing migration of the rural poor to the north and midwest are generally held responsible for the increase in welfare rolls in this same period. But possibly another way to account for the persistent one-third of America that remained poor throughout the fifties and sixties is to re-examine the opportunities for work and the average take-home pay for female heads of households in the period after World War II.

Notes

1. This is our conclusion based on research done so far. In an article entitled, "Women Discover Industry Is Hiring Men Only—And The Men Must Take Less Money," which appeared in the *Wall Street Journal* on November 15, 1945, the findings of an employment study made by the United States Employment Service and Social Security Board were reported: "Forty percent to 61% of the openings for women are clerical, sales, and service jobs but only 15% to 18% of the women claimants last worked in these fields." In the "Brief of the UAW-CIO Op-

posing the Proposed Equal Rights Amendment," the following commentary on postwar employment opportunities for women was made: "At the present time because of cutbacks in certain types of war production items, thousands of women members of the UAW-CIO have been laid off; thus the openings for women on war work are rapidly shrinking. These women have gone into other industries such as restaurants, motels, department stores, beauty parlors, etc."
2. "Report on Effect of Willow Run Bomber Plant Lay-Off," memorandum of

Director Cushman, War Manpower Commission, Michigan, to Detroit Area Labor Management Committee, May 1945.

3. Letter from Brendon Sexton, President, Local No. 50, Detroit, Michigan, to Victor Reuther, Assistant Director, War Policy Division, UAW, June 13, 1945.

4. Ibid.

5. Headline in a *Wall Street Journal* article, May 4, 1945: "Laid-Off Willow Run Workers 'Choosy' about New Jobs. Some Loafing."

6. Harold Pool and Lester M. Pearlman, "Recent Occupational Trends in the United States," *Monthly Labor Review*, Department of Labor, Bureau of Labor Statistics (August 1947), Vol. 65, No. 2, pp. 139ff. for information in this and preceding paragraphs.

7. "Sister Sue," *Ammunition*, March 1946. It should be noted that not all factory workers came from lower-level jobs. Edith Van Horn, an important contributor to this study, left Oberlin College to enter a factory during the war. Rockford and Mount Holyoke gave credit to students who spent time working in munitions factories. William H. Chafe, *The American Woman: Her Changing Social, Economic, and Political Roles, 1920–1970* (New York, 1972), pp. 138–42.

8. "Women Workers in Ten War Production Areas and Their Postwar Employment Plans," *Women's Bureau Bulletin* No. 209 (Washington, 1946), p. 27.

9. Chafe, pp. 142–43; "Negro Women War Workers," *Women's Bureau Bulletin* No. 205 (Washington, 1945), p. 18; "They Also Made Good," *Ammunition*, October 1945.

10. *Detroit News*, January 1945.

11. National War Labor Board, memorandum on equal pay, 1944.

12. Chafe, p. 159, and an unidentified newspaper story dated March 30, 1944.

13. *Detroit News*, November 7, 1944.

14. Chafe, p. 160.

15. *Detroit News*, November 26, 1943.

16. Frederick Crawford, "Women in Postwar Employment," *American Women in the Postwar World* (Newsweek Clubs Bureau, n.d.).

17. Frances Perkins, quoted by F. M. Brewer, "Women Workers after the War," *Editorial Research Report* 1, No. 16 (Washington, 1944).

18. "Women Workers in Ten War Production Areas and Their Postwar Employment Plans," pp. 5 and 45.

19. Statement of R. J. Thomas, President,

UAW-CIO, "On Employment of Women after the War," March 10, 1944. Further research on R. J. Thomas is required, since he is also known as having made public statements that were hostile to women. Walter Reuther's papers, which were not available to us at this time, may shed more light on the official and unofficial influence of the parent UAW on local unions in regard to sex discrimination.

20. A frequently appearing phrase in UAW propaganda is reference to the "Hitler" formula of no jobs for women. In an unpublished paper addressed to UAW women workers in UAW-CIO plants the following warning appears: "Fascism means degradation and misery for women workers. KKK—Kinder, Kirche, Kuche (Children, Church and Kitchen)—these are all the activities which Hitler says should be open to women."

21. *New York Times*, March 1, 1945, p. 26; "Women War Workers in Ten War Production Areas and Their Postwar Employment Plans," pp. 10 and 12.

22. "Why Women Work," Division of Industrial Relations, Department of Labor, New York (March 1946), p. 1.

23. Brewer, p. 286.

24. The National Federation of Business and Professional Women held a conference in July 1945 to study employment problems. Issues discussed were availability of counselling and permanent facilities, training of women for management positions, and discrimination against older women workers (*New York Times*, July 13, 1945, p. 8). In March of 1945 representatives from numerous women's groups and labor organizations convened in Indiana to draft "Reconversion blueprints." The blueprint called for analyzing job shifts, promoting fair layoff policies, fostering public employment service facilities, retraining women for postwar jobs, and promoting legislative programs to furnish these aims (*New York Times*, March 1, 1945, p. 18). A labor-management council was formed in Hartford (*New York Times*, August 24, 1945, p. 11). The YWCA held a conference in which representatives from industrial clubs in five states met to discuss retraining programs for women (*New York Times*, July 2, 1945, p. 12).

25. *Daily Worker*, December 1, 1944.

26. *Detroit News*; also, *UAW Policy Established by Convention Resolutions relative to Women Workers Rights, 1942–1968*, UAW, Women's Bureau, Detroit, Michigan, p. 19.

27. *Detroit News*, November 18, 1944.

28. "Why Women Work," p. 3.

29. See *Wall Street Journal* article, January 1, 1946.

30. Emil Mazey Collection, Archives of Labor History and Urban Affairs, Wayne State University, box 37 and box 39. Included in the boxes and filed by others throughout the Emil Mazey Collection are letters, committee proceedings, and other materials pertaining to the grievances filed by women.

31. Lucy Greenbaum, "Industries in U. S. Replacing Women," *New York Times*, February 19, 1946, p. 27.

32. Preliminary Inventory, Archives of Labor History and Urban Affairs, Wayne State University, folders entitled "Lay Offs." Reports for individual locals were filed for the years 1943 to 1945.

33. Letter from the president of the local union at Oliver Corporation, Springfield, Ohio, May 17, 1945.

34. "Agreement between International Union, United Automobile, Aircraft and Agricultural Implement Workers of America (UAW-CIO) and the Ford Motor Company, November 4, 1942 (Supplemental Agreements, May 10, 1943, and June 6, 1943)," Archives of Labor History, Wayne State University.

35. This clause and the others quoted below are taken from an interoffice communication from R. J. Thomas to Officers and Regional Directors, on the subject of "Seniority of Women Workers During the Reconversion Period," dated November 13, 1944. Archives of Labor History, Wayne State University. . . .

36. *Action Needed*, National Women's Trade Union of America League (Washington, 1944), p. 8.

37. *United Automobile Worker*, August 1, 1944. . . .

38. Letter, Victor Reuther, UAW, to Walter Reuther, UAW, March 16, 1944.

39. "Sister Sue," *Ammunition*, December 1945.

40. *UAW Fair Practices Sheet* 1:2 (May 1947).

41. Brewer, p. 297.

42. *New York Times*, February 13, 1945, p. 26.

43. Michigan Department of Labor and Industry, UAW-CIO Research Department report, November 1942.

44. From a private conversation with Lillian Hatcher, a staff member of the UAW Women's Bureau, in February 1973.

45. *Wall Street Journal*, January 22, 1946.

46. Brewer, p. 298.

47. Norman Hoffman Case, July 18, 1942, in Emil Mazey Collection.

48. UAW memorandum, "Early Decision on Women."

49. "Brown-Lipe Women Receive Big Checks Won by UAW-CIO," *United Automobile Worker*, July 15, 1945.

50. "Dorothy Scott at Hudson," *Ammunition*, September 1947.

51. *Congressional Record*, July 31, 1945, p. 10548. Refer also to Frieda Miller, "Equal Pay—Its Importance to the Nation," *Independent Woman*, November 1946; Lois Black Hunter, "Equal Pay at Work," *Independent Woman*, February 1948); and Carly R. Grantham, "Why Equal Pay Now?" *Independent Woman*, November 1945.

52. Chafe, p. 186.

53. *Wall Street Journal*, May 4, 1945; see also November 15, 1945.

54. *United Automobile Worker*, March 1, 1945.

55. "Women Workers in Ten War Production Areas and Their Postwar Employment Plans," p. 56.

56. Chafe, p. 164.

57. *United Automobile Worker*, July 1, 1945.

58. "Women's Bureau Conference," *Women's Bureau Bulletin* No. 224 (Washington, 1948).

59. Frieda Miller, "Employment Opportunities in Characteristic Industrial Occupations of Women," *Women's Bureau Bulletin* [no number] (Washington, January 1945).

60. "Advisory of War Manpower Commission Proposals: Post-war Employment Recommendations," *New York Times*, April 26, 1945.

61. "A Balance Sheet on Women's Employment," press release of Frieda Miller, Women's Bureau, January 12, 1947.

62. See UAW-CIO, 14th Convention Proceedings, Resolution 7 (1953).

DOCUMENTS: Minority Women—Work and Politics

ROBERT HAMBURGER
"My first job in New York"

As race relations deteriorated in the South at the turn of the century, blacks sought to escape racism, poverty, and the servitude of tenant farming by migrating north. When World Wars I and II created temporary jobs in industry, the migration increased. Between 1910 and 1920, for example, the number of southern-born blacks in the North jumped from 415,000 to 737,000. Women came north in even greater numbers than men, for employment agents traveled throughout the South recruiting black women for domestic work as immigrant women and their daughters moved on to other jobs. Statistics tell the story. In New York State alone black women made up 6 percent of the domestic workers in 1890, 21 percent in 1930, and 50 percent in 1970. Only in the last decade has this flow northward reversed as economic opportunities and race relations in the South improved.

As Robert Hamburger has pointed out, the decision of these women to migrate was a bold one, for the transition from the rural, small-town South to northern cities was not easy. Interviewing two of the more recent of these "new immigrants," Hamburger demonstrates through the stories of Roena Bethune and Rose Marie Hairston the lure of "the promised land," the discrepancy between promise and reality, and the capacity for survival that has distinguished generations of black women. Although some of these black domestics found work in homes pervaded by warmth and generosity, note how barriers of race and class could override the "bonds of womanhood" that black houseworkers presumably shared with the well-to-do white women for whom they often worked. To what extent has the job of domestic workers improved since the period described by David M. Katzman (part IIB)?

Excerpted from "A Stranger in the House" by Robert Hamburger, in *Southern Exposure* 5 (1977): 22–31. Copyright © 1977 by Robert Hamburger. Reprinted by permission of the author. An extended version of these narratives appears in Robert Hamburger, *A Stranger in the House* (New York: Macmillan, 1978).

ROENA BETHUNE

I was born the 14th of December, 1936, in a little small town called Fayetteville, North Carolina. Coming up as a child, I can remember us living in about a seven-room, white house on Merkson Road. My mother, she was a domestic worker. She worked in people's homes taking care of children and housekeeping. She could only do so much for us because she had to take care of all the bills and everything because our father had separated from us. My mother, she never received welfare checks. She always believed in going out and working and trying to take care of us herself. And I remembered the time that she would often tell us, "I don't know how I am going to make it, children, but by the help of the Lord we will make it."

She would earn something like $10 to $12 weekly, and we had to live off of this. She had very bad days and she had some good days. As for raising us, a daughter and a son, she would have to go out to work and leave us—and as me being the oldest child at home, I had a lot of work to do in the house. My mother would always tell me that I had to clean, and I had to cook if necessary. I was only about the age of nine years old when I started to learn about housekeeping. My mother had nobody to help her take care of us, but only herself.

Ever since I can remember, my mother worked for white families, but she never discussed with me about the hard times or nothing going on with the jobs. I was only a little girl; I can't remember so much about those times. The only thing that I know—she used to come in the house, and she'd be telling us, "Oh, my day was so hard. I had so much work to do, and I have to come home, and I have to do lots of things. You children have to help me out." That's about as much as I knew. I think my mother really didn't want us to know how hard times was.

But, you know, by looking on and observing you could see the expression on her face, you could tell when times come that wasn't so good.

I never went on the job with my mother. She used to work for this family —they had children growing up like me and my brother—and they would give my mother shoes and clothing for me and such things as that. When I was quite small, I didn't know no difference, but as I became to be a teenager I didn't like it because I wanted new clothes. My mother would bring things home, and I knew that she'd gotten them from someplace that she was working. I didn't want to wear them, cause in school the kids would laugh at you and say, "Ugh, your mother let you wear hand-me-down clothes." . . .

. . . After I was 15, things was better. And at 16, going on close to the age of 17, I was married. So that's about as much as I can say about coming up.

I met my husband in Fayetteville. We had an army base there which is called Fort Bragg. A lot of GIs was there, and my husband was a serviceman. We met each other downtown and we started talking. I was walking down the street and he was standing with some GIs at the corner. Myself and a couple of girl-friends was walking, and so the guys started talking, and so we just made a conversation, and he asked me if he could make a date with me. I hesitated, and we gossiped for a while. So I told him he could come back at Saturday afternoon. My mother didn't really approve of it. I started thinking about growing up and how you don't get things that you want, and I said, "Well I met this boy, a GI, and I know he have money, and he can maybe give you money sometimes and help out with, you know, if it might be something I wanted, he would get it for me." So we dated for about four months, and then we got married.

For five years we was very happy together, but then my husband—I really hate to say this—we started having trouble in the home. He started going outside, and he found something outside better than what he had in his home—or he thought he did. After that we separated and I came up to New York.

Believe me, I was here one week and I was ready to go back. I had heard a lot about the big city, and I had heard a lot about the bright lights. And when I came and I saw all the tall buildings and saw all the people moving in the streets, I said, "Who in the world could live in a place like this with the people in the street; they's pushing each other, it's overcrowded, and everybody's in a hurry, nobody have time to even speak to each other. How in the world can people live in a place like this?" And I was ready to go back home.

I was living with my brother and his wife. They had been living here already, about five years before I came to New York. So, my sister-in-law, she used to tell me, "Roena, you realize you never been in the city before, and the city is much different from just where you come from. You come from the South and you never seen a lot of people all in one place together like this. But if you stay here a while, you will like it. . . .

My first job in New York, I was a chambermaid doing household work at the Saint George Hotel in Brooklyn. As long as I worked in the hotel, the management was great. Dealing with the guests, that's where the little run-ins would come in. I would go in to make up the bed. As a routine, the customer occupying the room is supposed to be out of the room to let the maid make the room up. A couple of times when I'd go to the room the door would be unlocked—I'd go in the room and the man would be in the bathroom closed up, and he would say, "Come in, don't you like to make some fast money?" He'd be nude. I got very angry, very angry, and I

would run out of the room and go to the nearest telephone that was on the floor. I would call the desk and say, "The man in such-and-such a room, he's in the nude in the hotel, he's giving me a hard time, and I refuse to make this room up because he's not supposed to be in the room. He's offering me money, and I don't like to be going through stages like this because it's very terrible and embarrassing."

So the manager would say, "Well, just stand outside in the hallway, somebody'll be up in a few minutes and we'll get him out." So they'd come up and they'd talk to the guy and they'd get him to leave the room. Then I'd go in and make it up. Several times this happened.

There is a lot of things you go through working in a hotel. It was a very terrible embarrassment—some of the things, you wouldn't even want to approach nobody telling them about it. You try to get out of the room as fast as you can; you go down and make complaints. What can you do? These things happen living in a hotel.

I think it made a difference I was black —the way they would approach you, you know. You could read them, what they think, "Well, how much money can you be making for a job like this? I know that you will like to make extra money. You can't be making but so much, and nobody would never know about this but me and you. I can get over fast with you."

Now the way I feel about white people, I don't hate them or nothing, but I do have a little discrimination against them because, you know, it seems like they only class all the black people as one way. As far as I'm concerned with the white man or the white woman, when I go out there and I do a day's work for them, I just do my work. As far as I am concerned they don't love me and I cannot love them because I know that there is a space difference in between; there is a racial gap, because that white woman or white man that you go and work for in their house, when the time comes for them to serve dinner, they will not let you sit down at that dinner table and eat with them. They will tell you, "Serve us Roena, and then after you serve us you can have your dinner in the kitchen" where you do the cooking, not in the dining room where they sit down and eat their dinner themselves. So you know when things like this happen, there is a complex racial gap somewhere.

ROSE MARIE HAIRSTON

I was born in Martinsville, Virginia, 38 years ago. There's mostly furniture factories, farming, tobacco there. My family had their own house, but we didn't live there all the time. My parents moved to West Virginia, and my father was a coal miner. He was a motorman in the coal mine and a brakeman. A motorman drives down in the mine to bring the coal out. Sometimes he was a brakeman, and he would ride on the back of the little car, which was very dangerous. I forget what it's called, but from working in the mine he got fluid in his knees and elbows and up in his shoulder. And from getting his back hurt and his hip hurt six or seven times, it caused him to have a type of arthritis. My father started working at the coal mine at age 14, and he was retired about the time he got 40. He had been hurt a lot of times, you know; he was all broken up. . . .

In West Virginia we never knew anything about racial prejudice. Really, we never heard anything about that until we went back to the state of Virginia. Where we lived around the coal mine there was Jews, Italians, Hungarians, Poles and just about any race you could name. Everybody mingled together. When I was about 10, my brother Maurice and me went back to Virginia on the farm for a summer. We didn't know what they were talking about when they used to say "colored people." In West Virginia we didn't use the words. Everybody there was together. But when we were going to Virginia, we got off the bus to go to the bathroom, and we wanted something to eat, and we saw a sign said "Colored in the Rear." We went in there—it was a little, dirty, greasy room about the size of a good chicken house. It was so dirty in there. And then we wondered why all the white people were sitting up in the best part of the bus. Even the bathrooms said "No Colored." Even the telephones had big signs that said "No Colored." . . .

The schools was all black. We would get up at four o'clock and have breakfast and do some chores like milk the cows and feed the dogs and different little things like that. Then we would walk seven miles to catch a bus, and the bus would take us into town, and then after we got into town we would have about another mile to walk to school. . . .

When I was a little girl, I always had hopes of being a nurse or a doctor. I always wanted my husband to look like my father. I wanted my husband to be his height, his complexion. My daddy was not a big guy, but he was a handsome guy. I said if I ever married I wanted a big farm and a lot of children. One of my sisters, she wanted to be a doctor. Another one wanted to be a nurse, and one wanted to be a schoolteacher. We'd say that one day we'd be the Hairston clinic. We always wanted something that would help others. One time we said we'd work and make a lot of money, and then we'd go back to West Virginia and have an orphanage. Unfortunately, it never happened.

I was about sixteen-and-a-half, and I was reading a newspaper. It said, "Ladies and Girls 18 and over: Jobs in New York." And you didn't even have to pay to come to New York. And this ad said it paid $125 a week. I said, "Oh boy, that's good! I think I'll go up there and talk to this man." He was a preacher, too, and that's what made me mad. It was just another old gimmick. Anyway, I went up there and he interviewed me. He said, "How old are you?" I told him I was 18, and he kept looking at me.

He said, "I don't know, Rose, you look very young. Matter of fact, you look like you're no more than 12."

I said, "No, eighteen." So he told me to bring him proof that I was 18, or bring my mother. I told him all right. I caught the bus and went back home and got my cousin to come back with me. She was a much older lady than I was. She told them that she was my mother. She gave her consent for me to come to New York. So he said all right. He told me to come the next day and that he would meet me at the bus station. Then he described the persons that were to meet me in New York on 50th Street. So I met him the next day, and he gave me the bus ticket and he said, "Good luck, Rose." I said, "Yeah."

And he said, "When you make all that money, put it in the bank." I wasn't scared, I was determined because I thought $125 a week was a long ways from getting $7.50 a week.

I didn't tell my mother I was going. . . .

I went over to the bus station and met the preacher, Brother Plow. He was there with my bus ticket. I jumped on the bus. I was so excited. I was looking out the window, and I was listening good for the man to say New York. I was so excited. I said to myself, "Oooh, now I get to see the movie stars." I thought you'd probably see them on the streets. I had read a book about Harlem, and I was dying to see Harlem—125th Street, the Apollo Theater, and I was dying to see 42nd Street. I didn't understand what Wall Street was, you know. I thought it was somewhere all the rich people and celebrities be—that they'd be there just for you to look at.

When I got off in New York, I saw the people walking—it looked like everybody was walking fast and the cars was whizzing. I said, "Golly, if I get out there on this street, I'm gonna get hit by one of them cars. It's too crowded in New York." Then I saw there was two fellas, two Jewish fellas, there to meet me. I had a photograph of them. They told me that I should come with them, that they were there to meet me. While we were walking down the street, I would look up at the buildings and I ran into a stop-sign. After that I had a stiff neck from looking up at the buildings.

I got in their car and went out to the agency in Long Island. Leaving the city, I got disappointed. I said, "Oh my god, I just left the country and thought I was coming to the big city, and the man was trying to send me back to the country." The man in the agency would tell the people, "I have this nice girl here, she's very attractive, she's 18, and she's good with children." You know, they didn't know a thing about you. So they would say, "We'll bring her over in an hour, and when we get there, you have to give us $150." I said to myself, "He's selling the girls. I come all this way just to be bought and sold."

They took me out to this lady. I remember her well—Mrs. Burke at 250 Central Avenue in Cedarhurst. I got there and looked at this big old apartment building and I said, "It sure is a big old place." I had the idea that she lived there in that big old building all alone, and she expected me to clean it all by myself. I got in there in this little apartment, and she showed me through the rooms. I asked her, "Where do your children live?"

She said, "Here with me."

"Where would I live?"

"Here with me."

"Well, where?"

"You will live and sleep in this room with my children."

"I have to share this room with your children?"

I didn't like it because the little girl slept in a cradle and I slept in one bed and the little boy slept in one bed with me. I never liked to sleep with anybody. Then I had to get used to when the lady would get up early and leave, and you didn't see them no more til five or six or seven o'clock. Then she would come in and have something to eat. She didn't spend time with the children. I would think she don't love her children; she don't stay home. I wondered why.

I worked there about a month, and I kept asking her, "When is payday, when you going to pay me?" She said, "Oh, you'll get paid. Do you want me to give you money until you get paid?" So I said, "Yeah." So she gave me money. Her husband took me to Robert Hall's, and I think I bought a coat and two dresses and shoes. Anyway, I ran out of money, and he came over to the counter, and he asked me did I get everything I wanted, did I have enough money, and did I want anything else. I said no. The lady behind the counter said, "Gee, you have a good boss."

I said, "Boss?"

And she said, "Do you work for him? Is that your husband?"

"No, I work for him."

"Well, that's your boss."

I said, "Well, I just say it's somebody I work for."

When it came time to get paid, they didn't owe me, I owed them. It came up a big argument. I told her I was supposed to get $125 a week. She said, "No, I'll show you on the contract." So she went and got this contract, and she showed it to me. We was only supposed to get $100 a month.

I told her to get in touch with this agency. I told her, "I'm from the country, but I got sense enough not to work for $100 a month. I could stay at home and work for $100 a month." We called the agency, and the agency had went out of business.

She told me that she couldn't afford to pay $125 a week. She said, "You don't do a lot of cooking." I said, "Yeah, I understand that, but I sits here day and night taking care of your children, taking them to parks. I had to spend my money, cause when I take them to the store they be hollering about what they want. I didn't want to be embarrassed, so I used my money to buy them things."

She offered me $40 a week, and I told her I'd try it for awhile till I found something better.

After that she began to get very nasty and prejudiced. When her company came, she said she didn't want me to sit in the other room and watch TV. I would have to go back into my room until her company left. One day she asked me, "You wasn't used to eating steak and pork chops in West Virginia, were you?"

I told her, "Yes, I was used to good food in West Virignia."

So she said, "Well, the maids don't get treated like the family."

I said, "Well, I don't know what you mean by 'maid.' A maid is somebody who works in a hotel, right?"

"No, all of you that came up here are maids to us."

So I said, "Oh, you mean that this will be something like slavery time?"

She was from Georgia, and people were still treated like slaves in the Deep South till about 1960. I began to get very angry when she told me her parents had a lot of slaves. Then she said, "I wish it was slavery time, I'd make a good slave out of you." I got real mad and cursed her. One word followed another word, and then I got so mad that I slapped her. I slapped her hard as I could. I went into the bathroom, and the little boy came into the bathroom and bit me on the leg. I looked at him a long time and then I grabbed him. I started to throw him in the bathtub, but then I thought better of it. So I grabbed him and picked him up, and I turned him upside down by his feet and started to shake him. Then I just got so mad that I took his head and I put it in the commode.

She asked me was I crazy. I told her no. She said, "Well, you had better go back to West Virginia where they allow you to do that."

I told her that I was going to get me another job. I got my clothes and I went to a friend's house. Later, I called Mrs. Burke and asked her to pay me, and she said she would pay me when I stopped by. I felt a little uneasy going back, so I asked this boy, one of my friends to go with me. He went and got his two brothers and said, "Come on, go with me back to get the rest of Rose's things." They were great big guys, six foot four.

So I rang the doorbell, and she said, "Who is it?"

I said it was Rose.

She said, "Well come on in."

I started to open the door, and my boyfriend said, "Let me open it." So he opened the door, and when he opened the door, he looked behind the door, and Mr. Burke was standing behind it with a car jack. I guess he was going to hit me. And her mother, father and brother was standing there waiting for me.

I got my money and the rest of my things, and she tried to talk me into staying, but I didn't fall for it. I just laughed a lot. I guess it runs in my family, my mother laughs a lot too. So I got me another job.

ANNE MOODY
"Involved in the Movement"

For Afro-American women the politics of reform and the politics of inclusion merged. For most southern black women, the passage of the Equal Suffrage Amendment was meaningless because most blacks, especially in the deep South, were not permitted to vote whether male or female. Without political power they were unable to fight segregation laws, which consigned blacks to second-class citizenship and economic privation. The National Association for the Advancement of Colored People (NAACP), however, could do so. Founded in 1909, during the progressive era, by blacks and whites—many of the latter women associated with the settlement house movement—and based in New York, the NAACP established a Legal Defense Fund administered by a small staff of highly skilled lawyers who chipped away at *de jure* segregation in a series of important court cases. The 1954 Supreme Court decision, *Brown* v. *Board of Education*, which rejected as unconstitutional the doctrine of "separate but

Excerpted from "The Movement," pt. 4 of *Coming of Age in Mississippi* by Anne Moody (New York: Dial Press, 1968). Copyright © 1968 by Anne Moody. Reprinted by permission of The Dial Press.

equal" in the field of public education, marked the culmination of decades of litigation. By the mid-1950s blacks had reason to believe that the era of segregation and disfranchisement was coming to an end and that Afro-Americans could regain the political and civil rights that in the South especially had been so long denied.

When expectations aroused by the *Brown* decision were frustrated by white recalcitrance, blacks opted for a new strategy through which to attack segregation. That strategy was one of nonviolent direct action. Although the Montgomery bus boycott in 1956 marked the first such action involving thousands of protesters, the sit-ins that took place at a Woolworth lunch counter in Greensboro, North Carolina, in 1960 inaugurated a new stage in the struggle for equal rights. In the months that followed, thousands of young blacks and their white supporters engaged in sit-ins in restaurants, pray-ins at white churches, wade-ins at segregated beaches, and finally "freedom rides" and voter registration drives. Such massive protests prodded the conscience of the nation and resulted in passage of the Civil Rights Act of 1964 and a subsequent Voting Rights Act.

Anne Moody, the daughter of an impoverished black farm family in Mississippi, had worked as a domestic as a teen-ager. A student at Tougaloo College during the early 1960s, she became immersed in the struggle for racial justice. For her, as for many other women, white as well as black, participation in civil rights demonstrations meant risking family disapproval, physical violence, and the possibility of death. Her courage and her commitment to political change ultimately had economic overtones as well. Without gains brought about by the black revolution of the 1960s, Moody and countless women of her generation would have had little opportunity to escape the poverty and racism that had constrained the lives of their mothers and grandmothers. This struggle for freedom, equality, and autonomy on the part of black women in the civil rights movement would not be lost on their white counterparts, as birth of a new feminist movement would ultimately demonstrate.

I had counted on graduating in the spring of 1963, but as it turned out, I couldn't because some of my credits still had to be cleared with Natchez College. A year before, this would have seemed like a terrible disaster, but now I hardly even felt disappointed. I had a good excuse to stay on campus for the summer and work with the Movement, and this was what I really wanted to do. I couldn't go home again anyway, and I couldn't go to New Orleans—I didn't have money enough for bus fare.

During my senior year at Tougaloo, my family hadn't sent me one penny. I had only the small amount of money I had earned at Maple Hill. I couldn't afford to eat at school or live in the dorms, so I had gotten permission to move off campus. I had to prove that I could finish school, even if had to go hungry every day. I knew Raymond and Miss Pearl were just waiting to see me drop out. But something happened to me as I got more and more involved in the Movement. It no longer seemed important to prove anything. I had found something outside myself that gave meaning to my life.

I had become very friendly with my social science professor, John Salter, who was in charge of NAACP activities on campus. All during the year, while the NAACP conducted a boycott of the downtown stores in Jackson, I had been one of Salter's most faithful canvassers and church speakers. During the last week of school, he told me that sit-in demonstrations were about to start in Jackson and that he wanted me to be the spokesman for a team that would sit-in at Woolworth's lunch counter. The two other demonstrators would be classmates of mine, Memphis and Pearlena. Pearlena was a dedicated NAACP worker, but Memphis had not been very involved in the Movement on campus. It seemed that the organization had had a rough time finding students who were in a position to go to jail. I had nothing to lose one way or the other. Around ten o'clock the morning of the demonstrations, NAACP headquarters alerted the news services. As a result, the police department was also informed, but neither the policemen nor the newsmen knew exactly where or when the demonstrations would start. They stationed themselves along Capitol Street and waited.

To divert attention from the sit-in at Woolworth's, the picketing started at J. C. Penney's a good fifteen minutes before. The pickets were allowed to walk up and down in front of the store three or four times before they were arrested. At exactly 11 A.M., Pearlena, Memphis, and I entered Woolworth's from the rear entrance. We separated as soon as we stepped into the store, and made small purchases from various counters. Pearlena had given Memphis her watch. He was to let us know when it was 11:14. At 11:14 we were to join him near the lunch counter and at exactly 11:15 we were to take seats at it.

Seconds before 11:15 we were occupying three seats at the previously segregated Woolworth's lunch counter. In the beginning the waitresses seemed to ignore us, as if they really didn't know what was going on. Our waitress walked past us a couple of times before she noticed we had started to write our own orders down and realized we wanted service. She asked us what we wanted. We began to read to her from our order slips. She told us that we would be served at the back counter, which was for Negroes.

"We would like to be served here," I said.

The waitress started to repeat what she had said, then stopped in the middle of the sentence. She turned the lights out behind the counter, and she and the other waitresses almost ran to the back of the store, deserting all their white customers. I guess they thought that violence would start immediately after the whites at the counter realized what was going on. There were five or six other people at the counter. A couple of them just got up and walked away. A girl sitting next to me finished her banana split before leaving. A middle-aged white woman who had not yet been served rose from her seat and came over to us. "I'd like to stay here with you," she said, "but my husband is waiting."

The newsmen came in just as she was leaving. They must have discovered what was going on shortly after some of the people began to leave the store. One of the newsmen ran behind the woman who spoke to us and asked to identify herself. She refused to give her name, but said she was a native of Vicksburg and a former resident of California. When asked why she had said what she had said to us, she replied, "I am in sympathy with the Negro movement." By this time a crowd of cameramen and reporters had gathered around us taking pictures and asking questions, such as Where were we from? Why did we sit-in? What organization sponsored it? Were we students? From what school? How were we classified?

I told them that we were students at Tougaloo College, that we were represented by no particular organization, and that we planned to stay there even after the store closed. "All we want is service," was my reply to one of them. After they had finished probing for about twenty minutes, they were almost ready to leave.

At noon, students from a nearby white high school started pouring in to Woolworth's. When they first saw us they were sort of surprised. They didn't know how to react. A few started to heckle and the newsmen became interested again. Then the white students started chanting all kinds of anti-Negro slogans. We were called a little bit of everything. The rest of the seats except the three we were occupying had been roped off to prevent others from sitting down. A couple of the boys took one end of the rope and made it into hangman's noose. Several attempts were made to put it around our necks. The crowds grew as more students and adults came in for lunch.

We kept our eyes straight forward and did not look at the crowd except for occasional glances to see what was going on. All of a sudden I saw a face I remembered—the drunkard from the bus station sit-in. My eyes lingered on him just long enough for us to recognize each other. Today he was drunk too, so I don't think he remembered where he had seen me before. He took out a knife, opened it, put it in his pocket, and then began to pace the floor. At this point, I told Memphis and Pearlena what was going on. Memphis suggested that we pray. We bowed our heads, and all hell broke loose. A man rushed forward, threw Memphis from his seat, and slapped my face. Then another man who worked in the store threw me against an adjoining counter.

Down on my knees on the floor, I saw Memphis lying near the lunch counter with blood running out of the corners of his mouth. As he tried to protect his face, the man who'd thrown him down kept kicking him against the head. If he had worn hard-soled shoes instead of sneakers, the first kick probably would have killed Memphis. Finally a man dressed in plain clothes identified himself as a police officer and arrested Memphis and his attacker.

Pearlena had been thrown to the floor. She and I got back on our stools after Memphis was arrested. There were some white Tougaloo teachers in the crowd. They asked Pearlena and me if we wanted to leave. They said that things were getting too rough. We didn't know what to do. While we were trying to make up our minds, we were joined by Joan Trumpauer. Now there were three of us and we were integrated. The crowd began to chant, "Communists, Communists, Communists." Some old man in the crowd ordered the students to take us off the stools.

"Which one should I get first?" a big husky boy said.

"That white nigger," the old man said.

The boy lifted Joan from the counter by her waist and carried her out of the store. Simultaneously, I was snatched from my stool by two high school students. I was dragged about thirty feet toward the door by my hair when someone made them turn me loose. As I was getting up off the floor, I saw Joan coming back inside. We started back to the center of the counter to join Pearlena. Lois Chaffee, a white Tougaloo faculty member, was now sitting next to her. So Joan and I just climbed across the rope at the front end of the counter and sat down. There were now four of us, two whites and two Negroes, all women. The mob started smearing us with ketchup, mustard, sugar, pies, and everything on the counter. Soon Joan and I were joined by John Salter, but the moment he sat down he was hit on the jaw with what appeared to be brass knuckles. Blood gushed from his face and someone threw salt into the open wound. Ed King, Tougaloo's chaplain, rushed to him.

At the other end of the counter, Lois and Pearlena were joined by George Raymond, a CORE field worker and a student from Jackson State College. Then a Negro high school boy sat down next to me. The mob took spray paint from the counter and sprayed it on the new demonstrators. The high school student had on a white shirt; the word "nigger" was written on his back with red spray paint.

We sat there for three hours taking a beating when the manager decided to close the store because the mob had begun to go wild with stuff from other counters. He begged and begged everyone to leave. But even after fifteen minutes of begging, no one budged. They would not leave until we did. Then Dr. Beittel, the president of Tougaloo College, came running in. He said he had just heard what was happening.

About ninety policemen were standing outside the store; they had been watching the whole thing through the windows, but had not come in to stop the mob or do anything. President Beittel went outside and asked Captain Ray to come and escort us out. The captain refused, stating the manager had to invite him in before he could enter the premises, so Dr. Beittel himself brought us out. He had told the police that they had better protect us after we were outside the store. When we got outside, the policemen formed a single line that blocked the mob from us. However, they were allowed to throw at us everything they had collected. Within ten minutes, we were picked up by Reverend King in his station wagon and taken to the NAACP headquarters on Lynch Street.

After the sit-in, all I could think of was how sick Mississippi whites were. They believed so much in the segregated Southern way of life, they would kill to preserve it. I sat there in the NAACP office and thought of how many times they had killed when this way of life was threatened. I knew that the killing had just begun. "Many more will die before it is over with," I thought. Before the sit-in, I had always hated the whites in Mississippi. Now I knew it was impossible for me to hate sickness. The whites had a disease, an incurable disease in its final stage. What were our chances against such a disease? I thought of the students, the young Negroes who had just begun to protest, as young interns. When these young interns got older, I thought, they would be the best doctors in the world for social problems.

Before we were taken back to campus, I wanted to get my hair washed. It was stiff with dried mustard, ketchup and sugar. I stopped in at a beauty shop across the street from the NAACP office. I didn't have on any shoes because I had lost them when I was dragged across the floor at Woolworth's. My stockings were sticking to my legs from the mustard that had dried on them. The hairdresser took one look at me and said, "My land, you were in the sit-in, huh?"

"Yes," I answered. "Do you have time to wash and style it?"

"Right away," she said, and she meant right away. There were three other ladies already waiting, but they seemed glad to let me go ahead of them. The hairdresser was real nice. She even took my stockings off and washed my legs while my hair was drying.

There was a mass rally that night at the Pearl Street Church in Jackson, and the place was packed. People were standing two abreast in the aisles. Before the speakers began, all the sit-inners walked out on the stage and were introduced by Medgar Evers. People stood and applauded for what seemed like thirty minutes or more. Medgar told the audience that this was just the beginning of such demonstrations. He asked them to pledge themselves to unite in a massive offensive against segregation in Jackson, and throughout the state. The rally ended with "We shall Overcome" and sent home hundreds of determined people. It seemed as though Mississippi Negroes were about to get together at last.

Before I demonstrated, I had written Mama. She wrote me back a letter, begging me not to take part in the sit-in. She even sent ten dollars for bus fare to New Orleans. I didn't have one penny, so I kept the money. Mama's letter made me mad. I had to live my life as I saw fit. I had made that decision when I left home. But it hurt to have my family prove to me how scared they were. It hurt me more

than anything else—I knew the whites had already started the threats and intimidations. I was the first Negro from my hometown who had openly demonstrated, worked with the NAACP, or anything. When Negroes threatened to do anything in Centreville, they were either shot like Samuel O'Quinn or run out of town, like Reverend Dupree.

I didn't answer Mama's letter. Even if I had written one, she wouldn't have received it before she saw the news on TV or heard it on the radio. I waited to hear from her again. And I waited to hear in the news that someone in Centreville had been murdered. If so, I knew it would be a member of my family.

JESSIE LOPEZ de la CRUZ
"The first woman farmworker organizer out in the fields"

The tobacco and cotton fields of the rural Southeast were a continent away from the prune and apricot fields of San Jose, California; the ethnic and religious background of Mollie Goodwin equally distant from that of Jessie Lopez de la Cruz. Yet these two women had much in common during their early years: a strict upbringing, early marriage, and a constant struggle with poverty, pregnancy, and illness. That their lives subsequently diverged had much to do with the organizing activities of Cesar Chavez, whose drive to unionize farm workers received national attention in the 1960s. Note the similarities involved in the response to unionization by women workers described by Lopez de la Cruz and by Alice Kessler-Harris (part IIB) and the critical difference made by the contrasting attitudes of Gompers and Chavez. Note, too, the persistent opposition of employers to unionization, whether in 1900 or 1960. The movement of Jessie Lopez de la Cruz from farm worker to union organizer to community leader and Chicano spokeswoman to membership on the California Commission on the Status of Women makes her story not only a part of the long struggle of workers to organize but also of a more recent struggle of minorities and women to improve their position in American society. If Jessie Lopez de la Cruz shared much in terms of her early life with Mollie Goodwin, she also shared with Anne Moody a determination to change the conditions that had left her and so many women like her impoverished and powerless.

CHILDHOOD

My grandmother was born in Mexico in Aguas Calientes, near Guadalajara. She was raised by a very strict father and she married at thirteen. That was the custom. The girls, as soon as they were old enough to learn cooking and sewing, would get married. She had my mother and my oldest brother when she and my grandfather came across. My grandfather worked for the railroad laying the ties and tracks. Then he worked for a mining company. And after that we moved to Anaheim. We lived in a big four-bedroom house my grandfather built. With my grandparents and their children, three children of my mother's sister who had died, and the three of us, that made a big crowd.

My grandfather would get up Sunday mornings and start the fire in a great big wood-burning stove. He would wrap us up in blankets and seat us around that stove on chairs and say, "Now, don't get too close to the stove. Take care of the younger children." Then he would go out to the store and get bananas and oranges and cereal that he'd cook for us to eat, and milk, and he would feed us Sunday mornings. . . .

Then my grandfather had an accident. The middle fingers of his right hand was crushed and he couldn't work for about two weeks. When he went back he was told that he'd already been replaced by another worker. So he was out of a job.

He decided we'd better go on and pick the crops. We had done that before, during the summer. But this time we went for good.

We came North. The families got together; the women would start cooking at night, boiling eggs and potatoes and making piles of tortillas and tacos, and these lunches would be packed in pails and boxes. There was as much fruit as they could get together, and roasted pumpkin seeds. My uncle had a factory where he made Mexican candy in East Los Angeles. And he used to give us a lot of pumpkin seeds. So my mother dried these, and she roasted and salted them for the trip to keep the drivers awake. We'd start in a car caravan, six or seven families together, one car watching for the other, and when it got a little dark they'd pull onto the roadside and build a fire and start some cooking to feed us. Then they'd spread blankets and quilts on the ground and we would sleep there that night. The next morning the women and older children would get up first and start the breakfast. And we smaller children, it was our job to fold the blankets and put them back in the cars and trucks. Then my brothers and the men would check the cars over again, and after breakfast all the women would wash the dishes and pack them, get 'em in the cars, and we'd start again.

We'd finally get to Delano and we would work there a little. If work was scarce we would keep on going till San

Jose. I did the same thing my mother and my grandfather and my uncles did, picking prunes on our hands and knees off the ground, and putting them in the buckets. We were paid four dollars a ton and we had to fill forty boxes to make it a ton. They made us sign a contract that we would stay there until all the prunes were picked. When we would finish the prunes, in early September, we would start back. And stop on the way to Mendota to pick cotton.

When I was about 13, I used to lift a 12-foot sack of cotton with 104 or 112 pounds. When you're doing this work, you get to be an expert. I could get that sack and put it on my shoulder, and walk with that sack for about a city block or maybe a little less, to where the scale was. I could hook this sack up on the scale, have it weighed, take it off the hook and put it back on my shoulder and walk up a ladder about eight feet high and dump all that cotton in the trailer.

My brothers taught me how to do it. When I first started picking cotton, they had to untie their sack and go on my side of the row and help me put this sack on my shoulder, so they taught me how to do it when it was full. It's stiff. My brother said, "Just walk over it, pick up one end, and sort of pull it up, up, and then bend down, and when the middle of the sack hits your shoulder, you just stand up slowly. Then put your arm on your waist and the sack will sit on your shoulder and you can just walk with it." At 13, 14 I was lifting 104 and 112 pounds. I weighed 97, I guess!

As a child I remember we had tents without any floors. I think it was Giffen's Camp Number Nine. I remember the water coming from under the tent at night to where we were sleeping. My brothers would get up with shovels and put mud around the tent to keep the water out. But our blankets and our clothes were always damp during the winter. . . .

In thirty-three we came up North to follow the crops because my brothers couldn't find any work in Los Angeles during the Depression. I remember going hungry to school. I didn't have a sweater. I had nothing. I'd come to school and they'd want to know, "What did you have for breakfast?" They gave us a paper, to write down what we had! I *invented* things! We had eggs and milk, I'd say, and the same things the other kids would write, I'd write. There weren't many Mexican people at school, mostly whites, and I'd watch to see what they were writing or the pictures that they'd show. You know: glasses of milk, and toast, and oranges and bananas and cereal. I'd never had *anything*. . . .

COURTSHIP AND MARRIAGE

When I was a girl, boys were allowed to go out and have friends and visit there in camp, and even go to town. But the girls —my mother was always watching them. We couldn't talk to nobody. If I had a boyfriend he had to send me letters, drop notes on his way or send them along with somebody. We did no dating. If girls came to visit at my house, my grandmother sat right there to listen to what we were talking about. We weren't allowed to speak English because she couldn't understand. . . . We were allowed nowhere except out to the field, and then we always worked between my two older brothers. The only one they trusted was Arnold. He's the one I married! I was fourteen when I met Arnold, in 1933. We lived next door to his family, which was a big one. . . .

Arnold and I got married in 1938 in Firebaugh, where we'd all moved. We had a big party with an orchestra: some of Arnold's friends played the violin and guitar. But we had no honeymoon. On the second day after our wedding he went back to his job—irrigating. I'd get up at four o'clock in the morning to fix his breakfast and his lunch. He'd start the fire for me. I did the cooking in his mother's kitchen. In the morning I'd get up and run across and I'd fix his breakfast and his lunch and he'd go off and I'd go back to bed. There was no women's liberation at the time! I felt I was overworked in the house. . . . But I felt, "What can she (her mother-in-law) do without the help I'm giving her?" I felt sorry for her. She'd worked very hard and she had so many children, and had to wash her clothes in a tub with a rock board and do the ironing by heating the irons on top of the stove. All of us had to do this, but not many families had eight or nine little children.

I cooked with her until May. But I kept after Arnold: "I want my own kitchen!" So in May we drove all the way into Fresno. We got a few spoons and plates and pots and skillets and I started my own housekeeping. I still went to his mother's to help her during the day when Arnold was working. But I cooked in my own stove.

After I was married, sometime in May, my husband was chopping cotton and I said, "I want to go with you."

"You can't. You have to stay at home!"

"I just feel like going outside somewhere. I haven't gone anyplace. I want to at least go out to the fields. Take another hoe and I'll help you." I went, but only for one or two days. Then he refused to take me. He said, "You have to stay home and raise children." I was pregnant with my first one. "I want you to rest," he said. "You're not supposed to work. You worked ever since I can remember. Now that you're married, you are going to rest." So I stayed home but I didn't call it rest doing all the cooking for his mother.

Arnold was raised in the old Mexican custom—men on the one side, women on the other. Women couldn't do anything. Your husband would say, "Go here," you'd do it. You didn't dare go out without your husband saying you could. . . .

After a time I said, "I have really had it. Why do you have to go with your friends all the time when I'm being left alone?"

"Well, what's wrong with that? You can go visit my mother," I said, "Big deal, you want me to visit your mother and help make some tortillas." So he finally started giving me money, five or six dollars. He'd say, "My mother's going to Fresno. If you want to go with them you can go." Or he would say, "Donna Genoveva," a friend of ours, "is going to Fresno and she said you can come along." I'd get my two kids ready early in the morning and we'd go to Fresno or to visit her husband, who was up in the mountains in the hospital for TB. One day I just said, "Why do I have to depend on other people to take me out somewhere? I'm married, I have a husband—who should be taking me out." The next time he was home and said, "Here's the money," I said, "I don't want to go." He let it go at that and I did too, I didn't say another word. The following weekend he said, "Do you want to go to a show? My mother's going. They're going to Fresno." I said, "No." Then about the third time this happened he said, "Why don't you want to go anymore?"

"I do, I do want to go. I want to go somewhere, but not with anyone else. I want to go with you." So then he started staying home and he'd say, "Get ready, we're going into Fresno." And both of us would come in, bring the children, go to a show and eat, or just go to the park.

Arnold would never teach me how to drive. One day I asked him to. We were on a ditch bank about eight feet wide. He says, "Get on the driver's side. Now, turn around and go back." I got out. I said, "*You* do it! Just tell me you don't want me to learn if that's what you want." Then in 1947 I asked my sister, Margaret, and she showed me. We practiced in a field. After a few times she said, "Hey! You know how to drive! Let's go into town so you can buy your groceries."

So one day I said to Arnold, "I'm going out to get the groceries."

"Who's going to take you?"

"Me. I'm going to do the buying from now on."

I stopped working toward the last months of my pregnancies, but I would start again after they were born. When I was working and I couldn't find somebody I would take them with me. I started taking Ray with me when he wasn't a year old yet. I'd carry one of those big washtubs and put it under the vine and sit him there. I knew he was safe; he couldn't climb out. Arnold and I would move the tub along with us as we worked. I hated to leave him with somebody that probably wouldn't take care of him the way I could.

In 1944 we moved to a labor camp in Huron and we stayed there til 1956. But before that we had a single-room cabin. I used to separate the bed section from the kitchen by nailing blankets or pieces of canvas to divide. We had our bed and another bed for the children. All the boys slept in the bed and the girl slept with us in our bed. During the night Bobby being the youngest of the boys would wake up and be scared and he always ended up in our bed! It was pretty crowded, but what could you do? I was always nailing orange crates on the walls to use as cupboards for dishes. . . .

There was a lot of sickness. I remember when my kids got whooping cough. Arnold was sick, too, he was burning hot. During this time instead of staying in my own cabin at night I'd go to my mother-in-law's. The children would wake up at night coughing and there was blood coming out of their noses. I cried and cried, I was afraid they'd choke. I went to the clinic and they told me the children had whooping cough. That cough lasted six months.

It was like that for all of us. I would see babies who died. It was claimed if you lifted a young baby up fast, the soft spot would cave in and it would get diarrhea and dehydrate and die. After all these years, I know it wasn't that that killed them. It was hunger, malnutrition, no money to pay the doctors. When the union came, this was one of the things we fought against.

FIELD WORK

From 1939 until 1944 we stayed at Giffen's Camp Number Three. We were still following the crops. We would go out to pick cotton or apricots or grapes here near Fresno or we would go farther north to Tracey to pick peas. When there was no work chopping or picking cotton we'd go to Patterson or San Jose to pick apricots. Arnold did the picking and I did cutting for the drying-out in the sheds. . . .

We always went where we wanted to make sure the women and men were going to work because if it were just the men working it wasn't worth going out there because we wouldn't earn enough, to support a family. We would start early, around 6:30 A.M. and work for four or five hours, then walk home and eat and rest until about three-thirty in the afternoon when it cooled off. We would go back and work until we couldn't see. Then we'd get home and rest, visit, talk, then I'd clean up the kitchen. I was doing the housework and working out in the fields, and taking care of the kids. I had two children by this time. . . .

The hardest work we did was thinning beets. You were required to use a short-handled hoe. The cutting edge is about seven to eight inches wide and the handle is about a foot long. Then you have to be bent over with the hoe in one hand. You walk down the rows stooped over. You have to work hard, fast, as fast as you can because you were paid by the row, not by the hour. . . .

I used a short-handled hoe in the lettuce fields. The lettuce grows in a bed. You work in little furrows between two rows. First you thin them with the hoe, then you pick off the tops. My brothers-in-law and Arnold and I and some other friends worked there picking the tops off the lettuce. By the time they had taken up one row I had taken up two. The men would go between the two beds and take one row and break the little balls off. But I took two rows at a time, one with each hand. By the time I finished my two rows at the other end, it was close to a mile long, and my brother-in-law had only taken one row part-way. He said, "I'm quitting! If Jessie can beat me at this kind of work, I'm no good at it." So he never came back. About three or four other men wouldn't go back to work because they were beaten by a woman. They said, "I'm ashamed to have a woman even older than I am work faster than I can. This is women's job." I said, "Hey! What do you mean? You mean the men's job is washing dishes and baking tortillas?" They said working out in the fields was women's work because we were faster at it!

Out in the fields there were never any restrooms. We had to go eight or ten hours without relief. If there wasn't brush or a little ditch we were forced to wait until we got home! Just the women. The men didn't need to pull their clothes down. Later, when I worked for the Farmworkers, in a hearing I said, "I was working for Russell Giffen, the biggest grower in Huron. These big growers have a lot of money because we earned all that money for them. Because of our sweat and our labor that we put on the land. What they do instead of supplying restrooms and clean water where we can wash our hands, is put posts on the ground with a piece of gunny sack wound around them." That's where we went. And that thing was moved along with us. It was just four stakes stuck in the ground, and then there was canvas or a piece of gunny sack around it. You would be working and this restroom would be right there. The canvas didn't come up high enough in front for privacy.

We made it a practice to go two at a time. One would stand outdoors and watch outside that nobody came along. And then the other would do the same for the one inside.

LA CAUSA

One night in 1962 there was a knock at the door and there were three men. One of them was Cesar Chavez. And the next thing I knew, they were sitting around our table talking about a union. I made coffee. Arnold had already told me about a union for the farmworkers. He was attending their meetings in Fresno, but I didn't. I'd either stay home or stay outside in the car. But then Cesar said, "The women have to be involved. They're the ones working out in the fields with their husbands. If you can take the women out to the fields, you can certainly take them to meetings." So I sat up straight and said to myself, "*That's* what I want!"

When I became involved with the union, I felt I had to get other women involved. Women have been behind men all the time, always. In my sister-in-law and brother-in-law's families the women do a lot of shouting and cussing and they get slapped around. But that's not standing up for what you believe in. It's just trying to boss and not knowing how. I'd hear them scolding their kids and fighting their husbands and I'd say, "Gosh! Why don't you go after the people that have you living like this? Why don't you go after the growers that have you tired from working out in the fields at low wages and keep us poor all the time? . . . Then I would say we had to take a part in the things going on around us. "Women can no longer be taken for granted—that we're just going to stay home and do the cooking and cleaning. It's way past the time when our husbands could say, 'You stay home! You have to take care of the children. You have to do as I say.'"

Then some women I spoke to started attending the union meetings, and later they were out on the picket lines.

I was well-known in the small towns around Fresno. Wherever I went to speak to them, they listened. I told them about how we were excluded from the NLRB in 1935, how we had no benefits, no minimum wage, nothing out in the fields—no restrooms, nothing. I'd ask people how they felt about all these many years they had been working out in the fields, how they had been treated. And then we'd all talk about it. They would say, "I was working for so-and-so, and when I complained about something that happened there, I was fired." I said, "Well! Do you think we should be putting up with this in this modern age? You know, we're not back in the 20s. We can stand up! We can talk back! It's not like when I was a little kid and my grandmother used to say, 'You have to especially respect the Anglos, "Yessir," "Yes, Ma'am!" ' That's over. This country is very rich, and we want a share of the money these growers make of our sweat and our work by exploiting us and our children!" I'd have my sign-up book and I'd say, "If anyone wants to become a member of the union, I can make you a member right now." And they'd agree!

So I found out that I could organize them and make members of them. Then I offered to help them, like taking them to the doctor's and translating for them, filling out papers that they needed to fill out, writing their letters for those that couldn't write. A lot of people confided in me. Through the letter-writing, I knew a lot of the problems they were having back home, and they knew they could trust me, that I wouldn't tell anyone else about what I had written or read. So that's why they came to me.

I guess when the union found out how I was able to talk to people, I was called into Delano to one of the meetings, and they gave me my card as an organizer. I am very proud to say I was the first woman organizer out in the fields organizing the people. There have been Dolores Huerta and others, but they were in cities organizing the people, and I was the first woman farmworker organizer out in the fields. . . .

It was very hard being a woman organizer. Many of our people my age and older were raised with the old customs in Mexico: where the husband rules, he is the king of his house. The wife obeys, and the children, too. So when we first started it was very, very hard. Men gave us the most trouble—neighbors there in Parlier! They were for the union, but they were not taking orders from women, they said. When they formed the ranch committee at Christian Brothers—that's a big wine company, part of it is in Parlier—the ranch committee was all men. We were working under our first contract in Fresno County. The ranch committee had to enforce the contract. If there are any grievances they meet with us and the supervisors. But there were no women on that first committee.

That year, we'd have a union meeting every week. Men, women, and children would come. Women would ask questions and the men would just stand back. I guess they'd say to themselves, "I'll wait for someone to say something before I do." The women were more aggressive than the men.

When the first contract was up, we talked about there being no women on the ranch committee. I suggested they be on it, and the men went along with this. And so women were elected.

The women took the lead in calling for picketing and we would talk to the people. It got to the point that we would have to find them, because the men just wouldn't go and they wouldn't take their wives. So we would say, "We're having our picket line at the Safeway in Fresno, and those that don't show up are going to have to pay a five dollar fine." We couldn't have four or five come to a picket line and have the rest stay home and watch T.V. In the end, we had everybody out there. . . .

At White River Farms one morning very early, we were out there by the hundreds by the road, and these people got down and started working out there in the grapes. We were asking them not to work, telling them that there was a strike going on. The grower had two guards at the entrance and there was a helicopter above us. At other White River Farm ranches they had the sheriff, the county police, *everybody*. But there were pickets at three different ranches and where we were picketing there wasn't anybody except these two guards. So I said, "Hey! What about the women getting together and let's rush 'em!" And they said, "Do you think we could do that?" And I said, "Of course we can! Let's go in there. Let's get 'em out of there any way we can." So about fifty of us rushed. We went under the vines. We had our banners and you could see them bobbing up and down, up and down, and we'd go under those rows on our knees and roll over. When the scabs saw us coming they took off. All of them went and they got on the bus. The guards had guns that they would shoot, and something black like smoke or teargas would come out. That scared us, but we still kept on. After we saw all those workers get back on the busses, we went back. Instead of running this time, we rolled over and over all the way out. The vines are about four feet tall, and they have wire where you string up the vines. So you can't walk or run across one of these fences. You have to keep going under these wires. When I got out there on the road they were getting these big, hard dirty clods and throwing them at us. And then the pickets started doing the same thing. When the first police car came, somebody broke the windshield. We don't know if it was the scabs or someone on the picket lines, but the picketers were blamed.

When we women ran into the fields we knew we'd be arrested if they caught us. But we went in and we told the scabs, "If you're not coming out we're gonna pull you out!"

In Kern County we were sprayed with pesticides. They would come out there with their sprayers and spray us on the picket lines. They have these big tanks that are pulled by a tractor with hoses attached and they spray the trees with this. They are strong like a water hose, but wider. When we were picketing they came out there to spray the pickets. They had goons with these big police dogs on leashes.

One of the things the growers did to break our strikes was to bring in "illegal aliens." I would get a list of names of the scabs and give them to the border patrol. At that time, you see, we were pitted against each other, us and the people from Mexico, so it was either us or them. When I went to the border patrol office I'd go in and say, "Can I come in?" They'd say, "You can't come in. This is a very small office." They kept telling us they were short of men. But every time I went there, there were all of them with their feet up on the desks in their air-conditioned office. They told me they were under orders not to interfere with labor disputes. So I called Bernie Sisk's office and talked to them about it. Then I came home and called a lot of students who'd been helping us, and other people, and the next morning there we were at the border patrol. I said, "We're paying our tax money, but not for you to sit here while the illegal aliens are being used to break our strike."

While we were in Parlier, I was put in charge of the hiring hall. My house was right next to the office, and I had an extension to the office phone in my house. I could do the housework and take care of the children, but I could take care of the office, too. Before the contract, the hiring hall was just a union office where people came to learn about the union. When they got the first contracts we began dispatching people out to work. The hiring hall was also a place where people could meet and talk. A lot of people were migrants who needed to get to know each other. The people who were there all the time were against the migrants. I said, "We have to get these people together. We can't be divided." I was at the hall all day. People would drop by and I'd introduce them.

The second year we had a contract I started working for Christian Brothers. The men were doing the pruning on the grape vines. After they did the pruning the women's crew would come and tie the vines. (That was something we got changed; we made them give pruning jobs to women.) I was made a steward on the women's crew. . . . the first time we were paid when I started working, during the break the supervisor would come out there with our checks. It was our fifteen minute break, which the contract gave us the right to. We had to walk to the other end of the row; it took us about five minutes to get there, the rest of the fifteen to get our checks, and walk back, and we'd start working. This happened twice. The third time I said, "We're not going to go after our check this time. They always come during our break and we don't get to rest." So when we saw the pickup coming with the men who had the checks I said, "Nobody move. You just sit here." I walked over to the pickup. I said to the man inside. "Mr. Rager, these women refuse to come out here on their break time. It's their time to rest. So we're asking you, if you must come during our rest period, you take the checks to these ladies." From that day on, every payday he would come to us. That was the sort of thing you had to do to enforce the contract.

I became involved in many of the activities in the community—school board meetings, city council meetings, everything that I could get into. For example I went to fighting for bilingual education at Parlier, went to a lot of meetings about it and spoke about it. Parlier is over 85 percent Chicano, yet during that time there were no Chicanos on the school board, on the police force, nowhere. Now it's changed: we fought to get a Chicano mayor and officials. But then I was asking people, "Why are we always asked to go to the public school for our meetings? Why can't they come over to our side of town in Parlier?" So we began having meetings in *la colonia* at the Headstart Center, and there we pushed for bilingual education.

Fresno County didn't give food stamps to the people—only surplus food. There were no vegetables, no meat, just staples like whole powdered milk, cheese, butter. At the migrant camp in Parlier the people were there a month and a half before work started, and since they'd borrowed money to get to California they didn't have any food. I'd drive them into Fresno to the welfare department and translate for them and they'd get food, but half of it they didn't eat. We heard about other counties where they had food stamps to go to the store and buy meat and milk and fresh vegetables for the children. So we began talking about getting that in Fresno. Finally we had Senate hearings at the Convention Center in Fresno. There were hundreds of people listening. I started in Spanish, and the Senators were looking at each other, you know, saying, "What's going on?" So then I said, "Now, for the benefit of those who can't speak Spanish, I'll translate. If there is money enough to fight a war in Vietnam, and if there is money enough for Governor Reagan's wife to buy a $3000 dress for the Inauguration Ball, there should be money enough to feed these people. The nutrition experts say surplus food is full of vitamins. I've taken a look at that food, this corn meal, and I've seen them come up and down, but you know, we don't call them vita-mins, we call them weevils!" Everybody began laughing and whistling and shout-ing. In the end, we finally got food stamps.

BETTY FRIEDAN
The Feminine Mystique

If the lives of working-class women were still dominated by the struggle for eco-nomic survival, the same cannot be said of middle-class women who enjoyed unprecedented prosperity, especially in the years after World War II. Ensconced in their well-equipped homes in the suburbs, they flourished in an atmosphere of domesticity and affluence that characterized the new consumer culture. Such, at least, was the message of the women's magazines with their advertisements of the latest household appliances and advice columns on marriage and child care. Although there were rumblings of discontent in the 1950s, it was 1963 when Betty Friedan, a suburban housewife herself, exposed the triviality and frustra-tions of a resurgent domesticity. Friedan's indictment, a brief portion of which appears here, was the subject of much controversy. Women who found the grati-fication associated with child care and housework vastly overemphasized ap-plauded Friedan's forceful articulation of their own dissatisfactions. Other women objected vehemently, insisting that, as wives and mothers and perhaps community activists, they enjoyed a life style that not only benefited both their families and communities but provided them personally with freedom, pleasure, and a sense of self-worth. How are we to explain such different responses? Is the housewife described by Friedan foreshadowed in Ruth Schwartz Cowan's article on housework? In what sense is the role of housewife a product of the fusing of biology, economics, and ideology?

The problem lay buried, unspoken, for many years in the minds of American women. It was a strange stirring, a sense of dissatisfaction, a yearning that women suffered in the middle of the twentieth century in the United States. Each sub-urban wife struggled with it alone. As she made the beds, shopped for groceries, matched slipcover material, ate peanut but-ter sandwiches with her children, chauf-

Excerpted from "The Problem That Has No Name," chap. 1 of *The Feminine Mystique* by Betty Friedan (New York: W. W. Norton, 1963). Copyright © 1974, 1963 by Betty Friedan. Reprinted by permission of W. W. Norton & Company, Inc.

feured Cub Scouts and Brownies, lay beside her husband at night—she was afraid to ask even of herself the silent question—"Is this all?"

For over fifteen years there was no word of this yearning in the millions of words written about women, for women, in all the columns, books and articles by experts telling women their role was to seek fulfillment as wives and mothers. Over and over women heard in voices of tradition and of Freudian sophistication that they could desire no greater destiny than to glory in their own femininity. Experts told them how to catch a man and keep him, how to breastfeed children and handle their toilet training, how to cope with sibling rivalry and adolescent rebellion; how to buy a dishwasher, bake bread, cook gourmet snails, and build a swimming pool with their own hands; how to dress, look, and act more feminine and make marriage more exciting; how to keep their husbands from dying young and their sons from growing into delinquents. They were taught to pity the neurotic, unfeminine, unhappy women who wanted to be poets or physicists or presidents. They learned that truly feminine women do not want careers, higher education, political rights—the independence and the opportunities that the old-fashioned feminists fought for. Some women, in their forties and fifties, still remembered painfully giving up those dreams, but most of the younger women no longer even thought about them. A thousand expert voices applauded their femininity, their adjustment, their new maturity. All they had to do was devote their lives from earliest girlhood to finding a husband and bearing children.

By the end of the nineteen-fifties, the average marriage age of women in America dropped to 20, and was still dropping, into the teens. Fourteen million girls were engaged by 17. The proportion of women attending college in comparison with men dropped from 47 per cent in 1920 to 35 per cent in 1958. A century earlier, women had fought for higher education; now girls went to college to get a husband. By the mid-fifties, 60 per cent dropped out of college to marry, or because they were afraid too much education would be a marriage bar. Colleges built dormitories for "married students," but the students were almost always the husbands. A new degree was instituted for the wives—"Ph.T." (Putting Husband Through).

Then American girls began getting married in high school. And the women's magazines, deploring the unhappy statistics about these young marriages, urged that courses on marriage, and marriage counselors, be installed in the high schools. Girls started going steady at twelve and thirteen, in junior high. Manufacturers put out brassieres with false bosoms of foam rubber for little girls of ten. And an advertisement for a child's dress, size 3–6x, in the *New York Times* in the fall of 1960, said: "She Too Can Join the Man-Trap Set."

By the end of the fifties, the United States birthrate was overtaking India's. The birth-control movement, renamed Planned Parenthood, was asked to find a method whereby women who had been advised that a third or fourth baby would be born dead or defective might have it anyhow. Statisticians were especially astounded at the fantastic increase in the number of babies among college women. Where once they had two children, now they had four, five, six. Women who had once wanted careers were now making careers out of having babies. So rejoiced *Life* magazine in a 1956 paean to the movement of American women back to the home.

In a New York hospital, a woman had a nervous breakdown when she found she could not breastfeed her baby. In other hospitals, women dying of cancer refused a drug which research had proved might save their lives: its side effects were said to be unfeminine. "If I have only one life, let me live it as a blonde," a larger-than-life-sized picture of a pretty, vacuous woman proclaimed from newspaper, magazine, and drugstore ads. And across America, three out of every ten women dyed their hair blonde. They ate a chalk called Metrecal, instead of food, to shrink to the size of the thin young models. Department-store buyers reported that American women, since 1939, had become three and four sizes smaller. "Women are out to fit the clothes, instead of vice-versa," one buyer said.

Interior decorators were designing kitchens with mosaic murals and original paintings, for kitchens were once again the center of women's lives. Home sewing became a million-dollar industry. Many women no longer left their homes, except to shop, chauffeur their children, or attend a social engagement with their husbands. Girls were growing up in America without ever having jobs outside the home. In the late fifties, a sociological phenomenon was suddenly remarked: a third of American women now worked, but most were no longer young and very few were pursuing careers. They were married women who held part-time jobs, selling or secretarial, to put their husbands through school, their sons through college, or to help pay the mortgage. Or they were widows supporting families. Fewer and fewer women were entering professional work. The shortages in the nursing, social work, and teaching professions caused crises in almost every American city. Concerned over the Soviet Union's lead in the space race, scientists noted that America's greatest source of unused brainpower was women. But girls would not study physics: it was "unfeminine." A girl refused a science fellowship at Johns Hopkins to take a job in a real-estate office. All she wanted, she said, was what every other American girl wanted—to get married, have four children and live in a nice house in a nice suburb.

The suburban housewife—she was the dream image of the young American women and the envy, it was said, of women all over the world. The American housewife—freed by science and labor-saving appliances from the drudgery, the dangers of childbirth and the illnesses of her grandmother. She was healthy, beautiful, educated, concerned only about her husband, her children, her home. She had found true feminine fulfillment. As a housewife and mother, she was respected as a full and equal partner to man in his world. She was free to choose automobiles, clothes, appliances, supermarkets; she had everything that women ever dreamed of.

In the fifteen years after World War II, this mystique of feminine fulfillment became the cherished and self-perpetuating core of contemporary American culture. Millions of women lived their lives in the image of those pretty pictures of the American suburban housewife, kissing their husbands goodbye in front of the picture window, depositing their station-wagonsful of children at school, and smiling as they ran the new electric waxer over the spotless kitchen floor. They baked their own bread, sewed their own and their children's clothes, kept their new washing machines and dryers running all day. They changed the sheets on the beds twice a week instead of once, took the rug-hooking class in adult education, and pitied their poor frustrated mothers, who had dreamed of having a career. Their only dream was to be perfect wives and mothers; their highest ambition to have five children and a beautiful house, their only fight to get and keep their husbands. They had no thought for the unfeminine problems of the world outside the home; they wanted the men to make the major decisions. They gloried in their role as women, and wrote proudly on the census blank: "Occupation: housewife."

For over fifteen years, the words written for women, and the words women used when they talked to each other, while their husbands sat on the other side of the room and talked shop or politics or septic tanks, were about problems with their children, or how to keep their husbands happy, or improve their children's school, or cook chicken or make slipcovers. Nobody argued whether women were inferior or superior to men; they were simply different. Words like "emancipation" and "career" sounded strange and embarrassing; no one had used them for years. When a Frenchwoman named Simone de Beauvoir wrote a book called *The Second Sex*, an American critic commented that she obviously "didn't know what life was all about," and besides, she was talking about French women. The "woman problem" in America no longer existed.

If a woman had a problem in the 1950's and 1960's, she knew that something must be wrong with her marriage, or with herself. Other women were satisfied with their lives, she thought. What kind of a woman was she if she did not feel this mysterious fulfillment waxing the kitchen floor? She was so ashamed to admit her dissatisfaction that she never knew how many other women shared it. If she tried to tell her husband, he didn't understand what she was talking about. She did not really understand it herself. For over fifteen years women in America found it harder to talk about this problem than about sex. Even the psychoanalysts had no name for it. When a woman went to a psychiatrist for help, as many women did, she would say, "I'm so ashamed," or "I must be hopelessly neurotic." "I don't know what's wrong with women today," a suburban psychiatrist said uneasily. "I only know something is wrong because most of my patients happen to be women. And their problem isn't sexual." Most women with this problem did not go to see a psychoanalyst, however. "There's nothing wrong really," they kept telling themselves. "There isn't any problem."

JANE DE HART MATHEWS
The New Feminism and the Dynamics of Social Change

The resurgence of feminism in the late 1960s drew upon many sources. Some have been encountered in previous material in this part: the civil rights movement that enlisted Anne Moody and her white counterparts, the recognition of the inferior economic status of wage-earning women, and the attack on middle-class domesticity that Betty Friedan articulated with such force. There were other sources as well, among them issues left unresolved by an earlier generation of feminists. The following essay explores the origins of the new feminism, the growth and development of the movement, the ideas it generated and the oppo-

sition it incurred. Note in this essay how the four categories appearing throughout this book interact. Observe how *biology* (greater reproductive control and
longevity), *economics* (increasing numbers of wage-earning women and their marginality within the labor force), and *politics* (participation in various political efforts to obtain change) contributed in part to the development of a new *ideology*
(feminism.) Note, too, how the categories continued to interact as a new feminist
ideology generated political goals designed to achieve sexual equality—goals that
involved, among other things, greater reproductive freedom, economic parity,
and a new ideological formulation of what it means for women and men to become equal and autonomous persons in contemporary society.

Present-day feminists are separated by more than a century from their predecessors at Seneca Falls, while more than a half century separates them from
their early twentieth-century counterparts. Yet in what sense is the opposition
to the enlargement of women's sphere and the creation of a public role for
women that was encountered by these earlier generations of feminists paralleled
in the opposition that came to focus on ratification of the Equal Rights Amendment during the 1970s and early 1980s? What is at issue?

Fifty years after gaining the right to vote,
women who had been suffragists and
women young enough to be their great-
granddaughters embarked on a new quest.
Their motive: to change not only laws and
institutions, but values, patterns of behavior, personal relationships, and ultimately
themselves. Their goal: equality. This new
feminist movement was vigorous, diffuse,
and highly controversial. In order to understand its origins and goals, its opponents, and, most important, its potential
for changing society, it is necessary to
examine the long-term economic and social changes that created an environment
within which the movement could emerge.
It is important also to appreciate the ferment of the 1960s that provided feminism
with its ideological core, vitality, and impetus. To explore such origins is also to
explore the sense in which contemporary
feminists confronted issues an earlier generation had left unresolved.

UNFULFILLED EXPECTATIONS

By winning the vote in 1920, many women
believed that the decisive battle in the long

struggle for sexual equality had been won.
The atmosphere was electric with a sense
of achievement and expectation generated
by the euphoria of the moment. The fact
that enfranchisement had come on the
heels of other reforms identified with
women seemed evidence of their growing
influence. Congress had passed legislation
to protect women in industry, outlaw child
labor, and enact prohibition—measures
important to those who believed that
women and children were the primary
victims of exploitative employment and
alcohol-related abuse. Champions of wom-
en's rights also celebrated gains in education and employment. Since 1900 female
enrollment had shot up 100 percent in
public colleges and universities and nearly
500 percent in private ones. As ambitious
graduates gained access to advanced training, the proportion of women in the professions climbed by 1920 to an unprecedented 11.9 percent.[1] During World War I
women in record numbers had moved into
skilled jobs and administrative positions
formerly held by men.

These very real achievements had been
won by a movement that was successful

only so long as large numbers of women remained committed to each other and to common goals. This collective commitment had secured the vote and corrected some of the wrongs associated with women's exclusion from full participation in the public sphere of ballot box and marketplace. Few suffragists and reformers, however, were prepared to confront the barriers to equality in the domestic sphere of family. Most women as well as men still accepted as one of the few unchanging facts of life the conviction that woman's primary duty was to be "the helpmeet, the housewife, and the mother."[2] Feminists who hoped to provide additional, complementary, or alternative possibilities gradually found themselves a diminishing minority. Since their understanding of the many kinds of change yet required to ensure full emancipation was shared by so few women, enfranchisement failed to create a bloc of female voters prepared to use the ballot to remove additional barriers to equality. Like their male counterparts, they found issues of class, race, and ethnicity more compelling than the need to improve women's status. The collective power of the "woman's vote" through which suffragists had hoped to achieve further gains never fully materialized in the decade ahead.

Part of the reason for this failure lay in the physical and emotional fatigue of the suffragists themselves. The fight for the ballot, compounded by the stress of World War I, had taken its toll. As one suffragist explained: "After we [got] the vote, the crusade was over. It was peacetime and we went back to a hundred different causes and tasks that we'd been putting off all those years. We just demobilized."[3] For those who still had the energy, there were new causes. Pacifism and disarmament acquired an added urgency not only for prewar pacifists such as Crystal Eastman and Jane Addams but also for more recent enthusiasts such as suffragist leader Carrie Chapman Catt, who established the Na-

tional Conference on the Cause and Cure of War. Other women, whose feminist sympathies and political activism had been tenuous even in the yeasty reformist milieu of the progressive era, gradually yielded to the political conservatism of the 1920s. They could not be effectively mobilized for protest even when the Supreme Court in 1922 and 1923 invalidated two of the major legislative gains of the prewar women's movement—minimum wages for women and the abolition of child labor. Younger women who might have become new recruits found old visions of female equality less exciting than the personal gratification associated with the relaxed social and sexual mores and affluence of the new consumer culture.

As these and other disappointments mounted, divisions developed within the movement itself. The organizations most responsible for winning the vote, the National American Woman Suffrage Association (NAWSA) and its militant offshoot, the Congressional Union, had regrouped under new names. The Congressional Union, under Alice Paul's leadership, became the National Woman's Party. It enrolled between four and five thousand members, many of them professional women, whose first priority was improvement of women's status. Many NAWSA members moved in a different direction, finding their way into the new League of Women Voters created in 1919 to educate women for citizenship. The league represented the persistence of a broad progressive impulse along with the commitment to the advancement of women. Its bipartisan concern for "good government" and legislation protecting women and children made it the more broadly reformist of the two organizations. Disagreement over tactics during the suffrage campaign continued in the debate over the next tactic in the struggle for equality. The Woman's Party advocated a constitutional amendment to guarantee equality before the law. The league and other organizations—such as the General Federation of Women's Clubs, the Women's Trade Union League, the Young Women's Christian Association, and the American Association of University Women—preferred to deal with the many discriminatory aspects of the law through a state-by-state effort to change specific statutes.

The league's preference derived in part from fears that an equal rights amendment would jeopardize legislation regulating hours, wages, and working conditions for thousands of unskilled, nonunionized female workers. Their health and safety, insisted the league, required the special protection of government. The courts, having denied this legislation to men on the ground that such laws interfered with their "freedom of contract," permitted it to women workers only because of their traditional role as mothers. Women workers, opponents of the amendment argued, could ill afford to surrender their concrete gains for the abstract principle of equality.

By the end of the 1920s the league and its allies could point to a few transitory gains in the area of maternal and infant health care and to the easing of legal strictures affecting marriage, divorce, property holding, and contracts. But they failed to shake the unswerving conviction of Woman's Party loyalists that the key to equality lay in amending the Constitution. As a result of these disagreements, intense and acrimonious debate persisted throughout years of fragmentation and frustration. Feminism as an organized movement virtually disappeared. Individually feminists might cling to egalitarian goals. Collectively, however, they were simply too few and too powerless to achieve those goals. As a result, the fundamental circumstances of women's lives remained little changed.

For working-class women life was still one of constant toil—on farms, in factories and mills, or in other women's homes. The factory job that had promised escape from poverty or the drudgery of farm work or the servility of domestic service often car-

ried with it new problems. To be sure, increases in productivity during the 1920s allowed a handful of companies to initiate a five-day workweek, the eight-hour day, or a two-week annual vacation with pay. But low wages, long hours, frequent layoffs, monotony, noise, dirt, and danger still characterized many industrial jobs, especially in the nonunionized South. Moreover, wage work brought no escape from domestic duties.

For married women with children, the burden was especially heavy, as Grace Elliott's experience graphically demonstrates. An ambitious young textile worker, she worked as a weaver at the East Marion Manufacturing Company in Marion, North Carolina, during the 1920s. Earning $16 a week, she paid $5 for a cook and $2 for laundry. Because the $9 remaining seemed "such a slow path to home and furniture," she decided to do her own housework, getting up at 4:00 A.M., preparing breakfast and dinner, milking the cow, getting the children's clothes ready for them to wear to school before rushing to the mill for the 5:40 shift. Breaking at noon, she walked home for a cold lunch and then rushed back to the mill where she worked until 6:00 P.M. Returning home, she cooked supper, sometimes sewing after the children had gone to bed. Her schedule was "very hard" but, she insisted, "I had to keep the children in school." For all of her determination, the physical strain was too much. Like so many of her fellow workers, Grace Elliott was exhausted and ill at the end of four years. Struggling with wage labor, housework, illness, pregnancy, and poverty, such women seemed as powerless to control the conditions in which they lived and worked as did their voteless predecessors.[4]

Middle-class women fared better than their working-class counterparts. More advantaged economically, they had easier access to birth control devices and to the educational and professional opportunities that would equip them to function in the world outside the home. Yet if progress is measured by achievements in business, professional, and political life, middle-class women made few gains in the postsuffrage decades. The proportion of women attending colleges and universities actually declined between 1920 and 1960, as did the proportion of women on college faculties. In 1920, one out of every seven doctoral degrees was awarded to a woman; in 1956, only one in ten. By 1960 only 4 percent of the lawyers and judges in this nation were women, only 6 percent of the medical doctors, and less than 1 percent of the architects. Percentages, of course, can be misleading in that they indicate a share rather than absolute numbers. For example, although the percentage of women awarded the Ph.D. in 1920 was 15 percent as opposed to 10.5 percent in 1960, indicating a decline of one-third, the actual number of women receiving the doctorate had increased from 90 in 1920 to 1,090 in 1960. In certain areas of business, notably real estate, women had increased in both numbers and percentage.[5] In the final analysis, however, there was no escaping the fact that women were still excluded from the higher echelons of business, government, and the professions. The number of women elected to Congress throughout this entire forty-year period totaled a mere three in the Senate and forty-four in the House.[6] The number of female cabinet members was a scant two. A seat on the stock exchange was as difficult to come by as a seat on the president's cabinet. Boards of directors of major corporations were also a male preserve. Veteran champions of equality of the sexes had to admit a certain element of truth in the phrase that is the despair of radicals and the hope of conservatives: *plus ça change, plus c'est la même chose.*

UNRESOLVED ISSUES

The discrepancy between feminists' expectations and the actual accomplishments of women in the postsuffrage decades is a measure of how effectively internal and external barriers interacted to bind women to the traditional pattern of domesticity. That so many women rejected the new possibilities of public life for the old expectations of a private one when the former *seemingly* offered more challenging and potentially rewarding options is testimony both to the power of cultural constraints that undermined real freedom of choice and to the reality of external barriers that denied women equality in the workplace. Although women themselves may have thought they chose "freely," few were actually in a position to do so. Most had grown up in an atmosphere of profound conditioning that from infancy through adulthood assigned individuals of each sex social roles defined essentially by gender.

The cumulative impact of this socialization shaped young women's sense of themselves as females and the options open to them by the time they reached college. There, as in high school, the curriculum reinforced established patterns. Students taking home economics courses learned about the tasks that awaited them as consumer, homemaker, and mother. By the 1940s and 1950s many sociology courses portrayed the "normal" family as one based on a sexual division of labor and "sex-determined" behavioral characteristics. If the campus served as an environment within which to pursue a husband rather than an independent intellectual life or preprofessional training, that acknowledged a basic reality. Getting a man, especially one with bright prospects, was itself a vocational objective, one preferable to others.

The reason was that in a sexually segregated labor force positions filled predominantly by women carried little pay and prestige—to the financial detriment of the few males involved as well as the many females. Fields such as business, engineering, architecture, law, medicine, and university teaching were only slightly open to women. Female applicants to professional schools were usually confronted with admission quotas limiting the number of women, often to 5 percent. University faculties frequently assumed that female students would marry, get pregnant, and drop out, or, if they did graduate, never practice the profession for which they had been trained. Those young women who persisted, ultimately receiving the Ph.D. or the M.D., could expect continued discrimination in hiring, pay, or promotion once their active work life began.

They also had to face the problem of combining work and family in a society governed by traditional assumptions relating to both. Many business and professional women in the early years of the twentieth century solved the problem by staying single. Successive generations, less attracted to that option, had to find husbands willing to have a spouse pursue an active work life outside the home in an era in which a working wife was thought to reflect poorly on a man's ability to provide for his family. Even if husbands consented, those holding management positions in major corporations were expected by their companies to relocate frequently if they wished to move up the executive ladder. Wives of such men often found it difficult to establish their own vocational roots. Those who were able to do so had to contend with still other problems. Nagging fears that successful careers were inconsistent with marital happiness—at least for women—found reinforcement in Hollywood movies, women's magazines, and scholarly studies. The conventional assumption that an achieving woman would lose "her chance for the kind of love she wants" was criticized by the anthropologist Margaret Mead in 1935 to no avail.[7] Twelve years later the sociologist Ferdinand Lundberg and the psychiatrist Marynia Farnham were adamant in their insistence that "the 'successful woman' is only occasionally successful as a woman."[8] In this context, women whose personal and professional lives provided refutation of such assertions were simply too few to make a difference. For those younger women who did persist, the self-doubt and confusion that are a part of role conflict sometimes remained long after the conflict had been resolved.

Parenting complicated the situation even further, creating practical problems and compounding internal anxieties. To be a lawyer and a father in America was to be "normal"; to be a lawyer and a mother was to be "deviant" because motherhood was assumed to be a full-time occupation, especially in middle-class circles. How to cope with the physical and psychological demands of family while simultaneously meeting the performance criteria and competitive pressures of work challenged even the most dedicated and resourceful woman. Pregnancy and child care leaves, tax benefits for child care expenses, public day care centers with strong programs to encourage physical and intellectual growth: these measures had become well established in advanced European nations such as Sweden. But they were never fully incorporated into the structure of American society during the first three-quarters of this century.

Families, too, were ill prepared to accommodate the special needs of women who worked outside the home. With kin networks often scattered about in distant cities and towns, it was difficult to find a grandparent or aunt who could take care of children during an emergency. Husbands, even when supportive in principle, often proved reluctant in practice to assume additional responsibilities at home. To have done so would have pitted them against conventional expectations, especially if their own schedules were full and job-related responsibilities demanding. Energetic women motivated by ambition or poverty somehow managed. They devised suitable child care arrangements, revised household priorities, and balanced work demands and personal needs. That in the process they often acquired a reputation for being "superwomen" was itself indication of the inequities inherent in a sex role system that allowed men the option of combining career and family while denying it to women.

For the vast majority of middle-class women the problems of combining work and family were simply too great. Moreover, their social position was such that most of the working women they knew—clerks, beauticians, domestics—were lower-middle and working-class people. *Not* working for pay outside the home indicated the high status so important to millions of Americans. As internal constraints and external constraints reinforced each other, most middle-class women concluded that they would have a better chance for security and status as wives and mothers than as workers. Economic dependency seemed a small price to pay for the pleasures of domesticity and the rewards of community activism so integral to suburban life. Paying this price was not a conscious decision so much as the unconscious transaction of investing in roles patterned after those of their mothers. The little girls who donned women's clothes on rainy afternoons while "playing house" were also donning attitudes and habits. In doing so, they indicated their "agreement" to contracts yet to be made with little boys who were learning how to be aggressive, independent, and successful. The sentimental myths surrounding middle-class family life created an almost sacred place within which children could take an idyllic apprenticeship in adulthood. This inviolability protected the family from widespread criticism. Champions of women's rights, concentrating on legal and political disabilities that deprived women of a full public life, never effectively challenged the pervasive cultural constraints

binding women to dependency. To have raised such issues in the suffrage crusade would have been to play directly into the hands of opponents who were already predicting that giving women the vote would be the undoing of the family.[9]

There were, to be sure, achieving women whose lives were not defined only by domesticity—Helen Keller, Amelia Earhart, Mary McLeod Bethune, and Eleanor Roosevelt. But this was a culture that, while celebrating the "exceptional woman," endlessly romanticized domesticity, extolling the joys of the housewife-mother who lovingly tended her garden and a bumper crop of children. Even the heroines hawked by Hollywood fell into two categories: sex objects and wives. The former were voluptuous if vacuous—the sexually alluring blonde whom "gentlemen preferred," as Marilyn Monroe so sensationally demonstrated during what one film critic dubbed the "mammary madness" of the 1950s.[10] The latter, invariably played by Doris Day or Debbie Reynolds, were bland, childish, but amusing in a peppy, well-scrubbed, but unmistakably feminine way that projected them from girl-next-door to suburban wife. The message of the culture was clear. To be a woman in this society was to be "feminine"; to be a feminist was to be "neurotic."[11]

THE GROWING GAP BETWEEN IDEOLOGY AND REALITY

The apparent retreat from feminism into domesticity after 1920 hid a more complex reality. Impersonal economic, scientific, and demographic forces were subtly undermining old patterns and assumptions. Although in themselves these new developments did not produce a resurgence of feminism, they did add impetus to the growing gap between conventional attitudes and changing conditions. This in turn lent credibility to a feminist critique of society.

One of the economic realities of modern America has been that many women were never fully in their "place"—the home. They have long been part of a paid labor force. Their numbers increased significantly throughout the twentieth century. Even during the Depression the proportion of women in the work force remained constant. This occurred despite the fact that many employers, including local school boards and the federal civil service, sought to deny employment to married women, assuming, often mistakenly, that their husband's earnings were adequate to support the family and that, as working women, they took jobs away from other men with families to support. But if hard times forced some women back into the home, others were forced out. Many mothers desperately needed even meager wages to keep the family afloat at a time when one out of every five children in this country was not getting enough nourishing food to eat.

As the nation shifted from fighting economic depression to waging global war, women responded by the millions to patriotic appeals to get a war job so as to bring their men home sooner. Between 1940 and 1945 the proportion of women in the work force rose from 25 percent to 36 percent. Money as well as patriotism was involved. The women who flocked to factories were beneficiaries of New Deal legislation governing wages and hours for both sexes. They also benefited from the Congress of Industrial Organization's (CIO) successful unionization effort during the 1930s and became the first generation of female industrial employees to receive good wages. Not surprisingly many were reluctant to return home when "Rosie, the Riveter," that symbol of women war workers, was told to put down her riveting machine at the return of peace. Forced out of well-paying "male" jobs, many women returned to low-paying "female" jobs in restaurants, laundries, shops, and offices.[12] Moreover, their wartime experience seemingly had little impact on public attitudes. When asked whether married women whose husbands made enough to support them should be allowed to hold jobs if they wanted to, the majority of Americans responded with a resounding no.[13] Yet as white-collar and clerical jobs expanded rapidly in the postwar years, so did the number of working women.[14]

By 1960 some 40 percent of American women were employed in full- or part-time jobs. Moreover, those who worked outside the home were no longer predominantly young, single, or poor. Nearly half were mothers of school-age children; many of them were middle-class. When asked why they worked most responded that they regarded their jobs as an extension of family responsibilities as well as a matter of economic need. A second salary made possible a family vacation, a large home better suited to the children's needs, savings for college tuition, or simply a color television set for the family room. During the period when all America seemed about to become one great shopping mall, the definition of economic need was clearly changing. But even if one allows for a rising level of expectations consistent with the consumer culture of the 1950s, the fact remains that, while rhetoric still conformed to the old domestic ideology, the presence of women in the work force did not.[15]

The gap between the old ideology of home and family and the new reality of office and work widened still further as medical advances resulted in improved birth control devices and longer life expectancy. Referring to the extent to which women's lives had been determined by their reproductive role, Sigmund Freud had observed that "anatomy is destiny." But as women gained the ability to control "destiny"—to decide whether to have children, when and how many—they were no longer victims of biological processes. Use of condoms and diaphragms, widespread especially among middle-class couples, made birth control a reality even before the introduction in 1960 of an oral contraceptive—"the pill." As medical science also devised new weapons against disease, the years during which one could expect to function as a healthy, active adult increased accordingly. For example, the average woman in 1900, marrying at twenty-two years of age and having her last child at the age of thirty-two, could expect to live to fifty-one, which was about the time her youngest reached maturity. By 1960, however, the average woman, marrying at the age of twenty, could expect to live until she was sixty-five. If she completed childbearing by the age of thirty, staying home while her children were small, she faced by the age of thirty-five nearly half of her life ahead of her in a house empty of children—empty at first during school hours; empty ultimately for many years after the last child had moved out.

The implications were enormous. That they were not immediately grasped is not surprising for a generation seeking in the private world of home and family the security unavailable in a public world wracked successively by economic depression, world war, and the threat of global annihilation. Throughout the 1950s specialists in marketing techniques continued to fuse the role of homemaker and mother with that of consumer, stressing that true feminine fulfillment lay in maternity, domesticity, and purchase of the "right" products. Yet by glorifying women as homemakers and mothers at precisely the same time important changes were occurring that served to undermine those roles, advertising people were unwittingly helping to sharpen the discrepancy between the domestic myth and the new reality of many women's lives. The gap between reality (change) and ideology (popular notions) was not yet great enough in the early 1960s for large numbers of women to be shocked into recognition of it. But it was there.

The gap could be ignored initially because it was at first a "bad fit." It was an oval peg in a round hole, a size six foot in a five-and-one-half shoe—a small discomfort with which people thought they could live. Social scientists did report slight deviations in the domestic image: daughters tended to regard working mothers as positive role models; husbands were more likely to accord them a greater voice in financial decisions; and families provided more help with household chores.[16] But new developments were incorporated into old patterns even as women felt the pinch and stress. They still had difficulty seeing themselves as permanent members of the work force. Many seemed reluctant to join unions or press for equal pay, perhaps because they saw themselves as supplementary breadwinners or as housewives whom misfortune had trapped in monotonous, low-paying jobs.[17] That so many women continued to see themselves and their work primarily as serving family needs is hardly surprising in a culture in which homemaking was described as "the most important and difficult profession any woman can have."[18] But the bad fit was there: the unfairness of unequal pay for the same work, the low value placed on jobs women performed, the double burden of housework and wage work. Those women who sensed the growing discrepancy between the traditional private world of domesticity and new realities in the public world of work needed a new way of looking at things that would allow them to examine afresh the condition of their lives, moving from grudging acceptance to confrontation and change. They needed, in short, a feminist consciousness.

THE CREATION OF A FEMINIST CONSCIOUSNESS

Revolutions are seldom started by the powerless. The feminist revolution of the 1960s was no exception. It was begun largely by educated, middle-class women whose diverse experiences had sharpened

their sensitivity to the fundamental inequality between the sexes at a time when
America had been thrust into the throes of
self-examination by a movement for racial
equality. Some were young veterans of the
civil rights movement and the new left,
steeped in a commitment to equality and
the techniques of protest. Others were
young professionals increasingly aware of
their secondary status, and still others
were older women with distinguished careers as professionals or as activists. To
explore how they came self-consciously to
appraise women's condition as one demanding collective action is to explore
the process of radicalization that helped
to create a new feminist movement.

In its early state that movement consisted of two different groups—women's
rights advocates and women's liberationists. Although the differences between the
two groups began to blur as the movement matured, initial distinctions were
sharp. Women's rights advocates were
likely to have been older, to have had professional training or work experience, to
have been more inclined to form or join
organized feminist groups. Reform oriented, these organizations used traditional
pressure group tactics to achieve changes
in laws and public policy that would
guarantee women equal rights. Emphasis
on "rights" meant extending to women in
life outside the home the same "rights"
men had, granting them the same options,
privileges, and responsibilities that men
enjoyed. There was little suggestion initially of personal or cultural transformation.

Women's liberationists were younger
women, less highly educated, whose ideology and political style, shaped in the
dissent and violence of the 1960s, led
them to look at women's predicament differently. Instead of relying upon traditional organizational structure and lobbying techniques, they developed a new
style of politics. Instead of limiting their
goals to changes in public policy, they

embraced a transformation in private, domestic life as well. They sought liberation
from ways of thinking and behaving that
they believed stunted or distorted wom-
en's growth and kept them subordinate to
men. Through the extension of their own
personal liberation they hoped to remake
the male world, changing it as they had
changed themselves. For women's liberationists as for women's rights advocates,
however, the first step toward becoming
feminists demanded a clear statement of
women's position in society, one that
called attention to the gap between the
egalitarian ideal and the actual position of
women in American culture. There also
had to be a call to action from women
themselves, *for* women, *with* women,
through women. Redefining themselves,
they had to make being a woman a political fact; and, as they did so, they had to
live with the radical implications of what
could only be called a rebirth.

The Making of Feminists: Women's Rights Advocates

For some women, the process of radicalization began with the appointment of a
Presidential Commission on the Status of
Women in 1961. Presidents, Democrat
and Republican, customarily discharged
their political debt to female members of
the electorate, especially to those who had
loyally served the party, by appointing a
few token women, usually party stal-
warts, to highly visible posts. John Kennedy was no exception. He was, however,
convinced by Esther Petersen that the
vast majority of women would be better
served if he also appointed a commission
charged with investigating obstacles to
the full participation of women in society.
Assistant secretary of labor and head of
the Women's Bureau, Petersen believed
that the report of such a commission
could sensitize the public to barriers to
equality just as her own experience as a
labor organizer had sensitized her to the
particular problems confronting women

workers. Citizens thus informed could then be mobilized on behalf of governmental efforts at reform.[19] Accordingly, the commission was appointed with Eleanor Roosevelt serving as chair until her death a year later. Its report, *American Women* (1963), was conservative in tone, acknowledging the importance of women's traditional roles within the home and the progress they had made in a "free democratic society." It also provided extensive documentation of discriminatory practices in government, education, and employment, along with substantial recommendations for change.[20] Governors, replicating Kennedy's move, appointed state commissions on the status of women. In these commissions hundreds of men and women encountered further evidence of the economic, social, and legal disabilities that encumbered the nation's "second sex." For some, the statistics were old news; for others, they were a revelation.

Although there were variations from state to state, the pattern documented by the North Carolina Commission soon became increasingly familiar to a small but growing number of women throughout the nation. According to that commission's report, women workers, who made up over one-third of the state's labor force, suffered economically from job segregation and pay inequities. Of the 600,000 women employed outside the home in 1960, most (68 percent) were concentrated in blue-collar jobs or in traditionally low-paying "female" professions such as teaching and nursing. Whatever their occupational level, women earned significantly less than their male counterparts with comparable skills, experience, and responsibilities. They also had fewer opportunities for advancement. (Female mill operatives, for example, earned nearly 30 percent less than male operatives.)

Educational experience, seemingly more equitable, actually foreshadowed economic inequities. At the graduate level, women constituted only a tiny fraction of those enrolled in schools training future members of high-paying professions such as medicine. At the undergraduate level, female students clustered in the humanities, avoiding the math and science courses necessary for providing greater career choice. Whatever their educational level, most women lacked access to diversified vocational training, enlightened career guidance, and the kind of role models provided by women, especially minority women, holding important nontraditional jobs. Worse still, they lacked expert, readily available child care. (Licensed day care facilities had only one space available for every seventeen preschool children of working mothers.)

Legally women in North Carolina, as elsewhere, were handicapped not only by hundreds of discriminatory federal statutes but also by state laws denying them equal treatment under the law. For example, married women still lacked complete control over their own property; state law required the written assent of the husband before a wife could convey her real property to someone else. Nor did women function as political equals. In North Carolina, as in other states, women were less likely to vote than men and far less likely to hold elective office or significant policy-making jobs. Especially disturbing to the commission was the failure of most women to understand "the direct connection between their own active and informed participation in politics . . . and the solution to many of their most pressing problems."[21]

Some women, however, could make that connection. Aroused by growing evidence of "the enormity of our problem," members of state commissions gathered in Washington in 1966 for the Third National Conference of the Commissions on the Status of Women. Individuals who were coming to know and rely on one another as they pooled their growing knowledge of widespread inequities, they were a network in the making. They were also women who wanted something done. This time they encountered a situation that transformed at least some of those present into activists in a new movement for women's equality. The catalyst proved to be a struggle involving Representative Martha Griffiths and the Equal Employment Opportunity Commission (EEOC), the federal agency in charge of implementing the Civil Rights Act of 1964.

Despite the fact that the law proscribed discrimination on the basis of sex as well as race, the commission refused to take seriously the problem of sexual discrimination. The first executive director of EEOC, knowing that "sex" had been injected into the bill by opponents seeking to block its passage, regarded the sex provision as a "fluke" best ignored. Representative Griffiths from Michigan thought otherwise. While the bill was still in Congress she encouraged a small group of women in the House to become part of an unlikely alliance with legislative opponents of a federal civil rights act in order to keep the sex provision in the bill. Liberals objected, fearing that so encumbering a bill would prevent passage of much-needed legislation on behalf of racial equality. But despite such objections—and the ridicule of many of her male colleagues—Griffiths persisted. Once the bill passed she was determined to see the new law enforced in its entirety. When EEOC failed to do so, she lambasted the agency for its inaction in a biting speech delivered on the House floor only days before the Conference of the Commissions on the Status of Women met.

Griffiths's concern was shared by a group of women working within EEOC. They argued that the agency could be made to take gender-related discrimination more seriously if women had a civil rights organization as adept at applying pressure on their behalf as was the National Association for the Advancement of Colored People (NAACP) on behalf of blacks. Initially the idea was rejected. Conference participants most upset by EEOC's inaction decided instead to propose a resolution urging the agency to treat sexual discrimination with the same seriousness it applied to racial discrimination. When the resolution was ruled inappropriate by conference leaders, they were forced to reconsider. After a whispered conversation over lunch they concluded the time for discussion of the status of women was over. It was time for action. Before the day was out twenty-eight women had paid five dollars each to join the National Organization for Women (NOW), including author Betty Friedan who happened to be in Washington at the time of the conference.[22]

Friedan's presence in Washington was auspicious; her involvement in NOW, virtually inevitable. The author of a brilliant polemic published in 1963, she not only labeled the resurgent domestic ideology of recent decades but exposed the groups perpetuating it. Editors of women's magazines, advertising experts, Freudian psychologists, social scientists, and educators—all, according to Freidan, contributed to a romanticization of domesticity she termed "the feminine mystique." The result, she charged, was the infantilization of intelligent women and the transformation of the suburban home into a "comfortable concentration camp."[23] Harsh words, they rang true to those who found the creativity of homemaking and the joys of motherhood vastly exaggerated. Sales of the book ultimately zoomed past the million mark.

By articulating heretofore inarticulated grievances, The Feminine Mystique had advanced a process initiated by more dispassionate investigations of women's status and the discriminatory practices which made that status inferior. That process was the collective expression of discontent. It is not surprising that those who best expressed that discontent initially were overwhelmingly white, educated, and middle or upper middle class. College women who regarded themselves the equals of male classmates by virtue of intellect and training were, as Jo Freeman points out, more likely to develop expectations they saw realized by their male peers but not, in most cases, by themselves. The frustrations were even greater for women with professional training. The very fact that many had sought advanced training in fields not traditionally "female" meant that they were less likely to find in traditional sex roles the identity and self-esteem such roles provided other women. Moreover, when measuring themselves against fellow professionals who happened to be men, the greater rewards enjoyed by their male counterparts seemed especially galling. Privileged though they were, such women *felt* more deprived in many cases than did those women who were in reality less privileged. By 1966 this sense of deprivation had been sufficiently articulated and shared and the networks of like-minded women sufficiently developed so that collective discontent could be translated into collective action. The formation of NOW signaled the birth of a new feminist movement.[24]

The three hundred men and women who gathered in October for the organizational meeting of NOW were in the main professionals, some of them veterans of commissions on the status of women. Adopting bylaws and a statement of purpose, they elected officers, naming Friedan president. Her conviction that intelligent women needed purposeful, generative work of their own was reflected in NOW's statement of purpose, which attacked "the traditional assumption that a woman has to choose between marriage and motherhood on the one hand and serious participation in industry or the professions on the other." Determined that women should be allowed to develop their full potential as human beings, the organization's goal was to bring them into "full participation in the mainstream of American society NOW, exercising all the privileges and responsibilities thereof in truly equal partnership with men." To that end NOW developed a Bill of Rights, adopted at its 1967 meeting, that exhorted Congress to pass an equal rights amendment to the Constitution, called on EEOC to enforce antidiscrimination legislation, and urged federal and state legislators to guarantee equal and unsegregated education. To ensure women control over their reproductive lives, these new feminists called for removal of penal codes denying women contraceptive information and devices as well as safe, legal abortions. To ease the double burden of working mothers, they urged legislation that would ensure maternity leaves without jeopardizing job security or seniority, permit tax deductions for child care expenses, and create public, inexpensive day care centers. To improve the lot of poor women, they urged reform of the welfare system and equality with respect to benefits, including job-training programs.[25]

Not content simply to call for change, NOW leaders worked to make it happen. Using persuasion, pressure, and even litigation, they, with other newly formed women's rights groups such as the Women's Equity Action League (WEAL), launched a massive attack on sex discrimination. By the end of the 1960s NOW members had filed legal suits against newspapers listing jobs under the headings "Help Wanted: Male" and "Help Wanted: Female," successfully arguing that such headings discouraged women from applying for jobs they were perfectly capable of doing. Building on efforts begun in the Kennedy administration such as the passage of the Equal Pay Act, they pressured the federal government to intensify its commitment to equal opportunity. They urged congressmen and labor leaders to persuade the Department of Labor to include women in its guidelines designed to encourage the hiring and promotion of blacks in firms holding contracts with the federal government. They persuaded the Federal Communications Commission to open up new opportunities for women in broadcasting. Tackling the campus as well as the marketplace, WEAL filed suit against more than three hundred colleges and universities, ultimately securing millions of dollars in salary raises for women faculty members who had been victims of discrimination. To ensure that women receive the same pay men received for doing the same work, these new feminists lobbied for passage of a new Equal Employment Opportunity Act that would enable EEOC to fight discrimination more effectively.

NOW also scrutinized the discriminatory practices of financial institutions, persuading them to issue credit to single women and to married women in their own—not their husband's—name. WEAL, in turn, filed charges against banks and other lending institutions that refused to grant mortgages to single women, or in the case of married couples, refused to take into account the wife's earning in evaluating the couple's eligibility for a mortgage. Colleges and universities that discriminated against female students in their sports programs came under fire, as did fellowship programs that failed to give adequate consideration to female applicants.

While NOW and WEAL attacked barriers in industry and education, the National Women's Political Caucus (NWPC) focused on government and politics. Formed in 1971, the caucus was initiated by Friedan, New York congresswomen Bella Abzug and Shirley Chisholm—both outspoken champions of women's rights—and Gloria Steinem, soon to become founding editor of the new mass-circulation feminist magazine Ms. Especially concerned about the small numbers of women in government, the caucus concentrated on getting women elected and appointed to public office while also rallying support for issues such as the Equal

Rights Amendment (see document 12 in Essential Documents). Meanwhile women in the professions, aware of their small numbers and inferior status, began to organize as well. Physicians, lawyers, and university professors fought for equal opportunity in the meetings of such overwhelmingly male groups as the American Medical Association, the American Association of University Professors, and the American Historical Association.[26]

Collectively such protests served notice that more women were becoming feminists. The particular combination of events that transformed women into feminists varied with the individual. A southern legislator, describing the process that brought home the reality of her own second-class citizenship, wrote:

> As a State Senator, I succeeded in getting Mississippi women the right to sit on juries (1968); the opposition's arguments were appalling. When women began hiring me in order to get credit, I became upset at the discrimination I saw. After I was divorced in 1970, I was initially denied a home loan. The effect was one of the worst traumas I've suffered. Denial of a home loan to one who was both a professional and a member of the legislature brought things to a head.[27]

Although the number of women who understood what it meant to be the "second sex" were still only a tiny minority, they were nonetheless a minority whose energy, talents, and experience enabled them to work for changes necessary to ensure equal rights.

THE MAKING OF FEMINISTS: WOMEN'S LIBERATION

The process of radicalization that transformed some individuals into women's rights advocates occurred simultaneously—but in different fashion and with somewhat different results—among a younger generation of women. Many of them veterans of either the civil rights movement or the new left, these were the activists who would become identified with the women's liberation branch of the women's movement. Differing in perspective as well as style, they would ultimately push many of their older counterparts beyond the demand for equal rights to recognition that true emancipation would require a far-reaching transformation of society and culture.

The experiences awakening in this 1960s generation a feminist consciousness have been superbly described by Sara Evans in her book, *Personal Politics*.[28] "Freedom, equality, love and hope," the possibility of new human relationships, the importance of participatory democracy—letting the people decide—were, as Evans points out, part of an egalitarian ideology shared by both the southern-based Student Nonviolent Coordinating Committee (SNCC) in its struggle for racial equality and the Students for a Democratic Society (SDS) in its efforts to mobilize an interracial organization of the urban poor in northern ghettos. Membership in both organizations—"the movement"—thus reinforced commitment to these ideals among the women who joined. In order to translate ideals into reality, however, young, college-age women who had left the shelter of middle-class families for the hard and dangerous work of transforming society found themselves doing things that they would never have thought possible. Amidst the racial strife of the South, they joined picket lines, created freedom schools, and canvassed for voter registration among blacks, often enduring arrest and jailing. SDS women from affluent suburbs entered decaying tenements and were surrounded by the grim realities of the ghetto. They trudged door-to-door in an effort to reach women whose struggle to survive made many understandably suspicious of intruding strangers. Summing up the feelings of hundreds, one young woman wrote: "I learned a lot of respect for myself for having gone through all that." A height-

ened sense of self-worth and autonomy, Evans argues, was not all they acquired. They also learned the skills of movement building and the nuts and bolts of organizing.

Particularly important was the problem of getting people, long passive, to act on their own behalf. SDS women began by encouraging ghetto women together to talk about their problems. This sharing of experiences, they believed, would lead these women to recognize not only that their problems were common but that solutions required changes in the system. In the process of organizing, the organizers also learned. They began to understand the meaning of oppression and the valor required of those who fought it. They found new role models, Evans suggests, in extraordinary southern black women whose courage never waivered in the face of violence and in those welfare mothers of the North who confronted welfare bureaucrat and slum lord after years of passivity.

But if being in the movement brought a new understanding of equality, it also brought new problems. Men who were committed to equality for one group were not necessarily committed to equality for another group. Women in SNCC, as in SDS, found themselves frequently relegated to domestic chores and refused a key voice in the formulation of policy. Moreover, the sexual freedom that had been theirs as part of the cultural revolution taking place in the 1960s soon began to feel more like sexual exploitation as they saw their role in the movement spelled out in the draft resister's slogan: "Girls Say Yes to Guys Who Say No." Efforts to change the situation were firmly rebuffed. When SNCC leader Stokeley Carmichael announced, "The only position for women in SNCC is prone," he spoke for white males in the new left as well. Evans concludes: "The same movement that permitted women to grow and to develop self-esteem, energy, and skills generally kept women out of leadership roles and reinforced expectations that women would conform to tradition as houseworkers, nurturers, and sex objects." By 1967 the tensions had become so intense that women left the movement to organize on behalf of their own "liberation."

They did not leave empty handed. As radicals, they were accustomed to challenging prevailing ideas and practices. As movement veterans, they had acquired a language of protest, an organizing tactic, and a deep-seated conviction that the personal was political. How that legacy would shape this burgeoning new feminist movement became evident as small women's liberation groups began springing up spontaneously in major cities and university communities across the nation.

STRUCTURE, LEADERSHIP, AND CONSCIOUSNESS-RAISING

Initially, at least, the two branches of the new feminism seemed almost to be two different movements, so unlike were they in structure and style. Linked only by newsletters, notices in underground newspapers, and networks of friends, women's liberation groups rejected both traditional organizational structure and leadership. Unlike NOW and other women's rights groups, they had no central headquarters, no elected officers, no bylaws. There was no legislative agenda and little of the activism that transformed the more politically astute women's rights leaders into skilled lobbyists and tacticians. Instead this younger generation of feminists, organizing new groups wherever they found themselves, concentrated on a kind of personal politics rooted in movement days. Looking back on male-dominated meetings in which, however informal the gathering, a few highly verbal, aggressive men invariably controlled debate and dictated strategy and left less articulate and assertive women effectively excluded, they

recalled the technique they had used in organizing the poor. They remembered how they had encouraged those women to talk among themselves until the personal became political, that is, until problems which, at first glance, seemed to be personal were finally understood to be social in cause—rooted in society rather than in the individual—and political in solution. Applying this same process in their own informal "rap groups," women's liberationists developed the technique of "consciousness raising." Adopted by women's rights groups such as local chapters of NOW, consciousness-raising sessions became one of the most important innovations of the entire feminist movement.[29]

The immediate task of the consciousness-raising session was to bring together in a caring, supportive, noncompetitive setting women accustomed to relating most intimately not with other women but with men—husbands, lovers, "friends." As these women talked among themselves, exchanging confidences, reassessing old options, and mentally exploring new ones, a sense of shared problems began to emerge. The women themselves gradually gained greater understanding of how profoundly their lives had been shaped by the constraints of culture. Personal experience with those constraints merged with intellectual awareness of women's inferior status and the factors that made it so. By the same token, new understanding of problems generated new determination to resolve them. Anger, aggression, and frustration formerly turned inward in unconscious self-hatred began to be directed outward, becoming transformed into new energy directed toward constructive goals. If society and culture had defined who women were through their unconscious internalization of tradition, they could reverse the process, and, by redefining themselves, redefine society and culture. At work was a process of change so fundamental that the individuals undergoing it ultimately emerged in a very real sense as different people. Now feminists, these were women with a different understanding of reality—a new "consciousness," a new sense of "sisterhood," and a new commitment to change.

Consciousness raising was an invigorating and sometimes frightening experience. As one young woman wrote, "This whole movement is the most exhilarating thing of my life. The last eight months have been a personal revolution. Nonetheless, I recognize there is dynamite in this and I'm scared shitless."[30] "Scared" or not, such women could no longer be contained. Veterans of one rap group fanned out, creating others. For the feminist movement, this mushrooming of groups meant increased numbers and added momentum. For some of the women involved, it meant confronting and articulating theoretically as well as personally what "oppression," "sexism," and "liberation" really meant; in short, developing a feminist ideology.

TOWARD A FEMINIST IDEOLOGY: OPPRESSION, SEXISM, AND CHANGE

The development of feminist ideology was not a simple process. Women's rights advocates were essentially pragmatic, more interested in practical results than in theoretical explanations. Even among feminists who were more theoretically oriented, intellectual perspectives reflected differences in experience, temperament, style, and politics.[31] Manifestos, position papers, and books began to pile up as feminists searched for the historical origins of female oppression. Socialist feminists debated nonsocialist feminists as to whether socialism was a prerequisite for women's liberation. Lesbian feminists argued that the ultimate rejection of male domination meant the rejection of intimacy with men. Other feminists insisted that rigid sex-role differentiation op-

pressed men as well as women and that their goal should be restructuring male-female relations in ways that would encourage greater mutuality and fulfillment for both sexes in all aspects of life. Given such a variety of perspectives, it is almost impossible to talk about a feminist ideology in the sense of a unified theory to which all members of the women's movement subscribe. At the risk of considerable oversimplification, however, it is possible to talk about a critique of society. Owing much to the liberationists, this critique has come to be shared by many in the movement, including many women's rights advocates who started out with the initial belief that equality meant simply giving women the same "rights" men enjoyed.

Although feminists differ as to the historical roots of oppression, they agree that men have been the dominant sex and that women as a group are oppressed. Explanations for the perpetuation of oppression in present-day society also vary. Feminists whose socialism was forged in the new left of the 1960s see oppression as the inevitable result of a capitalist system that permits employers, in effect, to hire two workers for the price of one (men being paid wages with their unpaid wives performing the services necessary to enable them to perform their jobs). Women also working outside the home function as a cheap labor force enabling employers to keep wages low and profits high. Other feminists, including members of women's rights groups such as NOW, WEAL, and NWPC, believe the continuation of male domination and female oppression is perpetuated by sex role socialization and cultural values that continue to confer on males higher status, greater options, and greater power, by virtue of their sex. This preference, conscious and unconscious, for whatever is "masculine," feminists term *sexism*. Not surprisingly, they reject the traditional assumption that biology—sexual dichotomy—dictates distinct spheres, status, roles, or personality types. To put the matter most simply, feminists reject the notion that the bearing of children creates for women "natural" roles as wives and mothers, a rightful "place" limited to the home, a subordinate status, and behavior patterns of self-denying submissiveness and service to others. The persistence of gender-based determinism, they believe, continues to limit options resulting in female dependency and the vapid, trivialized image of femininity associated with such dependency—the femininity of the "Total Woman" with its mixture of sexuality and submissiveness. The fact that so many women continue to rely on men not only for financial support but also for social status and even self-esteem, feminists argue, deprives such women of the economic and psychological freedom to determine their own lives, to make real choices, to be judged as individuals on the basis of their own merit and accomplishments, not those of fathers or husbands.

Just as traditional male roles provide access to power and independence in a sexist society, whereas female roles do not, so masculine values define what attributes are admired and rewarded. Thus masculine qualities are associated with strength, competence, independence, and rationality, while female qualities are associated with fragility, dependence, passivity, and emotionalism. These qualities, however, are not intrinsically "male" or "female" in the sense that they are biologically inherent. Rather, feminists argue, they are an extension of the training that is part of sex role socialization. The very fact that masculine values are those Americans of both sexes regard more highly and also constitute the standard by which mental health is judged has implications feminists find distressing. Women, internalizing these sexist judgments and feeling themselves lacking in competence, tend to undervalue themselves (and women in general) and therefore lack

self-esteem. Moreover, society also undervalues the female qualities that are positive, such as nurturing, supportiveness, and empathy. *All* of these qualities—those considered "male" and those considered "female"—feminists insist are shared human qualities. Those that are desirable, such as competence, independence, supportiveness, and nurturing, should be encouraged in both men and women.

Such changes, however, demand the eradication of sexism. And sexism, feminists believe, is persistent, pervasive, and powerful. It is internalized by women as well as men. It is most dramatically evident in the programmed-to-please women who search for happiness through submissiveness to men and in the men who use their power to limit women's options and keep them dependent. It is also evident in a more subtle fashion among women who emulate male models and values, refusing to see those aspects of women's lives that are positive and life affirming, and among men who are unaware of the unconscious sexism permeating their attitudes and actions. Internalized in individuals, sexism is also embedded in institutions—the family, the educational system, the media, politics, the law, and even organized religion.

Given the pervasiveness of sexism, many feminists see no possibility for real equality short of transformation not only of individuals but also of social institutions and cultural values. Even what was once seen as the relatively simple demand of women's rights advocates for equal pay for equal work no longer seems so simple. What seemed to be a matter of obtaining equal rights *within* the existing system in reality demands changes that *transform* the system. Involved is:

a reevaluation of women as workers, of women as mothers, of mothers as workers, of work as suitable for one gender and not for the other. The demand implies equal opportunity and thus equal responsibilities. It implies a childhood in which girls are rewarded for competence, risk taking, achievement, competitiveness and independence—just like boys. Equal pay for equal work means a revision in our expectations about women as equal workers and it involves the institutional arrangements to make them so.

"There is nothing small here," observes a noted feminist scholar.[32] And indeed there is not.

FEMINISM IN ACTION

While the contemporary women's movement contains under its broad umbrella women who differ significantly in the degree of their radicalism, the changes implied in achieving sexual equality are of such scope as to make radical by definition those who genuinely understand what is involved in equality and, beyond that, emancipation.[33] Feminism is not for the fainthearted. To clarify frustration and rage so as to understand problems accurately and then to use that understanding in ways that permit growth and change in one's self are to engage in a process requiring considerable courage and energy. To reform society so that women can achieve legal, economic, and social parity requires even greater commitment—commitment that has to be sustained over time and through defeat. To work for cultural transformation of a patriarchal world in such a way as to benefit both men and women requires extraordinary breadth of vision as well as sustained energy and dedication. Yet despite the obstacles, thousands of women during the past decade have participated in the process.

For some the changes have consisted largely of private actions—relationships renegotiated, careers resumed. Others, preferring to make public statements of new commitments, used flamboyant methods to dramatize the subtle ways in which society so defined woman's place as to deny not only her full participation but

also her full humanity. As part of the confrontational politics of the 1960s, feminists picketed the 1968 Miss America contest, protesting our national preoccupation with bust size and "congeniality" rather than brain power and character. (In the process they were dubbed "bra burners," despite the fact that no bras were burned.) Activists pushed their way into all-male bars and restaurants as a way of forcing recognition of how these bastions of male exclusivity were themselves statements about "man's world/woman's place." They sat in at the offices of *Ladies' Home Journal* and *Newsweek* protesting the ways in which the media's depiction of women perpetuated old stereotypes at the expense of new realities.

Still other feminists chose to work for social change in a different fashion. They created nonsexist day care centers, wrote and published nonsexist children's books, monitored sex stereotyping in textbooks, lobbied for women's studies programs in high schools and colleges, and founded women's health clinics. They worked for reform of abortion laws so that women would not be forced to continue pregnancies that were physically or psychologically hazardous but could instead have the option of a safe, legal abortion. They formed rape crisis centers so that rape victims could be treated by caring females; they agitated for more informed, sympathetic treatment on the part of hospital staffs, the police, and the courts. Feminists also lobbied for programs to retrain displaced homemakers so that such women could move from economic dependency to self-support. Feminist scholars used their talents to recover and interpret women's experience, opening new areas for research and in the process furthering change. Feminist legislators sponsored bills, not always successful, to help housewives to secure some form of economic recognition for work performed, to enable women workers to obtain insurance that would give them the same degree of economic security afforded male coworkers, and to secure for battered wives protection from the physical violence that is the most blatant form of male oppression. Black feminists, speaking out on the "double jeopardy" of being black and female—"the most pressed down of us all"—lent their support to feminist measures of especial importance to minority women.[34] Actions, like voices, differed. Such diversity, however, was basic to the movement.

FEMINISM: THE PUBLIC IMPACT

In a society in which the media create instant awareness of social change, feminism burst upon the public consciousness with all the understated visibility of a fireworks display on the Fourth of July. The more radical elements of the movement with their talk of test tube conception, the slavery of marriage, and the downfall of capitalism might be dismissed out of hand. But it was hard to ignore the presence of *Ms.* magazine on newsstands, feminist books on the best-seller lists, women in hard hats on construction jobs or the government-mandated affirmative action programs that put them there. It was harder still to ignore the publicity that accompanied the appointment of women to the Carter cabinet, the enrollment of coeds in the nation's military academies, and the ordination of women to the ministry. A Harris poll of December 1975 reported that 63 percent of the women interviewed favored most changes designed to improve the status of women, although some were quick to insist that they were not "women's libbers."[35]

Evidence of changing views was everywhere. The list of organizations lined up in support of ratification of the Equal Rights Amendment included not only such avowedly feminist groups as NOW, WEAL, and NWPC as well as longtime supporters such as the National Woman's Party and the National Federation of Business and Professional Women's Clubs, but also "mainstream" women's organizations such as the General Federation of Women's Clubs, the American Association of University Women, the League of Women Voters, the National Council of Jewish Women, the National Council of Negro Women, and the YWCA. Included, too, were the Girl Scouts of America, along with a host of churches and labor organizations. Even more potent evidence that feminism had "arrived" was the 1977 National Women's Conference in Houston. Before over two thousand delegates from every state and territory in the United States and twenty thousand guests, three First Ladies—Lady Bird Johnson, Betty Ford, and Rosalynn Carter—endorsed the Equal Rights Amendment and the goals of the Houston Conference, their hands holding a lighted torch carried by women runners from Seneca Falls where, in 1848, the famous Declaration of Sentiments had been adopted. Confessing that she once thought the women's movement belonged more to her daughters than to herself, Lady Bird Johnson added, "I have come to know that it belongs to women of all ages." Such an admission, like the presence of these three women on the platform, proclaimed a message about feminists that was boldly printed on balloons throughout the convention hall: "We Are Everywhere!"[36]

OPPOSITION TO FEMINISM

For some women the slogan was not a sign of achievement but of threat. Gathered at a counter-convention in Houston and proudly wearing "Stop ERA" buttons were women who shared neither the critique nor the goals of the women's movement. They were an impressive reminder that social change generates opposition and that opposition to feminism had crystalized in the struggle for ratification of the Equal Rights Amendment. ERA—as the amendment is called—is a simple statement: "Equality of rights under the law shall not be denied or abridged by the United States or by any State on account of sex." It was first suggested in 1923 as the logical extension of suffrage. Not all feminists embraced the amendment, however. Some, fearing it would be used to strike down laws to protect women in the workplace, preferred to look for constitutional guarantees of equality through the extension of judicial interpretation of the Fifth and Fourteenth Amendments. By the 1960s sentiments had shifted. NOW called for passage of the amendment as part of its legislative agenda. The President's Task Force on the Status of Women and the Citizen's Advisory Council on the Status of Women endorsed the amendment, as did Presidents Johnson and Nixon. Persuasive feminists helped to bring aboard such historic opponents as the Women's Bureau and organized labor. Arguing in support of the amendment, they pointed out that New Deal legislation provided a basis for protection of both sexes that had not existed in the 1920s. They also pointed out that many state laws granting protection only to women had already been voided by Title VII of the Civil Rights Act of 1964. With unions and many women's organizations thus persuaded, NOW turned its attention to Congress itself, asking legislators to pass a constitutional amendment removing sexual bias from common, statutory, and constitutional law. In the spring of 1972 the Senate finally joined the House and sent ERA to the states for ratification by a lopsided vote of eighty-four to eight. Almost immediately twenty-one states rushed to ratify. By the spring of 1973, however, opponents of ratification had begun a counterattack that ultimately stalled the number of ratified states at thirty-five, three short of the needed three-fourths majority. They even induced

some ratifying states to rescind their approval. Early successes indicated that a majority of Americans favored ERA—but not a large enough majority.

Opposition to ERA is starkly paradoxical. A constitutional amendment proposed especially to benefit women was opposed by many of them. The dimensions of paradox are suggested by the reasons sometimes given for taking a position on the issue. Women opposed the amendment because they wanted to protect the family; other women supported it because they, too, wanted to protect the family. Women resisted ERA because some could not trust men to treat women fairly; and others supported it, giving precisely the same reason.

The paradox is resolved in part by remembering that conservatives of both sexes are often suspicious of the principle of equality, especially when identified with specific controversial federal policies. This is especially true of programs to bus school children in order to achieve equality through "racial balance" in the public schools. The policy was believed by some parents to be a denial of their right to educate their children how and where they pleased. Proponents of busing saw it as an issue of public policy, having nothing to do with private relationships. But opponents believed that education was an extension of the private relationships between parents and children. The moving of children literally from their parents' door to a faraway school was an act reinforcing the sense of losing one's children. Busing, therefore, was seen as an intrusion into the private domain of family, subverting the influence and values of parents. Other federal policies seemed to do the same thing. Attempts to break up segregated housing, for example, were seen as an assault on the right to live in neighborhoods that reflected the private, family lives of the people who lived there. Since ERA was perceived both as a continuation of previous governmental commitment to equality *and* as a symbol of feminism, it was attacked for attempting to give the federal bureaucracy power to change relationships within the family. Opposition to ERA expressed a diffuse anger with federal intervention in "private" relationships. As one woman wrote her U.S. senator: "Forced busing, forced mixing, forced housing. Now forced women! No thank you!"[37]

Opposition to ERA also expressed an elemental response to what many people believe to be a threat to cherished values. "The drug revolution, the sexual revolution, gay liberation, students' rights, children's rights, and the civil rights and the Native American and Latino movements"—to borrow the list of one observer—all challenged basic middle-class values.[38] Above all, there was the women's movement. Feminists believed that theirs was a struggle for justice and liberation— liberation from social roles and cultural values that denied rights and limited autonomy. To require all women to conform to patterns of behavior dictated not by biology but by culture was, from the standpoint of feminists, to deny freedom and self-determination to half the population simply because they were born female. To women who did not believe they were oppressed, however, feminists' efforts at liberation appeared *not* as an attack on unjust constraints but rather as an attack on familiar patterns that provide security. To women who had internalized traditional female roles, feminism, with its demands to rethink what it means to be a man or a woman, was perceived not just as an assault upon them personally but as symbolic of every other threat to their identity and traditions. Because ERA has been seen as the instrument through which feminists could achieve goals regarded by antifeminists as Utopian and threatening, the amendment itself has come to symbolize to its opponents both the danger and absurdity

inherent in this latest drive for equality of the sexes. Indeed the very idea of oppression seems preposterous to women who believe that they have benefited from being treated as "the fairer sex" and "the better half." Their experience, even if not the ideal of wedded bliss, nevertheless seems to them to be at odds with that of feminists who seem to antifeminists to be attacking women for behaving like women.

From this point of view feminists appear silly for wanting to use *Ms.* instead of the traditional *Mrs.* or *Miss*, tasteless for intruding where men do not want them to be, eccentric for celebrating the filly who won the Kentucky Derby. Worse still, feminists, in the eyes of antifeminists, appear to be women-who-want-to-be-men. The accusation that ERA would require men and women to use the same public toilets is not therefore to be taken literally so much as symbolically. It represents the intrusion of men and of women-who-want-to-be-men into the privacy of women-who-are-proud-to-be-women. The accusation that ERA would destroy the family should also be understood as a way of defending the social significance and indispensability of traditional female roles. Underlying everything is the theme of purity (traditional female roles) against danger and corruption (social disintegration). The result of this formulation of the issue of equality has been to enable antifeminist women to develop a consciousness of their own. The free-floating anxiety aroused by the enormity of the social change inherent in feminism thus acquired a concrete focus. ERA became an issue in which what seemed to be at stake for opponents was their very identity as women—and the fate of society.

Predictions of the terrible consequences that would result from ratification of the amendment were not so important as was the function such statements seemed to serve—that is, the reaffirmation of traditional sex roles identified with social stability. The indictment of feminism and of ERA is an indictment of what Phyllis Schlafly, the chief female opponent of ratification, persistently calls the "unisex society." By rallying women to this danger, Schlafly has revealed that the issue was not whether or not women should stay at home minding the children and cooking the food—Schlafly herself did not do that. The issue was the *meaning* of sexual differences between men and women.

Many feminists minimize those differences, believing that traditional roles are not only oppressive but outmoded because reproductive control and work in the public sector have made women's lives more like men's. Antifeminists inflate those differences. Their response is a measure both of their belief that women are "eternal in their attributes and unchanged by events" and their anger and distress at changes that have already occurred.[39] It is a reminder, too, of how far the feminist movement has still to go to achieve the political and legal reforms it seeks, much less its more far-reaching goals.[40]

NEW PROGRESS AND OLD PROBLEMS

There were gains during the 1970s to be sure. New reproductive freedom came with the Supreme Court's liberalization of abortion laws that removed the danger of the illegal, back alley abortions so long the recourse of desperate women. Sexual preference and practice became less an occasion for denial of civil rights and more a matter of individual choice. Evidence of expanding educational and employment opportunities seemed to be everywhere. Women assumed high level posts in government, the judiciary, the military, business, and labor. From an expanding population of female college graduates, younger women moved in record numbers into professional schools, dramatically changing enrollment patterns in such fields as law, medicine, and busi-

ness. Their blue-collar counterparts, completing job training programs, trickled into the construction industry and other trades, finding in those jobs the decent wage that had eluded them as waitresses, hairdressers, sales clerks, or domestics. Political participation also increased. Women emerged from years of lobbying for ERA with a new understanding of the political process. (So, too, did their opponents.) More female candidates filed for office and more female politicians worked themselves into positions of power. Revision of discriminatory statutes, while by no means completed, brought a greater measure of legal equality. A heightened public consciousness of sexism ushered in other changes. School officials began admitting boys to home economics classes, girls to shop. Some employers transformed maternity leaves into child care leaves, making them available to fathers as well as mothers. Liberal religious leaders talked of removing gender-related references from the Bible.[41]

Such gains, while in some cases smacking of tokenism, are not to be minimized. Most required persistent pressure from feminists, from government officials, and often from both. They were by no means comprehensive, however. As in the case of the civil rights movement, the initial beneficiaries of the feminist movement were predominantly middle-class, often highly educated, and relatively young. The increase in the number of single women, the older age at which women married for the first time, the declining birth rate—changes characteristic of the entire female population during the 1970s—were especially characteristic of a younger generation of career-oriented women.[42] But even for these women and their spouses, financial as well as personal costs were sometimes high: couples living apart for some portion of the week or year in order to take advantage of career opportunities; married women devoting virtually all of their salaries to domestic and child care costs, especially during their children's preschool years. Perhaps the personal recognition, independence, and sense of fulfillment associated with career success made the costs "affordable"—especially given the alternatives.

The women who stand to gain most from the implementation of feminists' efforts to change the nation's economic and social structure are not those who are young, talented, and educated but those who are less advantaged. Yet the latter could with good reason argue that over a decade of feminist activity had left their lives little changed in ways that really count. While the number of women in the work force continues to rise from less than 20 percent in 1920 to a projected 54 to 60 percent by 1990, working women in the 1970s saw the gap between male and female income widen rather than narrow.[43] Female workers earned 59 cents for every dollar earned by males. Although the gap is smaller among business and professional women than among blue-collar workers, a recent study of alumni of such prestigious graduate business schools as Stanford, Harvard, and the University of Pennsylvania indicated that women graduating in 1977 and 1978 were earning on the average $4,000 less a year than their male classmates.[44] Part of the explanation for this persistent gap lies in pay inequities. More fundamental, however, is the continuation of occupational segregation and the undervaluation of work done by women.[45] Around 80 percent of all working women still cluster in gender-segregated occupations in which wages are artificially low. At American Telephone and Telegraph, for example, a 1976 court case revealed that 97 percent of the middle management jobs were held by men, while 98 percent of all telephone operators and 94 percent of all clerical workers were women. Moreover, as inflationary pressures drive more women into the work force, competition for jobs in traditionally "female" fields enables employers to keep wages low.

With the dramatic rise in the number of female-headed households, the continuation of this occupational ghetto has disturbing implications not only for women workers but also for their children. Female heads of households, often lacking both child care facilities and skills that would equip them for better-paying jobs if such jobs were available, earn enough to enable only one in three to stay above the poverty level. Their struggle for economic survival is shared by other women, especially older women—widows or divorcees whose years of housework have left them without employable skills. Thus ironic as it may seem, the decade that witnessed the revival of the feminist movement also saw the feminization of poverty. By the end of the 1970s, two out of every three poor persons in the United States were female.[46]

Ironic, too, given the feminist insistence that child care and household responsibilities should be shared by working spouses, is the persistence of the double burden borne by women working outside the home. According to a recent national survey, in 53 percent of the couples interviewed both husband and wife agreed that, even though the wife held a job, she should also do the housework. Not surprisingly, working women continue to do 80 to 90 percent of the chores related to running a household, with husbands and children "helping out." For all the talk about the changing structure of family roles, major shifts occurred slowly, even in households in which women were informed and engaged enough to be familiar with current feminist views.[47] Although some fathers, especially among the middle class, have become more involved in parenting, the primary responsibility for children still remains the mother's. And working mothers still receive little institutional help despite the fact that by 1980 nearly half of all mothers with children under six worked outside the home. Without a fundamental rethinking of both work and family, women will continue to participate in the labor force in increasing numbers while, at the same time, remaining in its lower echelons as marginal members.[48]

In sum, economic and demographic change has been the basis of important changes in attitudes and behavior. As a result, life is more challenging for many women, but the feminization of poverty reminds the nation of its failures. We have yet to see the new social policies necessary to create the egalitarian and humane society envisioned by feminists. Indeed, in the climate of political conservatism of the 1980s feminists have had to fight hard to maintain gains already won. The reproductive freedom of poor women had already been eroded by limitations on federal funding of abortions, and the reproductive freedom of all women had been threatened by Congressional opponents of legalized abortion. Governmental enforcement of legislation mandating equal opportunity is effective only if a commitment to eradicate discrimination is backed with the funds and personnel necessary to do the job. Without an equal rights amendment requiring legislators to revise the discriminatory statutes that remain, the impetus will come not from the governments—state and local—but from individual women and men genuinely committed to equality before the law. Thus the need for collective action on the part of feminists is as great in the 1980s as it was in the 1970s.

Social change is complex and results from the interplay of many factors. No-where is this truer than in the women's movement. The swiftness with which a resurgent feminism captured the imagination of millions of American women dramatized the need for change. The inability of feminists to win ratification of ERA dramatized the limits of change. The irony of the polarization, however, was that the failure of ERA did not and could not stop feminism in its tracks and that antifeminist women, in mobilizing to fight the amendment, were themselves assuming a new role whether they acknowledged that fact or not. They organized lobbies, political action committees, and conventions; they also ran for and won public office. Where feminists have led, antifeminists would not be too far behind, defining themselves within the context of change they could not stop. But the rhetoric of liberation that had been so important to the awakening and maturation of women in the 1970s seemed by 1980 to be less appealing. Women could happily benefit from the achievements of feminism without understanding or embracing its critique and style. As a result, old patterns of sexual differentiation persisted. They had hindered efforts of women to establish a public role in the nineteenth century; they had restricted that public role once it was won. The same patterns, so indelible even under attack, continue to obstruct contemporary efforts to redefine social roles in the drive for equality. The tension between past position and future possibility, however, demands of all women—not merely feminists—a definition of self that extends beyond definitions of the past.

NOTES

I am especially indebted to William H. Chafe, Jacquelyn Dowd Hall, Linda K. Kerber, and Donald G. Mathews for their generous and helpful criticism of earlier drafts of this essay.

1. William H. Chafe, *The American Woman: Her Changing Social, Economic, and Political Roles, 1920–1970* (New York, 1972), p. 58.

2. Theodore Roosevelt, "The American Woman as Mother," in *The Journal of the Century* (New York, 1976), pp. 32–33.

3. Marion K. Sanders, *The Lady and the Vote* (Boston, 1956), p. 142.

4. For Elliott's account, see Marion W. Roydhouse, "The 'Universal Sisterhood of Women': Women and Labor Reform in North Carolina, 1900–1932" (Ph.D. dissertation, Duke University, 1980), pp. 91–92.

5. For a discussion of statistics relating to women in the professions as well as attitudes of college-educated women to careers, see Frank Stricker, "Cookbooks and Law Books: The Hidden History of Career Women in Twentieth Century America," *Journal of Social History* 10 (1976):1–19.

6. Excluded from this list are women who were appointed to congressional office simply to finish out the term of a deceased husband. Among these forty-seven, however, are women who were initially appointed or elected in a special election to fill the seat of a deceased incumbent, often a husband, and who went on to win election to a subsequent term—or terms—on their own. Figures were compiled from Rudolf Engelbart, *Women in the United States Congress, 1917–1972* (Littleton, Colo., 1974).

7. Margaret Mead, "Sex and Achievement," *Forum* 94 (1935):303.

8. Marynia F. Farnham and Ferdinand Lundberg, *Modern Woman: The Lost Sex* (New York, 1947), p. 202.

9. For an example of antisuffrage criticism on the dangers of suffrage to the family, see Anne F. Scott and Andrew M. Scott, *One Half the People: The Fight for Woman Suffrage* (New York, 1975), pp. 106–11.

10. Marjorie Rosen, *Popcorn Venus: Women, Movies, and the American Dream* (New York, 1973). Rosen uses the phrase as part of her title to chapter 18.

11. An excellent example of the antifeminist stance of many Freudian psychiatrists of the 1940s and 1950s is Helene Deutsch's *Psychology of Women* (New York, 1944). Typical is the statement: "Whenever the young girl exchanges a rich emotional life for scientific thinking, it is to be expected that later in her life sterility will take the place of motherliness even if she has given birth to many children" (2:67). Sports activities, greater intellectualization, and the one-child syndrome, according to Deutsch, were "visible forms in which the turning away from femininity manifested itself" (1: 303).

12. Sheila Tobias and Lisa Anderson, "What Really Happened to Rosie the Riveter? Demobilization and the Female Labor Force, 1944–47" MSS Modular Publications, Module

9 (1973), p. 3. Chafe argues in *The American Woman* (part 2) that World War II, nonetheless, represented a decisive break with traditional sex roles in that changes in women's economic roles provided a foundation for subsequent challenges to conventional definitions of women's place inasmuch as it helped to create a constituency for the contemporary women's movement.

13. According to a Gallup Poll, 86 percent of the American people objected to married women working; according to a *Fortune* poll, 67 percent. See Hadley Cantril, *Public Opinion, 1935–46* (Princeton, 1951), p. 1047, and "The *Fortune* Survey: Women in America," *Fortune* 34 (1946):8.

14. For a much more detailed analysis, see Valerie Kincade Oppenheimer, *The Female Labor Force in the United States: Demographic and Economic Factors Governing Its Growth and Changing Composition* (Berkeley, 1970).

15. For a fuller discussion of the way Americans and women in particular responded to this influx of married women in the work force, see Chafe, *The American Woman*, pp. 182–95, 218–19.

16. Lois Wladis Hoffman and F. Ivan Nye, *Working Mothers* (San Francisco, 1974), chaps. 6–7.

17. For a perceptive discussion of this issue, see Leslie Woodcock Tentler, *Wage-Earning Women: Industrial Work and Family Life in the United States, 1900–1930* (New York, 1979), pp. 180–85.

18. Quoted in Marguerite Wykoff Zapoleon, *The College Girl Looks Ahead to Her Career Opportunities* (New York, 1956), p. 9. See also Ashley Montagu, "The Triumph and Tragedy of the American Woman," *Saturday Review* 41 (1958):14.

19. Cynthia E. Harrison, "A 'New Frontier' for Women: The Public Policy of the Kennedy Administration," *Journal of American History* 67 (1980):630–46.

20. U.S. President's Commission on the Status of Women, *American Women* (Washington, D.C., 1963).

21. N.C., Governor's Commission on the Status of Women, *The Many Lives of North Carolina Women* (n.p., 1964). The report benefited from the fact that the study was funded—some state commissions were not—and from the expertise of some of its members among whom were then U.S. commissioner of welfare, Ellen Winston, and economist and later secretary of commerce, Juanita Kreps. The phrase quoted is that of Anne Firor Scott who chaired the commission. Al-

though none of these three found their involvement with the commission a "consciousness-raising" experience in that the data were already familiar, the findings were new to other members. Scott speculates that the many regional and national meetings attended by chairs of state commissions were important both for developing among those women involved a growing concern with women's issues and for network building. Interviews with Ellen Winston and Anne Firor Scott, December 7 and 8, 1980.

22. For events leading to the founding of NOW, see Jo Freeman, *The Politics of Women's Liberation: A Case Study of an Emerging Social Movement and Its Relation to the Social Policy Process* (New York, 1975), pp. 53–55. For a more detailed study of Title VII of the Civil Rights Act and its implementation, see Donald Allen Robinson, "Two Movements in Pursuit of Equal Employment Opportunity," *Signs: Journal of Women in Culture and Society* 4 (1979): 413–33.

23. Betty Friedan, *The Feminine Mystique* (New York, 1963).

24. Freeman, *Politics of Women's Liberation*, pp. 35–37.

25. National Organization for Women, Statement of Purpose, 1966, reprinted in *Up from the Pedestal*, ed. Aileen S. Kraditor (Chicago, 1968), pp. 363–64; National Organization for Women, Bill of Rights, 1967, reprinted in *Sisterhood Is Powerful: An Anthology of Writings on the Women's Liberation Movement*, ed. Robin Morgan (New York, 1970), pp. 512–14.

26. Freeman, *Politics of Women's Liberation*, chap. 3; Maren Lockwood Carden, *The New Feminist Movement* (New York, 1974), chaps. 8–10; also Gayle Graham Yates, *What Women Want: The Ideas of the Movement* (Cambridge, Mass., 1975), chap. 2.

27. Quoted in Carolyn Hadley, "Feminist Women in the Southeast," *Bulletin of the Center for the Study of Southern Culture and Religion* 3 (1979):10.

28. Sara Evans, *Personal Politics: The Roots of Women's Liberation in the Civil Rights Movement and the New Left* (New York, 1979); see also Evans, "Tomorrow's Yesterday: Feminist Consciousness and the Future of Women," in *Women of America: A History*, ed. Carol Ruth Berkin and Mary Beth Norton, (Boston, 1979), pp. 390–415. The following paragraphs rely heavily on this essay and Evans' *Personal Politics*.

29. For a discussion of women's liberation activities and ideas, see Carden, *New Feminist Movement*, chaps. 5–7, and Yates, *What Women Want*, chap. 3.

30. Quoted in Evans, "Tomorrow's Yesterday," p. 407.

31. The literature is extensive, beginning with Simone de Beauvoir, *The Second Sex*, trans. and ed. H. M. Parshley (New York, 1961). Alice Rossi's "Equality between the Sexes: An Immodest Proposal" in *The Woman in America*, ed. Robert Jay Lifton, *Daedalus* 93 (1964), 607–52, was especially important as an early statement by a feminist sociologist. Key works generated by the movement include Caroline Bird, *Born Female* (New York, 1969); Kate Millett, *Sexual Politics* (Garden City, N.Y., 1970); Shulamith Firestone, *The Dialectic of Sex: The Case for a Feminist Revolution* (New York, 1970); Judith Hole and Ellen Levine, *Rebirth of Feminism* (New York, 1971); Elizabeth Janeway, *Man's World/Woman's Place: A Study in Social Mythology* (New York, 1971); Juliet Mitchell, *Women's Estate* (New York, 1971); Evelyn Reed, *Problems of Women's Liberation: A Marxist Approach* (New York, 1971). Anthologies include Morgan, ed., *Sisterhood Is Powerful*; Toni Cade, ed. *The Black Woman: An Anthology* (New York, 1970); Deborah Babcox and Madeline Belkin, eds., *Liberation Now: Writings from the Women's Liberation Movement* (New York, 1971).

32. Judith M. Bardwick, *In Transition: How Feminism, Sexual Liberation and the Search for Self-Fulfillment Have Altered America* (New York, 1979), p. 26.

33. For a fuller discussion of what is meant by the term *emancipation*, see Gerda Lerner's statement in "Politics and Culture in Women's History," *Feminist Studies* 6 (1980): 50.

34. The phrases are those of Frances Beale in "Double Jeopardy: To Be Black and Female," in *The Black Woman*, ed. Cade, pp. 90–100, and of Patricia Haden, Donna Middleton, and Patricia Robinson in "A Historical and Critical Essay for Black Women," in *Voices from Women's Liberation*, ed. Leslie B. Tanner (New York, 1971), pp. 316–24. According to the 1972 Louis Harris Virginia Slims pool, a higher percentage of black women than white supported efforts to improve women's condition. Black feminists such as Pauli Murray, Elizabeth Koontz, Shirley Chisholm, and Florynce Kennedy have been important to the movement and black feminist groups have developed; the initial response of many black women, however, was to regard the women's movement as a white woman's movement. Freeman explores

some of the factors accounting for this initial reaction in *Politics of Women's Liberation*, pp. 37–43.

35. Louis Harris, "Changing Views on the Role of Women," *The Harris Survey*, December 11, 1975.

36. Caroline Bird and the Members and Staff of the National Commission on the Observance of International Woman's Year, *What Women Want: From the Official Report to the President, the Congress, and the People of the United States* (New York, 1979), p. 68 for Johnson's statement.

37. Violet S. Devieux to Senator Sam J. Ervin Jr., March 23, 1972, Samuel J. Ervin Papers, #3847 Southern Historical Collection, Library of the University of North Carolina, at Chapel Hill.

38. Bardwick, *In Transition*, p. 9. For a discussion of the impact of change involving values and the psychological resistance engendered, see pp. 9–20.

39. This apt characterization is William Chafe's; see *The American Woman*, p. 209. Chafe's *Women and Equality: Changing Patterns in American Culture* (New York, 1977) provides the most analytically sophisticated study thus far of the issue of women and equality. It explores the interrelation of economic, demographic, and legal changes that make possible the resonance of a feminist critique and hence the creation of a viable protest movement. Also useful is his exploration of the analogy between race and sex, particularly the patterns of control applied to both blacks and women.

40. For a fuller analysis of the significance of the struggle over ERA and the debate over feminism, see Donald G. Mathews and Jane De Hart Mathews, *The Equal Rights Amendment and the Politics of Cultural Conflict* (New York, forthcoming).

41. The percentage of female lawyers and judges has risen from 3.3 percent in 1960, to 4.7 percent in 1970, to 12.4 percent in 1979—an increase of 49,000 between 1970 and 1980. The percentage of female physicians also increased, although less dramatically, from 6.8 percent in 1960, to 8.9 percent in 1970, to 10.7 percent in 1979—a numerical increase during the same decade of 21,000. Women entering engineering, although still a tiny minority, did increase the percentage from less than 1 percent in 1960 to 1.6 percent in 1970, to 2.9 percent in 1979—for an increase of 20,000 during the 1970s. The number of female bank officials and financial managers also rose dramatically during that decade, from 17.6 percent in 1970 to 31.6 percent in 1979. The number of female college and university teachers rose much more slowly due to constricting job opportunities in the profession. By 1980, however, women made up about 31 percent of college and university faculties and were receiving about 25 percent of all Ph.D.'s awarded. The number and percentage of female college graduates also increased; by the end of the decade almost half of the graduating seniors were women. Women moving into traditionally "male" jobs at the blue-collar level showed greatest gains as transport equipment operatives (bus and cab drivers, for example). Making up 3.6 percent of the labor force in that occupation, they increased by 160,000. The number of female union members also rose during the 1970s by over a million. Another area showing gains was the military where, by 1980, women made up over 6 percent of the enlisted persons and of officers. See U.S. Bureau of the Census, *Statistical Abstract of the United States: 1979* (Washington, D.C., 1979), pp. 373, 629; U.S. Bureau of Labor Statistics, *Perspectives on Working Women: A Databook* (Washington, D.C., 1980), pp. 10–11.

The number of women elected to office rose throughout the 1970s with substantial gains during the last half of the decade. By 1979 there were 14,225 (9 percent) female elected officials as compared with 5,765 (4 percent) in 1975. Following the death of Eleanor Grasso of Connecticut in February 1981, there were no women governors; however, the number of women holding statewide elective office had risen to 32 (11 percent) in 1979. Following the 1980 elections, the number of women elected to Congress reached an all-time high of 21 (2 senators and 19 representatives), while the number of women elected to state legislatures rose to 880 (12 percent) as compared to 610 (8 percent) in 1975. Similar increases occurred at the county and local level. In 1979 women holding country offices numbered 947 (5 percent), while the number serving as mayor or as members of municipal councils numbered 12,459 (10 percent). The above figures were obtained from the National Information Bank on Women in Public Office, a Project of the Center for the American Woman and Politics, the Eagleton Institute for Politics, New Brunswick, N.J.

The first female Supreme Court Justice was appointed in 1981.

42. The number of single women, es-

pecially between the ages of twenty and twenty-four, has risen substantially—from 28.4 percent in 1960 to nearly 50 percent by 1980—while the birth rate has dropped from an average of over three children per family in 1960 to under two by 1980. See U.S. Bureau of the Census, *Statistical Abstract of the United States: 1979*, p. 43; U.S. Bureau of the Census, *Population Profile of the United States: 1979* (Washington, D.C., 1980), p. 5.

43. In 1960 median earnings for workers fourteen years old and over, working 50 to 52 weeks per year, were $5,307 for males and $3,118 for females. By 1970 that gap had widened, with males earning $8,529 and females earning $4,719; and by 1978 it had closed only slightly, with males earning $16,062 and females earning $9,641. See U.S. Bureau of the Census, *U.S. Census of the Population: 1960, Subject Reports, Occupational Characteristics* (Washington, D.C., 1963), pp. 232, 234; U.S. Bureau of the Census, *U.S. Census of the Population: 1970, Subject Reports, Occupational Characteristics* (Washington, D.C., 1973), pp. 280, 282; U.S. Bureau of the Census, *Population Profile of the United States: 1979* (Washington, D.C., 1980), p. 39.

44. Results of the Stanford survey appeared in the *Raleigh News and Observer*, February 1, 1981.

45. As late as 1979 nearly 80 percent of wage-earning women worked in sales, clerical, service, or factory jobs. Of those holding professional or managerial jobs, most are nurses or are teaching below the college level. See Bureau of Labor Statistics, *Perspectives on Working Women*, pp. 10–11.

College students continue to aim for traditionally defined jobs, a trend meaning that the earnings gap will persist. For example, in 1976 49 percent of all B.A. degrees, 72 percent of all M.A.'s, and 53 percent of all Ph.D.'s awarded to women were in six traditionally female fields: education, English and journalism, fine and applied arts, foreign language and literature, nursing, and library science. Yet the Bureau of Labor Statistics estimates that between 1976 and 1985 there will be only 70,000 new jobs in kindergarten and elementary school teaching, for which an estimated 99,000 teachers will be competing. In contrast, there will be 56,500 new jobs available to an estimated 49,800 graduates with a degree in engineering. See *New York Times*, May 11, 1980.

46. Diane Pearce, "The Feminization of Poverty: Women, Work, and Welfare," *Urban and Social Change Review* 11 (1978): 28–36.

47. Catherine White Berheide, Sarah Fenstermaker Berk, and Richard A. Berk, "Household Work in the Suburbs: The Job and Its Participants," *Pacific Sociological Review* 19 (1976): 491–518.

48. For a fuller discussion of these issues, see Carl Degler, *At Odds: Women and the Family in America from the Revolution to the Present* (New York, 1981), chap. 17, and Alice Kessler-Harris, *Women Have Always Worked* (New York, 1981), pp. 157–65.

Essential Documents

The law of the United States affects all inhabitants, but some statutes have had a special significance for women. This section includes the following selection of statutes, constitutional amendments, court decisions and other documents that have had important impact on the status of women in America:

1. Marriage, Divorce, Dower: Examples from Colonial Connecticut (1640, 1667, 1672)
2. Declaration of Sentiments (1848)
3. Married Women's Property Acts: Examples from New York State (1848, 1860)
4. Reconstruction Amendments (1868, 1870)
5. *Bradwell* v. *Illinois* (1873)
6. Comstock Law (1873)
7. *Minor* v. *Happersett* (1875)
8. *Muller* v. *Oregon* (1908)
9. Equal Suffrage Amendment (1920)
10. *Adkins* v. *Children's Hospital* (1923)
11. Civil Rights Act, Title VII (1964)
12. Equal Rights Amendment (1972)
13. *Frontiero* v. *Richardson* (1973)
14. *Roe* v. *Wade* (1973)
15. *Taylor* v. *Louisiana* (1975)

1

Marriage, Divorce, Dower:

Examples from Colonial Connecticut, 1640, 1667, 1672

MARRIAGE

Each American colony developed its own code of laws. There were major variations from colony to colony, but all drew on their memories of English example. All colonies placed in their statutes a law regulating marriage. This reflected a concern that marriages be celebrated publicly in order to guard against bigamy. Laws also guarded against marriages between close relatives; note the wide number of relatives under prohibition. In the course of the nineteenth century the list of prohibited relatives was shortened.

The statutes that follow are from the laws of the colony of Connecticut. The portion requiring the publication of intent to marry is one of the earliest passed in the colony (1640). The original version included the observation that "many persons, by rash and inconsiderate contracts for their future joining in marriage, involve themselves and their friends in great trouble and grief." Although the Connecticut statute listed degrees of kindred in terms of relationships among men, other colonies provided parallel lists for men and women. Connecticut did provide similar punishments for male and female transgressors.

Why might a woman be pleased that her colony had a law like the following one?

An Act for Regulating and Orderly Celebrating of Marriages . . . , 1640, with revisions 1672, 1702

Forasmuch as the ordinance of marriage is honourable amongst all; so it is meet it should be orderly and decently solemnized:

Be it therefore enacted . . . That no persons shall be joined in marriage, before the purpose or intention of the parties proceeding therein, hath been sufficiently published in some public meeting or congregation on the Lord's day, or on some public fast, thanksgiving, or lecture-day, in the town, parish, or society where the parties, or either of them do ordinarily reside; or such purpose or intention be set up in fair writing, upon some post or door of their meeting-house, or near the same, in public view, there to stand so as it may be read, eight days before such marriage.

. . . And in order to prevent incestu-

The Public Statute Laws of the State of Connecticut (Hartford, 1808), 1:477–79, 236, 239–40.

428

ous and unlawful marriages, be it further enacted, That no man shall marry . . . his grand-father's wife, wife's grand-mother, father's sister, mother's sister, father's brother's wife, mother's brother's wife, wife's father's sister, wife's mother's sister, father's wife, wife's mother, daughter, wife's daughter, son's wife, sister, brother's wife, son's daughter, daughter's daughter, son's son's wife, daughter's son's wife, wife's son's daughter, wife's daughter's daughter, brother's daughter, sister's daughter, brother's son's wife, sister's son's wife.

And if any man shall hereafter marry, or have carnal copulation with any woman who is within the degrees before recited in this act, every such marriage shall be . . . null and void; And all children that shall hereafter be born of such incestuous marriage or copulation, shall be forever disabled to inherit by descent, or by being generally named in any deed or will, by father or mother. . . .

And it shall be in the power of the superior court to assign unto any woman so separated, such reasonable part of the estate of her late husband, as in their discretion the circumstances of the estate may admit; not exceeding one third part thereof.

DIVORCE

Early America was a divorceless society. South Carolina boasted that it granted no divorce until 1868. Most colonies followed the British practice of treating marriage as a moral obligation for life. Occasional special dissolutions of a marriage were granted by legislatures in response to individual petitions or by courts of equity, but these were separations from bed and board, which normally did not carry with them freedom to marry again.

Colonial Connecticut was unusual in treating marriage as a civil contract, which might be broken if its terms were not carried out. Connecticut enacted the earliest divorce law in the colonies. It made divorce available after a simple petition to the superior court under certain circumstances. People who did not fit these circumstances were able to present special petitions to the legislature. Normally a divorce in Connecticut implied that the innocent party had the right to marry again.

Most petitioners for divorce in early America were women. On what grounds might Connecticut women petition for divorce?

An Act relating to Bills of Divorce, 1667

Be it enacted . . . that no bill of divorce shall be granted to any man or woman, lawfully married, but in case of adultery, or fraudulent contract, or wilful desertion for three years with total neglect of duty; or in case of seven years absence of one party not heard of: after due enquiry is made, and the matter certified to the superior court, in which case the other party may be deemed and accounted single and unmarried. And in that case, and in all other cases afore-mentioned, a bill of divorce may be granted by the superior court to the aggrieved party; who may then lawfully marry or be married again.

DOWER

Perhaps no statutes were more important to women in the first 250 years after settlement of the American colonies than the laws protecting their claims to dower. The "widow's dower" should be distinguished from the dowry a bride might bring with her into marriage. The "widow's dower" or the "widow's third" was the right of a widow to use one-third of the real estate that her husband held at the time of his death. It was an old English tradition that he might leave her more in his will, but he could not leave her less. If a man died without a will, the courts would ensure that his widow received her "third."

It is important to note that she only had the right to *use* the land and buildings. She might live on this property, rent it out, farm the land, and sell the produce. But she could not sell or bequeath it. After her death the property reverted to her husband's heirs, who normally would be their children, but in the case of a childless marriage it might go to others whom he identified.

In the Connecticut statute, printed below, note the provisions protecting the widow's interests. Normally colonial courts were scrupulous about assigning the widow's portion. Observe, however, that widows could not claim dower in "movable" property, which might represent a larger share of their husband's wealth than real estate. As time passed and the American economy became more complex, it became increasingly likely that a man's property would not be held in the form of land. If the land were heavily mortgaged, the widow's prior right to her "third" became a barrier to creditors seeking to collect their portion of a husband's debts. By the early nineteenth century courts were losing their enthusiasm for protecting widows' thirds.

By the middle of the century the married women's property acts began to reformulate a definition of the terms by which married women could claim their share of the property of wife and husband. But between 1790 and 1840, when the right to dower was more and more laxly enforced and the new married women's property acts had not yet been devised, married women were in a particularly vulnerable position.

An Act concerning the Dowry of Widows, 1672

That there may be suitable provision made for the maintenance and comfortable support of widows, after the decease of their husbands, Be it enacted . . . that every married woman, living with her husband in this state, or absent elsewhere from him with his consent, or through his mere default, or by inevitable providence; or in case of divorce where she is the innocent party, that shall not before marriage be estated by way of jointure in some houses, lands, tenements or hereditaments for term of life . . . shall immediately upon, and after the death of her husband, have right, title and interest by way of dower, in and unto one third part of the real estate of her said deceased husband, in houses and lands which he stood possessed of in his own right, at the time of his decease, to be to her during her natural life: the remainder of the estate shall be disposed of according to the will of the deceased. . . .

And for the more easy, and speedy ascertaining such rights of dower, It is further enacted, That upon the death of any man possessed of any real estate . . . which his widow . . . hath a right of dower in, if the person, or persons that by law have a right to inherit said estate, do not within sixty days next after the death of such husband, by three sufficient free-holders of the same county; to be appointed by the judge of probate . . . and sworn for that purpose, set out, and ascertain such right of dower, that then such widow may make her complaint to the judge of probate . . . which judge shall decree, and order that such woman's dowry shall be set out, and ascertained by three sufficient freeholders of the county . . . and upon approbation thereof by said judge, such dower shall remain fixed and certain. . . .

And every widow so endowed . . . shall maintain all such houses, buildings, fences, and inclosures as shall be assigned, and set out to her for her dowry; and shall leave the same in good and sufficient repair.

2

Declaration of Sentiments, 1848

The "Convention to discuss the social, civil, and religious condition and rights of women" that was announced by Elizabeth Cady Stanton, Lucretia Mott, and two of their friends in 1848 was simply an open meeting to which the public was invited. It provided an occasion for debating and publicizing a set of reform proposals. The meeting in Seneca Falls, New York, was followed by a series of other public meetings—in Rochester, New York; Akron, Ohio; and Worcester, Massachusetts. But the manifesto of the Seneca Falls Convention, written by Elizabeth Cady Stanton, remained the basic statement of reformers' goals throughout the nineteenth century.

The rhetoric of the Declaration of Sentiments was borrowed from the Declaration of Independence. Through its lines flowed the conviction that the Revolution had made implicit promises to women which had not been kept.

Seneca Falls, New York, July 19–20, 1848

When, in the course of human events, it becomes necessary for one portion of the family of man to assume among the people of the earth a position different from that which they have hitherto occupied, but one to which the laws of nature and

Declaration of Sentiments, in *History of Woman Suffrage*, edited by Elizabeth Cady Stanton, Susan B. Anthony, and Matilda Joslyn Gage, vol. 1 (New York: Fowler & Wells, 1881), pp. 70–71.

of nature's God entitle them, a decent respect to the opinions of mankind requires that they should declare the causes that impel them to such a course.

We hold these truths to be self-evident: that all men and women are created equal; that they are endowed by their Creator with certain inalienable rights; that among these are life, liberty, and the pursuit of happiness; that to secure these rights governments are instituted, deriving their just powers from the consent of the governed. Whenever any form of government becomes destructive of these ends, it is the right of those who suffer from it to refuse allegiance to it, and to insist upon the institution of a new government, laying its foundation on such principles, and organizing its powers in such form, as to them shall seem most likely to effect their safety and happiness. Prudence, indeed, will dictate that governments long established should not be changed for light and transient causes; and accordingly all experience hath shown that mankind are more disposed to suffer, while evils are sufferable, than to right themselves by abolishing the forms to which they were accustomed. But when a long train of abuses and usurpations, pursuing invariably the same object evinces a design to reduce them under absolute despotism, it is their duty to throw off such government, and to provide new guards for their future security. Such has been the patient sufferance of the women under this government, and such is now the necessity which constrains them to demand the equal station to which they are entitled.

The history of mankind is a history of repeated injuries and usurpations on the part of man toward woman, having in direct object the establishment of an absolute tyranny over her. To prove this, let facts be submitted to a candid world.

He has never permitted her to exercise her inalienable right to the elective franchise.

He has compelled her to submit to laws, in the formation of which she had no voice.

He has withheld from her rights which are given to the most ignorant and degraded men—both natives and foreigners.

Having deprived her of this first right of a citizen, the elective franchise, thereby leaving her without representation in the halls of legislation, he has oppressed her on all sides.

He has made her, if married, in the eye of the law, civilly dead.

He has taken from her all right in property, even to the wages she earns.

He has made her, morally, an irresponsible being, as she can commit many crimes with impunity, provided they be done in the presence of her husband. In the covenant of marriage, she is compelled to promise obedience to her husband, he becoming, to all intents and purposes, her master—the law giving him power to deprive her of her liberty, and to administer chastisement.

He has so framed the laws of divorce, as to what shall be the proper causes, and in case of separation, to whom the guardianship of the children shall be given, as to be wholly regardless of the happiness of women—the law, in all cases, going upon a false supposition of the supremacy of man, and giving all power into his hands.

After depriving her of all rights as a married woman, if single, and the owner of property, he has taxed her to support a government which recognizes her only when her property can be made profitable to it.

He has monopolized nearly all the profitable employments, and from those she is permitted to follow, she receives but a scanty remuneration. He closes against her all the avenues to wealth and distinction which he considers most honorable to himself. As a teacher of theology, medicine, or law, she is not known.

He has denied her the facilities for obtaining a thorough education, all colleges being closed against her.

He allows her in Church, as well as State, but a subordinate position, claiming Apostolic authority for her exclusion from the ministry, and, with some exceptions, from any public participation in the affairs of the Church.

He has created a false public sentiment by giving to the world a different code of morals for men and women, by which moral delinquencies which exclude women from society, are not only tolerated, but deemed of little account in man.

He has usurped the prerogative of Jehovah himself, claiming it as his right to assign for her a sphere of action, when that belongs to her conscience and to her God.

He has endeavored, in every way that he could, to destroy her confidence in her own powers, to lessen her self-respect, and to make her willing to lead a dependent and abject life.

Now, in view of this entire disfranchisement of one-half the people of this country, their social and religious degradation—in view of the unjust laws above mentioned, and because women do feel themselves aggrieved, oppressed, and fraudulently deprived of their most sacred rights, we insist that they have immediate admission to all the rights and privileges which belong to them as citizens of the United States.

In entering upon the great work before us, we anticipate no small amount of misconception, misrepresentation, and ridicule; but we shall use every instrumentality within our power to effect our object. We shall employ agents, circulate tracts, petition the State and National legislatures, and endeavor to enlist the pulpit and the press in our behalf. We hope this Convention will be followed by a series of Conventions embracing every part of the country.

3

Married Women's Property Acts:

Examples from New York State, 1848, 1860

Americans inherited the ancient English custom of *coverture*, by which the married woman's civil identity was covered by or absorbed into her husband's. By common law tradition a husband might spend his wife's property, punish her physically, and provide her with only minimal food, clothing, and shelter. The rigor of the common law was in fact substantially eased both in England and the colonies by courts of equity, which permitted more judicial discretion. The common law rights of the husband might, for example, be circumvented by premarital contracts or trusteeships.

But these options were most realistic for women who could obtain the benefit

Laws of the State of New-York, Passed at the Seventy-First Session of the Legislature . . . (Albany, 1848), pp. 307–308; *Laws of the State of New York, Passed at the Eighty-Third Session of the Legislature* . . . (Albany, 1860), pp. 157–59.

of sophisticated legal advice and who had substantial property to protect. They were not readily available to poorer women who needed them most. The Declaration of Sentiments sharply attacked contemporary practice as "civil death" for women. Reformers gave high priority to legislation that would confirm the right of married women to the property they had brought into their marriages and to wages and income they earned after marriage.

Ironically, the first married women's property acts, passed in Mississippi in 1839 and in New York in 1848, were supported by many male legislators out of a desire to preserve the estates of married daughters against spendthrift sons-in-law. Four out of the five sections of the Mississippi act broadened the rights of married women over their own slaves.

Note the limits of the 1848 New York law and the ways in which women's rights were extended by the 1860 revision. In 1860 married women were also confirmed in their guardianship of their children.

New York State Married Women's Property Acts

1848

The real and personal property of any female [now married and] who may hereafter marry, and which she shall own at the time of marriage, and the rents issues and profits thereof shall not be subject to the disposal of her husband, nor be liable for his debts, and shall continue her sole and separate property, as if she were a single female. . . .

It shall be lawful for any married female to receive, by gift, grant, devise or bequest, from any person other than her husband and hold to her sole and separate use, as if she were a single female, real and personal property, and the rents, issues and profits thereof, and the same shall not be subject to the disposal of her husband, nor be liable for his debts. . . .

1860

[The provisions of the law of 1848 were retained, and others were added:]
A married woman may bargain, sell, assign, and transfer her separate personal property, and carry on any trade or business, and perform any labor or services on her sole and separate account, and the earnings of any married woman from her trade . . . shall be her sole and separate property, and may be used or invested by her in her own name. . . .

Any married woman may, while married, sue and be sued in all matters having relation to her . . . sole and separate property . . . in the same manner as if she were sole. And any married woman may bring and maintain an action in her own name, for damages, against any person or body corporate, for any injury to her person or character, the same as if she were sole; and the money received upon the settlement . . . shall be her sole and separate property.

No bargain or contract made by any

married woman, in respect to her sole and separate property . . . shall be binding upon her husband, or render him or his property in any way liable therefor.

Every married woman is hereby consti-tuted and declared to be the joint guard-ian of her children, with her husband, with equal powers, rights, and duties in regard to them, with the husband. . . .

4

Reconstruction Amendments, 1868, 1870

Until 1868, the United States Constitution made no explicit distinctions on the basis of gender. Of qualifications for voters, it said only that "the electors in each State shall have the qualifications requisite for electors of the most numerous branch of the State legislature" (Article I, section 2). Reformers merely needed to persuade each state legislature to change its own rules in order to enfranchise women in national elections.

The word *male* was introduced into the Constitution in section 2 of the Fourteenth Amendment, as part of a complex provision—never enforced—intended to constrain former Confederates from interfering with the civil rights of newly freed slaves. Suffragists were bitterly disappointed at the failure to include sex as a category in the Fifteenth Amendment. But until the test case of *Minor v. Happersett* (document 7), they clung to the hope that the first article of the Fourteenth Amendment would be interpreted broadly enough to admit women to the polls.

Fourteenth Amendment, 1868

1. All persons born or naturalized in the United States, and subject to the jurisdiction thereof, are citizens of the United States and of the State wherein they reside. No State shall make or enforce any law which shall abridge the privileges or immunities of citizens of the United States; nor shall any State deprive any person of life, liberty, or property, without due process of law; nor deny to any person within its jurisdiction the equal protection of the laws.

2. Representatives shall be apportioned among the several States according to their respective numbers, counting the whole number of persons in each State, excluding Indians not taxed. But when the right to vote at any election for the choice of electors for President and Vice-President of the United States, Representatives in Congress, the executive and judicial officers of a State, or the members of the legislature thereof, is denied to any of the male inhabitants of such State, being twenty-one years of age and citizens of the United States, or in any way abridged, except for participation in rebellion, or other crime, the basis of repre-

sentation therein shall be reduced in the
proportion which the number of such
male citizens shall bear to the whole num-

ber of male citizens twenty-one years of
age in such State. . . .

Fifteenth Amendment, 1870

The right of citizens of the United States
to vote shall not be denied or abridged by
the United States or by any State on ac-

count of race, color, or previous condition
of servitude. . . .

5

Bradwell v. Illinois, 1873

Although she could not practice in the courts until the end of her career, Myra
Bradwell was perhaps the most notable female lawyer of the nineteenth century.
She read law in the office of her husband, a prominent Chicago attorney and
county judge. In 1868 she began to publish the *Chicago Legal News,* a weekly
newspaper covering developments in courts and legislatures throughout the
country. Because she had received a special charter from the state legislature
under which she was permitted to act without the usual legal disabilities of a
married woman, she ran the *News* as her own business. She wrote vigorous
editorials, evaluating legal opinions and new laws, assessing proposed state legislation, and supporting progressive developments like prison reform, the establishment of law schools, and women's rights. She drafted bills improving married women's rights to property and child custody.

It was only logical that she should seek admission to the bar. Although she
passed the entrance tests in 1869, she was rejected by the Illinois State Supreme
Court on the grounds that she was a married woman, and therefore not a fully
free agent. Appealing to the United States Supreme Court, her attorney argued
that among the "privileges and immunities" guaranteed to each citizen by the
Fourteenth Amendment was the right to pursue any honorable profession. "Intelligence, integrity and honor are the only qualifications that can be prescribed
. . . the broad shield of the Constitution is over all, and protects each in that
measure of success which his or her individual merits may secure."

The Court's decision came in two parts. Speaking for the majority and citing
the recent decision of the Supreme Court in the slaughterhouse cases, Justice
Samuel F. Miller held that the right to practice law in the courts of any particular

83 U.S. 130.

state was a right that might be granted by the individual state; it was not one of the "privileges and immunities" of citizenship. Then, in a concurring opinion, Justice Joseph P. Bradley offered an ideological justification for the Court's decision that was based on inherent differences between men and women and that was to be widely used thereafter to defend the exclusion of women from professional careers. (It should be added that in 1890, twenty years after her original application, the Illinois Supreme Court relented and admitted Bradwell to the bar.)

Mr. Justice Bradley:

The claim of the plaintiff, who is a married woman, to be admitted to practice as an attorney and counselor at law, is based upon the supposed right of every person, man or woman, to engage in any lawful employment for a livelihood. The supreme court of Illinois denied the application on the ground that, by the common law, which is the basis of the laws of Illinois, only men were admitted to the bar, and the legislature had not made any change in this respect. . . .

The claim that, under the 14th Amendment of the Constitution, which declares that no state shall make or enforce any law which shall abridge the privileges and immunities of citizens of the United States, and the statute law of Illinois, or the common law prevailing in that state, can no longer be set up as a barrier against the right of females to pursue any lawful employment . . . assumes that it is one of the privileges and immunities of women as citizens to engage in any and every profession, occupation or employment in civil life.

It certainly cannot be affirmed, as a historical fact, that this has ever been established as one of the fundamental privileges and immunities of the sex. On the contrary, the civil law, as well as nature herself, has always recognized a wide difference in the respective spheres and destinies of man and woman. Man is, or should be, woman's protector and defender. The natural and proper timidity and delicacy which belongs to the female sex evidently unfits it for many of the occupations of civil life. The constitution of the family organization, which is founded in the divine ordinance, as well as in the nature of things, indicates the domestic sphere as that which properly belongs to the domain and functions of womanhood. The harmony, not to say identity, of interests and views which belong or should belong to the family institution, is repugnant to the idea of a woman adopting a distinct and independent career from that of her husband. So firmly fixed was this sentiment in the founders of the common law that it became a maxim of that system of jurisprudence that a woman had no legal existence separate from her husband, who was regarded as her head and representative in the social state; and, notwithstanding some recent modifications of this civil status, many of the special rules of law flowing from and dependent upon this cardinal principle still exist in full force in most states. One of these is, that a married woman is incapable, without her husband's consent, of making contracts which shall be binding on her or him. This very incapacity was one circumstance which the supreme court of Illinois deemed important in rendering a married woman incompetent fully to perform the duties and trusts that belong to the office of an attorney and counselor.

It is true that many women are unmarried and not affected by any of the duties, complications, and incapacities arising out of the married state, but these are exceptions to the general rule. The paramount destiny and mission of woman are to fulfill the noble and benign offices of wife and mother. This is the law of the Creator. And the rules of civil society must be adapted to the general constitution of things, and cannot be based upon exceptional cases. . . .

6

Comstock Law, 1873

This "Act for the Suppression of Trade in, and Circulation of Obscene Literature and Articles of Immoral Use" was passed at the urging of Anthony Comstock, the head of the New York Society for the Suppression of Vice. The first section prohibited the sale of the described materials in the District of Columbia and the territories; subsequent sections prohibited the sending of these materials through the mails or their importation into the United States. In the 1870s many states passed their own versions of the federal law.

The law reflected a widespread belief that both contraception and abortion were acts of interference with the natural order and with God's intentions. No distinction was made between drugs used for abortion and materials used for contraception; all were treated in the same terms as pornographic materials. Note the heavy penalties provided.

Be it enacted . . . That whoever, within the District of Columbia or any of the Territories of the United States . . . shall sell . . . or shall offer to sell, or to lend, or to give away, or in any manner to exhibit, or shall otherwise publish or offer to publish in any manner, or shall have in his possession, for any such purpose or purposes, any obscene book, pamphlet, paper, writing, advertisement, circular, print, picture, drawing or other representation, figure, or image on or of paper or other material, or any cast, instrument, or other article of an immoral nature, or any drug or medicine, or any article whatever, for the prevention of conception, or for causing unlawful abortion, or shall advertize the same for sale, or shall write or print, or cause to be written or printed, any card, circular, book, pamphlet, advertisement, or notice of any kind, stating when, where, how, or of whom, or by what means, any of the articles in this section . . . can be purchased or obtained, or shall manufacture, draw, or print, or in any wise make any of such articles, shall be deemed guilty of a misdemeanor, and on conviction thereof in any court of the United States . . . he shall be imprisoned at hard labor in the penitentiary for not less than six months nor more than five years for each offense, or fined not less than one hundred dollars nor more than two thousand dollars, with costs of court. . . .

Public Laws of the United States of America, Passed at the Third Session of the Forty-Second Congress (Boston, 1873), p. 598.

7

Minor *v.* Happersett, *1875*

In 1872 suffragists in a number of places attempted to test the possibilities of the first section of the Fourteenth Amendment. "The power to regulate is one thing, the power to prevent is an entirely different thing," observed Virginia Minor, president of the Woman Suffrage Association of Missouri, and she presented herself at the polls in St. Louis in 1872. When the registrar refused to permit her to register to vote, she and her husband sued him for denying her one of the "privileges and immunities of citizenship"; when they lost the case they appealed to the Supreme Court.

In a unanimous opinion the justices held that if the authors of the Constitution had intended that women should vote, they would have said so explicitly. The decision of the Court meant that woman suffrage could not be developed by way of a quiet reinterpretation of the Constitution but would require an explicit amendment to the Constitution or a series of revisions in the laws of the states.

Mr. Chief Justice Morrison R. Waite delivered the opinion of the Court:

The question is presented in this case, whether, since the adoption of the fourteenth amendment, a woman, who is a citizen of the United States and of the State of Missouri, is a voter in that State, notwithstanding the provision of the constitution and laws of the State, which confine the right of suffrage to men alone. . . . The argument is, that as a woman, born or naturalized in the United States and subject to the jurisdiction thereof, is a citizen of the United States and of the State in which she resides, she has the right of suffrage as one of the privileges and immunities of her citizenship, which the State cannot by its laws or constitution abridge.

There is no doubt that women may be citizens. They are persons, and by the fourteenth amendment "all persons born or naturalized in the United States and subject to the jurisdiction thereof" are expressly declared to be "citizens of the United States and of the State wherein they reside." But, in our opinion, it did not need this amendment to give them that position . . . sex has never been made one of the elements of citizenship in the United States. In this respect men have never had an advantage over women. The same laws precisely apply to both. The fourteenth amendment did not affect the citizenship of women any more than it did of men. . . . Mrs. Minor . . . has always been a citizen from her birth, and entitled to all the privileges and immunities of citizenship. . . .

If the right of suffrage is one of the

88 U.S. 162.

necessary privileges of a citizen of the United States, then the constitution and laws of Missouri confining it to men are in violation of the Constitution of the United States, as amended, and consequently void. The direct question is, therefore, presented whether all citizens are necessarily voters.

The Constitution does not define the privileges and immunities of citizens. For that definition we must look elsewhere. In this case we need not determine what they are, but only whether suffrage is necessarily one of them.

It certainly is nowhere made so in express terms. The United States has no voters in the States of its own creation. The elective officers of the United States are all elected directly or indirectly by state voters. . . . it cannot for a moment be doubted that if it had been intended to make all citizens of the United States voters, the framers of the Constitution would not have left it to implication. . . .

It is true that the United States guarantees to every State a republican form of government. . . . No particular government is designated as republican, neither is the exact form to be guaranteed, in any manner especially designated. . . . When the Constitution was adopted . . . all the citizens of the States were not invested with the right of suffrage. In all, save perhaps New Jersey, this right was only bestowed upon men and not upon all of them. . . . Under these circumstances it is certainly now too late to contend that a government is not republican, within the meaning of this guaranty in the Constitution, because women are not made voters. . . . If suffrage was intended to be included within its obligations, language better adapted to express that intent would most certainly have been employed. . . .

. . . For nearly ninety years the people have acted upon the idea that the Constitution, when it conferred citizenship, did not necessarily confer the right of suffrage. If uniform practice long continued can settle the construction of so important an instrument as the Constitution of the United States confessedly is, most certainly it has been done here. Our province is to decide what the law is, not to declare what it should be.

We have given this case the careful consideration its importance demands. If the law is wrong, it ought to be changed; but the power for that is not with us. . . . No argument as to woman's need of suffrage can be considered. We can only act upon her rights as they exist. . . .

8

Muller *v.* Oregon, *1908*

The farmer's workday was sunrise to sunset. When the first factories were established in the early nineteenth century, they were operated for equally long hours. It was a particular interest of laborers and of progressive reformers to support enactment of limits on the workday. The ten-hour day was on the agenda of early labor unions, and the federal civil service adopted it shortly after the Civil War.

208 U.S. 412.

But in 1905 the United States Supreme Court refused to uphold a state law limiting the hours of bakers to ten hours a day. Ruling in *Lochner* v. *New York*, the Court held that such a law was not "a legitimate exercise of the police power of the State, but an unreasonable, unnecessary, and arbitrary interference with the right and liberty of the individual to contract in relation to his labor. . . ."

After the *Lochner* decision progressives were forced to conclude that it was impractical to support limitations on hours that applied to *all* workers. But it occurred to some that a special case might be made in defense of a limit on working hours for women.

When the constitutionality of the Oregon ten-hour law for women was challenged, the National Consumers' League undertook the defense of the statute and hired attorney Louis D. Brandeis to present the case before the Supreme Court. The brief he presented to the court in *Muller* v. *Oregon* was startling and unprecedented. It consisted of only two pages of legal argument and over one hundred pages describing the "world's experience regarding women's hours of labor." Although the document became known as the Brandeis Brief, it was prepared largely by his sister-in-law Josephine Goldmark, a social worker and a staff member of the Consumers' League. Goldmark wrote a closely reasoned monograph, drawing on reports of factory inspectors, bureaus of labor statistics, commissioners of hygiene, and on observations of physicians, and demonstrating that everywhere in the civilized world long hours had been shown to be detrimental to the health, safety, and morals of employed women. The style of argument, drawing as it did on social evidence as much as upon abstract legal reasoning, came to be known as "sociological jurisprudence." The style was widely employed; the government's case in 1954 in *Brown* v. *Board of Education*, on the desegregation of schools, had much in common with the Brandeis Brief.

In 1908 the Supreme Court upheld the constitutionality of the Oregon law, though making it clear that it was swayed primarily by the case made for women's physical vulnerability and couching the decision in terms of traditional sex roles. Compare the reasoning to that offered in the *Bradwell* case more than thirty-five years before.

Mr. Justice David J. Brewer:

. . . It may not be amiss, in the present case, before examining the constitutional question, to notice the course of legislation, as well as expressions of opinion from other than judicial sources. In the brief filed by Mr. Louis D. Brandeis for the defendant . . . is a very copious collection of all these matters. . . .

The legislation and opinions referred to . . . may not be, technically speaking, authorities, and in them is little or no discussion of the constitutional question presented to us for determination, yet, they are significant of a widespread belief that woman's physical structure, and the functions she performs in consequence thereof, justify special legislation restricting or qualifying the conditions under which she should be permitted to toil. . . .

That woman's physical structure and the performance of maternal functions place her at a disadvantage in the struggle for subsistence is obvious. This is especially true when the burdens of motherhood are upon her. Even when they are not, by abundant testimony of the medical fraternity continuance for a long time on her feet at work, repeating this from day to day, tends to injurious effects upon the body, and, as healthy mothers are essential to vigorous offspring, the physical well-being of woman becomes an object of public interest and care in order to preserve the strength and vigor of the race. . . . Differentiated by these matters from the other sex, she is properly placed in a class by herself, and legislation designed for her protection may be sustained, even when like legislation is not necessary for men, and could not be sustained. It is impossible to close one's eyes to the fact that she still looks to her brother and depends upon him. . . . her physical structure and a proper discharge of her maternal functions—having in view not merely her own health, but the well-being of the race —justify legislation to protect her from the greed as well as the passion of man. The limitations which this statute places upon her contractual powers, upon her right to agree with her employer as to the

time she shall labor, are not imposed solely for her benefit, but also largely for the benefit of all. Many words cannot make this plainer. The two sexes differ in structure of body, in the functions to be performed by each, in the amount of physical strength, in the capacity for long continued labor, particularly when done standing, the influence of vigorous health upon the future well-being of the race, the self-reliance which enables one to assert full rights, and in the capacity to maintain the struggle for subsistence. This difference justifies a difference in legislation, and upholds that which is designed to compensate for some of the burdens which rest upon her.

We have not referred in this discussion to the denial of the elective franchise in the State of Oregon, for while it may disclose a lack of political equality in all things with her brother, that is not of itself decisive. The reason runs deeper, and rests in the inherent difference between the two sexes.

For these reasons, and without questioning in any respect the decision in *Lochner* v. *New York*, we are of the opinion that it cannot be adjudged that the act in question is in conflict with the Federal Constitution, so far as it respects the work of a female in a laundry, and the judgment of the Supreme Court of Oregon is Affirmed.

9

Equal Suffrage Amendment, 1920

A federal woman suffrage amendment was introduced into the Senate by S. C. Pomeroy of Kansas in 1868 and into the House by George W. Julian of Indiana in March 1869. It seemed to suffragists to be a logical response to the refusal to include the word *sex* in the Fifteenth Amendment. "The same arguments made in this country," observed Elizabeth Cady Stanton, "for extending suffrage from time to time, to white men, native born citizens, without property and education, and to foreigners . . . the same used by the great Republican party to enfranchise a million black men in the South, all these arguments we have to-day to offer for woman. . . . This fundamental principle of our government—the equality of all the citizens of the republic—should be incorporated in the Federal Constitution, there to remain forever."

After several close votes the Nineteenth Amendment to the Constitution was approved by Congress in the spring of 1920 and was ratified by the necessary thirty-six states in August, just in time for women to register to vote in the 1920 presidential election.

Section 1. The right of the citizens of the United States to vote shall not be denied or abridged by the United States or by any State on account of sex.

Section 2. Congress shall have power to enforce this article by appropriate legislation.

10

Adkins *v.* Children's Hospital, *1923*

Minimum wage legislation was the counterpart to maximum hour laws. In 1918 Congress authorized the Wage Board of the District of Columbia to fix minimum wages for women and children in order to protect them "from conditions detrimental to their health and morals, resulting from wages which are inadequate to maintain decent standards of living."

This act was attacked, much as maximum hour legislation had been, as an interference with the right of the employer and employee to contract freely. Suit was brought against it by a hospital that employed many women at lower than minimum wages. Arguing for the Wage Board and on behalf of the Consumers' League was Felix Frankfurter, who used a Brandeis Brief researched by Molly Dewson that was a thousand pages long. He convinced Justices William Howard Taft and Oliver Wendell Holmes, Jr. that low wages and long hours were linked. In their dissenting opinion they stated that if Congress could regulate one it could regulate the other. Holmes also observed that the phrase "liberty of contract" did not appear in the Constitution.

The majority of the Court was not, however, persuaded. The members of the majority distinguished between maximum hour legislation, which they saw as

261 U.S. 525.

directly allied to health concerns, and minimum wage legislation, which they thought "simply and exclusively a price-fixing law." The majority also observed that the Nineteenth Amendment obviated the need for protective legislation for women.

The *Adkins* decision blocked progress in minimum wage legislation for fifteen years, until there was a new president (Franklin Roosevelt) and a number of new justices on the court. The 1937 decision in *West Coast Hotel* v. *Parrish* upheld the claim of Elsie Parrish, a chambermaid, to a minimum wage set by the state of Washington and explicitly overturned the *Adkins* decision, thus validating protective wage legislation for women.

Mr. Justice George Sutherland delivered the opinion of the Court:

. . . the ancient inequality of the sexes, otherwise than physical, as suggested in the *Muller Case* has continued "with diminishing intensity." In view of the great —not to say revolutionary—changes which have taken place since that utterance, in the contractual, political and civil status of women, culminating in the Nineteenth Amendment, it is not unreasonable to say that these differences have now come almost, if not quite, to the vanishing point. . . . we cannot accept the doctrine that women of mature age, . . . require or may be subjected to restrictions upon their liberty of contract which could not lawfully be imposed in the case of men under similar circumstances. To do so would be to ignore all the implications to be drawn from the present day trend of legislation, as well as that of common thought and usage, by which woman is accorded emancipation from the old doctrine that she must be given special protection or be subjected to special restraint in her contractual and civil relationships. . . .

. . . What is sufficient to supply the necessary cost of living for a woman worker and maintain her in good health and protect her morals is obviously not a precise or unvarying sum. . . . The amount will depend upon a variety of circumstances: the individual temperament, habits of thrift, care, ability to buy necessaries intelligently, and whether the woman live alone or with her family. . . . It cannot be shown that well paid women safeguard their morals more carefully than those who are poorly paid. Morality rests upon other considerations than wages. . . .

11

Civil Rights Act, Title VII, 1964

The Civil Rights Act of 1964 was a comprehensive law of enormous significance. It was a complex statute, twenty-eight printed pages long and divided into eleven major sections, or *Titles*. Title I dealt with voting rights; Title III with

U.S. Statutes at Large, 78:253–66. For a full discussion of Title VII, see Donald Allen Robinson, "Two Movements in Pursuit of Equal Employment Opportunity," *Signs: Journal of Women in Culture and Society* 4 (1979):413–33.

the desegregation of public facilities; Title V established a Commission on Civil Rights. Title VII defined a long list of practices that would be forbidden to employers and labor unions, obliged the federal government to undertake an "affirmative" program of equal employment opportunity for all employees and job applicants, and created an Equal Employment Opportunity Commission (EEOC) to monitor compliance with the law.

Title VII was notable in that it outlawed discrimination on the basis of gender as well as of race. *Sex* was added to the categories "race, color, religion and national origin" by Representative Martha Griffiths of Michigan shortly before the bill's final passage in the House. She received unexpected support from conservative colleagues who spoke on behalf of the amendment in the hope that the prospect of sexual equality might cause the entire bill to fail.

The Equal Employment Opportunity Commission, which began to operate in the summer of 1965, anticipated that virtually all its complaints would come from blacks. They were surprised to discover that 25 percent of the complaints received during the first year were from women. In the course of responding to these complaints, both the commission and the courts were driven to a more subtle analysis of female job categories and work patterns. Section 703(e)1 required that employers wishing to define a job category by sex had to show that sex was a "bona fide occupational qualification"; it was not enough to say that men or women had traditionally filled any given job.

The act was amended in 1972 and again in 1978; on both occasions the EEOC was given substantial additional powers and responsibilities. The three major areas of EEOC activity are: (1) furnishing assistance to comparable state agencies, (2) furnishing advice to employers and labor unions about compliance, and (3) enforcing compliance by conciliation and by legal action.

Sec. 703. (a) It shall be an unlawful employment practice for an employer—

(1) to fail or refuse to hire or to discharge any individual, or otherwise to discriminate against any individual with respect to his compensation, terms, conditions, or privileges of employment, because of such individual's race, color, religion, sex, or national origin; or

(2) to limit, segregate, or classify his employees in any way which would deprive or tend to deprive any individual of employment opportunities or otherwise adversely affect his status as an employee, because of such individual's race, color, religion, sex, or national origin.

(b) It shall be an unlawful employment practice for an employment agency to fail or refuse to refer for employment, or otherwise to discriminate against, any individual because of his race, color, religion, sex, or national origin, or to classify or refer for employment any individual on the basis of his race, color, religion, sex, or national origin.

(c) It shall be an unlawful employment practice for a labor organization—

(1) to exclude or to expel from its membership, or otherwise to discriminate against, any individual because of his race, color, religion, sex, or national origin;

(2) to limit, segregate, or classify its

membership, or to classify or fail or refuse to refer for employment any individual, in any way which would deprive or tend to deprive any individual of employment opportunities, or would limit such employment opportunities or otherwise adversely affect his status as an employee or as an applicant for employment, because of such individual's race, color, religion, sex, or national origin; or

(3) to cause or attempt to cause an employer to discriminate against an individual in violation of this section. . . .

(e) Notwithstanding any other provision of this title, (1) it shall not be an unlawful employment practice for an employer to hire and employ employees, for an employment agency to classify, or refer for employment any individual, for a labor organization to classify its membership or to classify or refer for employment any individual, or for an employer, labor organization, or joint labor-management committee controlling apprenticeship or other training or retraining programs to admit or employ any individual in any such program, on the basis of his religion, sex, or national origin in those certain instances where religion, sex, or national origin is a bona fide occupational qualification reasonably necessary to the normal operation of that particular business or enterprise. . . .

Sec. 705. (a) There is hereby created a Commission to be known as the Equal Employment Opportunity Commission, which shall be composed of five members,

not more than three of whom shall be members of the same political party, who shall be appointed by the President by and with the advice and consent of the Senate. . . .

(g) The Commission shall have power—

(1) to cooperate with and, with their consent, utilize regional, State, local, and other agencies, both public and private, and individuals; . . .

(3) to furnish to persons subject to this title such technical assistance as they may request to further their compliance with this title or an order issued thereunder;

(4) upon the request of (i) any employer, whose employees or some of them, or (ii) any labor organization, whose members or some of them, refuse or threaten to refuse to cooperate in effectuating the provisions of this title, to assist in such effectuation by conciliation or such other remedial action as is provided by this title;

(5) to make such technical studies as are appropriate to effectuate the purposes and policies of this title and to make the results of such studies available to the public;

(6) to refer matters to the Attorney General with recommendations for intervention in a civil action brought by an aggrieved party under section 706, or for the institution of a civil action by the Attorney General under section 707, and to advise, consult, and assist the Attorney General on such matters. . . .

12

Equal Rights Amendment, 1972

An Equal Rights Amendment (ERA), with slightly different wording than the one proposed in 1972, was sponsored in 1923 by the National Woman's Party. It seemed to them the logical corollary to suffrage. But that amendment was vigorously opposed by the League of Women Voters and other progressive reformers, lest it undermine the protective legislation for which they had fought so hard.

An ERA was introduced regularly in Congress virtually every year thereafter, but it received little attention until after World War II. In 1950 and 1953 it was passed by the Senate but ignored by the House.

By 1970 much protective legislation had been applied to both men and women. It was possible to support an ERA without risking the undoing of labor law reforms. The hope that the Supreme Court would apply the Fourteenth Amendment's "equal protection of the laws" clause to cases involving discrimination on the basis of sex as firmly as it applied the clause to cases involving racial discrimination had not been fulfilled. When the ERA was introduced in 1970 it was endorsed by a wide range of organizations, some of which had once opposed it; these organizations included groups as disparate as the United Automobile Workers and the Woman's Christian Temperance Union. Its main sponsor in the House was Martha Griffiths of Michigan; in the Senate, Birch Bayh of Indiana.

The ERA was passed by Congress on March 22, 1972, and sent to the states for ratification. There was much initial enthusiasm; within two days six states had ratified. But the pace of ratification slowed, and only thirty-five of the needed thirty-eight states had ratified it by 1978. (Four state legislatures voted to rescind ratification, although the legality of that move was open to question.) In October 1978 Congress extended the deadline for ratification from March 22, 1979, to June 30, 1982.

Section 1. Equality of rights under the law shall not be denied or abridged by the United States or by any State on account of sex.

Section 2. The Congress shall have the power to enforce, by appropriate legislation, the provisions of this article.

Section 3. The amendment shall take effect two years after the date of ratification.

13

Frontiero v. Richardson, 1973

Sharron A. Frontiero was an Air Force officer who was dismayed to discover that she could not claim dependent's benefits for her husband on the same terms that her male colleagues could for their wives. She and her husband brought suit, claiming that statutes requiring spouses of female members of the uni-

411 U.S. 677.

formed services to receive more than half of their support from their wives to be considered dependents, while all spouses of male members were treated as dependents, violated the due process clause of the Fifth Amendment and the equal protection clause of the Fourteenth Amendment.

The Supreme Court ruled in favor of the Frontieros in a complex decision that used statistical information about women's place in the work force in a manner reminiscent of the Brandeis Brief. Speaking for three of his colleagues Justice William J. Brennan, Jr. prepared a historically based argument, explaining the distance American public opinion had traveled since the *Bradwell* case. He drew analogies between discrimination on the basis of race, which the court subjected to strict scrutiny, and discrimination on the basis of sex.

In concurring with Brennan's opinion, three justices observed that although they agreed with the Frontieros in this particular case, they were not yet persuaded that sex ought to be regularly treated as a "suspect category." Only when—or if—the Equal Rights Amendment were passed could the Court be sure that the public agreed that discrimination on the basis of sex ought to be evaluated as critically as discrimination on the basis of race.

Note that the facts in *Frontiero* relate to discrimination against the husband of the wage earner, not directly against a woman. It is the family of a female wage earner that is discriminated against. A similar case is *Weinberger* v. *Weisenfeld* [420 U.S. 636 (1975)], in which the husband of a dead woman demanded survivor's benefits equal to those available to widows. A number of other sex discrimination cases have been brought by men, challenging older laws that were intended to protect women. *Reed* v. *Reed* [404 U.S. 71 (1971)], in which the Supreme Court struck down an explicit preference for males as administrators of a deceased person's estate, is unusual in that it is a straightforward example of an occasion on which a woman brought suit directly against a law that discriminated against her.

Mr. Justice William J. Brennan, Jr. announced the judgment of the Court:

The question before us concerns the right of a female member of the uniformed services to claim her spouse as a "dependent." . . .

At the outset, appellants contend that classifications based upon sex, like classifications based upon race, alienage, and national origin, are inherently suspect and must therefore be subjected to close judicial scrutiny. We agree. . . .

There can be no doubt that our Nation has had a long and unfortunate history of sex discrimination. Traditionally, such discrimination was rationalized by an attitude of "romantic paternalism" which, in practical effect, put women, not on a pedestal, but in a cage. Indeed, this paternalistic attitude became so firmly rooted in our national consciousness that, 100 years ago, a distinguished Member of this

Court was able to proclaim . . . "The natural and proper timidity and delicacy which belongs to the female sex evidently unfits it for many of the occupations of civil life." . . .

It is true, of course, that the position of women in America has improved markedly in recent decades. Nevertheless, it can hardly be doubted that, in part because of the high visibility of the sex characteristic, women still face pervasive, although at times more subtle, discrimination in our educational institutions, in the job market, and perhaps most conspicuously, in the political arena. . . .

Moreover, since sex, like race and national origin, is an immutable characteristic determined solely by the accident of birth, the imposition of special disabilities upon the member of a particular sex because of their sex would seem to violate "the basic concept of our system that legal burdens should bear some relationship to individual responsibility. . . ." And what differentiates sex from such non-suspect statuses as intelligence or physical disability, and aligns it with the recognized suspect criteria, is that the sex characteristic frequently bears no relation to ability to perform or contribute to society. . . .

. . . over the past decade, Congress has itself manifested an increasing sensitivity to sex-based classifications. In Tit[le] VII of the Civil Rights Act of 1964, for example, Congress expressly declared that no employer, labor union, or other organization subject to the provisions of the Act shall discriminate against any individual on the basis of "race, color, religion, *sex*, or national origin." Similarly, the Equal Pay Act of 1963 provides that no employer covered by the Act "shall discriminate . . . between employees on the basis of sex." . . .

With these considerations in mind, we can only conclude that classifications based upon sex, like classifications based upon race, alienage, or national origin, are inherently suspect, and must therefore be subjected to strict judicial scrutiny. Applying the analysis mandated by that stricter standard of review, it is clear that the statutory scheme now before us is constitutionally invalid. . . .

Mr. Justice Lewis F. Powell, Jr., with whom the Chief Justice and Mr. Justice Harry A. Blackmun join, concurring in the judgment.

I agree that the challenged statutes constitute an unconstitutional discrimination against servicewomen . . . but I cannot join the opinion of Mr. Justice Brennan, which would hold that all classifications based upon sex . . . are "inherently suspect and must therefore be subjected to close judicial scrutiny." . . . The Equal Rights Amendment, which if adopted will resolve the substance of this precise question, has been approved by the Congress and submitted for ratification by the States. If this Amendment is duly adopted, it will represent the will of the people accomplished in the manner prescribed by the constitution. . . . It seems to me that this reaching out to pre-empt by judicial action a major political decision which is currently in process of resolution does not reflect appropriate respect for duly prescribed legislative processes.

14

Roe *v.* Wade, *1973*

The Comstock Law had been echoed by a series of anticontraception and anti-abortion laws throughout the country. James Mohr observes, "Every state in the Union had [by 1900] an antiabortion law of some kind on its books . . . except Kentucky, where the state courts outlawed the practice anyway." The Texas law prohibited abortion except for the purpose of saving the mother's life. In 1970 a single pregnant woman, known as Jane Roe to protect her privacy, brought a class action suit challenging the constitutionality of that law as a violation of her right to liberty as guaranteed by the due process clause of the Fourteenth Amendment.

The Court's decision in *Roe* v. *Wade* marked a sharp change from long-established practice. As the opening lines of the majority decision make clear, the justices were aware they were making a sensitive decision. The issues that were raised by *Roe* v. *Wade* have not been settled and are not likely to be easily resolved, touching as they do on basic religious and ethical beliefs. Abortion is an issue of concern to men as well as to women. It is an issue on which women and men hold a wide variety of views. Among the questions raised are:

1. What are the limits of a woman's right to control of her own body?
2. Should the unborn be afforded legal rights?
3. What rights should the father have?
4. What rights does the community have to set general policy? What are the appropriate limits of government intervention? The state may not require a woman to conceive a child; can the state require a woman to bear a child?
5. Will any of these rights change as improvements are made in the technology for the discovery of birth defects and genetic abnormalities, and for caring for premature infants at earlier ages?

Mr. Justice Harry A. Blackmun delivered the opinion
of the Court:

We forthwith acknowledge our awareness of the sensitive and emotional nature of the abortion controversy, of the vigorous opposing views, even among physicians, and of the deep and seemingly absolute convictions that the subject inspires. One's philosophy, one's experiences, one's exposure to the raw edges of human exis-

410 U.S. 113. For the quotation given above, see James C. Mohr, *Abortion in America: The Origins and Evolution of National Policy, 1800–1900* (New York, 1978), 229–30.

tence, one's religious training, one's attitudes toward life and family and their values, and the moral standards one establishes and seeks to observe, are all likely to influence and to color one's thinking and conclusions about abortion.

In addition, population growth, pollution, poverty, and racial overtones tend to complicate and not to simplify the problem.

Our task, of course, is to resolve the issue by constitutional measurement, free of emotion and of predilection. We seek earnestly to do this. . . .

The principal thrust of the appellant's attack on the Texas statutes is that they improperly invade a right, said to be possessed by the pregnant woman, to choose to terminate her pregnancy. Appellant would discover this right in the concept of personal "liberty" embodied in the Fourteenth Amendment's Due Process Clause; or in personal, marital, familial and sexual privacy said to be protected by the Bill of Rights . . . or among those rights reserved to the people by the Ninth Amendment. . . .

It perhaps is not generally appreciated that the restrictive criminal abortion laws in effect in a majority of States today are of relatively recent vintage. Those laws, generally proscribing abortion or its attempt at any time during pregnancy except when necessary to preserve the pregnant woman's life, are not of ancient or even of common-law origin. Instead, they derive from statutory changes effected, for the most part, in the latter half of the nineteenth century. . . . At common law, at the time of the adoption of our Constitution, and throughout the major portion of the nineteenth century . . . a woman enjoyed a substantially broader right to terminate a pregnancy than she does in most states today. . . .

When most criminal abortion laws were first enacted, the procedure was a hazardous one for the woman. This was particularly true prior to the development of anti-

sepsis. . . . Abortion mortality was high. . . . Modern medical techniques have altered this situation. Appellants . . . refer to medical data indicating that abortion in early pregnancy, that is, prior to the end of the first trimester, although not without its risk, is now relatively safe. Mortality rates for women undergoing early abortions, where the procedure is legal, appear to be as low as or lower than the rates for normal childbirth. Consequently, any interest of the State in protecting the woman from an inherently hazardous procedure . . . has largely disappeared. . . . The State has a legitimate interest in seeing to it that abortion, like any other medical procedure, is performed under circumstances that insure maximum safety for the patient. . . .

The Constitution does not explicitly mention any right of privacy. In a line of decisions, however . . . the Court has recognized that a right of personal privacy, or a guarantee of certain areas or zones of privacy, does exist under the Constitution. . . . This right . . . whether it be founded in the Fourteenth Amendment's concept of personal liberty . . . or . . . in the Ninth Amendment's reservation of rights to the people, is broad enough to encompass a woman's decision whether or not to terminate her pregnancy. . . . We . . . conclude that the right of personal privacy includes the abortion decision, but that this right is not unqualified and must be considered against important state interests in regulation. . . .

. . . the State does have an important and legitimate interest in preserving and protecting the health of the pregnant woman . . . and . . . it has still *another* important and legitimate interest in protecting the potentiality of human life. These interests are separate and distinct. Each grows in substantiality as the woman approaches term, and, at a point during pregnancy, each becomes "compelling."

With respect to the State's important and legitimate interest in the health of the mother, the "compelling" point, in the light of present medical knowledge, is at approximately the end of the first trimester. This is so because of the now-established medical fact . . . that until the end of the first trimester mortality in abortion may be less than mortality in normal childbirth. It follows that . . . for the period of pregnancy prior to this "compelling" point, the attending physician, in consultation with his patient, is free to determine, without regulation by the State, that in his medical judgment, the patient's pregnancy should be terminated.

. . . For the state subsequent to approximately the end of the first trimester, the State, in promoting its interest in the health of the mother, may, if it chooses, regulate the abortion procedure in ways that are reasonably related to maternal health.

For the state subsequent to viability, the State in promoting its interest in the potentiality of human life may, if it chooses, regulate, and even proscribe, abortion except where it is necessary, in appropriate medical judgment, for the preservation of the life or health of the mother.

Our conclusion . . . is . . . that the Texas abortion statutes, as a unit, must fall. . . .

15

Taylor v. Louisiana, 1975

The first American women to qualify for jury service were citizens of Utah in 1898. Not until after the passage of the Nineteenth Amendment did service generally become available; even then it was common for states to exclude women from lists of possible jurors unless they specifically asked to be placed on the lists. Occasionally this practice had been questioned, but the Supreme Court had permitted states to treat all women differently from all men for the purpose of jury service, and to exclude women unless they volunteered, on the grounds that women were normally most needed at home.

Billy Taylor was convicted of kidnapping in 1972. After his jury was empaneled he appealed for a new trial on the ground that in Louisiana women had to volunteer to be eligible for jury service. Since women had been systematically excluded from the jury pool, Taylor claimed that he would be deprived of his federal constitutional right to a fair trial by a jury of his peers, that is, of a representative segment of the community as a whole.

The majority opinion made extensive use of an opinion written by Justice William O. Douglas in 1946. It upheld Taylor's claim. "Until today," it concluded, "no case had squarely held that the exclusion of women from jury venires [lists of eligible jurors] deprives a criminal defendant of his Sixth Amendment right to trial by an impartial jury drawn from a fair cross section of the community."

419 U.S. 522.

Mr. Justice Byron R. White delivered the opinion of the Court:

The Louisiana jury-selection system does not disqualify women from jury service, but in operation its conceded systematic impact is that only a very few women, grossly disproportionate to the number of eligible women in the community, are called for jury service. In this case, no women were on the venire from which the petit jury was drawn. . . .

The State first insists that Taylor, a male, has no standing to object to the exclusion of women from his jury. . . . Taylor was not a member of the excluded class; but there is no rule that claims such as Taylor presents may be made only by those defendants who are members of the group excluded from jury service. In *Peters* v. *Kiff* . . . (1972) . . . a white man challenged his conviction on the ground that Negroes had been systematically excluded from jury service. . . .

We are . . . persuaded that the fair-cross-section requirement is violated by the systematic exclusion of women, who in the judicial district involved here amounted to 53 percent of the citizens eligible for jury service. . . . This very matter was debated in *Ballard* v. *United States* [in 1946]. . . . The . . . view that an all-male panel drawn from various groups in the community would be as truly representative as if women were included, was firmly rejected:

. . . who would claim that a jury was truly representative of the community if all men were intentionally and systematically excluded from the panel? The truth is that the two sexes are not fungible; a community made up exclusively of one is different from a community composed of both; the subtle interplay of influence one on the other is among the imponderables. . . . The exclusion of one may indeed make the jury less representative of the community than would be true if an economic or racial group were excluded.

. . . The States are free to grant exemptions from jury service to individuals in case of special hardship or incapacity and to those engaged in particular occupations the uninterrupted performance of which is critical to the community's welfare. . . . A system excluding all women, however, is a wholly different matter. It is untenable to suggest these days that it would be a special hardship for each and every woman to perform jury service . . . it may be burdensome to sort out those who should be exempted from those who should serve. But that task is performed in the case of men, and the administrative convenience in dealing with women as a class is insufficient justification for diluting the quality of community judgment represented by the jury in criminal trials.

Further Reading

Part I

Traditional America, 1600–1820

BIOLOGY

Extracts from the Journal of Elizabeth Drinker, ed. H. D. Biddle (Philadelphia, 1889), includes extensive comments on Drinker's experience of childbearing and motherhood. For patterns of women's lives, see Robert V. Wells, "Demographic Change and the Life Cycle of American Families," *Journal of Interdisciplinary History* 2 (1971):273–82, and Daniel Scott Smith and Michael S. Hindus, "Premarital Pregnancy in America, 1640–1971: An Overview and Interpretation," *Journal of Interdisciplinary History* 5 (1975):537–70.

ECONOMICS

Lyle Koehler, *A Search for Power: The "Weaker Sex" in Seventeenth-Century New England* (Urbana, 1980), examines the work options open to women. See also John Demos, *A Little Commonwealth: Family Life in Plymouth Colony* (New York, 1970). For women's lives in the Chesapeake, see Lois Green Carr and Lorena Walsh, "The Planter's Wife: The Experience of White Women in Seventeenth-Century Maryland," *William and Mary Quarterly*, 3d ser., 34 (1977):542–71.

POLITICS

The witchcraft trials of 1692 were an occasion on which religious and political concerns mingled. The fact that the targets of the trials were, with few exceptions, female, makes them an important episode in women's history. Chadwick Hansen, *Witchcraft at Salem* (New York, 1969), treats the crisis in the context of seventeenth-century belief in folklore; Paul Boyer and Stephen Nissenbaum, *Salem Possessed: The Social Origins of Witchcraft* (Cambridge, Mass., 1974), treat it as an expression of social and economic tension in the community. John Demos, "Underlying Themes in the Witchcraft of Seventeenth-Century New England," *American Historical Review* 75 (1970):1311–26, reexamines the trial records for what they suggest about the roles of women in colonial New England.

IDEOLOGY

For the letters on which Anne Firor Scott drew for her portraits, see *The Letters of Benjamin Franklin and Jane Mecom,* ed. Carl Van Doren (Princeton, N.J., 1950), and *The Letterbook of Eliza Lucas Pinckney,* ed. Elise Pinckney (Chapel Hill, 1972). For the ways in which religious practices affected women's role and status, see Mary Maples Dunn, "Saints and Sinners: Congregational and Quaker Women in the Early Colonial Period," *American Quarterly* 30 (1978):582–601. For the response of American women to the Revolution, see Linda K. Kerber, *Women of the Republic: Intellect and Ideology in Revolutionary America* (Chapel Hill, 1980), and Mary Beth Norton, *Liberty's Daughters: The Revolutionary Experience of American Women 1750–1800* (Boston, 1980).

Part IIA

Industrializing America, 1820–80

BIOLOGY

For an important overview, see Carl N. Degler, *At Odds: Women and the Family in America from the Revolution to the Present* (New York, 1980), especially chaps. 2–9. For attempts to improve the general level of female health, see Regina Markell Morantz, "Making Women Modern: Middle-Class Women and Health Reform in 19th-Century America," *Journal of Social History* 10 (1977): 490–507.

ECONOMICS

Although the literature on slavery is large and complex, it rarely focuses on the distinctive experience of enslaved women. Willie Lee Rose, ed., *A Documentary History of Slavery in North America* (New York, 1976), and John Blassingame, ed., *Slave Testimony: Two Centuries of Letters, Speeches, Interviews and Autobiographies* (Baton Rouge, 1977), do include important material on women. Gerda Lerner, ed., *Black Women in White America* (New York, 1972), is a rich collection of primary sources. Richard S. Dunn, "A Tale of Two Plantations: Slave Life at Mesopotamia in Jamaica and Mount Airy in Virginia, 1799–1828," *William and Mary Quarterly,* 3d ser., 34 (1977):32–65, is a comparative study that provides a detailed reconstruction of the work lives of slave women and emphasizes the pressures under which they lived. Many elderly women who had been slaves when young were interviewed by the Federal Writers' Project in the 1930s. Selected interviews appear in B. A. Botkin, ed., *Lay My Burden Down: A Folk History of Slavery* (Chicago, 1945), and Norman R. Yetman, ed., *Voices from Slavery* (New York, 1970). Leon Litwack, *Been in the Storm So Long: The Aftermath of Slavery* (New York, 1979), pays substantial attention to the experience of black women during Reconstruction.

For women's work in the domestic economy, see Nancy F. Cott, *The Bonds of Womanhood: "Woman's Sphere" in New England* (New Haven, 1977), chap. 1. For the impact of industrialization, see Thomas Dublin, *Women at Work: The Transformation of Work and Community in Lowell, Massachusetts, 1826–1860* (New York, 1979), and Helen Sumner, *History of Women in Industry in the United States* (Washington, D.C., 1910).

For the feminization of schooling, see Richard M. Bernard and Maris A. Vinovskis, "The Female School Teacher in Ante-Bellum Massachusetts," *Journal of Social History* 10 (1977):332–45, and Anne Firor Scott, "What, Then, Is the American: This New Woman?" *Journal of American History* 65 (1978):679–703.

POLITICS

Estelle Freedman, *Their Sisters' Keepers: Women and Prison Reform in Nineteenth-Century America* (Ann Arbor, 1981), introduces an important reform movement. Gerda Lerner, *The Grimké Sisters from South Carolina: Rebels against Slavery* (Boston, 1967), is a readable biography that suggests the way in which abolitionism could lead to a concern for women's rights. Ellen C. Du Bois, *Feminism and Suffrage: The Emergence of an Independent Women's Movement in America, 1848–1869* (Ithaca, 1978), is an important interpretation that stresses the radicalism of the demand for suffrage. Five massive volumes of the basic sources on the suffrage movement have been conveniently abridged in *A Concise History of Woman Suffrage: Selections from the Classic Work of Stanton, Anthony, Gage and Harper*, ed. Mari Jo Buhle and Paul Buhle (Urbana, 1978). For women's involvement in the Civil War, the basic book remains Mary Elizabeth Massey, *Bonnet Brigades* (New York, 1966).

IDEOLOGY

The concept of "The Cult of True Womanhood" was given its name in an essay with the same title by Barbara Welter, *American Quarterly* 18 (1966):151–74. A different reading of some of the same sources is offered by Gerda Lerner, *The Majority Finds Its Past: Placing Women in History* (New York, 1979), chap. 2. See also Cott, *The Bonds of Womanhood,* and Kerber, *Women of the Republic,* chaps. 7, 8, and 9.

For the way in which religious beliefs affected women's role and behavior, see Mary Ryan, "A Woman's Awakening: Evangelical Religion and the Families of Utica, New York, 1800–1840," *American Quarterly* 30 (1978):602–33; Joan Jacobs Brumberg, *Mission for Life* (New York, 1980), and Donald G. Mathews, *Religion in the Old South* (Chicago, 1978), chap. 2.

Part IIB

Industrializing America, 1880–1920

BIOLOGY

Biology and ideology interacted in the medical treatment of women, a subject much discussed in scholarly articles. See, for example, Carroll Smith-Rosenberg and Charles Rosenberg, "The Female Animal: Medical and Biological Views of Woman and Her Role in Nineteenth-Century America," *Journal of American History* 60 (1973):332–56. Using data from hospital records Regina Markell Morantz and Sue Zschoche compare the treatment delivered by male and female physicians in "Professionalism, Feminism, and Gender Roles: A Comparative Study of Nineteenth-Century Medical Therapeutics," *Journal of American History* 67 (1980):568–88. For differing interpretations of Sanger and the birth control movement, see Linda Gordon, *Woman's Body, Woman's Right: Birth Control in America* (New York, 1977), James Reed, *From Private Vice to Public Virtue: The Birth Control Movement and American Society since 1830* (New York, 1978), and David M. Kennedy, *Birth Control in America: The Career of Margaret Sanger* (New Haven, 1970). For an overview of women's sexuality during this period, see Degler, *At Odds*, chaps. 11–12.

ECONOMICS

Family expectations and work options interacted in different ways with different ethnic groups. For a study of that interaction with respect to Italian women, see Virginia Yans-McLaughlin, *Family and Community: Italian Immigrants in Buffalo, 1880–1930* (Ithaca, 1977). Articles on other groups are in the *Journal of Urban History* 4 (1978). For a general study of working-class women, see Leslie Woodcock Tentler's *Wage-Earning Women: Industrial Work and Family Life in the United States, 1900–1930* (New York, 1979). Prostitution provided jobs for women whether they entered such work voluntarily or, as many did, involuntarily. See Lucie Cheng Hirata, "Free, Indentured, Enslaved: Chinese Prostitutes in Nineteenth-Century America," *Signs: Journal of Women in Culture and Society* 4 (1979):3–29. For the remarkable letters of Maimie Pinzer, a Philadelphia prostitute struggling to create a new life for herself, see *The Maimie Papers*, ed. Ruth Rosen (Old Westbury, N.Y., 1977). New employment opportunities for educated women developed in libraries with librarianship becoming feminized just as had schoolteaching. See Dee Garrison, *Apostles of Culture: The Public Librarian and American Society, 1876–1920* (New York, 1979).

Politics

Economics and politics overlapped as many middle-class women became involved in reforms affecting the lives of working-class women and children. In the process they created new alliances such as the Women's Trade Union League and a new career for women, social work. See Nancy Schrom Dye, *As Equals and as Sisters: Feminism, the Labor Movement, and the Women's Trade Union League of New York* (Columbia, Mo., 1980). On Jane Addams, see Allen Davis, *American Heroine: The Life and Legend of Jane Addams* (New York, 1973), and *The Social Thought of Jane Addams*, ed. Christopher Lasch (New York, 1965). Note the role of women in social service and social work in Clarke A. Chambers, *Seedtime of Reform: Social Service and Social Action, 1918–1933* (Ann Arbor, 1967).

The increasing activism of women helped prepare a prosuffrage constituency. For this development in the South, see Anne Firor Scott, *The Southern Lady: From Pedestal to Politics, 1830–1930* (Chicago, 1970), chap. 6. For the black woman's club movement, see Lerner, *The Majority Finds Its Past*, chap. 6. The standard history of suffrage remains Eleanor Flexner's *Century of Struggle: The Women's Rights Movement in the United States* (Cambridge, Mass., 1958). See also Sharon Hartman Strom, "Leadership and Tactics in the American Woman Suffrage Movement: A New Perspective from Massachusetts," *Journal of American History* 62 (1975):262–82.

Ideology

Attitudes about appropriate behavior for men as well as women are discussed by Peter Gabriel Filene, *Him/Her/Self: Sex Roles in Modern America* (New York, 1974), chaps. 1–4. On ideology and education, see Roberta Frankfort, *Collegiate Women: Domesticity and Career in Turn-of-the-Century America* (New York, 1977). The way ideology affected debate on changing divorce laws is evident in William L. O'Neill's *Divorce in the Progressive Era* (New Haven, 1967).

Part III

Modern America, 1920–80

Biology

See Paul A. Robinson, *The Modernization of Sex: Havelock Ellis, Alfred Kinsey, William Masters and Virginia Johnson* (New York, 1976). Sex and sexuality are the focus of two issues of *Signs: Journal of Women in Culture and Society* 5, 6 (1980). On childbirth practices, see Nancy Schrom Dye's review essay, "History of Childbirth in America," *Signs: Journal of Women in Culture and Society* 6 (1980):97–108. An important study of mothering by a social scientist is Nancy Chodorow's *Reproduction of Mothering: Psychoanalysis and the Sociology of Gender* (Berkeley, 1979). On the interaction of biology and ideology with respect to aging, see Susan Sontag, "The Double Standard of Aging," *Saturday Review* 55 (1972):29–38. A scholarly study of women and aging that looks to the future is Alice S. Rossi's "Life-Span Theories and Women's Lives," *Signs: Journal of Women in Culture and Society* 6 (1980):4–32. On rape, see Susan Brownmiller, *Against Our Will: Men, Women, and Rape* (New York, 1975).

Economics

For an overview, see William H. Chafe, *The American Woman: Her Changing Social, Economic, and Political Roles, 1920–1970* (New York, 1974). On the Depression, see Winifred Wandersee Bolin, "The Economics of Middle Income Family Life: Working Women during the Great Depression," *Journal of American History* 65 (1978):60–74; also Ruth Milkman, "Women's Work and the Economic Crisis: Some Lessons from the Great Depression," *Review of Radical Political Economics* 8 (1976):73–97. William L. O'Neill, *Women at Work* (Chicago, 1972), contains reprints of two very readable works that reveal the limited progress made by women in the work force during the twentieth century. The first is Dorothy Richardson's *Long Day* (1903) and the second is Elinor Langer's report "Inside the New York Telephone Company" (1970). For an example of the problems facing women seeking work in traditionally "male" professions, see Mary Roth Walsh, *Doctors Wanted, No Women Need Apply: Sexual Barriers in the Medical Profession, 1835–1975* (New Haven, 1977). Women's work in the home is explored in Helena Z. Lopata's *Occupation: Housewife* (New York, 1971). For recent efforts to improve the economic status and social role of the women whose main occupation is homemaking, see Rae Andre, *Homemakers: The Forgotten Workers* (Chicago, 1981). Lerner's *Black Women in White America* contains selections dealing with many facets of work performed by black women as well as other noneconomic issues. Those wishing to explore more fully the experience of women of racial and ethnic minorities should consult Gerda Lerner's *Teaching Women's History* (Washington, D.C., 1981), pp. 60–65, paying particular attention to the sources listed in the footnotes to these pages.

Politics

J. Stanley Lemons, *The Woman Citizen: Social Feminism in the 1920's* (Urbana, 1975) follows politically active reformers and feminists after suffrage. Important biographies of individual activists include Jacqueline Dowd Hall's *Revolt against Chivalry: Jessie Daniel Ames and the Women's Campaign against Lynching* (New York, 1974), and Joseph P. Lash's biography of Eleanor Roosevelt, *Eleanor and Franklin* (New York, 1971), and *Eleanor: The Years Alone* (New York, 1972). For the contemporary feminist movement, see Sara Evans, *Personal Politics: The Roots of Women's Liberation in the Civil Rights Movement and the New Left* (New York, 1979), and Jo Freeman, *The Politics of Women's Liberation: A Case Study of an Emerging Social Movement and Its Relation to the Social Policy Process* (New York, 1975). For an important discussion of sexual (and racial) equality, see William H. Chafe, *Women and Equality: Changing Patterns in American Culture* (New York, 1977).

IDEOLOGY

In addition to *Women and Equality,* in which Chafe discusses ideology as well as economics in his analysis of social change, see Filene, *Him/Her/Self*, chaps. 5–7. See also Sheila Rothman, *Woman's Proper Place: A History of Changing Ideals and Practices, 1870 to the Present* (New York, 1978). For feminist ideology, see notes to Mathews, "The New Feminism and the Dynamics of Social Change" (part III). For a discussion of the relationship between ideology, architecture, and urban design, see Dolores Hayden, "What Would a Non-Sexist City Be Like? Speculations on Housing, Urban Design, and Human Work," *Signs: Journal of Women in Culture and Society* 5 (Supp. 1980):s170–87. For the relationship between ideology and law, see Albie Sachs and Joan Hoff Wilson, *Sexism and the Law: A Study of Male Beliefs and Legal Bias in Britain and the United States* (Oxford, England, 1978).

An important reference containing excellent short biographies and a brief bibliography on many of the women appearing in this book is *Notable American Women, 1607–1950: A Biographical Dictionary*, ed. Edward T. James, Janet Wilson James, and Paul Boyer, 3 vols. (Cambridge, Mass., 1971), and *Notable American Women: The Modern Period*, ed. Barbara Sicherman and Carol Hurd Green (Cambridge, Mass., 1980).

Index

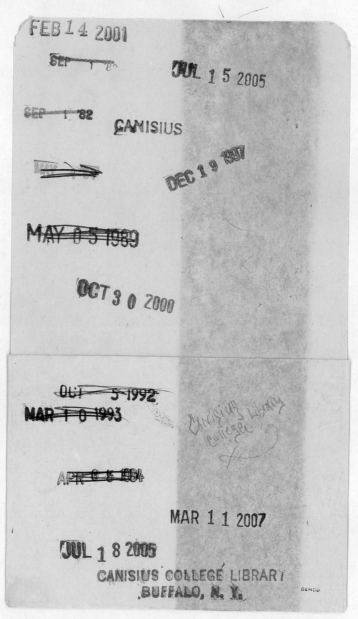